CW00920261

Palgrave Studies in Comparative Global History

Series Editors
Manuel Perez Garcia
Shanghai Jiao Tong University
Shanghai, China

Lucio De Sousa
Tokyo University of Foreign Studies
Tokyo, Japan

This series proposes a new geography of Global History research using Asian and Western sources, welcoming quality research and engaging outstanding scholarship from China, Europe and the Americas. Promoting academic excellence and critical intellectual analysis, it offers a rich source of global history research in sub-continental areas of Europe, Asia (notably China, Japan and the Philippines) and the Americas and aims to help understand the divergences and convergences between East and West.

Advisory Board:
Patrick O'Brien (London School of Economics)
Anne McCants (Massachusetts Institute of Technology)
Joe McDermott (University of Cambridge)
Pat Manning (Pittsburgh University)
Mihoko Oka (University of Tokyo)
Richard Von Glahn (University of California, Los Angeles)
Bartolomé Yun-Casalilla (Universidad Pablo de Olavide de Sevilla)
Shigeru Akita (Osaka University)
François Gipouloux (CNRS/FMSH)
Carlos Marichal (Colegio de Mexico)
Leonard Blusse (Leiden University)
Antonio Ibarra Romero (Universidad Nacional Autonoma de Mexico, UNAM)
Giorgio Riello (University of Warwick)
Nakajima Gakusho (Kyushu University)
Liu Beicheng (Tsinghua University)
Li Qingxin (Guangdong Academy of Social Sciences)
Dennis O. Flynn (University of the Pacific)
J. B. Owens (Idaho State University)

More information about this series at
http://www.palgrave.com/gp/series/15711

Bartolomé Yun-Casalilla

Iberian World Empires and the Globalization of Europe 1415–1668

palgrave
macmillan

Bartolomé Yun-Casalilla
Pablo de Olavide University
Sevilla, Spain

Palgrave Studies in Comparative Global History
ISBN 978-981-13-0832-1   ISBN 978-981-13-0833-8   (eBook)
https://doi.org/10.1007/978-981-13-0833-8

Library of Congress Control Number: 2018953325

© The Editor(s) (if applicable) and The Author(s) 2019. This book is an open access publication.
Open Access This book is licensed under the terms of the Creative Commons Attribution
4.0 International License (http://creativecommons.org/licenses/by/4.0/), which permits
use, sharing, adaptation, distribution and reproduction in any medium or format, as long as
you give appropriate credit to the original author(s) and the source, provide a link to the
Creative Commons licence and indicate if changes were made.
The images or other third party material in this book are included in the book's Creative
Commons licence, unless indicated otherwise in a credit line to the material. If material is not
included in the book's Creative Commons licence and your intended use is not permitted by
statutory regulation or exceeds the permitted use, you will need to obtain permission directly
from the copyright holder.
The use of general descriptive names, registered names, trademarks, service marks, etc. in this
publication does not imply, even in the absence of a specific statement, that such names are
exempt from the relevant protective laws and regulations and therefore free for general use.
The publisher, the authors and the editors are safe to assume that the advice and information
in this book are believed to be true and accurate at the date of publication. Neither the
publisher nor the authors or the editors give a warranty, express or implied, with respect to
the material contained herein or for any errors or omissions that may have been made. The
publisher remains neutral with regard to jurisdictional claims in published maps and
institutional affiliations.

Cover illustration: Heritage Image Partnership Ltd / Alamy Stock Photo

This Palgrave Macmillan imprint is published by the registered company Springer Nature
Singapore Pte Ltd.
The registered company address is: 152 Beach Road, #21-01/04 Gateway East, Singapore
189721, Singapore

The Open Access publication of this book has been financially supported by GECEM ('*Global Encounters between China and Europe: Trade Networks, Consumption and Cultural Exchanges in Macau and Marseille, 1680–1840*' http://www.gecem.eu), a project funded by the European Research Council-Starting Grant, ref. 679371 (under the European Union's Horizon 2020 Research and Innovation Programme) and of which the Principal Investigator is Professor Manuel Perez-Garcia.

Praise for *Iberian World Empires and the Globalization of Europe 1415–1668*

"In this important and ambitious book, based on the command of a massive literature and illuminated by shafts of insight, Bartolomé Yun-Casalilla challenges the stereotype of early modern Spain as a society incapable of responding to the demands of an increasingly globalized world. Using a comparative approach that embraces other European states of the period, he explores to striking effect what the joint Spanish-Portuguese possession of Europe's first global empire meant to the peoples of the Iberian peninsula."
—Sir John Elliott, *Regius Professor Emeritus, Oxford University, UK*

"This book is seminal. It provides the facts and the history required to rescue the histories of state formation, institutional development and imperial expansion in Iberia from the condescension displayed by neo-liberal economists and historians to the contributions of Southern Europe to the early modern preparations and pre-conditions for early breakthrough in the North to industrial market economies."
—Patrick Karl O'Brien, *FBA Emeritus of Oxford and London Universities, UK*

"A comparison that seemed obvious but that only now begins to be seriously made. Beyond similarities that seemed probable and imaginaries about mythic differences, the first two great European political spaces (the Iberian empires) of the early modern era are here studied in their complexity and multileveled interconnections."
—António Manuel Hespanha, *Instituto de Ciências Sociais, Universidade de Lisboa, Portugal*

"While the early modern history globalization has substantially progressed in recent years, there has been a surprising tendency to keep the Iberian Empires on the periphery. This new work by Bartolomé Yun-Casalilla corrects this view and puts them back in the center. His thesis is that both Spain and Portugal constructed the first world-wide empires and hence were fundamental actors in the political, military and economic foundations of early globalization."
—Carlos Marichal, *El Colegio de México, Mexico*

Acknowledgements

This book is a result of several years of work into and reflection upon Iberian societies in general and Castilian society in particular.[1] It began as an English translation of a study published in Spanish (Yun 2004) and took on a life of its own, expanding to offer new perspectives and to engage in debates with a broader literature, in particular in regard to the phenomenon of globalization. It is aimed at both specialists in the Iberian worlds and the general reading public and offers a general discussion and a critical perspective on these fields of study. It attempts to provide a basic narrative account of background events.

A long list of thanks is required for those with whom I have worked and collaborated, but here I can only mention Sir John Elliott, A. M. Hespanha, Carlos Marichal, P. O'Brien, H. Van der Wee, B. Aram, O. Svriz Wuchener, I. Pérez Tostado, L. M. Córdoba Ochoa, S. Serrano, M. Fabián Figueroa, A. Romano, L. Molá, J. Flores (who also read some parts of this work), I. A. A. Thompson, M. Soares Da Cunha, N. Monteiro,

[1] This work has been financed by the project 'Nuevos productos atlánticos, ciencia, guerra, economía y consumo en el Antiguo Régimen' (P09-HUM 5330) and by 'Globalización Ibérica: redes entre Asia y Europa y los cambios en las pautas de consumo en Latinoamérica' (HAR2014-53797-P), which is included in the activities of the PAIDI research group HUM 1000 "Historia de la Globalización: violencia, negociación e interculturalidad" of which the PI is Igor Pérez Tostado. I have also received the financial support of the ERC Starting Grant GECEM ('Global Encounters between China and Europe: Trade Networks, Consumption and Cultural Exchanges in Macau and Marseille, 1680–1840'). Principal investigator Manuel Pérez García.

P. Cardim, L. Ribot, R. Grafe, J. P. Dedieu, and J. Owens (these last four made some excellent criticisms of my book *Marte contra Minerva*), and F. Ramos and M. Diaz Ordóñez and M. J. Milán (to whom I am grateful for their help with the maps and graphs). I must thank my magnificent doctoral and post-doctoral students at the European University Institute in Florence (and the institution itself), among whom I should mention J. L. Gasch, A. García Montón, B. Lindorfer, I. Sosa, I. Pugliese, I. Fattacciu, M. Pérez García, B. Fernández de Castro, H. Silva, J. Gouveia, G. Almeida Borges, J. M. Escribano (who helped with the bibliography and footnotes), and I. López Martín (who helped with the maps on urban Europe). Mention should also be made of Phillip Williams, patient translator, with whom I have discussed some of the themes mentioned close to his field of study. And very special thanks is deserved again by B. Aram, who made a revision of the style of this book, helped with its editing, and advised on particular aspects of its content.

This book is dedicated to Angeles. Thanks a lot for the happy decades together.

CONTENTS

LIST OF MAPS

LIST OF GRAPHS

LIST OF TABLES

INTRODUCTION

Over the last few years, the history of empires has undergone something of a renaissance. This is due in part to the new interest in global history and the privileged status it has acquired in academic circles. This volume tries to explore the relations between globalization and empires, two developments or phenomena that are often considered complementary but should not be confused.

In recent years, economic historians have entered into debate about the degree of globalization prior to the late nineteenth century. For Williamson and O'Rourke, the late 1800s saw the beginning of this process, with an identifiable tendency towards the convergence of economic variables, especially prices.[1] Discussion has tended to turn on the use of terms such as hard or soft globalization, primitive globalization, the first globalization, and so on. These are debates of great interest.[2] But a few preliminary observations are needed. The first is that I find the definition of Flynn and Giráldez (also evident in Williamson and O'Rourke) to be somewhat restrictive, as they propose that the economic historian must define globalization primarily from the perspective of the 'exchange' of 'products' and 'its long-lasting impact' 'on all trading partners' (2002). While I agree with many of their statements about the importance of silver in this process, I have tried to demonstrate that although the economies of the

---

[1] See, among others, O'Rourke and Williamson (2002, 2005).
[2] In addition to the works of Williamson and his collaborators, see Jan De Vries (2003, 2010, 2011).

sixteenth and seventeenth centuries did not meet these criteria—as Williamson and O'Rourke argue—those economies did create connections that would be decisive for the political economies and the construction of the state and, in this way, the allocation of resources in Europe and its colonies. My approach also starts from the conviction that global history is not only important because of what it tells us about non-European worlds but also because it offers us a different perspective and overall context for Europe itself, and may even allow us to reinterpret it in light of the new vantage points thus acquired. Indeed, this may be its most important contribution (Yun 2007). These two presuppositions are the basis of the book, which attempts to employ them in a concrete form to understand the internal history of Spain and Portugal, drawing comparisons between them and other countries and exploring the way in which globalizing forces conditioned relations with other areas of Europe. For this reason, the debate is not always focused on the history of mercantile relations or the classic literature on 'world economies' of Wallenstein but also on some of the classics of the new institutional economics, such as Acemoglu, Johnson, and Robinson.

Another of the purposes of this book is to use this perspective to approach the history of empires and the processes of state building in Iberia, using the concepts of monarchies and composite states.[3] It also attempts to challenge some stereotypes and views that, although anachronistic, have resulted in a highly negative understanding of Iberian societies. To the extent that it looks at problems of statecraft, a basic purpose of this book is to analyse the effects of war on society. This aspect of *Marte contra Minerva* (Yun 2004) which was largely ignored by its readers is vital in understanding the pacts between elites and central power and the forms of organizing coercion and its effects on society.

Empires and the political formations of this period cannot be understood, however, by a study focusing exclusively on what we could call formal institutions. Above all, an analysis of informal institutions—and personal rules—is required, something which is not present in the studies of D. North and his co-authors but which remains essential from our point of view: the family, the extended lineage of family and the kinship relations it entailed, patronage and friendships, reciprocity, prestige, and so on. An analysis of these informal institutions is vital not only to understand political organizations and their dynamics but also the political economies of the time and the forms of

---

[3] Some ideas in Yun (1998).

resources allocation.[4] It may, of course, be difficult to distinguish between formal and informal institutions (Grafe 2012). This is even more the case when we deal with Old Regime societies in which the separation between the public and the private is not clear and in which institutions such as the family are very regulated by the law. The exercise is, however, without doubt of considerable heuristic value. This study will try to set out the internal dynamic of elites, in which reciprocity and conflict were two sides of the same coin and vital to any understanding of political dynamics as well as economic and territorial expansion, including the establishment and nature of empires. Also the relations between the different local and regional elites and the central power of the state is also constitutes a central part of my arguments. Another crucial argument is that these informal institutions developed in contexts of great political and jurisdictional fragmentation, which created enormous competition for resources. From this perspective, it becomes essential to discuss how the institutional framework affected the allocation of productive factors and economic growth or recession. The conclusion is paradoxical, because although this institutional framework explains some of the most negative aspects of the economic behaviour of these societies, it is obvious that the final effect of these (supposedly) inefficient institutions (inefficient, i.e. from the perspective of the new institutional economics) could very well be economic growth of a notable scale within the parameters of pre-industrial societies. Such was the case when the available resources and the ecosystems in which they were inserted acted positively. And this may be true not only for territories in Europe but also for the colonies.

From a heuristic and methodological point of view, a study of the sort undertaken here has obvious roots. Comparative history and what is somewhat unfortunately called 'transnational history' are undoubtedly among the creditors.[5] While the work of authors such as D. North appears continually as a point of discussion, this is only possible in the context of a critical use of their own concepts and ideas. Bourdieu's theory of capital reconversion has been useful to the extent that it allows us to link economic and political factors and explains the decision-making process of historical agents in general and of elites in particular (Yun 2011). And I have also found inspiration in the theory of organizations of H. Simon and others (Yun 2011).

---

[4] A good number of studies of political economies have focused only on mercantile institutions, the state, the judicial system, and the consulates. See, for example, the innovative book by Hough and Grier (2015).

[5] My theoretical approach in Yun (2007, 2014a).

I have adopted a narrative structure in order to provide the reader new to this area with the basic facts upon which my conclusions are based. I have also included conclusions from chapters and papers published elsewhere and focused on related phenomena. This is done in the hope that they broaden perspectives and tie in with important and ongoing debates but do not require a lengthy narrative description of these parallel processes and forces. I am aware that this narrative strategy can give place to some repetitions, but I also want to think that in many cases this is good for those readers who prefer to read only particular chapters of the volume. Lastly, this study approaches the life of the two empires from a top-down perspective, but there is a complementary perspective still to adopt by looking at the empires from below and by analysing how the different local societies established some of the limits for the elites' negotiations. Arguments are always based on choices, and I had to make mine. I do really hope that further research will address the problem from this other perspective and illuminate many aspects that are less explicit here.

PART I

The Iberian Grounds of the Early Modern Globalization of Europe

In or around 1450, Europe began to emerge from the ashes of the crisis of the fourteenth century. This recovery would be the result of a series of internal forces, the role of the institutions being perhaps the most significant of them. The process, moreover, would entail a fundamental qualitative leap forward in the long process of globalization, by which the different regions of the planet would come to be tied together by ever tighter bonds.

In light of this growth, an overly pessimistic and anachronistic vision of the Iberian economies has prevailed. This view underlined their archaic character and held that they were barely expansive. Such an interpretation is hardly surprising when many historians have worked backwards, influenced by very negative visions of the Iberian countries and their empires prevalent in the eighteenth and nineteenth centuries. Moreover, many scholars have subscribed to a simplistic idea of empires as a source of growth, and the result was—and is—a perception of the Iberian empires as historical anomalies (Yun 2010).

Some scholars, for example, wrote of the formation of a semi-peripheral economy, whose function was simply to construct a bridge for the transfer of primary materials from America to Europe, with manufactured products flowing back in the opposite direction (Wallerstein 1979; Frank 1978). A few years ago, it was even normal to think that America's riches had been bestowed upon a country lacking the technical and institutional means necessary to face the challenge of the New World, Castile being the domain of warriors and priests and therefore unable to take advantage of this gift from Providence. Spain, in other words, was not qualified to build a more dynamic economy capable of supporting the development of capitalism. Other scholars described the Spanish economy of this period as one unable to generate development and even growth (Cipolla 1976, p. 233; Kamen 1978, p. 25). Others, E. Hamilton prominent among them, considered that the flood of precious metals out of America caused ravages in the Spanish economy: it raised salaries—and, therefore, the costs of production—thus pushing back industrial investment, at the same time that it increased the price of Spanish manufactures, thus lowering their competitiveness in relation to those of other countries (Hamilton 1934, Spanish translation 1975). Even Keynes liked this opinion and made it his own (Keynes 1936). As perhaps had to be the case, some historians have seen this as evidence of the Spanish and Portuguese way of life—specifically, their alleged dedication to the culture of honour, disapproval of manual work, and even lack of entrepreneurial spirit—and argued that these cultural norms hindered a genuine long-term economic development.[1] For Pierre Vilar the Spanish empire embodied 'the superior phase of feudalism', one that necessarily led to a profound and enduring decadence (Vilar 1974). Working from the theories of Max Weber on the role of the Protestant ethic as a motor of capitalism, D. Landes has written of Spain's self-imposed intellectual isolation and its adherence to a form of Catholic intolerance that would have aborted any process of technical and economic developments (Landes 1998). This vision dovetails with the view of the Iberian economies as being subject to an iron law of decreasing agrarian returns due to the farming of increasingly poor soils and the inevitable contradiction that had to emerge with evidence of demographic growth and the development of cities (Braudel 1976; Anes 1994). More recently Acemoglu, Johnson, and Robinson have applied the ideas of the new institutional economy, already tested by Douglas North, to illustrate the supposedly predatory character of Spanish absolutism and underline the weakness of property rights and the lack of positive institutions. These features, they postulate, created high transaction

---

[1] This idea was present in the work of Sánchez Albornoz, in which the warrior condition of the Spanish in the Middle Ages was a 'psychosis' which was inherently inimical to the development of manual and commercial activities. His phrase 'neither feudalism nor bourgeoisie' neatly encapsulates many of these ideas (1976, vol. I, pp. 678–703). Echoes of Sánchez Albornoz's idea could be still noticed—albeit phrased more elegantly—in the work of leading historians such as Bennassar (1976).

costs and heightened levels of risk, both of which were very negative for economic development (Acemoglu et al. 2005).

Visions of this sort have led to exaggerations that recent research has either entirely dismissed or, at the very least, nuanced. Indeed, some of the above theories would be unacceptable today. This section proposes to revise many of these areas. It will focus on an analysis of the institutions and political systems that emerged from the crisis of the fourteenth century. To this end it aims to set out the most important of the dynamic forces in the development of feudal society, with special reference to the situation in the Iberian Peninsula (Chap. 1). In addition, an analysis of this sort requires us to consider the context of globalization, empire, and growth during the sixteenth century, thus providing a critical overview of a few of the old ideas and stereotypes (Chap. 2). This will also set out a new characterization of economic growth in the sixteenth century (Chap. 3). The basic thesis is that medieval societies were subject to an internal dynamic within their elites that obliged them to search for ever-greater resources. These tensions were the basis of the political instability of the fifteenth century; they would shape the transaction formulas at the heart of the dominant coalition[2] composed by the different elites and would result in the very different political systems that emerged in the Iberian Peninsula.

---

[2] I use the expression in the same way as North et al. (2009). Such a term does not mean here a complete political agreement among the elites but rather as a sort of pact that is not exempt of internal tensions, on the bases and general structures of the epoch's society (see Chap. 4).

CHAPTER 1

Global Context and the Rise of Europe: Iberia and the Atlantic

Historians remain convinced of the importance of the changes that occurred in the European economies between 1450 and 1550. Whether these processes are seen as the result of a partnership with Asia or as the beginning of the European miracle, the scale of the transformation is undeniable. It would affect the entire planet (Jones 1981). Changes such as these were the result of the convergence of global forces, manifested above all in the development of a technology that made possible the oceanic discoveries and overseas expansion. But, fundamentally, they were the outcome of internal transformations that took place in the institutions that regulated social life, in the structure of landlords' rents, property rights, and political systems. The coincidence of these two processes unleashed a series of unexpected opportunities.

GLOBAL LINKS AND INTERNATIONAL EXCHANGES IN EUROPE AND THE IBERIAN PENINSULA

The Global Forces and the Portuguese Atlantic Expansion

Ever since Marco Polo's famous voyages to China, the Italian city-states, and above all Venice and Genoa, had initiated a series of contacts with Asia whose effects in Europe were immediately felt (Fernández-Armesto 2006). Trade in silks, spices, and other products characterized by their

© The Author(s) 2019
B. Yun-Casalilla, *Iberian World Empires and the Globalization of Europe 1415–1668*, Palgrave Studies in Comparative Global History, https://doi.org/10.1007/978-981-13-0833-8_1

high price in relation to their weight would be one of the keys to the rebirth of the Mediterranean, the formation of banking capital, and the emergence and development of the techniques of commercial exchange. If the European elites fought among themselves on the battlefield, in their claims to prestige and in their efforts to immortalize their lineages, then equally they competed in their search for the exotic, their intention being to outstrip their rivals in the consumption of oriental spices and silks and in experimenting with the aesthetic and hedonistic effects of extremely expensive products imported from the Orient (Brotton 2002). In this way, and despite not being manifested in high volumes of trade, the demand for such goods would change the international commerce of this period. It would also spark oceanic exploration, which would be the result of the search for new sea routes by which to acquire these luxury products. Furthermore, Flynn and Giraldez (2002) have argued that the increasing value of precious metals, and particularly of silver, in Europe is due to the China's shift towards the collection of taxes in this metal, which increased the world demand for them.

Yet, it would be a mistake to reduce this primitive globalization of Europe to changes caused by contact with the Far East. Something more than the desire for these products was needed before the leap overseas could be made, and this was also related to the interchanges between civilizations. From the medieval period, contact between the different civilizations of the Mediterranean produced a range of cultural and scientific exchanges (Abulafia 2011). The Iberian Peninsula being the crossroad of Christian, Arabic, and Jewish cultures, it brought together the most advanced forms of knowledge of the age in the fields of arithmetic, trigonometry, and cartography. This cross-cultural fertilization was crucial for expansion. The knowledge acquired by the Mallorcan school of cartography; the science that was transmitted from the *Fenix de las Maravillas del Mundo*, written in 1268 by Ramón Lull; and the expertise of the Mallorcan Jew Abraham Cresques, among others, would pass to Lisbon, which at the time benefited from an effervescent intellectual atmosphere thanks to the enthusiasm of Henry the Navigator and a brilliant group of marine adventurers, Christopher Columbus among them. The cross-fertilization of ideas that flourished in Iberia resulted in developments such as the translation into Latin of the Ptolemy's *Geographia*; the progress made in the representation of meridian and parallel lines; the use of the compass and, shortly afterwards, of the astrolabe, which meant that it was easier to check and correct routes at sea; and the use of the Iberian caravel, a creative hybrid that mixed the advantages of the Northern and Southern European ship types.[1] Even inventions such as the printing press, of Chinese origin, helped to reduce the chances of error in the reproduction of maps (Bagrow 1964, pp. 65 and ff.). From the fourteenth century, Europe appropriated another Chinese invention, gunpowder, thus acquiring the military capability necessary to undertake its expansion.

The so-called rise of the West, which is often considered a unique phenomenon in human history, can be overrated. It was not an exceptional event. The world had lived through similar processes at other times—for example, in classical Rome, in the steppes of Mongolia—and on many occasions. Indeed, something similar was happening at the time. From the medieval period, Arab merchants had been systematically extending their reach into North Africa and towards South East Asia. From 'Asia Minor', the Ottomans expanded into the Maghreb and the Balkans (Casale 2010). Even in the sixteenth and seventeenth centuries, European expansion, always identified with the Atlantic navigation routes, had its counterweight in the extension of Moscow's territories towards the Ukraine and the Orient (Céspedes 1990; Kennedy 1988, Chap. 1; Darwin 2008, pp. 118–25). These processes were important, not only because they provide a relativist perspective that challenges the historical exceptionalism with which the history of Europe is sometimes viewed but also because they created the communication networks that made the old continent's expansion a step towards globalization.

So how, in this context of expansion, did Iberians venture into the Atlantic? An extraordinary array of resources available to the Portuguese and Castilians led to their voyages of discovery along the coastlines of Africa. Moreover, these ventures were also the result of local forces that connected to global developments.

Portugal's Atlantic vocation only began during the fourteenth-century crisis. It is not surprising, therefore, that the first significant leap from the Iberian coastlines, the natural frontier of these kingdoms, should have led to the conquest of Ceuta (1415). The Portuguese were seeking an entrepot much as they would in Ormuz or Macao more than a century later (Thomaz 1994, p. 23). Overseas expansion also entailed a way of continuing the *Reconquista*, which had transformed itself into a means of reproduction and social development in this society. Some historians have

---

[1] For the cartographical improvements, see Bagrow (1964, pp. 65–107). On the techniques of navigation, Chaunu (1977).

understood, therefore, that although these explorers were searching for wheat fishing banks and other primary materials (Godinho 1969), the true reason for their expansion cannot be found in the need for foodstuffs, as Portugal's population had been practically stagnant since the Black Death. (Thomaz 1994, p. 17; Mattoso 1997, p. 327).[2] Nor could early overseas expansion have been the enterprise of a nascent bourgeoisie taking its first commercial steps. Rather, above all else it entailed a way of giving free rein to the expansive needs of the nobility and the internal conflict that it was generating within Portuguese society during this period (Thomaz 1994, p. 27 and *passim*). This line of action, which remained important until the adventure launched from Ceuta that cost the life of King Sebastian (1578), would be completed with the exploration of the Saharan coasts and the Atlantic islands. To this end there existed incentives linked not only to local forces but also to globalization itself, such as the need for African gold and the desire to secure it directly, thus cutting out intermediaries, the Saharan traffickers; this option was ever more important as general prices were falling and so the purchasing power of gold was rising (Vilar 1969; Godinho 1969).

The phases of this expansion are well known, and there is no point in setting them out again here.[3] Often presented as private enterprises—and even as having a non-Portuguese component—Portuguese expansion would quickly assume a handful of definitive characteristics. It was frequently marked by a system of *razias* (very common during the *Reconquista* and based fundamentally upon piracy and raiding) in search of slaves, gold, malaguetta pepper, and other products. As was often the case in imperial ventures of the day, these *razias* were usually undertaken in the hope of securing concessions and privileges from the king who, from an early stage, reserved the so-called right of conquest and taxes levied on general commerce for himself. Moreover, at the same time, a peculiar phenomenon emerged—the 'merchant state' (Thomaz 1994). That is to say, the king assumed the role of trading directly and—it almost goes without saying—claimed for himself the monopoly over gold deposits, such as those of San Jorge da Mina. Moreover, if the monarch often offered concessions to trade, conquer or raid from points on the coast, from 1469

---

[2] This having been said, Thomaz proposes a close correlation between immigration from the north eastern zone of the country, the most highly populated, and the repopulation of the Atlantic islands (1994, p. 17).

[3] See Godinho (1969), Parry (1990, Chap. 6), and Chaunu (1977).

he also proceeded to lease royal rights to merchants. In this way he broke with the system that depended upon concessions to *fidalgos*, nobles in general, *escudeiros*, and adventurers who had not always been born in Portugal (Thomaz 1994, p. 137). This was a system that sought to externalize the costs of the enterprise to the king and addressed the difficulty of mobilizing human resources that were very limited but, at the same time, created many problems of control for the Crown.

The outcome would be a society of few ties or links that would seek stability by conceding advantages to the *casados*, that is, those men who contracted matrimony and settled down more or less definitively overseas. It was also one that intensively tested the social codes of the metropolis—above all else it challenged the traditional frontier between merchants and nobles, who were often all corsairs—and began a process of intermingling with local societies that would give rise to figures such as the famous *lançados*, armed men who undertook pillaging operations, usually by travelling on the great rivers (Disney 2009, vol. II, pp. 51–2). These groups came to exercise an enormous power of mediation between the metropolis and the local tribes, particularly with regard to commerce and piracy.

This rather unstructured system did not, however, prevent the formation of a genuine framework tying together the different points of this empire. Moreover, from the middle of the century, commerce began to impose itself upon the various raiding activities, to which it was, in any case, very closely related. By then, the Portuguese had arrived at Cape Verde and, thanks to the autonomy of navigation that the caravel bestowed upon them, were pressing ahead with the colonization of the Azores (Disney 2009, vol. II, pp. 32–3, 92–3). Indeed, on these islands they had begun to expand the cultivation of sugar cane, a luxury product in this period and a symbol of social distinction (Mintz 1986), as well as the production of wine in Madeira and other products in the different areas of the archipelago. These same forces built upon themselves: sugar further increased the need for slaves (Lisbon was an active market from the very beginning), who could be captured in the conquered territories or elsewhere along the African coastline, thus feeding the plantations and further strengthening the momentum towards exploration and conquest. At the same time, the increasing supply of gold fostered the development of trade in the area and also in Portugal, as well as stimulated commerce between Portugal and Europe. It has often been pointed out that products exported to the *feitorias* (enclaves for trade and military actions) did not constitute a large volume of commerce. Nevertheless, these exports, however limited, stimulated the trade in goods from Europe and, above all, Morocco; this situation particularly ensued with respect to the wealthier *feitorias* like San Jorge da Mina (Disney 2009, vol. II, pp. 60–1). By 1475 hopes were growing that Africa could be circumnavigated and Asia reached by sea (Thomaz 1994, pp. 142–5).

By this juncture—after 1478 and a long period in which the adventurers' actions were the norm—the Castilians controlled the Canary Islands and, with Genoese financial backing, began to extend the cultivation of sugar. As in other episodes of this age, this expansion responded to global stimuli and employed financial and technical resources with a markedly transnational component. In 1492, and above all thanks to Portugal, the Atlantic was opening up and becoming a dangerous but promising theatre of action for the Iberian peoples: its currents and winds were known; the economy which would later come to characterize it had begun to take shape; people, animals, and plants were now circulating among its seas and islands (Russell-Wood 1992). And the sea passage to Asia was open.

Towards a European Poly-nuclear Recovery

European Recovery and Property Rights

A large number of explanations have been advanced for Europe's economic recovery. During the last decades of the twentieth century, a debate took place that showcased unilateral explanations such as those of Postan (Malthusian), Wallerstein (Marxist with an accent on relations of commercial dependence), and Guy Bois or Brenner (also Marxist, with emphasis on the relations of production). All offered important insights.[4] Yet the most plausible general explanation should not only encompass a combination of them but also include the effects of institutional transformations and the evolution of agrarian property rights. The recovery, in any case, was based upon regional processes of different rhythms and intensities that only in their second phase created synergies sufficient to constitute a general phenomenon across the whole of Europe.

It was logical that from a very early stage, Lisbon, Seville, or Guadalquivir Valley, all of them linked to Atlantic commerce, should experience rapid growth. Toulouse, involved in the trade of *pastel* dyes since 1430 and also

[4] See Postan (1966), Bois (1976), Wallerstein (1979), and Brenner (1993).

connected to international trade, experienced significant expansion. In northern Italy the profits from this new commerce were invested in agricultural improvements and urban economies, such as those of Florence or Genoa, which expanded between 1444 and 1460 (Goldthwaite 1980, p. 33; Heers 1961, pp. 504–5). However, many other regions experienced serious problems. Immersed in the Hundred Years War, Normandy's agrarian production fell intermittently until 1450, while its commerce suffered 'alternative phases of depression and recovery'. Breton commerce went through a similar pattern of boom and bust, and Catalonia, ever more marginalized from the main maritime artery that ran from Genoa to Mallorca, Valencia, and Granada, could not react.[5] The Hundred Years War affected the volume of traffic in the English Channel, the very sea that was destined to serve as the great artery of European trade from the second half of the fifteenth century. The precariousness of the emergent fiscal systems forced governments to finance these wars by manipulating their currencies, thus provoking more uncertainties for commerce. Above all else Europe desperately needed more money. Specie was now required not only for long-distance commerce but also for more modest operations, even if in effect this meant using 'black money', copper coins of low value (Spufford 1988). In such a situation, monetary instability entailed negative consequences. Furthermore, the elites' demand for goods from the Orient provoked a continual drainage of metals away from Europe, the result of which was a serious monetary deficit that was impossible to overcome through the established channels of securing gold and silver.

From 1460 to 1470, a pattern of expansion can be discerned, although this was not yet a general one. Nevertheless, regional circuits had begun connecting to each other more firmly. Fear of social uprising had led to a highly sophisticated system for supplying food in many European cities, something which was also positive for growth. The agrarian multi-activity (domestic industry, the muleteer trade, local or low-scale peddling, etc.), and crop-diversification (i.e. the cultivation of products for the market combined with those destined for self-consumption), widened the spectrum of resources available to the peasantry, thus advancing demographic and economic recovery. As a result of these and other changes, in France

[5] On Normandy, see Bois (1976, pp. 63–4, 117–22) and Mollat (1952, p. 542). On Brittany, Touchard (1967, pp. 377–8); for Catalonia, Vilar (1962, vol. I, pp. 419–20).

the proportion of children per family rose from 1:1 in 1350–1410 to 1:4 in 1440–1510 (Neveux et al. 1975, p. 140).

Are we facing a situation of lower seigniorial pressure upon agrarian activities leading to an improving standard of living for the peasantry, as set out by G. Bois many years ago (1976)? It is probable that a change along these lines did occur in many areas. But the factors behind this situation were more complex than the French historian allowed. In addition to the burden of the rents and seigniorial taxes, the peasantry also faced new demands made by the monarchy, whose fiscal system was increasingly developed and effective in many regions. Moreover, landlords' incomes were also subject to a logic of extensive increase because of the foundation of new estates, which meant that the pressure fell on an increasing number of peasant families. And yet, notwithstanding these observations, we might also consider a series of factors which Bois did not contemplate and which might even lead us to strengthen his overall interpretation. The growth of seigniorial demands upon an ever-increasing number of vassals and peasants frequently affected a rural population that had been, until this point, free of seigniorial charges. Therefore, these new extractions perhaps had fewer detrimental effects, at least in the short term. Furthermore, if landlords and royal tax collectors now demanded to be paid in coin, then this encouraged the commercialization of agrarian products by the peasantry as a means of obtaining the cash needed to pay these new extractions. It must also have given impetus to the rural manufactures and their commercialization as well as to the transport systems—especially the carting sector. Additionally, there were many great nobles who actively sought to attract trade fairs and weekly markets to their domains as a source of income and, therefore, a means of sponsoring commercial and industrial activities.[6]

In this context the opening up of the German silver mines provoked a 'pre-revolution' of prices (Braudel and Spooner 1967). But, what could be the importance of a factor that affected only a marginal aspect of the economy of the time, such as prices and the circulation of high-quality specie? In reality, the flow of money acted in the context of an incipient urban network that would be decisive in providing dynamism to crucial zones of overland trade, such as those of the imperial territories. From this moment the Rhine artery served for the diffusion of English and Flemish textiles into the markets of central Europe. The valley of the Rhone and

[6]For Castile, see Ladero (1994) and Yun (1987). For England, Wilson (1959).

the fairs of Lyon served to unite Northern and Central Europe with the south of France and Catalonia, where Germans sought light dyes and saffron. The Central European region also developed, as German industries (fabrics, copper, and iron) expanded into Silesia and Bohemia.

This network gave rise to a system of fairs based upon centres such as Lyon, Nuremberg, Frankfurt, Vienna, or Krakow, which were also connected with the Brabant region, Castile, and Flanders (Pach 1968, pp. 310–1). The heart of Europe was recovering thanks to this more fluid overland commerce, and this energizing circuit was completed after the conclusion of the Hundred Years War (1453) and the pacification of Castile (1479), dragging in its wake goods such as Castilian wool, Ibizan salt, Biscayan iron, and the wines of Oporto. This trade brought the North Sea into closer contact with the Mediterranean (Childs 1978).

Europe witnessed the birth of a new model of economic expansion, one which had its roots in a closer linking of the peasant economies with the market; a broader spectrum of productive activities; a more fluid and better-organized overland commerce, which was completed by the inter-linking of decisive circuits of maritime trade; and the overall advances in the sophistication and security of international commerce as well as the mental apparatus and horizons of Europeans.

This expansion cannot be explained by subordinate economic relation-ships between the distinct regions. The European recovery appears in principle to be better explained by the model of poly-nuclear growth set out by H. Van der Wee (1990) or J. Israel (1990), than by a system of hierarchical relations, as Wallerstein suggested some time ago (1979).

The Iberian Peninsula
This broad tide had a dramatic impact upon the Iberian Peninsula, where growth was not delayed once the different forces began to combine and reinforce a series of arteries binding internal commerce with the zones of the coastal areas.

The Atlantic areas were, by now, exhibiting signs of incipient dyna-mism. In Andalusia, from the fifteenth century, the flow of Sudanese gold towards the coast of North Africa had attracted the Genoese who, pushed forward by their fierce rivalry with the Venetians, had established themselves in Malaga, Cadiz, and, later, Seville. The presence of the Ottoman Turk in Asia Minor and the reduction of the production of sugar in Egypt left the market open to the Genoese, who expanded into Madeira and the Canary Islands. On the coastal estates of Huelva's local aristocrats in southern Castile, nobles such as the Medinasidonia and Niebla gained access to abundant African fisheries and the wheat of the Maghreb. The Canaries, conquered by Castile, served as a magnificent bridgehead from which to extend the cultivation of sugar cane (Fernández Armesto 1982, pp. 13–5). The abundance of available lands in the Guadalquivir Valley fed continual emigration from the north and advanced the formation of great noble estates producing food crops for the swelling cities. But the Andalusian axis was nothing more than a part of a line of expansion that had another pivot on the Portuguese coasts and, more concretely, in Lisbon. In this way a tendency was carried out that led to a greater dependency upon Castile's economy and society, and that would be the basis for Portugal's political neutrality (Thomaz 1994). Here contacts with Africa and the Canary Islands fed the slave trade, while the docks saw the arrival of unprecedented quantities of wood, peppers, sugar, gold, wine, and other products coming not only from Africa but also now from the Madeira islands and the Azores (Disney 2009, vol. II, pp. 84–93). Lisbon and Oporto were becoming the most dynamic parts of the Portuguese economy; the products that passed through these hubs were found, in increasing numbers, in Antwerp (Van der Wee 1963). The Atlantic front, running from Cadiz to Oporto, was establishing itself as more and more relevant to European patterns of trade. A key factor in all of this was the gold brought from the Sudan to Portugal, which also fed trade with the north of Europe and was crucial for the strengthening of the Atlantic front of the Old World. Not only Portugal but the whole Luso-Atlantic area would be now more closely linked to the north of Europe.

This vitality was equally discernible in the strength and vigour of the Cantabrian ports, which served as arteries connecting the north of Europe with the interior dynamism of Castile and the Duero Valley.[7] Castilian merchants were favoured by changes in the Flemish markets and by the production of new and lighter cloth of a high quality (Van der Wee 1988, pp. 329–36). This thriving commerce, reflected in the foundation of the *Universidad de Mercaderes*, a trade guild, and, in 1494, in the *Consulado de Burgos* (Consulate of Burgos), would be accompanied by the development of maritime insurance and the export of wool, salt, wine and Basque iron

---

[7] On the connections with Britany, see Touchard (1967). Childs (1978) studies the links with England and Munro (1973) stressed the positive effects on Castilian wool trade of the English protectionist bullion acts.

to satisfy the increasing demand generated by the European economy's recovery. It was also accompanied by an ever-growing trade in the import of fabrics, artwork, and luxury items from Flanders.[8]

The activation of Mediterranean trade was accompanied by a displacement of the commercial centre of gravity from Barcelona to the Mallorca-Valencia axis and the increasing presence of the Genoese in these areas. This network incorporated two trade routes: one came from the East and the Near East; another ran from Genoa to North Africa. But the expansion of Genoese interests into Castile and Portugal would also enhance the connections between the western Mediterranean and the north of Europe (Iradiel and Sarasa 1989, pp. 103–6).

These axes of expansion linked to international commerce converged in the Iberian inlands and were the basis for an impressive development of commerce and financial techniques on the peninsula. Furthermore, this part of Europe was a crossroad that necessarily saw its dynamism reinforced.

Institutions, Political Economies, and Regional Forces

From the fourteenth century, the demographic problems derived from the Black Death tied into difficulties originating from the involvement of the Iberian kingdoms in various phases of the Hundred Years War, as well as a series of internal conflicts which, in turn, became mixed up with factional disputes.[9] But if the problems had common roots, the responses, set out in the respective polities' institutional systems, underlie their different patterns of economic recovery.

It should not surprise us that *Portugal* should be one of the first territories to recover economically. The stability of its political system was a decisive contributing factor to this recuperation. But behind this phenomenon there stood the imperial expansion itself, which strengthened the king economically, as he controlled taxes paid by the Cortes, another stabilizing factor. The abundance of African gold afforded the Crown a greater degree of monetary availability and helped to avoid currency devaluation, thus providing security to domestic commerce (Thomaz 1994). But, above all, such an expansion offered an outlet for aristocratic tensions, reduced the degree of internal conflict, and afforded the chance to reduce the pressure

---

[8] Bilbao (1987, pp. 51–2); Van der Wee (1988, p. 330) Childs (1978, p. 89 and Chap. 4).

[9] For a synthesis of the political history of this period and the role of war, see Mackay (1980).

on peasants and vassals (Thomaz 1994). At this moment the new property systems were consolidated: these were based on *enfiteusis* (in which land was conferred by estates through long-term lease agreements) which offered good farming conditions to peasants. Moreover, the development of Atlantic trade favoured the growth of population centres between Galicia and Lisbon, with the riverside settlements—above all, those of the Tagus—also benefitting. This also improved the conditions for commercialization of peasant produce, some of whose goods (above all, wine) were henceforth exported to the north of Europe.

This process did not lead to the disappearance of differences between the more populated region to the north of the Tagus and the more sparsely populated areas to the south, towards the Algarve, which were also positively affected by the new commerce and enjoyed climates and soils that were kinder than those of the Alentejo. Moreover, this pattern was consistent with a certain difference originating in the respective institutional systems: to the north, the seigniors wielded enormous authority; in the large zone to the south of the Tagus, the great councils, sometimes under the domination of the Military Orders, shaped the society and institutions that regulated the assignment of resources (Mattoso 1997, pp. 528 and ff.). From 1450 population began to grow for the first time since the Black Death, and by around 1500 it had superseded its levels in 1348 (Mattoso 1997, p. 333). From this point the growing workforce helped to maintain the expansive rhythm of the noble economies.

According to the most common interpretation, in the Crown of *Castile*, the abundance of available lands after the demographic crisis served to strengthen the development of sheep and livestock breeding and, consequently, of an economy based upon wool exports.[10] This is, however, only part of the picture. The recovery would depend to a great degree upon the institutional framework and how it came to regulate the assignment of economic resources. A key development was the rise of a new fiscal system based on two types of taxes: the *tercias* (the two ninths of the tithe ceded by the Church to the Crown) and the *alcabala* (a local tax of Muslim origin set in theory at 10% of commercial transactions). The latter was conceded initially only as an annual service by the Cortes but became permanent without ever being formally renewed by them. Contrary to what would happen in the Crown of Aragon, the King of Castile retained a high degree of freedom of action over both the collection and use of taxes of this sort.

[10] This traditional view is set out in the classic study of Klein (1979).

It was one thing to create laws, consolidate royal jurisdictions, and obtain taxes yet quite another to ensure their enforcement, integrity, and collection. In fact, since the fourteenth century, and in a climate characterized by continual conflict, the Castilian sovereigns had found themselves forced to alienate the right to collect *tercias* and *alcabalas* to the nobility; they were also compelled to create new seigniorial estates as a means of maintaining clients in this group. Thus, the royal demesne, theoretically inalienable, was progressively reduced. To exacerbate this situation, the collection of royal taxes was not at all easy on the noble estates. As a result, by 1450 the economic basis of the new nobility had been established: large-scale livestock herding, landownership, and alienated royal incomes.[11] And this pattern was not only applicable to the aristocracy but also to the ecclesiastical institutions. Moreover, in exchange for their help, a few monarchs had ceded privileges, jurisdictions, and even royal taxes to the cities.[12] Thus, the cities' rights of lordship (urban *señorío*) and their control over common lands and privileges became more defined. As might have been expected, many of these privileges and sources of income were acquired by towns represented in the Cortes, and many of these were cities situated in the Duero and Guadalquivir Valleys. The development of this institutional system helped to shape the patterns of economic growth. Even when facing considerable geographical obstacles, the emergent urban networks served to advance the greater integration of large economic spaces. The consequent links and connections were visible in commercial routes which, in turn, fed into the larger international networks described above. From the coasts of Cantabria trade flowed down, invigorating the economy of the Duero Valley. From Seville, the arteries ascended up to Toledo, passing through Córdoba and La Mancha. The commerce of Lisbon would tie in with the fairs of Medina del Campo and the Duero regions and with the traffic of Seville in the Guadalquivir Valley. A multitude of annual fairs and weekly markets scattered throughout these regions served to tie the local economies with the international circuits. The strengthening of the cities facilitated the concentration of agrarian incomes in them, which in turn fed their economic activities and thus benefited a growing group of artisans and businessmen.

---

[11] Suárez (1975), Martínez Sopena (1977), Quintanilla (1979), Cabrera (1977), Mata (1987), Atienza (1987).

[12] Rucquoi (1987, vol. I, pp. 293–310), Diago (1993, pp. 181–206), Sánchez (1989), Jara (2000).

The other side of Castile's institutional development—the strengthening of the seigniorial estates of the nobility and the Church—would also have positive effects for economic growth. The emigration of peasants towards the south obliged many landowners of the northern Meseta to try to retain their population; to this end they ceded the right to use extensive tracts of land to rural communities, a trend which would increase agrarian output. The possession of *alcabalas* and *tercias*, as well as the privileges to stage markets and fairs, redoubled the interest of the aristocracy in sponsoring trade and in settling populations in their lands. In Andalusia, the great estates situated near important urban centres took advantage of a more regular pattern of commercialization and benefited from the arrival of a workforce and the growing urban demand (Collantes 1977).

In addition to the increasing production of cereals, wine, olive oil, and other products, economic expansion was evident but the livestock economy. In the case of sheep, production was organized into local and regional guilds or unions (*mestas*), as well as in the great association called the Honourable Council of the Mesta (Bishko 1978). Economic growth took place in the industrial and commercial sectors. With regard to the first, change was evident in the potential of the urban guilds but also in the emergence in some areas of a rural and urban cycle often controlled by a merchant-businessman (a real *verlager*, in many senses). The flowering of these commercial and financial activities was evident in many cities. Burgos and Seville are the best known examples (Pike 1978; Casado 1987).

The evolution would be subtly different in the Crowns of *Navarre* and *Aragon*. The repopulation formulas applied there were similar to those of Castile and had given rise to the emergence, next to the feudal nobility, of towns with well-defined seigniorial jurisdictions and diverse ethnic and religious populations. But these regions' emergence from the crisis had been different, and some institutional variations are visible.

Navarre had been hemmed in between France, Castile, and Aragon, three of the most powerful political formations of the period, a fact that reduced its opportunities for overcoming the crisis through territorial expansion. Only a policy aimed at ensuring diplomatic equilibrium among its three neighbours—and, above all, between Castile and France—allowed the kingdom of Navarre to survive as an independent political entity until 1515. As a result of this inherent limitation, the fiscal capacity of the kingdom was lower. As in Castile, the *alcabalas* were appropriated by the high nobility (Usunáriz 1997, p. 71). But the difficulties in increasing the yield of these taxes limited the scope for the extension of the nobles' incomes, a trend which redoubled the conflict between the different factions of the kingdom, in which the nobility played an important part.

The territories of the Crown of Aragon (the kingdoms of Aragon, Mallorca, and Valencia and the principality of Catalonia) also displayed marked differences to those of Castile. The Cortes were characterized by a system of a balance of power between king and kingdom that was much more formalized institutionally than in Castile. These assemblies' greatest strength lay in their capacity to pass legislation and the fact that they were convened periodically and as separate assemblies representing the kingdoms or, as was the case in Catalonia, the principality. As in Castile, the royal patrimony had been exhausted, above all in Aragon. But the power of the Cortes and the Delegations of the Cortes (*Diputació*) would impose noticeable limitations on the monarchy's capacity to create an independent and efficient fiscal system. A good deal of royal income would come from the monarch's negotiations with cities such as Zaragoza, Barcelona, Valencia, or Palma de Mallorca to obtain cash advances in exchange for royal privileges, financed through the sale of municipal bonds (*censals*). These procedures would restrict the possibility of conferring royal incomes upon the nobility in the way that had occurred in Castile and led the Aragonese nobility to overcome the crisis by reinforcing its jurisdictional rights and its capacity to change the legal framework in the Cortes. In the kingdoms of Aragon and Valencia, the large size of the *Morisco* (originally Islamic) communities and their social weakness allowed landlords to increase peasant servitude and the duties on family production.[13] But the Christian vassals were not to escape the demands of the nobility either, as a good part of its income was based upon monopolies, tithes, and 'various other forms of payment and taxation, but always very high ones'. Likewise the landlord retained important privileges of precedence in the sale of products, which, in markets that were less developed than those of Castile, also had a negative effect on peasant commercialization of any surplus (Lacarra 1972, pp. 135–6, 175).

The effects of this institutional framework in shaping models of economic growth in the Crowns of Navarre and Aragon were obvious. As in nearly all of Europe, the very favourable relation between population and available land created adequate conditions for expansion. But formal

---

[13] The Cortes of 1423, 1436, and 1461 renewed the landlords' 'right to mistreat' their vassals and consecrated their judicial autonomy, which became the crucial part of the agreement between king and kingdom in some areas (Iradiel and Sarasa 1989, p. 648).

political institutions would shape the different patterns of development and the distinct political economies of each kingdom.

The strip of land that encompasses today's regions of Navarre and Aragon was perhaps the least dynamic in economic terms. In both territories the urban network was less developed or depended too heavily upon the macrocephaly of Zaragoza, around which it gravitated. The new aristocracies were not as active as their Castilian counterparts in promoting commerce, due to their incomes depending less heavily upon it. Agriculture had a number of strong points. A *Morisco* agriculture existed, often based upon irrigation systems and exhibiting high levels of productivity. The extension of the *enfiteusis* system fed peasant commercialization. But, in contrast to Castile, the payment of land rents in proportion to production, as well as the landlord's monopolies upon the sale of agrarian products, limited peasant commercialization and the chances of developing an agrarian and population growth cycle similar to that of Castile. The urban network was less dense in Navarre and Aragon than in Castile. This fact, together with a trade pattern based upon exports by major merchants of commodities obtained by leasing seigniorial rents, reduced the positive effects of commerce upon producers. Economic growth was palpable, and symptoms of improvement can be perceived in the living conditions of peasants and in the expansion of the livestock economy (Laliena 1987). But these areas' demographic and productive dynamism lagged behind that of Castile.

From the point of view of its resource endowment, Catalonia was one of the peninsula's areas with the greatest economic potential. Nevertheless, in Catalonia, an increase in the landlords' pressure upon vassals unleashed situations of social instability and had negative effects on economic growth even more serious than those of Castile. The issuing of municipal bonds diverted capital away from commercial development. The macrocephaly of Barcelona created provisioning problems and accentuated its dependence upon wheat imported by sea. This situation not only contributed to increase the city's debts due to the need to pay for foodstuffs but also encouraged the flight of money out of the principality and thus contributed to monetary instability. The shift of Genoese trade towards Valencia and Seville worsened the state of affairs. Moreover, as R. S. López and Vicens underlined years ago, Catalonia did not count upon a domestic market in its hinterland that would have allowed it to 'face the onslaught of the crisis' (Vicens Vives 1974, p. 213). The Catalan economy recovered, but the recession would last until the end of the fifteenth century.

In Valencia there existed the vestiges of serfdom—in particular this was true among the *Morisco* population—and a very solid pattern of seigniorial jurisdictions, even when set against the authority of king, had emerged as the solution to the problem of the maintenance of aristocratic power. As in the kingdom of Aragon, the relative autonomy guaranteed to the land-holders in the enforcement of the terms of contracts served as the basis for the collection of incomes derived from their lands. In addition to share cropping, the renting out of individual farms (by *enfiteusis*) and monopolies, as well as the *tercias*, constituted important parts of landlords' income. Some of these landlords, as was the case with the Gandía family, also received important incomes from sugar mills. As in Aragon, the crisis had helped to strengthen the position of a minority of well-off workers. The dimensions of the farms they owned were to increase, as did other factors or trends in their favour. But, above all, and in contrast to Aragon and Catalonia, the shift of international trade towards Valencia made it one of the peninsula's more important commercial and artisanal centres. With 70,000 inhabitants in 1480, its role as intermediary between the Mediterranean and the hinterlands of Castile and Aragon intensified, at the same time as its industrial base grew and expanded (to incorporate wool and silk textiles, paper, the printing press, and—of course—construction) (Furió 1995). In these circumstances a commercial agriculture developed which produced goods for both local markets and export. It was based on the direct commercialization of peasant production thanks in part to the favourable conditions created by the *enfiteusis*. Next to non-traded cultivation, the growth of market-oriented products such as sugar cane and the white mulberry tree (tied to the production of silk) also became stronger. This does not mean, however, that we can speak of a regional growth marked by harmony and balance. The capital's overwhelming demand for resources compelled the authority to source wheat from Castile and Sicily, and paying for these imports had to be met by the exportation of sugar and, above all, silk.

A similar combination of factors explains Mallorca's economic expansion. Even if a good part of the nobility had ploughed their investments into municipal debts, the crisis had favoured them by the formation of farmsteads of a considerable size which would give rise to a form of agriculture that was intensively commercialized and based upon a paid labour force, replacing obsolete and residual forms of slavery. As it became increasingly important to the Mediterranean trade systems thanks to the Genoese alliance, Mallorca appeared to have strengthened its (by now) traditional commerce with Africa and with areas of Italy and the Iberian Peninsula. In turn these links had positive consequences for its industry. Yet the Mallorca economy was a long way from being a balanced one. Exports seldom compensated for imports of Sicilian wheat and the acquisition of municipal bonds by Catalan merchants accentuated the flow of money out of the island.

SOCIAL CONFLICTS AND POLITICAL REGIMES

Aristocratic Lineages, Local Oligarchies, and Conflict

The great estates are preserved best by extending them, and since they cannot remain unchanged it is inevitable that they decline unless they are expanded.[14]

These were the words that an astute observer, don Pedro Pacheco, marquis of Villena and favourite of Henry IV of Castile (1424–1474), used to refer to a structural phenomenon in European societies of his time: the expansive logic of the aristocratic houses and estates. Several decades later, Nicolò Machiavelli devoted his *Il Principe* to the problem of the *stato* which had to be preserved (*conservato*) and often expanded in order to maintain the prince's status. This expansive dynamic was linked to the conflictive environment of the time, in which the only means of preserving bloodline, status, and prestige was through a continual struggle for power against peers. Events in France, and especially the process of the formation of great seigniorial estates, which were sometimes spread out or scattered over considerable distances, provide a good example of how families could accumulate new resources (Nassiet 2000). The Portuguese case (described above) provides further evidence of this dynamic. As in Castile, a crisis had emerged in the oldest aristocratic lineages (e.g. the Sousa) (Thomaz 1994, pp. 443, 458–9), but a new generation had emerged whose clashes would reach previously unseen proportions and would result in expansionist tensions.[15] If today's businesses live in a world of economic competition determined by market share and technological progress, the noble houses

---

[14] Del Pulgar, (1971, p. XIV).

[15] Mattoso (1997, p. 454) has pointed out that one of the keys of the noble houses' behaviour was their necessity to 'acrescentar' (expand) their dominions.

of the 1400s existed in a context of military-political conflict that drove them to expand their estates and to fight for political and economic resources. This was their way of avoiding extinction.

The historiography has also emphasized the political context, particularly the idea that in a highly fragmented institutional and jurisdictional system, maintaining status with respect to peers required violence, which therefore became normal. In this way, the political structure's main component, jurisdiction, overlapped with the lineages' internal conflicts. The study of these features of medieval societies shed new light on the dynamics of the epoch's political economy.

This expansionism was also rooted in the internal dynamics of the family and the lineage. Until well into the modern period, the seigniorial family had to live beneath the spectre of extinction. As in all classes wielding high disposable incomes in the ancien régime, birth rates were very high. But, at the same time, martial activities brought a high mortality rate, above all in sons, which resulted in a limited capacity for biological reproduction (Clark 2007). This having been said, it is now known that the need to guarantee masculine line of succession led to practices which markedly encouraged the birth rate, not only in regard to sex but also in the speed and frequency in the celebration of second nuptials. But, more important—and as happens in businesses today—the behaviour of these groups was determined by their perceptions and short-term anxieties and not by long-term statistics (which are of course the backbone of modern studies). It is known that many families found themselves having to provide new political and economic resources for their offspring, provisions made in the hope that they would live to inherit them. Quite frequently these arrangements were made during the childhood or even before the birth of a beneficiary. For these reasons there was, in the short term, a clear and recurring desire to ensure the expansion of estates and resources.[16]

The predominance of the extended family pattern among the aristocracy and the extension of its webs of kin solidarity towards distant relatives and social and political clients accentuated the desire to expand the patrimony as a way to satisfy the promotion of the collateral and secondary members of the lineage. The same effects drove the need to provide dowries and favourable marriage alliances for female members, who were also

---

[16] Many examples of these practices can be found in the collection of studies edited by Costa and Rodrigues (eds.) (2004).

crucial to the families' economic and political strategies. In the Iberian kingdoms, the institution of *mayorazgo* (entailed estate) or the *morgadio* in Portugal, aiming at preserving the patrimony intact for the eldest son, redoubled the desire to search for new estates with which to compensate second-born sons. These institutions also compelled families to pay higher dowries to facilitate favourable marriages or the entrance of daughters into the Church.[17] Lawsuits and disputes over rights of succession, a manifestation of this inner conflict, ate up increasing quantities of money and resources, thus feeding the need for more.[18] This dynamic within the ruling families unleashed friction for the control of areas of strategic importance.[19] Advances made in military techniques and fortifications, and the consequent increase in the cost of these technologies, reinforced the need for expansive policies (Cooper 1991, vol. I.1, pp. 83–6).

The political economy of the estates reinforced this outcome. The exercise of seigniorial power led to the cession of part of the seigniorial income to local forces or agents in order to cement alliances, thus enhancing the expansive logic of the estates and the conflict inherent in them. Increasingly widespread possessions led to greater monitoring and administration costs and so created a vicious cycle in the expansion of these estates.[20] Political and social competition entailed additional costs of legitimization and patronage, namely, expressions of cultural magnificence springing from the chivalric mentality displayed in concepts such as 'the life of fame' (*la vida de la fama*) and immortalized by the most cultured noble patrons, such as Jorge Manrique, in stunning works of art. This familial munificence also had to be manifested in artistic patronage and the foundation of religious establishments that could support relatives and clients within the household.[21] This spiral of escalating commitments, which reinforced the anxiety for expansion and the search for additional estates and resources, must have been quite common in this era. Around this time, another Castilian noble,

---

[17] Although from a later period, the dowry of 85,000 ducats that the *Almirante* of Castile paid to the Count of Benavente, setting this sum against his income, can be added to the previous example. *Osuna*, leg. 424, Archivo Histórico Nacional (hereafter AHN).

[18] See the case of the Mendoza family in Nader (1986, pp. 129–54).

[19] See the case of the conflict between the Stúñigas and Mendozas in Ladero (1982, p. 173).

[20] See the case of the Benavente and their need to multiply the number of administrative units (*mayordomías*) in *Osuna*, leg. 424. AHN.

[21] See Cabrera (1977, pp. 325–30) or the testament of the Duchess of Alburquerque in 1476 in *Diversos de Castilla*, leg. 37, n. 36, s.f. Archivo General de Simancas (hereafter AGS). Yarza (1993).

don Gómez Manrique, expressed the 'agony' of the lords and monarchs due to the fact that 'the more land/they have in more dominions/the more immense agonies/they face night and day with payments and wars'.[22]

One of the main outcomes of this need to expand estates was the noble's quest to secure royal demesne and voracity for the usurpation of Crown taxes which, as we have seen, were essential components of the political confrontation. This would be crucial to political developments.

These trends coincided with two convergent features of late medieval societies: first, the urban patriciate's involvement in a similar dynamic of conflict and its predisposition for expansion; and second, the increasing importance of urban government for the reproduction of the patriciate's status.

One could state that there were demographic reasons for this first feature, if we consider the high index of family turnover within wealthy nonaristocratic groups in Old Regime Europe and the pressure or need that it created for the expansion of their own patrimony.[23] But this was especially true when they had evolved more towards noble forms and felt the same types of social pressures and constraints as the high nobility, which was a normal process in fifteenth-century Castile and Europe in general.[24] Moreover, the process of internal change that this group was experiencing was in itself a source of tensions and a catalyst for internal conflicts. Though a uniform model of evolution never existed, the cases of Valladolid, Guadalajara, Segovia, and Córdoba offer good examples. Here the patriciate families lived in a state of permanent internal tension that very often superimposed itself upon aristocratic and dynastic rivalries and was also intimately linked to family or clientele strategies as well as to the need to increase their political and symbolic power within the *ayuntamientos* (town halls). The entrance of the Jewish *converso* families into the ranks of the patrician elite certainly did not smooth over these clashes but rather created new disputes.[25]

But this was just a part of the story. The strengthening of the towns and cities as they acted as agents for the *Reconquista* and the emergence of this

---

[22] 'Cuanto mayores tierras/tienen en más señoríos,/más inmensas agonías/sostienen noches e días con libranças e con guerras/'.

[23] This is the main argument of Clark (2007), which, as we will explain below, is taken here in a different way. The material and visual culture of the period, of which Memling's portrait of a merchant family is a good example, is very expressive in this respect.

[24] In the case of Castile, this social ascension was materialized in what Suárez (1975) called the formation of a 'new nobility'.

[25] See examples in Rucquoi (1987, vol. II, pp. 189–213), and Yun (1980).

urban elite had led to the growing importance of the urban *señorío* and the *ayuntamientos* as spaces of power and political action, as well as their serving as key factors for the preservation of the political and economic capital of the oligarchies and the middling nobility. Thus, the expansion and preservation of the urban *señorío* and its privileges also became the spigot for the patriciate's political conflicts with the big landlords and the king. Underpinning those conflicts, there was also a line of political thinking according to which the king's main obligation was the defence of the royal demesne and patrimony, including the taxes (principally the *alcabalas*) voted by the Cortes and paid mainly by the cities. This idea also explains the continuing protests made by the cities in the Cortes against the alienation of the demesne as well as their bargaining with the Crown over their eventual support for the concession of political and economic privileges in exchange of voting new services (Haliczer 1981). No doubt, this political position by the cities implied a contradiction of great impact and significance, in that the patriciate families were often allied with particular aristocratic households but collectively opposed their interests before the Crown. But this situation would also open up one of the most important lines of conflict until the end of the sixteenth century (Chap. 4).

A dynamic of this sort was not only the result of the needs of the great lay lords and the urban patriciate. It was also derived from the growth of ecclesiastical institutions. In order to understand this, it is necessary to consider that the church hierarchy was an institution in itself—with its own dynamic but also subject to specific interest groups—and, at the same time, a safety valve for tensions originating in the heart of the aristocracy and the urban elites. A large number of individuals from both groups entered into the great ecclesiastical institutions and through them, and their extraordinary influence, contributed not only to the reproduction of the interests of the different families but also to smooth over their own conflicts (see also Chaps. 4 and 5). The result was a high degree of tension: first, because, as we have seen, the need to support these institutions through donations further increased the basic imperative that drove forward both the patricians and aristocrats; and, second, because church institutions expanded not only by receiving donations but also by purchases or usurpations,[26] which clashed with the expansion of the noble estates and threatened the royal demesne, contributing in this way to cities' uneasiness (Cabrera 1977, pp. 140–72; Owens 1980, 2005).

---

[26] Gavilán (1986, pp. 185–225), Mata (1987, vol. I, pp. 145–71), Pérez-Embid (1986, pp. 371 and ff.).

A similar process was taking place in many rural communities where, at the same time as a system of power based upon the *concejo*, the peasant community, was being set in place, a group of well-off peasants was able to establish itself and to grow progressively stronger. From the *remensas*, the elite of the peasant society of Catalonia, to the Castilian *labradores* (a sort of yeomen) who enjoyed a strong degree of representation in the village town halls, this group extended its capacity for political action both within rural communities and beyond them. Its political activities were mainly directed to protecting the collective rights of communities, which of course guaranteed the *concejo* significant privileges or advantages. The importance of the right to use the communal village fields, in conjunction with the significant extension of these common lands in this period, bound these well-off peasants to the rest of the peasantry. At the same time, this defence of the commons also became the main reason for conflict with the landlords, who usurped these resources in spite of the specific alliances that they often established with the well-off peasants.

To complete this portrait, it has also been said that the growing dynamism of both urban and agrarian societies led to friction in the heart of the cities and mid-ranking towns. The gap between a highly dynamic minority on the one hand and the artisans and the overflow population of low-skilled or unskilled workers on the other created conditions ripe for uprisings. Above all this was the case in the populous cities of the south, such as Córdoba and Seville, and in centres such as Valencia, Barcelona, or Zaragoza. As we shall see, tensions resulted in conflicts involving accusations of ethnic or religious impurity; they also led to struggles between rival groups and lineages that challenged the traditions of coexistence and gave vent to popular demands manifested more or less explicitly (Mackay 1972).

Isabella and Fernando: From Crisis to War and Expansion

Bargaining Power

These tensions became more evident from the middle of the century when Henry IV (1425–1474) applied an erratic policy in Castile. Known as 'Henry of the Favours' (*Enrique de las Mercedes*), on account of his efforts to win over the high nobility by conceding taxes and parts of the realm, he also attempted to deal with the claims by the Cortes, taking measures to balance out the situation by introducing the so-called *tasa de señoríos*.[27] Yet these measures proved largely inadequate, and the king had to initiate a policy of monetary devaluation. The outcome was a reaction by the nobles, whose incomes in cash were depreciated, and the cities, whose commerce was adversely affected (Mackay 1981, pp. 87–104). He was also unable to control local revolts. In the cities of Andalusia and Galicia, a series of conflicts between urban or rural noble factions exploded and even paved the way to more radical peasant protests, leading the authorities to unite to suffocate the rebellion (Valdeón 1975, p. 171). Complaints about the usurpation of royal patrimony led to uprisings in many of the towns (Haliczer 1981).

In the Crown of Aragon, the tensions became very evident during the reign of John II (1398–1479). In Catalonia the rebellion of the *remensa* peasants, infuriated by the efforts of the landlords to overcome their problems by resurrecting the old feudal rights, superimposed itself upon the pre-existing conflict between the urban factions of Barcelona. Here, the tension was between the so-called *Busca*, mainly artisans, and the *Biga*, composed of members of the patriciate, financiers, and those whose incomes derived from the city's debts (*censals*). The former were in favour of a protectionist policy and monetary devaluation that ensured the competitiveness of their goods in the international markets. The latter were inclined to call for monetary stability, hoping to retain the value of their *censals*. Conflicts within the nobility and the patriciate were also seen in Zaragoza, Teruel, Huesca, Mallorca, and Valencia, where different factions locked horns to secure a slice of the available political and economic resources. In Navarre the tensions between different factions with a pronounced noble character (the *beamonteses* and the *agramonteses*) took the form of an authentic civil war that pitted prince Charles of Viana against his father, John II of Aragon.

Traditional historiography usually considers the marriage of Isabella and Ferdinand as a turning point in this process, the outcome of which was political order. Probably it was. Yet the 'Catholic monarchs' were not able to impose an unrestricted form of absolutism, as has sometimes been suggested. Political stability was rather the outcome of social transactions and bargaining with the elites.

---

[27] The 'tasa de señoríos', often considered a concession to the nobility on the grounds that the king acknowledged the landlords' right to collect the *alcabalas* within their *señoríos*, was in fact a mutual concession between king and nobles (Yun 2004, p. 62) See also *Nueva Recopilación*, lib. IX, tit. XV, f. 93 v.

Isabella and Ferdinand's arrival on the throne was the result of a long period of political instability and a civil war. By this juncture a sector of the aristocracy had taken to the idea that the only way out of the near-permanent chaos that threatened the established order was a strong monarchy. There were sound political reasons for this conclusion, but economic ones were also important. The civil war in Castile had demonstrated to many members of the elite the need for a strong monarchy that guaranteed the political and fiscal system (Haliczer 1975, 1981, pp. 56–8; Perez 1989). The same could be said of the Catalan nobility and the elites of Barcelona, who were ever more convinced of the need for the king's arbitration. Castilian cities were at this point convinced that they had to 'subordinate their own ambitions to the conservation of the "power and union of the royal crown"'.[28] The movement of the *Hermandades,* coalitions or 'brotherhoods' of cities that signed pacts for mutual defence, reflected the need for domestic pacification.

For these reasons the ability of the Crown to push through reforms depended upon a policy of negotiation and bargaining which was often twofold. In Castile the creation of the Royal Council consolidated the power of the king over the nobility. But this same council continued to protect the corporate jurisdictions of the nobles, Church, and cities. The creation of the regional courts, the *Audiencias* and the *Chancillerías* strengthened the superiority of the king's justice over the landlords' private jurisdictions. But, crucially, the lay and church estates retained their courts, and they continued, therefore, to exercise their power of enforcement as first instance courts. The reform of the Castilian fiscal system was also highly significant. In the Cortes of 1476, the kings managed to obtain a huge service, but they were again reminded of their duty to preserve the integrity of both the realm and royal taxes. The consequence was a series of measures aimed at the closer control of the royal debt and at limiting any further usurpation or donation of the royal patrimony.[29] These measures culminated in 1480 when the *juro*'s interest rates (paid by the Crown) were decreed and orders were given that all those who had

---

[28] González Alonso (1988, p. 254). This idea was made very clear in the reminder of the Cortes of Ocaña (1469) to the king that he was obliged to rule and keep peace in the kingdom. *Patronato Real,* 69, doc. 18. AGS. The idea was also very prominent in Castilian politics, as similar notions were expressed in the Cortes of 1455, ibid., 69, doc. 14, fol. 14. AGS.

[29] All grandees of the kingdom were obliged to swear that they would never usurp the royal patrimony, and it was also decided to limit the grants and concessions given by the kings (*Nueva Recopilación,* Lib. IX, Tit. VIII, ley XV and Lib. V, Tít. X ley III).

received or usurped the royal demesne since 1464 had to return it.[30] But, at the same time, this policy was a long way from proposing a complete break with the nobility or the erosion of its institutional and economic power. The application of these measures was done in a very selective way depending on the families involved. Moreover, acceptance of the restoration of the royal patrimony provided the nobility a means of consolidating part of its achievements over the previous decades, at the time that the kings increased their incomes and improved their means of collection while the cities achieved a political success that they could exhibit before the eyes of the kingdom.

The same was true in Catalonia. Here the uprisings that followed the Cortes of 1481 convinced Ferdinand that the only means of proceeding was through agreement. The so-called Sentence of Guadalupe (1486) recognized the right of the landlords to maintain their leasehold upon the land (*dominio eminente*) and jurisdictional control over their estates, thus guaranteeing them part of their income. But the same Sentence also recognized the freedom of the peasantry and abolished the landlords' so-called bad practices. Overall this measure resolved the conflict by benefitting the landlords and more powerful peasants and recognized the social changes that had occurred over the previous centuries at the expenses of the lower peasantry (Vilar 1962, vol. I, p. 509). Ferdinand was not, therefore, a liberator king who subjugated the nobility to the benefit of the peasants: rather he played the role of an arbiter who guarantied existing social relationships. Something similar happened in the kingdom of Aragon, where the Sentence of Celada (1497) consecrated the power of the landlords, recognizing their privileges and power to the detriment of the rights of the peasantry.

Royal policy with regard to cities was also double-edged. The kings employed all available means to increase their control over them. The institution of the *corregidor*, an official representing the king in the town councils, became a permanent feature of the political landscape and the Crown put in place a series of reforms aimed at limiting the involvement of the great nobility and restricting the penetration of local government by noble clienteles (Lunenfeld 1987). The intervention of the Crown was aimed at the appointment of skilled personnel to town and city offices, which was also a way to increase its power for arbitration among local factions (Belenguer 1976, pp. 197–201; Amelang 1986, p. 41). During most of the

[30] *Patronato Real*, Libro 15, AGS.

reign, the *alcabalas* were collected through their being rented out, a measure that demonstrated royal authority and exasperated local oligarchies who complained that it frequently resulted in excessive collections.[31] The *Santa Hermandad*, based on the model of the urban *hermandades*, was converted into an instrument under the ever more direct control of the monarchs (Lunenfeld 1987, pp. 47–9). But on the other hand, the cities and their oligarchies retained a high degree of autonomy. For this reason peace brought with it a sudden deluge of confirmations of city and town privileges.[32] Many *corregidores* fell into the subtle but complex networks of local factions, rivalries, and solidarities, and the power and influence of many aristocrats upon urban clientele networks were notable in big cities such as Córdoba, Seville, and Murcia, and others, particularly in the South. In the Crown of Aragon—and not only there—the overall consequence of these reforms was the strengthening of the oligarchies and of the direct channels of communication between the monarchy and the cities, something which served to strengthen both of them and allowed them to bypass the Cortes, which often were too slow and unwieldy in this regard.[33] In Castile the farming out of tax collection was to be selectively and gradually replaced by the *encabezamientos* of cities, a system by which the tax collection was ceded to the local councils which, therefore, gained fiscal autonomy. This system was destined to constitute one of the cornerstones of both the political system and of the patterns of economic behaviour over the coming decades (Chap. 4). All of this came accompanied by a strengthening of the power of the municipal authorities in the management and regulation of guilds and corporations, as is showed by the case of Cuenca (Iradiel 1974, pp. 86–97).

Foreign Wars for Domestic Peace

As important, if not more so, for political stability was the war against the *Nazarí* kingdom of Granada. The fact was perfectly understood at the time, to the extent that, as late as 1580, Jerónimo Zurita would write:

---

[31] See the case of Córdoba in *Actas Capitulares*, 12, 22 de mayo, 28 de junio, 5 de julio, Archivo Histórico Municipal de Córdoba (hereafter AHMC) and *Registro General del Sello*, julio 1506, s.f. AGS.

[32] *Registro General del Sello*, legs. 147501 to 147507 (from January to July 1475) *passim* AGS.

[33] See the case of Barcelona in Amelang (1986, pp. 41–2). In Zaragoza and Valencia, dialogue was crucial for the concession of subsidies paid by emitting more *censals* which were highly attractive to the patriciate (Belenguer 1976, p. 45).

> Princes ... should remember that this [domestic peace] can only be properly
> achieved by conquest and conflict, which have to be sustained perpetually for
> the glory and prosperity of their state and the growth of their dominions.[34]

With these words the chronicler and historian of the Crown of Aragon set down the expansive principle that Fernando del Pulgar had previously detected in many noble households. The difference was, of course, that Zurita was writing about the monarchy as a whole. What he possibly did not know was that this period—the conflicts that stretched from the War of Granada (1482–1492) to the arrival of Charles V in 1517—was to be decisive. Not only did this cycle of conflict, which continued with the Italian wars and the expansion into Africa, represent a key moment for the continuity and expansion of a seigniorial society. It would also be a key moment in the refinement of a theory about how to finance these wars and the role of the kingdom and of the king's patrimony to this end.

The effects of the war upon the relationship between the monarchy, the cities, the aristocracy, and the Church are difficult to exaggerate. The campaigning, in fact, began as a medieval conflict, with nobles and towns mobilizing troops and armed retinues and leading them on the battlefield. But this struggle also marks the beginning of the 'military revolution', the character and impact of which will be discussed below. Thus, in its last phase, the war would require unprecedented levels of expenditure, military technology, and manpower. It therefore presented the monarchy with what was to become the great problem facing the fiscal systems in the early modern period: the financing of a military apparatus that no longer was sustained purely by the nobility or the cities but rather depended upon a more sophisticated financial system and a more centralized logistical apparatus.

The immediate outcome was for the Crown to appeal to the *auxilium* of the nobility, consisting now not only of military assistance but also of the advancement of money, on the proviso that compensation would be made at the end of the war by the Crown's turning a blind eye to the taxes and lands usurped by the nobles. In this way, a system was established which kept some medieval features of the *auxilium* and subsequent royal

[34] Jerónimo Zurita, *Historia del rey don Hernando el Catolico: de las empresas y ligas de Italia*, Zaragoza, 1580, vol. 1, p. 5 (edition by A. Canellas López and revised by M. Canellas and A. López, Zaragoza, 1989, 6 vols.).

compensation. But this was done not only by conferring jurisdictions and feudal rights upon the nobles but also by recognizing the revenues and rights that they had misappropriated. With regard to the urban oligarchies, war presented a unique opportunity to establish a relationship of mutual commitment with the monarchy, thus opening the door to the possibility of the conferral of titles of nobility or even of estates in the new domains won in the fighting (Gerbert 1979).

The conflict also affected relations with the Church and led to the creation of new revenue streams. Preached as a crusade and in part financed by bulls sold and promoted in sermons by churchmen, it gave rise to the concession by Rome of two services that would continue after 1492, the 'crusade' (*cruzada*) and the 'tenth' or 'subsidy' (*décima* or *subsidio*). It is highly significant that, though they had to be negotiated with the Pope, both were beyond the control of the Cortes, meaning that they quickly became, in Ladero's words, 'the object of envy of the other European kings'. Moreover, to help finance the conflict, the Pope conceded to Ferdinand the title of Grand Master of the Military Orders and, with it, a basic source of patronage. This gave him the support of a nobility seeking to enjoy the estates and honours of these organizations. Thus, the war not only enhanced the alliance between the monarchy and Church but also led to new sources of income and patronage that 'overlapped with the previous one without replacing it' (Ladero 1973, pp. 238, 245) and that was at the free disposal of the Crown with no limit imposed by the Cortes.

The War of Granada was an episode in a much larger cycle of events, one which had already led to the conquest of the Canary Islands and which would also lead to the campaigns in North Africa. These conquests had a religious component but also were aimed at securing access to Africa's gold, slaves, and land, mainly for sugar production (Fernández-Armesto 1982). The outcome was, again, a reinforcement of the relations between the Crown, the nobility, the Church, and the towns. The former extended its domains. The Church again projected the conflict as a crusade, which brought it increasing economic and political resources and, in turn, justified the prolongation of the concession of the *tercias* to the Crown. The members of the urban patriciate found ways of achieving social and economic advancement in these campaigns. Accords were signed with the Genoese investors in sugar plantations, thus strengthening links to a group that was destined to serve as the financial nerve system of the empire.

This effort to project power abroad was extended from 1494 with involvement in the Italian Wars against France. Aimed at defending Aragonese interests, this conflict was in large part financed by Castilian funds and served as a way of testing the mettle of many second-born sons of the Castilian nobility. Thus the novelty in this cycle of war abroad lay not in its political or diplomatic consequences but rather in the justification for conflicts fought in distant lands whose purpose was not the defence of the kingdom of Castile itself nor the defence of Christendom. While the War of Granada was fully justified by the age-old duty of Christian kings to defend Christendom, the Italian campaigns did not appear to fall under the same umbrella. This difference was even more significant in that the wars of Italy were not at all cheap. Through them new military strategies led to long, expensive and exhausting conflicts (Hale 1985, pp. 48, 63).

A large part of the funds that paid for these campaigns came from the ecclesiastical subsidies and the *cruzada*. But one other important innovation emerged: now debts accumulated from contracts (*asientos*) for the payment of troops in Naples and Sicily, where in effect Aragonese interests were being defended, were being met with services voted by the Cortes of Castile. In other words, the cost of a conflict that was difficult to justify from a strictly religious perspective and went against constitutional principles established throughout Europe was being levied upon the kingdom of Castile (see Chap. 4). How were the wars of Italy helping to defend Castile or Christendom? Was the King of France really the enemy of Christendom?

The line of response to such questions was developed by Ferdinand himself, who in the text of the Holy League convened by the Pope expressed the notion that France was acting against the interest of Christendom, an argument that was to be repeated later on in the Cortes of 1512.[35] And a few years later, in 1515, the convocation of the Cortes once again turned on similar criteria and referred to the obligation to defend the Church of Rome, using ideas justified by a comparable conceptual framework. In this way, the war in Naples reinforced a series of inter-linked—but not always harmonious—interests and established an innovative line of argument that would be key to the political, institutional, and, therefore, economic evolution of Castile and, indeed, of Spain as a whole.

[35] *Patronato Real*, legs. 60, f.26 and 69, 49. AGS.

To recapitulate: Isabel and Fernando had arrived at a certain equilibrium—an unstable one, it is true, but an equilibrium nonetheless. Navigating through negotiations and pressures leading in different directions, they had succeeded in momentarily lessening the structural tensions within the elites. Their policies would result in different political systems. In Castile they had engineered one of relative fiscal centralization, with a certain capacity for obtaining funds from the Cortes. In Aragon, the fiscal system had evolved to a far lesser degree. War had been crucial in this process and had served to satisfy the expansive needs of the nobility, the urban patriciate, and, indeed, even the Church. But finally, it had not resolved the basic problem of the alienation of royal patrimony, and at the same time, it created a new series of tensions with the Cortes in Castile—the debate over the use of the taxes and services of the kingdom for campaigns which did not benefit it directly, a theme which would be central to subsequent Iberian history, as we shall see.

Portugal: The Bases for a Precocious and Enduring Political Stability

Between 1449, when the Crown managed to pacify the last concerted attempt at noble rebellion, and 1822, when Brazil was lost, Portugal lived the longest period of political stability enjoyed by any European country in the early modern period (Thomaz 1994, p. 131). This stability, largely due to the imperial regime, had some parallels in Castile. As we have just seen, this kingdom was not free from tensions similar—or even identical—to those seen in other polities of the time. Mattoso (1993, p. 459 and ff.) has even written that the coexistence of the nobility appears to have been based on the continuous discord. However, as in Castile, efforts had been made to channel existing tensions. From the end of the fifteenth century, the nobility's needs for social consolidation and extension started being satisfied by overseas campaigns initiated by the Crown and even by involvement in the Castilian wars on Granada (Thomaz 1994). At the same time, the Crown had made several attempts to satisfy the noble lineages' expansive tendencies by ceding possessions belonging to the royal demesne (Disney 2009, vol. I, pp. 132–40). But, above all, the involvement of many lineages in the imperial project had served to alleviate tensions; revealingly, many second-born sons—whose status was directly threatened by inheritance rules—were present in these wars of conquest (Thomaz 1994). To the extent that the empire was also a commercial venture, it also offered a considerable number of members of the urban classes ways to

satisfy their needs. The blurring of boundaries within the African ventures—
and, above all, in the colonies—served to dilute the frontier between these
groups, providing each with what it most desired: the merchants acquired
noble status, and the nobility obtained money and wealth. Portuguese
Atlantic expansion had thus served the same purposes as the War of
Granada, which it, in fact, predated.

In the overall Western European picture (see above), the Portuguese case
was also peculiar in certain regards. Here the 'domain state' continued to be
the outstanding feature of its development. A sizeable part of the Crown
lands was ceded and recovered in successive cycles, a process that created
tensions in the kingdom and its councils. But, much more important,
Atlantic expansion had allowed the amplification of this patrimony and
expanded the king's revenues. Around 1459, in response to the wars with
Castile, the Cortes had ceded to the king the *sisa* tax, very similar to the
Castilian *alcabala* and administered by the municipalities (Mattoso 1993,
pp. 521–4).[36] But colonial revenues allowed for the development of a fiscal
system that only demanded a limited commitment from the kingdom.

The result was a situation very similar to that of Castile, although some
important degrees of nuance are needed in our analysis. In these conditions, the monarch retained a high degree of power. This was consistent
with the efforts to strengthen royal justice (Mattoso 1997, p. 516). The
Cortes had become an integral part of the political system, but its advance
was less important in comparison with the situation in Castile, principally
because of the lesser development of the tax state in Portugal. This fact,
together with the expansion of foreign trade, helps to explain the very
limited evolution of the urban network and its polarization in Lisbon and
Oporto. The equilibrium between Crown and nobility was increasingly
obvious, even if the relationship was governed by tensions and periodic
concessions, above all after the series of crises and was periodically deepened by the temptation among the nobility to turn its loyalty towards the
Castilian monarch. The promulgation of the *Ley Mental* (1434), which
recognized that the seigniorial estates belonged in the final instance to the
king, who was periodically required to renew his conferral of them upon
the nobility, contributed to creating a difficult equilibrium but one which

---

[36] It is worthwhile underlining that one of the reasons for the cities believing that the king
was facing financial difficulties was not only his involvement in wars but also the concession
of his patrimony to the nobles.

led to overall stability. It is important to note that, in this context, the House of Braganza had distinguished itself and managed to be the exception to end-of-century attempts to recover parts of the royal patrimony that ceded over the previous decades (Disney 2009, vol. I, pp. 134–5). This reduced the gap with the ruling house of Avis and created a considerable distance between that family, the Braganza, and the rest of the *fidalguia*. But, in any case, the oppressive tendencies of the nobility towards its peasantry, if considerable, could be tempered, and, this being the case, it was possible to maintain forms of land cession and property rights similar to *enfiteusis*.

The resulting political economy would not lead to the disappearance of tensions which were, after all, structural. But it did create an institutional framework that was crucial to understanding the history of Portugal in the coming centuries. It is very revealing that, in contrast to other areas of the Iberian Peninsula, there were hardly any movements or protests resembling the *Comunidades* or *Germanías*.

IBERIAN STATE FORMATION IN EUROPEAN PERSPECTIVE

Comunidades *and* Germanías

The political equilibrium established by the Catholic Kings was broken by Isabella's death in 1504, and this rupture would unleash the *comunero* and the *agermanado* rebellions of the years 1519–1521.[37] These were not isolated events but rather sprang from constitutional problems that were present, in one form or another, across Europe. But, above all, they deserve to be considered from the perspective of the development and consolidation of the elites which have been mentioned previously, even if the historiography dedicated to them has almost always pointed in another direction.

The economic growth and the wars of the last decades of the fifteenth century alleviated the internal tensions. But these tensions, being structural in nature, had to manifest themselves in many ways. By 1500 it was again obvious that many aristocrats needed to expand their incomes and to obtain loans. They were involved in constant competition to secure revenues, sometimes even usurping the royal patrimony and the demesne

---

[37] For a detailed analysis of these movements, see Perez (1976) and Durán (1982).

lands held by the towns.[38] These abuses even provoked serious exchanges between the *corregidores* and the high nobility (Haliczer 1981, pp. 91–123). On many occasions struggles of this sort were extended into the cities through the noble clienteles and sometimes even involved the lowest social strata of the city.

In Castile, the instability was increased by the mounting burden of the monarchical apparatus, which had the same need to expand its income as did the nobility. These needs were aggravated by the campaigns in North Africa and the outbreak of war in Italy. Taking these factors into account, it is possible to explain not only the continual demands for the increase in taxes made on behalf of the Crown during the first decades of the century but also the resurgence among the cities of the doctrine stressing the absolute need to secure the restitution of royal patrimony.[39] In the Crown of Aragon, a similar increase in royal spending had led to a general rise in the 'services' (in effect, taxes) of cities such as Valencia, Barcelona, or Mallorca (Durán 1982).

Insofar as it had overseen an important phase of economic development, the reign of Ferdinand and Isabella had strengthened even further the tendency towards social change in some urban environments. Many cities had witnessed the strengthening of an urban elite formed not only by members of the lower nobility but also by merchants, lawyers, and university graduates, who were educated in a concept of legality which the monarchy itself sometimes failed to respect. Economic development had also reinforced a sector of artisans, a sort of middle class. But in all of these cities, the chasm between the rich and powerful on one side and the poor,

---

[38] See, for example, Aragon in Abadía (1998, p. 66) and some Castilians cases such as the Duke of the Infantado and the Count of Benavente in *Osuna*, leg. 410, exp. 58, and leg. 418, exp. 4, núm. 4; AHN. *Cámara de Castilla*, legs 3, f. 181 and 172, leg. 2, and others. AGS. On the usurpation of lands, see Cabrera (1977). For the particular case of Córdoba, see *Actas Capitulares*, 2 and 31 December 1518; 3 January 1519; 1 March and 27 April 1520; and 24 September 1522. AHMC. The fights between nobles were very well described by Corona (1958). For the Crown of Aragon, see Durán (1982), Serra (1988, pp. 49 and ff.), and Colás and Salas (1982, pp. 70–1).

[39] On her deathbed, Queen Isabella herself voiced her concern about the *alcabalas* that had not been reclaimed from the nobility (those of 'toleration or permission', as they would come to be known) and her desire for the rules of redemption set down in 1480 to be applied with rigour. *Patronato Real* (libros de copias) libro 18, ff. 192 v^a–194^a, AGS. The text is included in the famous *Cédula de Medina del Campo* of 24 November 1504. A complete version can also be found in *Nueva Recopilación*, Libro IV, titulo XV, ley, I.

vagabonds, and politically displaced on the other had grown alarmingly. This generated urban tensions which were often blended with anti-Jewish sentiments and actions and an increasing rejection of the *Morisco* minority (Yun 1980). All of these tensions contributed to an atmosphere of desperate millennialism that coincided with the strengthening of the theory that underlined the inalienability of the royal demesne and the need for collective action for the 'common good' and against tyranny (Maravall 1970, pp. 108–33).

Despite these similarities, the dynamic of the *Comunidades* and that of the *Germanías* was to be different.

The *Comunidades* of Castile reflected to a large degree the problems set out above. By 1520, the discontent expressed itself in demands for the reform of the fiscal system. But it was not only a question about the volume of taxes but also about their genesis and use. It is often forgotten that Charles V sought to claim services from the Cortes in order to pursue his dynastic and personal ambitions, something which, obviously, appeared to go against some crucial constitutional principles (Perez 1989, pp. 26, 33 and ff. and Chap. 4). On top of this came the dissatisfaction of the cities represented in the Cortes due to the interference of royal power in their affairs and the usurpation of the royal demesne over the previous years. Furthermore, many of the *alcabalas*, whose collection had been ceded to the cities since 1494, were again farmed out to the highest bidder, which provoked a storm of criticism not only from the urban elites but also from the lower ranks of craftsmen who had seen their taxes rise during a time of successive bad harvests and economic difficulties.

Moreover, Charles V had the dubious merit of radicalizing the discontent of the Cortes when, in 1518 and with the intention of attracting the nobility to him, he acknowledged the right of the 'great nobles and knights' to collect the *alcabalas* and sought to raise more taxes without attempting to reclaim a single square foot of the royal patrimony that had been usurped over the previous years. At the same time, his claim to be able to appoint foreigners to offices in the Castilian administration went not only against the interests of the nobility and the patriciate of the cities but also against the most deeply entrenched political principles of the time, while his absence from Castile could easily be interpreted as a separation between the king and his kingdom in the political sense—rather than in the physical one—of the term.

If these tensions provided the catalysts for rebellion, they were also extremely important in shaping events and the subsequent evolution of the conflicts. A rebellion that began with a certain aristocratic passivity quite quickly took a dramatic turn of events, with the popular mobilizations at municipal level, the creation of the *Junta*, a sort of council of towns, and a process of radicalization in both cities and countryside. During this initial phase, we see a divided aristocracy that, later on and with a few exceptions, quickly closed ranks when the rebellion assumed a markedly anti-seigniorial character (Gutiérrez Nieto 1973). But even this solidification of the nobility against the rebellion was marked by a certain reticence and hesitation, the intention being to prevent the king from triumphing immediately and to secure grants, favours, and reparations as rewards for their efforts on his behalf. We also see that the cities went as far as to organize an action in defence of the integrity of the 'kingdom' and were also clearly made nervous by the movement against the aristocracy, although they were carried along by the revolt and later revived their most trenchant criticisms of the nobility for its misappropriation of the royal patrimony. And, above all, we find that when the community, led by craftsmen and the urban middle class, became radical and conflicts began to emerge between cities, their urban estates, and their lands, and when the anti-landlord campaigns in the countryside became more virulent, the disquiet and unease began to spread among the very leaders of the *comuneros* themselves. These elites therefore acted against a movement that clearly threatened to subvert the established order—an order that they were not only duty-bound to defend but that it was also in their interests to protect.

The *comunero* movement might well have changed the balance of power and altered the course of history. In fact, when compared with the conflicts of the fifteenth century, what is surprising is the highly developed political theory espoused by its leaders. But, looking back at previous events, the eventual outcome cannot be said to have been a surprise: the great winner was the Crown, and the result was a new political equilibrium that consecrated the existing relationships of power and institutional systems. This would be decisive for the pattern of economic development.

The *Germanías* also revealed the basic problems of this society. The need to enlarge the incomes of the landowners had been manifested in the extension of the jurisdiction of the nobility and clergy. At the same time, in the absence of a fiscal apparatus as developed as that of Castile, the nobility had increasingly subscribed to the *censals* sold by the cities. The dynamic that it created had to be different to the one in Castile and, obviously, had to affect the physiognomy of the conflict in a different way (Durán 1982, p. 414). Industrial development—above all in Valencia and its surroundings—had reinforced the power of the artisans at a moment when municipal power was becoming increasingly elite in nature, thus creating a crucial tension. The coincidence of these factors with increasing fiscal demands paved the way for protest and a rebellion which invoked the need to sanitize public finances and to root out corruption in the administration.

This discontent coincided with rural upheavals against the landlords and was exacerbated by the effects of plague and the danger of attacks by pirates and bands of nobles. The wave of protest gave rise to several different movements in the areas around Valencia and Barcelona; Lerida and many other areas of Catalonia, as well as in the south of Aragon, were also affected. In these zones, where the municipal reforms begun by King Ferdinand were creating better conditions, the uprisings would take the form of violent but very localized episodes. In contrast, in the city of Valencia and in Mallorca, the movement of the *Germanías* would come close to being a genuine revolution. Here, the Council of the Thirteen, which basically represented the craftsmen, raised the flag of the *libertats* (freedom). Its programme aimed not only at municipal reform and the overhaul of the justice system, both of which, it was alleged, had become dominated by the gentlemen (*cavallers*), but also the re-establishment of the municipal patrimony on a healthy footing and the disappearance of the taxes created to deal with the accumulated debt.

All of this led to a revolutionary programme which had the Italian republics as its model and which also resulted in an attack upon the *Moriscos*, considered a pillar of the seigniorial machinery. The end came in the form of a seigniorial reaction that would crush the revolution. In Mallorca the diffusion of the movement into the rural areas appears to have been provoked by the demands of the *forans*, the rural population around the capital, to redistribute the payment of the taxes between the city and the surrounding countryside, which was also subject to these new impositions (Durán 1982, *passim*).

As with the *Comunidades*, the *Germanías* were the product of a society that had seen marked commercial growth and was searching for new formulas of political organization. Both led, essentially, to the same conclusion—the shoring up of the argument that the monarchy presented the solution to the problems of the time. However, to the extent that these were structural problems with very deep roots, neither conflict can be said to have been the solution to these difficulties but rather the clearest manifestation of them. They also presented, perhaps, a cause for reflection for the ruling groups in both kingdoms.

Western Monarchies. The Iberian Kingdoms in Comparative European Perspective

It is not difficult to recognize different models of political organization and institutional evolution in Western Europe around 1520. To a certain extent, all of the models can be seen as a means of overcoming the tensions of medieval societies, and all would leave their imprint on the political economies and, therefore, on the subsequent patterns of economic development of the different areas of the continent.

In *France* the monarchy was strengthened with a relatively efficient system for the mobilization of resources and as a result the Crown was capable of extending its patronage ties towards the ruling groups of society. The policy of territorial unification had led to the extension of the dominions of the king at the cost of the independent or semi-independent princes (Provence and Brittany, above all), at the same time that a new fiscal system had been established, developed, and linked to the needs of the army. Despite the complexity and territorial diversity of the system, a distinction can be made between direct taxes such as the *taille*, which fell on property, and indirect ones such as the *gabelles*, which were levied on the purchase of a handful of products. A large part of the tax collection system was, moreover, under the control of the *generaux des finances* and was controlled by the King's council.[40]

Yet a system of this sort was some way from serving as the basis for an unchallenged absolutism or a unified institutional system. Considerations of political theory and institutional framework compelled the Crown to enter into a series of pacts which were similar in form and scope to those of the Iberian Peninsula (see Chevalier 1994). The doctrine of Gallic Church, which protected the independence of the Church not only from the interference of the Pope but also from the meddling of the king and which had been consecrated in the Pragmatic Sanction of 1438, had set down the rules of this equilibrium. However, the king's ability to meddle in ecclesiastical patronage had increased considerably. The Concordat of 1516 had set down a new status quo with Rome. In this accord the Pope was freed of any theoretical subjection to conciliar authority, and the king increased his scope for patronage in the Church. The result would be an

[40] See Chevalier (1994). In 1524 Francis I created *Tresorier de l'Epargne* (1524), which would manage the incomes arriving to the central treasury and allocated financial administration to the *Conseil d'Etat*. More details in Wolfe (1972, pp. 86 and ff.).

ever greater involvement of the Church in the interests and programme of the Crown, which exercised its right to nominate clergy to benefices to favour the great families of the kingdom. The Gallic Church thus emerged as an institution in which the powers of the Crown on the theoretical and institutional levels were limited but which, in reality, was closely tied to the interests of the king.

Even more evident was the political and institutional *entente* with the urban patricians. The first step in understanding this must be to recognize that the authority of the king was not homogeneous. If he had ample powers in some areas, then in others—this was the case in Languedoc—the provincial estates not only voted the taxes, but they could also determine the form that they took; it was even quite usual for the collection of these revenues to be the responsibility of these local powers. From 1484 the King of France had to wrestle separately with this multitude of *états provinciales*, something which required considerable efforts and obliged him to make specific concessions from which the cities in general and the urban elites in particular often benefited. In addition, the sale of offices ended up creating another form of relationship (and balance) between the Crown and the urban elites, at the same time as the issuing of municipal *rentes*—debt bonds, very similar to *censales*—subscribed to in the majority of cases by the patricians increased their interests in the regular functioning of the fiscal-financial system which guaranteed them the collection of their yields.[41]

Nor were the high nobility alienated from the new political construction. As in Castile, the aristocracy had gained control of the collection of certain royal taxes during the reigns of Charles VI (1368–1422) and Charles VII (1403–1462); but, on the other hand, it was denied the right to collect the *taille* in many areas. This limitation did not deprive it, however, of the chance to profit from the process. Not only did the nobility consolidate its exemption from the payment of certain taxes, but very shortly it also converted itself into the principal beneficiary of the rafts of

---

[41] Russell Major spoke of 'an increase in popular participation in government' (1980, p. I), and B. Chevalier lucidly described the agreement between the king and the 'bonnes villes'. In his view the system was grounded on the king's respecting the autonomy of the cities when collecting taxes in exchange for cash advances. This system guaranteed the cash available to the king, lowered his tax collection costs, and reduced the jurisdictional conflicts. The cities, for their part, retained a part of the fiscal income and could shift the fiscal burden to the countryside (1987, pp. 144–9).

pensions and offices granted by the Crown; the payment of the salaries due to the holders of these positions depended, of course, on a healthy royal patrimony. From 1516, thanks to royal patronage, the great families also increased their presence in ecclesiastical offices. Given these developments, it is not surprising that historiography, led by the work of Russell Major (1981), has rejected the idea, proposed by M. Bloch, of the inexorable decline of the French aristocracy. The strength of the aristocrats is even more clear if we consider that, in addition to the extraordinary revenues derived from the Crown, many high nobles were able to increase their regular or ordinary incomes and to manage successfully their private patrimonies and estates.

As in many areas of Castile and Portugal, this interlinking of mutual interests at the summit of the monarchy would confer stability upon the political system and, therefore, support the established social order. The reinforcing of the rural community, the increasing economic power of a peasantry that had diversified its sources of income as it emerged from the crisis, and the formation of a peasant elite which found itself caught between the preservation of the forms of local government and an alliance with the great landlords halted the process of deterioration of rural society (Neveux et al. 1975, pp. 134–55).

Though things were quite different in *England*, a few determined early steps had also been made towards the process of political centralization. Whereas in France the Parliament (*États généraux*) had been unable to transcend regional interests, from a very early stage, the monarchy of England was required to form a relationship with its Parliament that represented 'the community of the kingdom'. But this difference did not imply that in England there had been a greater development of the kingdom as a fiscal unit nor that new and undreamt of possibilities now lay before the king, his high nobility, leading clergy, or urban *rentiers*.

The English Crown had maintained the greater part of its demesne estates and patrimony. Moreover, the incorporation into the Crown of the estates of extinguished noble families during the Wars of the Roses and the reorganization of the royal lands by Henry VII (1485–1509) served to keep it intact as a provider of considerable sources of income. At the same time, the lands of the Crown could be used as a fountain of royal patronage through their temporary cession to the nobility. However, the chances of exploiting the fiscal system of the kingdom and the development of the tax system were much smaller than in France or Castile. The king could recur to subsidies granted by Parliament, but these had to be approved and renewed by the assembly and were even controlled by it through its capacity to oversee the collection and use of these monies. In reality, in the fifteenth century, the financial resources of the Crown were comparatively meagre. Aside from the monies collected from the royal estates, its regular permanent revenues depended upon tolls and other impositions of a feudal type which did not provide the quantities—nor anything like them— that were collected in Castile through the *alcabalas* or in Portugal through the *sisas* and the empire (Russell 1988, pp. 31–8).

At the same time, the main forum for political relations between the king and the kingdom was Parliament. This had been the case since the time of the war with France. More than simply a gathering of delegates representing different cities and their urban patriciates, the House of Commons represented the kingdom as a whole. Given the very low level of development of the jurisdictional and fiscal functions of the cities and their relatively minor demographic importance, their relationship—direct or indirect—with the Crown was much less decisive for the political equilibrium of the kingdom than was the case in France or Castile. In the last instance, Parliament cannot be described as a gathering of deputies who were dependent upon and controlled by their respective local oligarchies but rather a group that made little or no effort to seek to increase the privileges of the municipalities. Although the political equilibrium and the reproduction of the social system depended to a large extent on the bilateral relationships that bound the king to the aristocracy, gentry, and Church, these relations were catalysed largely through Parliament. If Westminster was to see its political role diminished during the reign of Henry VII (1457–1509), the impact of this relationship upon the model of overcoming the medieval crisis was already established.

All of this created a situation that was subtly different from that of France. If, thanks to the improvements in the management of the Crown lands, the King of England had increased his chances of using patronage to control the nobility, then the limited character of this type of transaction (which, in any case, was not easily extended over time), the control of Parliament over a large portion of other royal finances and the very limited development of the royal bureaucracy—without doubt, England represented a much less evolved form of tax state than did Castile or France—made it very difficult for the monarchy to subsidize the nobility in a systematic and generous way. At least it could not do so to the point that the needs of this group were met during the fifteenth century (Dyer 1989, p. 47). It is very probable that this situation had been one of the causes of the attack launched by the English aristocracy upon the peasant and communal village economies in some parts of the countryside and whose most obvious manifestation lay in the enclosure of communal lands. The figures presented by R. Allen demonstrate that these enclosures were especially intense towards 1524. At the heart of all of these changes lay the fact that, in distinction to Castile and France, the English rural community had never developed its military powers.

From the perspectives of the kingdoms of France and England, the peculiarities of the Iberian Peninsula may be seen in a clearer light.

The parallels are obvious. As has been emphasized, the case of Castile offers some noticeable similarities with France. In both kingdoms relatively strong fiscal systems were emerging and would allow for a certain degree of royal autonomy (with the limitations that we will see). These fiscal systems also became a way to nurture aristocratic incomes.

But, even then, the differences between Castile and France were noticeable. In France these transfers to the nobility consisted mainly in the appointment to offices and the concession of temporary or lifetime grants. In Castile the contemporary equivalent was the *encomienda* of the military orders and the offices in the army and administration. But the lion's share of these transfers consisted in the more or less legal cession of *alcabalas*, *tercias*, and parts of the royal patrimony, which provided the nobility with a permanent and regular source of income. Thus, the economic bases of the Castilian aristocracy were to be even stronger than those of their French counterparts, and part of the agreement's renewal would consist in a pact of silence regarding the rents that had not in fact been given by the Crown but simply usurped by the nobles—and which were, therefore, of dubious legality in the eyes of the Cortes. (See Chap. 4 below.)

At the same time, the case of Castile goes against a certain number of the ideas set out a few years ago on the role of these extraordinary incomes as a mechanism that reduced the pressure of the landlords on the peasantry. Without doubt, these revenues and concessions did have this function at certain moments, but the history of Castile until (at least) 1520 demonstrates that access to the royal fiscal system did not prevent the nobles from trying to extend their lands by assuming control or ownership of soils belonging to communities or the royal estates themselves. In other words, the aristocrats sought revenues from additional sources.

Comparison of the models of the different polities of the Crown of Aragon and the kingdom of Navarre invites a number of observations. Looked at as fiscal systems, the similarities with England and, therefore, the differences from France and Castile are clear. In none of these kingdoms did the monarchy succeed in establishing a fiscal system that was as accessible (and as easily manipulated) and developed as was the case in France or Castile. In these polities, as in England, the most important source of income that the kingdom offered its ruler (the 'subsidies' of one kingdom; the 'services' of another) could not be alienated or conferred upon the aristocracy or could only be done so with considerable difficulty. Pensions and offices offered the best and, indeed, almost the only means of patronage and of overcoming the nobility's economic problems. But at the same time—and in contrast to the situation in England—the Crown of Aragon had established fiscal-financial relationships with a number of cities (above all Pamplona, Zaragoza, Barcelona, Valencia, and Palma de Mallorca) that clearly did provide the urban oligarchies with an additional source of income in the form of *censals*.

Nor can the relationships between landlords in these kingdoms and their vassals be easily identified with those of England. In all of these areas, the effort to overcome the difficulties faced by the nobility had been expressed in the pressure applied upon vassals and lands. But the results would be very different from what is usually referred to (although often debated) for England. In the kingdom of Aragon and, in certain respects, in Valencia, the power of the nobility would be directed not only towards the acquisition of additional land but also—and mainly—to deepening its existing rights of jurisdiction and even forms of forced labour, something which in turn was favoured by the presence and numerical importance of a *Morisco* minority, which was seriously disadvantaged in terms of its rights and legal conditions. In Catalonia the tensions in the heart of the aristocracy were overcome thanks to formulas designed to provide the nobles access to the ecclesiastic tithe (*diezmo*) and that led them to share cropping. These revenues, in contrast to the English model based upon the extension of aristocratic properties, would provide the predominant type of rent available to these groups. They would constitute along with the *censals* and a number of incomes derived from royal offices, the nobles' most important source of income. At the same time, the Sentence of Guadalupe had made it as difficult for the principality to follow the Aragonese model as the English or the Castilian ones. This was because it had allowed a free peasantry to consolidate itself, liberated from many of the landlords' demands and among whom it was possible to find a rural elite with rights over the soils that it farmed, a feature which would serve to paralyse any attempt by the great families to accumulate territories by force. The case of Mallorca also has its own specific characteristics. Here the possession of *censals* would give the nobility in general a significant portion of the revenues extracted by the centralized fiscal system and the municipal financial apparatus. But, progressively, the agrarian relationships pivoted upon the formation of large latifundia whose effective control would be ceded in the form of 'posesions', an arrangement that would lead to a limit on the availability of lands for the lords and nobles (Jover 1997).

The differences and contrasts between Portugal, France, and England also deserve attention. In Portugal the royal financial system had begun to develop, as in France and Castile, and the kingdom was increasingly involved in a tax system of notable proportions. But the development of the empire, and the funds obtained from it, would progressively marginalize the importance of the kingdom's contribution. Thanks to the empire, the needs of social reproduction of the *fidalgos* had been given an outlet, and this would limit their interest in strengthening their jurisdiction or acquiring peasant property (this does not, obviously, mean that no incentives existed for these actions). The Portuguese imperial venture also led to an urban jurisdictional network that was weaker than its counterpart in Castile and in which only some cities such as Lisbon and Porto exercised considerable force and weight.

This overview of the very different political, institutional, and economic trajectories found in the history of Western Europe makes clear that the Iberian kingdoms did not present any exceptional or unique paradigm. On the other hand, it is evident that a number of models emerged, each subtly different, even if many common denominators can be found.

*   *   *

The Iberian kingdoms had been the great protagonists of the phase of globalization that initiated the 'rise' of the West. This was in part due to the convergence of global forces (the circulation of technical knowledge and previous commercial development) but can be explained above all by the action of forces and needs that were present across all of Europe and that would materialize in Iberia in a very specific way. The elite's need for consolidation and extension, and in particular the needs of the nobility, had been at the root of the first leap into the Atlantic and can be seen as little more than a continuation of previous actions and practices typical of the *Reconquista*. The involvement of the peninsula in ever-expanding commercial routes, allied to changes in the institutional system and property rights, had helped the economic recovery and brought about a certain relaxation of the tensions between the social classes. At the same time, important lines of tension were emerging: the fight for the royal demesne, the debate over the use of the kingdom's resources, and the importance of royal patronage, thanks to its increased ability to capture resources and consequent tensions over their use, were among the most important of these points of prospective conflict. In any case, and despite the difference between them, two exceptional powers—Castile and Portugal—were emerging, both driven by clear expansive vocations and able to nullify internal tensions as they established their respective empires. The different institutional patterns that would condition the political economies of the Iberian World were more or less consolidated by 1520.

Open Access This chapter is licensed under the terms of the Creative Commons Attribution 4.0 International License (http://creativecommons.org/licenses/by/4.0/), which permits use, sharing, adaptation, distribution and reproduction in any medium or format, as long as you give appropriate credit to the original author(s) and the source, provide a link to the Creative Commons licence and indicate if changes were made.

The images or other third party material in this chapter are included in the chapter's Creative Commons licence, unless indicated otherwise in a credit line to the material. If material is not included in the chapter's Creative Commons licence and your intended use is not permitted by statutory regulation or exceeds the permitted use, you will need to obtain permission directly from the copyright holder.

CHAPTER 2

Iberian Overseas Expansion and European Trade Networks

In 1526, Charles V married Isabel of Portugal. In doing so he put in place the groundwork for the dynastic union with the last of the peninsular kingdom to have escaped the gravitational pull of the Habsburgs. At this point the Portuguese and Castilians were involved in collaborations, entanglements, and conflicts stretching from Asia to America, thus forging the foundations of a global system. Clearly, this system was precocious and sophisticated, simultaneously partitioned and interconnected (Subrahmanyam 2007; Bethencourt 2013). In spite of that sophistication, paradoxically, this imperial experience has provided the basis of a very negative interpretation of the history of the Iberian Peninsula. According to this interpretation, oceanic expansion converted Iberia a 'semi-periphery' within Europe, serving simply as a conduit for the export of raw materials, some of them obtained from their colonies, to the north of Europe, while industrial products manufactured in the 'centre' of this emergent world economy—in other words, in the north of the old continent—would flow in the opposite direction (Frank 1978; Wallerstein 1979).

SAILING THE ATLANTIC, CONQUERING AMERICA

In 1492, the Spaniards made the leap into America. In 1497–1499 Vasco da Gama rounded the Cape of Good Hope and reached India. In 1520, Ferdinand Magellan sailed through the straight that would take his name,

B. Yun-Casalilla, *Iberian World Empires and the Globalization of Europe 1415–1668*, Palgrave Studies in Comparative Global History, https://doi.org/10.1007/978-981-13-0833-8_2

and following his death Juan Sebastian Elcano returned to Spain as the first man to circumnavigate the world (1522). What was behind these names? Columbus was not of Castilian origin: he was Genoese and had acquired much of his knowledge in Portugal. Magellan, sailing on behalf of Charles V, was in fact a subject of the King of Portugal. If these details are apparently superficial, they should not blind us to the fact that from the very beginning of the primitive globalization, these initiatives were the result of cross-border entanglements and patterns of knowledge that were profoundly interrelated.

Challenges and Tools

When in 1519 Cortés landed in Mexico and began to take an interest in this 'second America', the gold reserves of the Caribbean were nearing exhaustion. The following years would see the conquest of both Mexico and Peru, where the Spanish found extensive political formations that were overcome so rapidly that one historian has observed that by the 1540s the New World 'was already conquered, in so far as Spain would conquer it' (Davis 1976, p. 52). But the extraordinary speed of the conquest should not lead us to forget the problems posed by it and by the control of these vast new domains.

America was, perhaps, seen by many as a promise. But it presented, to all and sundry, a challenge of dimensions that were difficult to imagine. This most definitely was the case for Castile, which faced not only the challenge of conquest but also the struggle to control and to exploit American peoples and wealth.[1] America was a distant continent of vast, unimagined proportions, with ecological and geographical conditions ranging from deserts to rainforests. Europe's best sailors and cartographers took some time to represent a geographical reality that was, in the first instance, unfathomable. After the exhaustion of Caribbean gold reserves, Spain faced the problem that some of the riches that the Spaniards were seeking, such as Inca gold and silver, were found in particularly remote and inhospitable areas. This having been said, the richest areas would turn out to be

---

[1] A definitive study of the global impact of what could be called the 'globalisation of America' has yet to be written. This is not the place to undertake any such effort. Here we can only underline a number of the most important aspects of it for the purposes of this book.

just to the north (the Aztec confederation) and to the south (the Inca Empire) of the Caribbean Sea, which quickly emerged as the cornerstone of interactions with the Iberian Peninsula.

Geography and environmental systems imposed serious constraints upon communication. Dependence upon the winds and the ocean currents led to long stationary periods during voyages and caused lengthy delays in travel across the oceans. Even after a communication system was organized, Chaunu has calculated that a round trip between Andalusia and Mexico took some eighteen and a half months, of which only five were actually spent in sailing. In the first place, this posed a political problem due to the delays affecting orders and communication between the metropolis and the colonies (Chap. 7). But it also constituted a serious financial drawback, resulting in a long period in which capital would be immobilized, with the subsequent high costs for traders. In addition, given the unpredictability of the weather, the inevitable and long delays, and the need for security, vessels were loaded with as many foodstuffs, weapons, and ammunitions as possible. While these measures represented sensible planning, they proportionally decreased the voyages' overall profitability. The increase in the vessels' dimensions, moreover, would bring new problems when the convoys came to pass over the sandbars at the mouth of the Guadalquivir River. In effect, they were often forced to wait for high tides near the Cape of San Vicente, the area of maximum danger for corsair attack. These were some of the reasons why trade was skewered towards goods that were very expensive relative to their weight, such as gold, silver, or slaves, and made use of others, such as hides and leathers, as a kind of very low-cost ballast freight, whose function was to balance outgoing loads (Chaunu 1977, p. 45).

There were also problems of a more strictly social—or human—origin. The conquest and organization of territory were relatively rapid in the areas where extant political structures were more advanced. In this regard it was important that the Aztec confederation and Inca Empire were minimally centralized and that, with the fall of their centres of power, Spaniards took control of extensive and efficient networks apt for the ruling of their territories. But the limitations on the control of territory were very considerable across much of the continent, where there remained many tribal societies in inhospitable areas that were very difficult to access (and often, also, these were of relatively little interest to the *conquistadores*). In any case, the problem lay not only in conquering distant regions but also in maintaining them. This is to say that the question was how to mobilize resources—human and technical—for conquest or how to incentivize this process without relinquishing control of these territories. But it also concerned how to maintain a small group of colonists in situ among a population that dwarfed them.

Yet even where conquest had been achieved, it was not always easy or possible to exploit the available resources. As the Portuguese had exploited well-established trade routes in the Indian Ocean, the Castilians took advantage of extant tributary networks. However it was difficult to force the population to toil for its conquerors. Moreover, no labour market existed to provide a workforce. Of course, Indian institutions existed for the use of forced labour in return for the exchange of gifts and compensations (Menegus 1991). But to get these to function on the necessary scale was a major problem. The most sought-after resources in the initial phase—gold and silver—were not easy to obtain and posed technological problems. During the first phase, in fact, the progress in mining was based upon a 'mixing of European techniques and those inherited from the old settlers'. But towards 1550, and despite the abundance of mineral deposits, 'diminishing returns' started to make themselves felt (Sánchez 1989, vol. I, pp. 311–2) that could only be overcome by a technological leap forward. For silver mining this meant addressing the basic technical problem of mineral amalgamation. This had to be done with mercury, a product then available only in Europe and China, which obviously increased the final cost of production (Sánchez 1989, vol. I, p. 324). And these are only a few of the examples of the difficulties faced by these crucial sectors during the conquest.

The situation can be better understood if we also consider the shock that the discovery of this New World was provoking among Europeans. As is well known, the mere existence of America and its inhabitants compelled Europeans to reject the authority of traditional ideas and start to envisage reality from a platform provided by empirical observation (Elliott 1972), as would the later discoveries of Kepler and Galileo. Over the course of the sixteenth century, empirical observations would progress in auxiliary sciences such as botany and through the collection of words or the study of languages such as Quechua.

The encounter between different civilizations also affected the concept of the Indian and led to discussions about his status as a human being. On the one hand, for the first Dominicans, the Amerindian embodied an unblemished soul, the clean slate (*tabula rasa*) described by Aristotle upon which the values of the most pristine forms of Christianity might be inculcated. On the other hand, for the *conquistadores* the indigenous communities represented mostly an untapped reservoir of expendable labour. In this sense, the challenge lay not in the existence of a new reality that needed to be understood but rather that it produced an array of interpretations that were seized upon in competing fields of interest. In juridical circles controversies of this sort were very prominent in what Tomás y Valiente (1992) called the 'critical stage' between 1511, when the first voices were raised against the exploitation and even the enslavement of the Indian, and 1566, with the death of Bartolomé de las Casas, who had been the most resourceful and committed defender of the rights of the indigenous population.

These challenges notwithstanding, until very recently scholars have held that Castilian society was poorly equipped for this endeavour. In this light, the negative effects of the conquest were easily explained.[2] But Castile was in fact one of the areas of Europe best prepared for a challenge of these proportions. It boasted human capital and institutions well-suited to such a gigantic undertaking. It stood in the vanguard of navigational advances and had seen the emergence of advanced forms of military organization that some historians have considered to be a key element in Europe's unique historical trajectory (Hale 1985, Chap. 2). Financial techniques and institutions were already highly developed and would shortly be supplemented by the emergence or adoption of systems such as the Italian *commenda* and *compagnia*, crucial to any drive to accrue the capital necessary for the colonial adventure (Macalister 1984, p. 98). Castile boasted a multitude of foreign merchants, with Italians and, specifically, Genoese, keen to become involved in Seville.

In addition, the Iberian Peninsula harboured local institutions that for centuries had overseen campaigns of military expansion and colonization that were almost unique in Europe (with the exception of expansion eastward from Germany). The control of territory in the New World came to be based upon municipalities very similar to those that had been formed in the Iberian Peninsula during the *Reconquista*, with the establishment of the town council (the *cabildo*), the local by-laws (*ordenanzas*), the municipal district (*alfoz*), and the extensive communal estate over which the

---

[2] John Elliott (2006), however, has recently called our attention on the pioneering character of this Castilian enterprise and underlined that the English expansion into the New World involved a high degree of imitation of it. See also Cañizares-Esguerra (2006).

town would exercise its jealously guarded jurisdiction (Weckmann 1993). As civic ceremonies and rituals emphasized, all of these bodies or institutions served the king and his justice (Macalister 1984). In contrast to the later English programme, Iberian colonization was very much directed from above (Elliott 2006, pp. 117–9). After the first problems with Columbus alerted the Crown to the need for caution in order to avoid any relative loss of power, Castile would resort to pre-existing formulas, such as *capitulationes*, a type of accord between the king and a conqueror that maintained royal sovereignty in exchange for the governmental and economic concessions in recently discovered lands (Aram 2008; Carrasco and Céspedes 1985, p. 291).

As we have seen, the monarchy maintained a fiscal apparatus rivalled only by France. The creation of the Council of the Indies (1524) gave it a central body capable of directing and controlling—or attempting to control—the New World's political organization. Castile had also overseen the development of judicial institutions that would become basic to the regulation of social relations in the New World. The Castilian *Chancillerías* served as a model for the *Audiencias* responsible for the administration of justice in America, while the Aragonese viceroyalties provided a template for a political figure—the viceroy—who might be seen as a kind of 'alter ego' of the king in the overseas dominions. Both institutions increased the government's ability to regulate social life and territory and thus its coercive power. They operated thanks to a bureaucracy of lawyers trained in some of the Old World's best universities (themselves representative of one of the earliest and most impressive manifestations of the 'educational revolution' sweeping over the continent) and whose judgements and interpretations would lead to the emergence of the so-called *Derecho Indiano* (Indian Law), a pioneering effort to adjust Castilian legal traditions to the specific circumstances of the Indies (Tomás y Valiente 1992, pp. 325–45). This group of royal officials and interpreters of the laws of the kingdom together with the *alcaldes mayores* and the *corregidores*, the main authorities at the municipal level, exercised judicial and governing powers. At an early point, the Crown obtained from the Pope the right to nominate bishops (*derecho de presentación*) in the Indies. In fact, Rome had previously allowed the Crown to claim all tithes paid by its American subjects. In addition to providing the Crown significant revenues, these measures gave it a valuable source of patronage and offered it a high degree of control over what was to be one of the main pillars of the colonization—religion and religiosity.

At the same time, the problems in establishing a labour market were overcome through the *repartimientos de indios*, that is, the temporary distribution of Indians as a workforce for the colonizers, and the *encomienda*, which saw a certain number of Indians given to the colonists on a permanent basis, with the natives being obliged to pay tribute or work in exchange for protection and being taught the Christian religion. Moreover, ownership formulas that were common on the peninsula, such as the *mayorazgo*, entailed ecclesiastical property and others, gradually extended to the New World, where they would have an enormous impact on institutional frameworks and property rights (Coatsworth 2008).

The basic infrastructure for the control and processing of information in this vast empire and in the European territories took the form of the creation of central archives such as that of Simancas, maps and geographical accounts (*Relaciones geográficas*) or descriptions of territories, and *memoriales* or reports. This information gathering occurred on a scale never before seen (Parker 2001). In addition to these surveys describing the new continent, *visitas*, or traditional visits involving the dispatch of officials to oversee the control of the administration, were undertaken. *Juicios de residencia* were also commonly used to evaluate the performance of officials at the moment of their replacement. All of these measures constituted a governmental attempt to achieve self-sufficiency in obtaining one of the most expensive resources of the time, information (Brendecke 2012). The 1560s and 1570s witnessed a genuine offensive on this front, with law graduates (*letrados*) providing coherence to the American legal system. Or, at least, this was the intention (Rivero 2011). From 1569 to 1571, Juan de Ovando was charged with reforming the Council of the Indies, the organism overseeing and upholding the laws of the Indies, with the aim of giving it a more central role. Parallel to this reform, the government created notary offices (*escribanías*) to register contracts and thus contributed to the regulation of economic and social relationships, something which at least offered the possibility of reducing transaction costs or, more accurately given the starting point, of converting an unmeasurable degree of insecurity into a risk that could at least be assessed with some degree of precision.

Over the century the fiscal system slowly was implemented within the apparatus for the mobilization of American resources. The collection of taxes such as the *alcabalas* and levies on alum, snow, playing cards, salt, and other goods proceeded at rates similar to those on the peninsula. This system was based around a growing number of *cajas*, treasury districts, established in the more important cities (TePaske and Klein 1982). In addition, the system for the transfer of funds from one *caja* to another (the so-called *situados*) was advanced. This arrangement, in turn, would become vital for the defence of territories and, in contrast to what occurred in Europe, based its efficiency on the absence of political and jurisdictional barriers between the different regions (Marichal and Souto 1994; Marichal and von Grafenstein 2012). The system stretched as far as Manila (Alonso 2012).

A sophisticated convoy system was also organized, combining warships and commercial freighters, aiming to guarantee the Crown's commercial monopoly and to resist attacks of corsairs from countries such as England and, later, Holland. Based upon a delicate balance between geography, climate, technology, and human and nautical resources, this system was organized from the House of Trade (*Casa de la Contratación*) in Seville (1503) (Parry 1990, pp. 53–6; García-Baquero 1986, pp. 23–30). The convoys would become the basis of the *Carrera de Indias*, a description of which gives a clear idea of the high degree of sophistication often present in the colonial system (Map 2.1).[3]

---

[3] The system, as it began to be regulated during the 1560s, was as follows: each year Sanlúcar de Barrameda witnessed the departure of two fleets, one in May and the other in August; both sailed with armed protection and were loaded with wine, oil, textiles, luxuries, swords, books, grains, and other goods sought by a colonial elite with high purchasing power. Their voyages lasted between five and six weeks. The May fleet headed to Vera Cruz (Mexico) and the August convoy towards Nombre de Dios and, after 1597, Portobello (Panama), where they unloaded their cargoes and retired to overwinter in Cartagena de Indias. The outward journey was relatively easy, all things considered; the real problems lay in coordinating the return to Spain, which depended upon uniting in Havana at the beginning of summer, before the arrival of the hurricane season. The fleet from New Spain, loaded with silver, cochineal, and other products, could do this quite easily, even though it had to set sail from Vera Cruz in February so as to take advantage of the trade winds. Its voyage lasted three to four weeks. Problems were greater for the galleons that had to collect the silver coming from the mines of Potosí to Panama; here precision and timing were crucial, and the whole operation depended on the co-ordination of many linked factors. Ideally, the linking up would be achieved in March, so that it would be back in Havana before the hurricanes. But for this to occur, it was necessary that it should rain early in Bolivia—an uncommon occurrence—so that the mills could prepare the ore and melt the silver into ingots. When this process was accomplished, a long chain of llamas carried it down from Potosí to the port of Arica (15 days), where it was sent to Callao in Lima and then loaded and shipped, aboard special vessels, to Panama (20 days). From there it was transported on the backs of mules across the isthmus to Nombre de Dios or Portobello (at least four days travelling), where the fleet awaited it.

If this delicate mechanism of synchronicity and co-ordination worked, the fleets could reach the sandbar that accumulates at the mouth of the Guadalquivir in August (the best

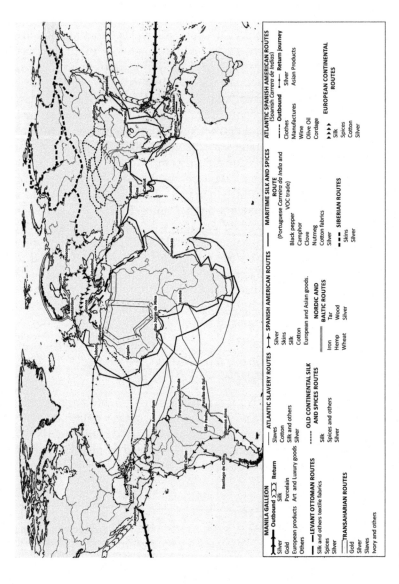

Map 2.1   Main commercial routes, c. 1640

The *Carrera de Indias* belies the old myth of Spain being a country with little organization or technological capacity; it also demonstrates the development of methods of observation and organization as a means of understanding nature, oceanic currents, and winds. This methodology was already evident in the process of oceanic expansion. But it developed even further thanks to the voyages and the foundation, in 1508, of the School of Pilots of Seville (Schäfer 2003). In this same period, medical doctors such as Monardes and theorists such as Arias Montano and Acosta would make a considerable contribution to the use of empirical observation as a means of understanding the New World (Aram and Yun 2014). New technologies in the mining sector would also be crucial. The exhaustion of ground-level deposits and the crisis in silver production based on the traditional smelting furnace were resolved by the development of a method for its amalgamation with mercury, which reduced costs and lessened the technological dependency on the peninsula, thanks to the exploitation of the mines of Huancavelica (Sánchez 1989, pp. 310–32). The Spanish empire was in reality a stage for scientific and technological development that barely resembled the pessimistic visions of it to which we have become accustomed (Barrera-Osorio 2006, pp. 6–12). This technical capacity quickly manifested itself in another series of advances that would have a marked effect upon the sixteenth century and ran from the use of animals such as mules to the introduction of sugar mills.

Political Control, Bargaining, Resistance, and Environmental Failures

Despite Iberian societies' extraordinary capacity to mobilize material, institutional, and human resources, the outcome would not be an American society that was tightly controlled from Castile. In the first place, the very means of financing the conquest led to forms of negotiation that would have an enormous impact upon the political economy of

---

time to cross it) and so enter into what was a very safe harbour. In fact the galleons often reached it between September and October and so were forced to wait for high tides or high river levels to overcome the bar; alternatively goods could be unloaded onto barges. This task was carried out near the Cape of San Vicente, the area of greatest danger for attacks from corsairs or pirates; this problem would be more common as the size of ships increased over the course of the second half of the sixteenth century.

Elliott (1990, pp. 41–3), on the basis of the reconstruction of Báncora (1959).

the colonies and the imperial system sensu lato (Chap. 7). Moreover, the conquest was a disaster and a failure in humanitarian, demographic, and ecological terms.

In distinction to modern empires of the nineteenth century, Iberia's sixteenth-century imperial enterprises were not paid for in economic currency dispatched from the metropolis or other colonies. Rather, they were financed through a multitude of accords made at the local level between the king and the conquerors and colonizers, including the religious orders. These negotiations had no jurisdictional framework as defined and formalized as in the composite monarchies of Europe, in which the cities, nobles, and Church exercised legal powers of coercion (Chap. 1). For reasons set out (above), the Crown took great care not to cede effective jurisdiction to private individuals. This has sometimes led to the impression that the government of America was based upon the unanswerable and absolute power of the king. Yet the very system of conquest, based on *capitulaciones* and general concessions of political rights and economic privileges by the Crown to the conquerors, created a form of *do ut des* and depended upon the exchange of privileges in the use of natural and political resources that from the very beginning nuanced the effective power of the king. What the conquistador—Columbus himself is the most evocative example—received was the recognition of his 'privileges' to use resources or to govern in return for his extending the dominions and resources of the king. The *encomiendas* and *repartimientos* of Indians also implied this type of transaction. Both were based on the Crown's ceding of tributary advantages or the use of a workforce in return for colonization. From this basis sprang the later problems faced by the monarchy in revising the conditions it had set down for the first *conquistadores*, as did the settlers' subsequent revolts and obstructionism, both of which were fully justified from their point of view. The empire was built on an exchange between the Crown, which saved the most precious of all resources—money—by conferring political and social capital, and the effective capacity for enforcement upon the colonists. This was done, however, on the grounds of the preservation of royal jurisdiction and the creation of formal institutions of government that were, in appearance, at least, dependent upon the king.

A process of this sort did not avoid permanent conflicts. An attempt to institute reforms in 1542 known as the *Leyes Nuevas* provoked settlers' rebellions. The policy on *encomiendas*, for instance, the suppression of vacant ones, triggered considerable resistance among their holders. In Peru things went as far as open conflict in 1544. It proved possible to avoid this outcome in New Spain thanks to the necessary adjustment being made in time, but in 1564 a new wave of discontent broke out and led the rebels to name the son of Cortés as their legitimate king.

The other step to the articulation of dominion, the relations between colonials and Amerindians, led to more than one flare-up and resulted in armed uprisings. As early as 1536, this difficult relationship led to the Peruvian rebellion of Manco Cápac, giving vent to forms of dissent that would last until 1572 and would lead to the foundation of the independent kingdom of Vilcabamba and the spread of millenarian beliefs that encouraged resistance. Attitudes were, clearly, changing. In this period, 'rebels' not only learnt to fight against horses by constructing pits or throwing balls at their legs but also, according to the account of Titu Cusi, son of Manco himself, reinforced their old religious beliefs by identifying the Christian deity as a false God consisting of nothing more than painted cloth and clearly bettered by the visible gods—the Sun and the Moon—who communicated with their people. The emergence, from 1564, of the religious movement of the Taqui Ongo was consistent with these developments and with the traditional cyclical conception of history. This programme assumed a messianic character and announced the resurrection of Pachacamac and a victorious revolution against the Spaniards. These beliefs would become so enduring and deep-rooted that they would resurface in the eighteenth century. The same could be said of the forms of frontier resistance, such as that of the *araucanos* (in today's Chile, and which lasted until the nineteenth century and displayed a remarkable degree of military adaptability), and uprisings in the humid zone of Mexico, among the Chichimeca, who would never in fact be conquered. Indeed, it has even been argued that 'the entire colonial history is marked by resistance and revolts' (Bennassar 1980, pp. 221–52).

In the midst of such unrest, the *encomenderos* certainly became progressively stronger and created the conditions for political bargaining with the Crown on a new basis. The demographic crisis, leaving huge unpopulated spaces, provided the *encomenderos* with a pretext to dominate peoples and to control their land. Some *encomenderos* proclaimed themselves owners of the possessions—principally the land—of greatly diminished or entirely absent communities. By the middle of century, 'much of the Mexican plateau had fallen into the hands of a few wealthy individuals' (Davis 1976, p. 57). In areas devoted to mining, which held such enormous interest for the Crown, the needs for labour led to similar processes and changes. With the demographic recession and technological innovations, mining became a high-cost activity that relatively few settlers could afford to enter. These developments were accompanied by a remarkable effort by the merchants of Lima and the ecclesiastical institutions to finance mining operations, making efforts that were decisive in providing liquid funds for a key sector of the colonial economy. Such developments cemented in place another important facet of the relationship between the monarchy and its subjects, the basis of which was a flexible application of the law and which allowed the Crown to claim its share—the 'royal fifth'—of production. This 'accord' would prove to be the basis of the great cycle of American silver flowing onto the peninsula between 1550 and 1600–1610. If it wanted to make the Indies a source of income, the Crown had to facilitate the work of these merchants and ecclesiastics. Its relationship with them, if usually marked by tensions, was always based upon reciprocal and mutual need.

The understanding between local authorities and the Crown was reflected in the decentralization of the *Derecho Indiano*, something which even permitted the survival of indigenous laws and customs. Common to all of these developments was recourse to the long-established Castilian tradition of 'obeying but not complying' with the law, a custom used by the municipal councils of many cities as a way to 'oppose the authoritarianism of the King and his officials' (Tomás y Valiente 1992, pp. 337–41).

This mixture of pressure, resistance, and asymmetric transaction was also clear in the process of the religious acculturation of the indigenous population—and, indeed, in the limits to this process. Anthropologists have shown that the efforts to change the culture and mental world of the Indians had certain limits, in large part because of the syncretic nature of many religious beliefs. As the case of the Maya makes clear, the outcome was often a hybrid type of religion that displayed on the one hand a capacity for resistance and, on the other, the negotiating structures that had to be adopted (Farris 1984, pp. 442–536). Religious syncretism entailed another way of compromising, one paid for in blood in many cases but not less important than the other accord with the king: this was the agreement that the local chiefs and indigenous lords should not only organize the collective tasks to pay the tribute but also its transfer, a part of which they duly retained for themselves (Menegus 1991). The relationship was also based upon the Church, whose expansion implied the development of another important actor in political and economic affairs as well as religious ones. The Franciscans, Dominicans, and Jesuits acted as mediators between colonists and Indians and were subject to the same exchange of forms of capital, including economic resources, with the monarchy.

From the demographic and humanitarian point of view, this system and the contact between these two worlds resulted in a catastrophe without precedent in the history of humanity. A key starting point to understand sixteenth-century America is the way the combination of ecological forces and institutions led to what Las Casas called the 'destruction of the Indies', the demographic catastrophe following the conquest. Whatever the population figures of America in 1491, it is clear that the indigenous population was sizeably reduced in the following decades. Thus, for central Mexico—a region that has generated considerable controversy—Borah and Cook postulate a fall from 25 million inhabitants in 1519 to 1.38 in 1595. This is, perhaps, overly dramatic. But, even taking more recent attempts at revision by scholars such as Zambardino (from between 5 and 10 million to 2.2 and 3 million in 1568), it is impossible to deny that the Amerindian population fell between 50% and 70%. This obviously entailed dramatic consequences for the economy of the area and workforce availability. Some calculations even suggest a fall of between 60 and 80 million inhabitants in 1500 to 10 million in 1600, including European immigrants.[4]

As it is well known, this breakdown in American history has been the cornerstone of the so-called Black Legend, which portrays Spain as a cruel country destroying not only American resources but above all native American populations and cultures.

Over the last few decades, however, a rich vision of the ecological clash of these two worlds has emerged and has gone a long way towards explaining the 'means' of conquest—in other words, the environmental factors that facilitated this process. The 'ecological imperialism' analysed by Crosby was, no doubt, a key factor (Crosby 1988). Diseases such as smallpox ruined the lives of thousands of Indians (and strengthened their belief in the divinity of the Spaniards, whose resistance to the epidemic was far higher). Focusing upon illnesses, John Elliott has written that 'the most effective of all the allies for the imposition of European supremacy was not human, but rather biological' (2006, p. 112). Plants such as white clover, which quickly spread through Peru as fodder, displaced the Incas from fields that had been vital for their livelihood. The pig, an omnivore requiring high quantities of carbohydrates, competed with the Indians for high-calorie foods. Semi-wild cattle spread very quickly throughout Mexico and other regions. Together with proliferating numbers of horses, they helped

---

[4] See figures in Maddison (1995) or some different but equally meaningful estimates in Romano (2004, Chap. 1).

destroy much of the foliage that was very delicately balanced in some zones.[5] This vision somewhat shifts the accent from human action and cruelty to more impersonal factors and, no doubt, contributes to a less maniquean view of the 'destrucción de las Indias'.

Yet one needs to consider ecological imperialism not only as the encounter of flora, fauna, and microorganisms, as is usual, but also in relation to the role played by the institutions, cultural beliefs, and patterns of knowledge regulating the uses of resources and ecosystems. Today it is clear that the logic of how the *encomienda* functioned would be crucial. Amerindians were awarded to the *encomenderos* as a workforce or as tributaries for a temporary period designed to be cancelled at some point, when the Indians would revert to the Crown. Hence there emerged a tendency towards the quickest possible exploitation of the Amerindian population as an essential part of this drama. In the same way, the *repartimientos* of indigenous peoples and the use of *mitas* (personal labour services that the Indians had to perform in the mines) involved the massive displacement of individuals from their communities to the mining areas, thus exerting a dramatic effect upon the original social structures and demographic equilibrium. These institutions, moreover, did not act in a vacuum but, rather, in combination with environmental forces. The settlers' efforts to maximize profits—an objective inherent to their cultural beliefs and aspirations—came on top of intensive rhythm of work that these institutions demanded of the Amerindians and for which the physiology of the native population was entirely unprepared. In many areas the diet of the Amerindian population—and diet is a crucial component of all living beings in any ecological system—was based on carbohydrates drawn from the manioc plant, maize, potato, and other crops; physiologically, such natives were unprepared for the *encomenderos*' demands for continuous exertions in the fields and mines (Bennassar 1980). On the other hand, the destruction of the original ecological systems combined with forms of social and institutional organization unprepared to confront the ensuing environmental challenges. The introduction, for example, of European crops and technologies associated with the new institutional frameworks created by the Spaniards arrived but spread too late to avoid the demographic catastrophe.[6]

---

[5] Crosby (1988), McNeill (1977, pp. 176–207).

[6] The results of the work in progress of Bethany Aram and her research group, 'ArtEmpire', should clarify many of these questions, which are often absent from the relevant bibliography.

The institutional component of this process, if often marginalized by historians, was highly significant. Legislative measures were clearly unable to stop or prevent the exploitation of the Amerindian population, nor was the medicine of the time capable of meeting the challenges posed by the 'microbial unification of the world', in Le Roy Ladurie's memorable expression (1973). Las Casas denounced this situation to Charles V at the very moment of the emission of the 'New Laws' (*Leyes Nuevas*, 1542), which sought to supress the *encomiendas* (and in fact did so in certain areas), and attempted to end the exploitation of the Indian. The logic of Las Casas' programme lay not only in human rights and religion, as has often been said. It was also based upon the peninsular experience of a continual stripping away and usurpation of the royal patrimony (Chaps. 1 and 4), it being somewhat of an obsession of the Crown to avert a similar process in the Americas. In fact, this was what was occurring from the very moment that subjects of the king—the Indians—died in harsh labour systems. But the remedy was worse than the illness. The new measures unleashed even more ferocious desires for exploitation of the workforce. Legislation camouflaged, but did not prevent, abuses in a distant world in which the capacity of enforcement of the royal courts—and, therefore, their ability to arrest abuses—was very limited (see below). The need for a labour force justified wars of conquest often based upon the idea of the existence of cannibalism (this was not always certain), which was seen as a symptom of barbarity. The notion of the barbarous served to justify not only war but also forced work systems such as the *repartimiento*, which were thought to offer the redemptive and civilizing power of work to the barbarian population (Córdoba 2013). As is well known, the New Laws were also the pretext for the trade in American slaves, something legal and consistent with the cultural beliefs of the period.

In this way and to an extent, the Black Legend emerges as a rhetorical excess that undervalue the context of events and with profound consequences on the image of Spain. Such is even more the case considering attempts to avert the catastrophe, at least on paper and in some of the Crown's acts. At the same time, a purely ecological vision, based solely on flora, fauna, microbes, and so on, overlooks the human and institutional components of the process, especially if the period's cultural beliefs, in which humanitarianism and human rights were much less developed than today but were already in the mind of people such as Las Casas, provided the foundations of this institutional framework. Between both extremes lies a third more complex, but also more realistic and less maniquean, possibility. The environmental problems, illnesses, interests, and abuses combined with certain political economies that neither acted nor were capable of acting to avoid a process of resource destruction that implied, even in the midterm, a disaster with characteristics new in the history of humanity.

The Portuguese Empire and Asia: Bargaining, Diversity, and Limits

At the conclusion of the reign of Manuel I of Portugal (1465–1521), the Portuguese were present on both the northern and eastern coasts of Africa, across the Indian Ocean, and even in the Chinese Sea. Moreover they had created a genuine Atlantic system that connected a range of archipelagos with the metropolis and with Africa and which was extended as far as Brazil.

Rounding the Cape of Good Hope early in 1498, Vasco Da Gama had sailed the coasts of East Africa with just two ships. Beyond this point the navigation became easier. Shortly afterwards he discovered that the coasts of the Indian Ocean were very navigable, although dangerous during the monsoon season. As with the great American empires—those of the Incas and Aztecs—the pre-existence of communication networks was vital to the giant strides subsequently made by the Europeans. Da Gama took more than a year to return to Lisbon with two great achievements (Parry 1990, Chap. 7).

The first of these was profit and, more important, he compiled information regarding the seas and coasts, language difficulties, societies, and religions. In Lisbon many intelligent Portuguese believed that, if conquered, India 'would weaken the forces of the kingdom to such an extent that it would be without those necessary for its conservation'.[7] But money and information was all that King Manuel—although partly mistaken—required to embark upon a campaign of conquest.

As we have seen, the Portuguese empire was certainly not a work of Minerva—no empire, in fact, has ever been. A mixture of violence, piracy, fortresses, and factories, it included, when necessary, a form of diplomacy that went as far as the formal submission to local kings or the provocation of a massacre as a lesson to the others. Such methods served to overcome

---

[7] 'Debilitaría tanto as forças do reino que ficaria ele sem as necessárias para a sua conservação'. Quoted by Romero Magalhães (1997, vol. III, p. 521).

the resistance of the Venetians, the Mamelukes of Egypt, and the Ottoman Turks, who looked unfavourably upon this new competitor—one who was, to make things worse, a Christian (Godinho 1982–1987). The strategy employed in these early phases demonstrated what would be the great strength and principal weakness of the Portuguese empire: the control of chain of key coastal positions, Goa (1510), Malacca (1511), and Ormuz (1515). Ormuz, an enclave ceded thanks to an agreement with the Safavid Persian dynasty that was confronting the Ottoman Empire, allowed for the control of the Persian Gulf and the chance to pressure the Turks in the Red Sea with the aim of cutting their involvement in Indian Ocean commerce. Goa opened up trade to India and constituted an excellent step towards the East. Malacca allowed Malaysia to be approached, thus making the Spice Islands (one of the principal foci of commerce in the area) reachable and allowing trade in the Chinese Sea, even touching Japan (Magalhães 1997, vol. III, p. 446). From the 1530s the expansion would be slowed and more focused on the consolidation of positions in this area. In 1529 the Portuguese had to recognize Castilian rights to the Moluccas (Indonesia). The Portuguese efforts against the Turk in the Red Sea ended in failure, and until 1555–1557 they were unable to establish themselves in Macao, where the Chinese reaction to the violence that they had used would stop them in their tracks (see the Portuguese routes in Map 2.1).

Enterprises of this sort capitalized Portugal's relatively few advantages, as a distant and small country with, consequently, very limited demographic resources. Nevertheless, to face the Muslim merchants connected to the Red Sea and Persian Gulf trade, the Portuguese called upon artillery-bearing ships of huge dimensions. The broadside (*andanadas*) tactic, consisting of bombarding enemy ships from the greatest possible distance, allowed the Europeans to sink or incapacitate their adversaries before direct hand-to-hand fighting—in which their adversaries' more numerous crews would have prevailed—could take place. This tactic also enabled the Europeans to sow panic in enemy ports and enclaves, sometimes with the aim of conquering them but, more often and simply, to make a show of strength. Obviously, the practice did not lead to the conquest of large territories, which would have been impossible from Portugal. The comparison with the Ottoman Empire, which had by this point conquered Mameluk Egypt, is revealing. The trade in spices in Antwerp afforded the Portuguese access to the timbers of the Baltic, while the Turk was making use of the woods of Anatolia and therefore facing extremely high transport costs (Headrick 2010, Chap. 2).

The development of the sugar economy in Madeira, the Azores, Santo Tomé, and Cape Verde was followed by the emergence of Brazil. On Vasco da Gama's return from India, King Manuel immediately charged Pedro Álvares Cabral, *un fidalgo da casa del rei*, to sail for Brazil, a zone to the east of the line drawn by the Treaty of Tordesillas and, therefore, a land recognized as belonging to Portugal for exploration. This was followed by later expeditions along the eastern shores of South America and brought about contact with the Amerindians. Although trading concessions were made and some factories (*feitorias*) were created, at this point the country was too committed to the Indian Ocean in order to make great progress elsewhere (Disney 2009, vol. II, pp. 204–12). The halt in Portuguese expansion in Asia in the 1530s may be the reason for its subsequent attention to South America, where the French were gaining territory and seeking to obtain the wood (*pao*) of Brazil, a dye product very much sought by the businessmen of Nantes and Brittany and by the tapestry producers and tailors of Europe (Lockhart and Schwartz 1983, p. 181).

After 1550, however, Portuguese expansion in Asia slowed down largely due to confrontations with highly developed states and empires that were absorbing some of the West's military techniques (Darwin 2008, p. 74). Attacks upon Turkish positions in the Red Sea did not bring about decisive conquests, and the Portuguese dream of reaching Suez disappeared for a period of time. Indian Ocean piracy marked the Portuguese system. A realistic policy had led Portugal to abandon enterprises in North Africa, which came to be dominated by the rivalry between Charles V and Süleyman (Disney 2009, vol. II, pp. 125–9). By the mid-century, the differences between the Portuguese empire in Africa and Asia and the Spanish in America (and, indeed, the Portuguese dominions in Brazil) were already very clear: the Portuguese had encountered very solid political formations, with highly developed military technology (at least in comparison with the Aztec and Inca empires) and highly evolved internal social and economic systems and ecosystems adapted to European illnesses after centuries of contact. Together with the scarce population of Portugal, these circumstances explain the empire's highly limited capacity for penetration and domination. All of these factors would be decisive for the history of the empire.

As was the case for Castile in America, the system for the acquisition and control of territory had been based upon ceding political capital to private agents who would conquer and exploit the lands on behalf of the monarch in Lisbon. That is to say that *feitorias* and *capitanias donatarias* were created (above all this was the case in Brazil, which was divided into 12 such districts) each with the prerogative to penetrate into the hinterland (Lockhart and Schwartz 1983, Chap. 6). These districts were very similar to the metropolitan *senhorios*, and the government ceded the right to govern them in return for the conquest (Weckmann 1993). Another option was to employ a system of *contrato* in which private individuals received privileges to make use of the land. These were negotiated relations (Hespanha and Santos 1998, vol. 5, pp. 351–66) characterized by their very low cost to the royal exchequer, although, of course, they had a high opportunity cost for it in terms of its capacity for political control. In the case of Brazil use was also made of the foundation of cities (usually coastal ones), the outcome being that the population density of the hinterland would be noticeably lower than in Spanish America. These arrangements were conditioned not only by the difficulties in penetrating the hinterland but also by their character as enclaves within export-orientated economies that acquired slave labour from abroad and in return sent practically all of their produce overseas. As a result, royal influence in the cities of the Portuguese colonial world would be less marked and slower to establish itself than was the case in the Castilian colonies (Lockhart and Schwartz 1983, Chap. 6).

This having been said, it was obvious that the proper exploitation of this extensive network of contacts depended upon certain regulatory efforts and government from above. As in Spanish America, institutions with a strong centralizing tendency were established above the rudimentary ones on the ground. In fact, the Portuguese oriental empire was divided into two differentiated zones (Boyajian 1993) with interdependent but individualized institutions. The *Casa da Índia*, founded in 1503 and later imitated in Castile, was charged with regulating maritime space and overseas commerce and oversaw the royal monopoly in trade between Lisbon and Goa. Moreover, in theory the Portuguese system had a clearer monopoly than the Castilian one: while in Seville the Crown only regulated the trade between private individuals and attempted to respect the privileges of each city as a commercial licence holder, in Lisbon the king himself reserved the right to trade in determined products. The second institution was the powerful *Estado da Índia*, whose governor or viceroy was appointed by the monarch, resided in Goa, and was charged with the costs of protection, diplomacy, and enforcement in the Asian colonies. The *Estado da Índia* was charged with controlling and regulating Asian trade, a very important part of which was in private hands (Boyajian 1993,

Introduction). Following the annexation of Portugal by the Habsburgs, Philip II (Philip I in Portugal) introduced centralizing projects in the *Estado da Índia*, with the creation of the *Conselho da Fazenda* (Miranda 2010) being of particular importance. In Brazil the office of the captaincy royal was created, with similar functions and its headquarters in *Todos os Santos* (Bahia), whence it governed Portuguese America. As in Spanish America, those captaincies that had been ceded in the phase of conquest were repurchased or redeemed to restore their government to the Crown (da Cunha and Monteiro 2005, p. 202). The Inquisition was used by the king to his own benefit and with an eye on the defence of his overarching or 'superior' authority (Bethencourt 2009). Equally the King of Portugal obtained from the Pope the right of patronage, known here as the 'presentation' of bishops, which conferred a notable power not only on political affairs but also, indirectly, on religious ones. And the King of Portugal also obtained the privilege to control the *Misericordias* in the empire and beyond it (Marcocci 2012, pp. 107–8).

Such methods are sometimes seen as a form of unconstrained absolutism that would shape the Portuguese empire: in reality, they were no such thing, and the system did not lead to the imposition of total or all-encompassing monarchical power and, as a result, to institutional unification. In the Indies and in Africa, the distances and frontier character of many territories obliged the Crown to bargain with local actors of Portuguese origin and to negotiate with them over the administration of coercion, taking as a starting point the very heterogeneity of these territories and, consequently, the mixed nature of the resulting administration (Hespanha and Santos 1998, pp. 351–8). The very administrative reform programme itself, and the creation of the *Conselho da Fazenda*, was unable to overcome the enormous differences between tax-collecting centres and so led to negotiations between Goa and the local administrators. As a result, they retained a high degree of autonomy that led to 'systematic' corruption being accepted (Miranda 2010). The outcome was a negotiated process in which powers were ceded, thus implying a certain degree of autonomy. The African coasts, for example, were often in the hands of *lançados*, *bandeirantes*, and slavers, mixed with local populations, who exercised considerable autonomy (Disney 2009, vol. II, pp. 49–54). This was also the outcome in the *capitanias donatarias*, whose officers enjoyed considerable room for manoeuvre. The cities founded in Brazil fell into the hands of groups that enjoyed a notable degree of freedom of action and who received their privileges in return for their governmental and tax-collecting functions (Fragoso 2001, p. 47). In distant frontier territories, such as Brazil, the slavers operated with a high degree of autonomy and a de facto scope for negotiation that even allowed them to compete with the coastal cities in their power relations with the Crown (Lockhart and Schwartz 1983, Chap. 6). Overall the system, being based on the concession of institutional advantages in return for services or the mobilization of material resources, tended towards the creation of privileges that limited the right of the newcomers in regard to the previous negotiations with the Crown (Fragoso 2001, pp. 44–5). The viceroys and governors themselves, supposedly conduits for the transmission of the king's power, exercised a high degree of freedom of manoeuvre. The same can be said of bishops and clergy and, especially in this period, of the Jesuits who often pursued their own interests rather than defend the authority of Madrid or Lisbon (Valladares 2001, *passim*). And this tendency was even clearer in cities such as Macao, where the Portuguese authorities shared and negotiated the decision-making process with the Chinese (Hespanha 2001, p. 171).

This flexible form of articulating the power of the king and his vassals in the colonies was completed with pliable formulas of negotiation between the Portuguese settlers and the original populations. Here one of the keys was the creation of informal and complex relations, which included good doses of both initial violence and later matrimonial alliances and *mestizaje* (Subrahmanyam 2005). This fact is evident in Asia, where one of the crucial reasons for the survival of the imperial system lay in the capacity of merchants to mix and communicate with local societies. The fact that the very term *casados* (married) was used to describe the permanent residents of the Portuguese enclaves gives us an idea of the importance of these arrangements (Disney 2009, vol. II, pp. 147–9; de Sousa 2010). In Brazil the success of the *capitanias*, many of which had disappeared within a few decades of their creation, depended upon the establishment of informal networks that generated solid pacts with the local societies (Lockhart and Schwartz 1983, pp. 184–90). And this not only afforded an enormous scope for mediation to those who formed these pacts: it also increased their capacity to establish accords with Lisbon.

To the extent that these negotiations were extended and became used in different contexts, the result was what L. F. Thomaz (1994) called the different status of the territories composing the *Estado da Índia* and A. M. Hespanha has called 'a multiple colonial state' (2001, p. 170) and the emergence of a society where diversity and transactions between diverse social and religious identities marked the political economy.

Apart from reasons rooted in the need to govern at long distance and over a society in which political negotiations largely depended upon privileges conceded by the king, this combination of negotiation and autonomy is due to the rise in the imperial sphere of informal global networks that generated a high degree of self-sufficiency. We will return to this point in Chap. 7. For the moment it is to be noted that the pattered applied to the case of the Jesuits, who by 1600 had created a global network and even were one of the solutions set upon by the Crown for the maintenance of Portuguese control in areas such as Brazil, China, and Japan. And this was also the case for merchant networks that, like the ones created by Jewish businessmen around their common identity and which gave them a presence in the colonies, took the form of well-forged grids that served to circulate news, information, capital (sometimes as dowries), and merchandise. These emerged at a very early moment and henceforth grew only in strength (Studnicki-Gizbert 2007).

OVERSEAS TRADE AND EUROPEAN ECONOMIES, 1492–1580

Silver and the Price Revolution

The establishment of the Spanish and Portuguese empires meant an enormous step forward for the process of globalization. But what were the consequences of this first phase of globalization for Europe?

The question of the impact of the American economy on the old continent entails consideration of the arrival of precious metals and the so-called price revolution, the inflationary process that existed across Europe during the sixteenth century. Studies have demonstrated the existence of two clear cycles, the first lasting until the middle of the sixteenth century and marked by the shipments of gold and a slow increase in silver imports. The second, running from 1560 onwards, saw significant amounts of precious metals and, above all, an explosion in the amount of silver entering Seville.[8] According to Barret, between 1492 and 1600, about 17,000 tons of silver and 280 tons of gold were produced in America, constituting, respectively, 74% and 39% of the world's total output between these dates (Barret 1990, p. 225). The impact, truly global, was particularly marked in Iberia.

---

[8] See above all Hamilton (1975), Attman (1986), Barret (1990), or TePaske (1998), Feliu (1991) and Reis (2016).

Contemporary thinkers such as Azpilcueta and Bodin explained that a greater amount of monetized silver necessarily made prices rise, and Hamilton's studies as well as a long list of works on all Europe, and more in particular on the different Iberian territories from Portugal to Castile, Valencia or Catalonia have pointed in the same direction.[9] Other historians have emphasized the importance, at least in Spain, of population growth as a key to inflation, underlining that prices grew faster in relative terms during the first half of the century and pointing out that in this timeframe the arrival of metals was proportionally lower, while population growth was pronounced.[10] This argument was challenged by Harry Miskimin on the basis that the growth of American remittances must also be understood in terms of their relative increase, which was higher in the first half of the century with regard to the existing stock of money than in the second half of the century.[11] Evidence for and against each one of these arguments has been presented in academic debates.[12]

Despite the huge interest of this debate from the perspective of economic theory, the most interesting element for many historians is not the question of whether or not the quantitative theory of money summed up in the Fisher equation is correct. As Miskimin himself has noted, this equation represents a tautology, and, consequently, it is 'fruitless to wonder whether or not it is the "truth" behind the European economy of the sixteenth century' (Miskimin 1989, vol. XIII, p. 181). The important thing is not so much to determine if inflation was the result of American treasure as to study how the increase in monetary circulation connected to other factors and developments.

A long time ago, authors such as Y. S. Brenner drew attention to the fact that, even while retaining the quantitativist paradigm by themselves,

---

[9] As is well known, the proponents of this theory have begun from the application of the equation of Fisher, which in its simplest form is usually set as $MV = PT$, where M is the monetary mass, V is the velocity of monetary circulation, P is prices, and T is transactions. The increase in the availability of metal would have been the basis for an increase in the monetary mass that would explain inflation. It would reach very low levels—around 2% annually—in comparison with today's rates, which proved, nevertheless, significant rate for the time (Hamilton 1975).

[10] Braudel and Spooner (1967), Nadal (1959), Vilar (1969, pp. 107–9).

[11] Harry Miskimin (1981). As (at least) a working hypothesis, Miskimin's argument can also be applied to the so-called pre-revolution of prices generated by the growing production of gold and silver in Central Europe.

[12] See a more developed version of these ideas in Yun (2004, pp. 128–38).

population growth and economic development in the sixteenth century could cause an escalation in monetary velocity and thus induce an increase in prices. This view has been subsequently developed through the consideration of urban growth, in principle an indicator of the existence of an increase in the technical division of labour. According to Goldstone (1991), the sixteenth century witnessed a growing specialization of labour, suggesting a higher degree of intensity in the exchange of goods and services and, therefore, an increasing monetary velocity which could have encouraged inflation.

To clarify the real situation requires, however, a series of preliminary remarks. It is quite possible that the importance of the currency and, in particular, of gold and silver coin is sometimes exaggerated. Copper coins were still often instrumental in small trade. In addition, the economy of sixteenth century moved, in many periods and in many regions, through transactions in which the intervention of cash was non-existent.[13] Moreover, the fact that at the highpoint of the century American treasures barely amounted to 7.5% of the gross domestic product of Castile—that is to say, possibly less than 0.5% of European total GDP—underlines that, in macroeconomic terms, its importance was lower than some have imagined (Yun 1998). However, the recognition of the marginal character of monetary circulation in some areas of Europe and in some segments of the economy does not imply that there was not a correlation between the variables set out above.

Although it can only be a suggestion, a comparison between New Castile, in the centre of the peninsula, and other areas of Europe is very indicative of the way in which these factors were intertwined. A comparative analysis shows how four variables, monetary circulation (measured both by the increase in the amount of silver in circulation and by currency devaluations), commercial and industrial development, and population growth, may very well explain the evolution of prices. In any of these different areas, they increased more when any one of these variables was combined with the others to provoke a rise in prices (Yun 2004, pp. 133–6). And, although this data may require a more robust quantitative exercise, everything suggests that in reality it was the different intensity with which

---

[13] Frequently, remuneration for rural and urban work, or part of it, was paid in specie. This also occurred with payment to servants and maids in the seigniorial houses and ecclesiastical institutions. In 1566 the Count of Benavente dedicated more than 60% of his wheat income to the payment of servants and similar costs. *Osuna*, legs. 242, 483, exp. 2, AHN.

these four factors combined that determined the rate of the evolution of prices in these disparate and distant regions.

The effects of this rise in prices on the Spanish economy will be considered later. Of immediate concern is the question of how the globalization promoted by the Iberian empires would encourage and transform trade between the regions of Europe.

Although its importance has been exaggerated, the world-wide increase in monetary circulation was clearly one of the reasons for the price revolution. Certainly money in itself did not create trade, nor was it the only thing that contributed to the improvement in methods of payment and facilitated transactions (this was still more true for 'good money' coined from silver or gold). Systems of compensation to account, letters of exchange, whose endorsement was extended, or the cheque, clearly more widely used during the century, helped to secure these outcomes. However, the abundance of good coin was undoubtedly a factor that cannot be overlooked in attempting to explain such a process; this is especially true if we consider that if many of these operations and methods of payment saved on the use of cash, in the end they also implied monetary transactions, even if these involved lower quantities.

In addition, and despite its limited use, the growing amount of good money led to the development of a form of international trade which, even though it was different from local commerce, was also closely related to it. Taking into account the interaction between the development of urban networks and the deepening of rural market circuits, the maintenance and development of these networks—encouraged by the more long-distance trade and, therefore, by the growing use of gold and silver coins—accelerated the economic changes that had been taking root among peasant families and had begun in the previous century. And this took place in spite of the fact that in many regions of Europe gold and silver were rarely used.

The abundance of precious metals and their steady flow into the coffers of the monarchies made it easier to achieve stability in the value of the European currencies against silver. In turn, this led to a greater degree of exchange rate stability among the different European currencies themselves.[14] Only France underwent repeated currency depreciations. This stability is important not because of the insights it offers into the relations

---

[14] See the chart of Braudel and Spooner for evidence that the sixteenth century, and specifically the first half of it, was a period of relative stability in this regard when compared to the seventeenth century (Braudel and Spooner 1967).

of currency exchanges. Rather, it is significant because it accustomed merchants to operate in a world where monetary manipulations, although in existence, were more exceptional, thus contributing to a certain sense of security which was a guarantee for the development of business.

If, as it has been said, the output of German mines had exerted a relative—but decisive—effect on the commercial growth of the last decades of the fifteenth century and the first of the following century, then so when, from 1530, the American mines began to take over, they would become a factor—not the unique one but certainly an important one—in bestowing upon an increasingly commercialized economy the means of payment that constituted the essential lubricant of this development.

Markets and Trade Networks

Due in part to eighteenth- and nineteenth-century theories, the possession of colonial empires has often been considered an important factor in economic growth and industrialization. According to these ideas, empires have played a crucial role in obtaining colonial raw goods and developing overseas markets for European industries. Fundamentally, Wallerstein (1979) continues this basic approach, although his vision is a much more refined one, and he and others have used dependency theory to interpret the sixteenth and seventeenth centuries. The Spanish and the Portuguese empires, in this long-standing paradigm, were missed opportunities already in the sixteenth century; dependency theory has strengthened even further this vision of the history of Iberia and Europe in general. The Castilian and Portuguese imperial ventures have, therefore, been seen as anomalies in the history of modern empires (Yun 2010).

The basis of this idea has been, however, highly criticized by some historians. Years ago, P. O'Brien (1980) drew attention to the extremely small size of colonial markets and the difficulty of attributing a decisive role to them before 1750. Whether or not this was a useful model for the British or European economy of the 1700s, its application to the situation of Castile and, indeed, to the old continent in general in the 1500s is very convincing. Indeed, for some time I have been arguing that something similar to this model is a good fit for the Spanish empire (Yun 1998, 2004, 2010).

Furthermore, in contrast to the common opinion among historians, the chances of the emergence of high demand for Castilian (or European) goods in America or in Asia were not that great. In order for a powerful colonial market for European products to emerge, it was first necessary for the local society to pass through a complex process of acculturalization, which matched local demand to the European patterns of consumption and industrial production. Moreover this change could only be achieved in the long term and by non-commercial mechanisms that were more closely connected to violence, war, and the creation of intra-colonial circuits of trade (Yun 2013). The demographic crisis brought about in America by contact and conquest further reduced the potential capacity of this market. Around 1580, when smuggling was only just beginning in earnest, annual shipments to the Indies were not greater than the internal trade of a city such as Córdoba. Quite possibly, the amount of textiles being exported to the overseas dominions did not reach the quantity sold on the market of this city (Yun 1998). Although often forgotten by economic historians, this is entirely logical: around 1580 only 250,000 white settlers lived in Spanish America, meaning that the potential demand for the products from the Old World was rather small. This signified the equivalent to between 4% and 5% of the existing theoretical additional demand of the Iberian Peninsula. At this juncture, a number of local industries in sectors such as textiles were also emerging, while construction (one of the most important) and other branches were largely tied to essentially regional circuits and had a very small impact upon the industrial sector of the metropolis. The rise of the American empire was not, therefore, an extraordinary missed panacea for Iberian industrial development, simply because the opportunity was rather small until around 1580 at the earliest.

And this context must inform our understanding of the evolution of the European economy in general and of the Spanish economy in particular during the sixteenth century.

In short, the first phase of this primitive globalization does not seem to have been based on the creation of very dynamic overseas markets for European (or Castilian) industrial products. Moreover, Europeans soon were able to use American silver to level their balance of trade with Asia—the true centre of the world economy, contrary to the preaching of an overly mechanical application of dependence theory—thus making it unnecessary to increase their exports to Far Eastern markets, and, therefore, the need to develop an industry able to balance or compensate its trade with the East.

But it is also obvious that, from a commercial point of view, there can be no doubt that this process saw an increase in the movement of goods at the global level and, in particular, a rise in those heading to Europe. Even scholars such as O'Rourke and Williamson (2002), who have

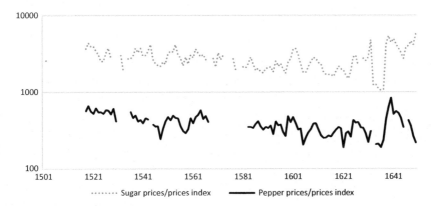

Graph 2.1   Sugar and pepper prices in regard the prices index in Castile
Sources: My own elaboration based on data from Hamilton (1975, Appendix III, IV and V) and Reher and Ballesteros (1993). Prices of sugar and pepper from Old Castile.

relativized the impact of this period's international trade in the process of globalization, have shown that the increasing flow of pepper into Europe was crucial for the fall in the real prices of this commodity, a trend that demonstrates the relevance of this commerce. Other products reveal the same pattern. In Graph 2.1 the evolution of sugar and pepper prices in relation to the price index in Andalusia shows a similar trend. It is also evident that globalization produced an exponential increase in the slave trade, and the same happened with products such as cacao, cochineal and other dyes, and many other goods.

This process also facilitated a growth in intra-European trade. A high proportion of the Portuguese cargoes that arrived in Lisbon from Asia and Africa to be re-exported to Northern Europe were compensated by an inverse trade of tin, copper, lead, mercury, wood, alum, and other goods towards Portugal. The arrival of American silver into Europe, via Spain, had similar effects. It not only enhanced previous trade from Northern Europe to the Iberian Peninsula but was also a positive factor in allowing for more Iberian, and in general Mediterranean, commodities, such as salt, wool, and others, to be exported to the north.

To what extent, then, did this commerce break with the poly-nuclear model of development that previously existed in Europe (Chap. 1)? The answer to this question allows us to provide a more in-depth analysis of the concrete effects on international commerce.

Spanish silver and the products of the Castilian and Portuguese Atlantic economy that arrived in the Low Countries and England also encouraged the connections with the faraway areas of the Baltic Sea.[15] Thus, Northern Europe, and, in particular, Antwerp, was greatly favoured by the commercial development of the Atlantic front and the Iberian trade with America, Africa and Asia (Van der Wee 1963, vol. II, Chap. 6). The beginning of the rise of the city was related to the arrival, from the start of the century, of Portuguese cargoes. Until the 1530s Lisbon merchants, many of them of *converso* origin, faced the problem of not having sufficient quantities of African gold to meet payments for spices and so sought in Antwerp the silver and copper that the Fugger and the Welser obtained through the lease of the royal mines of Tyrol. This also contributed to enhance the trade between Iberia and the north of Europe.

The first impact of this new connection was quick to make itself felt on the functioning of European commercial circuits. If until this juncture products from Asia were unloaded at Venice and then redistributed across Europe, now they would descend from the Low Countries, through the fairs in Lyon, while silver and copper from Central Europe was sent up to Antwerp in increasing quantities (Gascon 1972). This transformation was accompanied by a greater dynamism of overland continental trade, evident in the increase in the movement of cattle from Denmark, North Germany, Hungary, and Central Europe towards the Netherlands (for the European routes, Map 2.1).

The aftermath of the difficulties of the 1520s saw the decisive moment for Antwerp, a city which, despite the persistence of certain problems symptomatic of fluctuations in American trade, would now experience an unprecedented phase of expansion (Van der Wee 1963). It then forged increasingly close connections with England and developed its own luxury goods and linen industry, thanks largely to the Low Countries' growing links with Iberia, one of the main markets for its manufactures, which it exchanged for wool and other raw materials.[16] Mid-century Antwerp was,

---

[15] To give just one example, trade in rye rose from 20,900 tonnes in 1490 to 46,200 tonnes in 1557 (Zytkowicz 1985, p. 66). We might also consider the growing quantities of furs, wood, wax, salted-fish—Iberian salt was already common in the Dutch provinces—and many other heavy but widely dispersed items whose consumption was growing.

[16] Pach (1968). Van der Wee (1988) underlines the importance of the Castilian market for Flemish production (tapestries, high-quality fabrics, all types of artistic objects, etc.).

therefore, a commercial and industrial centre of the first rank. It was the meeting point for select and expensive products from the south and the heavy and popular products of the north. And it also served as a point of redistribution throughout Northern and Central Europe for Iberian silver; sugar, spices, and many other Atlantic, African, and Asian goods; and a sizeable part of Italian production. In addition, the city's economy was based on a powerful and diversified industry that was increasingly tied to the production of high-quality and artistic goods. Antwerp oversaw the emergence of certain trading techniques and financial developments (Van der Wee 1988, pp. 184 and ff.). From the beginning of the century, German houses (the Welser and the Fugger) had displayed through Antwerp their interest in financing businesses in the Portuguese and Castilian colonies and in advancing monies to Charles V; now the city saw the emergence of methods conducive to the streamlining of credit (Ehrenberg 1955).

Political factors were important to all of these changes. The formation of the dispersed composite monarchy of Charles V did not presage the disappearance of the numerous existing trade barriers among his territories. All were governed by different constitutions and a diverse array of commercial and political elites, and each one of them would retain its jurisdictional specificities. A genuine process of economic integration as it is understood today was all but inconceivable. The fiscal and monetary diversity of these territories and the existence of corporations of local merchants staunchly determined to maintain their privileges created barriers to outside penetration of many sectors and regions. However, the formation of this complex and dispersed political network in Western Europe also would have some positive effects for the internationalization of commercial networks and the integration of regional economies within this territorial mosaic. The consciousness of having a shared king gave an elite of businessmen close to the Court a certain security in regard to the stability of commercial links. That Charles implemented a policy of monetary stability in some of his domains no doubt helped deepen relationships between them. The case of Flanders and Castile and the relations of exchange in relation to silver is a good example. Although caution should be exercised in approaching this theme, Graph 7.2. demonstrates how, if the seventeenth century was characterized by both currencies being prone to considerable fluctuation, the sixteenth century, above all until 1569, would be marked by a high degree of stability and, therefore, predictability.

Political factors would also have a definite impact upon international trade for financial reasons. Despite the so-called Castilian monopoly on American trade, the Fugger penetrated into the colonial economy by contracting *asientos* with the king in exchange for the import of goods which were traded in Europe (Kellenbenz 2000). And the same can be said of the penetration of the Welser into the slave trade that was present across extensive areas of Europe (Kellenbenz 2000, p. 225). The growing ease with which Spanish wool was travelling to Flanders, and with it the ever more fluid trade of Flemish and German goods into Castile, was related to the loans that these bankers, together with the Genoese, provided to the Emperor and which, given the ban on exporting currency from this kingdom, led to the repatriation of their loans and the interests accrued on them by sending commodities to other areas of Europe (Ruiz Martín 1990a). The growing trade in silk between Granada and Italy originated in the lease that Charles, always needing money, conceded to the Genoese for this commerce.

But did the emergence of the Atlantic and this growing trade represent a setback for the Mediterranean economy? Did it lead to a more polarized economy with a dynamic North and a retarded South? It would appear that it did not. Certainly, there were some areas in the South that drew benefits from this process. Among them is the obvious case of Genoa. Favoured by the vacuum left by the expulsion of the Jews, and having gained access to monarchy's finances, the great bankers consolidated Genoa's fortune. If German bankers were able to capture part of the production of raw materials in Iberia, Genovese connections were not weaker—on the contrary (Carande 1987, vol. I, pp. 295–315). Their hand would be greatly strengthened after 1528, when Genoa in effect became a protectorate of Charles V, who, in turn, would create the fairs in Besançon as a means of counterbalancing the weight of the fairs of Lyon, while the Tuscans became the allies of the King of France. These developments would extend the influence of the Genoese into the North and the Netherlands, which would be decisive for the splendour of Genoese banking during the reign of Philip II and the establishment of a commercial and financial network unprecedented in Europe (De Maddalena and Kellenbenz 1986). As early as the 1540s, the Genoese were already the largest foreign colony in Flanders after the Castilians. Venice also resisted the pull of the North. From the 1520s it reacted with noticeable results in the spice trade, and the importance of the Venetians in Lyon's spice trade recovered up to 85% by 1533–1534 (Gascon 1972, p. 646), thanks to new routes through Asia Minor and Aleppo. In the lagoon city, many resources were ploughed into industry, a sector that would diversify in response to the demand for quality that would, in turn, encourage further industrial diversification and boost new and very dynamic sectors such as printing, glassware, and others (Sella 1957; Lane 1973, pp. 308–12). If the Genoese were able to cope with financial competition from German banking in the Court of the Habsburgs and even, through it, to control sectors strategic for trade, Tuscan banking would further strengthen its position in the market of Lyon, where it established strong bonds of financial and political complicity with the King of France (Gascon 1972). Such developments took place while the Florentine industry maintained a remarkable rate of growth that would reach its climax in the 1560s (Malanima 1982).

Despite the importance of colonial trade and the development of the Atlantic front with its links to the global economies of America, Africa and Asia, the European economy did not fit the model applied to it in a mechanical application of the theory of dependence. Far from leading a hierarchical relationship of subordination with regard to a central axis, the growth of the first decades of the century remained a process based upon various centres (see Chap. 1). One needs to think also that, despite the striking development of the Atlantic façade, the penetration of international trade into family economies and regional markets was still too small to determine the models of economic growth of large geographic areas.[17] This consideration, of course, does not preclude recognition of the crucial role of Atlantic trade in the working of the commercial networks within Europe.

These arguments lead to a consideration crucial for our case: the notable capacity that, from a relatively low level of use of resources, could be achieved by institutions that were apparently inefficient in generating growth according to the model of the new institutional economics. As a matter of fact, this international commerce, like the incipient trade with America, Africa and Asia was based on economic privileges and on the monopolistic access to resources and information.

---

[17] A comparison is instructive: the annual remittances of American silver that were paid to private individuals in Castile for commercial sales, services, and inheritance came to 2250 million maravedís in 1590–1591, when the gross domestic product of Castile was worth 30,000 million (Yun 1998, p. 131, n. 25).

IBERIA IN THE GLOBAL ECONOMY: LOWERING
TRANSACTION COSTS

An Export Economy?

The increasing role of the Iberian Peninsula in the expansion of foreign trade was clearly expressed by indicators such as the *almojarifazgo* of Seville or the *periatge* of Barcelona (Yun 2004, pp. 147–51). As was the case for Europe as a whole, incipient globalization may have induced a series of changes of great importance in patterns of consumption. The ever-easier access to foreign products, the expanding availability of methods of payment, and the increase of income derived from domestic economic growth would activate the demand for products of all kinds in the Iberian kingdoms. The rise of prices in the Iberian Peninsula must also have attracted foreign manufactured products. The fact that this economic growth was accompanied by the development of access to easy credit for privileged groups (see Chap. 4) would give further impetus to a form of ostentatious consumption that was already prominent in the societal mores of the time and which was satiated primarily with exotic, rare, or expensive goods usually sourced from abroad. The growing devotion of Iberian aristocracies and elites to the culture of the Italian and Flemish Renaissance would pull in the same direction (Brotton 2002). Partly as a result, a pattern of conspicuous consumption and ostentation took hold among the nobility and urban patriciate that was clearly linked to the cultural shifts experienced by these groups. As early as the reign of Charles V, many foreign travellers in Iberia referred not only to the spices consumed there but also to the rich clothes and the damask and taffeta that adorned the persons and homes of the nobles and great businessmen or to the ornamental richness of the churches and palaces.[18] Demand of this sort was met by the consumption of expensive fabrics and objets d'art imported from Italy and Flanders, whose industries quickly benefited from this demand,[19] as did

---

[18] N. Popielovo *Viaje de Nicolás de Popielovo*, in García Mercadal (1999, vol. I, p. 300), J. Munzer, *Viaje de Jerónimo Munzer*. Ibidem. p. 309, 310, 374–5. Guicciardini *Relación de España*, Ibidem, p. 585.

[19] Van der Wee (1988). Dámaso de Frías, a traveller of the epoch, refers to the 'alteration of the costumes, customs and manners of living that we see in all of Spain since the Flemmish entered into it', specifying the abandonment of 'temperance' and the 'old parsimony in eating habits of the Spaniards', *Diálogo de Alabanza de Valladolid* García Mercadal Ibidem. p. 247.

their counterparts in France (Rouen and Nantes above all). And it would seem that this process was increasingly influential as the reign wore on as new lifestyles, linked in part to the palace and the adoption of more refined habits, took root (Checa 1988, pp. 195–216).

This trend would even further encourage the reverse flow of exported raw materials from the peninsula to the rest of Europe. Wool shipments, undoubtedly the most important of all of the Spanish export products, increased threefold in volume during the first half of the century. The same thing occurred in Aragon where, in addition to wool, leathers and saffron were also prominent in exports (Gómez Zorraquino 1987, pp. 87–98). Sugar and silk were exported from Valencia in growing quantities, as was silk from Granada and Murcia and the alum of this latter region.[20] From the middle of the century (the start of the second cycle of the Atlantic economy), the role of Castile and Portugal as bridges in the trade of raw materials coming from the New World was accentuated as large quantities of cocoa, hides, sugar, cochineal, and other products arrived, part of which was exported to other areas of Europe (Phillips 1990, pp. 58, 80, 70).

Several factors contributed to these changes. In Castile, the improvement of the fairs system pivoting around Medina del Campo, Medina de Rioseco, and Villalón was, without doubt, one of them. These were institutions whose commercial regulation would help reduce an initially very high level of transaction costs and risks. For some time these fairs had constituted an important meeting point for foreign merchants and Castilians. During the sixteenth century, the co-ordination of payments between the Castilian fairs and those of Antwerp and Bergen op Zoom was established on near-perfect footing, as was the internal trade fair circuit within Spain (Carande 1987, vol. I, p. 331). Links of this kind further reduced information costs and uncertainty and guaranteed spatial and temporal convergence of supply and demand, thus allowing the establishment of a regular system (and therefore one of more predictable operations involving fewer risks) for transferring funds between them. The increasing importance of fairs allowed the monarchy to channel payments through them, thus permitting it to borrow from and make repayments to *asentistas* and bankers present at these gatherings. In turn this practice provided a stimulus to large-scale businessmen who, needing money to

---

[20] Furió (1995, pp. 244–5), Pérez and Lemeunier (1984, pp. 77–9). Cortés and Vincent (1986), Ruiz Martín (2005).

meet their commitments to the king, channelled growing quantities of products and bills of exchange through these meetings. (Abed Al-Hussein 1982). During the middle years of the century, the annual amount paid by the king in this way could even touch 2,000,000 ducats, a figure of signifi- cance if we consider the gross annual income of the monarchy in Castile might reach five or six million at this point (Yun 2004).[21] The impulse behind the fairs was also linked to the development of the American econ- omy that forged sudden, and intense, ties. Around 1520, of 186 letters negotiated with fairs from Seville, 107 referred to trade with Lyon and only 79 with the other fairs of Castile (Otte 1986). But this ratio, if itself of some importance in a year of civil war and intense conflicts in Medina del Campo, would rise during the following decades. The fairs became a circuit linking the whole global economy, from Southeast Asia to the Caribbean, Lisbon, Seville, and Antwerp, and reaching as far as the more developed areas of Italy. Its importance with regard to the development of foreign trade is therefore undeniable.

A similar result emerged from the foundation and development, begun in the fifteenth century, of consulates in Castile that were similar to the existing ones in the Crown of Aragon. The Consulate of Burgos was established in 1494. Bilbao followed suit in 1511. Seville, where by 1503 the *Casa de la Contratación* already existed, would have to wait for the *Real Provisión* of 1543 and the *ordenanzas* of 1556.[22] The effects of this type of institution would be immediate. Despite friction between them (especially between those of Bilbao and Burgos) and the not-so-positive future evolution (see Chap. 5), the consulates would initially improve the organization of the convoys and maritime insurance system. Above all, they enabled special courts and arbitration systems to reduce transaction costs by making judicial review a more agile, rapid process (as is specifically clear from the *ordenanzas* of Burgos and Seville) and so increased guaran- tees of responsibility and agreement among their members.[23] Membership in a consulate created bonds of trust and even, in some cases, of shared responsibility among merchants, traits which were especially valuable in

[21] *Dirección General del Tesoro*, Inv° 24, legs. 490, 1299, 1458, 815, 1432, 491, 492, 494, 495, 561, 561 bis, 562, 563, 564, 565, 566, 567, 568, 569, 570, 571, 572, 573, 574, 575, AGS.

[22] Basas (1994, pp. 25–40) and García-Baquero (1992, pp. 57–84).

[23] Basas (1994, pp. 33–6) and García-Baquero (1992, pp. 74–9).

the operation of trading diasporas. While networks such as that of Burgos (active across Europe and particularly in the north of the continent) had been created much earlier, there are good reasons for thinking that these organizational improvements substantially increased their projection into the Netherlands during the first half of the sixteenth century.

The development of powerful financial networks across the peninsula would also contribute to the expansion of international trade. Here it is worth repeating that the export of wool, silk, and colonial products was activated by the advancing of money in the form of the renting out of royal incomes and taxes by merchants and bankers. The same happened with alum, a mordant necessary for the production of fabrics, which was purchased by the Genoese from the marquis of Vélez and the duke of Escalona through similar mechanisms (Ruiz Martín 2005). Sugar was purchased from the duke of Gandia in Valencia, as was the saffron, wool, and other products that formed part of the seigniorial rights of Aragonese nobles, who rented them out to financiers in return for the loans necessary to overcome their liquidity problems.[24] Even without these institutional advantages, these networks were able to absorb a large part of production. Thus, the merchants of Burgos acquired wool through a system of advancing credit to the shepherds when they were most in need of money—that was before the wool itself had even been shorn from their sheep. The Genoese not only used mechanisms of credit based upon the king's revenues or those of the aristocratic houses. Their loans to the banks and merchants of Seville involved in the *Carrera de Indias* also served to give them indirect access to goods from America.[25] On the east coast, the Genoese not only secured the purchase of Granada silk through financial mechanisms. They also purchased wine, raisins, barilla, sugar, and other products sold to them by growers in need of cash; their actions were clearly favoured by lower costs achieved through well-established, well-oiled networks and their control of these trade circuits (Pérez and Lemeunier 1984).

These ties (accords between businessmen and the monarchy or with individuals through the leasing out of rents or simple credits) also explain the erection of entry barriers and the consolidation of oligopolistic mechanisms that reduced the capacity for the distribution of wealth of this trade. This would become notorious later on. But, again, for the moment and

---

[24] Carande (1987, vol. III), Halperin (1980, p. 27), and Gómez Zorraquino (1987).
[25] Edwards (1977) and Fortea (1981, pp. 341–5).

under certain conditions, such connections could lower transaction costs and risk in the context of institutions that the new institutional economics considers inefficient.

A Semi-periphery of Europe? Domestic Trade and Institutional Improvements

The development of foreign trade and the export of raw materials created significant tensions within the peninsular economies. Many sectors of it, such as high-quality textile production, found themselves having to compete with powerful importers of goods of a similar—or, indeed, higher—quality and with exporters of raw materials essential for the elaboration of their own merchandise. Likewise, the barriers to entrance created by the groups of contractors and financiers who secured a large share of raw materials through financial mechanisms further reinforced this situation and were conducive to the financial subordination of Iberian banking by the great cosmopolitan international financial houses (Ruiz Martín 1990b). But does this situation justify reference to a 'semi-periphery'?

There are reasons to think that it does not. Castilian bankers were mainly focused on the internal market. But it is also true that, thanks to their international links and the commercial expansion, some of them were able to operate in cross-border spaces and to use more modern techniques to that end. They developed considerably during the first half of the century, as is demonstrated by the rise to prominence of families such as the Ruiz, the Maluenda, the Bernuy, the Salamanca, or the Calatayud and many others (Carande 1987, vol. III). Some, like the financiers of Seville, did so in collaboration with the Genoese. Others, like the young Simón Ruiz who, according to his brother, Andrew, 'would not confine himself to having all the treasure of the world', acted independently in the international arena (Lapeyre 1955, p. 74, n. 176). All of them mastered the art of the letter of exchange and the account books (Lapeyre 1955). And a similar development occurred in Portugal. Certainly, the role of international bankers in providing loans to the king in the Low Countries was crucial and was going to condition the development of the Portuguese banking system. But, at the same time, these decades witnessed the development of international commercial and financial networks through the agency of the Portuguese Jewish merchants, which would be very relevant after 1580 (Boyajian 1983).

Though we will come back to the manufactures' development below, it is important to note here that there were also industrial sectors within Iberia that would take advantage of international ties. Córdoba leathers and other embossed leather goods were exported by the Genoese themselves and even arrived in significant quantities in Flanders, where they would be much imitated (Van der Wee 1963). The textile industries of Córdoba and Segovia were able to begin to adapt to demand for higher-quality merchandise thanks to the replacement of cruder dyes (sourced within Spain) by pastel (an import) and thanks to the alum extracted by the Genoese capital in Murcia (Fortea 1981). Cochineal, brought from America, would bring noticeable improvements to fabrics and light cloths (Marichal 2014). The Basque iron industry faced intractable problems due to competition from other areas after 1550, but its expansion to reach 'optimal production' seems undeniable up until that date—an expansion for which domestic demand was partially responsible but which, in view of exports to England, should also be seen as the effect of external demand favoured by the increasingly close relationship between the economies of the peninsula and Europe (Bilbao 1987, pp. 49–57). One manifestation of the expansive capacity of domestic industry can be found in the petition made to Charles V in the Cortes asking him to raise the quota of wool that had to remain in Castile in 1552. This was precisely the moment at which, in Córdoba, the growth of the textile industry meant that 'the tensions in the wool market took on a whole new dimension' (Fortea 1981, p. 350).

The expansion of ties with the international and colonial economies was, together with the military needs of the Crown, the fundamental cause of the development of both the military and merchant navy, which had been growing since the fifteenth century and which enhanced the naval industry and the demand for wood, iron, copper hemp and other industrial products. This fact, though poorly known, is no longer in doubt. The idea of a limited and insufficiently developed Spanish navy can no longer be sustained, although it has been reiterated in a great deal of the international literature (Casado Soto 1998). It was always supported by the Crown, which above all else was interested in the construction of successively larger vessels (Carande 1987, vol. I, pp. 351–414). In the Crown of Aragon, Barcelona became the most important construction centre for galleys in the peninsula (Goodman 1988, p. 96). By the mid-century it was already facing a crisis of 'accelerating demand' for maritime transport vehicles (Casado Soto 1998, p. 353). This explains the expansion of this industrial sector in cities such as Seville, Bilbao, and the aforementioned

Barcelona. The Iberian countries became central points for the development of naval technology. This was even clearer in Portugal, where the size of the navy increased dramatically between 1500 and 1560 (Costa 1997, p. 265). In the Portuguese capital, this sector also activated demand for industrial products, above all in the cities of the lower Tagus and the zones between Porto and the Galicia frontier. For these reasons it has been even possible to speak of a 'state capitalism', due to the direct involvement of the Crown in these businesses, which were crucial for its trade monopoly (Costa 1997, p. 262).

While encouraging the export of raw materials and the import of industrial products, the Castilian fairs also had positive effects on the domestic economy which gained in consistency and internal coherence. The trading system based upon synchronized periods between meetings held in the different places served, moreover, to reduce transaction costs and transport risks also for products moving within the internal market too. Many merchants from different regions of the peninsula, including Portugal, approached these gatherings with the guarantee that they could securely buy and sell their products in an environment of intense commercial activity and relatively abundant liquidity and with the confidence that they could defer part of their payments if necessary (Yun 1987, pp. 186–95).

The fairs were a stimulus for the development of agriculture and animal husbandry. The benefits were felt from the vineyards of Medina del Campo to the wheat fields of the Tierra de Campos and across the northern plateau where livestock herds grazed (Yun 1987). And they also sparked many other commercial sectors. The effect of these developments was to boost interregional trade between the plateau of Castile and the snow-topped mountains of Cantabria. Areas such as La Rioja awoke to their industrial vocation thanks to the effects of these periodic reunions.[26] And they had the same effect as had on the textiles of Segovia and even, further afield, those of Cuenca. Fair meetings carried forward the creation of the internal market, as is demonstrated by the presence at them of merchants from as

---

[26] Although little studied, this theme is mentioned in numerous references found in the Archivo Histórico Municipal de Medina de Rioseco, hereafter AHMMR. See, for example, leg.13 (ant.) exp.298 (especially, the *Memorial del pleito de Medina del Rioseco contra el Conde de Benavente*).

far afield as Córdoba, Seville, and Granada and the regular circulation of bills of exchange originating in these cities (Fortea 1981, pp. 395, 398). During this period, the financial market of Medina del Campo continued to serve the industry of Granada by advancing capital to it (Abed Al-Hussein 1982). The contribution of the fairs system to the formation of the Iberian trading network can also be shown in regard to Portugal, whose traders sold sugar, spices, and other overseas products into it; they also purchased cloth, not all of which was manufactured abroad, with considerable quantities produced in Segovia or Cuenca. Some time ago, P. Vilar provided an account of the intensification of traffic between Barcelona and Medina del Campo, explaining how the latter served as a staging post for the fabrics and leathers which the Catalans exported to America and how soap carried to Portugal through Castile was exchanged for 'brazil', a dye that undoubtedly helped to boost the textile industry (Vilar 1962, vol I, pp. 333–4).

The increasing interconnection of the domestic market was also the result of many other currents and flows that bound different circuits together. Relations between Andalusia and Portugal, and Lisbon in particular, appear to have been established before the annexation of 1580, as is demonstrated by not only the increasingly important role of the Portuguese in Seville but also their presence in Córdoba. Toledo acquired its 'role of regional redistribution centre', where the markets sold textile products from the northern and southern plateaux and even from Valencia and the kingdom of Aragon; and this came at a time when its relations with Andalusia and Portugal also intensified through the supply of Atlantic and Asian products in exchange for products coming from different mainland areas (Montemayor 1996, pp. 238, 255–61). Trade between Castile and Aragon was also reinforced. Isolated data provided by Lapeyre on Castilian customs has revealed that Catalan fabrics and Perpignan cloth were both imported and, moreover, that an intense trade was maintained with Valencia, where Castilian wheat was sold in exchange for goods including silks, citrus fruits, and rice (Lapeyre 1981, pp. 47–9). These expansive trends in internal trade are clearly visible in some commercial indicators of a more quantitative character (Yun 1987; Montemayor 1996).

Political and institutional reasons also pulled in this same direction and contributed to the reduction of risks and costs of transaction in long-distance commercial operations within the Peninsula. In regard to the currency, the Emperor's reluctance to undertake devaluations is well known.

He was loathed to introduce measures that, indirectly, would have meant a certain convergence of the monetary systems of the various kingdoms during the first third of the century.[27] There were sound financial reasons for this policy. However, Charles V's reluctance disappeared in 1537 with the order to issue *escudos* of 22 carats equivalent to 350 maravedís, which seems to have positive effects.[28] In a similar vein, the reduction of the *vellón* to 5.5 grains in 1552 facilitated lower-level trade and the circulation of fractional currency, vital for local and regional trades and the development of commercial and artisanal activities, in which this type of coin was commonly used (Hamilton 1975, pp. 69–70). The beneficial effects of these operations are better understood in light of the reflections of Sargent and Velde on 'small change' (2002).

Another important advance was found in the policy of appointments and the creation of notaries. This phenomenon, always interpreted from the perspective of power relations and whose limits we will study, has a certain relevance as means of guaranteeing contracts in a society that until this point had based its guarantee on personal knowledge or the endorsement of intermediaries known by both the seller and buyer. In these years the role of the notary or scribe came to be defined in great detail, although this policy actually stretched back into the fifteenth century.[29] In 1503 the Crown sought control of the appointment system, with the aim of ensuring the competence of the office holder,[30] while Charles V was concerned because the appointments of these officials were approved by the justice of

[27] See Hamilton (1975, pp. 67–8). The requests of the Cortes for the reduction of the quantities of silver and gold in the different coins (the ducat or *ducado y la blanca*, above all) can be found in *Actas de las Cortes de Castilla* (hereafter *ACC*), M. Danvila (ed.) (1861), vol. IV, p. 328 y 388–93, among others.

[28] This measure brought the currency into line with the monies then circulating in France and Italy, thus limiting its outward flow towards these countries and improving its interior circulation in more important transactions. At the same time, it also served as an incentive to trade between Castile and Aragon, as there was now a standard measure with the money that had been circulating in Catalonia since 1535 (Hamilton 1975, p. 69).

[29] In order to prevent the appointment being made by arbitrary methods that might result in the naming of unqualified individuals, in 1480 the Catholic Kings decreed that 'no title of scribe of the chamber, nor of public scribe, should be given to anyone other than a qualified person, one examined in the council and with licence from the king'. At the same time, their duties and requirements were defined (*Nueva Recopilación*, libro IV, Tit. XV, ley I).

[30] This was done at the same time as appointments made by other means were revoked. *Nueva Recopilación*, libro IV, Tit. XV, ley V.

the town or city in question.[31] Yet, piecemeal legislation was handed down that regulated the formal conduct of these officials, with the aim of improving their status as bondsmen for contracts, something which was in principle positive for trade and transactions in general.[32]

Although the regulation of notaries and scribes produced no decisive qualitative change, this sort of measure may well have had some positive effects, especially if we consider the relatively insecure initial situation.[33] This policy would strengthen with the improvement of the *Chancillerias*, whose support for the fulfilment of contracts and judicial functions is well known (Kagan 1991). It resulted in legislation that provided guarantees on commercial transactions, contracts, and compliance,[34] with

---

[31] In this regard, see law III (of 1534), or law XVIII, in which an order is given with the aim of extending the scope of action of the scribes, with the corresponding effect of enlarging their role as guarantors and so reducing uncertainty in transactions. Specifically it states that 'we order the *corregidores* and justices of cities and towns of these our kingdoms that they should compel and reward the scribes of a number of them that go out into the land to take writs and despositions as they are asked [to do]'. *Nueva Recopilación*, Libro IV, Tit. XXV, ley XVIII.

[32] An attempt was made to avoid nepotism in the actions of the scribes, who often fell into this trap when dealing with the networks of monasteries and religious institutions. New norms were set down, with annual checks, new protocols, and norms of behaviour stipulated for testimonies, and writs, with the aim being to guarantee the efficacy of the system. See *Nueva Recopilación*, Libro IV, Tit. XXV, *passim*.

[33] The importance of the measures introduced in regard to scribes should be underlined. They were not brought about by a new drive by the Crown to set down rules and control social life, although at times the towns criticized these measures on these grounds. On the contrary, on more than one occasion, the Crown asked for the extension and strengthening of the powers of these officials, without doubt because of their quest to inculcate greater respect among private individuals, a quality that was increasingly important for the urban oligarchies as a means of reducing risks and increasing security in economic relationships of an ever more impersonal and market-orientated nature. Thus the City of Granada included among its petitions of 1542 that the clause should be respected that anyone using his property for a *censo* should register it before a scribe of the council and that no alternative arrangement should be allowed. It is very necessary, it went on to note, for the good of these kingdoms that those who engage in contracts should not be misled. *Patronato Real*, 69–82, AGS.

[34] Aside from the *Nueva Recopilación*, other collections of legislation of this period can be found. See the wealth of norms and rules on companies that are found in Hugo de Celso, *Repertorio de las Leyes de Castilla*, Madrid, 2000 (edited by Alvarado Planas), specifically, f. LXXV ff.

provisions that aimed to standardize weights and measurements[35] and the publication of compendia of laws.[36] Although these measures were apparently aimed specifically at lawyers and men of justice, in all cases they sought to improve the legal system with the aim of building confidence in commercial activities and achieving a quicker settlement of disputes—a trait which, as is well known, is one of the keys to the development of trade.

All of these measures, in themselves conducive to the integration of markets, were accompanied by a fall in the costs of transport. The phenomenon is difficult to measure, and, indeed, no series of prices for transport costs can be given. But the signs are very clear. In the first place, prices were clearly rising, and, on the other, the supply of transportation was evidently expanding, trends which will be explained later (see Chap. 3). These circumstances must have led to a decline in relative prices of transport.

In conclusion, the formation of vibrant internal commercial networks could be interpreted as a negative phenomenon for endogenous development if it had served only to encourage the penetration and distribution of industrial products and the export of raw materials. But there certainly were industries which, although they had to suffer foreign competition, also drew benefits from the abundance of raw materials or the commercial advantages drawn from the expansion of the external sector. In addition there were sectors that were able to undertake a process of technical

---

[35] According to Hamilton (1975, pp. 168–9), the real advances in this regard were achieved during the reign of the Catholic Kings, while Charles, 'weighed down by the burden of the Empire and the cares of state, had hardly any time to devote to such prosaic tasks' (p. 169). We do not know the extent to which the reign of the Emperor saw an advance in this regard. As late as the 1570s, there were some who stated that in Salamanca a number of figures were 'somewhat lacking in their measurements and weights', 'pesas y medidas algo faltas', *Cámara de Castilla, Libros de Cédulas*, lib. 62, AGS.

[36] The collections of laws cited in this chapter should be seen in the same light. Their very survival implies a greater capacity to apply laws dealing with responsibility, commerce, risk, guarantees, and so on. As set down in the *Nueva Recopilación* of 1571, the new volumes use and cite pre-existing texts such as that of Diego Pérez de Salamanca, *Repertorio de todas las Leyes y pragmáticas y Bulas...*, Medina del Campo, 1549, or that of Hugo de Celso cited above (*Repertorio de las leyes de Castilla... Op. cit.*). In turn, this tome was first printed in Valladolid in 1538 and included new norms, rules, or guidelines on a wide number of matters such as 'debts and debtor' (*deudas y deudor*) f. XCII, 'contracts' f. LXXVII, 'guarantor and guarantee' (*fiador y fiaduría*) f. CXLV–CXLVII, 'buying and selling', f. LXXV, and so on.

development and import substitution. As we will see in the next chapter, the expansion of urban networks and industrial development were both very consistent with such developments.

* * *

Spain and Portugal created a highly complex system in their colonies. Certainly it is problematic to describe it as an absolutist one (meaning one in which the king's authority was unchallenged and unrestrained), much as this has been the view of many scholars. Far from being a monolithic, well-controlled instrument whose logic can only be explained by the decisions taken in its hierarchical vertex, the Spanish and Portuguese colonial systems emerged as a complex binding of powers and working interests, simultaneously delicate and characterized by relatively decentralized decision-making processes. This is not to deny that major efforts at centralization and control were undertaken from the Lisbon and Madrid or that, as we shall see, these attempts became even more frequent from the end of the sixteenth century. The juridical code itself helped towards this, in part because it considered the colonies as belonging to the Crown (nor should it be forgotten that the king continued to hold rights over the land). The result was a high degree of autonomy, with a diverse number of decision-making centres but the existence of a central power that took responsibility for the government and regulation of social and commercial relations. In societies as complex as these, where the presence of the Crown and its degree of penetration into the social fabric varied, these arrangements would lead to levels and forms of negotiation that were very different from one another and which are difficult to set within the (usual) formulas of polycentrism and centralism.

Spanish and Portuguese institutions in both empires had in fact provided positive results for economic growth and expansion in the peninsula. But, being also appropriate to a society whose development had been based upon war and conquest, they also had a notable capacity for destruction. In other words, the rules of play were shaped by mechanisms leading to both the capture and destruction of wealth. At times, they were highly inefficient in replacing lost resources, largely due to the extremely limited development of medicine and the other tools necessary to resist death, which was the main challenge to emerge from the conquest. This fact was also seen in the way that the Spanish adapted existing American institutions to their use.

The impact of all of this in the colonies and therefore in the different patterns of empire had to be, however, very uneven. After 1492 a period

of ecological imperialism took place in America, and the European institutional systems were to prove more adept at destroying the existing productive systems than at reconfiguring them rapidly with a more effective
apparatus. Few episodes in the history of humanity have had such dramatic effects or such long-lasting ones. On the contrary, the effects in
Africa and Asia were different. In the former, the slave trade, developing
with Atlantic expansion, would lead to convulsions within the original
societies. But the lower degree of penetration of the Europeans until the
nineteenth century and their greater resistance to disease produced less
profound social changes in Africa than in America (Headrick 2010). The
population would even continue to grow throughout the sixteenth century. But in regard to Asia, the scope for the decomposition of the original
societies and the establishment of destructive (European) institutions was
also highly reduced. This was, moreover, a world with a microbial system
close to that of the old continent and more resistant to diseases brought
by the Europeans.

On the other side of globalization, Europe was affected as, especially,
was Spain but not in the way we have supposed for years. The growth of
trade to which America, the African coast, and Asia contributed did not
break the model of poly-nuclear development of the fifteenth century, and
the Iberian societies did not move to the semi-periphery of this New
World economy. In this regard the institutional framework was crucial.
The informal mechanisms for the creation of confidence and the reduction
of risk appear to have been efficient, as can be seen in the trading networks
based upon personal accords, familial ties, and reputation. The expansion
of international trade is incomprehensible if we fail to understand this.
And these institutions overlapped with the formal institutions created by
the monarchy in both countries in a way that was beneficial for economic
growth. This was not because of the intrinsic nature of these institutions
but rather because of the huge number of resources available to them. The
benefits were manifested in improvements to the system of justice, contracts, the use of money, international commercial organization, and interregional trade. Attention should also be placed upon the fact that even
institutions based upon privilege, the use of the monopoly or expensive
and asymmetrical information, appear to have had positive outcomes. To
put this another way, they did not abort the capacity for growth prevalent
in a society of abundant but unexploited resources.

This leads us not only to relativize the impact of political or formal institutions on economic growth but also to think that their effects depend directly upon the context and the quantity of available resources. These conclusions will only gain strength in the following chapters, which examine the internal evolution of Iberian societies.

Open Access This chapter is licensed under the terms of the Creative Commons Attribution 4.0 International License (http://creativecommons.org/licenses/by/4.0/), which permits use, sharing, adaptation, distribution and reproduction in any medium or format, as long as you give appropriate credit to the original author(s) and the source, provide a link to the Creative Commons licence and indicate if changes were made.

The images or other third party material in this chapter are included in the chapter's Creative Commons licence, unless indicated otherwise in a credit line to the material. If material is not included in the chapter's Creative Commons licence and your intended use is not permitted by statutory regulation or exceeds the permitted use, you will need to obtain permission directly from the copyright holder.

CHAPTER 3

Domestic Expansion in the Iberian Kingdoms

During the last decades of the twentieth century, historians became convinced by the model of the *economie immobile*. This interpretation, heavily influenced by the Annales school, postulated an almost total absence of economic growth prior to the Industrial Revolution.[1] The application of this model to the Iberian kingdoms—sometimes even avant la lettre—presented a highly negative interpretation of their economic development in the early modern period. Indeed, some authors even argued that the economy was dominated by an extensive agriculture which was fundamentally incapable of increasing its levels of productivity. The result was, it has been argued, a demographic increase that absorbed any expansion in production and which unleashed a crisis of Malthusian proportions at the end of the sixteenth century that was followed by recession. According to the assumptions of the new institutional economics as practiced by Douglas North, this outcome was also the inevitable result of the imperfect development of property rights in Spain; this imperfection was, in North's view, linked to the absence or extremely limited development of the capitalist system of land ownership (North 1981). Yet the realities of the 'Spanish case', which have so often been taken as irrefutable proof of these theories or models, in fact constitute excellent examples of

[1] See, for example, Le Roy Ladurie (1966). But the idea has been taken up again recently in a more sophisticated way by Clark (2007).

© The Author(s) 2019
B. Yun-Casalilla, *Iberian World Empires and the Globalization of Europe 1415–1668*, Palgrave Studies in Comparative Global History, https://doi.org/10.1007/978-981-13-0833-8_3

the limits of these visions in explaining the behaviour of the economy. Above all, this is true in regard to Castile but also for most of the Crown of Portugal.

A TECHNOLOGICAL CROSSROAD[2]

Beyond economic considerations, a negative and pessimistic vision has long been very present in the different views on Iberian technological development. It is as if the technological delay characteristic of the Spanish and Portuguese industrial revolution of the nineteenth century had been projected retrospectively, giving rise to a sort of black legend according to which the development of useful knowledge had been always impossible in the Iberian countries. It is in part a consequence of the Enlightenment view of Spain and Portugal, expressed by Masson de Morvillers who, in a famous article in the *L'Encyclopédie Méthodique*, inquired: 'In two centuries, in four, or even in six, what has Spain done for Europe?' Spain, he added, is a country where it is necessary 'to ask priests for permission to read and think?' (Eamon 2009). In the last few years, however, historians of both science and technology have drawn attention to the capacity of sixteenth-century Spain and Portugal—frontiers in this aspect did not exist—to expand in these fields.[3] They have also underlined the capacity of the peninsula to transfer this type of knowledge to the American colonies, with emphasis falling on the idea that these advances were vital to the control, conquest, and exploitation of these territories. But this process had its origins in Europe. Some of the keys to it will be developed in this chapter: the use of the mule, of agrarian instruments made from iron, leather, esparto grass, and canvass, all of which were to be evident in the development of rural industries in the Old and New Worlds. These were not revolutionary technologies but did take their place in this process of piecemeal, widely dispersed improvement whose overall impact would be important. Although no diachronic studies have been attempted, it is evident that the use of mills to grind flour advanced, with windmills being very prominent. Very probably Cervantes was venturing beyond the anecdotal when he set technology and knightly ideals as opponents and rivals in his two great

[2] A more elaborated and detailed version of what follows in Yun (2017). After writing these lines, I could read Cañizares-Esguerra (2017) who goes in depth on these ideas.
[3] See the cases studied in López Piñero (1979), Goodman (1988), and Barrera-Osorio (2006). For a brilliant defence, Eamon (2009).

scenes evoking the windmill and fulling hammer: logically, *don Quijote*, a noble himself, identified these two monsters as his natural enemies. As we have seen, improvements were also made in the field of iron production. The introduction of techniques borrowed from German mining in the quarrying of silver and other sectors was a part of this process (Sánchez 1989). For obvious reasons, Iberian societies quickly adopted American dye products (indigo, the Campeche stick, or cochineal) that allowed it to make changes in the textile production processes.

If maritime expansion cannot be explained without reference to the technological and scientific progress achieved in fifteenth-century Iberian countries, then additional improvements in these fields were also the cause of the qualitative leap forwards made in the sixteenth century. The creation of the School of Pilots and Cartography in Seville, the Academy of Mathematics (founded by Philip II), the treaties on cartography such as those of Francisco Faleiro or Pedro de Medina and many other initiatives give the lie to the old stereotype of sixteenth-century Iberia being a society disinterested in technology (Goodman 1988). Something similar can be said of figures such as Juan de Monardes, a medic from Seville whose relatives were merchants involved in the *Carrera de Indias* and who brought him grasses from the New World so that he could study them and test their medicinal qualities. But this was just one part of a broader trend. What was really going on was the systematic amplification of forms of empirical knowledge gathering that would shortly culminate in Sir Francis Bacon's consecration of this type of scientific knowledge as a crucial part of modern thinking. In reality, Monardes' contemporaries included figures such as García de Orta, a converted Jew, medical doctor, and botanist from Portugal whose works would go around the world (Boxer 1963).[4] Something similar could be said of engineering and hydraulics, which were set out in the works of Juanello Turriano (Zanetti 2012). The numerous proposals of the *arbitristas* were comparable in scope to modern patent applications (García Tapia 1990).

Though there are several examples in Joan Thirsk's influential study on English projectors (1978), scholars have systematically overlooked the fact that some English proposals for economic improvement and the modernization of its industry and mining sector depended upon introducing changes whose origins lay in Spain or Portugal.[5] Perhaps not too many

---

[4] García de Orta, *Tratado de las drogas, y medicinas de las Indias Orientales*, Burgos, 1578.
[5] See, for example, some cases quoted by the author (Thirsk 1978): stockings knitted of silk (p. 45), hard white soap (pp. 53–4), and Spanish leather (p. 55).

hasty conclusions should be drawn from an area that still requires more in-depth and detailed study, but it is important not to forget the known contributions when attempting to reach a balanced assessment of the technological evolution of early modern Iberian Peninsula.

It is also worthwhile to remember that Iberian naval technology was crucial to Dutch maritime development and that Castilian financial techniques—with marked Italian roots—would spread in Europe in the sixteenth century (de Vries and Van der Woude 1997; Van der Wee 1967).

Though, as we will see, important advances took place, it is quite possible that a weak point of this technological development lay in the failure to adapt agrarian techniques, crucial for the economy of the time. Here, perhaps, improvements in organization were more important, even if they are sometimes difficult to separate from technological improvements, with which they often went hand in hand. In any case, it is important to remember the reasons for this progress, although here, again, more research is needed. A hypothesis can at least be presented. The Iberian Peninsula combined two necessary conditions: it was, first, the crossroads of technological development and cultural cross-fertilization; and, second, technology was vital to maintaining the empire. Oceanic expansion had been possible thanks to the meeting of different cultures (Chap. 1). And this continued to be the case. Being the centre of a composite monarchy spread out across Europe, the enormous power of the King of Spain and his needs generated a strong gravitational pull upon 'mechanics', inventors, and intellectuals from across the world. Juanello Turriano was from Cremona. Monardes had one eye on America and the other on Castile. De Orta was born in Castile, emigrated to Portugal, and travelled to Goa. The Welser and the Fugger, who carried American and Iberian mining forward, gathered their knowledge in Germany, the most advanced country of its time in this sector. Even the procedure for the amalgamation of mercury came from a German, who put it into practice in America (Sánchez 1989). And we cannot overlook the fact that many of those who proposed 'remedies', reforms, and patents—sometimes it is difficult to differentiate between them (Yun 2016)—were Italians and Germans, Flemish, and French. Not all of these proposals had much sense, of course. The term 'arbitrista' carried the connotation of madness or opportunism (Yun 2016). But the very fact of their existence demonstrates an intellectual effervescence. This circulation of techniques and inventions, the sponsorship of hybrid forms that brought about new knowledge, is typical of the period in which the word 'invention' was not taken to be that different from the term 'imitation' and was understood as such in many areas of Europe, where what was presented as an invention in one country was very often merely a copy of something common elsewhere.

The type of networks that allowed these new inventions and forms of knowledge and expertise to circulate was also highly important for other activities. In part they were similar to the webs through which artisans moved (Epstein 2002). These would be very prominent in relation to mining, which benefited from being a sector with an almost non-existent degree of guild governance, thus ensuring a higher degree of receptivity when faced with innovation. But this was also true in relation to the circulation of men, science, and ideas through princely courts and noble households. This was the case in the circuits that spread the new knowledge on mining, hydraulics, mathematics, and watchmaking and in which Juanello Turriano moved (Zanetti 2012). The same was true of many other specialists and inventors who proposed patents to the monarchy. But the king was also concerned, as were institutions such as the Council of the Indies, to develop new types and fields of knowledge, often being conscious that these areas were very poorly represented in the universities. The transfrontier character of the monarchy and its elites (Chap. 4) pulled in this same direction, favouring the circulation of knowledge. The presence of books on geometry, mathematics, geography, and history (disciplines intimately linked to war and to natural philosophy) in noble libraries is eyecatching. Questions of personal and familial prestige aside, this was a type of knowledge that was not confined to the nobles and that, moreover, revealed an interaction with the 'mechanics' and other intellectuals who played such a role in the art of war. These contacts were especially intense with Italy, the most important centre for the production of scientific and technical knowledge of the time. And this helps us to understand a phenomenon that until recently was largely overlooked by scholars.

LOCAL INSTITUTIONS, REGIONAL ECOSYSTEMS, AND LAND PROPERTY RIGHTS

But if the capacity to produce and, above all, to adapt and recycle technology was one of the keys to Iberia's economic and geographic expansion, then this growth can only be understood through a description of the different regional economies and land property rights. In the end, this economy was fundamentally a regional one conditioned by its physical characteristics.

In an area marked by an enormous diversity of geographical and institutional features, it perhaps makes sense to begin with an idea of the vast differences that existed between productive ecosystems and regional institutions, many of which had emerged during the centuries of the *Reconquista*. This disparity was manifested in many different forms of productive organization, wealth distribution, and social domination which were to a large degree the result of the interplay of the three basic institutions in rural life: the peasant family, the rural community (often organized in *concejos* and *cámaras* in Castile and Portugal, respectively), and the *señorío*.

The so-called Atlantic Spain, the area from Galicia to Navarre in the north of the country, was an ecological unit. These mountainous regions all shared a climate of mild temperatures and frequent rainfall spread over the calendar year. Their abundant water supply, extensive natural grasslands, and thick woodland meant that they were very different from the Spanish and Portuguese interiors (García Fernández 1975). Yet, these general features notwithstanding, this was a very heterogeneous region. In Galicia and Asturias, the peasant community had converted itself into the basic unit for regulating and exploiting agrarian resources (Saavedra 1983, p. 17, 1993, pp. 428–51). This function was performed by the *concejos*, or rural communities sometimes made up of a number of different villages or settlements and sometimes by one single nucleus that organized social and economic life in its territory. The *concejos* regulated crop rotation patterns and controlled the exploitation of the ample and leafy woodlands, which were often held as communal property. With certain logical differences, this situation was reproduced in Navarre and in the Pyrenean valleys, where communities frequently grouped together to exploit the available resources (Zabalza 1994, pp. 65–7). The Basque Country was, however, slightly different in this regard, even if it did not break with the model entirely. Here the extended family unit was crucial—in many senses even more than the rural community—and the majority of these functions were organized around the farmhouse and on a smaller scale.[6]

In spite of the role of the *concejos*, and in marked difference to the situation on the Meseta, it is clear that the role of the peasant community as a mediator in the distribution of products between the peasantry and its land-

[6] Even in the fifteenth century, this area had seen the emergence of ties of association between different towns, guaranteeing a better defence of their common interests and a better regulation of the mountainside spaces (Fernández de Pinedo 1974, p. 62).

lords had been reduced. In Galicia the *concejos*' struggle against the rights of the landlords had led the latter to prefer to receive payment of rents in *enfiteusis* on a lifetime basis or even as a perpetual lease, with the individual famers paying them directly (Saavedra 1985, p. 443; García Fernández 1975, pp. 190–7). Here, again, the Basque Country was the exception to the rule, as almost half of its peasants were landowners and farms were generally rented on shorter-term leases.[7] The result across Atlantic Spain and the western Pyrenees was the stability of the peasant exploitation, based on extended family networks that were strengthened by the proclivity of the landlords, who were predominantly ecclesiastical institutions, to rent lands as units with all of their attributes (houses, space for livestock, etc.) to families and married couples. This created rural communities in which social inequalities were much less pronounced than on the flatlands of the Meseta. But at the same time, these conditions strengthened the position of a middling group of *hidalgos* and intermediate nobility that lived in the more important centres such as Oviedo and Santiago. Shortly this social group would benefit from lands ceded also *a foro* (through *enfiteusis*) from the great ecclesiastical institutions and lay landowners. This development allowed such middling aristocrats to take part in agrarian production and converted them into a fundamental link in the chain of power and the exercise of coercion on the local level. Even in the Basque Country, a mid-ranking sector, whose fortunes originated in commerce, was consolidating its position in networks that distributed agricultural products (Villares 1982, pp. 77–95; Fernández de Pinedo 1974, pp. 58–9).

This being a zone of abundant year-round rains, these factors led to demographic and productive growth. In some areas this growth was based upon a 'pre-revolution' of millet, which supplemented the cultivation of other cereals such as wheat, barley, and spelt. Moreover, the abundance of woodlands and mountain pasture, together with the precise regulation of the use of farmable soils, allowed agriculture and livestock farming to thrive side by side, a development which the consequent high quantities of animal effluent further encouraged. The high quantity of woodland resources and the resulting opportunity to feed both livestock and people provided a large number of additional assets to these peasant economies and limited the effects of bad harvests (García Fernández 1975). A number of auxiliary activities, some of them encouraged by the urban development of the Meseta,

---

[7] For the Basque Country, García de Cortázar (1988, pp. 262–3).

Table 3.1   Demographic growth in sixteenth-century Iberia

	1530	1590	% growth per year
	0.000 inhabitants	0.000 inhabitants	
Crown of Castile			
Andalusia	762	1067	0.7
Asturias	81	133	1.1
New Castile	614	1145	1.4
Old Castile	1049	1254	0.3
Extremadura	305	451	0.8
Galicia	263	504	1.5
Leon	503	633	0.4
Murcia	74	115	0.9
Basque Country and Navarre	268	296	0.2
Total	**3919**	**5598**	**0.7**
Crown of Aragon			
Aragon	255	310	0.4
Catalonia	251	364	0.8
Valencia	273	360	0.5
Total	**779**	**1034**	**0.5**
Continental Spain	**4698**	**6632**	**0.7**
Portugal	**1162**	**1550**	**0.6**

Sources: My own elaboration from Nadal (1984) and Miranda (2016), applying to Portugal the ratio *vecino*/inhabitant of Nadal: 4 instead of 4.3

supplemented incomes: transport; short-term migration to the peninsular interior in search of wages during the harvest of cereals and viticulture (from July to September), iron and carbon production, and trade in leather, woods, fish, and other local products to the more urbanized areas of the interior.[8] Population growth, if quite meagre in the Basque Country and Navarre, was highly notable in Asturias and Galicia, where clear demographic spurts occurred between 1530 and 1580, despite this being a period of considerable emigration (see Table 3.1 and Map 3.1).

These characteristics, common across Atlantic Spain, were also present in some of the foothills and more humid climates with a rich vegetal cover of the Duero Valley, such as the sierras of Sanabria, the mountains of León and Burgos, the high regions of Soria, or the foothills of the north of the central system (above all Ávila and Segovia). But overall the *central plateau*

---

[8] Saavedra (1983, p. 50, 1985, p. 18), Anes (1988, p. 39), Lanza (1991, pp. 121, 143–8).

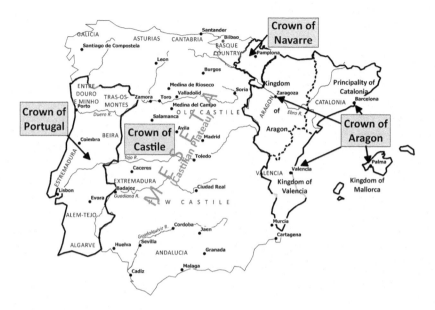

Map 3.1   Iberia in the sixteenth century

(the *Meseta*)—the extensive flatlands of drier climate and more extreme temperatures that stretched from the mountains of Cantabria and the Sierra Morena through the valleys of the Duero, Tajo, and Guadiana rivers—presented a very different panorama. Having said this, allowance must be made for the diversity of such a big region.

The mononuclear *concejos* that dominated the north of the Duero were succeeded by the poly-nuclear 'communities of town and land' (*comunidades de villa y tierra*) to the south of the river. The latter were extremely hierarchical organizations where the 'town' controlled economic activities not only within its own estate but also within those of the surrounding rural communities. Here the rural community played also a crucial role, organizing and regulating the exploitation of natural resources, setting the crop rotation patterns (normally based on a cycle of just over a calendar year and in which cereals were the staple crop), and alternating between sheep farming and the cultivation of the vine and the system of rotating cornfields (*derrota de mieses*). This entailed the opening up of the agricultural farmland immediately after the cereal harvest by August so that local herds could graze on the stems and stubble and fertilize the land with their excrement. The result was an open field system organized by the community that both defended vineyards and oversaw systems of local transhumance running to the nearby mountains. In many cases a number of councils or communities of one *comunidad de villa y tierra* formed alliances in order to exploit their pastures and woodlands, thus increasing their economies of scale. Moreover, many of these communities counted upon extensive tracts of unfarmed lands within their municipal estates; these terrains either had no owner or belonged to the king and thus could be used by farmers or livestock breeders with the council's permission (Vassberg 1983).

The role of the rural council was also significant in the distribution of wealth between landlords and peasants. The quantities of wealth channelled through them on the Meseta were far greater than in their equivalents in Atlantic Spain. These institutions often undertook to collect the royal or seigniorial taxes such as the *alcabalas* and the *tercias* from the inhabitants. Frequently the community, as a corporation, had obtained the right to use seigniorial lands and was charged with organizing their use and transferring the tribute or payment to the landowner for these privileges. The community operated, therefore, as the basic intermediary between the rural society and the landlords, who in many cases enjoyed the right to appoint to local authorities and to administer justice at a basic level—in other words, they exercised coercive power.[9]

This is not to deny, however, the existence of a direct relationship between great lords on the one hand and individual farmers on the other. On the contrary, this arrangement was common and even led to the emergence of a wide variety of forms of direct relationships between the tenant and the landlord, running from *enfiteusis* to the short-term renting of properties belonging to the nobility or Church. Many seigniorial properties included pasturelands and woodlands that were never rented or ceded to councils but instead exploited directly by their owners for their livestock economy.[10] This system was even more common in the extensive zone to the south of the Tajo, where large landowners controlled huge flocks (particularly sheep)

---

[9] In Castile at this time, 'the farmers did not speak individually, but instead as natives of a municipal corporation; kings and lords communicated with their mayors more than with individual subjects' (Nader 1990, p. 18).

[10] See the case of Guadalajara in Gómez Mendoza (1978, pp. 88–92) or, for a different form, the case of the county of Feria in Badajoz and the pasturelands of the count of Belalcázar in la Puebla (Cabrera 1977, pp. 277–9).

and enormous grazing lands. Many proprietors of this sort—the Monastery of Guadalupe, the archbishopric of Toledo, or the Military Orders—were closely tied to the Honoured Council of the Mesta (see Chap. 1).[11]

Further to the south, this large-scale property ownership and, therefore, social inequalities became increasingly common. Although the ecological possibilities of this zone, in which summers are considerably warmer and rains more scarce, were more limited, these high levels of inequality compelled the peasantry to diversify its economic undertakings, resulting in the development of domestic industry, transport activities, and alternative agriculture in general. These adaptations provided families with additional incomes and allowed them to overcome the basic inequality in land ownership. These forms of alternative agriculture or peasant industries were viable thanks to the emergence of peasant markets regulated by the more important towns using privileges conceded by the local lord or the king himself.[12] Markets of this sort constituted centres of commercialization for the wools of small local herds as well as for linen, esparto grass, hemp, and basic crude cloths. Finally, these rural markets also served as the focal points for myriad transport activities (Vassberg 1986, p. 238).

The Mediterranean and continental climate of the interior had lower rainfall levels than Atlantic Spain. Nevertheless, in these zones there thrived a cereal agriculture whose yields matched the European average and existed side by side with exceptional numbers of livestock, particularly sheep, which were grazed not only through transhumance between different ecosystems but also (and above all) between different municipalities (Bishko 1978). This agro-pastoral economy was noticeable for forms of communal organization and the co-ordination of resources in both the low hills and flatlands. Furthermore, despite the false stereotype of this being a zone completely dominated by the designs of the all-powerful Honoured Council of the Mesta, it is clear that, the main transhumance routes and certain pasturelands excepted, it was the local community that exercised the greatest influence over land use. This was also, of course, an important area for vineyards,

---

[11] Ruiz Rodríguez (1993, p. 27); Klein (1979, p. 73); López-Salazar (1987, pp. 9–18).

[12] The term *alternative agriculture* alludes to a series of non-basic crops of considerable, if ultimately marginal, importance and which became a valuable source of income for many peasants in early modern Europe (Thirsk 1997). Noel Salomon refers to a similar phenomenon, placing emphasis upon artisanal production, viticulture, and transport as 'peasant industries', activities providing auxiliary incomes to peasant economies (1982, pp. 33, 111, 291–301).

a labour-intensive crop, whose cultivation was undertaken thanks to the protectionist by-laws of the rural centres. The greater cities further to the south, where considerable distances separated the inhabited centres from the farming areas, saw important changes. These were brought about by the replacement of the ox by the mule, a quicker beast of burden and so one capable of ploughing more rapidly and travelling to more distant areas—an important consideration given the progressive concentration of property and the dispersion of plots of cultivated land. The diffussion of the mule constituted, probably, one of the more important technical advances implemented from the fifteenth century.

The predominance of hereditary systems based upon the division of property among all of the peasant family's sons resulted in patterns of early marriage. Unfarmed and communal lands were widely accessible; many councils specifically reserved these for local married couples or widows. These conditions resulted in a zone of unquestionable demographic vigour, with high levels of population mobility.

Seigniorial incomes, boosted by their jurisdictional rights and the consequent increase in landlords' capacity to collect excises, were enhanced by lands rented on short-term, renegotiable leases and, at times, as *enfiteusis*. In some cases, owners directly exploited their estates (above all, this was true for pastureland and meadows). But the basis of their income lay in the *tercias* and *alcabalas* paid by the peasant communities as institutions.[13] In many cases the uneven division of productive resources had created a rural elite of farm workers (*labradores*, a sort of yeomen) who regulated the use of resources belonging to the municipal institutions.

Thus, the Meseta was a dynamic and growing region. The solidity of peasant economies in the Duero Valley and mounting urban development favoured the growth of production and population, which was only limited by its high demographic density and elevated rates of land occupancy (see Table 3.1).[14] Further south, in New Castile, Extremadura, and Murcia, less solid peasant economies, with lower levels of urban density, were blessed with

---

[13] As it has been said before (Chap. 1), the *tercias* were the 2/9 of the ecclesiastic tithes and the *alcabala* an ad valorem tax on commercial transactions. Both were often ceded to the jurisdictional seigniors.

[14] With demographic densities of 16 inhabitants per square kilometre, the highest of the peninsula in 1530, the population growth would have been 0.3% annually (Table 3.1).

enormous quantities of exploitable land as yet unfarmed (their densities around 1530 were 8.4, 7.3 and 2.8 inhabitants per square kilometre, respectively), and this would attract new settlers from the northern areas who sought small plots, a salaries, or, more commonly, both. Commercial development, which in Murcia's case depended upon distant and sometimes even foreign markets, would be one of the keys to growth across this broad swathe of territory, as can be understood through an analysis of population figures.

From a political and institutional perspective, the rural communities of *Andalusia* also enjoyed extensive legal and coercive powers. With a more concentrated urban and semi-urban population, the ample communal estates offered abundant opportunities in the foothills to the north of the region and, indeed, in upper Andalusia in general; but there were also many opportunities in the lowlands of the Guadalquivir. These lands were allocated as small plots, thus lending a degree of solidarity to the humbler peasant families and anchoring the population to the soils.[15] In addition there were a large number of unfarmed and council lands, communally owned and managed by the municipalities. These were dedicated to livestock farming or the production of wool. The community constituted, therefore, an important element in the exploitation of resources in Andalusia. It also played a significant role in the transfer of incomes to the landlords, who claimed *alcabalas*, and monopolies on slaughterhouses, flour and oil mills, and taverns, as well as taxes on the passage of commodities. The collection of these revenues was entrusted to the municipal authorities or controlled through the jurisdiction that the seigniors exercised over rural centres.[16]

Yet, this region had the most highly developed forms of large estates (*latifundia*) belonging to the great lords, the clergy, and even the mid-ranking nobility. From the fifteenth century onwards, the organizational basis of these *latifundia* was the country house or *cortijo*, the centre of an extensive farmstead boasting granaries, various kinds of mills, stables, a courtyard, pens, and a residence where the proprietor or tenant would live (Collantes 1977, p. 115). Large enterprises of this kind were usually leased out over six-year periods in exchange for rents paid in specie or coin. In some cases they were directly farmed by the landowner. Their logic was

---

[15] Cabrera (1977, p. 350), Vassberg (1986, pp. 168–9), and Mata (1987, vol. I, pp. 180–6).

[16] Atienza (1987, pp. 234–79). For areas of the Sierra Morena, see Cabrera (1977, pp. 250–330).

therefore very different from those of the family units that distinguished other areas to the north. In Andalusia, and more in particular in the Guadalquivir Valley, on the other hand, salaried seasonal work predominated; agricultural surpluses were sold in the highly populated urban centres or even sent to foreign markets. But there also existed a network of smallholdings; additionally, many small plots of land belonging to the local lord or municipality were leased out. These smaller exploitations supported a working population employed seasonally on the great estates, thus serving as a means of externalizing maintenance costs.

It would, however, be wrong to speak of uniform conditions across the region. On the contrary, a wide range of characteristics were found in lower and upper Andalusia. In general terms, however, Andalusia appeared to be a society characterized by levels of inequality that were even more marked than those of the north of the peninsula, and this was true not just in economic terms. Because its population was continually augmented by immigration, the lower strata of peasants played a relatively insignificant role in local government. Above all, this was the case in the large towns, where the councils were controlled by local oligarchies that were never entirely independent of the nobility. Familial or client relationships united these different factions with the great nobles, creating a very fluid and complex dynamic.

As in the zones of La Mancha and Extremadura analysed above, the abundance of both available land and salaried work in the great estates attracted immigrants from the north of the peninsula. The constitution of the great cities stimulated both the commercialization of the surpluses of these huge estates and their dynamism in attracting settlers. The resulting demographic growth, if less dramatic than in New Castile (in part because of the loss of people sailing for America), was nevertheless clearly evident in the economic dynamism of this large region (Table 3.1).

An advanced form of rural council organization that formed an important link in the regulation of productive resources and the transfer of landlord incomes had also developed in the region of *Aragon*. The *concejos* collected the *pechos*, taxes on the members of the peasant community, on behalf of the landlord. They also collected the symbolic rights inherent in the lord's jurisdiction as well as monopoly rights on slaughterhouses and mills. Often councils had been granted the control of communal lands conceded by the seignior in exchange for a *censo enfitéutico* or 'treudo' (Colás and Salas 1982, pp. 33–42; Colás 1988, pp. 24–6). However, in Aragon the lords' income also included revenue streams derived from a more direct and unmediated relationship with their vassals in which the councils often played little or no part. There were also full or allodial properties, rented to peasant families or farmed directly by the landlord using hired workers and, in the case of the *Moriscos*, groups who were compelled to serve their lord with personal labour whenever this custom had not been commuted to direct payment in money. But this type of property, fully owned by the seignior, was less developed than in Castile, and, whether it was with the intervention of the community or without it, Aragon was 'the world of shared proprietorship'. A long time previously, the lords had handed over their lands in return for a 'censo enfitéutico' or 'treudo', sometimes contracted out in perpetuity and paid in money, coin, or by a portion of the yield (Colás 1994).

The vestiges of servitude and the importance of shared property differentiated Aragonese from contemporary Castilian landownership, but the major difference stemmed from the evolution of the jurisdictional power of the lords. Jurisdictional prerogatives in themselves hardly generated any economic income; however, here, as in Castile, certain landlords' possession of absolute jurisdiction converted them into judges whose decision could not be appealed, thus marginalizing the authority of the king himself. The lords' capacity for enforcement and the control of violence was even more marked in Aragon than in the Crowns of Portugal and Castile.

Shared property, which acknowledged the peasants' right to cultivate the land, and the abundance of communal lands helped to stabilize both Christian and *Morisco* peasant family economy. Yet peasant society remained characterized by marked internal differences, with many farmers continuing to live in small holdings often based upon an intensive agriculture depending upon irrigation systems and auxiliary activities directed towards the market (crops such as saffron, the vine and olive, etc.) (Atienza 1988, p. 147; Colás and Salas 1982, p. 38).

The combination of absolute seigniorial jurisdiction and the presence of the *Morisco* population, whose legal status was weaker, contributed to the formation of a society in which the power of the nobility was almost unlimited in terms of both its control over vassals and its capacity to interfere with the organization of the economy.

Growth was, therefore, limited in Aragon by its relatively inflexible economy, which in turn can be understood as a result of the shackles of feudal origin, the exercise of noble jurisdiction, and the minimal level of urban development. Annual demographic growth was thus restricted in the kingdom to rates of around 0.4%—and this despite its low demographic densities (5.3 habitants per km squared) (Yun 2004). These characteristics may be seen, in part, as a consequence of the juridical insecurity of peasant existence and the extremely arbitrary justice to which seigniorial authorities submitted rural communities.

The communities of the *kingdom of Valencia* also 'possessed a great vitality' (Ardit 1994, vol. II, p. 190). They constituted centres around which social and economic life was organized. But, at the same time, the majority of the land belonging to the seigniors and to the large ecclesiastical institutions was rented out, either in *enfiteusis* or as leases, directly to farmers with no form of intermediation by the community (Peris 1989, p. 86). In some areas, such as those around the Huerta, a region where the irrigation network had been extended, the use of plots of land conceded in *enfiteusis* served to reduce the differences that had emerged from the inequitable division of peasant property. The result was a situation of great variety in the distribution and structure of farmlands (Furió 1995, p. 308).

In general the coastal zones and those near the capital witnessed a form of agriculture that was highly influenced by the market and consequently was dedicated to commercial products. This was especially true in areas around the region of Huerta, where an intensive farming of fruit, mulberry trees, and vegetables predominated, and in the coastal zones and those near the capital. From the sixteenth century, viticulture was spreading into the dry lands (those without guaranteed irrigation), producing raisins, almonds, and crops exported for industrial use (Halperin 1980, pp. 21–2, 26). These trends contributed to the diversification of peasant incomes and fed economic growth. In many areas, the 'decision on the use of the fallow land was made by individuals, not collectives, and depended on the quality of the terrain'. Farmers who directly exploited their soils possessed thus 'an unlimited degree of control over their lands' and 'an almost-absolute liberty in deciding which crops to grow' (Ciscar 1977, p. 44; Peris 1989, p. 37). This progress was fed by the availability of capital from cities, merchants, and even the aristocracy, as in the case of the Genoese interested in sugar cane production, silk, and other products or the duke of Gandia, who invested with the aim of expanding the cultivation of these crops. Another positive factor lay in the need to provision the capital, Valencia, which was growing because of international commerce (Chap. 1) and the exploitation of crops such as sugar, silk, and other products. Cereals were sourced from across the Mediterranean (and especially from Sicily) and from Old Castile.

As in Aragon, the jurisdiction of the landlords had developed significantly in Valencia and even offered a certain degree of autonomy from the king's legal authority. This jurisdiction was wielded through the authorities named by the community government and played an important role in the transfer of rents to the landlords who received part of their income from their land through direct exploitation but whose principal income derived from lands conferred upon tenants in *censos*. Another of the most important income streams was the *tercio diezmo* and *regalías* (rights of the king ceded to the landlords) and privileges linked to jurisdiction that were paid by the community as a whole.[17]

These trends resulted in highly diverse agrarian systems, ranging from the extensive exploitation of livestock (in the interior uplands) to the intensive agriculture of the meadow or *huerta*. In all cases they were exercised with vigorous forms of feudal jurisdiction. But this was also a highly flexible agrarian economy, very much orientated towards the market, where *enfiteusis* served as the basis for improvements in production undertaken by the peasants enjoying perpetual use of the land that they farmed. In this context, the region's commercial development around the capital sparked a growth surge that was clearly manifested in the figures detailing demographic progress.[18]

Similar paradoxes can be found in *Catalonia*, where, nevertheless, the landowners' vigour was considerably less noticeable. The idea first outlined by Pierre Vilar (1962, vol. I, p. 562), that the Sentence of Guadalupe brought about 'a feudal restoration and a social pact that confirmed feudal revenues' (Serra 1988, pp. 46–9) and created a new social equilibrium in the countryside (see Chap. 1) has been widely accepted.

The basic motor of late fifteenth-century growth does not appear to have been the rural community. As in all of Europe, it continued to be the fundamental unit upon which the jurisdictional power of the landlord and king was exercised through local authorities and delegated legal representatives. But, in general, their involvement in economic life was less common than was that of their counterparts in Castile or the region of Aragon. On the contrary, the key to both the rural economy and Catalan agrarian expansion was the family, always tightly tied to the land through the *mas* (Elliott 1963, pp. 28–31) and whose role had been strengthened by the Sentence of Guadalupe to the

---

[17] Ciscar (1977, pp. 228–35), Ardit (1994, vol. I, pp. 92–3).

[18] According to Ardit, the population may have increased between 0.25% and 0.41% annually between 1510 and 1609, depending on the population at the starting point (1994, vol. I, p. 19).

extent that it consecrated the property rights of the peasant elite and established the precedent that only by its abandonment could a property return into the hands of the landlord. The crisis of the fourteenth century and the subsequent concentration of lands appear to have led to the increase in the habitual size of the *mas* (Vilar 1962, vol. I, p. 577). These larger dimensions brought about an improvement in their capacity to mobilize productive resources. Inheritance rights tended to reserve the lion's share of goods for one of the sons (usually the eldest), and this custom also favoured the stability of the family farm, even if it prejudiced the other children. This explains the coexistence beneath the same roof of not only the head of the family but also a number of his brothers and sisters, who thus constituted a complex variant of the family unity and one capable of mobilizing a large amount of labour (Elliott 1963, pp. 28–31). But this was not the only consequence of the Sentence of Guadalupe. At the same time, the establishment of this strata of *masovers* (an elite of property owners exploiting its rights over the *mas*) had contributed to the crystallization of another wider sector of small peasants—the other side of the coin—who found themselves compelled to rent the plots of the *mas* or to work upon them for a salary during the periods of greatest agricultural activity (Elliott 1963, p. 30).

These conditions gave rise to a form of peasant society with a high capacity for production. From an early point, it supported the emergence of *masías*, assisted by the security and permanence of property rights. In many cases this was fed by important investments in fixed capital (buildings, granaries, and stables) and brought about a reorganization of farms which, in turn, would have an impact upon production. The renting out in *enfiteusis* of plots of the *mas* to small peasants served to tie the workforce to the land and consolidated the position of the humblest groups in rural society, thus feeding demographic and agrarian growth. These developments were accompanied by the expansion of industrial and market-orientated crops that diversified both resources and sources of income for the rural population. The result of all of these changes was the expansion of the vineyard, or the increasing exploitation of millet, rice and vegetables, dry fruits, hemp, silk, and saffron (the latter products tied to the commercial networks established by German merchants trading through Perpignan and the fairs of Lyon). Catalonia, therefore, supported relatively dynamic and flexible agrarian systems, in which polyculture was made possible around the *masía*, whose prosperity was based 'upon the *size* and the *variety* of its production' (Vilar 1962, vol. I, p. 584).

The collection of revenues was very seldom channelled through the community as such, and by the sixteenth century, all prospect of resurrecting the personal *remensa* (the payment due to the lord for the chance to leave the land) and many of the feudal rights claimed by landlords in the previous century had vanished. This led to a higher degree of security for their vassals and tenants (see Chap. 1). But, at the same time, the landlord claimed a number of important prerogatives which allowed him to seize an important part of the surplus production and to participate in the agrarian growth brought about by the extension of this ever-more flexible and varied agriculture (Duran 1982). Yet the overall equilibrium was not threatened by the enforcement powers wielded by the landowners; on the contrary, and in comparison with previous periods, these seigniorial prerogatives in fact limited the landowner's propensity to commit abuses and so came to form the basis of a new period of demographic and economic growth. Catalonia's population grew at an annual rate of 0.8% from 1530 to 1590 (Table 3.1). As was the case in other southern zones of the Iberian Peninsula, one of the reasons for its attractiveness to settlers from the north—in this case, the French side of the Pyrenees—lay in a combination of institutions, natural resources, and economic factors.

More than an ecological unity, *Portugal* was a set of regions made up of very distinct physical components. The differences are very marked: from the mountainous zones of the north, such as the provinces of Entre-Douro-e-Minho and Tras-os-Montes, with their Atlantic climate, to the plains of the Alentejo and even the more mountainous zone with the highest rates of precipitation, such as the Algarve in the South. The role of the *concelho* (equivalent to the Castilian and Aragonese rural council or *concejo*) was important across the country. The system for the concession of privileges established by the Portuguese kings was governed by the idea that the monarchy should not grant excessive power to any one nucleus. It had, however, given rise to a more homogenous and less hierarchical political sphere than in Castile, as above all differences were caused by economic activities (Mattoso 1997, pp. 205–40). Moreover, in overall terms long-term leasehold (*enfiteusis*) had developed to a significant extent during the last centuries of the Middle Ages, to a considerable degree due to the stagnation of the population at very low levels between 1350 and 1450 and the consequent need to attract settlers to many zones of the country (Mattoso 1997). The north of the country had seen the establishment of more seigniorial estates, while in the south the great councils were abundant, with extensive municipal estates and sometimes existing under the jurisdiction of the Military Orders. This difference between the north and south—and above all between the north and south of the Tagus River—was perhaps one of the most important traits of the Portuguese economy. In any case, the farming system regulated by councils predominated across the country, with rotation timetables for cereals, at times combined with the vine, olive, and ovine livestock. The north, being more populated, was characterized by a variety of crops and natural resources that permitted a higher density of population, which was well above the peninsular average. This being the case, it witnessed the strongest forms of emigration, above all towards the Tagus Valley, Lisbon, the settlements of the lower Tagus Valley, and even in part towards Alentejo, to the extent that its poor soils allowed such a movement. Moreover, in addition to the diversity of resources, the north of Portugal was more open to the Atlantic through Lisbon and the cities and towns between Porto and the frontier with Galicia. This was a region where the impact of the oceanic and commercial expansion would have a notable effect.

The poor soils and arid summer climate of Alentejo between the Tagus and the Guadiana meant that it was less conducive to economic activities. Its very low demographic densities (among the lowest of the peninsula), the concentration of commercial activities to the north of Lisbon, and the coastal characteristics meant that its openness to and interaction with the sea were very limited, despite its boasting almost 300 km of shoreline between Lisbon and the Cape of St. Vincent. Here wheat and transhumance livestock farming (above all in the frontier zones with Castile) had a relatively greater importance (Magalhães 1997, pp. 230, 239), and it is not surprising that pasturelands were hired out to Castilian shepherds. But the chances of the commercialization of peasant production were very modest, not only because of the absence of an attractive outside market but also because of the low density of the urban mesh that was, in Castile, a crucial factor in growth.

ECONOMIC EXPANSION IN A PRE-INDUSTRIAL SOCIETY

The expansive cycle that had begun in the last decades of the 1400s was sustained throughout the following century. But what type of expansion was achieved? What were its dimensions and limits? Did it fit the model of an extensive agriculture surrender to diminishing marginal returns or yields whose surplus production is systematically absorbed by the upward evolution of land rents or seigniorial extractions, the result of which is a debilitating tension between resources and population?

Growth and Development

It should immediately be stated that the present-day definition of modern economic growth, based upon a continuous process of expansion in per capita product, must be applied with great caution to pre-industrial economies. Even if they did not achieve this increase of income per inhabitant, in economies which existed on the margins of subsistence, success lay in the simple production of more foodstuffs that allowed them to support more inhabitants. But the Iberian cases allow us to go further than this.

The population increase in Spain is, without doubt, evident and even more accelerated than in most parts of Europe, as can be seen from Table 3.2, which presents some corrected numbers for Spain, following the calculations of J. De Vries and my own estimates by using data from Nadal (1984) and Miranda (2016). The population of Portugal also had risen from some 1.2 million inhabitant households around 1527 to some 1.5–1.6 million inhabitants at the end of the century (See Serrão and Marques 1998, p. 44, Graph 1; Miranda 2016). Whatever the point of reference, it is clear that the Spanish and Portuguese population increased

Table 3.2 Demographic growth in sixteenth-century Europe

	(Millions of inhabitants)					% growth per year
	1500	1530	1550	1590	1600	
Scandinavia	1.5		1.7		2	0.28
England	2.3		3.1		4.2	0.86
Scotland	0.8		0.9		1	0.22
Ireland	0.8		0.9		1	0.22
Holland	0.95		1.25		1.5	0.45
Belgium	1.25		1.65		1.3	0.04
Germany	12		14		16	0.28
France	16.4		19		20	0.19
Switzerland	0.6		0.75		0.9	0.4
Italy	10.5		11.4		13.1	0.22
Spain		4.69		6.63		0.7
Portugal		1.2		1.5		0.6
Austria-Bohemia	3.5		3.6		4.3	0.2
Poland	2.5		3		3.4	0.3

Sources: My own elaboration from De Vries (1994, p. 13) and Nadal (1984, p. 74, Table 9) and Miranda (2016), using a ratio vecino/inhabitant of 4 for Portugal (see Table 3.1)

noticeably even in comparative terms with Europe from 1530 to 1590.[19] As matter of fact historians agree that in both cases the demographic growth was particularly intensive until 1570.

The same impression emerges when we turn from population to the main indicators of cereal production (Yun 2004, pp. 199–200, Graphs 4.1 to 4.4). Even when allowance is made for the purely approximate nature of these figures, it is clear that the 1500s continued the long phase of expansion begun during the previous century. Abundant references can be found to indicate the expansion of other products, such as wine and olive oil in both countries.[20] Probably this dynamism was less noticeable in the case of sheep, for which our data is less solid and convincing, but the overall conclusion must be positive.[21] In regard to the secondary and tertiary sectors, if inherently more difficult to measure, the figures provided on urban and industrial developments are highly indicative of commercial and industrial growth in the northern Meseta and Andalusia and even in Catalonia, Valencia, and the coastal areas of Portugal.[22]

As traditional historiography has underlined, there can be no doubt that, aside from the commercial development described above, this general economic expansion was made possible by an increase in agrarian production derived from the extension of cultivated lands, to which many contemporary sources allude.[23] This is evident at a local level in the permissive policy of many towns and councils with regard to the breaking of

[19] The figures given for Spain by De Vries (1984) (6.8 and 8.1 million inhabitants in 1500 and 1600, respectively) appear less trustworthy than those of Nadal (1984, p. 74). Spain witnessed the second largest growth in all of Europe after England (0.86). Portugal is also in the most dynamic group with a 0.6% of growth per year.

[20] In Valencia, Cáceres, and Catalonia, the data sets refer to overall production of cereals, wines, and other goods, which are representative of the majority of agrarian production (Yun 2004). For other regions, see Casey (1983, pp. 266–7), Ibáñez (1995, p. 244), Huetz de Lemps (1967), Ponsot (1986, XIX, see chart 4.6), Pérez and Lemeunier (1984, Graph. 1), and Latorre (1989).

[21] The number of livestock in the Mesta appears to have fallen noticeably from 1520 (Le Flem 1972), but it does not appear that this contraction could have been sharp enough to bring down the overall agrarian product. A number of cases confirm this thesis (Lemeunier (1977, p. 327), Halperin (1980, p. 25)). Moreover there are reasons for thinking that this reduction was compensated by higher levels of stationary livestock farming and short-distance transhumance (Ruiz Martín 1990a).

[22] Bennassar (1983, pp. 324–28), Pulido (1993), Elliott (1963, p. 56), García Espuche (1998).

[23] See, for example, López-Salazar (1986, pp. 151–252). For Portugal, (Magalhães, 1997).

new soils and the need to attract settlers by conceding fiscal exemptions and access to unfarmed land (Pérez and Lemeunier 1984, pp. 63, 66, 69–72; Yun 1987, pp. 120–3). But the extension of cultivated land is also evident in the fact that those regions where the population density was lower in 1530, such as New Castile, Asturias, Galicia, Murcia, Andalusia, the lower Mondego, the areas around Lisbon, Alentejo, and other zones, were generally those that made the greatest progress over the course of the century. Only the kingdom of Aragon fell outside of this paradigm, for the reasons outlined above.

If very difficult to measure, intense bursts of interregional migration stood at the heart of this dynamic. Notwithstanding its notable potential for growth, the north-western area of the peninsula appears to have been sending inhabitants to the Duero and Tagus valleys for much of the sixteenth century both in Portugal and Castile.[24] At the same time, the northern Meseta was providing settlers for Extremadura, New Castile, Andalusia, and Murcia. This same pattern is also found in the eastern regions, where the kingdom of Aragon hardly grew despite its low initial population densities, although it clearly helped to feed the notable expansion of Catalonia, even if the principal factor in the growth of the principality was the arrival of French settlers, while the kingdom of Valencia attracted immigrants from France, Gascony, Aragon, and Castile.[25]

But does the extensive character of the agrarian system mean that it makes no sense to speak of a growth in per capita income and productivity in the sixteenth century? This is in fact the most common idea among economic historians, and there are even those who, like Cipolla (1976) or H. Kamen (1978), denied some decades ago not only the existence of economic development but also, implicitly, the idea of genuine growth.

There exists, however, a great deal of evidence that allow us to be more positive and even to support a more critical view of the image of an *economie immobile*, as Hoffman did for the case of France (1996). As I think I have proved (Yun 2004, pp. 211–4) by using estimates of different regions such as New Castile, Catalonia, and Andalusia, there are many reasons to

---

[24] See the case of the migration flows to Medina del Campo in Marcos (1978, p. 272).

[25] For Catalonia, see Nadal (1984, pp. 74–82). For Valencia, attention falls on the annual accumulative growth rates of 0.47%, and it can be supposed that these would have been still greater in the first half of the century. Ardit proposes a general rate of growth between 0.51% and 0.82% between 1530 and 1580 (1994, vol. I, p. 19). See also Furió (1995, pp. 271–4).

think that the agrarian output increased faster than the population at least until the 1570s (Yun 2004, p. 213). In other words, it is more than probable that total population growth in the kingdom fell beneath the expansion of production for several decades.

We are faced, therefore, with an unmistakable agrarian expansion, meaning an increase in the agrarian product 'per capita'. Beyond this, insofar as the primary sector generated a significant portion of the total product and was accompanied by a phase of industrial and commercial developments, it is clear that this trend represented a phase of real economic growth in all senses. For this reason, it should not be surprising that, at the end of the century, the indicators for the consumption of meat among the Spanish should be very close to those of areas of notable economic vitality, such as Italy. And if, regrettably, there are only a few studies on the material culture of the period, it is nonetheless clear that a certain increase of production of consumer or industrial goods aimed at the domestic market took place, above all among certain sectors of the better-off peasantry, a trend that corroborates the overall pattern of changes (Livi-Bacci 1988, pp. 144–5).

But the most reliable indicator of economic growth in pre-industrial societies is, without doubt, the coefficient of urbanization which, in effect, represents the proportion of the total population that does not live off agriculture. Growing urban population rates therefore unequivocally indicate the increasing productivity of the rural sector, which was able to feed a higher proportion of people living in towns. This form of growth is undeniable across Spain and Portugal. As Map 3.2 shows the urbanization rates in both countries and in Castile in particular were already quite high by 1550 (the figures for Castile correspond in fact to 1530). Furthermore, the urban population not only grew more quickly than the rural one but did so in eye-catching proportions. An analysis of the figures provided by Jan De Vries shows that in Spain the percentage of the population living in urban nuclei with more than 10,000 inhabitants passed from 6.1% in 1500 to 8.6% in 1550 and 11.4% in 1600; whereas the overall development of urban centres within Europe went from 5.6% to 6.3% and 7.6%, respectively. This rhythm is even faster in Portugal, where, thanks in part to the expansion of Lisbon, the figures were of 3%, 11%, and 14.1% of the population in centres of more than 10,000 inhabitants (De Vries 1984, p. 146, Table 3.7). If we take the centres with more than 5000 inhabitants in England, France, Holland, and Castile, we find that one of the areas where this portion of the population had most quickly grown is Castile (Table 3.3). It had risen from an index of 62 in 1530 to 100 in 1600

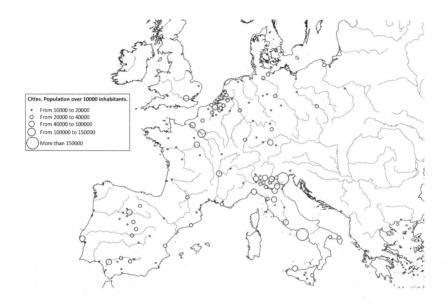

Map 3.2   European urban networks, 1550

Table 3.3   Urban population in Western Europe

	France		England		Holland		Castile	
(% of inhabitants in centres of more than 5000)								
	%	Index	%	Index	%	Index	%	Index
1500	9.1	105	5.3	66				
1530							13	62
1550					20.8	72		
1600	8.7	100	8	100	29	100	21	100
1650					37	128		
1700	10.9	125	17	213	39	134		

Sources: My own elaboration with data from Wrigley (1987) and Fortea (1995)

(1591 to be exact). Castile therefore exhibits, with England, the fastest rate of urban growth (Table 3.3). This urban development is even more meaningful if one considers that Castile, which represented more than the 80% of the Spanish population, was already by 1530 one of the more urbanized areas of Europe with 13% of its inhabitants living in centres of more than 5000 people (more than in France or England) (see above Table 3.3). Likewise, by the same epoch, the 8.6% of the Portuguese lived in towns of more than 10,000, which is even more than in England and France too. It is not surprising that the most recent estimates of Spanish and Portuguese economic growth in terms of GDP per capita shed also a positive image (Álvarez Nogal and Prados de la Escosura 2013; Costa, Palma and Reis 2015).[26]

The Advantages of Peasant Economies and Increasing Productivity

What were the causes of this increase in per capita productivity that belie, at least in its most simplistic and absolute formulations, the argument for the *economie immobile* as well as the idea of an increasing pressure through rents that would swallow up any increase in production?[27] Recent studies draw attention to the strictly relative nature of this immobility and provide reasons for thinking that interpretations such as those of G. Bois (1985) and R. H. Hilton (1985) that used to place emphasis on seigniorial extractions may need considerable modification. It may be worthwhile, therefore, to reconsider the peninsula's agriculture from the viewpoint of property rights and ensuing balance between land and labour.[28]

---

[26] Gelabert (1994, p. 184). The theme was set out and quantified by Prados de la Escosura and Álvarez Nogal after the first version of this idea had been developed in Yun (2004).

[27] The most complete vision is probably offered by Le Roy Ladurie, who coined the concept. See (1966, vol. I, pp. 226–35).

[28] It may seem strange to those scholars, such as North and Thomas, who have postulated a close correlation between individual property and agrarian growth (and, logically, by extension shared ownership and economic stagnation), but a more precise organization of the various ways by which soils were owned and a perfection of community practices was in fact positive in creating growth in the productivity levels of peasant labour. The theories of North and Thomas and their vision of Spain can be found in North (1981, p. 150). The passage above having been written for the first edition (Yun 2004), a number of colleagues have drawn my attention to parallels with the excellent work of Horden and Purcell (2000). Probably some parallels do exist. However, I would place emphasis on institutions and property rights and their interaction with connections between regions and their respective ecological systems. In any case, Horden and Purcell attempt to provide a very generic model of the Mediterranean (probably not unique and exclusive to the Mediterranean), while here I aim to study the specific key factors that allow us to define a particular phase of expansion on the sixteenth-century Iberian Peninsula.

Everything indicates that the fixing of local by-laws (*ordenanzas*) of towns and villages in the fifteenth and early sixteenth centuries led to a greater balance and complementarity between agriculture and livestock breeding and, above all, extended the advantages of this equilibrium to ever-greater surface spaces. Many measures were introduced to clarify not only property rights but also the use of the land, with the aim of attaining greater security in farming: the clearer demarcation of spaces over the seasons within the municipal estates, the appointment of guards to watch the vines and livestock, the creation of institutions such as the town shepherd, and other similar measures. In many cases, these initiatives were successful, with communal fields being used to benefit both agriculture and pastoralism at different times in the agrarian calendar, given the different potential uses of soils and the ecological conditions of each unit or area.[29] Rural communities not only improved the productive conditions of their estates but also, from the fifteenth century onwards, were keen to forge agreements and accords with other communities. The resulting sharing of pastures among councils, frequent in the Castilian *Meseta*, allowed cycles of transhumance between different municipal areas, as well as the short-distance displacement of livestock and general co-ordination of the demands of cattle rising with those of agriculture. Moreover landowners themselves were keen to implement this type of improvement, thus achieving a greater balance and complementarity between different agricultural zones which, without doubt, would contribute to heightening overall productivity.[30] In some areas the community coordinated the use of resources that were inherently difficult to regulate without collective oversight, such as water; in some areas of Aragon, the Spanish Levante, and the Portuguese banks of the Tagus River, the community would even undertake to dig and maintain

[29] The positive effects of greater security and the reduction of risks through measures of this sort with regard to crops were especially important for the extension of vineyards and other arboreal products. These were always highly vulnerable to the destructive incursion of livestock, above all at moments of flowering and fructification of the plant which, moreover, required significant investment, sometimes over several years, in work and care. See the case of the Tierra de Campos in Yun (1987).

[30] This long phase of productive expansion contemplated the increase in Castilian and Aragonese livestock, which would be directed towards the zones of poorer soils, Murcia and Valencia (Lemeunier 1977, pp. 338–9; Ardit 1994, pp. 56–7). In Aragon local- and interregional-level cycles of transhumance developed under the auspices of the landlords, which increased the complementarity of resources between the highlands of Teruel or the lands of Tierra del Moncayo, Pyrenees, and the banks of the Ebro river (Abadía 1993).

irrigation ditches.[31] In many regions, from Malaga to Mallorca and Valencia to Lisbon or Cáceres, the municipal by-laws prompted and regulated the expansion of fruit and mulberry trees in combination with other forms of activity and in harmony with the cycles of agricultural farming.[32] This complementary balance in exploiting resources was also found in the trend towards the specialization of products on the local level. In the Duero Valley, areas such as the Tierra de Medina, to the south of Valladolid, took steps towards specializing in viticulture, while the nearby area around Tierra de Campos began to focus on cereal production. This complementarity was determined not so much by the connections between these regions as by the effects of the growth of Valladolid, equidistant between both regions, due to its different ecological and institutional conditions. Similar movements were found in the Rioja region or in Murcia (Pérez and Lemeunier 1984, pp. 69, 78–9). Indeed, these regions were not so different from many areas around Lisbon where complementarity led to more interregional trends: here the chance to import cheap wheat over several decades allowed for the extension of the vine and other products in the regional hinterland.

All of this brought about a more efficient and secure use of the land. It also led to a greater efficiency in the use of labour and in the balance between soil and labour. In fact, this equilibrium adapted to the different agrarian cycles throughout the year and, by mobilizing hands at times previously marked by relative idleness, forged a more efficient work cycle over the year.[33]

---

[31] Apart from the examples cited above, see those for Valencia in Peris (1989, p. 255) and Murcia in Pérez and Lemeunier (1984, p. 84) or the form by which *Morisco* agricultural techniques were blended into the systems of Christian communities, bringing about notable advances in Ponsot (1986).

[32] See the surprising case of Cáceres, where the *ordenanzas* or by-laws brought about the expansion of mulberry tree groves and fruit trees (Pereira 1991, pp. 128–32). On the development of this type of products in Portugal, very much connected to what Thirsk called alternative agriculture, see Magalhães (1997, pp. 234–9).

[33] The example of the peasants of Murcia is illustrative in this regard. They cared for the vines in March and collected the leaves of mulberry trees so that between April and June, the silkworms could feed on them while the labourers were cutting the barley and leaving it to dry between June and July. Wheat was then also harvested. Some could even work in the salt farms from May to September and in the trap nets in June and September; from the latter month, it was possible to sell some products in local fairs, before harvesting the wine in

The intensification of work patterns in combination with the agrarian cycles was often accompanied by the interregional migration of temporary workers. The peasants of the north of the peninsula, highlanders, Galicians, and Asturians were increasingly present in the Castilian Meseta during the harvest weeks, after which they gradually made their way back towards their homes in a rhythm set by the ripening wheat, taking employment in each region for a few weeks at a time as they steadily moved northwards. Of course some labourers did remain in the Duero Valley for the grape and olive harvests in September and, after this, to work as peddlers and in the transport of goods to their homelands, carrying with them a variety of products acquired or commissioned in Castile's summer fairs (Vassberg 1996, pp. 67–77). Equally important were the short-distance movements, such as those of the settlers of the Castilian Extremadura who went down to harvest olives in Seville and of the people of La Mancha who farmed their lands during nearly the entire year but descended upon Murcia between April and June to farm the silkworms and harvest the wheat.[34]

The permanent migration of people indicated the existence of a surplus workforce and, therefore, a decreasing marginal productivity in the zones of the north of the Central System (both in Portugal and in Castile), in France, or in upper Aragon; labour moved from these areas to ones where high-quality soils could be farmed and, consequently, where labour's marginal productivity was higher. The result of a reallocation of this sort between land and labour could only be an overall increase in productivity per person.[35]

Despite there being very few incentives for investment for many landlords, there were some improvements in fixed capital and agrarian techniques. As we have seen, in Galicia and Mallorca, the tendency among proprietors was to rent lands as units of production with everything necessary

October. From this point to the end of the year, the cereal fields could be prepared, but, in addition, in December and January, the olive harvest had to be collected. Peasants might still be involved in the storage of olives or the shovelling of snow. See Pérez and Lemeunier (1984, p. 89).

[34] Herrera (1980, p. 232), Pérez and Lemeunier (1984, p. 90).

[35] This is more important if we take into account that in many areas of the South, which had low densities in the first half of the century, there must still have been an abundance of good lands which had yet to be farmed.

on them, something which shows an interest in agrarian equipment as the base for cultivation. As we have seen, in Catalonia the *masía*, whose basic construction represented the investment of fixed capital, was emerging as a productive unit in which the weight of the buildings, installations, and means of production increased, thus sparking a concomitant proportional improvement in peasant labour productivity. In Andalusia they were now building small cottages in the fields where the journeymen could spend the night in order to save time by avoiding long-distance displacements during periods of work (the sewing and harvest of olives and grapes), thus allowing the farming of lands which were not necessarily poorer but, more simply, had gone unused for centuries. The *cortijos* not only offered the necessary buildings, stables, or areas of temporary lodgings for the seasonal workers but also increased the number of mills for cereal and olive oil production in proportion to the expansion of olive farming (Herrera 1980, p. 232; Elliott 1963, p. 30).

There were technical advances in farming that, despite their relatively limited impact, should not be dismissed entirely. These improvements represented modest, but accumulative, advances. As we have seen, in Galicia and Asturias, a sort of pre-revolution of maize was brought about by millet. If the cultivation of millet had relatively modest beginnings in Spanish Galicia, its introduction into many regions of Portugal would be extensive and important. In the humid areas of the Atlantic North, the new species of African maize were really successful, in part due to the endemic scarcity of wheat, which was more apt for the plateau of the South, while rye was extended in the hills of the interior (Magalhães 1997, p. 231 and ff.). The spread of new crops such as sugar, rice, and the mulberry tree in many areas of Valencia, Aragon, or Granada and Malaga represented a decisive step forward that, moreover, often took place in the gaps between farmed fields and could be combined with other crops in the irrigated meadows as a form of alternative agriculture. In Murcia some of these small advances—significant due to their accumulative effect—ran from improvements in the measurement systems to the diffusion of waterwheels as a method of raising water in the irrigation ditches (Pérez and Lemeunier 1984, p. 65). And, if the effects of these improvements were most spectacular in the irrigated zones, there was no shortage of progress in the dry lands, manifested, for example, in the system of 'pasture and crop' and in the progress made in the enclosure of pastureland and use of fallow in combination with cereal cropping and the winter grazing of livestock in oakland (*adehesamientos*).[36] This system had a parallel in the combination of olive and cereal cultivation in some zones of Coimbra (Magalhães 1997, p. 245). Of course, specific forms of property and seigniorial rent were sometimes behind these advances. As said above, while a good deal of landlord revenue was not usually ploughed back into productive investment, in the context of a growing population and demographic mobility, it often created the institutional conditions that allowed peasant initiatives to have free reign. Some of these improvements—above all those implemented in lands rented out as *enfiteusis* for a lifetime or in perpetuity—were tied to the interests of the peasant to optimize the productivity of soils over which he enjoyed complete control. There were also forms of renting land, such as letting in return for a proportion of the products (share cropping), which created a positive stimulus towards improvement in some areas of the peninsula, specifically when guarantees were given that the landlord's portion or share would not be increased (Miranda 2017). In some areas the growth of seigniorial income could be achieved by rolling out new crops or using new technology. One example of this was the duke of Gandía's interest in expanding the growth of sugar cane and installing *trapiches*, mills to grind it, in his estates; many other landowners were keen to produce silk. And, of course, in all estates there was a clear movement towards the repopulation of the land, something which lay behind the productive enhancements of the century.

As agrarian historians have often remarked, the substitution of oxen for mules in some areas reduced the soil yields but was compensated by a resultant increase in the level of human productivity per hour worked. In many regions overall factor productivity must have increased until the top

---

[36] For example, in many regions of southern Spain, the system of 'pasture and crops' was extended, generally in the 'mountains of holm oaks', (*monte hueco de encinas*), meaning on one surface or area, a number of different forms of farming were undertaken, ranging from grazing lands to cereals, thus generating a wide range of products—woods, firewood, acorns, and so on (Pereira 1991, p. 99). In Salamanca, Extremadura, and Andalusia, examples of creating enclosed pasture (*adehesamiento*) have been found, which do not necessarily mean the displacement of cereal by livestock. On the contrary, it probably represented a more efficient form of combining both practices within large estates reserved for communal use and in which integrated systems for the use of soils were in place, 'to the great improvement of the ecological components of some zones' (Valle 1985, pp. 536–8).

earth was finally exhausted. The development of complementary activities outside of agriculture entailed the mobilization of otherwise idle hands. This resulted in the expanding use of female and male labours. David Vassberg has written that 'many peasants, especially those resident in the mountains, spent two or three months a year as itinerant merchants, or as muleteers or transporters, earning extra money'. Certain towns and areas of course played a prominent role in these networks, above all those situated in or near the frontier mountain ranges that separated these natural regions.[37] Equally important was the development of activities to transform agrarian products. The production of charcoal from wood was common from the meadows of the south to the mountain economies further north. But in some zones, it became a decisive activity, as was the case in the Basque Country and Navarre. For some of these peasants (above all those of the Basque Country), agrarian pursuits and the commercial exploitation of the mountain were combined with involvement in the iron industry (Bilbao 1987). For similar reasons, the development of this type of activity was also clear in Catalonia: 'forges and mills multiplied in the sixteenth century along the banks of the rivers and mountain streams' (Vilar 1962, vol. I, p. 545). Above all else this increase in peasant multi-activity was important in producing textiles and in manufacturing clay objects and leather goods and a multitude of other niche crafts. In many towns the production and sale of wool textiles, straps, farming tools, leather, clay, and linen products developed apace. And in some areas, such as the Rioja region, Segovia, Córdoba, the Algarve, Beira, between the Duero and the Portuguese side of the Miño region, and many others, the development of the domestic textile industry had the same effect of mobilizing unemployed workers, while something similar occurred in many Morisco areas of Aragon and Castile.[38]

The more pessimistic models and interpretations cannot be supported either by the available data on the evolution of rents or seigniorial demands. Certainly, the extension of the farmed area and pressure on land entailed

[37] Vassberg (1986, p. 3), Ortega (1974), Salomon (1982), and da Silva (1967). On the role of the *Moriscos* in transport activities and commercialization, see Halperin (1980, p. 73).

[38] Brumont (1993, pp. 135–6), da Silva (1967, pp. 29–31, 112), Fortea (1981, pp. 281–8). In the *Morisco* communities of Valencia, 'entire villages' of the duke of Gandía were employed in sugar cane cutting and the mills dedicated to its grinding, in making esparto and linen products, shoes, and mats (Halperin 1980, pp. 66, 70–1). For the Portuguese regions, see Magalhães (1997, pp. 254 and ff.).

an increase in payments for the use of the soil. But this process was thoroughly shaped and delayed by forms of ownership and property rights that, as we saw in Chap. 1, were directed at the building up of the seigniorial estate's population and the development of peasant economies.

In Galicia, Castile, Valencia, Catalonia, and other areas, the extensive properties let out in *enfiteusis* to families or communities created relatively secure conditions for their exploitation. The fact that they paid fixed (and predictable) sums for the use of the land encouraged peasants to take advantage of productive improvements. Even when the lands were given on short-term or revisable leases, the terms of contracts included fixed clauses or conditions of considerable importance: one such accord from Andalusia relaxed the rent payment in case of natural catastrophes. Frequently lands were exploited over long periods by tenants belonging to one family group, with successive generations forging a personal relationship with the proprietor; for his part the landowner gained additional security in rent payments, a trade-off which tended to lessen the tendency to increase these demands. In this way the restriction of the number of potential tenants to the inhabitants of a small town or village limited the possibility of raising land rents (Lemeunier 1998; Sebastián 1999, pp. 335–6). This and other similar forms of behaviour appear to have been especially important in the renting out of meadows and large properties for payment in coin, something which explains the barely noticeable increase in rents paid and even their diminution in real terms (Yun 2004; Miranda 2017). The abundance of unused lands (*baldíos*) or council lands (*tierras concejiles*) for which either no or very low rents had to be paid had a similar effect. And, on top of this, the first 40 years of the century witnessed a marked effort to extend communal rights on the royal estates, with the implicit permission of the Crown.

Of course, mechanisms existed for the adjustment of land rents. From the end of the fifteenth century, landowners began to take an interest in revising the *foros* and *censos entifeuticos* sometimes in perpetuity, hoping to rent lands on short-term, revisable contracts and in return for direct payment in specie. It is also clear that many nobles and powerful estate owners were tempted to claim royal lands where doubt existed over proprietorship, and this trend clearly reduced the ability of small holders to expand their farms without renting. But this land grab not only allowed for a period of readjustment but was also at times difficult to accomplish. Contrary to what was occurring in other areas of Europe (e.g. those zones of England where claims of full ownership were being advanced to change the terms of leases), many peninsular landlords had to face not simply isolated peasant families or small alliances of them but entire communities. In cases of this sort, peasant settlements not only resisted the ambitions of their lord by force but also—and before arriving at this extreme solution—enjoyed a notable capacity to recur to the royal law courts (the cases in the archives of Chancelleries are indicative of this facility; see Chap. 5), a practice that generated considerable additional cost to the landlord and served as a reminder of the value of prudence before entering into such costly lawsuits. The idea was that the justice system should maintain the laws of the kingdom, and it, in conjunction with the health and resilience of the municipal estates, played in favour of many communities over long periods.

Even for those owners of lands ceded in *enfiteusis* (these were very often nobles and ecclesiastical institutions), there was not always much sense in compelling the peasants to revise rents which, aside from not being easily modified, were tied to other more important forms of income, such as the *tercias, alcabalas,* and others. If we take into account that many noble families could overcome their income deficits through favourable credit arrangements in the form of *censos consignativos* (mortgages endorsed by their *mayorazgos*—Chap. 4), it is easy to understand why, despite the structural tendency to revise land property rights, there were also considerable practical reasons mitigating against any such alteration.

The results of these developments were widely evident. Even in areas of strong demographic pressure—such as in the Tierra de Santiago or Jaén—it was sometimes the case that the available rise in the revisable rents on lands was not automatically applied by landlords.[39] Moreover some of these mechanisms could, in the final instance, be beneficial for quite a few of the farmers. This was because the increase in rents and the pressure of demand upon lower-quality lands, together with the increasing money supply, brought about a rise in prices which in the end benefited the more efficient farms and those that were less exposed to this type of burden. Certainly, the inflation of the sixteenth century should not be explained in these rather Ricardian terms; nor were prices the most important variables in peasant incomes. But many farmers with surpluses which were not subject to higher rents were able to obtain this benefit through the market. It

---

[39] Yun (2004). It should be noted how, in the cases cited, the variable remained almost static until at least 1540. Overall, within this expansive tendency set out according to theoretical formulations, the trend of this form of extraction on produce should have been stable until the early sixteenth century.

is, moreover, evident that the effects of this change, if marginal, increased over the course of the century.

In this way, the fixed nature of seigniorial land rents created better conditions for peasant businesses for several decades, while the increase in the productivity of work over a long period compensated for any rise in payments to landlords. The combination of factors was favourable for economic growth and even for an increase in the levels of productivity. However, the theme should also be approached with an eye on other forms of extraction levelled on production, such as the fiscal burden. To understand this fully, a more general perspective is needed.

The Final Test: Industrial Development and Regional Urban Systems

The final and perhaps the most decisive proof of the consistence of the sixteenth-century Iberian economic expansion—that is, of its non-semi-peripheral character and of the strength of its agrarian and general domestic forces—can be found in the evolution of the changes taking place in the industrial sector and the regional urban networks. Though some ideas have already been advanced (Chap. 3), these aspects deserve additional reflection.

The textile industry, which was to be the most affected by the importation of foreign goods, underwent changes and introduced productive improvements which were intended to allow it to adapt to demands for higher-quality goods and that were characteristics of a vigorous and dynamic process of import substitution. In Cuenca, for example, we know of the dissemination of the *verlagssystem* and the merchant-manufacturers who came to 'put workshops in their homes'. Enjoying annual profits that averaged 15% in 1553, this sector had, since the end of the previous century, been adopting itself to the 'new draperies' (Iradiel 1974, pp. 232–3; Reher 1990, pp. 27, 30). Córdoba also overcame the sector's purely artisanal structure in order to facilitate the development of the 'new draperies' and the products' adaptation to the ever-changing demands of a market of greater dimensions and quality (Fortea 1981, pp. 271–2). This development was possible thanks to the introduction of agro-urban production circuits (Fortea 1981, pp. 279–80). A process of this sort also led to significant progress in the silk industry. A number of factors were behind it: the greater availability of raw materials, easier access to dyes, and improvements in the workforce, largely as a result of the efforts of the *Moriscos* (Fortea 1981; Aranda 1984).

In Segovia the growing weight of a new type of merchant acting as a *verlaguer* was significant. The result would be an increase in the quality and the wider dispersion of light cloths, which were even adapted to American demands (García Sanz 1987; Lorenzo 1979, p. 435). The *verlagssystem*, based upon an agrarian-urban cycle, developed in Toledo, advancing both the woollen cloth and silk industries. The wool industry also developed in the hinterland zones of Portugal, near the great livestock tracks. But the most dynamic sector was perhaps the one that produced cloth and linen fabrics, tied to domestic consumption but also—importantly—to the production of naval canvas (Costa 1997, pp. 253–81). Across the entire peninsula, a trend towards the production of high-quality items (and even the imitation of foreign fashions) can also be discerned, particularly in the silk industry. This was possible thanks to access to dyes and colourants through the international commercial circuits. Something similar happened in Valencia, whose production was strongly linked to demand in Castile ('the main customer for Valencian silk fabrics'), or in Barcelona, where the weight of the artisan sector grew thanks largely to domestic demand.[40]

We do not have in-depth studies of the functioning of the guilds, but everything indicates that, at least during the first half of the century, these would have been more open than has sometimes been believed. Where it has been possible to make accurate measurements, such as in Valladolid, it has been found that only 30% of apprentices came from the city itself (Bennassar 1983, pp. 217–21)—and it can be assumed that of these only a fraction came from the families of the masters who did the hiring. Despite later problems, many sectors displayed a certain permissiveness with regard to the activities of the *Morisco* population, whose technical expertise was of great importance in areas such as the production of silk fabrics (Aranda 1984). Thus, some sectors at least responded positively to some of the variables that elicited such pessimism from Ogilvie (2011), who has been highly sceptical of the capacity of Old Regime guilds to introduce productive improvements.

A comparison of the textile production figures for a number of Castilian cities against those of their most active rivals in Italy is very meaningful. This is especially true in light of the former's low points of departure. If, by 1560, 20,000 pieces of cloth were produced in Venice, Córdoba reached the

---

[40] Montemayor (1996, pp. 201–33), Casey (1983, pp. 88–90), and Vilar (1962, vol. I).

figure of 18,000, to which might be added the 7000 of the surrounding areas, while in Segovia some 16,000 were manufactured. It must, of course, be added that these figures can only take us so far and that the great Italian centres of production in Venice and Tuscany definitely produced goods of a higher quality and, therefore, of higher monetary value.

Moreover, the development of other industries should also be noted. This is true, for example, for the construction industry and associated sectors. Behind its dynamism there was the growth of population, the main roots of which are to be found in the expansion of the primary sector. But also significant was the new conception of the home and the spread among elites of tastes and lifestyles imported from abroad and, above all, from Flanders and Italy (Yun 1999c). By the 1540s the notion of the 'nobility of a city' had clearly won many minds and hearts, becoming an increasingly important facet of the political culture of the time and manifested 'in the people and buildings and memorable things that there are in a place, with temples, hospitals, bridges, castles, public buildings and private homes'.[41] The result was the development of a range of industries related to construction, including metalwork and carpentry.[42] The fact that construction developed in productive circuits restricted and closed in on themselves helps us to understand the huge impact of this sector on the domestic and local economies.

This change in the habits of consumption, coming on top of demand for cheaper, less sophisticated goods, also lay behind the expansion of the goldsmith (from candlesticks to cutlery), leather, and embossed-leather trades, the latter two being important in Córdoba (Fortea 1981, p. 243). New eating habits, which encouraged the use of cutlery and tableware, gave impetus to the porcelain industries of Talavera de la Reina or Triana (Seville), while more popular tastes encouraged the clay furnaces that sprang up in many villages and cities across Spain (Sánchez 1989, vol. I, p. 151). Toledo also boasted industries dedicated to silverware and jewellery (also extremely important in Córdoba) and the production of swords, musical instruments, sculpture, and painting. Demand for these artistic products often came from churches and clergymen (Montemayor 1996, pp. 201–6).

---

[41] *Diálogo en Alabanza de Valladolid*, en Alonso Cortés (1955, p. 250).
[42] See the importance of these sectors in Medina del Campo (Marcos 1978, pp. 312–20), Cordoba (Fortea 1981, p. 243), or Seville (Bernal et al. 1978).

This development was not confined to industry. Progress was achieved in mining thanks to technical advances of the first magnitude, linked both to government and private demands. The demands generated by trade, the army, construction, the textile, leather, food, and paper industries—all of these sectors fed a remarkable drive to farm unused fields; to advance the mining of iron, copper, tin, sulphur, and lead; to make better use of forests; and to produce dyes, lime, plaster, and brick (Sánchez 1989, vol. I, pp. 119–65).

Mining was a productive branch also tied to one of the most dynamic sectors—naval construction. And the development of this activity was undeniable. It would expand significantly in the north of the peninsula, in certain areas of Catalonia, and, above all, in Seville and Lisbon.

These observations explain why, in spite of the development of the export economy, urban growth did not conform in any way to patterns deemed typical of 'peripheral economies', which are generally taken to have low rates of urbanization, with the major centres found in the geographical periphery of the country. Regarding urbanization rates, we have already shown that they were high. But what about the regional distribution? Though one cannot speak of a peninsula urban system—that is, one stretching across Iberia—but rather of regional systems, the great dynamism of the hinterland is very meaningful. Areas of coastal development existed since the fifteenth century (Chap. 1), such as the shoreline from Barcelona to Valencia and Murcia/Cartagena. Seville provides another example of an expansive city, being tied to maritime activities for commercial exchange. Furthermore, the growth of the Portuguese cities from Lisbon to Porto (including those of the lower Tagus near the capital) was certainly very notable (Costa 1997). But the Iberian urban networks were more complex.

As regards Portugal (Table 3.4), around 1527 the number of Portuguese centres that passed 5000 inhabitants was very small when compared with Castile and the urban pattern, with the fast growth of Lisbon, reminds that of a peripheral economy.[43] On the one side, Portugal's cities' growth

---

[43] The great difference, however, was in the very physiognomy of the urban network. The gap between Lisbon and the rest of the country was not only greater—for example, in comparison with the difference between Seville and the rest of Castile—but also grew during the century. It would be necessary to wait until 1600—with the boom of Madrid—to encounter a similar breach or imbalance in Castile. In 1527 Lisbon already boasted 55–65,000 inhabitants and was the most populous city on the peninsula (Seville had hardly reached 50,000). In 1550, Lisbon may have reached 100,000. Porto had fewer, 13,000; by the midpoint of the century, this number had risen to 15,000 (Disney 2009, vol. I, p. 145).

Table 3.4   Urban population in Portugal, c. 1530

	1530		
	Moradores	*Inhabitants*	*% urb. pop/tot. pop*
Lisbon	13,010	55,943	
Porto	3006	12,926	
Evora	2813	12,096	
Santarem	1988	8548	
Elvas	1916	8239	
Tavira	1547	6652	
Guimaraes	1405	6042	
Coimbra	1329	5715	
Lagos	1310	5633	
Portalegre	1224	5263	
Setubal	1220	5246	
Total urban pop.		132,302	11
Total population		1,200,000	

N. B. towns with more than 5000 inhabitants

Sources: Teresa Ferreira Rodriguez (1997, p. 185) and Miranda (2016), using the coefficient 1:4.3 for the ratio morador/inhabitants

was based upon long-distance relations. Lisbon—and more and more Porto—was involved commercially with the fairs of Castile, with Seville, Flanders (highly significant), and, above all, Antwerp. They had also growing commercial connections with the African coasts, Asia, and Brazil. The dynamism of these cities was based upon their role in the process of re-exporting goods, as well as upon the arrival of wheat from North Africa: for the entire century, Lisbon became the redistribution centre of the country at times of dearth. But, on the other side, the oceanic expansion allowed cities such as Lisbon and Porto to have a marked impact upon their respective hinterlands, in which they would generate growth. The series of city ports that dotted the lower Tagus and, to a lesser extent, the Duero were further proof of positive effects of Lisbon and Porto on nearby centres, as was the growth of settlements on the Atlantic seaboard and as of towns of the interior such as Portalegre, Evora and Elvas, connected to the trade with Castile (Table 3.4 and Magalhães 1997, pp. 206 and ff.). Hence, this urban network, while, indeed, coastal and very much dependent of international trade, was not necessarily proof of a dependent economy as it is defined today.

In Spain the most dynamic towns remained those of the interior of Castile. The high degree of urbanization of the Crown of Castile and particularly of Extremadura, the Upper Guadalquivir Valley, New Castile, and Old Castile, in 1600 is very visible in Maps 3.2 and 8.1. That same impression emerges from an analysis of the active population of some of the Castilian cities already mentioned, among which the primary sector hardly reaches 20% of the active population and craftsmen are always above 50% of the total (Yun 2004, pp. 170–2). Particularly in the Duero Valley, these were mostly urban centres in the interior of the country, where the percentage of inhabitants working in industry and services was very high.

In conclusion, market integration and the dynamism of the agrarian and industrial sectors had not led to the formation of a pan-Iberian urban network. Rather, there had emerged a series of regional urban systems tied to the development of the exterior sector—and not always due to dependency relations—as well as an urban network in the centre of the Crown of Castile with degree of dynamism comparable to that of the most developed zones of Europe. Thus, there emerges the question: how can the economic and institutional model that stood behind this situation be characterized?

PATTERNS OF ECONOMIC GROWTH, MARKET, AND INSTITUTIONS

The answer to this question is complex: rather than an economic model, it involves regional models that developed links among themselves. Growth was largely based upon regional dynamics and was also made possible by the connections of each of these regional ecosystems to the outside world. The structure of these regional economies had not changed substantively in regard to the situation established in the fifteenth century (Chap. 1). On the Mediterranean front, however, Barcelona had reacted to Valencia's stealing a march; the Atlantic economy was now bound together more forcefully around Lisbon and Seville; the corridor joining the Basque towns to Burgos and the Duero Valley was also strengthened. The zones of the hinterland, which had been the most powerful motor for growth, were centred on the area from Duero Valley to Toledo, sometimes extending their ties towards the southern *Meseta* and even Andalusia (Ringrose 1983b).

The key was the existence of regional economies that did not constitute a completely integrated interior market but nevertheless created enough synergies among themselves to push forward growth. This development was the fruit of their more thorough insertion into international and even global economic circuits, as well as of a number of additional factors: a more efficient agriculture, the existence of complementary elements in the use of factors such as labour (with both definitive and seasonal emigrations providing positive stimuli), the synchronization of crops, the growing commercialization of the peasant production (very dependent upon the density of the urban networks), the complementary and connected nature of the ecological systems, and organization and technical improvements in the productive process.

In these circumstances, property rights that were very much at odds with those considered optimal by the theorists of the new institutional economics, in combination with moderate levels of land rent pressure on peasants, in fact had positive effects. All of these factors coincided (and dovetailed) with a very moderate level of fiscal pressure, a variable which, if inherently difficult to measure on account of the enormous disparity between actual and theoretical rates of taxation, appears to have evolved below real-term values for several decades, judging by the trend of the most important exactions. This occurred (see Chap. 4) in the Crowns of Portugal, Aragon, and Castile, above all from 1530 until 1560–1570. With regard to the latter period, where taxes increased noticeably in the course of the century, it is important to note that they hardly increased in real terms. But this was also the case of the *sisas* of Portugal, where fiscal pressure swiftly led to customs and duties being levied on foreign trade. Taking into account the upward evolution of agrarian production and population, it is obvious that the relative fiscal burden of the state on economic activities in general, and agrarian activities in particular, fell until at least 1570.[44]

So, if at some point during the first half of the century—very possibly in the first 30 years of it—some burdens were increased, then it is certain that this change could have had only a limited impact upon the overall expansive trend. These years were marked by an abundance of lands and labour mobility, with growing productivity in levels of both agricultural work and

---

[44] See the case of Córdoba in Fortea (1986, p. 76); for more general estimates, see also Bilbao (1987).

land productivity, and successful resistance to any increase in seigniorial rents; they also witnessed a burgeoning array of auxiliary peasant activities, marked urban expansion, and even some degree of specialization in the role of the cities, with a balance of commerce that had yet to be destroyed by the massive importation of high-quality industrial products. If, from the 1530s, land rents began to lose part of their rigidity, this was a slow process offset—above all in Castile—by a lower burden in real terms of other types of impositions, both in the countryside and in the city.

This pattern of economic growth logically suffered from blockages: yet, by the same standard, it grew to historically unprecedented proportions. Nothing similar would occur again in inland Spain and Portugal until the nineteenth century. As a matter of fact, viewed in perspective, this phase of growth reached rates (understood in terms of product per capita) that were close to those achieved in some areas of nineteenth-century Spain and Portugal (Álvarez Nogal and Prados de la Escosura 2013; Costa, Palma and Reis 2015).

Looking at this development, some historians have written of a 'failed transition' to capitalism (Casey 1985); others have postulated an agrarian capitalism—a dubious term in my opinion—in regions such as Andalusia. Moreover, the notable development of the market makes it tempting to consider it a central element in the working of the economy. A more detailed analysis of the institutional framework demonstrates, however, that the political economy behind this process corresponded to institutional systems that are normally considered very inefficient for economic growth within the schemes and paradigms of the new institutional economics (more on it in Chap. 5).

One of the best signals or indicators of this argument is found in the fact that an important part of the incomes of the seigniorial class and the great ecclesiastical institutions came through taxes rooted in privilege and coercion and not in the direct commercialization of the landlords production. In this situation there were stimuli for productive improvements but the limits of the system would depend on to what extent there was a radical change in the institutional framework.

As regards peasant economies, a number of families' distribution of work over the year were affected by the market, and their sale of commodities and labour increased. Hence, the market augmented and diversified the incomes of many families, contributed to the division of work, and, to a certain extent, encouraged a form of specialization not entirely unrelated to economic growth. Yet, in comparison to today's capitalist economies, the market was highly limited as a mechanism for the assignation of productive resources. In other words, the market was a very important force, but its impact upon the family economies and on the productive specialization and on the combination among land, labour, and technology will remain relatively small in comparison to what happens in our current economies.

The cities themselves were, in spite of their commercial and industrial development, units of jurisdiction, genuine urban seigniorial estates. Their status and character affected not only the lands under their control but also the organization of industrial and commercial activities in them, which were strongly regulated by criteria far from the optimization of the efficiency of productive factors and closer to those of reciprocity and social assistance given to the guilds and confraternities (Chap. 5). These criteria even affected the specialization of functions in the cities, which, by their very nature, had to be limited, because, in effect, urban jurisdiction and the capacity for enforcement that it gave the cities implied the establishment of limits to commercial activities and products from other centres, something which, obviously, limited the transfer of goods and services between them and, consequently, the productive specialization inherent in all urban systems in the strictest sense of the word. It was logical that in many zones, and in the heart of Castile, above all, cities were highly developed, as they constituted nuclei that concentrated land incomes and a diversified demand for goods and services that could only be met by the development of the tertiary and secondary sectors. Some of these cities therefore produced goods and services that could be exchanged beyond their jurisdictional frontiers, giving rise to a certain form of specialization.

*   *   *

This was not an economy where institutions and property rights led to higher levels of economic efficiency in the way new institutional economics postulates. It could even be said that, from this perspective, it is odd that such a significant period of expansion had taken place. But the remarkable phase of expansion—remarkable, that is, on the scale of pre-industrial economies—has an explanation.

This explanation must be found in the fact that the institutions' efficiency did not depend upon their apparent similarity to those of advanced capitalism but rather upon how they operated in specific historical contexts and, above all, upon the availability of resources whose assignment they regulated. In other words, the efficiency of institutions resided not in the fact that they were good or bad per se but in the way in which they positively combined with ecological factors and external changes tied to international commerce. The Iberian sixteenth century economic growth shows the role of the village communities and their forms of organizing agrarian systems and commercial circuits were positive in a world in which the availability of land and other natural resources was high and the possibilities of combining labour, migrations, agrarian seasonal complementarities, space, and commercialization were many. In this context, exclusive and very precise property rights (those that reserved all rights upon the use of land to individual proprietors) were not indispensable, as some visions derived from the new institutional history have presumed (North and Thomas 1973). Even communal properties, when combined with the regulation of the *concejos* or when in a scenario of land abundance, had positive effects for agrarian expansion.

It is even possible to argue that economic growth was only possible because of the inability of some institutions (the councils, towns, and landlord, above all) to control population movements and interior migrations, two forces that contributed to the reallocation of land and labour in order to generate greater productivity. Behind everything lay the conditions set by regional ecological systems that allowed both long- and short-term emigrations to the south. Agrarian institutions were incapable of controlling and absorbing all of the wealth generated by the marginal activities such as the domestic production of manufactures and alternative agriculture. Equally, it should not be forgotten that if in theory landlords controlled the use of violence, then they had to exercise this right with moderation in areas where they encountered solid agrarian communities and where the development of royal justice balanced the scope for abuse by the mighty. The result was highly irregular, with numerous local and regional variations. The difference, for example, between the areas of the Crowns of Castile and Aragon, or even between regions such as the Ebro Valley and the fertile regions of Valencia (areas characterized by very different forms of property rights), was highly noticeable.

It is therefore necessary to set out the processes of political and institutional evolution that lay behind these changes and that, in part, explain them. An understanding of this sort is also crucial to describe the limits of this expansive wave.

Open Access This chapter is licensed under the terms of the Creative Commons Attribution 4.0 International License (http://creativecommons.org/licenses/by/4.0/), which permits use, sharing, adaptation, distribution and reproduction in any medium or format, as long as you give appropriate credit to the original author(s) and the source, provide a link to the Creative Commons licence and indicate if changes were made.

The images or other third party material in this chapter are included in the chapter's Creative Commons licence, unless indicated otherwise in a credit line to the material. If material is not included in the chapter's Creative Commons licence and your intended use is not permitted by statutory regulation or exceeds the permitted use, you will need to obtain permission directly from the copyright holder.

Conclusions Part I

THE IBERIAN GROUNDS OF THE EARLY MODERN GLOBALIZATION OF EUROPE

In the classical view of globalization as 'the Rise of the West', Iberian empires are taken to have generated world economies in which these two countries—both of them economically backward, it is said—were unable to take advantage of the possibilities offered to them by the new markets of America and Asia (Wallerstein 1979; Frank 1978). Today this model is very much under review. This is not only because of doubts concerning the size of these markets, which appear to have been considerably smaller than was once thought (O'Brien 1980). It is also because what might be termed 'Iberian globalization' is now recognized as one of several such processes. Similar transformations had taken place in other areas of the world, from Anatolia to India, Russia, and even China (up to the fifteenth century) (Findlay and O'Rourke 2007; Darwin 2008).

The reasons for this burst of Iberian expansion are well known—commercial growth, the search for gold and new routes to Asia, the evangelizing impulse, and so on. Equally famous is the sophisticated maritime technology and weaponry of the Iberian peoples; this can be linked to the meeting of cultures and the transcultural processes and knowledge transfers that had taken place in Iberia during the Middle Ages. These societies therefore formed the embryo of European expansion, with the birth of naval superiority perhaps being the key to it—indeed, it was also the main limitation, to the extent that no such advance was made in the military control of territories (Headrick 2010; Findlay and O'Rourke 2007). And it is also clear that the analysis provided by E. Jones (1981), who underlined the decisive role of competition among states for European political and economic development, was very applicable to Iberia. The competition between Castile and Portugal, and the need of both to assert their rights in areas like the Canaries and the African coast, where their subjects had been both collaborators and rivals from the very beginning, is a good example of this.

But, this having been said, this conflict was rather different from what is commonly imagined. Both the King of Portugal and his rival and counterpart in Castile were trying to channel, and thus control, internal tensions in their respective kingdoms. This struggle was in reality the fruit of the relations of solidarity and conflict that existed among the nobilities, aristocracies, the cities, and the Church, all of whom competed with each other and with the Crown for the control of resources. This was to a large extent due to the context of jurisdictional and political fragmentation of the societies of the time. In fact, if advanced capitalist economies are characterized by a state that regulates market competition, then early modern ones were shaped by political 'competition' among social agents for the control and expansion of their economic, political, military, and (even) religious resources. In this game, the king was not an impartial referee but rather an agent who had to defend his interests and present himself as a third party at one and the same time. And it is very important to emphasize—in contrast to Jones's interpretation and the others most frequently advanced by scholars—that the background to this dynamic was formed by relations of tension and reciprocity existing within each of these social agents and, in particular, in the family, lineage, and kinship relations that characterized them and which they tried to solve by expanding the resources available to each one of them. Institutions such as *mayorazgo*, important in all societies of Southern Europe, were a means of preserving the lineage from dissolution and thus to maintain and keep together a series of resources that were vital in this confrontation. But this institution also further sparked and sought expansion, insofar as it required an increase in family resources to meet the needs of the secondary branches of the family and the extended lineage and, consequently, the collateral payments upon which these organizations depended. Yet these kinds of needs were not only found among the aristocracy but also in the nobility at large and even among the urban classes, who sometimes projected them into the expansive policies and politics of the cities themselves. The entrance of family members into the Church, a Malthusian practice for combating this situation at the level of the individual, could in turn redouble this expansive dynamic and deepen the conflict within elites on a more general scale. Although J. Schumpeter (1955) suggested something like this view of elites when he spoke of the processes of social ascension of the former, the argument set out here goes a step further. In any case, the result was a process of 'imperial' construction that would have a unique and special stage in Iberia and that was manifested in the fight against Islam and, often, in the usurpation of the royal patrimony that had been at the eye of the storm during the fifteenth century. As a result of all this, by 1238 Aragon had completed its 're-conquest' in Iberia and built an ephemeral—but impressive—'empire' in the Mediterranean that was the fruit of the Crown's ability to coordinate and direct the internal dynamics of the nobility and mercantile groups (Gerbet 1994). In 1249 the Crown of Portugal had conquered the Algarve, and its nobility and monarchy—supported by the Portuguese and Genoese mercantile classes—threw themselves into the African and Atlantic expansion that the king tried, with relative success, to control. In Castile, these same energies threatened the king's patrimony and created internal tensions that would lead to the conquest of Granada and the expansion into Africa and America.

All this would shape the imperial adventure. In terms of their organizational capacity, these were not archaic empires of medieval character: on the contrary, though the medieval component is obvious, the Iberian empires saw determined attempts at centralization made by their respective monarchies, a continuation of the medieval struggles. This was possible thanks to their institutional and military development and to the educational revolution that was taking place in Iberia (Chap. 4). Without these components, the empire would not have been possible—this was especially true for the one that would revolve around Castile—nor would it have taken the very complex form that it would eventually adopt. But without considering the forces behind the colonization programme, we cannot understand the dynamics of these empires. Originating in the needs of elites and their internal dynamics, with Crown finance often playing a limited role in their construction, the conquest instead tended to be characterized by the conferral of political capital and spheres of self-government upon the colonizers in exchange for their campaigns of conquest undertaken on behalf of the king and the resources that they won for him. For this reason, these two empires would soon be grounded on a vast number of micro-negotiations that counterbalanced attempts at control by the central apparatuses of these monarchies. Scholars often forget, even when they speak of the importance of religion in Iberian imperial enlargement, that the prodigious expansion of religious orders and institutions in the new territories implied an externalization of the costs and risks of colonization by the Crown. Costs of this sort were in fact met by a plethora of clerics who preached Christ with one hand and won subjects for the monarchs of Madrid and

Lisbon with the other. The agreements between the Habsburgs and the Pope, on the one hand, and the Avis and the Pope, on the other, to increase the monarchs' participation and control of the resources generated by the Church (patronage rights, the granting of tithes to the king, etc.) are a manifestation of the intention of these dynasties to intervene in this process and the resources it generated. But this entente implied that the Crown recognized the wide influence of the religious orders and even of the secular church in the New Worlds. The Jesuits would perhaps be the best example of the tension implicit in this relationship, and their expulsion from both empires in the eighteenth century was a manifestation of the risk of rupture that had always threatened this process.

The results of all this were varied: on the one hand, the Crown obtained enormous resources that it would try to control through a centralized bureaucracy based in the metropolis. On the other hand, another outcome was the emergence of a system in which the centralization and autonomy of the various social and institutional agents were mixed. Given the vast extent of empires and the wide variety of these conditions and situations in them, this balance between centralization and autonomy was very diverse indeed. These were not centralized empires; but neither were they simply a chain of decision-making centres of equal importance within the hierarchy and capable of imposing their agenda upon the centre. The urban or enclave character of some colonial areas facilitated attempts at central control based on the use of these nodes as centres of dominium and negotiation with the elites. But these were—obviously—immense territories, where the exercise of power was often difficult. The ethnic, social, and cultural diversity of these empires, immersed in one of the greatest globalizing explosions in history, would further complicate their monitoring and exercise of authority. An attempt was made to combine the difficult equilibrium that arose from this situation with a policy that, while it did not exclude violence, attempted to be inclusive and, in the long run, would maintain and even increase the levels of diversity. It is not surprising that J. H. Elliott has emphasized that this was one of the great differences with the English empire in America, where an exclusive, rather than inclusive, approach predominated (2006, Epilogue, pp. 594–595).

Empires such as these were able to wage war successfully on other empires that had begun similar processes. They did so in America and on the African coast, and despite a greater degree of parity, their efforts in Asia were relentless; here the Portuguese exercised some initial advantages in the techniques of naval combat, although rather fewer in terms of land warfare and the control of territory (Headrick 2010).

In America, the struggle for colonial resources, the difficulty in regulation, and the remarkable Iberian superiority in the exercise of violence over conquered peoples led to a capacity to destroy the original ecosystems that was unprecedented in history. The impact on the globalization process is hard to exaggerate. Looked at only from the demographic perspective, a global population of around 430 million inhabitants saw some 60–70 million disappear in just 60 years, that is, about 15% of humanity. And if we extrapolate the growth figures of the rest of the world between 1500 and 1600 (around 32%) and calculate the world population on this basis, the result would be that it would have stopped growing at around 80–90 million inhabitants. Even considering the major past pandemics such as the outbreak of the Black Death in Europe, it is difficult to imagine phenomena so devastating and of such great impact in the long term.[1] Furthermore, the transformation of American ecosystems should also be taken into consideration. An institutional perspective may offer important insights into this facet of the 'Columbian encounters', as ecological imperialism was clearly highly significant in them. Moreover, if by ecosystem we mean a set of relationships between social and natural agents that include the institutions of different societies, as in the preceding pages, it can well be said that what was being demonstrated was the inefficiency of the Iberian institutions when it came to preserving and replenishing many of the resources that were being systematically destroyed. The demographic crisis in America coincided with the enormous cultural distance that separated the existing American societies and those of Europe. In turn, this cultural gulf created great differences in its material culture and consumption patterns. All of these factors meant that it was thus very difficult for dynamic markets to emerge for European products in general, and for Iberian goods in particular, and it would take a long time to generate world economies that would lead to relations of centre-periphery domination in the two banks of the Atlantic world. Indeed, everything indicates that, following the logic of a pre-mercantilist ideology, this was not the fundamental aim or assumption of the metropolis in framing its policies.

In a world with many centres of economic globalization, areas were found—the Indian Ocean and Asian regions in general—that were capable of bombarding Castile and Portugal, and through them Europe as a whole, with highly expensive products with high added value. This favoured a neg-

---

[1] Obviously, these calculations are purely guidelines. The figures of Findlay and O'Rourke (2007, p. 161) come from Maddison (1995). See also Chap. 2.

ative trade balance between Europe and Asia. If centre-periphery economic relations existed—a very dubious proposition that we have refuted at the European level—these were the very opposite of the model presented in the literature of the 1970s. As a consequence, the effects on trade integration on a global scale were limited as the goods sent to Europe from the Asian areas constituted a very small part of its overall production; in turn, this perspective explains why some authors have found data that supports the absence of an early commercial globalization (O'Rourke and Williamson 2002, 2005).

Given that American markets had yet to be developed and imports from Asia were very much focused on luxury products that were still sold in small quantities in relation to the size of the European economy, it is understandable that the poly-nuclear character of fifteenth-century European growth was also maintained. As far as the Iberian kingdoms are concerned, they could take advantage of the new resources and the price differential with Asia, but also that relations on a global and imperial scale were not primarily responsible for improvements in their productive systems. This does not mean—despite a strong historiographic tradition to the contrary—that productive advancements did not occur in Iberia. On the contrary, these clearly did occur and were remarkable precisely because there was no hint of an international economic subordination and the economic growth at European level remained poly-nuclear in character.

Contrary to what has often been said about Iberian technological backwardness, important advances were clearly behind this growth, based upon the circulation of knowledge and expertise in the region. In spite of the fact that the composite monarchy implied the institutional diversity of the different states of the Habsburg dominions, the simple fact that many polities belonged to the same dynasty favoured the circulation of technology among them. Undoubtedly, the porous borders of the time were not an obstacle to the circulation of technological practices, but this network of polities accelerated it to the extent that it included areas such as Italy and the imperial territories of Central Europe, while both the king and elites were powerful agents of transmission of knowledge (Yun 2017). Likewise, there was a growing connection between the different regional ecosystems within the peninsula. These would not produce an integration of the internal markets similar to the one that would serve as the basis of industrialization in England after 1750. On the contrary, a series of economic regions were strengthened by their links with the sea; however, most decisive in this regard were ties in the interior lands, which increased the domestic connections but failed to create an urban system or an integrated market on a peninsular scale. The limitations of the transport system and the composite character of the monarchy—and, therefore, the need to respect the borders between the various Iberian kingdoms—also limited market integration. But growing interregional connectivity was encouraged by the boom in the cities of the interior as political centres from the fifteenth century onwards, which in turn triggered the commercialization of domestic production and encouraged ties between neighbouring areas. In this context of a certain mercantile development, it is understandable that American silver, combined with the growth in population and the division of labour (parallel to urbanization), should have produced the most intense and genuine price revolution in Europe of this time. Had this occurred in an economy with hardly any mercantile development, the effects of the flow of silver would have been very different.

Moreover, growth was especially encouraged by the existence of property rights that were apparently inefficient—at least, according to the model of the new institutional economics—but which, thanks to the regional ecological systems in which they thrived, the abundance of resources and the complex factors that generated them turned out to be highly positive throughout most of the century. It might, indeed, be possible to talk of growth and development in a pre-industrial economy such as this one.

The internal confrontations among elites, and the limits placed upon their capacity to extract resources from society—and in the case of Portugal, the empire—were set down in the different political systems seen in the many Iberian kingdoms towards the end of the fifteenth century. Although all typology is a simplification, the models conformed to different patterns also present in other areas of Europe. Across the peninsula—if more slowly in Aragon—the strengthening of the power of the king, the market, and the cities had paralysed any development that would have led to a greater seigniorial control of the peasant labour force, and, of course, this had reduced the chances of developing a peasant servitude system. Portugal and Castile in fact gave rise to forms of absolutism characterized by a high degree of manoeuvrability of the central power (this was very close to the French model), which did not imply a reduction of the enormous power of the regional and local elites and their capacity to monopolize the economic, political, and military resources. The expansion of such elites had been based on increasing the size of the pie rather than on substantial changes on how it was distributed; this having been said, by the end of the fifteenth century, Portugal was already advancing towards a system in which the monarch exercised a remarkable degree of power thanks to colonial revenues. The territories of the Crowns of Aragon and Navarre evolved towards forms of absolutism combined with more solid parliamentary systems that, although very different to it, are more reminiscent of the English model in terms of its effectiveness in containing the power of the king. In all cases it proved very difficult to expand the resources of the nobles, elites, and king at the same time; in Castile this was for geostrategic reasons and in Aragon because its expansive cycle had been consummated much earlier. In short, then, Castile and Portugal were creating powerful systems for pumping resources and opportunities for elites through state and fiscal apparatuses that were, by the standards of the time, remarkably efficient. In the Crown of Aragon, it was impossible for the nobility and elites to benefit from comparable mechanisms. This meant that seigniorial jurisdiction became an essential consideration and factor for them, particularly in the kingdom of Aragon itself, which also shied away from the English model.

Of course, the different characteristics of these polities varied in proportion to each case. But the most important thing is the diversity of the constitutions and political practices of these territories. This was all the greater if we take into account that within each of these political formations, there coexisted very different legal systems and a wide variety of customary norms. When comparing the Iberian Peninsula's political formations with those found in the Holy Roman Empire or the Italian Peninsula, we tend to emphasize the proto-national character of Iberian states. But internal diversity and jurisdictional fragmentation were also very prevalent in the peninsula. This would be decisive—even more so when the inheritance of Charles V is taken into account—for their government and, this is often forgotten, for their respective imperial ventures. These empires would become the solution to the problem of the elites' social consolidation and expansion. In other words, globalization—and the way in which European globalization was taking place—would have a decisive impact not only upon the models of economic development but also upon the state-building processes and the reproduction of asymmetries that would leave an indelible mark on the history of Europe. This does not mean that these elites and the social and economic systems on which they were based were going to remain immutable; if anything, the very opposite was the case. And this is the subject of the next chapters.

PART II

State Building and Institutions

Even if it did not create voluminous colonial markets for most of the sixteenth century, the first wave of globalization was crucial for its impact upon institutional and social fabrics. Also crucial in this regard were empire, war, and the establishment of a composite monarchy spread out over a good part of Europe.

From a general perspective, it is usual to speak of a military revolution that brought about profound changes in the financial and political structure. Usually viewed in terms of the process of modernization, this transformation supposedly paved the way for a centralization of the state systems for resource extraction and led to the appearance of fiscal states that heralded a leap forward for Europe (Yun 2012). Very interestingly, these two processes have been stressed often in the Castilian (Spanish) case. This section aims at discussing these aspects of European history by considering the case of Iberia. In doing so—and more importantly for our arguments—we will also consider the role of the empires and the composite monarchy in the reproduction and evolution of the peninsula's political economies and social fabric, as well as their possible effects on the institutional framework which regulated the allocation of resources. Our starting point is that the historical changes associated with this situation need to be studied from the consideration of the conflicts and the redistribution of power at the heart of these states.

CHAPTER 4

The Empires of a Composite Monarchy, 1521–1598: Problem or Solution?

The purpose of this chapter is to explain how the Iberian kingdoms' involvement in a complex and global composite monarchy affected the structural social tensions within the elites studied in Chap. 1. It will also discuss to what extent the resolution of the internal conflicts within the different kingdoms, and particularly within Castile and Portugal, led to a centralized military fiscal state, as is usually thought to have happened. It is, therefore, necessary to consider not only the fiscal apparatus but also the whole system for resource mobilization, thus challenging the vision that places emphasis only on taxes. In other words, we need to follow the arguments of J. Schumpeter, according to which tax systems (and by extension the mobilization of resources for war) are in fact a subproduct of social structures.

This line of thought leads us to reject the old stereotype of a society dominated by obedience to the king but also to question the model (popular in the 1980s) that emphasizes the high number and intensity of clashes between the monarchy and the Cortes, the cities, the aristocracy, and even the Church.[1]

---

[1] See part of this literature in Fernández Albaladejo (1992) and Owens (1980) for Castile. For the Aragonese territories, Colás y Salas (1982), Solano (2001), and Gil (1988).

© The Author(s) 2019
B. Yun-Casalilla, *Iberian World Empires and the Globalization of Europe 1415–1668*, Palgrave Studies in Comparative Global History, https://doi.org/10.1007/978-981-13-0833-8_4

WHY CASTILE?

The Problems of a European Composite Monarchy

Charles V (1500–1558) inherited a collection of very different territories dotted across Central and Western Europe.[2] His patrimony was probably the most extensive European political enterprise ruled in Europe by one person since the Romans. When the sprawling American territories and Portugal and its empire were added to this inheritance (in 1580), it became the most far-reaching territorial amalgamation known to history. The division of the Habsburg dominions between the two branches of the House in 1556, with the split of the Austrian (Ferdinand and his successors) and Spanish lines (Philip and his heirs), had not significantly diminished the dimensions of this dynastic conglomeration and the problems that ruling it entailed (Bérenger 1990).

This 'collection of kingdoms' created a 'problem without precedent' as far as it involved conflicts between logics derived from very different political agendas (Koenigsberger 1971, p. 4). Charles V understood that God had placed such vast terrains in the hands of his family 'for the good and universal peace of Christendom'[3] and, it might be added, for the advancement of the House of Habsburg. But in each one of his territories, there were political projects framed according to its own internal interests and which did not fit in the Emperor's plan. It is understandable that he attempted to move according to 'the line of least resistance' (Koenigsberger 1971). But it was, however, inevitable that, given the dispersion of his states, their status as frontier regions scattered across Europe, and the multiple forms of power expressed in them, they would be the main reason for the 'mounting tension' that marked the history of the continent from the sixteenth century onwards (Rabb 1975).

First the Italian Wars against the French Valois; then the religious conflicts against the German princes, with the rebellion of the Netherlands

---

[2] To be more precise, this composite monarchy included the Low Countries, the Franche-Comté, Tyrol, Austria and the states of today's southern Germany, Castile (and its conquered territories in America), Navarre, Aragon and the Italian states (Naples, Sicily, and Sardinia), the *presidios* or coastal forts of North Africa, and, later, the state of Milan. Bohemia and Hungary, inherited by his bother Ferdinand, were also associated directly or indirectly.

[3] This is the way Charles V expressed the idea in the Cortes of Castile. *Patronato Real*, 70–19, AGS.

from the 1560s; and finally the campaigns against England, exponentially increased the demands and costs of conflict and transformed the character of war and the means of waging it in Europe. But, more important, the military tensions in which Charles V and Philip II were involved coincided with the apogee of another global polity: the Ottoman Empire. After taking Constantinople in 1453, the Turks had advanced into the western Mediterranean and the Balkans; to the East, they had moved into the Red Sea and as far as the Persian Gulf and the Indian Ocean (Casale 2010). In parallel, they took the North Africa thus building up 'a vast tri-continental empire' (Darwin 2008, p. 73). Based on reconciliation between Islamic traditions and dynastic absolutism, as well as on equilibrium between regional powers and centralization, the Ottoman Empire became the main enemy for Christendom and a problem for the economic contacts with Asia and within the Mediterranean. It was a power, therefore, which the Habsburgs simply could not ignore and one of the main reasons for warfare in Europe and religious rearming in the Mediterranean. This was even more so as long as the sultans were able to form temporary alliances with the French Valois (Braudel 1976, vol. 2).

The challenges facing the European states, and the Iberian monarchies in particular, must be understood in this context. On the one side, the 'military revolution', even if it remains a debatable concept, obliged them to instigate profound changes in the extant political and fiscal architecture (Parker 1995), which also affected the internal distribution of power. It also implied—it is said—what Joseph Schumpeter called the transition from the 'domain state' to the 'tax state': that is, to a state based not only upon the resources of the prince but also the greater commitment of the different kingdoms to tax payments.[4] However—and this is often forgotten by economic historians—this shift had to be achieved in the context of a fiscal theory that was based upon four pillars, all of which had been manifested in the *comuneros* revolt: that the king should pursue his dynastic and personal policies with his own means (what the English referred to in the formula 'to live off his own'); that he could not collect taxes without the consent of his subjects; that fiscal contributions should only be spent to benefit the kingdoms that approved them, and not others; and that the royal patrimony could not be alienated without the kingdom's permission (Gilbert 1972, pp. 101–10).

---

[4] Schumpeter (1991). The ideas of J. Schumpeter have here a heuristic value rather than a historical one. But their explicative potential is important (Yun 2012).

All these principles, on their own a problem for the rulers, interlinked with some technical difficulties, the most important being the need for credit to finance war or, in other words, the need to get loans situated upon future income. Furthermore, borrowing large sums of money on short-term repayment schemes involved punitively high rates of interest or non-monetary compensations in the form of privileges. The solution to this situation lay in obtaining a stable and predictable source of income, one that permitted the consolidation of short-term loans in longer-term repayment schemes at lower interest rates. But, in addition to this consolidation of loans and since most of them were used to pay for faraway campaigns, it was also crucial to be able to transfer funds across borders, which on many occasions entailed contravening the states' fiscal constitutions.

The Habsburgs were not, of course, the only dynasty to experience credit problems. As we shall see, similar troubles beset the rulers of France, England, and many other polities. But for the Habsburgs, these difficulties were a case apart. The dispersion of their domains and the Habsburg's geopolitical strategy led them to require more money than any other ruler. They had to negotiate with a large number of distinct assemblies, all of them of very different ilk; finally, not only did they need stable and reliable incomes, but it was also essential to arrange and, if possible, justify the transfer of funds between distant polities whose interests were difficult to coordinate.[5]

Contrary to what has often been thought, the process by which Castile became the fiscal and military backbone of the empire was not linear. It is also doubtful that everything depended upon the availability of men and a population easily recruited for war.[6] Moreover, around 1520 Flanders and the southern German territories offered potentially greater financial resources than did Castile. In these regions, advanced financial systems had emerged thanks to market-oriented economies, which enabled them to provide the state military and fiscal resources.[7]

---

[5] This was recognized by contemporary observers, such as the traveller M. Suriano, 'Relación de España. Hecha al regreso de su embajada cerca de Felipe II en 1559', in García Mercadal (1999, vol. II, p. 305).

[6] As is well known, most of the soldiers fighting in Europe were not Spanish but Swedish, German, Flemish, and so on (Hale 1985).

[7] According to Tilly, this was important for state formation in the early modern period (Tilly 1990).

The states of Burgundy and Flanders, tied to the imperial territories of Germany by strong economic bonds, had emerged at a very early stage as the pillars of Charles V's power. Here a dense web of patronage was extended, bringing enormous social, political, and even economic advantages to the Burgundian and Flemish nobles. Antwerp's commercial and financial development during the first half of the sixteenth century was one of the bases for the collection of funds (Braudel 1996, pp. 270–1). The connection between Flemish banks and German banking houses would allow the Emperor to make use of the services of families such as the Fugger and the Welser, who were also tied to him by their interest in exploiting mines (Carande 1987, vol. III, pp. 33–5). This axis, however, suffered a number of fiscal deficiencies. Like his uncle the Emperor Maximilian—who liked to laugh at the French and their fiscal subjugation by their king—Charles V had to base his finances in these states on incomes derived from renting out mines, which were used both as guarantees and to consign payments (Ehrenberg 1955, pp. 31–42). The proposals of the Estates General of the Low Countries always had to be discussed and approved by the provincial estates, and their final vote required unanimity, meaning that opposition from any one of a number of parties could become an obstacle to the Emperor's ambitions (Koenigsberger 1971, pp. 27–33; Tracy 1985, pp. 29–69). Furthermore, in all of these territories, the local assemblies were charged with collecting the monies they had voted through a convention that ensured that they kept part of these taxes.

Conditions were even more complex in the Mediterranean theatre. In Aragon, Catalonia, and Valencia, the contributions depended above all on the voting of extraordinary subsidies for specified purposes or campaigns and were very much controlled by the *Diputaciones* and *Generalidades* (see Chap. 1). It was, therefore, very difficult to use revenues secured in this way for operations that might involve the transfer of funds from one state to another (Tomás y Valiente 1982, pp. 41–50). In Navarre a number of additional problems emerged. The proximity of France, the almost continual conflict experienced after 1524, and the affection felt by a sector of the nobility for the Valois cause created conditions that made the Crown's appeal for contributions even more problematic.

In Sicily and Naples, similar circumstances prevailed. In spite of attempts to introduce reforms, marked limitations on the availability of funds existed (Muto 1980, pp. 28–35; Calabria 1991, pp. 42–5). A large chunk of the contributions were based on the system of *donativos*, basically forced loans that also had a negotiated element. These contributions were seldom extended for more than three years and therefore relatively unstable; moreover, they were always made in return for important concessions by the Crown. Furthermore, both kingdoms—and Sicily above all—lived under the continual threat of Turkish attack, thus making them very vulnerable while also obliging the Crown not to burden them excessively in order to preserve their political loyalty and stability.[8]

The situation in Castile was not noticeably better. Although often forgotten, there in fact existed very large fiscal demarcations (Yun 2004). Moreover, a degree of confusion reigned over rents, on where and how they were collected and from whom, above all when the seigniorial estates and royal demesne were concerned. Duties such as the crusade service (*cruzada*) easily ran into problems and local resistance. Further complicating matters, these taxes had to be negotiated with the Pope, which created a certain instability. The resulting irregularities created disputes between the different social orders and were exacerbated by abuses in revenue collection. On Charles V's arrival, some revenues were *encabezados* (granted by the cities at a fixed amount in exchange for the right to collect them), but many others were not, leading to problems in execution.[9] This situation created a swarm of collectors, taxmen, and treasurers, few of them averse to lining their own pockets, while the local authorities often also retained a healthy share for themselves (Carretero 2000). These problems were aggravated by a great number and forms of overlapping jurisdictions. Moreover the monarchy's organization, based upon *Consejos* (Councils) with two crucial, but sometimes clashing, duties—the oversight of the king's authority and upholding the laws and customs of the many kingdoms over which he ruled—further limited the Crown's effective executive power (Fernández Albaladejo 1992).

Castile, we have seen, was a relatively rich kingdom, with a developing economy. But even in 1520–1530, its economy was very different from the more market-oriented economies of Flanders or Italy. Moreover, after the expulsion of the Jews, Castile clearly lacked great financiers capable of arranging the transfer of large funds from one dominion to another. Those groups who would later be capable of doing this had not yet reached a sufficient level of organizational maturity. And the Indies were not yet able to provide the funds necessary to establish and maintain the king's credit.

---

[8] According to Koenigsberger, the island was the 'most lightly-taxed of the kingdoms of the emperor' (1971, pp. 47–9).

[9] See, for more details based on primary sources, Yun (2004, pp. 261–3).

As the *comuneros'* conflict had made clear, Castile was no less insistent than Christendom's other kingdoms that its resources should not be used for nondomestic causes or distant foreign wars waged in the defence of Habsburg interests (Perez 1976, pp. 546–7, 550–4). Pointedly, the *comuneros* had reminded Charles V that 'the monarch cannot use at his will the possessions of the crown that do not belong to him as his private property'. Furthermore, very much in tune with medieval theory (Chap. 1), the *comuneros* had reminded Charles V that it was his duty to ensure that 'all that is alienated from the royal crown should be returned to it'.[10]

These arguments did not disappear in 1521; rather they survived at a subaltern level and certainly complicated the mutual understanding between king and kingdom (Carande 1987, vol. II, pp. 49–50). Indeed, a number of old problems linked to the alienation of the royal patrimony returned to the spotlight. In its meetings of 1523, 1524, and 1528, the Cortes complained about royal taxes that had been illicitly alienated to (or by) the nobility; they also railed against what they considered the fiscal disadvantages of the royal demesne in regard to private seigniorial estates. As we shall see, these petitions for redress would not be entirely ignored.

Aristocratic discontent must also be considered. Having been the great ally of the Crown against the *comuneros*, the aristocrats found that their financial difficulties could not be properly addressed simply by a distribution of the booty captured from the rebels. The situation was very fluid. In 1524 Charles V, pressured by the great estate holders on one side and the cities on the other, revalidated the 1504 legislation about the reversion of alienated incomes to the Crown. This measure was not likely to improve relations between nobility and king. The Church also failed to provide a network for the secure, reliable, and efficient collection of hefty funds. True, these years witnessed the establishment of the Council of the Crusade (*Consejo de Cruzada*), in part in response to the demands of the campaigns in North Africa. But the King of Castile had not only to negotiate the payment of sums with the Pope but also the precise figures to be collected from each diocese, monastery, and abbey (Perrone 1998). For all these drawbacks, the ecclesiastical services did in fact become an important financial resource, even being included in a number of *asientos*. But these services were neither reliable or predictable nor easily collected.

---

[10] See *Patronato Real*, 4, 84. AGS. and Perez (1976, pp. 548, 549, n. 129).

Castile was not compliant or docile; nor was it particularly enthusiastic about Habsburg strategy. It was not the great panacea to the king's problems in 1517, or even in 1521, in the wake of Villalar. In short, contrary to an old view that only underlines a relation of obedience and agreement between kingdom and king, the monarch's margin for manoeuvre was quite limited.

Castile, a Nervus Belli

And yet, despite all of these factors, Castile became the backbone of the Habsburg empire for many decades.

A precise reconstruction of what the Habsburgs secured from their respective territories is very difficult. The rulers themselves would have been hard-pressed to present a clear idea of these contributions—an indication of the enormous difficulties that the dynasty had to face (Comín and Yun 2012). This having been said, the facts and figures that can be reconstructed speak for themselves. By the 1530s Castile was providing some 70% of the Habsburgs' resources in Western Europe (Comín and Yun 2012). Naples and the Duchy of Milan were the next most important contributors (Table 4.1). Even allowing for a healthy margin of error, these figures demonstrate the enormous burden that fell on these kingdoms. When they are viewed in the long term, the conclusions are no less striking. In real terms the incomes collected from Castile multiplied by more than a factor of ten between 1500 and 1600.[11] This rise had been much quicker than in the other polities for which figures are available, such as England, France, or Holland (although calculations here are a matter of complexity the outcome can be easily accepted as an order of magnitude. See Graph 4.1). This growth was rapid until the 1560s, when the treasures arriving from America first came to make their presence felt. But they continued throughout the reign of Philip II, thanks to the increasing fiscal pressure and the second cycle of receipts of American silver brought about by the improvements in amalgamation techniques. This period also witnessed a more rapid increase in the contributions of other kingdoms, such as Navarre, Catalonia, and Naples, although everything indicates that the share of the royal income provided by Castile continued to be higher. In comparison with Naples, for example, the proportion

---

[11] See Comín and Yun (2012, p. 237, Table 10.2).

Table 4.1 Charles V's incomes in different territories of the Habsburg composite monarchy

	(Data in grams of silver, circa 1535)	
	c. 1535	% of the total
Iberian estates		
Castile	50,394,883	69.1
Catalonia	1,948,750	2.7
Aragon	397,236	0.5
Valencia	658,480	0.9
Navarre	672,819	0.9
Total	54,072,168	74.2
Italian estates		
Naples	10,103,783	13.9
Sicily	1,747,266	2.4
Milan	6,994,121	9.6
Total	18,845,170	25.8
Low Countries	7,234,405	9.9
Total	72,917,338	100.0

Sources: Comín and Yun (2012)

between Castile and the Italian kingdom had been something like 5:1 in the middle of the century; by the end of the century, it was around 3.5 to 1.[12] This trend was important (see below), as it provided an indication of the tendency in the next century (Chap. 8); but it does not, fundamentally, challenge the idea that in the sixteenth century Castile (and the Indies) had become the sinews of war.

This pattern helps to explain the increase, still more difficult to measure, of debt (meaning *asientos*, short-term loans taken at high rates of interest, as well as borrowing consolidated as *juros*) (Yun 2004, p. 318, Graph 5.7). This rise was also noticeable during the time of the Emperor but continued to grow throughout the second half of the century, as A. Castillo showed a few decades ago (1963). In particular, it led to a considerable increase in the amount of consolidated debt.

This helps to explain the increase in the size of military forces and war spending, another variable that is notoriously difficult to pinpoint. In regard to Castile, we know that the 'ordinary' budget for defence passed

[12] Data from Thompson (1976, p. 288) and Calabria (1991, p. 134).

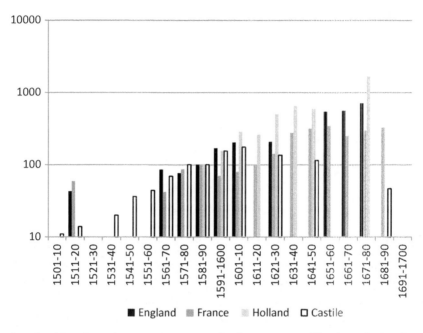

Graph 4.1 Crown's revenues in England, France, Holland, and Castile, 1500–1701 (current English pounds. Index: 1581–90 = 100)
Sources: My own elaboration from Comín and Yun (2012).

from some 740,000 ducats in 1559 to 3.4 million in 1598. To this sum we should add the 3.45 million ducats assigned to pay for the war in Flanders (Thompson 1976, p. 288). This trend suggests a ninefold increase in costs, which is maybe exaggerated but which far outstrips any rise in prices. The military budget therefore increased in both real and nominal terms, even without taking spending in Flanders into account. Again, Castile paid the lion's share. More than 50% of its budget was spent on war; in contrast Naples spent something like 30% (six million against one million).[13] The

[13] See Thompson (1976) and Calabria (1991). For Castile, only the budget for Flanders and defence is included here. Military costs in Naples increased from 1.3 to 3.5 and 3.3 million ducats between 1550, 1574, and 1600.

difficulties of these calculations notwithstanding, the Low Countries, Sicily, or Milan operated on a similar scale but with lower overall budgets (Parker 1972, pp. 139–57).

By the end of the century, the Habsburgs had established a system that transferred funds from one state to distant theatres of war. By this juncture a multitude of loans, including many raised in Flanders, had been set on the incomes of Castile, which was now financing campaigns in Portugal or the Azores, while other kingdoms, such as Naples, were paying for troops deployed on the Iberian Peninsula itself (Rodríguez-Salgado 1992, pp. 85–116). This development did not mean that the Castilians had forgotten their basic constitutional principles, of which they continued to remind the king whenever they could.[14] These same practices were also evident in Naples and Milan (Calabria 1991, p. 55). Indeed, sometimes the Castilian assembly could see the value of financing a frontier conflict that did not affect Castile directly. Thus, during the War of Navarre against France and the conquest of Fuenterrabía, the Cortes and public opinion were entirely convinced by strategic concerns (Navarre was seen as the gateway to Castile) and the need to defend the Pyrenees frontier.[15] On other occasions arguments of a religious kind were used, although these were often clumsy or forced.[16] And there was no shortage of reasons why it was necessary to offer a hand to Hungary or to arm the fleet of Genoa.[17]

[14] In its petitions to the Cortes of 1542, Córdoba alluded to the 'war of our holy faith against infidels' as 'the office and exercise of kings' and the only justification for the collection of taxes raised for this purpose. *Patronato Real*, 69, 61 AGS. Fray Antonio de Guevara justified war only when it was undertaken for 'that which for us He wanted to offer his blood on the Cross' ('Aquel que por nosotros quiso su sangre en la Cruz ofrecer' (*Relox de Príncipes*, 1994 [1529], 757).

[15] In 1523, when the recovery of Fuenterrabía was being planned, Carlos alluded to the fact that the King of France had 'attempted to occupy its lands for the discord that there was in these kingdoms at that time'. *Patronato Real*, 70, 22. AGS.

[16] Even if it proved impossible to hide the true reasons for it, this served as the means for justifying the continuation of campaigns in Italy against Francis I: 'the need to provide for the good and universal peace of Christendom and the conservation of his imperial authority, of his kingdoms and estates'; all of which, our source concludes, 'is necessary for the service of God, His Majesty and Christendom'. *Patronato Real*, 70, 19. AGS.

[17] On 5 December 1526, the Emperor summoned the Cortes to ask for extraordinary taxes in order to help his brother; the argument was that the Turk 'wants to overcome and subject

Similar lines of argument had first been deployed in 1544, when it was deemed necessary to provide an extraordinary tax (*servicio*) to counter the alliance between the Turk and the King of France.[18] Castilian society found more than a grain of truth in the king's plea for assistance. Indeed, this argument was precisely why this particular appeal proved so effective.[19]

The monarchy's composite character and its collateral effects would also prove decisive. These mechanisms were linked to the development of powerful commercial and banking networks within this political complex, which created political ties between the monarchy and the bankers and facilitated the transfer of funds to distant theatres of arms. The first of these conduits to emerge belonged to the leading German families, such as the Fugger and the Welser; later the Genoese rose to prominence, although they had actually begun earlier. The Centurione, the Balbi, the Spinola, the Sauli, and others advanced funds in return for access to the economy of Castile and America and for *asientos* offering high rates of interest.[20] These great houses acted in coalition and had acquired or established networks spanning across the old continent, something that allowed them to achieve more than even the increasingly powerful Castilian bankers: to transfer funds across Europe with a certain degree of alacrity and a high level of security, making use of letters of exchange linking the great fairs of Castile, Seville, Flanders, and Italy.

These families—this is important in order to avoid erroneous arguments—were closely tied to the Habsburg dynasty and to its monarchical imperial

---

the Christians' and what he did was 'a very great offense to God, Our Lord, and his holy Christian religion by taking and occupying the lands and estates of the Church and of the Christian princes'. The Emperor also reminded the deputies of his responsibility before God, who 'put us here to reign over the Earth and gave us this Empire and estate, with which we serve him'. He also appealed to 'these kingdoms of Spain' that 'were among the first to believe in the faith of Our Redeemer and Saviour Jesus Christ and baptised by the water of the Holy Spirit and are so zealous for our Holy Catholic Faith', *Patronato Real,* 69. 63. AGS. In regard to the armada of Genoa, he placed emphasis on its strategic importance, alluding to its 'proximity to Africa and Turks that live there and come [here] every day'. *Patronato Real,* 69, 74, AGS.

[18] *Patronato Real,* lib. XVIII, ff. 29v°-37r°. AGS.

[19] In 1539 cities such as Jaen recognized the Emperor's 'enterprises in the defence of our holy Catholic faith and the good of these kingdoms' and thanked him for them. *Patronato Real,* 69. 80. AGS.

[20] See the variety of these relationships in the different case studies presented in Herrero et al. (2011).

system through bonds that were not simply economic (Herrero et al. 2011). The Genoese links, for example, were founded on the political settlement arrived at in 1528: here the families that controlled power in the republic made a pact with the Emperor, who became the referee of the internal relationships between the old and the new nobles (*nobili vecchi* and the *nobili nuovi*) in order to guarantee the political status quo of the city as well as his alliances with it (Canosa 1998). Genoa thus remained an independent republic although, in reality, it existed as a satellite state of the Habsburg conglomerate thanks to a collaboration based on the interlinking of both political agreements and financial services. Furthermore, for the Genoese the alliance with the Habsburgs, renewed in 1575, was founded upon the possibility of obtaining political and social capital, in part through a long process of fusion with the Castilian nobility, a trend that would in turn shape the history of the kingdom, as we shall see (Canosa 1998).[21] Genuine clientele networks formed among financiers who were capable of circulating political and economic capital between areas. This trait goes a long way towards explaining the effectiveness of these networks, as these were not simply families but rather coalitions of *alberghi*, densely configured and close-knit associations with a very strong political component (Grendi 1997). In other words, to study the financial relationships between the Crown and the Genoese *asentistas* purely in terms of interest rates and other economic variables is to simplify things and to adopt an erroneous rationale.

The establishment of this system for the transfer of resources can be explained as a sort "primitive" financial revolution beginning in the 1530s and set down in the general agreement for the *alcabalas*. As we shall see, this financial revolution was, in reality, a process that would take shape in the second half of the sixteenth century in Holland but would reach its maximum expression in England after 1688 (Brewer 1990). In the first case, it would consist of a process in which representative assemblies would achieve control over the budget and, by extension, over state spending and the consignment and repayment of debt (Tracy 1985). It would allow 'the contracting of long-term loans and the development of a consolidated debt, guaranteed by the authorities'. The system served to offer guaran-

---

[21] Among the Genoese families that established strong links with the Castilian aristocracy, one could underline the Spínola, very tied to the dukes of Albuquerque (Rodríguez Villa 1905).

tees to subscribers with a consequent fall in interest rates ('T Hart et al. 1997, pp. 18 and ss.). What happened in Castile was very different, but it at least shared some of these traits. The situation was not entirely new, as from before 1530 the services voted by the Cortes to the Crown were used as a guarantee to the *asentistas*, who obtained a monopoly over their exploitation. Indeed, loans were even taken out against the guaranty of the 'ordinary' services or those made by the ecclesiastical institutions.[22] But the *encabezamiento* of 1538 represented a clear step forward. In that year, the king and the Cortes finally agreed that a fixed sum would be decided upon and set down for a long period of time. In exchange for these concessions, Charles V agreed that the collection of taxes was to be administered by the cities according to quotas shared out among them. Obviously, this accord was favourable to the cities and the kingdom in general (and has always been seen as such), as it conceded them a margin for manoeuvre, and the quantities to be levied would fall in real terms due to inflation. But this agreement—and this has often been forgotten—also meant that the king obtained a secure, reliable, and predictable source of income, allowing him to win the confidence of lenders and to consolidate his debts upon it. As a result, the monarch gained an unprecedented capacity to assume debts, thus permitting him to raise the *situado*, the quantities paid as interest on loans, to above 8000 million maravedís by the end of his reign.[23]

During the following decades—and above all during the reign of Philip II—the figures for the *encabezamiento de alcabalas* would form the basis for discussions between king and kingdom (for this reason they were closely monitored by the *asentistas*). It should be stressed that the Cortes of 1559, 1563, and 1575–1577, meeting in the aftermath of royal bankruptcies, presented moments when institutional breakdown was a genuine possibility. But the upward revision of figures on these occasions allowed the consolidation of debts and permitted the system to function once again. Even at the end of the century, when in the 1590s the *millones* system was established, the eventual solution followed similar lines: the cities assumed responsibility for the collection and administration of the tax through rates which they themselves created and set (Fortea 1990).

---

[22] The Cortes alluded to how the service of 1525 was requested to meet 'debts of very great quantities of gold'. See *Patronato Real*, 70, 19, AGS.

[23] These ideas were developed in detail in Yun (2004), but had previously been presented in Yun (1998, 2000).

The system could be implemented thanks also in part to the treasures coming to the king from America. These shipments allowed the Crown to take *asientos*, short-term loans, with the guaranty of the American silver and then, in a second step, to consolidate those loans as *juros* (long-term public debt) endorsed by the *alcabalas* and other incomes. This meant a crucial step forward in another (neglected) dimension: since the warranty for the *asientos* was the American treasure, which belonged to the king, this operation escaped the control of the Cortes and could be used for any purposes. But, the second step also implied that the incomes of the kingdom—the *alcabalas* endorsing the *juros*—were also used to finance campaigns that had little or nothing to do with the interest of the kingdom but rather originated in the king's personal agenda. Though the cause of continuous complaint, this system thus camouflaged a crucial problem that was both technical and constitutional.

These developments also allowed the Crown to proceed to reduce its levels of interest payment on *juros*, which were to become (and remained until 1700) one of the cheapest forms of public debt in Europe. At their emission, they were, in fact, cheaper than English and Dutch debts (at least until the middle of the seventeenth century) and they were at the same level as some of the more economical debts emitted by the solvent city-republics of Italy (see Graph 4.2).[24] The south of Europe was in fact precocious in achieving a reduction of the nominal interest rates levied on consolidated debt without proceeding to a fully fledged financial revolution (Yun and Ramos 2012, pp. 20–5).

This (apparent) long-term efficiency has recently inspired some (highly) optimistic assessments from the macroeconomic perspective (Drelichman and Voth 2014). However, and even if we accept many of the nuances proposed by these studies (see also the same revisionist line in Comín and Yun 2012), the macroeconomic perspective and the principal figures of income, debt, and expenditure are not sufficient in themselves. Furthermore, this view does not capture all of the sharp edges, drawbacks, and catches which are crucial to any genuine understanding of what happened. In fact, even leaving aside for one moment the effects (nearly always negative) of fiscal extraction on the economy (although these are often exaggerated), there are many obscure tones and shades to our canvass. Thus Castilian

---

[24] On the *juros'* interest rates and its evolution, see Álvarez Nogal (2009).

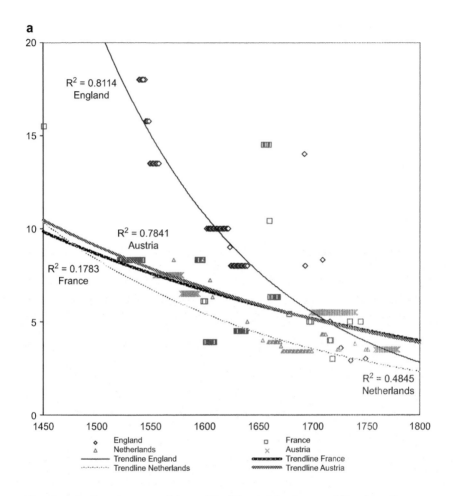

Graph 4.2 Interest rates of the public debts in Northern and Southern Europe, 1450–1800. (**a**) England, France, the Netherlands, and Austria. (**b**) Bologna, Florence, and Venice. (**c**) Milan, Naples, and Castile

Sources: My own elaboration from Epstein (2002, Table 2.1, nominal interest rates on public debt in Europe, c. 1270–1750) and Pezzolo (2012, Table 11.1, interest rates on government loans in Italy, 1450–1799). All trend lines correspond to an exponential adjustment.

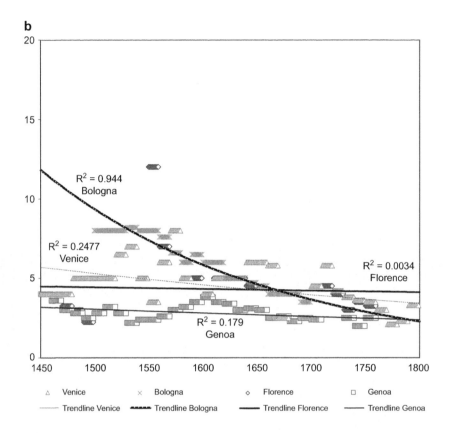

b

R² = 0.944
Bologna

R² = 0.2477
Venice

R² = 0.0034
Florence

R² = 0.179
Genoa

| △ Venice | × Bologna | ◇ Florence | □ Genoa |

Trendline Venice   Trendline Bologna   Trendline Florence   Trendline Genoa

Graph 4.2   (continued)

debt increased more quickly than did incomes throughout much of the century—a factor leading to instability. Things were even worse in the short term, when war needs created genuine traumas for the functioning of the financial system. Moreover any study of debt and of the quantities involved in it is highly unlikely to paint a general picture of sustainability (needless to say, comparisons with today's ideas of sustainability are misleading.)[25] The frequent royal bankruptcies were the result of the

[25] Drelichman and Voth (2014, p. 33) have even spoken of a relatively low volume of debt in respect to the GDP of Castile (not more than 60%). Even beyond the weakness of their figures on GDP in terms of measuring sustainability, their estimate is difficult to accept

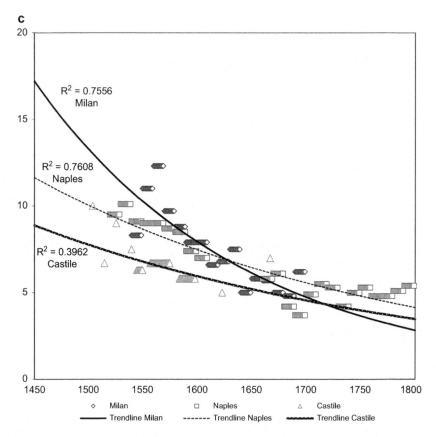

Graph 4.2   (continued)

periodical imbalance between debts and incomes. These were often accompanied by—sometimes heralded by—the recurrence to forced loans, the seizure of American treasure belonging to private individuals, or the Crown's delay of payments scheduled in the fairs of Castile.

(pp. 34–35, 116–25). The problem lies in estimating the total debt beyond the *juros*. This debt was, without doubt, small in relation to today's economies and had limited effects upon growth, to the extent that not all of the economy was monetarized. But taking into account the part of the economy that worked through monetary transactions, it has to be concluded that it had much more negative effects, in particular on the money market.

It is true that the bankruptcies and the requisitions of American treasure were not the unmitigated catastrophe of legend, as they subsequently led to negotiations and agreements with the bankers and businessmen (the *medios generales*, in which both sides sought a compromise) (Sardone 2018). This should not surprise us. For a long time, historians have been aware of the negotiated character of the royal bankruptcies.[26] But these manoeuvres and talks did not prevent moments of high risk for the financial and commercial economy in general and the relevant businessmen in particular, who were the most exposed and vulnerable within the financial system to violent jolts of this sort.[27] It should be added that the entire system functioned through frequent negotiations with elites for ever-greater services to the Crown, as was the case, for instance, with the ecclesiastical institutions: these talks also created uncertainty. At heart—and in spite of the figures—the fiscal system of the kingdom was more or less efficient but also very weak. In the end this ship, whose sustainability had been sublimated, was re-floated—or, more precisely, the inevitable shipwreck was averted for another day—by burning a few more of its planks of wood. It survived, in other words, thanks to the constant alienation of the three elements—royal patrimony, state structures, and royal sovereignty—that it was supposed to sustain and protect (Chap. 1). The sale of *alcabalas*, *tercias*, jurisdictions, noble titles and offices, and unfarmed or common land belonging to rural communities became a slow, but unstoppable, drip feed over many decades, despite the complaints of the Cortes and the kingdom in general. And although a degree of legal subterfuge was introduced into most sales (it was commonly stated that the Crown could repurchase the rights or goods in question whenever it so desired), these clauses were never activated.

All in all, the fiscal system had been effective for the Crown but very demanding for the kingdom and the elites. But the whole picture cannot be understood if we do not consider it in a wider perspective which takes into account its social context, although this has often been ignored by recent studies on financial history. This will also help to situate finances in a broader scenario which is crucial for this book: the system of mobilizing resources in general and its implications for the political economy.

---

[26] See Lovett (1977) and Rodríguez-Salgado (1992).

[27] The fact (mentioned above) may have been important on account of its producing short-term alterations in the money market. This effect got worse from the 1550s. According to Abed Al-Hussein's figures (1982, appendix 2, pp. 365–6), a greater quantity of delay in fair payments, and a longer period of payment, can be found as the century progresses, something which obviously provoked reasons for uncertainty.

A CONFLICTIVE PACT

The Challenges of a Dynamic Society

From 1521 the cycles of great upheavals and civil wars that affected France, the German territories, or the Low Countries were absent from Castile. As we shall see, religious reasons in part explain this divergence (Chap. 6). Yet the social tensions derived from the dynamics within elites (Chap. 1) and from social and economic change were a day-to-day reality.

Documents detailing the popular political culture of the Castilian and Aragonese towns make it very clear that for many peasants the most important values were not necessarily those of obedience to the king. Ideas such as the 'zealous service of God and the republic of the poor' could come to be more crucial and might even collide with the demands for loyalty (Yun 2004). The conflict against the seignior, which burst forth during the revolts of the *Comunidades* and *Germanías*, was ever present in the Chancelleries of Castile throughout the sixteenth century and emerged not infrequently in Aragon (Kagan 1991). And this legal confrontation was just one facet of a sort of shadow boxing which sometimes even spilled out into actual violence and encompassed everything from collective disobedience to disputes over the use of agrarian resources.

All European societies of this period were characterized by a high degree of mobility (Vassberg 1996). But a case might be made for the Iberian states being above average in this regard, as regular and seasonal emigrations were extremely important for the peasant economies of the peninsula (Chap. 3). Another key factor, common to all European continental societies, was the multitude of jurisdictions. The result of mobility and the plurality of jurisdictions presented difficulties in maintaining social control. The inherent anonymity of a population working far from home or its place of origin created significant problems for the authorities, as did popular forms of socialization. Those who migrated from one place to another were often poor or vagabonds, who constituted a source of concern and conflict. The growth of the cities ensured that their internal social relations were increasingly tense and more difficult to control and order. Figures from picaresque literature such as *Rinconete and Cortadillo* or *Lazarillo de Tormes* reflected a reality that has shone through many historical studies.

But the internal tensions of this society were not limited to problems of this sort. The need for expansion felt by the lineages and the urban elites remained present during the sixteenth century.

Many noble households found that their status maintenance costs grew more quickly than did their disposable incomes. This was especially true for those lineages whose revenues were badly adapted to the general increase in prices (Yun 2002a). The strengthening of the judicial system—above all in Castile—and the solidity of the rural community in many areas made it more expensive and difficult to revert to force and to the usurpation of lands and taxes as a means of expanding seigniorial rents at the expense of the royal patrimony (Kagan 1991; Owens 2005). The tension between spending and incomes was becoming increasingly marked.[28] If in the fifteenth century the seigniors had had to build fortresses and equip and arm retinues, now they had even more reasons to spend money, military burdens aside. Matrimony had become a way of obviating and resolving conflicts and forming alliances between nobles: as a result 'the number of dowries shot through the roof' (Atienza and Simón 1989).[29] The establishment of cadet branches was another significant expenditure. The expansion of the seigneurial domains to provide collateral branches with a property and so avoid interfamilial tensions also required investment and spending. Royal service, which was essential for the social promotion of both first- and second-born sons, constituted another significant form of spending. The Renaissance lifestyle entailed a need for ever-more expensive and luxurious palaces, thus pushing up the costs of social legitimization; similar programmes might also lead to altruistic spending on welfare, charitable institutions, and religious foundations.[30] The result, in both Castile and Aragon, was an increase in nobles' debt from the 1520s, which threatened to dissolve both inherited patrimonies and 'free' possessions (those that were not entitled and therefore not subject to the *mayorazgo*) (Yun 1987; Abadía 1993, 1998).

The expansionist dynamic felt by the second-rank nobility and the urban oligarchies would be no less decisive than in the previous century and led to a policy designed to capture political and economic resources (Casey 1989, pp. 52 and ff.). The result was, once again, a fight for the amplification of patrimony or for the control of the key positions in the administrative and political systems, none of which could be acquired without expenditure. The growing prevalence of the *mayorazgo* increased

---

[28] See the case of Castile in Jago (1982) and Atienza (1987) and that of Valencia in Casey (1983). For more details from a general perspective, Yun (2004).

[29] See also the complains of the Almirante de Castilla in *Diversos de Castilla*, 37, n. 36, sf. AGS.

[30] Viñas (1970) and Checa (1988).

these needs to the extent that, as for the high nobility, it required them to enlarge their patrimonies to compensate the lesser branches of the family in one way or another. The increasingly elitist nature of local government added pressure on rival factions to place their clients and creatures in the mayoral offices at a time when these institutions were gaining political relevance (Yun 2004). Although self-regulating mechanisms existed, these tensions were manifested in bitter factional and group conflicts over the control of municipal offices.[31] A wave of banditry swept through many of the rural zones of Aragon, Catalonia, Valencia, and Navarre, often encouraged or sponsored by groups of local nobles.[32]

A further additional tension in the cities was the rise of businessmen who sought to gain access to the *mayorazgos* and town councils. Families such as the Dueñas and the Salamanca in Burgos, the Espinosa of Medina de Rioseco, and the Alcázar of Seville provided good examples of this sort. Bernabé Ortega represented this impulse in Medina del Campo. This trend was more destabilizing when it became mixed up in the religious problem. Spanish society decisively rejected crypto-Judaism, and any manifestation of it might be considered as evidence of tainted lineage. Together with the notion of purity of blood, this rejection created a model of conformity upon which the ideal of an imagined community was formed. These developments would convert these themes into a source of discord among the elites. An accusation of crypto-Judaism or impure blood—whether true or not—might act as a corrosive poison that would end up affecting all members of an urban oligarchy and, in particular, their ability to reproduce their status through matrimony. That is to say, any such allegation would hit the key social capital that was crucial for the reproduction of the group. The case of the dispute between the Sotos and the Riquelmes in Murcia, explored in an excellent study by J. Contreras, demonstrates that quarrels of this kind were not simply evidence of social and religious discrimination against a minority.[33] They were much more than this, producing enormous tensions in the very heart of the oligarchies and affecting the very consolidation of the dominant coalition.

---

[31] See, for example, the case of Murcia in Contreras (1992) and Ruiz Ibáñez (1995).

[32] Elliott (1963), Torres (1994, pp. 103–19), Reglá (1966), Vilar (1962), Colás y Salas (1982, pp. 159–81, 208–76).

[33] The studies on the subject are many. For the families cited as examples, see Yun (1987), Lohman (1968), Pike (1966, 1978), Abed Al-Hussein (1982), and Contreras (1992).

Absolutism As a Threat to the Dominant Coalition

The development of absolutism would accentuate two forms of conflict—the first within the dominant elite and the second between its different social sectors and the king.[34]

As we have seen, the evolution of royal authority reduced the nobility's chances of recurring to violence or to the usurpation of lands. Its problems would have to be addressed with other solutions. During the first years of Charles V's reign, the Crown's policy of trying to reclaim alienated rents gained momentum. In 1524 measures that had been favourable to the aristocracy in Castile were revoked. Something similar happened in Navarre. Both Charles and his son repeatedly appealed to their nobility for military help, thus obliging them to meet additional military costs, at least in principle. The campaign against Tunis (1535), the repression of the *Moriscos* in Granada (1568–1571), the annexation of Portugal (1580), and even *auxilium* requests in specific instances compelled many nobles to mobilize troops and incur costs that threatened their economies. The advance and improvement in the organization of royal justice also posed a threat to the seigniorial jurisdictions. This was the case not only in Castile but also in Aragon, Valencia, and Catalonia, where seigniorial jurisdiction was even stronger but where a new generation of jurists and judges sought a balance of legal power that was more favourable to the king. Philip II even used the Inquisition in Aragon against the elites of the kingdom and, more generally, its laws and customs. He applied laws regarding the ownership of salt mines and undersoil wealth that went directly against the interests of the seigniors and in favour of those of the Crown.

The conflict between, on the one side, the urban oligarchies and the Cortes and, on the other, the king has assumed a crucial role in recent interpretations of this period. The increase in fiscal pressure was, without doubt, the most important—or most visible—cause of these tensions. Each round of negotiations over taxes was accompanied by a din of complaints and grievances. In Castile one of the worst moments came with the revision of the *alcabalas* in the 1560s and 1570s and actually resulted in armed conflicts in some cities (Jago 1981, 1985, 1989). Debates over the *millones* tax in the 1590s were equally fraught (Fortea 1990). Despite the manoeuvres to hide or justify it, the fact that some of these funds were used to pursue interests outside the kingdom further aggravated the situation.

---

[34] For what follows, see Yun (2004, Chaps. 5 and 6).

The efforts by Philip II to make use of the Inquisition against his rebel secretary, Antonio Pérez, unleashed an open conflict between the Crown and the *Justicia*, a sort of chief magistrate, and the city of Zaragoza.[35] Mention should also be made of the Catalan Cortes of 1585, which were especially difficult. Justified as a reform to end fraud and maladministration, a new tax (the fifth, *el quinto*) would further intensify the stand-off between the Catalan elites and the monarchy (Hernández 1996, *passim*).

The growing fiscal pressure on the Church and the continual demand for services provoked conflicts not only with Rome but also with the Assembly of the Clergy of Spain. Episodes such as the interruption of the ecclesiastical services (in 1519, 1533 and 1556) and the excommunication of Charles V by the assembly indicated an undeniable degree of tension (Perrone 1997). And the difficulties between Philip II and the clergy and, indeed, with Rome were even more keenly felt. The Crown's demands on the Church also increased during the second half of the century (Ulloa 1977). By this period some of the services demanded of the clergy had become so regular that, despite being subject to negotiations, they were used to endorse the *asientos* and even to consolidate *juros* (Ulloa 1977, p. 567). The increase in tax collection is all the more significant to the extent that by this time there emerged symptoms of a slowing down of the overall growth of Church income (Yun 2004). For this reason, the tensions between the ecclesiastical institutions and the Crown did not come to an end, above all during the negotiations over the *subsidio*. Furthermore, even if many of these concessions were justified by the need to defend Christendom, there remained a notable unwillingness to deploy the forces and funds of the kingdom in wars fought far from its borders or for the sole furtherance of dynastic interests. This was even the case when funds were collected by, or from, the clergy.[36]

---

[35] Colás and Salas (1982) and Gil (1988). A more detailed version of this conflict within the argument of this book, in Yun (2004, pp. 364–76).

[36] Already during the *Comunidades*, Augustinian and Dominicans friars in Salamancas complained that 'it is unreasonable that His Caesarian Majesty should spend the incomes of these kingdoms in the other lands that he has, as each one of them is enough for itself and this kingdom is not obliged to any of the others, nor subject [to them], nor conquered nor defended by foreign men', *Estado*, 16, 416, AGS.

A Crucial do ut des

Conflict is, however, just one side of the story. The relationship between the Crown and the elites was in fact twofold. The other side of the coin was the pact between the elites and the Crown that facilitated the former's social consolidation and resilience, as well as the maintenance of mutually beneficial relationships.

For the Castilian aristocracy, many of the new measures, like the plans for the reversion of *alcabalas* to the Crown, ended in nothing more than the paper on which they were written. Moreover, the demands of the Crown gave rise to a new system for financing noble debts, one that allowed them to mortgage the incomes of the *mayorazgo* through *censos*. This was, in reality, a legal fiction as in theory possessions tied to the *mayorazgo* were inalienable and therefore could not be used as collateral for borrowing. The formula that came to be used, therefore, was that it was the rents generated by these possessions that served as payments and as a collateral for the capital taken out in *censos*. This allowed them to replace short-term borrowing taken out at high interest levels for long-term loans given on much more favourable terms (Yun 1987). This manoeuvre relaxed the pressure on debts and was similar to the effects obtained with *asientos* and *juros* by the Crown. In fact the rate of interest charged on *censos* was set as equal to that on *juros*.

The adoption of this system is highly indicative of underlying developments. In effect the king granted permits to use the *censo* to encourage the nobility to continue to play its part in the *auxilium* of the Crown (Yun 1987). This *auxilium*, moreover, quickly came to be understood in the broadest terms, including diplomatic service (habitually paid for by the diplomats themselves), their presence at court, and participation in royal tours. But, from the very beginning, these permits were granted to resolve the problems of the noble family, whose stability was understood to be important for the health of the kingdom. Thus, *censos* were used for a wide variety of purposes: to pay for dowries, to cement matrimonial agreements approved by the king, to finance the careers of second-born sons, to buy rents sold by the Crown and so expand the incomes and dominions of the lineage. All in all, these were uses that served the expansive dynamic of the seigniorial households and relaxed their inner tensions.

Of course, *censos* did not solve all of the nobility's debt problems, which continued to grow on account of being a substantial part of the logic of aristocratic economies. But things did not stop there. From the last decades of the century, the king, taking advantage of the growing circulation of money, proceeded to lower the interest rates on *juros*, which also affected the official interest rates levied on *censos* and allowed many noble families to reduce their borrowing costs (Yun 1987). When these debts led to unsustainable situations, they resulted in the seizure and management of the seigniorial estate by royal officials. Although these arrangements have been considered another absolutist attack on the nobility, they only lasted until the financial health of the *mayorazgo* was restored; furthermore, the seigniors retained full legal ownership of the estate and received a pension from its revenues throughout the period of royal management (Atienza 1987). The king's intervention in the *señoríos* was the opposite: a crutch to allow them to keep walking. It is to be noted that, contrary to the arguments that view absolutism as a simple means for the reduction of the power of the nobles, all these measures were taken while invoking the *plenitudo potestatis* of the king and justifying the importance of the *mayorazgos* as institutions that preserved the correct order of the 'republic' (Yun 2004).

The *auxilium* was also a motive—when not the pretext—for the granting to the nobility of favours, grants, salaries, and assistance that raised their political and social capital as well as their incomes. Often these rewards came together. In 1600 the Count of Benavente obtained an annual salary of 60,000 ducats as viceroy of Naples, the equivalent of the revenues of his estates at this time. And to this we might add additional sources of income, not all of them easily located or entirely licit, as well as the political power which this office entailed. The king also took advantage of other instruments to help good relations with the nobles. The Military Orders were exploited as a means of patronage, with the concession of their *encomiendas* and military habits used to confer prestige, influence, and income (Yun 2004).

This *do ut des* was also clearly manifested in the overall relationship with the urban oligarchies. Despite the bitter negotiations over precise figures, both the system for the setting of *alcabalas* in Castile and the increase in ordinary services across the kingdoms framed obvious fiscal pacts between the Crown and local oligarchies. The fact that the *alcabalas* were maintained for long periods beneath the rate of inflation contributed to the calming of tempers. But, above all, even in the most tense moments, the rise in taxes was implemented while respecting and even increasing the autonomy of the cities that collected them, thus benefitting the oligarchies. The forms generally chosen for collection—the renting out of rights to persons close to the oligarchy or the division of taxes through branches of economic activity—gave a big power to local elites. Even the service of the *millones* in the 1590s, which provoked a wave of protest, was finally approved in Castile thanks to the cession to the cities of the rights to collect and manage this new duty (Fortea 1990).

The *millones* and other forms of taxation compelled the Crown to concede rights for the emission of city debts, which allowed the cities to make advance payments on the promised sums. Opportunities such as these were accompanied by permits for the creation of municipal taxes to pay these debts with the money collected (Ruiz Martín 1994). This facilitated the control of municipal properties by the loaners, who were none other than the members of the urban oligarchy itself and the powerful local ecclesiastical institutions (Yun 1990). Moreover, one of the results of this system was to justify debts that were taken advantage of by the cities and the local elites, who were able to buy offices from the king, acquire jurisdictions and privileges, take possession of unfarmed land, and so on. In this regard there were certain parallels with the profits taken by the nobility on the *censos* levied on *mayorazgos*. The result of all of this was, in the first place, a greater meshing and dependence of the destinies of the monarchy and those of the oligarchies. Another consequence was their enhanced capacity for renovation without this leading to great changes in their internal dynamic (Soria 2000).

Something similar happened in the Crowns of Aragon and Navarre, although some important points of divergence should be noted. As we have seen, here tensions coalesced into violent conflicts.[37] But the eventual resolution of the crisis is in itself evidence of the intense relationships forming between the elites and the monarchy. It also underlines the role of these ties in facilitating the elites' social consolidation and extension.

In Aragon, as elsewhere, the political theory of the period reflected this union with the king. According to this ideology, the 'embodiment of the body politic as a whole' resided in the 'union of king and kingdom' or the 'king with Parliament'—this was a chamber very much dominated by the high nobility (and in this respect substantially different from its counterpart in Castile).[38] In conformity with this representation, the collection of

---

[37] The literature on this theme is extensive. An overview, with some modifications of previous arguments, is provided in Yun (2004, Chap. 6).

[38] Though these expressions refer to the Crown of Aragon (Gil 1991, p. 80), the fact is even clearer in Castile (Fernández Albaladejo 1992). In Valencia 'un recíproco y mutuo contrato entre vuestra majestad y dicho reino' ('a mutual and reciprocal contract between Your Majesty and his kingdom') was also acknowledged (Casey 1983, p. 243).

services voted in their respective Cortes fell to the *Generalidades* and *Diputaciones*, for their own benefit and that of the elites.[39] The balance between the king and kingdom was also maintained thanks to the *Audiencias* and, above all, the survival of the Council of Aragon which, like the other councils, represented the laws and customs of the kingdom before the king himself. The very organization of judicial power itself, established in institutions such as the *Justicia de Aragón* which defended the rights and by-laws of the kingdom against royal aggrandizement, demonstrated the limits of the king's power and would end up producing an equilibrium. In the aftermath of the conflict of 1591, the king sought to make an example of Aragon and introduced reforms to both the Cortes and the *Diputación*. These measures meant that the monarch could now appoint the *Justicia de Aragón* and a 'foreign viceroy' (meaning a non-Aragonese person). But, far from proceeding to suppress the privileges upon which the jurisdictions of seigniors and cities depended, a new equilibrium was sought between local powers and the monarchy. Therefore, despite the appointment of viceroys born outside the kingdom, this institution exercised an important role as an intermediary between local elites and the royal Court.

The nobility was not seriously prejudiced. In Aragon the king's permission was not as indispensable as it was for the management of *censos* taken out on *mayorazgos* in Castile. But the system, applied in a way that was not dissimilar to that of Castile, also allowed seigniorial economies to resist (Abadía 1993, 1998). In Aragon *censos* on their own benefit were generally set down by noble households on the incomes of the towns and villages within their seigniorial estates: the fact that the nobles exercised a high degree of control over these settlements was decisive in this regard. On the whole the Aragonese nobles were less involved in the 'enterprises' or campaigns of the Habsburgs than their Castilian counterparts: their rewards and remuneration were correspondingly smaller. But their involvement not only increased over time but also drew in a disproportional number of the greater houses, like the Requesens and the Gandía. Some of these families came to intertwine themselves to such a high degree with their Castilian counterparts that it becomes pointless to speak of any distinction or division between them. True, they maintained many rivalries over jurisdiction (indeed some disputes were even of a judicial nature), although these tended to be limited in scope.

[39] Gonzalez Antón (1989, pp. 664, 666) and García Cárcel (1989, p. 685).

The elites of the most important cities, such as Zaragoza, Barcelona, Valencia, and Pamplona, found their situations moderately favoured and improved across a range of issues. The system for the collection of taxes was itself based upon the cities' marked autonomy, which reinforced the oligarchy's political capital. The growing emission of municipal debt, nearly all of which was purchased by the oligarchies, increased their political and economic power. These developments were reflected in the elites' increasing domination of the urban governments, a trend that in turn favoured understanding between the Crown and the oligarchies by creating channels for better communication (Amelang 1986, pp. 45–6; Furió 1995, p. 256). Moreover, after the uprisings of 1580, the urban elites of the kingdom of Aragon increasingly integrated themselves into the monarchy's judicial and bureaucratic apparatus (Gil 1988). The fact that this trend was much clearer in the ecclesiastical administration resulted in there being no effective structural division between the Church in Castile and Aragon. Individuals drawn from these elites moved seamlessly between the two realms: this, again, was an important factor.

In Castile, as in the territories of the Crown of Aragon, the sale of jurisdictions, noble titles, unfarmed lands, rents, and *censos* and *juros* set on municipal finances served to satisfy the needs for social promotion and consolidation of many members of these families (the sums involved were rather different across these kingdoms). The growth of the royal bureaucracy also created employment opportunities for them. The granting of military habits and the enrolment in royal armies, in whose regiments more and more Spaniards were active, had a similar effect (see the data given by Wright 1982). Another opportunity—the chance to seek office within the ranks of one of the most expansive churches in Europe—further eased the fortunes of the oligarchies, who provided many members of the ecclesiastical elites.[40]

The opportunities open to the oligarchies to take advantage of the growth of the ecclesiastical institutions were just one part of a broader process: despite the pressures exerted by the Crown, the Habsburgs were able to renew their pact with the Catholic Church and thus to provide it with an outlet for expansion as an institution of power with an economic character. The Catholic policies of the Habsburgs led to the growth of the number of institutions and offices, as did the stream of donations and

[40] We will return to this matter in the next chapter; see also the case of Córdoba in Soria (2000).

endowments made by the faithful and the related rise in ecclesiastical revenues. America was essential to this process. It was a vast virgin territory into which the ecclesiastical economy rapidly expanded, with the religious orders (the Dominicans, Franciscans, Hieronymites) being particularly voracious colonizers from the first moments. But it was the Jesuits, active from the second half of the century and in whom the presence of the low nobility and the oligarchies was important from the very beginning, who expanded at an unprecedented rate. America was also crucial to the growth of the secular clergy and led to an intense relationship between it and the monarchy, one that reinforced the bonds of mutual interest. From 1508, when the Crown obtained the right to 'present' (in effect, to appoint) all ecclesiastical benefices from parishes to bishoprics, its control over the life of the Church was combined with a unique capacity for patronage. In 1543 the monarchy won the right to set episcopal jurisdictions, thus reinforcing and extending its powers in America. Between 1511 and 1564, it created 22 dioceses; appointments in them were controlled by the Council of Indies. Clergy even had to swear loyalty to the king. Ecclesiastical patronage over the Indies (the right to name bishops) was considered the 'richest stone, the most beautiful pearl, in the royal diadem'. Apart from wealth, this right gave the Crown the ability to create ecclesiastical clientele networks that were unparalleled in Christendom. It was a form of reaching a general deal with the clergy and the elites, from whose number the clerical elite was recruited (McAlister 1984, pp. 94–7).

To understand the 'contract' between Crown and Church, it is important to note that some of the services rendered by it, such as the Bull of the Crusade (the source of tax income that most grew in this period), were not in reality paid from the pockets of the clergy but by the faithful, who were encouraged by the clergy to acquire these Bulls. Moreover, as with the cities, the churchmen did not always offer their resources free of charge. For example, the negotiation over the *excusado* allowed the ecclesiastical institutions to strengthen or obtain certain economic privileges, principally in relation to the 'sale of cereals without any limitation' (Álvarez 1990, p. 125).

The relationship with the Crown and the image of a common enterprise in defence of the faith increased the Church's spiritual capital and prestige. The country's growing identification with the anti-Protestant and Counter-Reformation causes enhanced cultural beliefs that were highly positive in respect to the Catholic Church. The result was a flow of donations and charity from the faithful, who saw it as the principal bastion in the defence of Christendom.[41] Thanks to all of this, the entailed properties in the clergy's hands were extended, and overall ecclesiastical incomes increased even more quickly than the Church's contributions to the king.[42]

Philip II has passed into history as a king in constant tension with Rome, a staunch defender of his right of 'presentation' of bishops and indefatigable in his efforts to control the Inquisition. But his relations with the Catholic Church in Spain and America were decisive in allowing this institution to prosper and to continue to be the receptacle of a large number of members of the elites. This fact relaxed the tensions generated among the nobles by their need for social expansion and would be crucial for the social consolidation of the dominant coalition in spite of its internal structural tensions.

In conclusion, absolutism did cut off some of this dominant coalition's opportunities for expansion. But in other ways, it helped and favoured its members by creating channels apt for their forms of social expansion, thus reinforcing a difficult but solid agreement between the Crown and the elites.

This was evident in many different developments. No records have been found of the collapse, extinction, or ruin of a single great seigniorial house during these years. Protected by the *mayorazgo*, their extraordinary incomes, and access to credit, their patrimonies did not dissolve; at most, they passed to other lineages through political marriages and inheritances. Many secondary branches of these houses satisfied their needs for promotion and increased their power and wealth to the point that they were actually able to complete with the central trunks of these lineages. The case of the Count Duke of Olivares, who belonged to a lateral branch of the Guzmán, is perhaps the most eye-catching example (Chap. 8). But something very similar happened with the house of Sandoval. Beginning at a relatively secondary position, with limited economic resources, this Castilian-Aragonese house not only rode out a number of storms but even became one of the most powerful in Castile by the early seventeenth century through the person of the duke of Lerma, favourite of Philip III. The security offered by the *mayorazgo* was instrumental to this rise, as was the matrimonial policy that allowed it to form ties with powerful lineages such

---

[41] Sermons on the Bull of Crusade were preached in the hope of encouraging poplar passion for this institution. For ironic comments, see Leonardo Donato's view in García Mercadal (1999, vol. II, 360).

[42] See the example of Madrid in López ed. (1998, pp. 82–7). For a wider vision, Atienza (1988), whose figures are presented in the following chapter below.

as the Gandía; also important was the decisive intervention of members of the ecclesiastical hierarchy—indeed, one such figure, Cristóbal de Sandoval, was illegitimate. The house's capacity for promotion is eloquently demonstrated by the fact that in the early 1600s three of its members possessed the ducal dignity (Williams 2006, pp. 15–30).

Between 1520 and 1631, more than 600 new titles were created, the vast majority being conferred upon individuals drawn from the high nobility, its lower ranks, and the urban elites. Obviously, if these titles represented the avidity of the Crown to satisfy the desire to purchase dignity and to reward service, then this was just the tip of the iceberg in terms of the capacity for social ascent. An understanding of the role and influence of urban oligarchies in this sector can be gleaned from the fact that of the bishops of Castile, more than 50% came from an urban background—a vastly disproportionate percentage in relation to the overall population. Between 85% and 90% were nobles—an indication of the elites' enormous capacity for promotion and ability to overcome problems.[43] It is not, therefore, surprising that open conflict and factional disputes in cities should have practically disappeared, being replaced by more pacific means of conflict resolution. The resources of the judicial system and matrimony allowed families to overcome tensions by sealing alliances. In Murcia, for example, the conflict between the Sotos and Riquelmes was largely resolved by fear of a total rupture involving allegations of impurity of blood—this was a form of self-enforcement between clashing groups who, in the end, had similar interests (Contreras 1992).

More widely the process by which elites had become involved in the monarchy and empire, and the capacity of both to offer an outlet for their needs for social consolidation and promotion, also contributed to a certain degree of stability in the political system and social order. In this way many of the fifteenth-century phantoms that had led to rebellions and civil strife—here Spain can be profitably compared to other areas of Europe (Chap. 6)—were palliated.

Global Forces and the Mobilization of Resources

The process described above should be understood in the context of the globalization and the incorporation of the Iberian kingdoms into an enormous imperial system.

---

[43] See the figures provided by Barrio in his various studies (2001 and 2004).

Silver and the Circulation of Elites Within the Empire

American silver and the inflationary process it fed had a corrosive effect on some seigniorial economies. Moreover, to the extent that it was accompanied by broader changes in mercantile development, it accentuated a number of social imbalances. But it also exerted a stabilizing effect on institutions, an outcome that is often forgotten (Yun 1998).

The quantities of silver arriving from America never constituted more than 25% of the total income of the Crown (Flynn 1982). This was not, of course, a small proportion. Many European princes could only have dreamed of something similar, especially as this was a source of revenue that was not under the control of the Cortes of Castile. But it is even more important to underline that American silver made possible the use of mechanisms for the conversion and consolidation of debt described above which was the cornerstone of the whole financial system, as well as the series of 'contracts' between the Court and the different factions of the elites. The subjects of Castile paid for a good part of the costs of the imperial system in Europe with their taxes. But it was the forced labour in the American mines and the taxes levied on their silver that made possible the pact between the monarchy and the elites, thus converting Castile into the backbone of the monarchy's imperial complex. Other countries of course underwent similar processes (see Chap. 6), but the arrival of silver marked a fundamental difference in the case of Spain.

Also the policy of the Crown with regard to the Iberian aristocracies was especially effective thanks to the arrival of Indies treasure fleets. The precious white metal facilitated a level of fiscal extraction and a type of involvement of the kingdom in the tax system that meant that the pressures on the nobility remained reasonable. The expansion of the amount of money in circulation was behind a process seldom remarked upon: it meant that nobles could now borrow to perform services requiring their direct mobilization, such as their deployment in the war against the *Moriscos* of Granada. Had credit not been available, their only means of providing these services would have been through immediately extorting their vassals and tenants or by using very painful lines of credit. Furthermore, the increase of available specie and the security in the repayment of the public debt that it generated help to explain (they were not the only reason) the lowering of interest rates that allowed the Crown to decrease rates charged on both *juros* and *censos*, whose weight fell upon the nobility. Without America, not only the stability of the monarchy but also the financial steadiness of the aristocracy and the opportunity to apply the credit policy described above would have been very difficult.

American silver was also crucial for the formation of the powerful network of financiers serving the king, something which contributed decisively to the creation of the Habsburg system and the conflictive pacts within it. Captured in America or Seville by the Italian or German families, silver energized their financial circuits in a way that would have been unthinkable in the fifteenth century.[44] As we have seen, American silver made possible the circuits between *asientos* and *juros* upon the royal taxes that characterized the financial system, as well as the mechanisms that allowed Madrid to 'camouflage' the operations for the transfer of funds from Castile to the European theatres of war. American silver was, therefore, crucial to overcome the technical and institutional constrictions of the composite monarchy.

The flow of silver and the expansion of American commerce were also relevant for the consolidation of the urban oligarchies, even if that commerce was smaller than usually thought. Global commerce, with the American trade as its vertebral column, and the growth of the class of merchants tied to it, created tensions in the very heart of the settled society. But these developments had an impact on the expansion of the elites. Though it was not the main factor, the arrival of the migrant's remittances could not but help to alleviate their internal tensions. Official figures—substantially less than the real total, without doubt—come to 1.3% of the GDP by 1591–1600.[45] This is not a huge proportion, but it needs to be remembered that an important part of it fell into the hands of a tiny amount of the overall population. Since part of this amount was made up of payments for exports from the peninsula, it seems logical to think that it also enhanced the conditions for the success of a merchant class that was able to mix with the old families of the urban elite, thus favouring their social and economic reproduction. The impact in Seville is, logically, the most evident phenomenon. Not only merchants—some of them of *converso* origin—but also a good number of mid-ranking nobles and even some aristocrats dedicated their time to commerce and made headway in this city of blue bloods (Pike 1978). This was often achieved by taking

[44] Although the literature on the matter is huge, a useful synthesis can be found in Ruiz Martín (1990a, pp. 16–23).

[45] These estimates are based on Hamilton (1975, p. 47) and Yun (1998, Table 2).

advantage of the noble status enjoyed by certain Genoese families involved, directly or indirectly, in American commerce.

Also highly significant were the opportunities the Empire offered its elites for circulation and promotion in America and Europe. As a result, these dominant groups enjoyed extraordinary geopolitical advantages, an exceptional factor—if we compare them with their European peers, with the possible exception of the Genoese, who constituted one of the epoch's most stable elites, due to the solidity of their pact with the Crown.

An analysis of emigration to the Indies and of the domestic life of the great noble houses might well demonstrate that very few of their members went to live in the New World. Certainly there were very few cases of mixed marriages with the 'indigenous nobility'.[46] This is logical, given that aristocrats sought to marry reflections of themselves that might not be perceived in American elites. However, from the end of Philip II's reign, many viceroys—perhaps, indeed, all of them—belonged to these great families (Schäfer 2003, vol. II, Appendix I, pp. 381–4). This form of service brought in large sums of money as extraordinary incomes, being one of the most sought-after benefits of the *auxilium*. Office holding certainly served to soften the so-called crisis of the aristocracy—this was a very mild crisis in Iberia—and to confront the internal aspirations within these families. In turn this affected not only the leading members of lineages but also their collateral branches, many of whose members travelled abroad to serve to their great profit and benefit. There are also a few fascinating cases of Iberian families creating American branches. The Borja-Gandía lineage provides one such example, as does the second branch of the Velasco, who created a whole dynasty in México after D. Luis de Velasco y Ruiz de Alarcón served as viceroy of New Spain. But these cases are surely symptomatic of a broader trend (Redondo and Yun 2008). The part of the aristocracy most affected by this process was, by some margin, the Castilian lineages. Yet a number of families of Valencian origin (such as the Borgia-Gandía) were progressively tied to the Castilian clans forging ties in Aragon and even in Italy. In this way the positive effects of the empire were transmitted through these families into and towards an aristocratic elite that was increasingly marked by a transnational component and that was becoming Spanish more than Castilian, Aragonese, and so on (Redondo and Yun 2009).

---

[46] See the case of Moctezuma's descendants in Hernández Franco (2006).

Nobles were most commonly employed on the European side of this empire. Forever conscious of the dynastic component and wary of the multiple layers of opposition to foreign elements, the Habsburgs seldom sought to employ subjects from one kingdom in the local administration of another state. However, from the second half of the sixteenth century, many members of noble families came to serve as viceroys or pursued military careers in Europe. Well-known cases such as that of the duke of Alba were not unique or exceptional (Maltby 1983). Careers of this sort allow us to trace family strategies, as in this case not only the 'Iron Duke' himself but all the Álvarez de Toledo lineage became active in the European theatre acquiring offices, promoting second-born sons, discharging military and diplomatic commands, or marrying daughters with prominent families in Italy or elsewhere.[47] The monarchy of the Habsburgs of Spain required an efficient and stable diplomatic service: by the end of the century, the ambassadorships dotted across Europe were generally in the hands of members of families of this sort (Redondo and Yun 2009). In turn nobles came to assume that this type of office was something like a birthright; on the other hand, this kind of position required an initial burst of expenditure by the office holder, who usually made use of *censos* to cover this outlay (Yun 2004). Nobles, in other words, were the most logical incumbents of this sort of office.

The employment of the Iberian nobilities in the imperial system further accentuated their ties with other European aristocracies. Families of Aragonese origin (the Riquelmes, the Santa Coloma, the Denia, and others) and Portuguese origin (the Castro and Silva) used these bonds to achieve forms of promotion that relaxed the internal tensions mentioned above and which, in time, changed their very nature and relationships with their places of origin (Redondo and Yun 2008). This transformation offered certain economic advantages and opportunities (noticeably honours and military habits), thus reinforcing both the alliance that connected Castilian nobles to the Crown and the opportunities for promotion of this social group. An analysis of the marriages of the members of the Order of the Golden Fleece between 1575 and 1600 demonstrates that the Castilian families had become the marriage partners of choice for many European nobilities (Yun 2016). This matrimonial market opened up avenues for

---

[47]The clearest case is that of the viceroy Don Pedro de Toledo, whose daughter, Doña Leonor de Toledo, married Cosimo de Medici, duke of Florence (Hernando 1994; Palos 2016). More examples can be found in Redondo and Yun (2009).

promotion and unblocked the internal tensions of these lineages. While the links were weaker with the Flemish houses, an entire chapter might be written on their marriages with the Italian lineages of Roman, Genoese, Sicilian, or Neapolitan origin. These interactions afforded them not only political and social capital but also the economic fluidity that allowed the high and mid-ranking aristocracy to face their domestic difficulties. Genoese marriages were particularly beneficial—and lucrative—in this regard.[48]

This imperial complex stood at the heart of the relationship between the Crown and the elites, in large part because of its capacity to satisfy those elites' needs for social and financial capital. Many members of this social sector assumed military offices and followed careers that offered the chance of social promotion or of avoiding the negative effects of the *mayorazgo* system. Figures such as Garcilaso de la Vega, Juan Boscán, and many members of the intermediate nobility ended up obtaining habits in the Military Orders (Postigo 1988). The martial professions (fighting and its related logistical and bureaucratic machinery) and the waging of war in America also provided a fertile terrain for these groups (Martínez 1993, vol. I, pp. 118–26), which shortly came to see the New World as a promising area for expansion. The known cases are highly evocative in this regard. These elites served as members of aristocratic retinues, as officers in the royal bureaucracy, or as businessmen who decided to remain in America. These were men drawn from the ranks of the *hidalgos*, or members of the middle classes in danger of falling into poverty (Martínez 1993, pp. 120–3). Families such as the Espinosa provide an excellent example of how dynasties incorporated merchants, businessmen, clergymen, and nobles, thus establishing transatlantic ties and so taking full advantage of the enormous advantages conferred by the empire (Lohman 1968). This social class provided many of the university students who created the dynasties of functionaries and lawyers who made their living in the New World (Pelorson 1980).[49] These (often temporary) emigrants not only sent money back to the Iberian Peninsula; those returning from the New World also brought back wealth that also alleviated the internal tensions within this group. Waves of emigration were therefore crucial to the process that, whether it ended in premature death or fabulous fortune, freed the Iberian political theatre of a great deal of pressure.

---

[48] See, for example, the case of Ambrosio de Spinola in Rodríguez Villa (1905) and Herrero (2009).

[49] For detailed studies, see Hampe and Honores (2004).

As it has been said, another important absorbent of the tensions within the Iberian elites and within the whole society was the ecclesial structure in America. Indeed, the expansion of the Church into the New World might be considered one of the most significant consequences of this emergent global empire. The emigration of churchmen, among them many lateral members of noble lineages, to the Indies was perhaps one of the most important means of reducing peninsular tensions. No exact figures can be provided, but it has been estimated that during the sixteenth century, some 6000 clerics crossed the Atlantic; this was a significant number if we remember that a number of them belonged to the tiny middling ranks and oligarchies of this society (Borges 1983). And so, aside from the fortunes involved, America was used to win over the clergy and to ensure the circulation of elites, from whose rank the Church assiduously recruited part of its members (McAlister 1984, pp. 94–7).

Mobilization of Resources and the Limits of the System

The status quo established between the Crown and the elites served to frustrate profound changes in the central finances. As pointed out before, the process was, of course, very far from a financial revolution of the sort taking place in Holland. But, more important and against an implicit idea very much accepted for years, the outcome, on the other hand, was clearly not a prototype for a centralized fiscal state that would allow the total concentration of military power and social coercion in the hands of an absolute king, as was believed until relatively recently.

In regard to the former, it has to be said that, despite its technical and constitutional sophistication, the Castilian financial system differed from that of Holland after the 1580s and from that of England after 1688.[50] The key to what happened in these countries was the development of parliamentary systems characterized by a relatively high degree of political representativeness, which gained control over the budget and public debt. In 1688 this system was accompanied by the creation of the Bank of England (in 1694) that would advance money to the treasury and, indeed, would end up controlling the money supply. Logically, this has been considered a key step in the development of institutions that allowed a marked increase in the capacity to sell state debt bonds (North and Weingast 1989). The situation of Castile (let alone the other kingdoms) was very different.

---

[50] Tracy (1985), 'T Hart et al. (1997), and Brewer (1990).

It is evident that the Castilian political model was very far from achieving the optimal conditions for a financial revolution. The Cortes suffered from a lack of representativeness, and some scholars have even questioned the ability of the city and town councils to control their own representatives in the assembly (Thompson 1989). The Cortes could rail against the costs of war and the transfer of money from the kingdom but had no control over expenditures. On the other hand, the development of the American-Genoese axis (mentioned above) placed the function that central banks would later perform (the management of debt) in the hands of an international corporation, which did not seek to benefit the kingdom but only to secure its own private interest. Here it is worthwhile remembering that in reality the Bank of England emerged as an institution offering annuities to subscribers, something that set it very much apart from the corporation of bankers who advanced short-term loans at high rates of interest to the King of Spain.[51] Behind this there stood the fact that the conflictive pact with the Crown was leading to a situation in which neither of the twin fiscal and financial poles of the monarchy—the cities and the Genoese—wanted to introduce substantial changes unless it was clearly in their interest to do so. And their interests were the opposite (Ruiz Martín 1990b). They therefore created a sort of paralysing equilibrium. This was for a variety of reasons and despite the fact that the Crown sought to take advantage of any dispute between them.

Quite a few of the Crown's efforts to reform the financial fiscal machinery sought to give it the very thing it most urgently lacked: a banking system that would allow cheaper credit and, as a result, the replacement of the Genoese. The project to convert the House of Trade (*Casa de la Contratación*) of Seville into 'a commercial bank and, at the same time, a deposit bank for the public debt of the Spanish Monarchy' is one of the most significant of these efforts (Ruiz Martín 1965). This scheme sought to attract private savings, some of them tied to the American trade, and so reduce both the high interest rates charged in the *asientos* and the role of the Genoese. The same might be said of the project of Valle de la Cerda and Oudegherste. Inspired by developments in Holland, which now stood on the brink of a genuine

---

[51] See the synthesis on the Bank of England of Van der Wee et al. (1991, pp. 246–53).

financial revolution, the intention was to create a network of local public banks. The idea was to attract savings by the granting of *censos* and the negotiation over *juros*: deposits obtained in this way would be advanced as loans to the king, thus displacing the hated Genoese (Dubet 2003).

Problems were compounded by the fact that this fiscal system lacked a genuine central treasury that would have permitted officials to make a precise estimate of its possibilities. Moreover, the behaviour described above (the management of the debt through *asientos* based upon incomes which were more or less known and secure) was just one part of the system. Many *juros* were sold directly by the Crown officials, and many investors and businessmen had to accept *juros* as compensation for seized Indies cargoes or Crown bankruptcies. Nothing could be imagined further from a system of debt based only upon the confidence of subscribers guaranteed by the control of the budget by the parliament.

What emerged in Castile—and in the other kingdoms under the Habsburgs—was very far from the model of a unified fiscal system that might serve as the basis of a centralized military state.

There was (for the epoch) a quite evolved royal fiscal and financial system, which was the pillar of the important development of military technologies (Parker 1972). Thanks to the former, thousands of soldiers—most of them mercenaries and not Castilians (Ribot 2008)—were paid in Flanders, Milan, and other areas of the composite monarchy. Even the American incomes were more and more used to pay for the different bodies of the navy there. But due to financial and logistic problems, theses armies were often decentralized in their logistic support, and contractors and *asentistas* played a very important role to the extent that it has been possible to identify a 'decentralization' that shifted the management of the army from the central government to the periphery and from the public administration to the private one (Thompson 1976: conclusions). It is not odd that some historians have recalled that the empire's bureaucracy in fact involved of a very tiny group of people (see, e.g. Stradling 1981: General Introduction).

Furthermore, the relation of tense cooperation that had emerged between the Crown and the elites also had a dimension outside of the fiscal system, one which is important for the understanding of the specific (and relatively limited) role of public finances in the mobilization of resources. The *auxilium* of nobles and aristocrats fed military and bureaucratic systems that had emerged in the Middle Ages and had a marked private and decentralized character. This involved direct military action by nobles or aristocrats who, having usually obtained financing through *censos* and credits, carried out missions on behalf of the Crown. This was a common occurrence in frontier areas like Murcia, where the military function of nobles such as the Marquises of los Vélez had been maintained during the fifteenth century (Owens 1980). This is just one case among many. The various forms of noble mobilization (cited above) maintained the military role of the aristocracy. This was especially commonplace in those regions which had close links with areas directly involved in military conflict of one sort or another and would become even more usual in the seventeenth century. Of course, the nobility was not the only active participant in practices of this sort. The cities, in reality collective seigniorial estates that are, therefore, also obliged to *auxilium* and military service, performed a very similar function. Seville, Granada, Valencia, La Coruña, Murcia, Cartagena, and many others found themselves compelled to carry out levies of soldiers and to maintain high levels of direct spending and/ or to assume debts for defence purposes.[52]

This picture should not surprise us, even though it breaks with the traditional and overly simplistic view of centralized fiscal systems of military mobilization. Recent research on other countries has also shown the importance of military entrepreneurs and private armies and mobilizations (though in Spain this was not strictly the case, since the *señoríos* of nobles or cities cannot be considered to be private) (Parrott 2012). Perhaps these private operations, for all that they attract the attention of specialists, have been viewed as less significant in the overall tapestry. It is to be noted that these methods and mechanisms, although widely divergent in themselves, bear many similarities to those employed in the conquest of the Americas (Chap. 2). They were based on a codex of *auxilium* and an ethos of personal initiative in exchange for the promise of later compensation.

It is impossible, for the moment at least, to calculate the economic value of these mobilizations and the debts they generated. Perhaps their overall significance was slight in quantitative terms. But we know, for example, that during the years 1589–1593, the *censos* subscribed by nobles to cover services

---

[52] Thompson (1976, pp. 11–37). The *Morisco* rebellion was largely fought with local levies and contributions from the cities of the south and eastern regions of the country. Seville paid 61,000 ducats (p. 18). Valencia came to pay 50,000, and cities in Catalonia, Sardinia, and Mallorca had to do the same on a number of occasions (pp. 19, 23). The same happened on the Cantabrian coast, which contributed 60,000 ducats 'with no cost to the royal patrimony' (p. 24).

(principally military) to the Crown rose to 1.6 million ducats, which represented 18% of the income collected in *asientos* in these years.[53] And it seems probable that the cities made military contributions and efforts of a similar or greater scale. Though maybe exaggerated, the case of Seville is very meaningful. To give an idea, the principal of the *censos* imposed upon the city's budget by 1595 was about 1.1 million ducats, which, extrapolating to the whole kingdom of Castile, would mean the equivalent of the *juros*' principal at the end of the century. Even taking into account that this is (probably) too high a figure and that more than half of it was the result of municipal expenses, it represents a large amount that cannot be forgotten in any study of the debt of the composite monarchy.[54]

Mobilizations of this sort worked within the existing fiscal arrangements and demonstrated the reality of conflictive cooperation: they served as one of the pillars of the political and social agreement between elites and the Crown. They would have a significant impact on the political economy of the empire and the process of state building. From the viewpoint of fiscal affairs, taxes were generated as a cascade: many of the fiscal impositions of the Crown upon the towns were paid by them by advancing to the king money which they obtained thanks to the subscription of *censos* on their municipal finances. And this was also the case for the payment of the local militias: to finance them the municipalities asked the king for permission to take *censos* and to create new taxes to make interest payments. Thus noble and town debts are important, and any definition of the 'public debt of Castile' needs to include not only the *juros*—that is the royal debt—but also the *censos* created for the accomplishment of the public tasks and functions (military commitments included) that these arms of the state were obliged to carry out.[55]

---

[53] According to my calculations, the average annual figures in ducats for various periods and years are 43,000 (1565–1569); 5400 (1574–1578); 77,500 (1579–1583); 25,000 (1584–1588); 330,000 (1589–1593); and 96,000 (1594–1598). *Cámara de Castilla, Libros de Relación*, libs. 14, 18, 21, 25 y 26, AGS. The calculation must be taken with some precautions. Probably, the nobles spent important quantities without previously asking for either a *censo* or a mortgage on their *mayorazgos*. And, in another sense, not all costs derived from war spending.

[54] See the figures in Martínez Ruiz (1992). I have extrapolated this onto the entire kingdom by taking into account the population of Castile.

[55] See these mechanisms in Ruiz Martín (1994) and in my 'Introduction' to Ruiz de Celada's book (Yun 1990).

The machinery for the mobilization of resources was, therefore, more far-reaching than has sometimes been supposed. The same could be said about its debts. It is quite possible that, taking all the contributions and exactions into account, recent optimistic estimates on the weight of taxes and the sustainability of the debt may have to be revised. As we shall see, this is also crucial to understand the state-building process.

One result of all of this was that military administration came to be characterized by a high degree of decentralization resulting in relatively poor performance and fraud. This would proceed to the extent that it resulted in what I. A. A. Thompson called the 'devolution of functions', in which military administration and even the conduct of war were placed in private hands. As a whole this system created a complicated and conflictive machinery, whose deployment was made more costly by its very character and which was permanently marked by clientelism, patronage, nepotism, misadministration, fraud, and corruption. This would be as much the case in Flanders as in Castile itself, and it was equally evident in the relationships between the various theatres of action and the functioning of the fiscal and financial system that fed the logistical apparatus.[56] Similar patterns were, of course, frequently found in other territories of the monarchy. The contracts for the maintenance of galleys in Genoa (especially those signed with Andrea Doria) provide a good example; again, arrangements of this sort would become more common from 1600 (see Chap. 8) (Williams 2014). In regard to the military system as a whole, it has been said that the 'centralisation of the Spanish administration was purely personal. In the same way that the monarchy was the sum of autonomous and privileged nations, united only by their loyalty to the same sovereign, the internal constitution of Castile was a conglomeration of liberties and independent jurisdictions centralised in the person of the king' (Thompson 1976, p. 42). Moreover, the Council of War was a 'Cretan labyrinth' and highly ineffective. Controlled by the aristocracy until the reforms of the end of the century, it was engaged in continuous rivalries with other councils. It exercised judicial responsibilities that weakened its capacity for quick responses and never managed to secure a monopoly over the control of military affairs.

All of these failures had their origins in 'profoundly structural weaknesses'. As in all monarchies of the time, at its heart lay a system of patronage for the conferment of offices and loyalties, one entirely consistent with

---

[56] For these territories, see Parker (1979) and Thompson (1976).

the principle of *do ut des*. Patronage did not, to be certain, necessarily involve the king (it was often a relationship between nobles involved in war and their subjects) or function according to the idea of office as a source of benefit typical of the period. As a result, the working of the administrative system was clumsy and costly to maintain, functioning according to a series of highly complex codes in regard to what today would be considered corruption (Yun 1994a). Furthermore, local authorities played a vital role in the collection of monies destined for war. For this reason much of the royal revenue ended up being lost on the wayside.[57] Finally, the mobilization system did not serve exclusively military ends, in part because of its institutional and social limitations. It was also used to feed the machinery of distribution of resources that came to be set out in the *situados* and *libranzas* claimed by nobles, patricians, and ecclesiastics, who absorbed the royal taxes at their very point of collection, thus reducing the remittances to the king. The result, again, was to broaden the disparity between the theoretical funds and the actual amounts.[58]

The Empire As a Solution in Portugal

Overseas expansion provoked important social tensions but also served to stabilize Portuguese society.

If a sizeable number of the merchants and financiers were of Italian origin (specifically Genoese), the Portuguese group (especially New Christians) was also notable. It became even more so following the expulsion of the Jews from the Crowns of Castile and Aragon in 1492. As in the rest of the peninsula, this was the origin of considerable tension that was manifested as a rejection of religious beliefs but which betrayed an ever more pronounced ethnic element. In some way these tensions were an Iberian materialization of the more general clash between nobility and

---

[57] As is well known, this is not a trait exclusive to Castile or to Iberian financial systems in general. See Collins (1988).

[58] In 1572, the Venetian ambassador Leonardo Donato estimated the income of the King of Spain as some 5.6 million *escudos* but believed that debt interest repayments absorbed 2.2 million and 'ordinary spending' (including the *situados* and running costs) 2 million. 1.4 million was, therefore, the net available sum: this was, very probably, highly optimistic. He believed that the situation was even worse in the Low Countries, where 'nothing comes out clean', L. Donato, 'Relación de España' (1573), in García Mercadal (1999, quoted on pp. 362, 386).

businessmen. But commercial development and economic growth also fed pressure for the social advancement of the urban oligarchies and merchants, which increased tensions within these elites. As in the other Iberian kingdoms, the nobility was compelled to increase military costs on the peninsula—less so, perhaps, than in Castile—as much as in the colonies (Vila-Santa 2015, pp. 71, 77, 85, 94, 113–5). And the development of royal justice clashed with the expansion of the jurisdiction of the seigniors (Hespanha 1989, pp. 414 and ff.), while a mentality of patronage increased their social obligations and prestige costs (Da Cunha 2003). The Portuguese nobility even came to apply forms of Malthusian self-control that, perhaps because they have passed under the historians' radar, are unknown in the other Iberian kingdoms (Carvalhal 2016, pp. 5–6; Boone 1986). This phenomenon, closely associated with a masculine hierarchy of ever-greater intensity in the houses of *fidalgos* and an extension of the *morgadio*, the equivalent of the Spanish *mayorazgo* (Monteiro 2003), led to the increasing entrance of daughters and second-born sons in the Church, this being a way of reducing internal tensions within the lineages (Boone 1986).

But, as in Castile, the overseas expansion favoured the consolidation and social promotion of elites (the early forms of this development have been described above). A considerable number of *fidalgos* (many of them belonging to secondary branches in the lineage or second-born sons), mid-ranking nobles, and even traders found that conquest served as a form of social development and gave an outlet to the internal tensions and family aspirations. This fact was manifested in what Magalhães Godinho (1963, pp. 213–4) called the *cavaleiro-mercador*, a noble dedicated to commerce who, in many senses, can be seen as the updated version of the knight errant of the Middle Ages, who had used foreign wars as an instrument of social promotion. Given the mixing of military violence and commerce—more often than not, extortion—which marked Portuguese actions on coastlines from Morocco to China, the figure of the *cavaleiro-mercador* was not necessarily or inherently contradictory (other countries were, of course, equally violent or exploitative). Beyond this oligarchy consisting of the intermediate nobility, some members of the great aristocratic dynasties could also find an outlet for their desire to reproduce their lineage and family through the empire. This was, however, a numerically small group. In fact the offices of governor and viceroy in the *Estado da Índia* were divided almost entirely between five families (Da Cunha and Monteiro 2005). But the cases are highly significant. The most eye-catching example is that of the governor Alburquerque, but he was followed by a considerable number of captains general, governors, and viceroys of the *Estado da Índia*, such as the different members of the Telles, Ataíde, or the Sousas Chichorro (Da Cunha 2005; Vila-Santa 2015; Pelúcia 2009). With regard to Brazil, families such as the Alburquerque and the Sá were prominent also in this process (Boxer 1952; Norton 1965; Viana 1968). And, of course, the Church, both secular and regular, offered another means of expansion. If only a few bishoprics were created, the Portuguese orders in general and the Jesuits in particular were able to impose themselves upon both Asia and Brazil, thus becoming a channel for the expansion of the elites. The Crown's right to *padroado* (similar to that of *patronato* in Castile) served to satisfy the elites' need for social reproduction and the projection of their clients into an ecclesiastical system that by now was acquiring global dimensions. The Military Orders created the social space fitting for the entrance of members of the nobility and the *fidalguia*—and even, indeed, for commoners (Olival 2001).

As Subrahmanyam and Thomaz have shown, noble emigration was small in absolute numbers (1991, p. 319). This is logical given the size of the group. But the impact of the empire should not be overlooked. To understand this, a wider perspective has to be adopted. As in the Spanish case, the empire bestowed upon the kings an extra income that allowed them to reduce the pressure of the Crown upon the aristocracy, *fidalgos*, and merchants, which in turn may have reduced tensions within the dominant elites. At the same time, this income extended the Crown's capacity for patronage towards these groups, not only in the colonies but also in Portugal itself. It is important to note that, from 1555, the Crown obtained from the Pope the titular leadership of the Portuguese Military Orders, something which allowed it to intervene in the conferral of habits and estates and so became a crucial method of ascent within the nobility (Olival 2004). This implied a notable increase in the Crown's capacity to offer patronage to the elites at the same time that it took possession of a fundamental tool for the regulation of the internal tensions of this group. And it should be remembered that this pontifical concession was consistent with the function of the empire—in Africa and India—as a means of propagating the Catholic faith.

This permitted the aristocracy to abstain from a systematic revision of the system of *enfiteusis* which, having created favourable conditions for the farmers, was one of the pillars of the agrarian growth achieved in the sixteenth century. Any attempt to understand the positive medium-term effect of the colonies must also take into account the broadening of the ecclesiastical structures within them. This was another balm that facilitated the consolidation and resilience of elites. A study of the Portuguese ecclesiastical chapter houses has underlined that the situation was very similar to that of Castile: the basis of a genuine church patriciate, they served as spaces for the projection and social development of families belonging to the local oligarchy (da Silva 2013). Portugal, in distinction to France, England, and even the Low Countries, hardly saw any big social conflict in the sixteenth century nor indeed until 1637–1640. This can be explained partly by religious factors but also by economic and social ones and more in particular by its elite's capacity for reproducing themselves.

This dynamic would not be broken in 1581. The annexation of Portugal by the House of Habsburg may have been violent, but it also meant that Portuguese elites could continue with their model of social reproduction. As the historiography of both countries has underlined, the Dutch and English attacks upon Portuguese possessions after 1580 certainly entailed a cost for these elites. But it is also worthwhile remembering that before the union of the Crowns—indeed since the 1540s—expansion in Asia had been slowed and the defence of the empire rendered increasingly difficult. In this light it is not surprising that a large part of these elites saw Philip II (Philip I in Portugal) as a solution to both their problems and those of the empire (Disney 2009, vol. I, Chap. 10). This is especially true when we factor into consideration the indebtedness of some of them as a result of their efforts to follow King Sebastian in his extremely expensive and disastrous African campaign, which ended in his death and that of many of his greatest nobles (Disney 2009, vol. I, p. 179). Many families belonging to the high nobility, whose position can be explained also by their previous links with their Castilian counterparts, henceforth adopted policies that clearly aimed at their mingling not only with their peers from over the border but also with groups from other regions of the monarchy, including Italy (Da Cunha 2009; Redondo and Yun 2009). And this did not entail losing their scope to project themselves on the empire, where viceroyalties were becoming ever more the preserve of the aristocracy, as were the governorships within the *Estado da Índia* (Da Cunha and Monteiro 2005). The empire was not only a source of offices and royal charity but also of profitable commercial licences granted to many *fidalgos* and, above all, the Braganza (Boyajian 1993, p. 34). This fact allowed these families to expand their political capital and even their economic potential. As we shall see, the economic upsurge that the Portuguese empire experienced thanks to its connections with the Spanish favoured the circulation of elites throughout this colonial system.

Even the commercial bourgeoisie and the New Christians, who may not have entertained high hopes for the intolerant fervour of Philip II, came to experience an important advance after 1580 (Boyajian 1983). The creation of titles—accelerated between 1580 and 1640—would be a cause of discontent for some of the old lineages but also an escape valve for the ambitions of others. The augmentation of the ecclesiastical institutions was continued, while Philip II further strengthened the growth of the Society of Jesus, known for its capacity to recruit young *fidalgos* and aristocrats from both kingdoms (Lockhart and Schwartz 1983).

The Crown's increased scope for patronage also reinforced these trends. As in the other Iberian kingdoms, the king's power of arbitration was strengthened. In Castile this process reinforced the dedication of resources to what has been called the economy of legitimation, which in turn contributed to social stability (Chap. 6). This was fed from the private accounts of the elites. But, above all, it was given a more visible expression through the development of the *Misericórdias*. While similar to confraternities and institutions providing social security in other areas of Europe, these represented a more advanced model. They were institutions that, depending upon the king, brought together initiatives aimed at fostering solidarity between their members, such as charity and alms to the poor (Bethencourt 2009; Sá 1997). Thus empire—and the union of the Crowns—had exerted the same effect as on the Castilian elites. Certainly, the court and the metropolitan administration were, more than the colonies, the most important spaces for social promotion (Da Cunha 2009). But this phenomenon was, at the same time, also the consequence of the growing revenues of the king, which mostly came from the colonies. In this way, the empire was a significant safety valve to advance and favour the consolidation and development of elites, while the king increased his scope for patronage: in this way a dominant coalition was reinforced, in which the role of the king was fundamental.

The Portuguese fiscal organization, which brought balance to the dominant coalition, also supported the reproduction of the social system. A form of tax state (Schumpeter 1955) emerged which was broadly similar to that of Castile but in which the majority of the king's income originated in his dominions and in the imperial monopoly over the trade of the most important products, as well as in the toll revenues. As in Castile, the fluctuations in expenditure had compelled the Portuguese Crown to search for a secure and reliable income (even though Lisbon was not saddled with the enormous debts of Madrid), and the *sisas* were used as the *alcabalas encabezadas* in Castile—as a fixed and more or less predictable income useful to endorse long-term public debt (Hespanha 1993a). Thus the Portuguese system also worked as a means of creating stable and predictable revenues upon which floating debts could be consolidated, crucial for dealing with fluctuations in receipts. The consequence was an increase in the *sisas*—or taxes upon the sale of products—administered by the town halls (*câmaras*), which enhanced the urban oligarchies' fiscal protagonism. Thus in Portugal, as in Castile, it has become common to talk of a devolution of functions referred to as *neomunicipalismo* in relation to the increasing relevance of the cities, whose role and responsibilities grew from the 1550s (Magalhães 1997). It is possible that, as in Castile, what was occurring in Portugal was a strengthening of an institutional role that had never truly been lost rather than an outright devolution of responsibilities. In any event, all of this allowed for a notable increase in the royal income during the sixteenth century, with a peak being reached at the end of it (Hespanha 1989, pp. 110–1). It also allowed for a non-written pact between the Crown and the urban oligarchies, which strengthened their political and fiscal influence within the towns.

A similar deal was also evident in the more general governance of the kingdom. In parallel, and despite the better organization of the central finances, government was and remained based upon the *Consejos* (Councils), central institutions that defended not only the rights of the king but also those of the kingdom, thus preserving a high degree of decentralization and agreement at the same time (Hespanha 1989). Thanks to the *Ley Mental* (1434), the tense pact between king and kingdom represented in the Cortes was accompanied by a greater resistance to the nobles' efforts to usurp the Crown's patrimony without eliminating each other's privileges and spheres of power. At the same time, thanks to the growing power of the *corregidores* and royal judges, the king's justice was strengthened. But it should be stressed that private jurisdictions were not eliminated (Magalhães 1997). Thus, in spite of increasing absolutism, the king and the kingdom were able to find a point of agreement.

But the differences with Castile were also important. Most of them could be found in questions of proportion and political structure. Income from the King of Portugal's imperial monopoly ranged from 60% to 68% in 1520 (Godinho 1968), a quantity that bears no relation to the 25% that the American treasures constituted in their peak years to the incomes of the Crown of Castile. The second most important contributor to royal incomes came from the import tolls, and to a large extent, these were tied to foreign commerce. In this way the *sisas* constituted a proportionally smaller part, and, consequently, the Crown's financial dependence upon local elites was proportionally lessened. The tax state, defined by J. Schumpeter as one involving a high degree of fiscal involvement of the kingdom in the state income, was less developed in Portugal than in Castile, while its component of rentier state (a state financed by other territories) was far greater than was the case in Castile (Yun 2012). Moreover, in contrast to what would occur in Habsburg territories, the Avis dynasty ruled only in Portugal and tensions over the use of resources to benefit other dynastic territories were almost non-existent. Another difference lay in patterns of borrowing. In Castile debts had been generated not only by the disparity between incomes and expenditure but also by the need to pay for distant campaigns that required that funds be sent in advance. Furthermore, the much-praised realism of the Portuguese monarchs, who did not hesitate to abandon their interests in North Africa in the mid-century (Dom Sebastião's disastrous expedition of 1578 being the only exception to this rule), did the rest. Debt never came to exert as much pressure in Portugal as in Castile, thus avoiding many problems. Money was not devalued, nor was there any need to declare bankruptcy, if we except the suspension of payments in 1560, which can hardly be considered as such (Godinho 1982–1987, vol. IV, pp. 215–6).

Peninsular Trends

Some time ago historians such as, first, H. Hauser and then F. Braudel and I. Wallerstein described the years after the breakdown of 1558 as a period of European-wide crisis and transformation. In light of Castile's financial problems, and those of Portugal in Asia, this idea appears to be corroborated.[59] These difficulties affected exterior commerce, whose crisis was deepened by the Dutch Revolt (1566) that destabilized Castilian connections with the north of Europe as much as those of the Portuguese markets and financiers (Phillips 1990; Boyajian 1983). During these years Seville's commerce also suffered, and the crisis of the fairs system and of Burgos trade began (Lorenzo 1979, vol. I, p. 199; Basas 1994).

[59]Of the 15 times that Indies cargoes were seized by the monarchy during the century (1523, 1535, 1538, 1545, 1553, 1555, 1556, 1557, 1558, 1566, 1577, 1583, 1587, 1590, y 1596), five were in the 1550s, and these unblocked the financial crisis of 1556–1558 (Carande 1987, vol. III, pp. 353–469).

The domestic economy would also go through problems. Efforts have been made to reduce the importance of the bankruptcies of this period—these were, of course, negotiated, like all of them (Lovett 1980)—but all indicators lead us to think that the effects on the financial economy were negative in the short term: they produced a breakdown in the credits chain, contributing to immobilize capital, and even affected certain industries.[60] Even admitting a reduced level of debt in relation to the GDP of Castile—our doubts on this matter have been set out above—the effects of the crisis should be measured in regard to the size of the monetized section of domestic wealth, which was a fraction of the GDP.

The financial problems coincided with a challenging situation in some regions. Since the 1560s the symptoms of a slowing down of agrarian and demographic growth had been perceptible in some regions of Castile, and in the Duero Valley in particular (Yun 2004, pp. 417–28), while agrarian growth in Portugal also tended to slow down (Miranda 2017). Though, as was the case of Castile (see below), tax pressure was not great in macroeconomic terms, the type of taxes created in this period, and particularly the *sisas* levied on basic goods, would also have negative effects on artisans' workshops (2004, p. 344).[61]

---

[60] As Drelichman and Voth (2014) say, there are good reasons for it. The argument is that in all cases they led to renegotiations of debt or compensation paid by the monarch, measures which, in truth, have been known about for much time. Still there are reasons to think that the effects on the financial economy were not negligible. Not only did these measures create uncertainty, but they also could have been a negative factor for transaction costs. They also delayed the payments made at fairs at precisely the moment when these gatherings had become more dependent upon the injection of money by the Crown at Medina del Campo (Abed Al-Hussein 1982, Appendix 2). See also Carande (1987, vol. I, pp. 325–6, 329–40). Precisely because the Genoese had constructed a cascade system that absorbed the negative effects of the monarchy's failure to make payment (Drelichman and Voth 2014, pp. 160–6), when they themselves were affected, it was difficult for them to satisfy their creditors on time, and these, in turn, found themselves in a similarly dire situation. This extended the effects throughout all productive branches and even hit the owners of *juros* (for more detail based on primary sources, see Yun (2004, p. 338)).

[61] Though some researchers have attributed to us a too strong emphasis on taxes as a factor for Castilian decay, we already gave a very nuanced opinion on this in Yun (1990).

Recently scholars have even come to speak of a variant of the 'Dutch disease' (Drelichman 2005): a greater rise in price of the most commercialized goods, which would have made them less competitive in relation to foreign imports. Here, however, comparisons remain to be fully demonstrated, as wheat can hardly be considered as some of the more commercialized products as Drelichman does (Table, p. 359). It would be more important to consider that the rise in wheat prices and other primary goods implied an increase in costs relative to

This having been said, the difficulties, if considerable, did not bring about an immediate change in the course of the economy. For at least 20 years (until 1580 or so), most of the regional economies of Castile and Portugal continued to grow thanks to a series of readjustments in the agrarian sector, as well as thanks to the positive medium-term effects of the process of globalization.

In Seville the beginning of a second Atlantic cycle in the 1570s led to an unprecedented period of growth, in part as a result of commercial diversification. This growth occurred as Portuguese trade with Asia was recovering, the trade with Brazil was enhancing the economy of towns such as Porto, and its commerce with the North was reconstructed (Boyajian 1983; Phillips 1990). Sevillian imports of products such as dyes, leathers, and pearls rose quickly (Lorenzo 1979). In turn the emergence in America of markets for Castilian commodities and the development of mines facilitated the exportation of industrial goods. Nor did the crisis of the payment fairs lead to a commercial recession in Castile, thanks in part to the increasing connections with Portugal and Seville (Yun 1987). At the same time, the development of Seville was happening while the financial axis was being shifted from the Castilian fairs towards Madrid (Ruiz Martín 1990a). The growth of Seville and Madrid partially compensated for the problems of the Duero Valley's fairs.

Similar trends were found in the agrarian sector and demographic evolution. The interruption of population growth and agricultural expansion in the Duero Valley and in the interior of Aragon was compensated for by the continuation of the expansive movement in the regions of the South. The model of growth continued to function, being based on demographic expansion and the colonization of southern regions as well as a high degree of connectivity.[62] At this point the structures and urban networks of Castile remained relatively solid. As a consequence, the problems raised by demographic pressure and the increase of land rent were mitigated by the peasants' capacity to maintain strong links with urban markets and to recur to

---

maintenance of workshops, thus limiting their competitiveness in relation to foreign goods. But since Vilar's called attention on it, this has been a frequently repeated argument that has slowly taken different meaning (Vilar 1974). This can be seen in a comparison of prices of goods, like wheat, and those of fabrics, for example (Yun 2004, p. 464, Graph 7.6).

[62] This appears to be demonstrated by the figures on urban and agrarian population (Yun 2004, Chap. 4). It is also shown by French emigration into Catalonia which contributed to the population growth at the end of the century (Nadal and Giralt 1960; Durán 1998, pp. 128–31). The population of Valencia continued to increase (Casey 1983, p. 62).

auxiliary activities associated with commerce (transport services, the production of coarse cloth and crockery, leather goods). All of this was facilitated by the continued abundance of common lands (the selling off of which would be moderate until the 1580s). The farming of intensive crops (such as the vine, silkworm, hemp, and linen), nearly always undertaken in small holdings, was also positive, above all when production was geared towards the market. Nor did the great estates and farms in the South, which benefited from the lowering of real wages paid in cash, collapse overnight. Some areas of Andalusia saw an expansion of olive oil exports to America, while the Catalan nobles invested in iron production, and the Valencian landowners splurged on sugar mills and silk production.[63]

The rise of agrarian prices and of land rents increased the elite's income and their demand for urban products. The overcoming of the elite's economic and social problems thanks to the empire enhanced their consumption of luxury goods. In many towns, the building sector (the construction of palaces in general and ecclesiastic buildings in particular) seems to have increased. The growth during this period of industries such as the textile sector of Segovia was closely tied to the production of high-quality goods consumed by well-off groups, now including the American elites. Moreover, an important feature of this activity was based on the use of raw materials whose prices increased very slowly.[64] In Catalonia the reorientation of the textile industry was even more intense and decisive from the 1550s, when a tendency towards a more efficient cycle of agrarian-urban interaction was established. A similar dynamism was exhibited by the silk industry in Murcia, Toledo, or Córdoba, these latter two being noticeable for their progress in adapting to the changing whims of fashion and demand.[65]

The figures and geography for the arrival of American silver, as well as of the types of merchandise purchased with it in 1570–1571, demonstrate that the colonial market was now positively affecting some industries.[66] Sectors such as naval construction and related industries (wood felling)

[63] Pérez and Lemeunier (1984), Jover (1997), Herrera (1980), Fortea (1981), Halperin (1980).

[64] On wool prices, Brumont (1984b) and Pereira (1991, pp. 229–30). The same happened with dyes, like cochineal until the 1580s (Yun 2004, p. 428, Graph 7.5).

[65] García Espuche (1998), Montemayor (1996, pp. 223–8), Fortea (1981, p. 327), Pérez Picazo y Lemeunier (1984).

[66] Da Silva (1967, pp. 65–101). On the presence of manufactured goods in the American cargos, see (Lorenzo 1979).

were favoured by the growing demand, above all in Vizcaya, Lisbon, Seville, and Porto. The spending of the monarchy clearly contributed to this trend as it built a fleet to meet the extravagant demands of its international strategy. In Catalonia this led to the development of a fleet of smaller vessels serving the Mediterranean ports, a change that demonstrates the relative vitality of the principality's economy.[67]

* * *

That the two imperial systems were factors for stability in the Iberian societies is accepted by most historians. Moreover, from a very teleological perspective of state building, it has been taken for granted that that process was accompanied by the formation of more centralized tax systems associated with the military revolution. In other words, it has been supposed that the so-called tax state and military state had to be coincident and convergent phenomena.

We have shown here that the empires and, more in particular, the process of globalization were not only factors of stability. In many ways, they were eroding the social fabrics of both Castilian and Portuguese societies and indirectly affecting the other territories. From that perspective the way the empires created political and social stability looks a bit different, and we need to explain why the stabilizing forces prevailed.

Political and social stability and, therefore, the consolidation and slow transformation of the institutional frameworks were the outcomes of mechanisms linked to the way the new fiscal system was organized (above all in Castile) and the way new opportunities in the credit market were used, the opportunities that the empires gave to elites to satisfy their need for expansion and, all in all, for reformulation of the 'contract' they had among themselves and with the Crown. Of course that contract was different in the monarchy's different spaces. By focusing on the case of Spain, we can see that, though contrary to a commonplace, the contribution of other kingdoms (viz. Naples and the Low Countries) increased, the development of a new fiscal system in Castile created a sort of umbrella that allowed other parts of the composite monarchy to preserve their fiscal systems almost intact. Portugal, not being a spread-out composite monarchy, was slightly different.

---

[67] Goodman (1997) and García Espuche (1998).

But this perspective of analysis also explains (better than previous approaches, I hope) that the outcome of these tensions in Castile was not a 'centralized' tax state. The reformulation of the agreement between the Crown and the elites, as well as among those elites, paved the way for a consolidation—not without evolution—of the old institutions. It also contributed to enhance a decentralized system of mobilization of resources for war of which the outcome was the elite's great capacity for exercising coercion, control of violence, and capability of enforcement. Though it is possible that in economic terms the size of the central tax state's budget was higher than that of all of the other corporations combined, the effects from the perspective of the political economy and on state building would be noticeable in all the territories of the composite monarchy. We will return to this.

Open Access This chapter is licensed under the terms of the Creative Commons Attribution 4.0 International License (http://creativecommons.org/licenses/by/4.0/), which permits use, sharing, adaptation, distribution and reproduction in any medium or format, as long as you give appropriate credit to the original author(s) and the source, provide a link to the Creative Commons licence and indicate if changes were made.

The images or other third party material in this chapter are included in the chapter's Creative Commons licence, unless indicated otherwise in a credit line to the material. If material is not included in the chapter's Creative Commons licence and your intended use is not permitted by statutory regulation or exceeds the permitted use, you will need to obtain permission directly from the copyright holder.

CHAPTER 5

The Crystallization of a Political Economy, c. 1580–1630

Most of the traditional explanations for the so-called decline of Spain have been based on—and sometimes encouraged by—a series of stereotypes about its social values and cultural beliefs. These attitudes have been studied as derived from the mere existence of a society of orders, without considering the formal institutions in which they were based. There is, therefore, a clear danger of anachronism when speaking about the institutions and political economies of the early modern period. It is quite common to refer to the central institutions of the monarchy and the way that they interacted with local powers in order to administer violence.[1] The analysis of commercial institutions has also become very common among historians.[2] And, even if it is obvious that the number of institutions that can be studied here is not limited—above all if we adopt what is apparently becoming the standard definition of institutions, 'the rules of the game' so to speak—too often scholars forget to examine in any detail or depth the effects that some of the more important of those institutions (the Court, the *señoríos*, the ecclesiastical corporations, the judicial system, and even the municipalities) had on the allocation of economic resources, to say

---

[1] See Tilly (1990). This chapter is, however, principally an attempt to enter into debate with the ideas of the new institutional economics and in particular with North et al. (2009), especially Chaps. 2 and 3.

[2] See Acemoglu et al. (2005) and Hough and Grier (2015).

© The Author(s) 2019
B. Yun-Casalilla, *Iberian World Empires and the Globalization of Europe 1415–1668*, Palgrave Studies in Comparative Global History, https://doi.org/10.1007/978-981-13-0833-8_5

nothing of the historiographical obliteration of the role of informal institutions (personal rules in many cases) both in state building and in shaping economic performance.[3]

This chapter aims to set Spanish early modern values and cultural beliefs in their institutional context at the end of the sixteenth century. Old stereotypes will be challenged, and the moral economy of the period will be considered as derived from a political economy and a system of institutions and personal rules. This will allow a more complete and balanced vision of the effects of all of this upon economic development.

IBERIAN STEREOTYPES AND CULTURAL BELIEFS IN EUROPEAN PERSPECTIVE

For many years the so-called decline of Spain has played a major role in reinforcing a range of stereotypes, some of which have become so pervasive as to assume the role of 'national character'.[4] As is often the case, some of these clichés have a basis in reality. Yet, as is always the case, they also represent a distortion of it.

The seigniorial lifestyle, a supposed aversion to commerce, and even a reputed abhorrence of manual labour and practical knowledge have been presented as causes of decline (Defourneaux 1983). Even more damning has been the use of these stereotypes to describe a turning point in the history of the country and to extrapolate supposedly national characteristics from them and from an essentialist narrative ('the Black Legend'), with the old clichés presented as crucial features of the 'Spanish way of life'.

These visions can, of course, be supported from contemporary evidence. The economy of legitimation practiced by the aristocracy (Chap. 1) has been presented as a highly irrational use of resources for families

---

[3] The economic action of the royal Court has been studied (Rodríguez-Salgado 1992, 1998), but emphasis has fallen on its impact upon economies and its impact on the rule of the game has been completely obliterated (Ringrose 1983a or López ed. 1998). In regard to the *señoríos*, much of what is known is derived from the Enlightenment. For an attempt at revision, see Yun (2002a). To an even greater extent, the ecclesiastical economies have been the victims of these interpretations: while this view cannot be said to be entirely erroneous in its analysis and criticism, a greater refinement and balance are clearly needed. The same is true for the municipal institutions. To my knowledge no study has dealt with them from this perspective despite their importance. On the role of informal institution in other areas see Rosenthal and Wong (2011). Also P. Vries (2015).

[4] In reference to these questions, Sánchez Albornoz came to speak of a supposedly *homo hispanicus* (1976), and Defourneaux (1983) referred to the 'Spanish soul'.

indebted up to their eyeballs. The spending on culture, patronage, charity, pageantry, and court luxury has been seen as proof of the truth of these stereotypes.[5] In fact, many writers of the day, such as Domingo de Soto, Luis Vives, and Pérez de Angulo, underlined the prevalent ethos of the aristocracy and the employment of wealth, which was channelled into the aforementioned 'economy of legitimation': help to the poor; the foundation of religious institutions; and patronage and the demonstration—and celebration—of status through conspicuous consumption (Yun 2004, pp. 56, 269). With respect to businessmen and businesses, the impression is often very similar, and the study of middle-class families has tended to underline their attraction towards a noble way of life and even—on first impression—their desire to abandon trade.[6] The famous (or infamous) prohibition issued by Philip II on foreign study, the general attempt at ideological control, and the Inquisition's efforts to censor publications lie behind the interpretation of a rejection of knowledge and learning (Kamen 1965). The picaresque and the so-called noble lifestyle have been seen as proof of the rejection of work and labour.

Yet a comparative context inevitably adds balance and proportion to this image. Many of these traits can be found in countries other than Spain (and Portugal, of course). The so-called noble way of life also existed in England, France, and even, indeed, in Holland, whose society is usually taken to embody precisely the opposite stereotype.[7] The other side of the coin, the supposed rejection of commerce, can be traced back to Braudel's idea of the 'betrayal of the bourgeoisie', a phenomenon that might be found equally in these countries and, of course, in Italy.[8] The rejection of

[5] An excellent description can be found in the handwritten manuscript *Avisos políticos, históricos y morales*. I am grateful to Fernando Bouza for this reference.

[6] See the cases of Medina del Campo, Valladolid, and Segovia, respectively, in Abed Al-Hussein (1982), Bennassar (1983), and Ródenas (1990). Rodrigo de Dueñas, of Jewish descent, was a businessman and alderman of Medina del Campo and would later be called the 'Medicis castellano'—the Castilian Medici, Caro Baroja (1978, pp. 376–887).

[7] For the English nobility, L. Stone (1979, p. 251) speaks of the need to lead 'a lifestyle in accordance with one's dignity' as being one of the most important factors in spending. For Holland, Van Nierop (1984, pp. 19–34). For France, Jouanna (1991, p. 44) and Gascon (1994, pp. 357–68). See also Schalk (1986).

[8] Braudel (1976, vol. II, 99–110). For France, Jouanna (1991) and Gascon (1977, pp. 303–22 y 357–68). Roland Gascon has written that the purchase of offices 'drained capital to the detriment of businesses' and weakened 'the great commercial dynasties'. What Stone calls 'the inflation of honours', with marriages between nobles and the daughters of

manual labour—or the marked preference for the noble lifestyle—formed part of the era's value system. Even the phenomenon of the closing off of the guilds can be found in other regions of Europe.[9]

These interpretations and concepts must therefore be nuanced and balanced within quite specific historical contexts. The noble lifestyle was also part of a process that had emerged from the *auxilium*, including royal favours, court patronage, and the capture of political incomes in order to overcome central tensions within the dynamic of aristocratic families and networks (Chap. 4 above) (Yun 2002a, 2005a and 2005b). The economic trajectory seen from the middle of the fifteenth century demonstrated the scope for development of merchant groups of undoubted potential. Families such as the Ruíz, the Dueñas, and the Espinosa, and many others, proved not only their trading spirit but also their skills and aptitudes as businessmen and bankers.[10] As was the case for their counterparts across the continent, investments in rents (*juros* and *censos*) and land were part of strategies aimed at the diversification of business and risk.[11] And, as in other countries, these families employed matrimonial and familial policies that allowed them to establish their businesses, reduce transaction costs, gain access to privileged sources of information, create flexible and far-reaching commercial networks, reduce barriers on access to certain areas, and achieve social promotion for themselves and their relatives.[12] The purchase of noble titles was a means of acquiring the sort of political capital that would be useful for their true interest and purpose—the reproduction of their families—which was a priority far above and beyond the financial success of their businesses. In a brilliant book, Michel Cavaillac has demonstrated the existence of what he labels 'a bourgeois spirit', a term whose value

businessmen can be considered the 'betrayal of the bourgeoisie' (Stone 1979, chapter 11). Something similar happened in Holland (Burke 1974).

[9] In France the artisan masters tended to consider their trade as 'a patrimony to be reserved for their sons' and sought to prevent the entrance of new members into guilds by a variety of means. In Holland the guilds also practiced restrictive measures to keep out newcomers (De Vries y Van der Woude 1997, pp. 174–6).

[10] Lohman (1968), Lapeyre (1955). On the diffusion of Castilian financial techniques in Europe, Van der Wee (1967).

[11] Lapeyre (1955), Abed Al-Hussein (1982), Carande (1987, vol. I), Casado (1997) among others.

[12] Abed Al-Hussein (1982), Casado (1987, p. 220). On the role of the merchants as consuls and a means to obtaining information, see the case of the Florentine Ginori, Zamora (2014), and Lobato (2013).

might be debated but that perfectly reflects the ideal of a group that valued merit and championed commerce and work and even advocated an anti-war policy in the hope that it might help the development of business (Cavillac 1994, pp. 256–410).

Something similar might be said about the myth of there existing widespread prejudice against practical knowledge and work in Spain. The capacity for technological development offers considerable proof of how mistaken this interpretation is, although it might be added that advances were largely achieved through the influence of foreign technicians and the assimilation of new knowledge (Chap. 3). Furthermore, it is very significant that the majority of the topics discussed in the preceding pages have been taken from the works of the *arbitristas*, the reform-minded writers of the early seventeenth century. From 1550 to 1630, men such as Cellorigo, Mercado, Caxa de Leruela, and Diego de Deza channelled their energies into criticizing the vices of the noble lifestyle—its luxury, indulgence, and rejection of manual labour. Yet the true value of these arguments, and the reason why they were enthusiastically welcomed, was that their readers shared the authors' revulsion at noble tastes and pretensions in general and specifically their rejection of manual labour (Mackay 2006). This positive assessment of work—and in particular artisans' work—permeated many ranks of society (Yun 2007).

All of this demonstrates the futility of studying the world of social values as a self-contained reality of permanent, monolithic, and uniform concepts characteristic of national identities. This society cannot have been said to have been shaped by either a noble ethic or bourgeois spirit: neither model advances any serious attempt to understand it, as it was characterized by competing values and ideals that were often applied flexibly and pragmatically according to circumstances and conditions, which were many and varied. Cultural beliefs were not homogeneous but rather were made up by a range of rival visions, each one exerting its influence at different times and to varying degrees.

This starting point affords us a better understanding of both formal and informal institutions and the way they strengthened specific cultural beliefs.

FORMAL INSTITUTIONS

The development of what A. M. Hespanha called 'the official law' was evident in sixteenth-century Spain and Portugal (Hespanha 1989, p. 376). This was, without doubt, a step towards the standardization of laws, an objective which, at least theoretically, could affect transaction costs and reduce risks. The growing importance of 'official law' was manifested in a number of developments already mentioned (Chap. 2), such as the compilation of laws or the increasing role and relevance of *Chancillerías* and provincial courts.[13] In Portugal, the appointment of non-residential judges (usually trained in official law) in the municipalities can be considered a manifestation of the same phenomenon (Magalhães 1997, p. 162). A system of royal *corregidores* and other types of local delegates of the king charged with the application of the law had also been extended across the Iberian kingdoms.[14] In Portugal, the *Ordenações Manuelinas* of 1514 and the *Filipinas* (1595) sought to impose a greater degree of uniformity upon the town councils (Magalhães 1997, p. 162; Neto 1997, p. 152). Some examples can even be found of the growing role of official law in the enforcement of existing adherent organizations by which traders guarantied internal agreements. The *Casa de la Contratación* of Seville and the *Casa da Índia* in Lisbon represent the clearest examples of this trend.[15] The training of skilled jurists and lawyers advanced quickly and even led to the emergence of a small army of law graduates dedicated to the application of the law across the entire empire.[16] The compilation and diffusion of juridical norms continued throughout the reign of Philip II and resulted in compendia that would enjoy a long life in all of the Iberian kingdoms (Tomás y Valiente 1992, pp. 263–81). Very often these regiments of experts, armed with voluminous legal compilations, did not in fact engineer an unconditional support for royal absolutism; on the contrary, they underlined the need for the king to respect and uphold the rights of the kingdom in question.[17] Moreover, a number of publications circulated that set out the ideal behavioural norms of the *corregidores* and specified how they should administer royal and seigniorial justice. The *Política para Corregidores* of Castillo de Bovadilla (1597) was one of the most notable and influential of these works.

---

[13] Kagan (1981), MacAlister (1984), Casey (1983), and, for a synthesis including America, Tomás y Valiente (1992). On Portugal's judicial system, see Hespanha (1989).

[14] For Castile, see Lunenfeld (1987) and for Portugal, Magalhães (1997, p. 161).

[15] For an empirical basis for these arguments, see Fernández de Castro (2015), and for Portugal, see Ferreira (2015, pp. 82–5).

[16] Pelorson (1980), Rivero (2011).

[17] See, for example, the case of Juan Bautista Larrea in Volpini (2004).

The increase in the number of cases brought before the regional court or *Chancillería* of Valladolid (Kagan 1981), which proportionally far out-stripped population growth, constitutes one of the best pieces of evidence for the development of the system of impersonal enforcement under the authority of judges. An eloquent demonstration of the character of this system can be found in the sociology of the cases brought before the *Chancillería* of Valladolid. According to figures presented by Richard L. Kagan, the most common target of litigation was the king himself, something which can be interpreted in principle as evidence of the development of a third-party system in which the so-called parasitic absolutist king had to play by (at least) some of the rules of the game.[18] After the king, the Castilian aristocracy were the group that most frequently recurred to judicial intervention, usually as the third party in a system of incentive-compatible agreements dealing in matters of dowries and matrimonial ties, transfers of inheritances, and questions related to the *mayorazgo*, dona-tions, and—finally but obviously of great importance in light of what has been set out above—debts (Kagan 1981, pp. 11–2). All of this demon-strates the insufficiency and failings of the system of self-enforcement and internal agreements, which had been predominant over the previous cen-turies and which had often led to violent feudal confrontations (Chap. 1). In Kagan's figures the aristocracy was followed by the cities, which liti-gated over questions of privileges, municipal lands, and, of course, debts (the greatest single cause of hearings in Castile). Finally it can be no sur-prise to find ordinary subjects and peasants, the latter suing their landlords (Kagan 1981, p. 12).

As we have seen (Chap. 2), the registering of written contracts increased, as thousands of documents in Castilian, Portuguese, and Aragonese archives prove. This development was manifested in the dense network of notaries and clerks that had emerged in all of the Iberian kingdoms at the end of the century.[19] They registered all types of agreements: accords for large-scale sales and purchases; contracts for the formation of companies; pledges and commitments to marry and, above all, to pay dowries (even in rural areas), both of which proved crucial for the economies of aristocrats,

---

[18] Significantly, many of the 'thousands of lawsuits' in which the king was a party were due to his duty 'to protect his vast personal patrimony' (Kagan 1981, p. 11).

[19] For Portugal, see Hespanha (1989, pp. 140–4). Like in the case of the judges, they were local offices.

patricians, and merchants; the *cartas de poder* (letters conferring power of attorney for collecting specific debts or acting on behalf of a trader in general matters) exchanged between businessmen operating in distant areas; post-death inventories of goods and their division between families; and even contracts to postpone or divide the payment of debts or to arrange their repayment in distant towns.

For this reason, notarial registers were increasingly used in the Atlantic and were established in America as a means of enforcing payments and debts (Cachero 2010). The use of identical formats and structures in the documents generated on both sides of the Atlantic was indicative of a movement towards the globalization of the rules of play. It is also interesting that this type of bureaucrat, in principle dependent upon the Crown— something which was not the case in other European regions (Yun and Ramos 2012)—emerged not only in the royal demesne lands but also in the towns under noble, ecclesiastical, and municipal jurisdiction.

As we will see further in this chapter, many of these trends created positive conditions for economic activities. But this view does not fit a reality that was much more complex.

The pact within elites and between them and the king guaranteed and even, in certain respects, reinforced both the jurisdictional role of these seigniorial estates and the private jurisdictions in general. In Castile, Aragon, and Portugal, noble and ecclesiastical estates retained some capacity of enforcement, despite the development of royal justice in the *Chancillerías* (Guilarte 1987, p. 203). At the root of everything was the superimposition of different laws and legal codes, which often operated in competition with one another (Hespanha 1989). Though the approval of the Crown was sometimes needed, the great aristocrats and leading ecclesiastical institutions retained their capacity of coercion and right to promulgate council by-laws (*ordenanzas*) that regulated social life and the exploitation of resources (García Hernán 2010). They also had the power to nominate local authorities and judges. In the Crown of Aragon, the exercise of 'absolute' jurisdiction extended the seigniors' enormous day-to-day power. Even in Catalonia, where the process was more ambiguous and nuanced, the authority of the jurisdictional landlords continued to be highly influential (Serra 1988). In Portugal things were not very different. Here, as in the rest of the peninsula, the seigniors retained an enormous jurisdictional capacity and powers of enforcement (Hespanha 1989, pp. 307–63). The importance of the nobles as nuclei for the mobilization of troops or credit (by setting debts in their *mayorazgos*) only strengthened this situation across the peninsula. The sale of jurisdictions—something inexistent in Portugal, although the alienation of royal lands had been significant in the fifteenth century—multiplied the number of social actors who held private jurisdictions in such a way that it advanced the fragmentation of the jurisdictional map and who mediated in the Crown's capacity to apply the law, at least in the first instance (Nader 1990).

A similar process took place in the cities despite their more direct dependency upon the king. The growing power of the king through his judges or mayors (*corregidores*) supposed a limitation to both their autonomous capacity of enforcement and the extrajudicial imposition of the wishes of the oligarchy. But, for reasons set out above (Chap. 4), the cities and municipalities retained great control over their fiscal systems, which was decisive for economic activity. And they also maintained their capacity for coercion and even, in the final instance, for the exercise of violence, in part because of their role in military mobilizations. All of this allowed the cities to strengthen their economic activities, a process which was accompanied by the reinforcing of the ideological justification for their privileges.

Given the similarities between changes in the towns and the system of *auxilium* exercised by the nobility, these trends reinforced the notion of the noble status of the city as a counterweight to the more republican vision that had previously been prevalent.[20] Aware of their character as a sort of collective *señorío*, the cities came to see themselves as a manifestation of nobility and so advanced rival claims over their ancestry and antiquity.[21] This same impulse strengthened the medieval vision of the city as being responsible for the common good, a trend which reinforced a political economy which was theoretically directed to this end.[22] This served as a justification for a city's economic resources and jurisdictions and strengthened its capacity for coercion.[23] And the cities clearly retained

---

[20] See the case of Salamanca—many others might be mentioned—in G. Gómez Dávila, *Historia de las Antigüedades de la ciudad de Salamanca*, ed. Facsímil de Salamanca, 1994 [Prologue of B. Cuart; of the original edition of 1606].

[21] The nobility of the city was, by extension, a reflection of the noble status of its families, something which consecrated the mimicry between a city and its patriciate. See G. Argote de Molina, *Nobleza de Andalucía* Riquelme y Vargas ediciones: Jaén, 1991 [original edition, Jaén 1866].

[22] On that vision in the context of an idea of republicanism, see Skinner (2002, pp. 39–117). On the urban *señorío*, Castillo de Bovadilla (1640).

[23] The concern for the wellbeing of the poor was very clear, as was the commitment to the general good and public services (teaching, health, cleanliness), or religious observance, all of which were undertaken with the aim of creating social cohesion and a sort of collective

a vigorous array of privileges and coercive prerogatives: the right to prohibit and regulate markets, such as that of wine; the power to police
weights and measures; and control over prices (Hamilton 1975). Another
significant right was the regulation of commerce through local intermediaries, a prerogative which was decisive for the collection of both *alcabalas*
and *millones* (Chacón 1979, pp. 342–54). Especially important was the
system for provisioning the city, which attempted to guaranteed the supply of bread, meat, and fish through the creation of communal granaries
and the public management of grain exchanges or through the establishment of a system of contractors who, in exchange for deals with the council or mayor's office, obtained the monopoly on the trade in the product
in question (see below). Moreover, the publicly funded purchase of common lands or municipal offices allowed the local oligarchies to control the
use of considerable resources and functions (De Bernardo 1994).

Many cities also maintained their regulatory capacity over industrial and
guild activities, which was crucial for economic development. This function
became more significant when the right to allocate or distribute taxes through
the branches of industry afforded it a greater degree of interventionism. In
Seville the 'municipal council was increasingly responsible for the approval of
the guild by-laws' until, well into the seventeenth century, this activity began
to fall under the control of the Royal Council (Bernal et al. 1978, p. 100).
Scholars have spoken of a growing 'municipal interventionism' in Córdoba
throughout the sixteenth century (Fortea 1981, pp. 381–8).

In the short term, the institutional evolution described in previous
chapters tended to preserve the rural councils (*concejos*) in their different
juridical formats. Yet here variation was considerable. There were areas—
such as Salamanca and Extremadura—where depopulation took place,
with the disappearance of small villages and hamlets: this was usually
caused by the expansion of the livestock economy, the interest of the
nobility and big ecclesiastic landlords in increasing their direct access to

catharsis (through great processions like those of Corpus Christi, feast days, and public acts).
The same can be said of the use of charity, the creation of confraternities, care for orphans,
or the efforts to implant a civilizing process of courtesy or urbanity through the control over
time, which led to the widespread purchase and installation of clocks in public spaces (Castillo
de Bovadilla 1597). In Castile policing was important, but much more so in Aragon, largely
because of the fight against banditry by cities or unions of cities (Colás and Salas 1982,
pp. 289–322; Torres 1994, chap. IV). All developments were very similar to what was happening in Portugal, where the *Ordenaçoes Filipinas* set down functions and similar ideological programmes (Hespanha 1989, pp. 132 and ff.).

land, or the reconsolidation of settlements. In the Crown of Castile, however, this process was not prevalent or common in many areas where the interest of the jurisdictional landlords—and specifically the importance of the *tercias* and *alcabalas* to their incomes—led them to support the survival of communities. Furthermore, the opportunities available to the seigniorial landlords to overcome financial difficulties through access to favours generated by the *auxilium* or easy credit may have acted as a safety valve for the pressure exerted on the peasant collectives (Yun 2002a).

These institutions underwent considerable change as a result of a combination of factors: the atomization of community relations brought about by the purchase of jurisdictions and the fragmentation of wider spaces of shared common land, a growing internal social differentiation, the concentration of property within the higher echelons of local society, the increasing domination of municipal government by elites, the ever-more common ownership of offices by leading families, and so on. But it is certain that they survived as an essential part of society and the institutional and economic arrangements described above (Chap. 3). For this reason, the rural community remained an institution that was vital to any understanding of the rules of coercion, the informal mechanisms of enforcement, and the regulation of economic activity and allocation of productive factors. This is particularly important to remember, as their domains saw the most frequent overlapping and clashes of official law and the myriad of 'non-official laws' and customs. Studies for Portugal (which cannot have been substantially different from the rest of Europe) show that it was at the level of the rural community that the various forms of law and models of enforcement (very much based upon compromise) had the greatest impact and importance (Hespanha 1989, pp. 363–77).

The process described in the previous chapters explains the survival of ecclesiastical justice and juridical autonomy. While remaining dependent upon Rome, ecclesiastical justice was faced with an increase in the capacity of royal justice to intervene, while the king's powers of mediation were also growing. At times, ecclesiastical institutions themselves required the king's intercession as a third party in their internal relations and disputes or in those with members of other religious orders. But the independence of ecclesiastical justice over the clergy remained untouched (Domínguez 1985, pp. 335–440). Moreover, the very fact that there existed such controversy over the ability of the Church to impose corporal punishment upon those members of the laity who broke its rules provides clear evidence that the ecclesiastical courts kept a good deal of their capacity for enforcement. Some contemporaries even justified the right of the clerics to impose these punishments for infringements such as the sale of substandard merchandise or the charging of excessive prices for goods (Domínguez 1985). A good number of institutions conceded *donativos* to the king—as we will see, this tendency became paramount in the seventeenth century—and even became involved in military levies, trends which reinforced their power within their domains or allowed them to obtain new privileges. In some cases, institutions obtained exemption from the *sisas de millones*, or were compensated for having to pay them, concessions which reinforced their capacity for fiscal autonomy. And there was general agreement that the Church's temporal jurisdiction might be used to punish those who lent money—not only ecclesiastics—at excessive rates of interest (usury). The opposition put up by the Cathedral of Zamora to laws about contraband trade with Portugal is indicative of its institutional power to resist the king's justice (Álvarez 1987). The Church continued to wield powerful religious censures and punishments; indeed, it even threatened excommunication for economic infractions such as the failure to pay the tithe (see Chap. 4).

The developments described in the previous chapter also explain the changes and continuities in the guild system. The expansion of the urban economies reinforced artisan activities and led to the framing of guild by-laws by many artisan corporations. In this respect, cases such as those of Seville and Toledo are significant.[24] It is very possible that a factor in these developments was the fiscal system (and the *encabezamientos*), which distributed fiscal burdens upon offices and branches of activity.[25] For this reason, the continued existence of these corporations could be vital to the ability of the cities to meet their fiscal quota. In order to understand the political economy of these institutions, it is important to consider that they were not corporations dedicated to a purely economic purpose or end; rather, their primary function was to guarantee the social interests of the group from which they were formed and to ensure reciprocity between them, despite the inevitable rivalries between members of different guilds. They had many other functions beyond mere economic regulation: support

[24] Bernal et al. (1978) and Montemayor (1996, p. 208).

[25] This connection between corporations and the fiscal system deserves better study. In any case, some authors such as Nieto (2006, p. 200) have established that it was reinforced when, in the seventeenth century, the corporations made *donativos* to the Crown, which therefore had a great interest in their survival.

was given to widows; assistance was provided for the burial of members; and the benefits of membership of these corporations were frequently projected into the public space through a rich visual and symbolic culture. But even more important, though in most of the towns corporations were under the city authorities' supervision, they had the function of controlling and regulating the production process, which gave them a high capacity of enforcement and coercion (see, e.g. Fortea 1981; Nieto 2006). The predominance of these functions—not only on the peninsula—explains an important feature of these corporations: their great interest in limiting competition from external competitors and in erecting entry barriers for them.

The consulates were to merchants what guilds were to artisans. The most interesting of them was, without doubt, that of Seville. As always with these institutions, the Seville consulate exercised a notable power of regulation over merchant relationships and was important in creating mechanisms of confidence—sometimes, informal ones—between its members. It was also active in resolving conflicts through nonjudicial means. This was achieved through self-enforcement and by forging private accords within the mercantile community. Of course, these arrangements existed beyond the consulates' members and their fields of operation. But the Consulate of Seville, like its counterpart in Burgos, which it imitated in many regards, also had its own justice mechanisms adjusted to the nascent Castilian commercial legal code and its growing transnational component (Smith 1978, chapters VI and VII). When traders did not reach an agreement through the Consulate—or the House of Trade (Fernández de Castro 2015)—mediation, the judges of these institutions also applied the laws of Castile in combination with more general customs and practices. They exercised a form of justice that was similar to that of the *Chancillerías*, above which there was only the Council of Indies and of the king himself; but they also heard cases brought against the king and, most often, against the abusive application of his fiscal measures and in many occasions the judges of the Consulate acted as 'watchful dogs' of the trader's economic interests' (Smith 1978, p. 147).

Although the Court exhibited the characteristics of a highly informal institution, it constituted one of the most important spaces for social and economic regulation in this period. The processes described in previous chapters led to the emergence of the Court as a political space in which patronage was administered and power exercised (Rodríguez-Salgado 1992, 1998). It became a decisive institution for the administration of violence and law, both of which would shape the management of the great patrimonies and, indirectly, the country's economy.

The composite monarchy of the Spanish Habsburgs had been constructed as a constellation of Courts. This having been said, clearly Philip II, Philip III, and Philip IV reinforced the role of Madrid Court and capital within the empire, even above the interests of Lisbon, to the great discontent of the Portuguese.[26] Madrid Court was in fact the crucible where huge economic, social, and political resources were distributed and, therefore, the main arena in which the conflictive pact was substantiated. In this political space, royal grace was dispensed, and appointments (for viceroyalties, embassies, military commands, etc.) could be obtained. These conferrals constituted the other side of the *auxilium* and were vital to elite groups.[27] Moreover, the Court was the arena where vital questions about seigniorial estates were resolved, where permissions for *censos* were obtained, and where contact could be made with the governmental councils, through which an array of favours could be secured for courtiers and their clients. Here the institution of marriage—determinative for the management of all estates and for noble patrimonies in particular—was arranged. And Madrid was, with Vienna, the most developed matrimonial market in Europe. Information on the political, social, and economic capital of prospective partners was available at these nodes. Three-party negotiations were entered into (with the king's involvement) over the terms and conditions of ties. In a sense, Madrid's king was the greatest 'matchmaker' in the world, as the ties decided here were questions of state, and for this reason the Habsburgs, like the Stuart kings of England (Stone 1979), had acquired the right to allow—or forbid—any prospective marriage (Atienza and Simón 1989, pp. 39–40). The Court was also a complex world of secrets and intrigues, in which the price of information, itself vital for the aristocratic economies and measurable in the cost of keeping a large numbers of clients, minions, and servants, was very high. Here accords were negotiated and strategies formed, often forcing the parties into a direct and personal relationship with the king's secretaries, administrators, and lawyers, who themselves habitually made valuable clients (Rodríguez-Salgado 1992). The rituals of power, and the need to generate the political and social capital necessary to secure the confidence

---

[26]The political and social processes can be found in different works of J. Mártinez Millán (e.g. Martínez and Morales (1998)). See also Lisón (1991) and Del Río (2000).

[27]See the cases of the house of Alba and Medinasidonia in Maltby (1983) and Pierson (1989).

and reciprocity appropriate to informal institutional relationships mediated though the social ciphers of the court and its arcane manners, compelled the high nobility and those above it to maintain a continuous presence in Madrid.[28]

Across Europe patronage and the king's capacity to distribute economic and social resources to clients and lineages would be one of the keys to political stability. In this sense Madrid Court was unique.[29] In fact, it was the balsam that made possible the relations of self-enforcement intrinsic to closed societies and that cemented the accord at the heart of the dominant coalition.[30] Here the effects of globalization and empire were evident. Despite the remarkable differences between the multinational elites that converged on Madrid, this was the Court of the 'greatest lord of the world', as the Venetian ambassador, Simon Contarini, remarked in relation to Philip III, adding that these characteristics increased the king's ability to temper political ruptures.[31] As an institution the Court even helped to crystallize relationships between the various nobilities of the empire (Yun 2009).

---

[28] This case is very similar to Greif's description of the great Genoese merchants and bankers (Greif 2006). Pinheiro da Veiga, a Portuguese noble in the Court of Valladolid at the beginning of the seventeenth century, described the conflict between the marquis of Tavara, 'who is very much a youth', and the duke of Infantado, 'who is very pro-Portuguese', over errors committed in the use of term of address 'señoría' and the expression 'merced' (1989 [1605–1606], pp. 115–6).

[29] For a very different view, see N. Elias (2000), who attributed 'the civilizing process' to the control of violence imposed upon the nobility of Louis XIV at Versailles. Here the aim is to study the court as a redistributor of incomes that palliated factional conflicts and its contribution to the consolidation of the political and social system (chapter 9).

[30] As elsewhere in this study, the terms employed here follow the usage of North et al. (2009), who do not, however, dedicate much attention to the court.

[31] 'Without touching his estate', Contarini wrote, the king 'has much to give in two ways; on the one hand, for distribution as a reward for the monetary services destined to this end; on the other, when he pays and rewards with the exercise of the offices given him, because he appoints twenty and more Viceroys [...] forty-six general captains [...] Distributes military orders, *encomiendas* [grants in rights to land and the services of their inhabitants] [...] those being are more than five hundred *encomiendas*, some worth twenty thousand ducats and the smallest five hundred [...] eight or more Archbishoprics [...] the least of which renders five thousand ducats; seventy-three bishoprics [...] most of them worth twenty thousand ducats, and none less than three thousand'. 'Relación que hizo a la República de Venecia, Simón Contarini, al fin del año 1605 de la Embajada que había hecho en España', in L. Cabrera de Córdoba, *Relaciones de las cosas sucedidas en la Corte de España desde 1591 a 1614*, Madrid, 1857.

The Crown might also be referred to as an institution. It was to a large extent responsible for the progress of the *Chancillerías* and the juridical systems that allowed litigants to appeal to official law. At the same time, the monarchs sponsored the emergence of the scribe system, the compilation of law codes, and other changes that took place across the Iberian kingdoms. The legal treatises of the time also emphasized the importance of presenting the king as the final legal authority—that is, above the private jurisdictions—and the sponsor of these new compilations of legal codes and customs.[32] The pact with the elites had helped to give political stability to the different kingdoms. The maintenance of social order, of which the king was the final guarantee, helped to create good conditions for many economic activities.[33] The ability to channel the internal dynamics of the elites and deal with their need for social promotion also contributed to social stability in the cities as in the countryside.

FAMILY AND SOCIAL NETWORKS

All Iberian societies—indeed, all European societies—were marked by tensions that originated in the relationships within families and extended families, lineage, and clients (Chap. 1). Family and kin relations were, without doubt, the informal institution par excellence of this society.[34] Furthermore, they were important in themselves but often also the pivotal point of wider informal social networks, constructed on the base of friendship, patronage, clienteles, common local origin (*paisanaje*), and so on. The influence and role of the family remained very important as a result of the evolution of the elites, which allowed for its consolidation as their basic fabric.

---

[32] See the case of the *Mental* Law and the *Ordenações Manuelinas* in Portugal (Neto 1997, pp. 152–4). For Castile, the most well-known case is the (very meaningfully) so-called *Recopilación de Felipe II* (Philip II compilation), previously discussed. But this is one example among many others. It is interesting to note that, unlike compilations of Castile, the other kingdoms' repertoires were published with no alteration at all. That is also the reason why the Castilian ones included a mandate of enforcement in the case that they were not identical to the previous laws.

[33] For the same argument applied to England, see Slack (2015).

[34] On the internal dynamics of the family in the Mediterranean area, see Delille (2003, Chap. 4).

As an institution of this kind, family, kin relations, and clientele networks (above all else, the patronage system strengthened these for both the nobility and the Crown) complied with fundamental functions. Familial networks were key to obtaining information. Nobles, like the Ataíde of Portugal, the patricians of cities such as Barcelona, or merchants, such as the Bernuy or the Ruiz of Burgos and the Echávarri of Bilbao, to say nothing of Catalan bandits such as the Nyeros and Caldells, used other members of their families to obtain information on court intrigues, city conflicts, the movements of adversaries, market conditions, and so on.[35] The personal ties binding them formed the basis of the confidence relationships that allowed them to operate in various political, social, and economic circles with a degree of risk reduction and a guarantee of success.[36] Institutions directly associated with familial relationships, such as matrimony, were the key to the transfer of political, social, and economic resources (this was usually achieved as dowries.) At the same time, matrimony and, specifically, the dowry served to put in motion mechanisms of self-enforcement aimed at sealing pacts or closing conflicts, sometimes ancestral in origin, between families (Yun 2002a). In all cases the family and kin ties were vital to the circulation of forms of capital through these webs. Using money to situate a son in the imperial, municipal, or ecclesiastic administration by the purchase of an office or by the foundation of a *capellanía* (a chapel) was, for example, a way of obtaining political or cultural capital that could subsequently revert to the group in the form of incomes or the amplification of properties (Yun 2011). It may be interesting to underline that this type of practice was not exclusive to the elites. The artisans and peasants also maintained links of confidence based on familial relationships or used matrimony with very similar aims.

Family, extended blood and kin relations, and client networks, and the informal ties that accompanied them, such as friendship, permeated the entire system of formal institutions. If this is perhaps obvious, it is worth

[35] These areas have been studied in great depth. For some examples, see Costa and Da Cunha (2006), Vila-Santa (2015), Ruspio (2007), Casey (2007), Priotti (2004, pp. 185–95), Casado (1997), Amelang (1986), and Torres (1994, *passim* and pp. 163 and ff.). On family in the Crowns of Castile and Aragon in this period, the pages written in general studies by James Casey are essential reading, above all (1989 y 1999), and his analysis of the case of Granada is excellent (2007), as are a number of works written or directed by F. Chacón; in example Chacón and Bertran (2011).

[36] For empirical support of this affirmation, see Casey (2007, Chap. 5).

dwelling on, as it will be vital to our later discussions. The king was a 'public' institution but also a member of a lineage and a dynasty, something which affected the government of the state in many important ways. The cities and seigniorial estates were criss-crossed by, and depended upon, bloodline and affinity relationships that bound those who governed them. The same was true of the guilds and rural communities. For this reason, neither nature nor the working of these institutions can be understood without this component. That the public and private domains were so indistinct—or difficult to separate—in this society contributed to it. To give one example, in certain cases the services of a city might be rewarded by conferring privileges upon its aldermen and officials rather than upon it as an institution (see examples in Martínez Ruiz 1992). Another example: the seigniorial estate, ruled by a lineage whose interests it served, was also an essential piece in the systems for the maintenance of law, military organization, and the government of the 'republic'. The presence of familial and kin relationships within an institutional framework that was, on the face of it, modern—sometimes, indeed, erroneously studied through Weberian parameters—formed part of the symbolic projection and political language of the time. Beyond being simply a metaphor, this provided a portrait of the reality and behaviour that was expected of persons. Some time ago Otto Brunner underlined this question, placing attention on the *oeconomia* (literally, the ruling of the household) of the seigniorial class and the need to understand it as a form of domestic relationship (1992). In 1651 the Portuguese Francisco Manuel de Melo wrote 'that the city is a large family and the family a city in miniature' (Casey 1999, p. 192). The metaphor of the king as the father is extremely well known, as is the assimilation of the political community to the family (Walzer 1965, chapter 5).

For a long time, it has been believed that, in common with its counterparts across Europe, the aristocracy was a group subject to irrational forms of management and disinterested in its lands and possessions.[37] Here it will be proposed that it is better to see it as a social group composed of individuals who operated within networks, and particularly family and lineage networks, dedicated to the reconversion of different forms of capital (Yun 2011). It is important to stress that the survival of these networks depended upon a properly functioning system of collateral payments and solidarity, as this smoothed internal tensions (Chap. 1 and Yun 1994b).

---

[37] Macfarlane (1973) and Baudrillart (1878–1880).

The aristocratic households were in fact organizations—in the sense applied to modern firms by Simon, Cyer, and March (Yun 2011, pp. 329–32)—whose main aim was not, as classical economics would have it, economic profit maximization but rather the consolidation, coherence, and expansion of the family and lineage itself, as behavioural economics would in fact imply (Yun 1994a, 2005a and 2005b).[38] The involvement of the great houses in the political system offered them enormous possibilities for that reconversion of social, cultural, and economic capital, which creates our impression of irrationality. In a context in which social capital was of such great importance, the investment in matrimonial alliances (dowries), in political clients (patronage), and in the promotion of the second-born sons so as to extend the power of the familial networks would be crucial (Yun 1994a). The increasing value of merit as a means of admission into this closed elite made it more necessary to invest in the promotion of military and diplomatic careers of the different members of the family and the lineage, at the same time as the acquisition of *habitus* that demonstrated status became more valuable, something which would also give impetus to investment in political capital for those members (Yun 2011). The increase in the king's ability to regulate relations within the nobility, manifested in his control of grace, favour, credit arrangements, and the management of the *mayorazgo*, made social and political resources more necessary than ever. This situation also encouraged investment in collateral payments within the lineages and the clientele networks in the forms of dowries, assistance to second-born sons, and so on, as a means of promoting members and maintaining unity by overcoming structural tensions. All of these developments combined with the dynamic created by the *mayorazgo*, which made family possessions inalienable and provided a shield against the dissolution of patrimonies by debt payments.

If different in important respects, the logic governing the management of ecclesiastical patrimonies displayed certain similarities. Logically, the central concern for these estates was not the family, or, to put it in a better way: the role of the family was set in different parameters. For most of the sixteenth century, the pressure created by the need for land, as well as the increase in agrarian production (and with it, a growth in tithe payments) and land rent, had allowed these ecclesiastical economies to reproduce and expand. But studies of the internal workings of the ecclesiastical corporations demonstrate that the involvement of members of noble, patrician,

[38] For all this, see Chap. 1 and Yun (2011).

and merchant lineages became especially frequent in the sixteenth and seventeenth centuries (Cabeza 1996; Irigoyen 2001). In many cases the entrance of new members brought ecclesiastical dowries and economic contributions, sometimes in the form of lands or rents (including *censos*). Chapel-building and the establishment of charitable institutions and other foundations fed this trend, often being done *ad personem*: that is to say, a member of an important family, often a less prominent one within the lineage (a woman or second-born or illegitimate son), entered into an ecclesiastical institution bringing with him or her an economic patrimony. This was an attractive outcome for both family and ecclesiastic institutions, as it extended the patrimony of the latter and offered an outlet to internal tensions within the former, as well as adding to its symbolic capital. Consequently, the family power and prestige was subtly extended: a prominent ecclesiastical career, membership in a cathedral chapter with a significant spiritual and economic patrimony, discharging the profession of public preacher, obtaining access to consciences through confession, and so on. It is highly symptomatic that donations and foundations frequently included clauses that specifically reserved their use for a family member or for future entrants from the lineage. In this way many ecclesiastical institutions acquired possessions as an organization while surrounding themselves with a genuine constellation of donated properties that operated according to their own logic and management rules. The explosion of possessions of this sort was often predicated upon saying a set number of Masses, attracting charity or preserving capital for future relatives, priorities which were very distant from the search for productive improvements. Frequently, these foundations even drew upon resources that uncles of entrants had acquired by discharging religious functions and, in particular, by securing payments for sermons, Masses, and religious services performed on behalf of the congregations of believers (Irigoyen 2001; Latorre 1992). Graphs 5.1 and 5.2 set out the total number of foundations and those established by the high nobility. The increasing transfer of economic resources to ecclesiastic institutions—to put it the other way round, the capacity of these institutions to absorb economic resources from noble, and nonnoble, families—is impressive. This was more so if we consider that the phenomenon was not confined to elites. It can also be found among peasant families and well-off *labradores* (yeomen) who, on a lower scale, saw these foundations as a means of accommodating their relatives, thus smoothing internal tensions (Brumont 1984a).

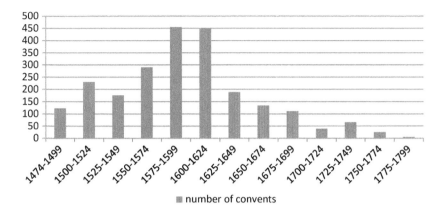

Graph 5.1 Convents founded in Spain, 1474–1799
Sources: My own elaboration with data of A. Atienza (2008, p. 33).

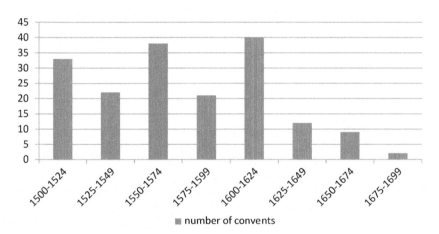

Graph 5.2 Convents founded in Spain by the main aristocratic families
Sources: My own elaboration with data of A. Atienza (2008, pp. 496–519). As the author clarifies, they are approximative.

The way large merchants and urban elites in general managed their resources is also better understood if we consider them within the context of their family relations. As already explained, networks, which were also based upon family relationships, had been highly efficient in generating economic expansion. It should be no surprise, therefore, that the historical analysis of events following the commercial crises of the epoch has led to emphasis falling on the purchase of public debt, jurisdictions, lands, and offices, all of which is taken to be a perversion ('betrayal') of the merchants as a social group (Braudel 1976). It is easily forgotten, however, that this type of investment was structural and formed part of practices that stretched back to the medieval period (Casado 1985, 1987, pp. 485–510). These practices obeyed social values but also responded to the need to combine risky investments with more secure ones or to control spheres of power that could be decisive for businesses. In reality this meant the circulation of different forms of capital within family constellations. Cases such as those of the Burgos-Maluenda, studied by H. Casado, and the Espinosa of Medina de Rioseco (both mentioned above), or even the *converso* merchants who controlled silk incomes studied by E. Soria (2016), demonstrate that investments in political rents or in symbolic capital—be at the level of the kingdom or at local level—seigniorial states, lands, or municipal offices were part of a family strategy.[39] Often these merchants used their daughters to transfer money through dowries, as well as to form alliances with oligarchies, patricians, and bureaucrats. For this same reason, they invested a fortune in training their sons, particularly second-born ones, who could subsequently obtain positions in the royal or municipal administration.[40] This investment allowed them to place members in decisive positions and constituted a collective strategy of diversification in the forms of capital and risk, one that also sought a certain complementarity within the family as it exchanged influence for trade and then traded so as to have influence and power.

We, historians, have too often forgotten that the basic unit of management was the family rather than the business company. For this reason it was important to repeat alliances with families of other merchants, as this was their fundamental activity—hence their interest in forming matrimonial ties with other businessmen or members of the elite. Within the extended family and its multiple kin ties, there were businessmen, scribes, bureaucrats, aldermen, consuls, and even royal secretaries: in short, this was a form of establishing pathways for the circulation of influence, money,

---

[39] See the case of the Córdoba's oligarchy in Soria (2000).

[40] In cities such as Seville, the majority of university students came from families of lawyers or rich businessmen (Pike 1978, pp. 77, 116).

prestige, security, and so on within these networks of kinship. Looked at in this light, there was a certain logic to the abandonment of business or trade based upon the forms of reconverting capital and calculating risk, not to mention the cultural beliefs of the day; when these conditions aligned, giving up 'the manual professions' by some members of these coalitions was a logical and rational move in the use of the group's resources. This having been said, in seventeenth-century Spain and Portugal, it was not easy to row back, although there certainly were those who, having adopted a noble lifestyle, continued to invest in business (Pike 1978, p. 119).

Family relationships were also crucial among artisans. As a matter of fact, their kinship dynamics, together with corporatist solidarity, were at the base of the tendency to closure of the guilds. This point deserves, however, some considerations. In many cases, the productive unit, that is the workshop, was a family unit and even part of the household. Though the studies on the interplay between family and workshops are not many for this epoch, this is evident, for example, in the case of the tanners of Madrid (Nieto 2006, p. 111), in which kin relationships were part of the managerial logic and could affect the credit system (see also Zofío 2005, chapter 5). It is not odd at all that fighting for the promotion of their sons within the profession was an important part of these families' strategies (Fortea 1981). The recent literature has also emphasized the importance of the female members of the family in the workshop. The interference of family solidarity (and not only of the family) in the guilds materialized in the purity of blood statutes (*estatutos de limpieza de sangre*) increasingly adopted by a number of guilds and corporations from the second half of the sixteenth century onwards in order to avoid the entrance of *conversos* and New Christians in general. Such prohibitions were not important because it was entirely impossible for a New Christian (and even more important for our arguments, for any person) to reinvent oneself and one's family's past or even to acquire documentary 'proof' of old Christian status. Rather it was because, regardless of the social condition of the person, the verification of any claim had to pass through a complex bureaucratic mechanism and required the mobilization of social networks to prove the absence of Jewish ancestors in two, three, or more generations. In the words of Dedieu, the statutes 'in reality served as the pretext for a test which, rather than focusing on origins, submitted the social power of the candidate to a severe examination' (Dedieu 1986). In fact, this institution must be understood in the context of a powerful collective movement in which the solidarity within the artisan families (and other social groups) was leading to the formulation of arguments based on a religious—and even racist—rationale, which, as a matter of fact, affected not only New Christians.

Like in many other institutions, the way family and the institution of guilds interlinked would be decisive.

Probably the most important institution of the day—the peasant family—has received the least amount of attention from the theoreticians of the new institutional economics. Its working logic could vary greatly according to local contexts: the character and availability of resources, local customs, and norms; village institutions; and income levels and patrimony. But overall, the outlines are relatively evident.

First of all, we need to make clear that, as D. Reher (1990) has shown for the case of the Iberian Peninsula, the family was not in economic terms the nuclear family composed only by the couple and their sons. It is however very common to see that there were very strong personal links joining this nucleus to other relatives with whom they could often carry out economic activities.

In contrast to the elites, the principal aim of these coalitions of kinship and friendship was not the promotion of their members, although this objective might be found among the well-off (which we will see was important). Nor was the basic ambition to obtain profits, manifested in monetary stock (savings), directed to a possible investment in productive improvements. Their principal aims were subsistence and the physical reproduction of the family. This was very difficult, given the conditions of limited resources and the frequency of epidemics and famines that might easily carry away some of its members and break the family unit that constituted the basic decision-making cell. The (regionally) very different inheritance patterns were vital to the hierarchical relations with the family or community. In general, like other social groups, the family was highly hierarchical, with the men's and paterfamilias' position being decisive, although the women played a fundamental role. Women and their reproductive capability were the pivot upon which family unity turned—demographers have shown that families broke up more easily when the mother died. Given the high level of post-childbirth mortality, women were also vital in providing an abundance of workhands for the family and the assignment of its productive factors. They also constituted a crucial stock of work which, when used to produce for the market, was essential as a component of economic growth.

Precisely for these reasons, the peasant family faced its own fragility in two challenges: to ensure that the rural community maintained a resource management policy that guaranteed subsistence; and to take maximum advantage of the available resources, sometimes in competition with other family units. Peasant solidarity, which had shone through the religious manifestations of the period (Christian 1989), has perhaps been idealized and exaggerated; nevertheless, it stood as an antidote to the enormous degree of conflict within the rural community. Trust between families, which also served to palliate conflicts, depended upon a range of qualities or conditions: good personal relationships, reputation (often based upon compliance with non-written contracts), the ability to heal wounds by recurring to forms of self-enforcement, the application of local community customs, and an appeal to the 'non-material inheritance' of some members of the community (Levi 1985). But the key point for the family economy was in fact the availability of resources, which depended on both institutions and environmental factors, as well as the economic situation of each region. These reserves were crucial during the crises provoked by bad harvests and epidemics but also depended very much on demographic pressure at a regional level.

This dependence upon factors exogenous to the family had increased due to changes in the rural community, mainly its increasing insertion in a state system and the growing influence of the more powerful rural elites who claimed a larger share of the community resources and a more strict intervention on markets' regulation.

Transaction Costs, Rent-Seeking, and Allocation of Resources: A Qualitative Approach

All of this leads to a reflection. Important steps forward had been made in the creation of enforcement systems that were increasingly uniform and that, making the application of laws more predictable across broader spaces where information on the legal rules was, normally, more expensive, could lead to a greater security in economic and social relations. A number of developments give us reason to believe in institutional advances that would be important in regard to a more rational and homogenous application of the law: the king's growing monopoly over violence, his capacity to impose himself upon other powers through patronage, and the continual presence of royal authority in important cities and councils in the person of the *corregidor*.

The rolling out of written contracts, logically, led to levels of compliance and a greater probability of their being used in accords between individuals who did not know each other personally and therefore lacked guarantees based on previous personal relationships to draw upon. This development was particularly important for commerce. The written register of contracts provided the fundamental support in the expansion of institutions, such as the *compagnia* and the *commenda*, that would take root across all of Iberia and in America and which served as a formula to contribute capital and share risks.

The king's authority and agreement with elites upon the existent status quo guaranteed a higher degree of political and social stability which was very positive for the reduction of risk and transaction costs. The development of militias and the Holy Brotherhood (*Santa Hermandad*) contributed to the maintenance of the internal social order, thus favouring economic activities as well. The very pact with the elites and the survival of the local militias allowed the monarch to mobilize these troops against potential risings in these territories, as was made clear in the use of Castilian elites and cities in the annexation of Portugal, in the risings in Aragon, and, in the seventeenth century, in the Catalan rebellion. It is significant that Castile experienced no general social convulsions after 1521 and those that did occur were merely local conflicts. If Aragon did face internal tensions and local rebellions, then these were contained in the 1580s. As it has been said, after the fifteenth century, Portugal would be free from great domestic troubles. Banditry did not disappear from the peninsula and was very prominent in the Crown of Aragon, but in Castile and Portugal, it would be much less significant or intense.[41] The cities were, of course, marked by poverty and delinquency, but they played a very minor role in the internal convulsions and kept a relatively low level of internal conflict compared to other areas of Europe (see Chap. 6). The growth of the king's powers of patronage also increased his ability to regulate social relationships and extended his capacity for enforcement; at the same time, in quite a few cases, the monarch played the role of a third party that regulated the relations between his subjects.

---

[41] The importance of banditry in early modern Castile was rightly stressed by Santos Madrazo (2000). What we want to underline here is the progress taking place during the sixteenth century. Furthermore, as long as the author considers the nobility the main protagonist of banditry, the social changes of the epoch suggest some improvements. As we will see, this is compatible with the existence of seigniorial jurisdictional coercion.

As we said before, a new spirit of intervention and improvement of its possessions was spreading among the aristocracy (Chap. 4).[42] In many areas of Castile, the seigniorial domain was not only a jurisdictional entity but more and more a set of properties in which economic improvements were possible under some circumstances. Not only the members of the high nobility but also the urban patricians and middle-rank nobles had obtained the absolute property of *baldíos* and council lands that might be improved. In those cases in which they did not have the jurisdiction or the possibility of collecting taxes, the possibility for an amplified reproduction of capital—not based in the simple extraction of surplus—through technological or organizational innovation existed.[43]

The ecclesiastical institutions were not completely devoid of efforts at improvement, above all from rural convents and monasteries that were sometimes managed by 'farming monks'. In fact investments in fixed capital in the form of granaries, windmills (of flour, paper, and olives trees), and other means of production facilitating the commercialization, transformation, storage, or sale of products were far from rare (López 1990). Nor, indeed, was there an absolute lack of investment in irrigation systems or in the development of crops directed towards commercialization, such as olive trees. There were even moves towards a more rational exploitation of mountain spaces and/or livestock (this was especially true for the vocational agrarian orders, such as the Cistercians and others) (López 1990).

The development of the consulates and towns' authority could have had positive effects too. Thanks to their justice systems and capability to mediate in conflicts, both developments may have paved the way for a justice closer to the subjects and able to generate trust. The rise of a group

---

[42] This is evident in the treatises dealing with the management of aristocratic patrimonies, such as Pérez del Barrio, *Dirección de Secretarios de señores y las materias, cuydados y obligaciones que les tocan* (Madrid, 1613). Dedicated to the marquis of Cañete, the text explicitly sought to 'increase the estate and property' and devoted great attention to the need to administer haciendas with great care. 'They were always,' it reads, 'administered with enormous curiosity and labour, being cultivated and favoured as if a principal means of support, and enjoyed great prosperity and fruitfulness' (p. 224). The author dealt with how to 'fertilise the land', rules for extending possessions, administering offices, appointing groundsmen and keepers, book-keeping, and so on (pp. 226v–9v).

[43] The process, very similar in some cases to the English enclosure movement, seems in principle that could produce economic improvements.

of *letrados*, trained in the Roman and common law in the universities and many of them working within these institutions (Kagan 1981), was in principle a positive development as long as it contributed to create a more homogenous system of enforcement also within consulates and cities. As a matter of fact, these *letrados* were the responsible for the introduction and emergence of a mercantile law with a very strong international component (Fernández de Castro 2015). As we will see, the urban autonomy might have negative effects, but it is also true that the cities' capacity to regulate the economic life within them might have been also positive for economic activities, as long as they were—or could have been—a third party in the administration of the law.

The guilds could also be less obstructive of economic change than usually thought. Over the last few years, scholars have engaged in an intense debate about European guilds, their capacity for innovation, and the reasons for their survival. This discussion has underlined their general efficiency, a characteristic that had featured in few, if any, previous assessments (Epstein 1998, 2002 among others and Ogilvie 2007). One of the arguments for the historiographical rehabilitation of the guilds in some European countries has been their ability to introduce technological innovations derived from the circulation of human capital and, therefore, to acquire technical knowledge and know-how, something which supposes a certain degree of willingness of guild corporations to allow the entrance of new members, who, of course, in principle did not have family relations with the members of the guild. Although we lack an in-depth study of the Spanish and Portuguese guilds of this period, recent research on the Iberian Peninsula tends to corroborate this revisionism. It is now clear that many guild regulations were applied with great discretion and lenience—or simply not enforced at all—thus indicating far greater flexibility than has previously been thought. This was also the case with those rules that regulated the minimum age of apprentices on their admittance to the workshop (Hernández 2007). The available figures, provided in studies such as Montemayor's work on Toledo, reveal that the by-laws might be revised and adapted to changing circumstances (Montemayor 1996, p. 208).[44] There was no shortage, moreover, of evi-

---

[44] Of the 30 by-laws emitted in Toledo between 1500 and 1626, 18, more than a half, were updated during the same period and, of them 10 were revised more than once. The years between the first drafts and the first revision spanned from 5 to 98, but changes in fewer than

dence of highly positive adaptations in some corporations until well into the seventeenth century—another indicator of greater flexibility and evidence that these guilds were more efficient in reducing transaction costs than was previously thought (Casado 2004). Above all else (Chap. 2), the development of the *verlagssystem* itself and the opportunities for the employment of merchant capital were considerable and suggest a more malleable system. The case of Madrid demonstrates that the number of guilds subject to the statutes of purity of blood was lower than was once thought (Nieto and Zofío 2016, p. 259). The available figures (admittedly, too few studies have been written) on the degree of openness of the guilds in the seventeenth century may be interpreted in the same way. The excellent work of Nieto and Zofío shows that 75% of the artisan masters of Madrid between 1561 and 1601 came from other provinces; in 1643–1649 this figure reached 68.2%. The interpretation of these figures remains problematic, but, as the above-cited authors argue, the fact that by this date many artisans coming from outside regions did not even have to register is indicative that access to the guild was even easier than it appears.

Nieto has also underlined that there were ways of adapting to increasing demand and changes in the demand structure. The development of the *verlagssystem* that we have described for some towns such as Córdoba and Segovia for the sixteenth century was also present in Madrid during the seventeenth century (Nieto 2006). This change indicates also to what extent the rigidity of the guild system was not so strict and the most prominent members of the mercantile community were able to introduce changes in the productive process. Furthermore, the artisan workshop implemented a system of subcontracts to face changes and increasing demand. This system consisted in the use of specialists, sometimes belonging to other offices, in exchange for a salary to produce goods or parts of the final product for the members of the guild. The method, very rudimentary on the other side, shows in our view a certain flexibility as long as it allowed for a temporary increase in supply beyond the productive limits of the family workshops at moments of peak demand, and this was done without incurring in structural costs.

30 years were quite common. I took these data from Montemayor (1996: table of pp. 208), Of course, these figures only call for a more detailed study since it is not certain that some of the reforms served not to open or improve the workshops' economic efficiency but, rather, the opposite effect.

From the side of the rural communities, it is also possible to find potentially positive developments. The maintenance of the rural community and the administrative structure of the *concejos* with their regulatory activity of the crop system kept the possibility to reduce risks and transaction costs in the use of the land. Some villages, though not many, were able to buy and to keep, which was the most difficult thing, *baldíos* and councils' lands and incorporate them as *propios* that belonged to the town hall and could be used by community members in different ways. The relation between economic resources and the available land could change to a more positive equation—as it did in many regions, particularly in the interior of Castile—and pave the way for an intensive use of them. In this light, it is easy to understand why the peasantry was an active agent for economic growth when there existed available productive factors at hand—including possibilities of commercialization of their surplus. These advances could be achieved by making use of the ties of confidence and solidarity that were based upon family relationships.

Therefore, the political and social development did not destroy all the possibilities of the institutional system to generate economic growth and an efficient use of resources. The key point would be in the balance between this positive side and a more negative one that we will study below.

As a matter of fact, political and social evolution would have also a less positive side. As long as it also reproduced the private jurisdictions of the nobility, the Church, and the cities, as well as their capacity of coercion, use of violence, and regulation of economic life, the outcome was also a plurality of superimposed powers, often resulting in conflict. The result could be a situation very similar to the one North et al. have defined as a closed society (2009).

This was a society of orders, with a corporate character and a huge variety of individual juridical statutes, which were, obviously, a source of fragmentation and uncertainty in social and economic relations between the different social groups. To litigate against a noble or clergyman could entail different implications, something which created marked uncertainty, as is demonstrated by the case between Belalcázar and Toledo. This was, moreover, a society with a plurality of law codes. As A. M. Hespanha has underlined for Portugal, the so-called official law was still a long way from displacing local and consensual laws: indeed, in some cases they imposed themselves upon and contradicted each other (1989). Furthermore the multiplication of laws created a certain degree of chaos. Sancho de

Moncada dedicated some memorable pages in which he underlined the excessive number of laws ('there must be more than 5000') and their cryptic character ('they speak erroneous words'), which left a wide margin for arbitrariness for the judges, 'so that they can squeeze whoever they want' (Moncada 1974 [1619], pp. 201–2). Jerónimo de Ceballos was very probably right when he asked in 1623:

> Where has one seen, in all the countries, so many tribunals and so little justice? Where so many judges and less regard for the state? Where more laws but lawsuits settled unevenly? And where such multitude of lawyers, notaries, and scribes, but so little attention paid to the causes of the poor, the young, and the widowed?[45]

The old custom of 'obeying but not complying' created limits on the king's capacity of enforcement and transferred decisions to corporations of citizens, above all to the cities and the Cortes, thus adding some additional uncertainties. Many conflicts were in the end resolved by systems of self-regulation before arriving before the tribunals and even, indeed, after having done so. As R. Kagan has written, this society was litigious to the point of exhaustion and might recur to the tribunals—and the cases brought before the House of Trade of Seville give grounds for suspecting the same (Fernández de Castro 2015)—not to resolve a conflict but simply to put off decisions. For this reason it is not unreasonable to suppose that going before the chancelleries in search of justice was, despite being increasingly frequent, bitterly criticized by a part of contemporary society and that 'an arbitrated settlement within the confines of the community was the preferred mechanism for ending disputes' (Kagan 1981, p. 18). In other words, a system of corporative self-enforcement was very often preferable to a decision reached by judges and the use of official law. Moreover, when trying to make use of the tribunals, the important thing in many cases was to decide the court or third party before which the suit would be brought, as this detail could be decisive in the application of the law rather than the letter of it. And the collision of laws and the superimposition and confrontation of juridical spaces could only increase uncertainty. Even if the decision remained in the hands of the judge, the effect of precedent or unwritten law in shaping decisions was inherent to the system itself. This meant that the circumstances of the case—the personality, merits, prior

---

[45] *Arte real para el buen gobierno*, 1623 (quoted in Kagan 1981, p. 210).

services and lineage of the parties, and many other factors besides—that were very difficult to foresee could have a marked effect on the verdict, and so the application of the law was unpredictable ex ante.[46]

The problems are evident in relation to the fiscal system. If in one town a certain tax had been levied in *sisas* upon a product, in the next town it might be set upon another product. Such a disparity was the outcome of a growing degree of local-level autonomy in the management of taxes. In many cases—the *millones*, for example—the methods for the collection of services conceded by the Cortes had to be approved by the king, but the proposals from the towns could differ. Likewise, what in the final instance mattered most was not so much how revenues were collected but rather the enormous variety of collection methods that appeared on the economic and fiscal map. There were even those towns that complied with the *servicios* by using their own municipal budgets (sometimes renting the *propios* or municipal goods, usually lands), whereas in other villages new taxes on consumables paid by commoners had to be introduced and collected.[47] Furthermore the collection of taxes was shaped by informal networks of local oligarchies, which meant that a situation of 'unpredictable arbitrariness' for any outsider arose, with a very noticeable tendency towards heightened risks.[48] This situation very clearly became worse during the seventeenth century as we will see (Chap. 8) and would be denounced as such in the 1700s. Vicente Alcalá Galiano described it in a book whose very title is highly expressive of the problems and which concluded with this advice:

> The contribution paid to the State by each one of its individuals should be clear and set out, not arbitrary. The time and means of payment should also be specified, and the tax payers should be informed of both of these details. Because, without this knowledge, he is exposed to the injustice of the tax collector, who can raise and lower the tax when it suits his interests and caprices. Any uncertainty in the imposition of taxes encourages the insolence and corruption of those who depend upon the collection of the royal patrimony and can take hold of it without any fear; [and it is clear] that the

---

[46] See also in this respect Fernández de Castro (2015).

[47] The leeway enjoyed by rural communities that controlled their own *alcabalas* was proportionate to their ability to pay the quantities allocated to them by using their own possessions; this was the case until the 1570s, at least (García Sanz 1987, pp. 333–5).

[48] I discussed this in the context of the theories of a new institutional economics in Yun (2001).

uneven level of contributions will not bring about nor can have such a prejudicial effect to the people as can that uncertainty.[49]

The problem was even worse for interregional trade, where the distance increased the difficulties in acquiring the correct information about local markets, which were very heterogeneous and opaque, as Regina Grafe has demonstrated (Grafe 2012). The aims of social and (above all) commercial networks were to reduce costs, to facilitate the transfer of information, and to create the confidence that the formal institutions could not provide. But the difficulties posed by the kaleidoscopic array of local laws and taxes are more than obvious.

Finally, it is worthwhile remembering that the progress in the implantation of 'official law' ran parallel in the different kingdoms. In other words, the plurality of pacts between the Crown and each one of its kingdoms led to the preservation of a mosaic of jurisdictional systems, all of them highly different. Sometime previously the various legal systems had borrowed or stolen from one another, but all retained their previous characteristics (Tomás y Valiente 1992, pp. 232–97). This meant that the prospect of the creation of a homogenous juridical-economical space was increasingly distant, something which affected transaction costs in operations conducted across their political borders.

Some details, moreover, suggest that much of the progress achieved in sixteenth-century Castile was reversed relatively quickly from the end of the century. From 1580 the activity and efficiency of the *Chancillerías* were clearly reduced. This growing ineffectiveness can be measured in the number of decisions passed down by the best-known example (the *Chancillería* of Valladolid), which fell from around 1400 in 1580 to between 200 and 400 in 1640–1660.[50] And if part of this reduction evidently was due to the interest in presenting great lawsuits in the Court or before the Council of Castile, it is worthwhile taking into account that there were relatively few of these major cases and that this fall was even more rapid than the decline in population. Furthermore, a study of the

---

[49] V. Alcalá Galiano, *Sobre la economía política y los impuestos*. Academia de Artillería de Segovia, Segovia: 1992, facsimile edition, p. 321. [original edition, Segovia 1781–1788].

[50] According to Kagan (1981), the phenomenon was in part due to the progressive replacement of the Chancellery by the Council of Castile after the transfer of the Court to Madrid. But even then, the facts are highly suggestive, as the same conclusion appears from calculations made by subtracting the cases generated in the city itself from the total number.

delays in law cases demonstrates that those of less than two years' duration fell by a notable proportion from 1560 to 1620 (from almost 50% to 34%), whereas the proportion of cases that lasted for eight years or more did not fall and may well have risen.[51]

What were the causes of this process? From its inception, the chancellery system was highly criticized, with elites and the aristocracy being both vocal and active in protesting against lawyers and this new judicial order.[52] Around 1600 this opinion had taken root among the *arbitristas*, many of whom represented the concepts of the urban patriciate. As many of them rightly pointed out, the costs incurred in law cases were bankrupting peasants, businessmen, seigniors, and, of course, cities (Moncada 1974 [1619], pp. 201–4). But these criticisms do not appear to have weakened the justice system. As J. Owens has underlined, the problem lay in the contradiction between the wish for a solid and efficient judicial system and the fact that the king could not maintain himself without the backing of the aristocracy on the one side and the mid-ranking nobility and urban patriciate on the other (Owens 2005, pp. 182 ff.). Indeed, this argument might be taken further than Owens himself allows. After 1580 the powerful private jurisdictions, consolidated within the conflictive pact between Crown and elites, were able to compete with royal jurisdiction (Thompson 1993, vol. II, p. 223).

The crisis of the chancellery system was, very possibly, the result of a combination of factors: the growing inefficiency of these courts due to the difficult relationships between their judges and the monarch (Kagan 1981);[53] economic problems and the spiralling debts of cities, seigniors, municipalities, and private individuals, which meant that recurring to slow-moving and inefficient tribunals was an ever less attractive option; and—highly important—the continued vigour of the city and seigniorial

---

[51] Kagan (1981, p. 7, Fig. 1). These figures must be treated with care, as the final judgement was emitted 'only upon request of the victorious party'. But it is very important that the figures of the author show that from 1620 the royal arrangements worked out as cheaper than the *cartas ejecutorias*. In spite of this, there occurred a reduction in numbers at least until 1660.

[52] Kagan (1981). For Quevedo's criticism of the lawyers, pp. 72–3.

[53] Although this area remains (unfortunately) poorly studied, it is obvious that many judges and lawyers entered into the dynamic of clientele systems, which also allowed them to achieve social ascent and to be promoted to other positions offering greater remuneration outside of the judiciary (Kagan 1981).

jurisdictions, a lasting feature of the conflictive pact, and the recourse to informal accords between parties.

The monarch himself was also a source of instability and violence that might run against the common law and create uncertainty and risks for economic activities. Despite the nuances introduced above, the reasons and arguments of Acemoglu, Johnson and Robinson (Chap. 4) are basically correct as it comes to the negative effects of bankruptcies and the seizure of American cargoes and treasures (2005). Obviously, the Habsburgs were not exceptional in many of these measures, and it is even possible that other monarchs were more arbitrary or less sensitive than them (see Sardone 2018). It is also important to remember that, after these measures, there were negotiations that alleviated the financial damage they induced.[54] But it is difficult to believe that they could not affect ex ante the feeling of risk and uncertainty, since those negotiations were always fraught and of an uncertain end.

This negative side of absolutism will become even more evident during the seventeenth century with the repeated devaluations of money, an action that, as theologians like Mariana denounced, was a gesture of tyranny that went against the kingdom's laws. The authority of the king, moreover, and his absolute power might serve as a brake on the positive effects caused by the development of justice and the chancellery courts, even in Castile itself. The exercise of *absoluta potestas* by the king over the chancelleries could be the cause of arbitrary actions. It was on behalf of his *absoluta potestas* that Philip II could settle an important lawsuit in Toledo in favour of the count of Belalcázar against the Archbishop of Toledo, without paying heed to previous judicial decisions and acting solely as a result of the political alliances at Court (Owens 2005). Moreover, it is possible to think that Philip II was much less given to this type of interference than his sons, above all Philip III. But all that was needed to create a sense of risks and higher transaction costs was the feeling that the lawsuits would be resolved not according to the letter of the law but in reference to the person against whom one litigated.

Though a relatively high degree of social order was a goal of the monarchy and its agreements with elites, the differences among the distinct

---

[54] Years ago historians such as Lovett (1977), Ruiz Martín (1990b), and Rodríguez-Salgado (1992) devoted very detailed studies to the way the big Genoese bankers got compensations for these actions.

kingdoms were many. In Aragon, the pact with elites was made in more challenging conditions because of the absence of American silver and the improbability of establishing fiscal-financial relationships similar to those in Castile (Yun 2004). This had made the Crown fiscally weaker and reduced its capacity of enforcement, resulting in positive effects in some cases. The reduced ability to palliate internal conflicts within the Aragonese, Valencian, and Catalan nobility was one of the reasons for the persistence of banditry and the related difficulty in maintaining law and order. In proportion to the development of seigniorial jurisdiction, this created a higher degree of insecurity whose impact upon economic activity is not known but—according to contemporary evidence—appears to have been negative until well into the seventeenth century (Chap. 8) (Torres 1994).

But the way laws and customs were enforced is not enough to understand the allocation of resources. We also need to consider other less positive aspects of the institutional development and to what extent they also effected the criteria for the management of those resources—above all, after having previously pointed out some possible positive effects.

Regarding the *señorío*, and in spite of the changes, efforts to improve the methods of collecting rents and monitoring patrimonies were still more important than organizational or technical advances.[55] As a general rule, the forms or types of property rights were also influential. Lands ceded in *enfiteusis* could not be the object of any (legal) productive improvement from the lords' side, and in a moment of demographic crisis, the actions from the peasants' side would not be frequent for several decades.[56] In areas such as Valencia and Aragon, the seigniors wielded considerable juridical rights and enforcement powers. These prerogatives guaranteed the collection of their rents and the defence of their economic privileges and so lessened the need to recur to formulas for the amplified reproduction of capital.[57]

The development of the Court had similar effects. Rather than investing in their properties, for many aristocrats a more rational policy was to

[55] Pérez del Barrio (1613, p. 235).

[56] Here the role of the *señor* might be simply to promote the actions of his vassals (Pérez del Barrio 1613, pp. 226v–9v), although this might be increasingly difficult in a moment of demographic recession.

[57] On the role of privilege and coercion in preventing economic improvements, see North et al. (2009).

redouble the amount of attention paid to the Court and intensify efforts to acquire extraordinary resources through political action, a determination that would elevate the practices of rent-seeking to a prevalent feature of the management of the great houses.[58] Moreover, aristocratic economies came to be based on an essential duality that explained the strange combination of luxury and indebtedness into which many of them fell. The aristocratic patrimonies were made up of two interconnected but different parts. On one side, there were the *mayorazgos* (composed mainly of seigniorial estates) whose incomes and management were subject to requirements and rules set down by the king. These were possessions whose use was restricted in the sense that they were tied down and almost always unmoveable; they could not be sold off or alienated in any way, and their capacity for generating liquid incomes could also be very limited. On the other side, there existed the favours, offices, pensions, and extraordinary incomes conceded by the Crown to the aristocrats, which constituted disposable sources of revenue that could be used immediately.

The result was a very asymmetric form of management. Being the *mayorazgo*, a non-alienable and subject to the king's unpredictable requirements and exigencies, the interest of the landlords in the improvement of their productivity was very limited. At the same time, the incomes provided by the *mayorazgo* were used as a means of obtaining political incomes and power, while the extraordinary incomes derived from royal grace and favour were only used in exceptional circumstances to improve the entitled properties. Such management criteria were the key to the coexistence of luxury and need that, in our eyes, appears an open contradiction but which served as a basis for a moral economy whose overall consequences would be decisive (Yun 1994a). A moral economy of this kind, tied to a series of increasingly firmly rooted cultural beliefs, existed throughout Europe. But it was manifested in Spain, above all in Castile, in a more pronounced way and with more evident consequences.

As has been said, forces to reduce incentives for improvements existed also among the ecclesiastic institutions. The exercise of privilege and specific property rights over land and rents held by these institutions would

---

[58] See the account records held in Simancas. According to my calculations, the count of Lemos, for example, enjoyed 'extraordinary' (additional) income, which came on top of those 'normal' ones derived from his seigniorial estates: the former brought in around 440,000 ducats in 1630 (*Dirección General del Tesoro*, inv. 1, lib. 5, exp. 81. AGS). These extraordinary revenues were numerous. See Yun (2002a).

also affect their management criteria. As had occurred with the *mayor-azgo*, the very character of ecclesiastical property—also, by definition, inalienable—led to *rentier* forms of management, in which important improvements were not necessary to maintain the patrimony intact. Privilege, in this case embodied in an exclusive type of property right, played a fundamental role. As in the lay *señoríos*, the notable capacity for enforcement wielded by many of these institutions allowed them to collect their incomes and, in some cases, led to the use of (not necessarily physical) coercion as a substitute for investment. Moreover, the make-up and nature of their incomes could also further reduce the attraction of introducing improvements: the collection of *foros*, of tithes, and of other *gabelles* required improvements in the forms of monitoring rather than advances in the productive system. The extension of ecclesiastical properties and their tax privileges reinforced the monopolistic advantages of some institutions in the local markets, therefore increasing their temptation for speculative management rather than for economic investments (Álvarez 1987).

In many regions such as the Duero Valley or Galicia, ecclesiastical prop-erties were made up of small plots of land dispersed over considerable distances (the result of unordered and unplanned donations) which were rented out on short-term leases. This greatly complicated the introduction of improvements for both the farmers themselves and the institutions that owned them. From the end of the sixteenth century, the control of rural credit in the form of *censos consignativos* gave rise to mechanisms for the extraction of peasant income that made agrarian improvements even more unnecessary from the clerics' side. Moreover, these *censos consignativos* became a way of obtaining the ownership of the land itself when borrow-ers defaulted on their repayments, thus achieving an 'extensive' (simple) reproduction of capital. This became especially clear when the brutal series of epidemics and poor harvests that began in the 1590s combined with the sale of common lands and resulted in the ruin of many farmhands and workers. At least until economic conditions changed at the end of the century, the way many ecclesiastical institution managed credit could be negative for economic growth, and that seems to have been the case. The model of economic expansion of these institutions based on donations from the society and in particular from the elites constituted a form of rent-seeking, in this case one that was not orientated towards the Court and the state (as was that of the aristocracy) but rather towards society as a whole. Family strategies also became incrusted or fossilized, therefore, in the economic management of ecclesiastical patrimonies and encouraged a simple form of reproduction for these institutions. The extension of the ecclesiastic patrimony through these strategies was more important than investment in productive improvements.[59] It is worthwhile remembering that war stood at the basis of all of these developments and that armed conflict was presented in religious terms as the only way to justify the taxes derived from it and the efforts and sacrifices demanded from society.

Regarding the commercial institutions, if the consulates could have positive effects in reducing risks and transaction costs among their members, the opposite effect was also very much present. This would be patent in the evolution of both the Consulate of Seville and the *Casa da Índia* of Lisbon. One of the keys to this was found in the systems for the control of colonial commerce associated with both empires.

When trade with America boomed from the last third of the sixteenth century, it became necessary to compensate the very high value of the silver cargoes and the arrival of other commodities with a balancing flow of exports to the New World (Hough and Grier 2015). Given the difficulties in meeting this demand with peninsular production alone (Chap. 7), the result was the massive entry of foreign goods, channelled through Seville, into America (Oliva 2004). It should be emphasized that this process was only made possible through the informal and family ties between Seville businessmen and foreign merchant communities. At the same time, this situation created the basis for a new relationship between Crown and Consulate. The Seville merchants—and the Consulate of the city, above all—had long provided financial assistance to the king in the form of fiscal 'advantages'; from the end of the sixteenth century, contributions of this kind would become regular (Oliva 2004). This arrangement led to forms of commercial management that were largely based on advantages derived from privileges and forms of rent-seeking. In this context, and in light of the notable benefit of intermediation with foreign industrial products, another salient aspect of commercial management is easily explainable: the reduced interest of merchant capital in general and of Seville capital in particular, to invest to dynamize industrial production in Spain. Furthermore, this combination of institutional restrictions based upon the

---

[59] The fact may be seen in the scarce, if not non-existent, quantities that were dedicated to these effects in the Cathedral of Huesca (Latorre, 1992). For the cathedral chapels of Portugal, see da Silva (2013).

use of privilege and the permeability of the system to the informal institutions like the family created significant entry barriers for non-members of the merchant coalition that pivoted upon Seville. Acemoglu, Johnson, and Robinson are probably correct when arguing that the Seville monopoly served to slow down the institutional development of the country and prevented the establishment of positive institutions. But, having said this, what is certain is that emphasis should fall on the image of a parasitical yet weak king rather than on an all-powerful one.

Something similar happened with the Lisbon merchant communities, although their point of departure was different. As in Castile, the Crown had established control mechanisms for trade with the colonies, particularly with Africa and Asia. This meant establishing taxes through the control of commerce. For this reason, the monopoly meant the king's direct involvement in commerce and especially the pepper trade. By the second half of the century, however, it was becoming clear that this control was insufficient and that, moreover, fraud, contraband, and Dutch commerce could not be constrained. This led to the introduction of a system for the licencing of commerce. In exchange for a set payment, permission was granted to private businessmen to trade with Asia and Africa. This arrangement brought two advantages for the Crown (or, at least this was the hope): it obtained funds derived from the payment of the licence and fiscal yields based upon this commerce. But, as in Castile, the intrusion of informal family networks into the system ended up perverting it. In a very short space of time, a large number of non-Portuguese families became involved in this commerce; these traders were often associated with dense international networks of Jewish businessmen originating in Portugal. As in the case of the Castilian monopoly, it was an 'international monopoly' (or, in other words, it was not a monopoly), in which merchants from many countries were involved, and the commercial management was based upon the exploitation of privileges and institutional advantages that rendered unnecessary any forms of investment designed to make the country's economy more dynamic. Equally and, again, as in Castile, these practices were brought about by a weak political system that was incapable of imposing institutions upon dynamic international commercial networks rather than by a parasitical monarchical absolutism that allowed no right of appeal against its mandates and structures.

Also a good part of the urban elites were tempted by ways of management that were in principle less propitious for the general efficiency of the economy. This situation is partly explained by the development of the political system and the methods chosen for the promotion of relatives within the family networks. Some of these families enhanced their relations with the Crown, thus acquiring the chance to obtain a position within the empire and the formidable array of political incomes that it offered. Emigration to America and Asia (in the case of Portugal), which was especially marked among the middle class, also played a role in permitting this group access to additional (and expanding) resources, thus reproducing a scheme little conducive to economic improvements in the peninsula. Many members of the rising urban classes saw the foundation of *mayorazgos* as a means of not only obtaining security for them and their families but also of enlarging their social and cultural capital.[60] The reinforcement of the city as a political organism, and the influence of these elites in the town councils, allowed them to apply practices of rent-seeking and so take advantage of this institution and the privileges it conferred. The investment in political capital was often more profitable than in productive improvements, which were always risky and uncertain; moreover, they were not easy to achieve, as in many cases they implied a challenge to the status quo and entrenched rights—for example, in the forms of land use, the cultivation system, and artisanal regulations.

In these circumstances, a logical and attractive policy for the local elites was to regulate the local market and the use of the recently purchased communal lands in their own benefit. Another option was the advantageous sale of goods in local markets that were heavily controlled by the town, thus creating important entrance barriers to potential competitors.[61] The private use of the public domain, directly or by an intermediary, might allow elites not to embark themselves in forms of production that involved greater risks and higher transaction and monitoring costs.[62]

Artisan families and the way they acted within corporations could also lead to not very much fertilizing management. Their attempts to limit competition among them and with outsiders could have that effect.

---

[60] See Guerrero Mayllo (1993), Hernández (1995), Soria (2000), Ruíz Ibáñez (1995), Owens (1980), Gutiérrez (1989), and De Bernardo (1994).

[61] Castillo de Bovadilla recognized that entrance barriers and the high degree of privilege that local powers wielded on behalf of oligarchies were prejudicial to external agents, citing in particular the justifications given for the conferral of offices (1597).

[62] See many of these practices in Ruiz de Celada's book, *El estado de la Bolsa. Op. cit* [1777]; see Yun (1990) and also De Bernardo (1994).

In many Castilian guilds, it was normal to restrict the number of apprentices that each master could take on and train. The temptation to impose restrictive policies by creating entry barriers and opposition to innovation was also present. Furthermore, the most dynamic craftsmen in seventeenth-century Castile, those of Madrid, found in a corporatist closure the best way to fight against the economic crisis after 1630 (Nieto 2006, pp. 205). The tendency to increase the money paid by the officials for the fees of the exam to become masters was also among the usual management practices, as was the tendency to reserve this status for the sons of the masters (Nieto 2006, chapter 11), to the extent that an author has spoken of endogamy and 'endotechnology' (Nieto 2006). In Córdoba the reaction against the arrival of *Morisco* artisans (who were especially skilled in silk production) appears to have been entirely negative, and not only because of religious prejudices, despite the prior existence of a considerable group of *Moriscos* in the city.[63] Such an event is also a proof of the many obstructive ways that might characterize the guild's policy. Furthermore the case of Madrid on which this revisionism is based so far can be also considered as a special case as long as, at least until 1630, it was the most dynamic centre of the peninsula thanks to the installation there of the Court. The figures of newcomers to the capital's workshops must have been an exception to the peninsular rule, and the low percentage of foreigners (6.6% in 1643–1649) is indicative of a relatively limited capacity

---

[63] In the aftermath of the *Morisco* rebellion, an important part of this minority, employed in activities of an industrial kind, was transferred to the city, creating a range of problems. Without doubt these difficulties had a religious motif, but they were also economic in nature. In certain sectors, such as silk weaving (which represented a long tradition within the history of the *Moriscos* of Granada), opposition among the Córdoba guilds to the newcomers was entrenched (it was extremely strong among the Old Christians). As is ever the case, the newcomers were criticized for their lack of knowledge, their production of low-quality goods (accusations which it is difficult to take seriously, as the very opposite was probably true), and, very significantly, for allowing women to work, an accusation that has been considered by Ogilvie as a proof of the closing—off of the guilds. Purely fiscal considerations (a large portion of the taxes collected by the city depended on them) meant that the *Moriscos* could always count upon the support of the mayor's office and the Chancellery of Granada, while the king was generally supportive of them. Yet one thing is certain: the *Moriscos* were expelled from Córdoba in 1609 with great clamour and popular celebration. The same was true across Castile and Aragon, but this form of mass rejection was not simply religious in origin: apart from other things, these 'new Christians' were also an economic threat to many craftsmen who defended themselves with their guild privileges.

to absorb technical advances originating from outside the country. But even in Madrid, the conflicts among the different professions and workshops—sometimes in the king's courts—reflect a high level of tension that also leads one to suspect high transaction costs in litigation and fights. As we said previously, the case of Madrid is also meaningful in that it is not entirely implausible to think that, at least in Castile, the forms of tax collection favoured sclerosis in the corporations. Some technological advances or profound organizational change could alter the basic niches of tax collection and even lead to the disappearance of some of the corporations, something which could result in a problem for the city authorities. The result was a tendency to defend, at least in the short term, the different corporations (each of them normally associated with a phase of the productive process), which in effect reduced the possibility of major increases in productivity and which, moreover, could be easily presented as a measure introduced for the common good.[64]

Also among peasants and rural communities, there were ways of using resources that were not so positive. Moreover, the evolution of the rural councils, which previously had been highly dynamic institutions supporting economic growth, could now rebound to the detriment of their members. Highly refined devices and systems for the exploitation of land and property rights, upon which a very fragile balance of resources had been based, might now serve as an obstacle to the introduction of qualitative changes capable of meeting the challenge posed by a larger population. And this was also largely because these changes threatened to rupture the social equilibrium and the rules of community. For the well-off peasants it was now easier to recur to the use of communal regulations to serve their own interests than to initiate uncertain processes requiring massive change. Their ambitions to

---

[64] The most eye-catching case is that of Córdoba, where opposition among local patricians and merchants involved in the *verlagssystem* served as a brake on innovations that were proposed to control and transform the phases of the process of production. As Fortea showed (1981), this was one of the keys to the disruption of the development of 'capitalist' (*sic*) forms of productive organization and the final crisis of the sector. Even in Toledo interesting innovations and adaptations occurred in certain sectors (such as silk production), and it has been possible to affirm that the office system, being well structured and organized, 'consolidated the established situation, encouraged parasitism, but discouraged new initiatives. In this way, it ended by depriving Toledo of all chance of recovery' (Montemayor 1996, p. 214).

control municipal positions, to link with families of *letrados* and bureaucrats, or their habit to transfer resources to the Church by funding *capellanías, obras pías,* and so on, has been clearly demonstrated (Brumont 1993, pp. 321–36). In other words, for elites, to convert economic into political and cultural capital was also a way to manage their patrimonies. This habit has even a rationale: by controlling municipal offices and enhancing their own prestige, they had the opportunity to mediate in the councils and in the regulation of resources in their own profit. For the peasant elites, market regulations, the use of the *propios* or municipal goods, and the administration of taxes were sometimes better and for sure less risky than the introduction of agrarian improvements. They could not even imagine— as historians sometimes appear to want them to—the development of agrarian capitalism, which historians have often linked to the emergence of large farms or estates. But, on the other hand, this limitation meant that the communitarian system itself lost much of the productive potential that brought considerable benefits in the sixteenth century.

The institution, established to try to engineer reciprocity and maintain a sort of zero equilibrium among peasants based upon a previous status quo and formal property rights, was decisive in limiting any profound change. As we shall see, only by taking into account economic variables such as demographic pressure, the demand to buy and rent land, the development of rural markets, and so on can the different degrees of efficiency of the distinct agrarian systems be explained. Only when these variables combined in such a way that it proved possible to increase quantities of labour and natural resources without breaking the community rules was it possible for millions of individual decisions to lead to a greater degree of efficiency in the fight against death. As we shall see, the situation would be very different to that of the sixteenth century; moreover, each region would be a law unto itself.

* * *

One of the most frequent errors made when analysing the institutions of the *ancien régime* is to classify them as inefficient in relation to those of today's capitalist economy; another is to judge them purely by their similarity to the ideal model we have of them. There can be no doubt that, from this perspective, the study of the reigning political economy in the Iberian Peninsula around 1600 leads inexorably to a negative conclusion.

Even when they do not accept the stereotypes and values of the new institutional economics, many historians of early modern Spain have arrived at similar conclusions. In reality, this is a legacy of Enlightenment thinking, a key moment in the development of the political economy, which saw the birth of concepts of progress and economic growth and reflections on the role of institutions that fed it. Until very recently, these perspectives and assumptions survived largely unchallenged.

But viewed from the perspective of the period, the panorama must be not only more complex but also more open in explaining efficiency quotas and growth that, obviously, belonged to a galaxy very far removed from those of the nineteenth and twentieth centuries. What emerges from the previous pages is that formal institutions and informal institutions, like the family and kinship relations, matter to explain economic behaviour and the reduction of transaction costs. But that analysis also shows that the institutions per se are not the sole point for the explanation of economic efficiency.[65] They were in many occasions twofold and could lead to different behaviours of the economic agents (Helpman 2004). The crucial point would lay in the circumstances that gave preference to individual decisions with more positive effects for the whole economy—often based on individual choices whose end was not at all economic development.

Many of the affirmations set out in the previous pages might be applied to other countries. The key point, therefore, is not that the Iberian political economy was ill and, therefore, inefficient but to what extent it was competitive in a more and more integrated world. The crucial aspect is to define to what extent these institutions were able to satisfy the needs of countries that had to defend their empires and also to what extent they were able to compete in a world in which both political and economic rivalries were becoming more severe and global. To look at the problem in this way also demands a regional perspective, as does consideration of the extent to which the positive and negative potentialities of the institutional system were more or less prevalent. This task will be undertaken in the following chapters.

---

[65] For a more quantitative analysis that reinforces this idea, see Ramos (2012).

Open Access This chapter is licensed under the terms of the Creative Commons Attribution 4.0 International License (http://creativecommons.org/licenses/by/4.0/), which permits use, sharing, adaptation, distribution and reproduction in any medium or format, as long as you give appropriate credit to the original author(s) and the source, provide a link to the Creative Commons licence and indicate if changes were made.

The images or other third party material in this chapter are included in the chapter's Creative Commons licence, unless indicated otherwise in a credit line to the material. If material is not included in the chapter's Creative Commons licence and your intended use is not permitted by statutory regulation or exceeds the permitted use, you will need to obtain permission directly from the copyright holder.

Conclusions Part II

STATE BUILDING AND INSTITUTIONS

The schools or disciplines of historical sociology, history, and the new institutional economics have shown particular interest in the state-building process that took place in Europe from the fifteenth century. In general, they have attempted to determine how medieval political formations lead to a type of modern state in which the central power monopolizes coercion and administration through a professional bureaucracy that governs a geographically coherent territory. In particular, scholars have noted how war brought about the construction of a military fiscal system that, in part by overcoming other corporate powers, was able to achieve centralization of resources and of coercive capacity in the hands of the central power, thus serving as a preliminary step towards Weber's model of the modern state. This narrative has almost always been compiled by projecting backwards the boundaries of the nation states that were consolidated during— and as a result of—the Congress of Vienna (1815) and have served as fundamental units of analysis for the early modern period. The perspective has certain logic if we consider that this type of state is, above all, a territorial one whose evolution we want to analyse retrospectively.

The problem emerges in another light if we follow the arguments set out in the above pages, through the analysis of the way in which the territorially dispersed composite monarchy developed, a network of geographically separated polities in which the relationship between the prince and each of the polities was based on a series of conflicts and agreements, with jurisdiction shared with (or delegated to) elites, cities, and the Church, who in turn maintained horizontal relations—often conflictive—with each other.[1]

Although his pivotal study hardly touches upon the Iberian countries, Downing (1992) provides some perspectives that may be useful to our understanding of composite monarchies.[2] Building on Tilly's argument for the 'exceptional case'—that in a context of sustained military pressure, access to abundant commercial income could cause a polity to avoid bureaucratization and even absolutism—Downing adds that the income extracted from conquered territories and external subsidies can have similar effects (Downing 1992, p. 9). These variables, and their very asymmetric forms, would create an enormous unevenness between the states of the Habsburg monarchy.

Around 1530, when Charles V was crowned Emperor at Bologna, the Habsburgs had established an unprecedented dynastic complex. In an area that was as politically fragmented as Europe, whose dynamics were governed by conflict and the balance between different polities (Jones 1981), this composite state posed a genuine threat to all. Within it, some states—including Castile, although this has not been recognized by historical sociology—had the requisites to create incipient bureaucratized and centralized systems: a relatively developed university system that allowed the Crown to recruit specialized personnel, an economy with a certain level of commercial development that created the bases of an efficient fiscal framework by the standards of the time, and a dynamic commerce and a customs regime that seemed to favour tax collection according to Tilly's model (1990).[3] But to understand subsequent developments, it is necessary to take into account other aspects and factors.

In this respect, it is important to underline that—in contrast with the prevailing image that only emphasized the negative aspects—there was an evident complementarity between the various parts of this composite monarchy. Indeed, this complementarity created the conditions for the survival of this system. Thus, the fiscal possibilities of Castile and America were really made to work thanks to the financial skills of Genoa—a decisive

---

[1] The idea of the composite monarchy encompasses two separate concepts or models: for Koenigsberger it was a polity 'including more than one country under the sovereignty of one ruler' (1986, p. 12); but this also implied a 'profound respect for corporate structures and for traditional rights, privileges and customs' (Elliott 1992, pp. 68–69).

[2] For an overview and discussion, see Ertman (1997, pp. 1–34)

[3] These are keys to a branch of historical sociology, Ertman (1997) or Tilly (1990), to justify the greater capacity to levy taxes in early modern states.

ally since 1528—and the German territories. In addition, this complementarity was possible insofar as these financial services were provided not by states (whose institutional impediments would have been very great) but by families such as the Welser, Fugger, Doria, or Spinola; that is to say, by informal networks whose cross-border character was an essential feature of their functioning. To this end, the role of the cash provided by the American mines was also vital. Flanders, Castile, Aragon, Naples, and Milan (from 1540) had very dynamic and growing populations, which enhanced the system's political and economic vitality. In the previous pages, we have emphasized the difficulties involved in the transfer of resources, a central argument in our reasoning, but it is obvious that technically the scope for the mobilization of capital and men was very developed for the standards of the time and that, in regard to previous arrangements, the composite monarchy signified a remarkable step forward. Soon the Habsburgs created a defensive barrier against their most important enemy, the Ottoman Empire. This firewall ran from Gibraltar to North Africa, Sicily, and Naples and stretched up to Vienna and the imperial territories, Bohemia and Hungary, with the complicity of Genoa and Venice. Both Venice and Genoa were independent republics whose policies fluctuated between obedience and disobedience, depending on circumstances. True, Muslim *corso* often penetrated this barrier, but the military capacity of this complex would be demonstrated at Lepanto: the forests of the Mediterranean; the iron of Iberia; the taxes of Castile, Naples, and Milan; the finances of Genoa, and soldiers and mercenaries from Castile, Switzerland, and the imperial territories; wheat from Sicily, Italian military, and naval technology; German mining technology; and so on. And, above all, the capacity with which the Habsburgs were able to combine these resources and tools was perhaps the ultimate expression of the strength of a system whose weaknesses are always stressed in relation to its distance from a modern state model.

This ensemble of dispersed polities was woven into a highly adaptive system, with an awareness of dynastic legitimacy and the notable flexibility offered by the family as a system of government. The latter had its great weakness in the unpredictable vicissitudes of the life—or death—of its members and, consequently, of inheritances. But the dynastic family was also a very extensive and flexible institution that could prove to be efficient, as is clearly demonstrated by the division of the two branches of the House of Habsburg in 1558. This was plainly a proof of (obligatory) strategy if one takes into account the solidity of these personal bonds and the chance to use them to maintain dominion in the territories governed by each of these two branches which were now united by bonds of solidarity and reciprocity as a way of facing their internal conflicts. The annexation of Portugal, again propitiated by the efficiency and fortune of family policy, would take this mosaic of states to an unprecedented situation: a territorial expansion perhaps only comparable to that of the Mongol empire in the thirteenth century. The system would be efficient for the Habsburgs and would last for decades; it was founded upon negotiations with the local political constitutions of the composite states, its remarkable capacity for propaganda, the imperial ideal (Dandelet 2014), and the very solid kinship ties that justified the existence of this network. In short, the familial character of the composite monarchy was both the strength and weakness of this system.

But it had another strength and weakness that was sometimes forgotten: this was the confessional character that the Habsburgs would soon impose upon their dominions; this ethos was derived from their own political justification as heirs to both the empire of Charlemagne and the reconquest of the Iberian Peninsula. That they could present themselves, thanks to their policy of alliances with the Pope, as defenders of Christianity and the faith was important in holding together this federation of patrimonial states; no doubt, the fear caused by the Turks on the shores of the Mediterranean helped. This fact, much commented upon by historiography, has one crucial dimension. The Habsburg imperial complex lies between those empires in which political power and religious power are separated but are inextricably linked and depend on agents with not-always-identical agendas: the pontificate and the House of Habsburg, in this case. The monotheistic character of Christianity and the dogmatic component within it would be decisive in this context. The difference, for example, with the Ottoman Empire, is very illustrative. The Sultan exercised both religious duties and authority within Islam (Burbank and Cooper 2010) and could, therefore, complement them even by implementing some degree of tolerance if it was needed (Barkey 2008). But this division of powers would be the grounds for crucial tensions for the Habsburgs. The attempts of Charles V, influenced by Erasmus, to reach agreement with the German princes and the way in which they clashed with papal religious policy are very significant in this regard and represent the first line of rupture of the monarchical complex. When Philip II ascended the throne, the respective positions had been radicalized to such a degree that religion, up to that time the crucial cement of this composite monarchy, was henceforth also one of the most important causes of conflict, as would be demonstrated by the rebellion of the Netherlands. By this juncture, the defence of 'Christendom' (but, to be more precise, Catholicism) had become enmeshed

CONCLUSIONS PART II   261

with political and, above all, fiscal theory, to the point that it was henceforth the only way to overcome what was the principal obstacle to the
government of this dynastic complex—the transfer of funds from one state
to another. The religious component, in turn, had reinforced the religious
character of the political economy of states such as Castile, where the confessional argument justifying this transfer of funds had to be rehearsed
exhaustively and so became part of the cultural beliefs that mediated the
use of financial and military resources.

In this context, the standard national histories are of very little use to
any understanding of the political economy of the Habsburg domains.
Today the aberrations and anomalies that can lead to a simplistic analysis of
the tax revenues of the states of the Old Regime are widely appreciated.
Although we cannot confuse the gross income and the net income of the
state, it is significant that the gross entries of it is significant that the net
income of the Habsburgs in Castile had not only grown faster than that of
any other European country in the sixteenth century, but by 1600 it were
twice the size of that of the King of France. If we add in the incomes of
Naples and Milan, it turns out that these three states alone enjoyed gross
incomes superior to those of their three principal rivals: France, England,
and Holland combined.[4] The costs of the Castilian debt also create the
appearance of an efficient complex (Drelichman and Voth 2014; Yun and
Ramos 2012). Portugal had followed a very different path. The House of
Avis had remained a secondary lineage in European politics, partly because
after the Catholic Kings the policy of the Habsburgs had been to 'neutral-
ize Portugal and isolate France' (Maltby 2011, p. 29), by seeking an Iberian
union that the avatars would delay to 1580 and that would only be possible
through violence. The result was a composite monarchy in Portugal but
not in the sense commonly used by Machiavelli, who emphasized the variety of distant and separate states under one dynasty: rather, what emerged
here was a kingdom made up of superimposed jurisdictional corporations
that were often in conflict with one another. Portugal would not become
an element of instability in Europe. Looking at the Atlantic, Portugal's
great competitors (and potential ally) were Castile and, by extension, the
Habsburgs. As we have seen, following Tilly's model, the chances of building a military fiscal state in Portugal were considerable. And if we allow
ourselves to be carried away by some of the ideals that are now frequently
enunciated by certain historians of the economy, it could be argued that

[4] These calculations, very approximate, are based on Comín and Yun (2012, pp. 235–238)
and the previous pages above.

this was the most 'absolutist' state in Europe: the parliament met only rarely in the sixteenth century, and yet the system of resource mobilization functioned with considerable efficiency. But Portugal is really more a case of external resources that fits some of Downing's reasoning and model. The first steps towards European globalization—manifested in the expansion into the Atlantic—endowed the king with abundant resources, but, critically, these originated from outside the kingdom and for a long time rendered unnecessary the transformation from a domain state to a tax state; rather, Portugal remained a *rentier* state until well into the sixteenth century (Yun 2012). It helped that its military needs in Europe were smaller in relation to its income, and, therefore, the system of indebtedness that forced other states to obtain taxes with which to attend to the imbalances between the king's income and his military needs did not lead to an extraction of fiscal resources as massive as that of Castile.

Portugal, on the other hand, is the counterexample that allows us to better understand Castile and the composite monarchy of the Habsburgs, to which it would be incorporated in 1580, increasing Madrid's power but also its problems. In fact, the Habsburg complex was only possible thanks to the impact of globalization. American silver allowed the operation of the international financing system (while putting it to the test at the constitutional level). But this was not because of the availability of silver in itself but because Castile found a way of converting silver into military spending by resorting to the loans taken out from contractors (*asentistas*), and this allowed it to consolidate its debt, which would not have been possible had the Castilian economy not been a relatively advanced mercantile one. This would, in any case, be the most important factor in understanding the military fiscal state in Iberia and in the Habsburg domains. In Portugal, the local power of the cities and seigniorial lordships and their autonomy with respect to the Crown would be notable, but this did not translate into an increase in incomes similar to that of Castile in terms of its fiscal capacity and the extraction of resources. In Castile, this fiscal state operated through a conflictive pact with the elites, the cities, and the Church that resulted in the enduring—indeed, even growing—power of the urban oligarchies. At the same time, local defensive needs brought about a reinforcement of local (seigniorial and urban) militias, which contributed to maintaining a system of dispersed coercion and permanent negotiation and overlap with the king's own forces. This political system had little or nothing in common with the model of the centralized military state and the uncontested imposition of its authority. And this process created a model that was different from the image of Iberian absolutism described by Acemoglu, Johnson, and Robinson.

But, above all, this conjunction of global and local forces increased the asymmetry in the Habsburg composite monarchy. States such as the Crown of Aragon or Sicily and some imperial polities evolved towards 'rentier states' and experienced few changes in their political-fiscal contexture. In the imperial territories, 'the fiscal and political structures remained stable from the sixteenth-century to the early eighteenth-century' (Pieper 2012, p. 168), and the kingdom of Hungary remained under the control of the 'states' until the end of the empire. Although these were not immobile structures, the shift from the domain state to the tax state (as defined by Schumpeter) was postponed (not coincidentally, Schumpeter was working on the Austrian case). However, the escalation of war costs meant that this situation could not last forever, and, above all, it signified that other polities more exposed to military conflicts for geostrategic reasons or with more favourable constitutions and more scope to forge different pacts with their respective elites found themselves compelled to pay more. One recurring tradition in Spanish historiography is to think that only Castile contributed to the war efforts. Nothing could be further from the truth. Certainly, Castile became the backbone of the empire. But Naples had to contribute with increasing amounts during the sixteenth century and after 1600 (Chap. 8), and the pressure on Flanders was unrelenting, which meant that their contributions continued to grow even in relative terms to those of Castile. Along with the fact that the pact with Castile was not at all stable, due in part to rising costs and the decline in the marginal profitability of taxes everything led to the first breakdown of the system in Flanders. It is very significant that the rebellion of the Netherlands coincided with the resistance of the Cortes of Castile to the revision of certain taxes (the *encabezamientos*), the bankruptcy of 1557, and, very importantly, the diffusion of Calvinism that put to the test one of the crucial elements of the Habsburg system: the religious rigidity that it had acquired and which made it impossible to maintain the dialogue and pact with elites, the two pillars of its existence. It is in this context that the most important reconversion in the history of this system took place: the division of domains between the two branches of the family.

It is very important to consider that the study of political formations and political economies of the time cannot be undertaken simply from the perspective of formal institutions (states, courts, cities, etc.) that maintained sovereignty and projected it. Any study must also take into account relationships that appear to be informal (family, dynasty, fidelity, patronage, etc.) but that were as important as formal institutions when determining political behaviour, state-building processes, and the use of resources. As much as a system of cities, principalities, and dominions, composite states were a network of informal but decisive families, lineages, and social networks (Yun 2009). Although implicit in Ertman's (1997) vision of patrimonial state or Mousnier's work on the venality of offices (1971), not many authors interested in state building have taken time to explore this aspect of them. An exception is J. Adams (2005), who has emphasized the interest of elite families in converting 'positions of sovereignty into the prosperity of their descendants' (2005, p. 81). This is explained in reference to the relations of conflict and solidarity that occurred within these family formations and were manifested in the need to find an outlet for younger sons, women, and even bastards.[5] One of the most interesting aspects of Adams's study is that she refers mainly to Holland, apparently a modern republic state, and focuses not only upon the aristocracy but also on the commercial bourgeoisie that would control the VOC and was a group in which the nuclear family was predominant.

The above pages have explored a double—and different—direction. They wanted to demonstrate that the state and in particular the empires were in part areas into which these elites projected themselves and that this method allowed them to overcome the depreciation of a part of their income (this was the case for quite a few aristocratic families) and, on the other hand, also advanced their efforts at social consolidation and expansion. This also implied a series of agreements with, in spite of the structural conflicts also inherent to those agreements, the Crown that bound them to it by relational ties that would facilitate the maintenance of the social order and the political system and that would also condition the changes within the latter. It is to be remembered that a good number of these conflictive pacts, which implied the assignment of quotas of coercion on behalf of the king, were made thanks to *absoluta potestas* and the supreme power of the monarch (this was even set down in the documents and licences granted to the nobles and aristocracy for these measures). Absolutism as a political practice was not necessarily alien to the multiplication and reinforcement of corporate powers. It is these kinds of processes that would explain what Ertman called the 'patrimonial state', regardless of the appropriateness of this term (1997, pp. 110–125). On the other hand, none of these processes were at odds with practices of

---

[5] See also Adams (2005, pp. 84–85).

restricting tension within the elites that were mostly achieved by celibacy and membership in the Church, a trend whose effects on the economy would be decisive.

But, above all, I have wanted to show that such developments, although asymmetrical according to imperial spaces and social groups, led to the reinforcement of the cross-border character of the elites. They found very different spaces in which to expand themselves. America could not become the most important area for the promotion and projection of Castilian aristocratic houses, although it offered them notable economic benefits and additions to their social and political capital. Indeed, the empire provided their Portuguese counterparts similar benefits overseas. In both cases, the chances of fusing the great families with local elites were very limited, and this would lead to the formation of colonial elites who, for a long time, were well outside the dynamics of the European aristocracies. This process of fusion, slow and really based on the reaching out of American families to peninsular ones rather than on an expansion of the Iberian aristocracies towards the colonies, would not occur until the emergence of an American nobility, which was only beginning to be noted at the end of the period under study and whose ability to link with the old Castilian families would be limited (Maruri 2007). In the meantime, America certainly would provide an outlet—sometimes only temporarily but often by creating transatlantic families for a couple of generations—for many mid-ranking nobles, bastards, clerics, lawyers, and even some heads of lineages; a similar process was also present in Portugal with the peculiarity that the number would have to be smaller given the size of the empire and the country itself.

From the perspective of the composite monarchy, this phenomenon would accentuate the asymmetry within it. The families of the Castilian high nobility became the hierarchical centre of the European Catholic nobility and its marital market. But this relationship would not—and could not—become a definitive or homogeneous system of links and ties. Where these links were intense, bonds were created that tended to stability; where they were not, things tended to be more precarious. Looked at this way, a rupture was almost inevitable with areas such as the Protestant United Provinces, where marriage ties with the Castilian nobility were more tenuous in contrast to those with the leading Flemish families (Vermeir 2009; Fagel 2009). Moreover, we must suspect that the distance between the great Castilian families and the nobility of the northern Netherlands—and with it, the obstacles to their incorporation into the imperial system as a whole—may have been one of the keys that led to a rapid change within the latter and the development of bourgeois forms of management to overcome their problems of social consolidation and expansion, with everything that this would mean and entail for the country's economy (see Van Nierop (1984) and the next chapter). At perhaps the opposite end of the scale was the Neapolitan nobility. With their old connections to the Aragonese families, they found in the monarchy an important support and a guarantor of their forms of social dominion to the extent that these cross-border relationships were increasingly directed towards the great families of Old Castile (Muto 2009). In the Iberian kingdoms themselves—increasingly, this included Portugal—the marital entanglement of aristocratic elites was a way of bringing these societies closer together and a factor in the process of state formation and the establishment of relationships between the various centres of the composite monarchy (Yun 2009). And this was not because it was a frictionless process, as it often led to divisions within the regional nobility or between it and local society. It should be borne in mind that these cross-border aristocracies did not have as their basic agenda the formation of political states; rather they sought principally to serve their own house and lineage and, in cross-border situations, would seek to secure resources and to send out free riders, as would be evident on many different occasions.

The conflictive pact in tax matters and the elites' ability to overcome their problems through various procedures ranging from the obtaining of royal *mercedes* to the use of privileged forms of credit and admission to the Church largely explain the political stability of those states upon which the weight of the empire fell most heavily, in particular Castile. This was also the case in Portugal. Catholic orthodoxy pointed in the same direction, until becoming an essential element of the political economy of the time and of the patrimonial management norms and guidelines. In the case of these families, entry into the ranks of the Church was at the same time a strategy of reproduction for the elites, a part of their moral economy, and a component of what we have defined as their economy of legitimization. All this resulted in a permanent jurisdictional fragmentation and the survival of private militias and armies, which reproduced the capacity of elites to exercise coercion.

It is not, therefore, surprising that all of this propitiated a series of characteristics in Spanish and Portuguese societies that have reinforced an image of exceptionalism. But such images do not stand up to comparison. On the other hand, the result of these developments was that these informal institutions and the internal solidarities of the elites permeated the entire institutional system. Thus, forms of wealth management would be created and reinforced: these were not aimed at wealth creation but rather at rent-seeking, or, at least, those institutions could lead to any outcome. And while these institutions would not themselves determine the course of economic development, they would have a significant bearing on it at a time when productive resources were becoming less abundant in relative terms. In turn, this would have an impact on the formation of the market, investment and the forms of seigneurial management, and so on, especially in the centre of the monarchy.

The internal dynamics of the composite monarchy were thus reaching a certain blockage point. The pacts between the elites had made it possible to overcome the structural tensions of the political and social system. But they had consolidated a political fragmentation that absolutism, itself a part of the process, could not easily overcome in its attempt at centralization. Moreover, institutions once taken by historians to renovate or renew society—above all, the king's justice—actually emerged in a way that did not conform to the model of a third party capable of making decisions on the basis of a strict and impartial application of the law. It is worth remembering that Iberian historiography has long drawn attention to the difficulties of applying the term 'modern state' in this period (Clavero 1981, 1986). The capacity of these networks to exercise family solidarity, kinship, patronage, and friendship would pervert—a loaded term, it is true—an institutional system whose very nature was far from that of modern societies. The king's own justice would itself fall prey to this situation, as is shown by the evolution of the *Chancillerías*. And, importantly, the 'military revolution' had not given rise to a state that monopolized the exercise of violence. The most effective armies, like the famous Spanish *tercios*, were sometimes dependent on private contractors like Ambrosio Spinola. But, furthermore, they were contemporaries—and sometimes complementary—of local armies of a stately or urban character. Nor did the military revolution lead to a military tax state that would completely control the tax collection system. The result was a set of political economies that were far from the ideal type of open society designed as *desideratum* by the new institutional economics (North, Wallis and Weingast 2009).

PART III

Organizing and Paying for Global Empire, 1598–1668

Since the last decades of the sixteenth century, Europe's insertion in the process of globalization intensified. It did so as a consequence of Iberian empires' development. But—this is important to consider—they were not alone in this process. On the contrary, it was a poly-nuclear development that had important consequences both in Europe and the Iberian world.

In macroeconomic terms, the figures of international trade were still small in regard to the size of the European economy. But the direct and indirect effects were notable from the perspective of the political economies of the distinct European regions. This section investigates those effects as well as the different patterns of political development that explain institutional trends in Western Europe and their economic consequences. The different trajectories, we propose, will be important to understand the consequences of globalization for Europe and the commercial and industrial competitiveness within it. But external factors, such as religion, also would be important in this process.

The question to deal with, however, is to what extent the union among the different polities that composed the Habsburgs' composite monarchy and more in particular Portugal and Castile—and, therefore, what we could consider the composite empire—would resist the pressure of globalization. To answer such a question, we also need to consider the way those empires were constructed and the relationship between formal institutions and the social networks on which they were based. From this perspective—I hope—some common places regarding the history of Iberia, Iberian empires, and globalization, as well as their economic trajectories and the concept of their decadence, will be clarified.

CHAPTER 6

Global Forces and European Competition

The elites of the Iberian kingdoms had been able to confront the problems of reproduction that faced them in the fifteenth century. As has been said, the empire was both the problem and solution, particularly for Castilian and Portuguese societies. But other areas of Europe confronted similar challenges, the main difference being the way they were approached and resolved. The results would be varied and decisive for Europe, as they would shape the different political economies of the continent. In all these cases, and sometimes in an indirect way, these outcomes were also conditioned by the process of globalization itself and by transnational factors, above all the wars into which the global Iberian empires would be drawn and the flows and currents of wealth and silver that they produced. The indirect result would be a first, if somewhat uncertain, step towards a model of greater polarization of growth which gravitated towards the north of Europe and linked it to a cycle of the longue durée in the relationship between resources and population.[1] This

---

[1] See Braudel (1976, vol. II, p. 791), among others. According to Braudel, the greater level of tension between resources and population in the south ended up facilitating the introduction of wheat by the Dutch and English in the Mediterranean, which they would then supplement with a growing trade in industrial products from the North. His thesis was later criticized by J. Israel, who drew attention to the need to avoid speaking of the north of Europe but rather about 'a tiny fringe, the extreme north western corner of the continent' (1989, pp. 5–11, 1990, pp. 133–161).

© The Author(s) 2019   271
B. Yun-Casalilla, *Iberian World Empires and the Globalization of Europe 1415–1668*, Palgrave Studies in Comparative Global History, https://doi.org/10.1007/978-981-13-0833-8_6

chapter aims at analysing how, in a context of increasing globalization—for the epoch's standards—silver flows associated with warfare, market integration within Europe, and political-religious developments affected the different institutional frameworks and consequently the economic competition among distinct Western European regions.

RELIGION AS A FACTOR: WESTERN EUROPEAN PATTERNS OF DEVELOPMENT

Economic historians are increasingly interested in the impact and influence of religion upon institutions and material development. They have usually contented themselves with examining how beliefs had economic effects, thinking along lines first suggested by Max Weber (Grier 1997). However, it is worthwhile underlining that its effects should also be considered from the viewpoint of the functioning of the institutions in question. As we have seen (Chap. 5), the influence of religiosity through the specific management criteria that it introduced into ecclesiastical institutions was notable. Moreover, its impact on political economies that so much depended upon social and political stability also should be considered. To this end, it is important to remember that sixteenth-century religion meant something more than individual and private sentiment with limited effects or impact upon public life. Political theory as much as political practices had sacred roots and origins as, therefore, did the functioning of the institutions. The former was based on the vision of the body politic as a community of religious ideas. From this concept sprang the idea of *cuius regio eius religio*. The spread of different forms of interpretation of devotion implied a rupture of the political and social body. This was a break that could be manifested at the level of the body politic and society as a whole, at the level of the state as an articulation of different powers and at the very level of coexistence and local politics and that above all affected the chances of reproduction of the elites' conflictive pacts.

A brief examination of events in other countries and the means of consolidation—or rupture—of institutional systems may cast light on this fact and on fundamental differences in the history of Europe.

Economic growth continued in France throughout the sixteenth century. If agrarian expansion was extensive, the spread of métayage and farms rented by well-off peasants allowed for improvements and investment in working tools and organizational innovations that improved the total factor productivity (Hoffman 1996, pp. 98–107). International commerce and the political solidity of the cities favoured the development of a urban network, with crucial nodes in the coastal areas but a strong penetration of the interior (Benedict 1989). This fact enhanced the development of rural markets and the commercialization of peasant production.

But this growth did not bring about a profound change in the political economy that governed the relations between the cities, the aristocracy, the Church, and the king. Until well into the century, the French Crown was unable to perfect its tax system and so create a fiscal state that involved the entire kingdom in tax collection; only some steps were taken towards the centralization and co-ordination of this system (Wolfe 1972, p. 104). The composite character of the monarchy and its system of checks and balances, similar to that of Castile, was maintained (Chap. 1). The cities not only retained their autonomy but even increased it to the extent that they became the credit bases of the Crown and assumed a sizeable portion of its debts (Chevalier 1987, pp. 150–151). Both the *états provinciales*, provincial representative assemblies, and the negotiating power of the urban oligarchies remained intact. Moreover, the *États généraux*", in which the kingdom used to meet, also retained scope for manoeuvre. As in the Iberian territories, the aristocratic families faced considerable difficulties in reproducing the social control of their lineages. We know today that the vigour of this group did not fall in general. Royal service allowed its members access to the wealth extracted by the fiscal system, and its incomes could be adapted to the depreciation brought about by the price revolution (Russell Major 1981; Salmon 1975, pp. 81–84). The military contributions of the 'second nobility' created channels for social advancement that contributed to overcome the internal tensions of the patriciate and the lower ranks of the aristocratic lineages (Bourquin 1994, pp. 24–58). The purchase of fiefs and seigniorial estates from both private individuals and the Crown allowed magistrates and businessmen to satisfy the need for expansion felt by the urban oligarchies (Salmon 1975, p. 42). At the same time, this trend increased the monarch's capacity for arbitration, set down in the growing influence and number of the 'men of the king' in the provinces (Jouanna 1989, pp. 80–90) and in their growing role as administrators of the condition of the noble. As in the Iberian kingdoms, the Church served as the machinery for absorption of this dynamic of social promotion. This came at the time that its jurisdictional autonomy and powers in relation to the king were retained to the extent that French royal absolutism has been seen as a relatively well-balanced political system (Beik 1985).

Towards 1550 agriculture entered a phase characterized by falling yields while the fragmentation of many farms lowered overall land productivity. Fiscal pressure was transferred onto the countryside, and urban salaries fell (Neveux et al. 1975, pp. 151–155). War with the Habsburgs led to an unprecedented increase in fiscal pressure and a reduction of the percentage of the royal taxes that remained in the hands of the cities charged with their collection, thus creating even more conflicts. Crown debts, which impacted cities such as Lyon and Paris, led to the bankruptcy of 1557–1558 (Chevalier 1987, pp. 150–151; Wolfe 1972, pp. 104–118). While unthinkable in Castile, the displacement of part of the fiscal burden towards the Church forced it to sell off ecclesiastical properties (Wolfe 1972, pp. 118–123). According to some calculations, during the sixteenth century, some 50% of ecclesiastical possessions were sold off. Nothing similar happened in Castile, although the seigniorial estates of some clergy were alienated. Moreover, the development of the French royal fiscal system threatened to break relations with the aristocracy (Chaunu 1977, pp. 166–167). This came at a moment at which families such as La Trémouille and others had problems achieving the extension of their lineages. The tension among noble households, structural to the system, increased.[2]

For these reasons the differences in regard to the Spanish Habsburg dominions were very clear. In geographical terms France was a geopolitically unified monarchy boasting a high density of population. On the other hand, it did not possess an empire with which to offer an outlet for the dominant coalition's needs for consolidation and extension. Nor could it count upon a stream of American silver to allow it to form an efficient system for assuming and consolidating debts (see Chap. 4). This having been said, the breakdown of the medieval model would be brought about by an external factor that was totally alien to the previous institutional framework and largely absent in Castile: religious division. If the Catholic Church had exercised less influence upon the French monarchs' international politics, the religious rupture would be a key factor in the history of the country.

The spread of Calvinism among society in general and the nobility in particular (leading to the rapid 'contamination' of its clients), and the subtlety of its doctrine on the subject of resistance to the king, fell upon a

---

[2] See the cases of the Guise, Montmorency, and the Bourbons (Knecht 1996, pp. 15–18).

receptive terrain marked by the growing discontent over the Crown's fiscal policies (Jouanna 1989; Wood 1980, p. 169). This was happening at
the same time that the 'aristocratic structure of power was converting a
civil war into a drama of a religious nature' (Chevalier 1994, p. 391).
Coming on top of the radicalization of court factions, religious confrontation would lead France into one of the most tragic periods of its history.

The subsequent conflicts brought into the open problems in the stability of the social system and, in particular, of the noble economies within it.
The 'state of finances' that had served as a basis for the continuity of the
social system was falling apart, and taxes were replaced on both sides by
pillaging and sacking (Chaunu 1977, pp. 170–175). And with the collapse
of the old arrangements, the social equilibrium achieved in the previous
century also disintegrated. The nobility sought to overcome its needs by
seizing communal lands and extending its dominions, as it had done during the Middle Ages. Many cities claimed greater degrees of autonomy or,
as was the case where the Protestants formed the majority, boosted and
extended their self-government (Knecht 1996, pp. 53–54). All of this was
combined with peasant uprisings against taxes, resistance to payment of
the tithe, and even the radicalization of popular groups in the cities.

As had been the case for the war of the *Comunidades* of Castile and the
Germanías of Valencia, the wars of religion brought to the light grave
problems within the existing social system. But, in the same way as in the
Iberian kingdoms, the wars convinced the nobility, magistrates, the
Church, the Catholics, Huguenots, and all the well-off sectors of French
society that the only way out was order and political stability. And this
order could only be achieved with a strong and absolute monarch ('an
official of God on the Earth'). This figure was finally embodied in Henry
of Bourbon, King of Navarre, proclaimed King of France after his renun-
ciation of Protestantism in 1594. From this moment, the political rhetoric
changed in respect to the theories—tyrannicide included—of the sixteenth
century (Holt 1995, pp. 213–216). The treasury reforms of Sully strengthened royal power and gave it new resources of patronage that allowed it
both to attract elites and to oversee the restructuring of the dominant
coalition (Salmon 1975, pp. 276–308). If religious conflict did not entirely
disappear, the confrontation over different creeds was overcome for the
moment. This supposed a decisive step forward for order and the reproduction of the social and political systems. The economic consequences of
this situation would be crucial.

In England the institutional system that emerged from the medieval crisis had less scope to redistribute rents and revenues among the elites (Chap. 1). A large part of the Crown's income came from its own royal patrimony or from import and export duties.[3] The social dominium of aristocratic lineages was maintained by extending their possessions and the establishment of great estates (Brenner 1993). Given the limits of the fiscal system, the urban oligarchies enjoyed fewer chances to exploit their autonomy or to mediate the collection of taxes. Shortly, they found themselves committed to the consolidation of their agrarian properties or to commerce as a means of expansion. Although this was a zone of very low levels of urbanization at the start of the century, the town oligarchies achieved very noticeable levels of economic and demographic growth based upon significant improvements in commerce, urbanization, and extensive agriculture that brought about an increase in productivity.[4] Probably this growth is most clearly reflected in the accelerating rhythms of urbanization. Moreover, these rates may be underrepresenting economic progress, if we take into account the extension of the *putting out system* which led to a high level of industrial productivity without a proportional development of the major cities.

The institutional system suffered from crucial problems. As in Castile, the aristocracy had to make assiduous use of credit (Stone 1979, p. 509). The growth of the regular income of the Crown was being steadily mitigated by the rise in prices, while royal expenditure shot through the roof at each and every moment of tension in foreign affairs. The Crown's capacity to increase its core revenue in England was lower than in Castile (see Graph 4.1). The origin of this limitation lay in part in the difficulties and costs involved in the management of the Crown lands (Russell 1988, pp. 31–33) and the slow increase in import and export duties, as well as in the stagnation in real terms of tax receipts (O'Brien and Hunt 1993). Henry VIII governed thanks to the support of the gentry in Parliament and the use of *statutes* that strengthened his absolute authority (Loades 1994, p. 411); but a system of this kind also increased the demands of patronage, manifested, for example, in a certain level of permissiveness in the cession of Crown lands to the nobility (Russell 1988, p. 32). As in other areas of Europe, the power system was already driven by grave tensions in the first half of the century.

---

[3] See figures in Hough and Grier (2015, p. 144) that come from Cunningham (2007).

[4] For this, see De Vries (1994, p. 13), De Vries (1984, p. 56), O'Brien (1996, p. 216), Overton (1996, p. 82), and Snooks (1994, p. 41).

The fortuitous factor that would most affect the reproduction of the social and institutional model would be Henry VIII's break with Rome and the creation of the Church of England. Despite the personal origins of this decision, it must be seen in the general European context, marked by tensions between monarchy and pontificate, as well as the Crown's need for increasing resources. Perhaps for these reasons, the effects upon the institutional system were crucial. The Reformation allowed the seizure and sale by the Crown of extensive ecclesiastical possessions during the reign of Henry VIII (monastery lands constituted one-fifth of the total land under cultivation) and then under Elizabeth I (the estates of the bishops).[5] This decision broke decisively with the model as it developed in Castile, which was based upon the amplification of ecclesiastical properties, and would have enormous impact upon the assignation of productive factors and the political economy (Chaps. 4 and 5).

The English Reformation also turned out to be crucial for economic and social development. It fed the expansion of the noble and gentry estates, the principal purchasers of the church lands. It permitted the promotion and reproduction of both social groups upon the basis of the establishment of extensive properties and, moreover, strengthened their affinities with the Crown as a result of the rupture with Rome, leading to a corresponding tightening of Crown control over this new nobility of proprietors (Hill 1969, p. 35; Stone 1979).

During the reign of Elizabeth (1558–1603), the rise of the gentry, the purchase of honours, and the problems of the old aristocratic lineages became more noticeable (Stone 1979, pp. 250–257). Unable to exert a firm grip over their possessions as enjoyed by their counterparts in Castile (achieved through the semi-public institution of the *mayorazgos*, combined with the peculiar system of mortgages taken out on possessions tied to them), denied access to a highly evolved fiscal apparatus such as that of Castile and even France, and without an empire and an international composite monarchy, such as the Spanish one that would allow the nobility to enjoy both massive incomes from the state and political space in which to expand, the English aristocrats' indebtedness would lead them to sell their possessions, a measure that successively renewed and changed their social group.

---

[5] Hough and Grier (2015, pp. 144–145), based mainly on Elton (1953, pp. 247–249) and Black (1959, pp. 14–34).

The social role of the high nobility began to change from the last years of the sixteenth century. The need to exploit its estates more intensively and efficiently and to invest in different sectors of the economy reduced the importance of the economy of legitimation (Chaps. 1 and 4) of many families (Stone 1979). The military character of the class disappeared almost entirely to the extent that war now depended upon the navy, an institution relatively highly controlled by the monarch and therefore crucial for state building (Glete 2000, pp. 67 and 147). If the cities maintained functions of social legitimation similar to those of Castile or France, their involvement in the fiscal system and in the distribution of resources was much less pronounced than in these countries, a factor that would affect their role in the institutional system (Chap. 4).

In some regards the political economy of England at the end of the century was similar to that of Castile or France. The judicial system had certainly developed, but corporative institutions controlled by merchants, such as the Merchant Adventurer Companies (Brenner 1993), the cities, or the old nobility, created forms of self-enforcement that limited the monarch's capacity for arbitration and juridical coercion. But in this regard, the evolution was very different, and, more important, the elites' coalition had been broken, and this led the country along a road of no return (in distinction to France), thus making it an exceptional case in the history of Europe. Despite the court corruption and patronage denounced during the reigns of James I (1603–1625) and Charles I (1625–1649), the merchant classes and the high nobility continued to enjoy far fewer chances to consolidate and extend its power though the institutions, access to political incomes or patronage, and corruption than their counterparts in Castile and Portugal—with all their empires—or even France. For the English nobles, it was necessary to return to overseas commerce while exerting pressure upon Parliament for a foreign policy that ranked commerce above dynastic or noble interests and that would override the concerns of those corporations that were constituted as the Merchant Adventurers (Brenner 1993). These overseas merchants retained a number of powers and even enjoyed a noticeable degree of access to violence that would afford them a certain advantage in the use of methods of enforcement. But they would slowly convert themselves into great agricultural proprietors and mine-owners, while their jurisdictional powers were steadily reduced. For this reason, they found it increasingly important to introduce productive improvements that would increase the efficiency of their mines and farming estates, even if this entailed rising social tensions with their subjects that came to cost them their image as paternalists and defenders of the traditional order (Stone 1979). Nothing like a double economy as described or as could be found in Castile was discernible in the isles, at least not with similar dimensions (Yun 2002a). In contrast to the *mayorazgos*, the English *strict settlements* were not adorned with any institutional mechanism that prevented the dissolution of patrimonies, and, consequently, they were not effective in this sense (Habakkuk 1994). And nothing like a network of ecclesiastical institutions governed by criteria of pure social profitability and legitimation existed in dimensions comparable to those of Castile, France, or even Portugal. Although what is referred to in this study as the economy of legitimation appears to be highly developed to English historians, who use the term 'economy of welfare', it is almost certain that English provision and spending would not resist comparison with the figures from the continent (Archer 1991; Slack 2015, p. 64).

Yet if this process had produced only partial effects, the outcome of this rupture was evident before the changes usually dated to 1688 (North and Weingast 1989): it would be manifested in social instability and political tensions leading to the decisive breakdown of 1640.[6]

The development of the Low Countries during the Middle Ages had been based upon commercial and industrial growth. The nobility, if present and significant in many areas, had much less economic, social, and—above all—jurisdictional power than in Castile or France (Van Nierop 1984, pp. 38–39; Israel 1995). Political fragmentation was reflected in considerable fiscal segmentation, and this compelled Charles V to enter into a seemingly endless round of separate negotiations (Chap. 4). Like his grandfather, the Emperor Maximilian, Charles V did not attempt to introduce radical changes in political and institutional organizations (Koenigsberger 1971, pp. 125–143). Despite reforming the treasury and arrangements governing the central finances, he did not carry out changes that would have resolved tensions between the Crown and the estates or between the provinces. The fiscal needs of the kingdom were covered largely by credit agreements set upon Crown possessions. But, given their

---

[6] These arguments, first presented in a more intuitive way in Yun (2004), have been clarified and given depth by Hough and Grier (2015, pp. 137–149) from whom some of these ideas are borrowed. Some nuance should be introduced to the vision presented by North and Weingast (1989) where the change is dated to the transformations of 1640 and more specifically 1688. Both visions are not mutually exclusive.

decline and indebtedness—in the 1520s they barely brought in 16% of overall income—it was impossible not to recur to voted subsidies from the estates and the development of the fiscal state.[7] The outcome would be a marked dependence upon the parliamentary assemblies that controlled not only the vote on the services but also the collection of these incomes and the emission of *renten*, debt bonds that allowed money to be advanced to the Crown (Tracy 1985). As in other kingdoms, a system of this sort brought with it the risk of corruption and bribery that would reduce the final amount collected (Koenigsberger 1971, pp. 166–175).

Set in the most dynamic area of European poly-nuclear economic growth, and with an ever-more intensive agriculture, the economic expansion of this region was very impressive, as can be seen from its high rates of urbanization (Van der Wee and Blomme 1994; Klep 1988; Israel 1995, pp. 113–116). This model, however, created important tendencies towards social instability. The scope for development of an aristocracy that might exercise coercion in alliance with the Crown, and so guarantee social order, was minimal. Moreover this group, which also had considerable debts, quickly overcame them through improvements in its productive system (Van Nierop 1984). In reality, this was the only viable option in light of the limits of the system for the redistribution of incomes, given the overall curbs on a system fully controlled by the states and the extent to which Castilian families were displacing their Flemish and Dutch peers in the government of the monarchy (Koenigsberger 1971). And something similar might be said of the businessmen and artisans whose social reproduction depended upon their involvement in the international market rather than upon political or fiscal incomes that could be obtained at the local level. If the cities maintained and even strengthened their fiscal autonomy, the urban economy rested upon other pillars that rendered it less dependent upon this fact.

Taxes upon commerce and consumption, the Habsburg wars—above all those with France—and fiscal demands had a destabilizing effect (Tracy 1985, pp. 75–107). The preoccupation in Madrid with religious 'contamination' led to the establishment of the Inquisition, a measure that alarmed and enraged the Protestants for obvious reasons and others on the grounds of foreign political interference. The reform of the bishoprics and the control that the Crown sought to exercise through them strengthened the resolve of the aristocracy, traditionally favoured by the status

---

[7] In fact, these subsidies accounted for more than 60% of income (Tracy 1985, pp. 30–31).

quo, at the same time that a number of leading families were replaced by the king's men, thus generating a widespread concern about the reproduction of this social group through the two usual channels, the Church and the court.

In this context the decisive external factor would be, as in France and England, religion. Calvinism, gaining strength over the previous years, unleashed a conflict across the Low Countries in 1566 whose intensity would previously have been unthinkable. The repression enacted by the duke of Alba, together with his efforts to introduce the *alcabala*, gave even greater strength and impetus to the movement (Maltby 1983).

The result of the conflict would be a society very different from its predecessors, in which the division between North and South was clearer.

In the southern provinces, existing economic growth would be slowed down.[8] The role of Antwerp in the international economy would be temporarily reduced. The Habsburgs sought the creation of a semi-independent political entity, in which the patronage of the Crown in relation to the aristocracy was strengthened and with it the chances of reproduction of a dominant coalition more similar to that of France or Castile.[9] The reform of the clergy served to consolidate the ecclesiastical institutions (Parker 1981, pp. 163–164). But favourable conditions for agrarian development, the advance of the *verlagssystem* and of luxury industries (a good part of them aimed at the markets of Brussels and Madrid), and the tendency to subsidize the fiscal shortfall from Castile favoured economic growth that would continue until 1650 and which, as we shall see, would be helped by the Habsburg monarchy's increasing expenditures (Van der Wee 1988, pp. 347–351).[10]

In the northern provinces, the outcome of the rebellion was even more positive in economic terms. Despite the leadership of Holland, the United Provinces continued to be a fragile confederation and did not even establish shared fiscal apparatus (Israel 1995, pp. 276–306; 'T Hart et al. 1997).

---

[8] Van der Wee and Blomme (1994). The same impression is gained from the population figures or the coefficient of urbanization of the whole area (De Vries 1984, p. 46; Van der Wee 1978).

[9] The previous explanation can be seen in Janssens (1998) and Degryse and Janssens (2005).

[10] According to the figures of Van der Wee and Blomme for Brabante and Flanders, the growth of income per capita may have accelerated to 0.22% between 1610 and 1660 (1994, p. 91). For the evolution of the urban population between 1550 and 1650, see Klep (1988, p. 267).

But war—and by implication the external threat—together with Calvinism and republicanism, provided the mortar that would bind this society together above the pacts among the elites that were very different from those of France and Spain. Moreover, the clamour of war was assisted by a genuine financial revolution. Although no central bank was created (as occurred in England after 1688), the representative assemblies were able to control the cost and central budget, something which served to increase confidence in the public debt and the state's ability to generate income through the sale of bonds (Tracy 1985; and 'T Hart et al. 1997). Within the space of just a few years, the *renten* were being sold at interest rates lower than those of the *juros* of Castile (Graph 4.2a and c).

Obviously this society was not immune to a degree of political corruption or the practices of rent-seeking (Adams 2005). But the scope for the noble classes and merchant patricians to make use of patronage at the expense of the state was reduced. Intensive agriculture, commerce, global expansion through the VOC and WIC, and the export of artisan goods were the only way out: these were, above all else, the bases for the country's prosperity. In fact, the trading companies implied a different model for the devolution of functions. These were institutions that obtained delegated sovereignty from central power. But they were semi-private institutions that lived by their own capacity to obtain investment and impose themselves upon international markets and not by the udders of a state that captured and redistributed funds from the kingdom as a whole. The key to mercantilism was set down in this way (Adams 2005).

Italy cannot be approached as a whole in economic, social, or political terms. It was, with the Low Countries, the most highly urbanized zone of Europe, and the poly-nuclear growth of the century would only serve to reinforce this tendency. But it had one of the most solid seigneurial systems in Europe. This was the case in both 'republic states', such as Genoa, Florence, or Venice, and dynastic polities, such as Naples, Sicily, and Milan. Even in the Papal States, the cities and nobles exercised jurisdictions over large seigniorial estates. In the merchant republics, such as Genoa and Venice, the capacity to exercise jurisdiction through their central administrations had been one of the keys to the success of the merchants and financiers (Greif 2006; González de Lara 2008). In all districts political control and the incomes that they generated were crucial to social success and to the capacity for reproduction of both the urban patriciate and the aristocracy (this was the case even if, as in Genoa or Venice, this had a financial basis).

As in all of Europe, the problems of falling salaries, poverty, the rising cost of land, and farm evictions were evident across the Italian Peninsula

(Braudel 1976, vol. I, pp. 602–604). And not a few problems originated in the rigidities of feudal rents, the need for expansion of the lineages, and the social ambitions of the patricians. In the South, banditry, nurtured in part by the local nobilities, was increasingly noticeable, and the rising levels of debt began to be a feature of the existence of many families (Villari 1973; Cancila 2013). This tension was also evident within the commercial and financial aristocracy of Genoa, where the fight between the *nobili nuovi* and *nobili vecchi* in 1575 laid bare to the world the conflicts originating in the dynamism of these elites (Savelli 1981). War and the demands of the Habsburgs accentuated the instability at crucial moments.

Italy, however, would witness the reproduction of the basic institutional framework. Religious stability, closely tied to the presence of the papacy, was doubtlessly one of the key factors in achieving this. Political fragmentation and the abundance of small states meant that social and political conflicts retained a predominantly local character and were controlled by the local oligarchies or by the Habsburgs, who presided over key territories.

The incorporation of a number of these states into the Habsburg domains had a destabilizing effect at a number of specific junctures. However, in the long term, it facilitated the survival of the social structures. The southern nobilities of Naples and Sicily, indebted and beset by problems of one sort or another, benefited from the patronage of the viceroyal courts (Muto 2005, p. 93; Galasso 1994). This also allowed them to form ties with the leading Castilian and Aragonese families, without doubt the most stable in Europe, and thus to secure a share in the political and economic capital which was to be the basis of the consolidation and extension of the elites (Muto 2009). This tie was also evident in the case of the Genoese families who provided financial services to the Habsbourg and discovered a form of social expansion—and, indeed, even ennoblement was possible in Castile—even if this meant exchanging financial capital for political and social capital in Madrid. Yet the court was not the only space within the monarchy that served this purpose. From the beginning of the sixteenth century, a tendency was established of marriages across frontiers within Italy or with French or imperial families; families such as the Gonzaga, the Colonna, the Visconti, the Spínola, and many others fully took advantage of such practices in order to enhance their power (see the case of Savoy in Osborne 2002). The proximity of the papacy and the Curia, whose membership was fed by these families during the century (Po-Chia 1998; O'Malley 1981), exponentially increased their capacity to overcome their own conflicts and accede to the immense possibilities of patronage that the papacy and the Curia offered (Donati 1995, pp. 250–257). The Habsburgs (in Madrid and Vienna), the Church, the empire, and even France offered local patricians and oligarchies the chances of stability and social advancement that were so important to them. The case of the Genoese *nobili nuovi* who were able to gain access to the financial services of the Habsburg empire is just one example. Their functions for the monarchy were considerable (Arrighi 1994, pp. 127–129).

The corollary of such service to the Hispanic monarchy was the enhancement of seigniorial jurisdictions and urban estates (in some cases, this took the form of the city-state) in many regions of Italy, something which went hand in hand with decentralized principles of enforcement. It is also evident that the development of the economy of legitimation in Florence, Rome, Genoa, or Venice would bequeath to humanity some of Europe's most superb examples of conspicuous consumption and artistic creation. This was not an obstacle to investment in the repopulation of territories in Sicily or to subsidizing those in Lombardy. But it would end by creating rigidities in the productive system. Nevertheless, these developments did not disturb the Italian Peninsula's complex political mosaic, which remained intact, as, indeed, did the jurisdictional fragmentation of each of these political units; at the same time, an urban industrial system with a marked corporative element was consecrated.

To the extent that the prosperity of the elites of Italy was founded upon providing financial services to the great powers, or in the vitality of the artisan sector of the cities, economic growth would continue to be noticeable. But the political and institutional evolution of the peninsula strengthened forms of political economy that were to be less efficient in the very long run.

Globalizing Agents

The world of 1600 was very different from that of a hundred years earlier, and globalization itself was changing.

Informal Globalizing Networks

Looking at the world in 1600–1630, what is striking is how it had generated forms of integration, control, rejection, and even ecological imperialism that would affect the European political economies in a decisive way. Primitive globalization came hand in hand with the development of informal transnational networks, often based upon what Granovetter (1973) called weak ties, which, if not necessarily Eurocentric, certainly would be decisive for the history of Europe.

From the sixteenth century, a process of Catholic renovation, in Po-Chia's phrase (1998), took place. It was to have a global dimension. The arrival of the Spanish in America and the Portuguese in Africa provided the framework that allowed for the global enlargement of the religious orders in particular and the Catholic religion in general. This process, whose only parallel in western civilization is found in the events of the decades following the life of Christ, was just another step in the expansion of medieval Christianity, including not only the continuation of the *Reconquista*, the eastward expansion of German society, the conversion of Northern Europe and Russia, and the movement known as the crusades. From the fifteenth century, the religious orders were active in Africa, following the Portuguese lead, the Atlantic, and, from 1500, America and Asia. Dominicans, Franciscans, and Augustinians from all Europe found a vast area of evangelization in America. They learnt languages, changed cultures, created forms of religious syncretism that attracted the indigenous populations, and introduced 'civilization' (often in a violent way).[11]

The Council of Trent and the Counter-Reformation accelerated this process. The Jesuits were already in the Orient. But now they began to attach themselves to the centres of power in Japan and China. (Céspedes 1990; Po-Chia Sia 2010). In spite of their recent ubiquity in current literature, they were really very few in number and came above all from Iberia. In parallel, the Augustinians expanded into the Philippines and South Eastern Asia. The establishment of the Spanish and Portuguese empires came to be inextricably tied to the expansion of the secular church and a network of ecclesiastical institutions that, like the monasteries and convents of the religious and missionary orders, established the nodes upon which systems of communication, cultural transferal, and hybridization would be based. These networks served to move persons and even—as the letters of the Jesuits illustrate well—dispatches, news, reports, and books. They advanced the cause of cultural integration and created and circulated images and stereotypes about different areas; in some cases they even led to the rejection of recurrent ideas and descriptions (Gruzinski 2004). These networks were even used to spread formulas for religious homogenization and cultural control, as was the case for the Inquisition, which was soon to

---

[11] The literature is vast. See, for example, Disney (2009), Boxer (1969), Russell-Wood (1992), and Parry (1990).

become a global institution (Bethencourt 2009). But, fundamentally, these networks, persons, and institutions retained a large margin of manoeuvre with respect to the monarchs' temporal power and, to be specific, to the Spanish imperial structure of Philip II and his successors, despite the kings' attempts to control them. European expansion was therefore marked by something that has often passed unremarked. Despite the proximity of temporal and spiritual power, it was based upon a dualism of powers, the spiritual authority of Rome and the temporal power of the monarchs. For all the involvement of the latter in the appointment of bishops and the exercise of patronage, this was to be a lasting and important dichotomy.

Catholic expansion did not come alone, nor did it represent all of the agencies involved in the process. Very shortly the Protestant societies created in North America their own nuclei of expansion. At the other extreme of Christendom, the Orthodox Byzantine Church was involving itself in Russia and the oriental frontiers of Europe. The same could be said of Judaism, whose development and expansion can be linked to the continuation of the process of expansion. These years witnessed what J. Israel called the 'revolution in Jewish life', 'the decisive change'. Spread across all of Europe, and often boasting Spanish origins, the Jews knitted together dense networks of cultural and commercial relations. Faced with attempts to contain them, these networks expanded into America and Asia (Israel 1985). Meanwhile, the expansion of Islam through Asia, towards Indonesia, the Philippines, and Malacca, and along Africa's east coast, the Sudan, parts of Ethiopia, and Indian ocean would continue throughout the century, being closely linked to the growth of Muslim commercial networks in these areas (Céspedes 1990, p. 57). It is also worthwhile remembering that, if religious identity formed the basis of these systems, these networks were the ideal stage for agents and mediators whose influence was not confined to a confessional programme. Once the contact among different cultural worlds was established, these agents transmitted many different types of messages (Cools et al. 2006).

To the extent that the Iberian empires became a platform for the internationalization and globalization of their elites, these institutions reinforced a process (mentioned above) that saw the emergence of global networks. And this process was more intensive from 1580. As occurred with the religious orders, this phenomenon was not limited to the relations between the metropolis and the colonies. As it also projected itself upon Europe as a whole, it bound the old continent and the New Worlds together in inextricable ways, with the areas of the south of Europe being especially affected.

These trends were not confined to the elites. According to official figures, about 130,000 Castilians emigrated to America between 1500 and 1580, many of them artisans (Romano 2004, p. 64; Martínez Shaw 1994). As their correspondence clearly demonstrates, these globetrotting elites took with them many servants and maids, members of their retinues, and even their friends and relatives belonging to the lowest social strata, all of whom contributed to creating global ties at all levels of the social hierarchy. And, importantly, the correspondence and testamentary records also show that many did not break entirely with the peninsula but rather maintained genuine links and networks (Otte 1986; Redondo and Yun 2008). Military officials, technicians, miners, and sailors, who had been trained in Europe, found in America, Asia, and Africa an area of action and even a theatre into which they could introduce and spread their knowledge, cultural habits, patterns of consumption, and so on (Centenero 2009, Altman 2000, Yun 2012). The 'oceanic world' (the Atlantic) was populated by slaves from Africa, many of them blacks, who, at the end of the sixteenth century, were already numerous in the Caribbean (as is widely known, New Guinea acquired its name as an allusion to the origin of its population). What is less well known is that they often lived side by side with Asians, some of whom were also slaves (De Sousa 2015). A respectable community of Chinese existed in Puebla, fed by Jewish merchants who forged links in Asia and the Philippines (Altman 2000 and Seijas 2014). This case provides a study of social groups who rapidly lost contact with their original societies but who were highly active in the process of cultural cross-fertilization and globalization that marked this period.

Commerce and merchant networks were especially active in the forming of this mesh of social and cultural agents. In spite of the attempt to control migration by the Spanish Crown, Italian families—above all the Genoese—followed their Castilian and Portuguese counterparts in expanding into America, often retaining a transnational component that defies any narrow national or political description (Subrahmanyam 2007; Bethencourt 2013; Kellenbenz 2000). By the mid-seventeenth century, the mixing of Europeans of very different origins was so advanced that contemporaries were unable to differentiate among them. This is what happened, for instance, in the Río de la Plata (Trujillo 2009), where Castilian and Portuguese groups settled. The last decades of the sixteenth century saw the flow of Portuguese businessmen into Brazil and the extension of their activities towards Argentina, whose direct connections with Africa consequently increased (Boyajian 1983). The entrance of the

Dutch, and subsequently the English, into the Caribbean and Asia is a symptom of this mercantile globalization (Boxer 1965). At the beginning of the seventeenth century, French skin traders made contact with the Iroquois and Huron in North America (Curtin 1984, p. 226).

This global expansion is just another manifestation of changes occurring in the old continent. Here the Jewish commercial diaspora drew in communities stretching from Poland to Central Europe to the Near East (Israel 1985). The Jews of the Low Countries strengthened their links with Lisbon and even with Burgos; from Lisbon they extended their ties with Italy (Ruspio 2007). In the other extreme of the commercial network, in the Mediterranean, 'the "Spanish Jews", spread out through Salonica and Constantinople, or through Ragusa, Split and Valona, taking control of the commercial routes of the Balkans' (Israel 1985, chapters I and II). The English, meanwhile, were increasingly active in the Eastern Mediterranean, in Venice and Greece (Fusaro 2015), and even in Safavid Persia. The Genoese could be found across the Habsburg territories, and families of noble financiers, such as the Spínola, the Gonzaga, and others, even established French and Austrian branches. During the second half of the century, the Flemish presence in Seville increased, while Italian activities in distant areas such as Gdańsk were growing (Samsonowicz 1973, pp. 538–539).

The ensuing and expanding webs of individuals displayed characteristics that are worthy of consideration. The first of these is that the political frontiers of empires were no obstacle to these personal connections. This would be more and more the case, as the analysis of Portuguese and Spanish empires (below) will show. But, perhaps more interestingly, though the different groups defined their particular identities according to their origin, religion, and family links, it is impossible to describe them in terms of 'national' networks, even in the case of Europe. This mixing of 'nations' was equally present within the old continent and was projected upon it. A Valencian noble family that achieved fame in Rome, such as the Borgia (mentioned above), demonstrates this point if we consider its American branches (Redondo and Yun 2008). The same could be said of the Corzo and the Mañara, both of Italian origin, that established deep roots in Castile and extended their reach into America, which in turn became decisive for their businesses (Vila 1991). In other words, these were not 'national' networks spread across the globe but rather a globalization or extension across the world of Europeans who, in many cases, were often already involved in 'transnational' practices. Some scholars might argue that Henry Kamen perhaps exaggerated in his interpretation, in which the Spanish empire emerges as not exactly Spanish (Kamen 2002). Nevertheless, an undeniable sociological basis sustains this view on, although the empire was far from singular in displaying these traits.

European Integration

Around 1600, these global networks served as channels for the transferal of products, patterns of consumption, and ways of life—and also for their combination and rejection (Yun 2014b). This reality was to have important effects on the economy. The population of African and European origin, as well as their mix with the remaining Amerindians, also grew— meaning both *mestizos*, the offspring of Spanish men and Indian women, and *mulatos* or 'mulattos' of black and white parentage. As a matter of fact, these groups grew in size during the sixteenth century and continued proportionally to do so in the following century, while the Amerindian population practically stagnated between 1600 and 1700 and so lost weight as a percentage of the total.[12] Obviously, the type and origin of a population cannot be identified with its norms of consumption. But, this having been said, it is evident that if this remained a small population in comparison with that of Europe, the number of inhabitants who sought goods and products from the old continent was growing, while demand for hybrid commodities and wares was also gradually increasing. And we should also remember that, aside from the 'whites', 'blacks', *'mestizos'*, and 'mulattos', the native Amerindian population was also adapting its patterns of consumption. Looked at from the perspective of the circulation of products moving in both directions, it is clear that, together with the extension of

---

[12] It has been calculated that around 1570–1600, Latin America had approximately 10 million to 10.2 million inhabitants (Romano 2004, p. 61), around 25% more than the Iberian Peninsula. Of these, the whites accounted for around 130,000 (between 1.2% and 1.3%); blacks, *mestizos*, and mulattos probably came to 260,000 (2.3%–2.5%) (Konetzke 1976, pp. 92 and 93). The rest, 9.8 million (95%), are Amerindians. By 1600 some 120,000 African slaves had been transported, and European emigration had reached 139,000 to Spanish America and 93,000 to Brazil; these figures reached 188,000 and 110,000, respectively, between 1580 and 1640 (Curtin 1969; Romano 2004, p. 64). By 1650 the black population had reached 830,000, the *mestizos* 400,000, and mulattos 269,000; the Amerindian population had fallen to 9,175,000, while Europeans had risen to 730,000, a considerable increase in both number and proportion (Konetzke 1976, pp. 92–93).

informal networks (in reality, both developments were part of the same phenomena), the empires began to promote patterns of consumption of a globalizing character (Kupperman 2012). This process was not easy, being marked by rejections, and often depended upon processes that were not purely economic in nature (Yun 2012). The diffusion of non-American patterns of consumption and hybridization was very often manifested in cultural, rather than commercial, processes and even in violence, which tended to follow in the footsteps of mercantile dissemination (Yun 2012). But, all in all, networks formed in this way accelerated the commercial relationship between the different areas of the New and Old Worlds. And this came at the same time that the presence of Europeans, and the processes of conquest and internal emigration associated with them, invigorated the spread of local American products (Saldarriaga 2011), and the arrival of Asian products also increased (Gasch 2014).

America began to export dye products, sugar, leathers, and other goods; true, the scale of this trade remains difficult to assess due to smuggling, but without doubt it grew from the middle of the sixteenth century and—something not to be overlooked—underwent diversification. Something similar was happening with the Asian trade controlled by the Portuguese and, increasingly, the Dutch, which also diversified. Pepper was followed by other spices and products, such as silk and cotton, indigo, clove, and nutmeg, among others (Boyajian 1993, p. 44 and *passim*). The processes ran parallel to the intensification of Atlantic commerce—and in particular of African trade—with America and Europe. Not only did the trade in slaves expand, but so did the trafficking of exotic products, fish, wine, grapes, dyes, ivory, and many others. And this was matched by the exportation of European products to Africa, with zones such as Morocco, Senegambia, Sierra Leone, Benin, and the Congo benefiting, while the commerce between the Gulf of Guinea and Brazil grew in vigour, and the Río de la Plata became more active (Russell-Wood 1992, chapter IV).

These ties not only brought distant continents closer together, but they also had a special effect upon trade within Europe. The result was a greater interconnection between the European economies. The evolution of urban networks is perhaps one of the clearest indirect indicators of this. It did not, of course, simply reflect the impulses of international trade. On the contrary, these links were closely tied to agrarian development and increases in local productivity that allowed for the emergence and advancement of urban industry. But it is very interesting to remember that around 1600, the process of urbanization was creating 'a unique urban hierarchy that was going to begin the fusion of the numerous European systems of urban' development (De Vries 1984, pp. 126–128). And even more important, between 1600 and 1650, a Europe-wide model of urban development was established that was increasingly linked to the advancement of the coastal zones and in particular to those of Atlantic Europe that were most closely connected to colonial commerce. If this cannot be considered to be the only cause of this change, it is evident that this was a factor in it.

The increase in the global circulation of silver gave further impetus to this process. As Attman (1986, p. 35) wrote, 'the enormous quantities of precious metals that the Spanish empire in America transferred to Europe ... were of the greatest importance for global commerce'.[13] The development of commercial techniques and the means of payment, as well as the increasing speed of transmission of commercial knowledge, had positive effects (Van der Wee 1978, pp. 306–332). Financial techniques developed in the south were adopted in the north, which hitherto had lagged far behind. As a result, deposit banks proliferated. The *ricorsa*, endorsement of a bill of exchange, became an even more common practice among the leading European businessmen (Van der Wee et al. 1991). The development of the printing press led to the dissemination of treatises on commercial techniques that facilitated the circulation of information on weights, measurements, and book-keeping or accounting, with similar effects (Hoock and Jeannin 1991, pp. 373–382). The expansion of insurance techniques was helping to reduce risks and transaction costs. Business networks further advanced these changes, lowering the costs of both transaction and information and making it possible to circulate goods between ever-more-distant centres. This was important for the extension of commerce into markets as imperfect and as different as those of the time.

If qualitative improvements in land transport remain difficult to pinpoint, it is very clear that ever-larger quantities of livestock were used, with the number of mules in particular increasing (Braudel 1976, pp. 375–376). Changes were also manifested in the growing repertoire of roads and journey routes; the inn system was improved, as were the available descriptions

---

[13] The European net monetary stock had passed from some 1021 tonnes of silver equivalent in 1570–1580 to around 2510 in 1590–1600. In this way the monetary mass in silver had multiplied by 2.5. Calculations are based above all on Morineau (1985, pp. 581–583) and obviously are very tentative. They do not take into account, for example, the melting of gold and silver to produce jewellery, which undoubtedly rose in this period.

of regions and roadways (Maczak 1996, pp. 37–53). But the most relevant changes took place in maritime transport, something which would be important in the displacement of the great axis of the economy towards the littoral zones in general and those of the Atlantic in particular. The pioneering techniques of naval construction of the south were spread across Europe and adopted and improved. In Holland this process led to the reduction of the sailing time between the Baltic and Spain; it also led to an increase in the size of the ships and their holds (De Vries and Van der Woude 1997, pp. 355–357). Other significant improvements continued to be made in the instruments of navigation and cartographical representation (Parry 1990, chap. 6). Oceanic navigation improved thanks to both institutional and organizational planning, developments that were manifested in the application of the sciences to the training of sailors in institutions such as the Portuguese *Casa da Índia* or the Castilian Council of the Indies (Chaunu 1959; Schäfer 2003). In the second half of the century, galleons and ships began to replace the old caravels, and both the number of merchantmen and their overall tonnage increased dramatically (Chaunu 1977, pp. 242–243 and 271). Writing of the Portuguese case, Godinho speaks of a recession after the crisis of the mid-century (1982–1987). But it is probable that the increase in the size of design of the ships soon compensated for this contraction to the extent that the highest figures of the century were registered in the decade 1581–1590 (Duncan 1986, pp. 3–25). This conclusion is strengthened if we take into account the upward trend found in the toll registers of both Malacca and Ormuz (Subrahmanyam and Thomaz 1991, p. 313 and *passim*). In this context it is not surprising that recent research on Portuguese cultural and political history in this period has moved from speaking of a 'crisis' to a 'reformation' of the empire (Barreto 2015, chapter 1).

By 1600 the growing quantities of spices (already a well-established phenomenon) and new colonial products arriving in the Old World were having a dynamic effect on other branches of trade. By this point European consumption of classical spices (pepper or products such as sugar) was rising, and new colonial products were bringing about changes in European (mainly European elites) patterns of consumption.[14] At the same time, the circulation of those products within Europe was encouraging new return

---

[14] The global production of sugar would rise thanks to the establishment of sugar refineries in Brazil, where output went up from 60 in 1570 to 230 in 1610 (Bennassar 1980, p. 158) and from 180,000 *arrobas* imported in 1560 to 600,000 in 1600 (Phillips 1990, p. 56). See also Mintz (1986).

trade routes between diverse regions and, with them, international market integration. Around 1567, for example, the imports of Spanish cochineal or Portuguese spices and sugar were already worth around half the overall trade between Spain and Portugal and the Low Countries (De Vries and Van der Woude 1997, p. 360). This commerce stimulated a reciprocal trade in other products, some traditional such as Iberian salt, and even reinforced return sales from the Low Countries, whose costs of distribution fell in line with the growing commercial complementarity between these two regions. All of this trade united with the inverse tide of merchandise that paid for the flow of Spanish silver towards the north of Europe.

It is not, therefore, surprising that even those scholars who have denied the existence of a 'revolution in transport' (understood as a continual reduction in costs from 1300 to 1800) have underlined the importance of the fall in freight costs in European commerce between 1550 and 1600 (Menard 1991, pp. 228–275).

All of these developments lead to a point for reflection. The process described above implied a long-term movement of merchandise that remained at a very modest level in terms of the GDP of the countries involved in it—above all Italy, Spain, Portugal, France, the Low Countries, and England. Moreover, the extent of American demand for European products should not be exaggerated compared to present-day standards. At the same time, it was a twofold phenomenon. The size of the white population in the Americas in 1600 (120,000–130,000) was not much greater than that of a city like Seville, which, as we said, still did not entail a big market for European products. But, on the other hand, that population grew to 730,000 by 1650. This is to say that during the first decades of the seventeenth century, America was still a relatively modest market but also an extremely expansive one. The outcome was clear: on the one hand, there existed ferocious competition for the control of this market on the European side, which can be fully understood in light of the colonies' high purchasing power; on the other hand, the market was already too large and dynamic for the countries that sought to monopolize it, Spain and Portugal, to be able to do so with their domestic production. And this situation leads to another consideration: despite the reduced size of this market and even of overall colonial commerce, its impact on the European mercantile economies would be quite significant. In fact, this expansion of international commerce and globalization brought with it the possibility that the more flexible and efficient economies would impose themselves upon the more rigid and weaker ones and also paved the way for increasing political and economic tension among Western European polities. In this context the impact of religious wars and the circulation of silver within Europe, partially associated with Spanish expenditure, would be crucial.

Habsburg Wars, American Silver, and the European Trends

In many ways the Spanish and Portuguese empires provided the crucial machinery for the transformation of the European economies.

Before 1566, when the rebellion of the Low Countries first broke out, the Habsburg wars had led to a concentration of war spending outside the peninsula. Moreover, the intense commercial relationships with the north and the Mediterranean also encouraged the flow of silver to these areas and the greater connection between them (Chap. 3). But these developments assumed hitherto unsuspected dimensions from the decade 1560–1570 thanks to the 'War of Flanders' (as it came to be known in Castile) and its tendency to drain away from Spain the silver brought in by the second cycle of American precious metals (Chaunu 1959).

It is important to emphasize that most military spending on the Iberian Peninsula was concentrated 'on the periphery' and, specifically, in the areas of Catalonia, Navarre, Gipuzkoa, Aragon, on the French frontier, Andalusia, Portugal, Galicia, and the Cantabrian coast (Thompson 1992, II, p. 11). The flow of silver in the form of military expenditure into these regions favoured their incorporation into the international commercial routes, the case of Catalonia being a good example (Vilar 1962). In this regard, the case of Portugal is also demonstrative. The increasing role of the Portuguese in the development of the commercial centres of Castile ensured that the Portuguese economy came to depend upon that of its Iberian neighbour and American silver—as well as Castilian currency—flowed in growing quantities to Portugal (Disney 2009), so affecting this economy and enhancing its links with international routes. It is worthwhile taking into account that part of the cost was spent on imported commodities, such as the woods of the north for ship construction, iron, and other goods.

But, moreover, the foreign wars of the Habsburgs affected, in a broad sense, the economic relationships between these areas.

Antwerp's fall was not a sudden one, as has often been claimed (Van der Wee 1963). But, this having been said, there can be few doubts about the negative effects of the conflict on the southern provinces of the Low Countries (Parker 1979, pp. 177–179). It was, moreover, exacerbated by a number of related developments: fiscal pressure was intensified, and the blockades imposed by the Sea Beggars affected another pillar of the Antwerp economy, its links with the south of Europe. The overall result was the dislocation of the system that had been so effective until the 1560s (Van der Wee 1963). English cloth would henceforth be directed towards other areas, and German commerce would flow towards the Hanseatic ports. Portuguese spices and Castilian wool would also be temporarily withdrawn from the Flanders route (Phillips and Phillips 1997, pp. 254–255). The trade of Lyon with Antwerp was also adversely affected by the French wars of religion and the shift of a range of Flemish industrial activities towards France (Van der Wee 1963). Antwerp's links with Italy were reduced by the fall in the overall volume of cross-continental commerce and the new links emerging between the subalpine peninsula and Castile, thus reorientating towards Iberia a significant portion of the shipments which previously had been sent over the Alps.

This succession of reverses would also affect the northern provinces of the Low Countries, although in this case the consequences were positive. Trade between Holland and the Baltic was negatively affected from 1569, confirming the difficulties facing the region and the deleterious effects of war (De Vries and Van der Woude 1997, pp. 363–364). Philip II's embargoes on Dutch trade had a short-term impact, in part because from 1580 he was able to use Portugal against the northerners. The war effort forced the rebellious provinces into a fiscal policy (resulting, inevitably, in higher taxation) that, (again) in the short term, had negative consequences on its economy.[15] Yet the downturn was only temporary. From the last years of the 1580s, the recovery of Dutch commerce and industry became evident. The destruction of the Spanish Armada, including many merchantships, made the Dutch indispensable in the Spanish traffic between Northern and Southern Europe at precisely the moment when they were re-establishing their influence in the Baltic, where they gained a foothold in the routes to Asia through Archangel; Spanish silver was, of course, vital

---

[15] Between 1552–1560 and 1588, fiscal pressure, measured as a percentage of an unskilled worker's salary, increased three-fold in Holland. The scale of this change was unique in Europe (De Vries and Van der Woude 1997, p. 97).

to Dutch transactions in both the Baltic and Far East (Israel 1989, p. 44). Moreover, a series of poor Mediterranean harvests allowed the Dutch to penetrate into the inland sea, thus offering them access to markets of ever-increasing size and value.

As a consequence, Holland and Spain, while still at war, came to find that their respective international economies could not work without each other—this was, in fact, highly significant for the strength of international commerce. Dutch merchants knew that Spanish and Mediterranean markets were vital for the wheat that they shipped from the Baltic; in turn this supply system was rapidly becoming a provisioning lifeline to the cities of southern Spain.[16] Fish (a staple food during the long Easter of the Counter-Reformation), light cloths (ever more adapted to suit the demands of the sweltering regions of southern Iberia), and other Dutch and Northern European products were becoming more and more sought-after in Iberia. Dutch shipping was also becoming vital to the export of Iberian goods to the north. In turn Holland needed ever greater quantities of Mediterranean salt, not to forget cochineal and spices from America, Africa and Asia. Above all else, the Dutch depended upon American silver, without which it would have been impossible to pay for their purchases in the Baltic regions and more and more in Asia. Little by little, these demands fed and merged into the Spanish need for Swedish copper with which to mint *vellón* coins in Castile (coin minting was rising from 1610 to 1620).

But it was not only the trade of the north of Europe that benefited from the flow of silver and the expenditure on war. In Italy the effects were twofold and very complex. The interruption of the axis between Burgos and Antwerp after 1566 caused a shift of the wool trade towards Italy and, especially, Florence (Ruiz Martín 1990a). The emergence of the 'Spanish road', a very narrow strip of territory between France and Germany that allowed Castilian silver to be carried to the northern theatre of arms, reinforced the position of the Genoese, who now controlled the finances of Philip II as never before (Parker 1972). The resultant changes left a trail of silver across northern Italy, whose businessmen were also able to take advantage of Lyon's problems to give impetus to the fairs of Piacenza. Spanish military spending in Lombardy, and the emergence of the Baroque court in Madrid, reinforced that region's connections with international routes (Braudel 1976; Sella and Capra 1984, pp. 109–115). American

---

[16] See the case of in Seville in *Cámara de Castilla, Libros de la Relación*, lib. 23, pp. 293 and ff. AGS.

silver flowing towards Italy must have been a positive factor for the integration of the regional economies of the Italian Peninsula's many states. Links such as those between Genoa and Naples or Sicily were strengthened by the purchase of large estates in the *Mezzogiorno* by the great merchants and bankers of northern Italy, who saw them as a means of investing in guarantied incomes and a way of acquiring wheat that could later be sold in the Mediterranean (Delille 1988). In Venice these changes coincided with a new flow of spices exchanged for silver in the Mediterranean and a general increase of Venetian participation in commerce from Sweden to Poland. This trend coincided with an increasing volume of trade from the Eastern Mediterranean areas to Asia through Safavid Persia.

War and silver, two phenomena that were always difficult to separate and were linked to the global broadening of economic and political relations, were becoming relevant to both the functioning of the European international economy and changes in it. These flows of silver sparked inflationary tensions in Northern Europe. But they also resulted in a proliferation of the means of payment, and this was beneficial to economies characterized by a strong commercial sector (at least, by the standards of the age).

By this time the trade between Holland and the Iberian Peninsula was restored, in spite of the increasingly ineffective attempts to impose a blockade. Annual transfers to the Low Countries grew to almost 4,000,000 ducats (Thompson 1976), meaning 1.4 ducats per capita each year. To this figure should be added the profits from commerce with Spain in the 1590s, when Dutch and Flemish merchants (the former illegally pretending to be Flemish) expanded their activities, mainly in Andalusia. The strength of economic links between the north and the south of Europe had become so important that the city of Seville itself complained about the reprisals, both fiscal and military, to which these 'nations' were subjected. Contraband and smuggling were the inevitable manifestations of this desire to trade (Gómez-Centurión 1988, pp. 257–317).[17] And though we do not have precise figures, we can assume that these activities sparked sectors of the Northern European economy and enhanced the international links between the different regions, thus smoothing out the negative

---

[17] No reliable figures can be given, but a memorandum on the import tolls of Seville put the value of the products unloaded at the docks between January 1593 and April 1595 at some 3.6 million ducats (Gómez-Centurión 1988, p. 295)—almost 1.5 million ducats each year, a figure that represented no more than the tip of the iceberg, given the level of smuggling and fraud.

effects of many political events. To a lesser degree, the new situation was also perceptible in the north of France. Here the arrivals of Spanish silver and the expenditure inherent to it were lower: 2.8 million ducats per year, according to Attman, which meant just 0.14 ducats per inhabitant or 1.8% of the agrarian product in 1588 (Morineau 1977, p. 979). Before the 1590s the positive effects of this commerce with the southern Netherlands had begun to be felt in England. From the 1540s trade with the Iberian Peninsula had remained relatively resilient; at the very least it remained stable and was perhaps growing, buttressed by the foundation of the Spanish Company (Brenner 1993, p. 12; and Croft 1989). Again, war and embargo did not have a genuinely tragic impact, and so vital were these trade lines that rivalries emerged between the merchant groups who operated in the Spanish Netherlands and the Merchant Adventurers, who traded in the Dutch provinces and claimed the right to control both routes (Croft 1989; Brenner 1993, p. 15). Another spur to commerce came with the foundation of the Turkish Company, the Venice Company, and the Levant Company, all of which took advantage of the growing connections of Spain with the Mediterranean and the experience of English traders in the Iberian Peninsula (Brenner 1993, pp. 16–23). After the disaster of the Invincible Armada, this activity grew quickly and even encouraged a greater interest in Atlantic commerce.[18] Two vital characteristics of this trade should be underlined. First, it was increasingly in the hands of the English themselves, meaning that an increasing proportion of it fed back into the domestic economy. Second, this trade was based not only on the expansion of the market for English products in the south of Europe but also on the importation of raw silk, woven Italian silks, spices coming through the Mediterranean, raisins from Greece, and American products (Brenner 1993, pp. 25–27).

The process—very much linked to the first globalization—in which Spain's foreign policy and economy served to spark commercial links elsewhere was even more pronounced in Italy. Here political and financial events came to oxygenize the economy, ensuring that many regions enjoyed a significant scope for expansion and their connections to international trade and finance were enhanced. The victory of Genoa in the financial battle for Madrid, and the continued vitality of the Piacenza fairs until 1621, meant that the Genoese maintained 'control over the world's wealth

---

[18] See Brenner (1993, pp. 26, 17, 30, 45–50) and Gómez-Centurión (1988, pp. 241–255).

for a long time' (Braudel 1976, vol. I, p. 671). This was despite the Spanish royal bankruptcies of 1596 and 1607. The need to feed the Spanish road also had a crucial impact on Italian trade with Europe for a long period (Parker 1972), and, as we shall see, it also benefited its industry until at least the 1610s.[19]

Several decades of warfare therefore favoured the redirection of trade networks in different areas of Europe. More importantly, the Habsburg empire and the first primitive globalization with their two main features, war and silver, had exerted a strong impact in enhancing a number of specific trade connections. Such connections were often interrupted but remained resilient and vigorous in the long term. But to fully understand their different histories, we need also to consider the local conditions and the political economies and institutions in which war and silver expenditure were acting.

THE GRADUAL SHIFT TO THE NORTH

The ways in which different countries faced the challenges and new international economic context at the end of the sixteenth century would be decisive. But this depended upon their respective political economies and upon the endowment of productive factors, the position of each country in the international economy, and their capacity to compete in more integrated markets. Competition among them also had become increasingly decisive on account of this process of economic integration that bound the areas of Europe and those of the rest of the planet.

1600: The Problems of Europe

In order to understand the consequences of this competition among economies, it is, however, important to consider the context that gave rise to it and the general problems facing them.

If regional differences were very marked—more so, indeed than national ones—by 1600 European society as a whole was facing a problem of

---

[19] Figures given by Parker leave no room for doubt about the relative importance of Italy in the payments made by the monarchy. If 11.7 million had been spent in Flanders between 1571 and 1577, some 7 million had been invested in the Mediterranean fleet, a considerable sum (Parker 1972, p. 232–236).

resources. The rapid increase of population (from some 80 to 100 million inhabitants from 1500 to 1600) and the accelerated rhythm of urbanization created evident Malthusian and provisioning tensions in Italy (Braudel 1976). But similar problems were emerging in France and England, where poor harvests and epidemics began a cycle of hardship that would last until 1630 (Wrightson 1982, pp. 122–123, and 142–148).[20] Even in the Low Countries, characterized by a form of highly intensive agriculture by the standards of the time, growth was based upon the extension of cultivated land (De Vries and Van der Woude 1997, pp. 27–28). And in Brabant it was possible to perceive a certain degree of agrarian stagnation by the 1550s (Van der Wee 1963, pp. 209–213). The higher rates of urbanization of these areas—a trait shared above all by Italy, the Low Countries, and some regions of France and England—created provisioning problems for the cities that sometimes threatened their economies and, in particular, their industrial sectors.

The increase in land rent accentuated this disequilibrium by reducing many peasants' margin of subsistence. To the extent that in many zones of Europe this came on top of a process of property concentration and caused a degree of social instability, it also brought about a number of productive adjustments. Although it remains difficult to measure social inequality, the figures produced by O'Rourke and Williamson on wage-rent relations demonstrate that the period 1500–1600 witnessed the fastest increase in inequalities in the entire early modern period (2005).

Trends in real wages are also downwards in countries such as England or Castile (Yun 2004, p. 425, Graph 7.3). If these figures should be used with caution, since in many areas of Europe cash salaries formed just a part of the incomes of peasants and members of the lower classes, this trend brought with it the permanent danger of reducing the purchasing power of many families. The result was the social uprooting and indebtedness of many peasants (Braudel 1976, vol. II, pp. 117–134). And with this outcome came the danger that poverty, Malthusian tensions, and social inequality would end economic growth.

In the same way as was happening in the Iberian countries, in many other areas, the development of the market and the juridical differences over the form of access to land provoked an increasing divergence within the peasantry. One of its manifestations was the emergence of a genuine

---

[20] Le Roy Ladurie (1977, pp. 576–585); Clay (1984, p. 126); Overton (1996, p. 79).

'peasant aristocracy', increasingly differentiated from the rest of its community. This change was evident in France and England, where authors such as R. Allen have underlined the growing inequality within the rural community.[21]

The inequality in the distribution of income undermined the chances of maintaining social stability within the rural community. Europe, and above all its cities, became full of poor and migrants from the rural areas (Geremek 1987). This was advanced by certain measures, such as the increase in the power of the seignior or the pressure of the *taille* and other taxes (Salmon 1975). At the same time, the development of the artisan sector, seldom achieved in direct proportion to the recognition of its political rights, created a number of tensions within the cities (Israel 1995, pp. 119–122, Lane 1973, pp. 318–319.)

The review of the different Western European economies (above) makes clear that tensions were also perceptible within the aristocracy and the seigniorial class. Even in those areas where seigniorial estates had been more resilient, structural tensions arose on account of the diminution of the rate of seigniorial extraction and the increasing expenditures to meet military and social requirements (Bois 1976; Asch 2003). True, European aristocracies were not ruined, as has sometimes been suggested. But this was a group subject to internal changes and in need of transformation. In the final analysis, the class that constituted the pillar of the social order was changing, a shift that, in turn, altered the basic structure of society.

From 1500 the escalating cost of war made everything worse. Historians continue to discuss the validity of the term 'military revolution', first coined by Roberts (Parker 1995). But what is clear is that the dimensions and demands of armed conflicts were growing across Europe, whether we accept a centralization of warfare or not. Bureaucratic costs and the need to feed the pacts of the dominant coalition increased expenditures, while the collection of taxes continued to depend upon highly consolidated local powers.

It is in this context that competition among the continent's different economies would act and be decisive. And this was because in these difficult moments, competition in international markets—including the limited but dynamic American market—would become very tough and crucial for the different regional economies.

---

[21] Neveux et al. (1975, pp. 134–135); Jacquart (1974); Allen (1992, pp. 66–67).

The Peninsular Interior by 1590–1600: The Limits of a More Rigid Economy[22]

The model for social development, characterized by the consolidation of the dominant coalition (Chap. 4) that had configured the political econo-mies of the Iberian kingdoms (Chap. 5), would make its impact felt from 1580. If all the Iberian kingdoms experienced similar problems, the impact would be different in each region. The peninsula's heartlands—a wide bank of land running from the Duero Valley to the banks of the Guadalquivir and from the Iberian System to the Alentejo region of Portugal—would suffer the most from this international competition. This was also because, leaving aside other conditions that will be examined below, it was here where the more negative components for economic growth would have greater impact. Since the last decades of the century, the more negative side of the institutional system (Chap. 5) would become predominant in the allocation of productive factors, which would reduce the competitiveness of the economy in a context of epidemic and economic crisis.

Long-Term Changes

By the sixteenth century, decisive long-term structural changes had taken place in this area. Many of the problems examined thus far for Europe in general were also present here: the tension between resources and popula-tion, the rising price of land rents, the fall of urban salaries and the imbal-ances in the distribution of income, tensions within the aristocracy, fiscal pressure, and so on.

But the situation would become even worse in many ways. The prolif-eration of entailed properties was reaching a very high level across the Iberian Peninsula but more in particular in this area. This fact is evident not only in the available data series on the foundation of *mayorazgos* (Yun 2004, p. 277, Chart 5.2) but also in the case studies of ecclesiastical institutions.[23] This irreversible trend obviously had strong accumulative

---

[22] The bibliographic apparatus and figures for this section can be seen in Yun (2004).

[23] Marcos (1985, vol. I, pp. 128 and 178); Yun (1987); Mata (1987); López (1998, p. 226); Pérez Picazo and Lemeunier (1984, p. 101). One of the evils of the kingdom, said a royal official (*corregidor*) of Seville in 1591 in an observation often repeated by the *arbitris-tas*, is that 'a great deal of property is being incorporated into the clergy and the religious orders by donations, chaplaincy foundations and the testaments of friars and nuns' (*Cámara de Castilla*, leg. 716. AGS).

effects and consequences.[24] The situation was made worse to the extent that the growth of the incomes of some seigniorial houses and religious institutions was very slow or even saw falls (Yun 2004, pp. 457–458). And all of this was happening while costs were rising and the economy of legitimation was gaining strength, propelled forward by the march of the Counter-Reformation spirit and the demands of court life.[25]

All of this had important consequences. One of them was that a greater proportion of the surface area and a greater share of the means of production were in the hands of the privileged and therefore subject to management criteria that, as we have seen, were now not always aimed at the introduction of improvements but rather at augmenting the reproduction of the political capital of the elites. Consequently, moreover, the rise in the price of land rents—a normal feature of the management of these patrimonies and one commonly employed over the previous generations (Chap. 3)—would affect an ever-larger share of the land surface and reach exhausting quotas.[26] Some seigniors even proceeded to raise other extractions, including the *alcabalas*.[27]

As everywhere in Europe, the long-term tendency was towards the polarization of incomes and a growing social inequality. This resulted in a range of consequences, such as inflation, the fall in real salaries, the rise of land rents, demographic pressure, and the shifting of fiscal burdens onto basic consumption goods that negatively affected a large part of the population. The same processes, together with the consolidation of entailed and mortgaged properties and bumper commercial profits, increased the wealth of elites. This phenomenon tended towards more progressive effects on consumption. On the one hand, conspicuous and luxury consumption was developing, tied as it was to the economy of legitimation, court lifestyles, and the double economy of *mayorazgos* and credit system

---

[24] See Yun (2004, p. 277, Table 5.2). Some concrete examples in Yun (1987, pp. 254–255), Basas (1994), and Gómez Zorraquino (1987, pp. 147–148). *Libros de Relación*, 18, 21, and 25 AGS.

[25] López (1990, pp. 79–80); Martz (1983, p. 172); Latorre (1992, pp. 209–211).

[26] Moreover, many seigniors and ecclesiastical institutions had to recur to tougher, more demanding rental formulas that would break with the criteria of the *enfiteusis* previously employed (Álvarez 1987, pp. 37–38).

[27] A variety of cases can be found in Pérez Picazo and Lemeunier (1984, pp. 98–99), Yun (1987), and López-Salazar (1987, pp. 101–102). The *Almirante* of Castile's *alcabalas* exceeded 1.3 million maravedís in 1568 and rose to 5.8 million in 1583–1588 and 6.7 million in 1589–1596. Libros de Acuerdos (respective years), AHMMR.

that allowed the nobles to assume debts without running the danger of seeing their patrimonies dissolved. On the other hand, the popular classes had to orient their preferences towards cheap and accessible products. Logically, these changes in demand constituted a challenge to industrial production, which had to become more specialized either in the production of luxury goods or in the most popular items and thus to compete in flexibility with foreign manufacturers.

A great deal has been said about the negative effect of fiscal pressure, which undoubtedly was increasing from the 1560s (Chap. 4 above). However, it is clear that, in macroeconomic terms, such pressure was not excessive, even at the end of the century. Moreover, public spending was also increasing (Yun 1998). But these perspectives do not exempt the state—or, in particular, the fiscal system—from blame for the coming economic difficulties. Taxes in the form of *sisas* and burdens on the consumption of basic goods (in part a consequence of the conflictive pact) limited the capacity of the artisan workshops to meet costs of maintenance and reproduction, above all because these ateliers depended upon forms of familial economy and apprenticeship. Here it is interesting to underline that, as we have seen, public spending was directed above all towards regions on the periphery—where wars tended to be fought—or resulted in purchases or forced requisitions that were often negative for economic activity. Moreover, the fragmentation of the fiscal map, which was a result of the pact between the oligarchies and the Crown over the matter of resource mobilization, was reaching peak levels.[28] And this same fiscal system was a background factor in the tendency towards rigidity of the artisan structures (Chap. 5). The sale of common lands accelerated from the 1570s to 1580s and had negative effects in the lands of the Meseta—or, at least, in some zones of the Duero Valley.

All of this was concurrently producing a transcendental and progressive change in the credit circuits in a way which has no parallel in other European regions. In the fifteenth century, the accumulation of incomes by the elites had had as a corollary a growing flow of loans towards the countryside and the productive sectors in areas such as the Duero Valley (Bennassar 1983). Now a sizeable share of this tide of money was going in

---

[28] The purchase of offices dedicated to the regulation of the local market and taxes collected on merchandise by cities and towns contributed to this process. See the case of Salamanca in 1577 in *Consejo y Juntas de Hacienda*, Libros Registro, leg. 41, sf. AGS.

the other direction and in particular towards the debts of the state and cities. We know, for example, that a new emission of *juros* doubled the consolidated debt between 1566 and 1577 and that by 1587 it had reached some 65 million ducats. It is probable that this would grow by almost 50 million ducats between 1566 and 1598, around 1.4 million ducats a year (Ruiz Martín 1975, p. 739). The overall consolidated debt in 1598 had risen, according to the figures (again, somewhat questionable) of F. Ruiz, by 80 million ducats. Another 20 million or more should be added to this figure to account for *censos* taken out on *mayorazgos*. This is to say that, without even factoring in the rising levels of municipal borrowing, state debt was above 100 million ducats, a figure superior to the available estimates of Castilian GDP (Cfr, Drelichman and Voth 2014). This is important in itself but is even more decisive if we add that this sum was already far above the size of the monetized part of the economy and, therefore, would exert a notable weight upon the cash flow and the chances of investing in the real economy.[29]

These developments were to have considerable consequences.

The peasant economies were also gradually losing degrees of resource elasticity, a quality that had been crucial to the economic expansion of some regions and strongly conditioned their management (Chaps. 3 and 5). The sale of wastelands (*baldíos*) and communal terrain was progressively reducing the versatility of the peasant economies, a key feature in the previous expansion in certain regions of the Duero Valley (Yun 1987). At the same time, access to wild fruits, wood, firewood, and other primary materials was becoming more difficult, as was the use of pasturelands that allowed the peasants to maintain small flocks (Aranda 1984, p. 143). These sales often ended jointly owned or collaborative agrarian land use arrangements that had been crucial to the previous growth (Yun 2004, p. 466). Many settlements found themselves unable to make use of the opportunities that the 'peasant industries' had previously offered them, manifested in the sale of small numbers of such products or of the goods manufactured from them (Chap. 3).

The sale of jurisdictions was creating uncertainties about the use of waters and soils (Nader 1990) that affected peasant markets and, consequently,

---

[29] On the way these calculations have been produced, see Yun (2004, pp. 464–465). More recently Drelichman and Voth have provided other figures, probably more accurate and based upon the *asientos*, but they do not change the argument.

the flexibility of family economies. Peasant commercialization of industrial products was rendered more difficult, due to the increasing fiscal pressure on these activities. Another of the conditions that had guaranteed agrarian growth and improvements in work productivity was threatened (Yun 2004, pp. 466–467).

It is possible to imagine in this context that the merchants developing the *verlagssystem* could take advantage of this situation by involving peasants in industrial activities, thus improving living conditions for the rural masses. But one needs to think that their capital was flowing in another direction and that quite probably the growing jurisdictional fragmentation increased problems by creating more barriers between the urban businessmen and the rural peasants. But the fundamental cause appears to have lain in the above-mentioned changes brought about in the credit circuits and the burgeoning fiscal pressure, as is clearly seen in the case of Córdoba (Fortea 1981).

This was, then, an economy that was progressively less flexible, in which credit circulated in a way that very often was not conducive to productive activities, where the land was subject to management guidelines that were increasingly rigid and where patterns of consumption were changing as the result of two fundamental phenomena: the impact of the crisis that would overcome the country at the end of the century and its capacity to face a series of problems that were met with greater success in other areas of Europe.

The End of Century Crisis in Castile

This scenario would be affected by a series of precipitating forces that, if not always negative, would severely test the productive system from the 1580s onward.

The wars in the north, the campaign for Portugal, and the problems in Aragon would oblige Castile to make unprecedented efforts that resulted in the increase in public spending to mobilize and provision armies and would have negative effects (Thompson 1992). The sale of jurisdictions and communal lands now reached unprecedented levels. The communities, already heavily indebted, that sought to buy them in competition with nobles and businessmen, found themselves compelled to increase the taxation on consumable goods.[30] Many of those peasants who were able to

---

[30] Soria (1995, p. 87); Nader (1990, pp.175–179); Pérez and Lemeunier (1984, p. 105); Kagan (1991, pp. 136–138).

assume control of lands had to support debts for many years. The new service of the *millones* would double the fiscal pressure. And, last but not least, the century's final was marked by a cycle of bad harvests and epidemics of unprecedented severity (Pérez Moreda 1980). Many small farms, and not a few large ones, were affected by similar pressures, as was the urban and industrial system itself. With regard to the former, some had to pay as much as 30% of their produce.[31] Factoring in tithes (10%), and seed costs (25% in the case of wheat), these detractions could easily entail 50% of the net product.[32] Given the high degree of land occupation achieved in 1580, the violent fluctuation of harvests, and the difficulty in emigrating to unfarmed soils, this tax burden meant that one of the most important pillars for expansion had come to an end (Chap. 3). This situation was made worse by the increase in land costs and their stabilization at the highest level ever reached during the century in the zones of the south, habitually welcoming to immigrants, something which demonstrated the difficulties in continuing the reoccupation of lands at low cost. The imbalance between pastureland and farmland, with a consequent effect in the availability of fertilizer, appears to have gotten worse (Anes 1994), and the increase, until at least 1580, of the price of beasts of burden and transport considerably complicated any prospective response to this problem (Yun 2004, p. 473, table 7.3). This came in the context of rising fiscal and seigniorial pressures, with difficulties in securing access to other resources and growing rigidities in family economies for the reasons mentioned above. In such difficult circumstances, the loans made available to these peasants in forms of *censos*, rather than acting as a stimulus to production and the mobilization of factors (as had occurred in the fifteenth century), constituted a form of credit on consumption that was vital for their very survival but could be lethal if, as often happened, they were unable to meet interest payments (Vassberg 1986, pp. 262 and ff.). All of this reduced the margin of subsistence and reproduction of the peasant family and rendered it more vulnerable to poor harvests and epidemics. And it also produced a reduction of both rural work productivity and the range of available resources, thus making it impossible to compensate for falling land yields as had been possible until the third quarter of the century (Chap. 3).

---

[31] As a result, land rent went up until it reached a century high point in the 1580s (Yun, 2004, p. 209, Graphs 4.5 and 4.6).

[32] Figures based on López (1990), Brumont (1984), and Vassberg (1986, pp. 224 and ff.).

If such hardships confronted the small- and medium-sized farms that predominated in the northern part of the *Meseta*, the situation was also challenging and no more positive for economic growth for the great tenants, who were more important in the southern *Meseta* and Andalusia. Rent from the *cortijos* (big farms) and pastureland had grown noticeably but had tended to level off from 1570 to 1580. Furthermore, a reduction had occurred in the real value of daily wages, and rents paid in coin fell in real terms. But it is no less certain that these farms were negatively affected by the increase in the cost of beasts of burden, which constituted a very important and inelastic part of the exploitation costs (López-Salazar 1986). Moreover, the difficulties involved in the commercialization of certain goods produced by the great farms (such as wool, whose price stabilized and then began to fall from the 1580s) were notable (Yun 2004, p. 74, Graph 7.4; López-Salazar 1987, pp. 30–31). The compulsory purchases for armies increased the insecurity of markets in many areas (Thompson 1976). And this came at a time that the large tenants found themselves facing stiff competition from the great rent collectors, the ecclesiastical and high nobility, when getting their products to the market. This also minimalized the potential positive effects of Madrid on their economies and on the agrarian development in general or had consequences that were so positive at the same time for Paris and London (Ringrose 1983a; Izquierdo 2001; Jacquart 1974).

This is not to say that there were not stimuli in this sense pointing towards the development of a new model of expansion based upon the great farms. As we have said, the very sale of wastelands and communal lands provided the basis for an agrarian capitalism in many areas of Castile and Andalusia in particular, similar to what was taking root in England. But, as we have said (Chap. 5), the result was that in many cases the process encouraged a type of management that was based upon the use of privileges derived from the control of local power or in the double economy of the *mayorazgos* and did not induce processes of innovation on a large scale. It is not that the big farms were untouched by changes. Considerable innovation was visible in the management of the great olive-growing estates dedicated to serve the growing demand from America. But, even in this case, this was really a form of farming that was not intensive in terms of local work (rather it depended upon seasonal bursts of a couple of months) and did not encourage immigration from the north to the south as had been the case in the previous phase of expansion. Of the distinct possibilities created by the institutional framework (Chap. 5), the less positive ones for economic growth were becoming the most common, and many of the most positive aspects of the sixteenth-century model of agrarian development were running into the sand.

The situation was no better for the urban economies. The problems of provisioning and the high price of foodstuffs posed certain difficulties for the cities. Taking as the point of comparison the relative prices of wheat and canvas, we can see that in the period 1550–1590, the relationship between the former, a basic article for the subsistence of artisans, and an item of merchandise that they sold was increasingly less favourable for them (Yun 2004, p. 464, Graph 7.6). With an agriculture that had reached peak productivity—and, therefore, very high prices of basic products—and with a tax system whose weight fell on foodstuffs, the artisans' margin for manoeuvre was decreasing. Of course, a few factors were in their favour, such as the stabilization of prices of certain primary materials such as wool or the fall of labour pay rates in the case of industry (Yun 2004, pp. 473–474, Charts 7.4 and 7.3). But even then the positive relationship was highly selective, because, in effect, other raw materials, such as cochineal, increased noticeably in price (Yun 2004, p. 428, Graph 7.5).

Tax increases during these years made things even worse. This rise in duties was not greater than in countries such as Holland where, moreover, a large part of taxes were collected as *sisas* on consumption (Yun 2004, p. 474, Chart 7.4). But, as we will see, Holland had clear advantages in this sense,[33] and, as we have just seen, *sisas* levied on the consumption of basic products at a moment of negative terms of trade between agrarian and industrial products could only have negative effects upon artisan workshops.

Clearly, the urban industries were passing through very difficult moments, but—equally evident—different areas had different capacities for reaction to these problems. The textile sector of Segovia was able to resist thanks to its growing specialization in high-quality woollen cloth (they were even exported to America) and to the use of a salaried labour force in some phases of production, which would permit it to externalize the maintenance costs of the workforce (García Sanz 1987). Toledo did

---

[33] It is fairly probable that an unqualified construction worker in Valladolid would have dedicated around 30% of his annual income to pay taxes, while his Dutch equivalent would have hardly had to contribute more than 20% (Yun 1999c; De Vries and Van der Woude 1997, p. 97).

the same, producing high-quality goods (silk fabrics) to meet elite demand (Montemayor 1996). But the problems were very considerable in cities such as Córdoba, subject to important rigidities and to local negotiations about taxes that did not always favour the artisans or their ability to adapt to new patterns of consumption (Fortea 1981).

The rigidity of the commercial circuits was also to have very negative effects at the end of the century. The problem would also become manifest in the wheat market. The imbalance between supply and demand would get worse when, on each bad harvest, the cities proceeded to prohibit 'exports' or to seize the cereal passing through their jurisdictions. The practice of compulsory purchases and seizures at the price of cost (Thompson 1976), understandable and necessary, further increased the rigidity of the market and, as usual in these cases, had repercussions in the price of industrial products (Yun 1980). Far from fomenting a system of multilateral interchange, the outcomes were a greater opacity and a number of new risks that delayed the adjustment between supply and demand.

In a large and mountainous country, with highly populated cities in the interior, effective and flexible networks of distribution that could adapt to all circumstances were necessary. But this need did not necessarily ensure their existence. The situation has been described by A. Sen in relation to hunger in the contemporary Third World: there existed a problem of supply and a concentration of demand in the cities; in addition, there existed problems of distribution that were related to the institutional framework and the network of local interests in this society (Sen 1981). In this context the transfer of the court to Madrid was a significant event. The positive effects of this move should not be forgotten. The capital was established far from the fertile soils of the Duero Valley, and in the heartlands of southern *Meseta*, still highly expansive in terms of its agrarian resources. From 1560 to 1600, the population of Madrid passed from 12,000 to almost 90,000 inhabitants (Carbajo 1987, pp. 132–138). Its positive impact upon the market and the surrounding areas was quickly felt. Madrid's demand contributed to maintaining New Castile's expansive wave of agriculture until the last decade of the century. Many nobles with possessions in zones near Madrid began to invest in agriculture. Cities such as Toledo or Segovia found a vibrant market for their products (Montemayor 1996). But Madrid was a strange addition to the established urban networks. Rather than grow and simultaneously provoke the reconfiguration of the urban system, Madrid attracted artisans and population from its surroundings, creating a vacuum in these satellites (Ringrose 1983a). The urban network of the *Meseta* would now enter into a process of crisis, which would last throughout the first decades of the seventeenth century (Chap. 8).

In these ways the impulses towards agrarian and urban growth of the sixteenth century were rapidly diminishing. Many of these problems also existed in other regions. But it was the centre of Castile, the region that had been an epicentre of economic growth, which was suffering the most from the negative impact of the institutions and management criteria created by the conflictive pact among the elites. The relative delay that would overcome the economies of the centre of the peninsula can, however, only be understood in relation to the comparative advantages of other areas of Europe.

The Advantages of the Enemies

The degree of flexibility of the different economies and their capacity to take advantage of international relationships were crucial. Both factors were tied to the institutional frameworks and political economies that resulted from the way the different regions faced the century's structural tensions.

In the 1590s the receipts of American treasure peaked at 11 million ducats a year, a figure which would not be surpassed for decades to come. At the same moment that the Spanish expenditure and the transfer of silver to the rest of Europe were increasing, the peace treaties of the early seventeenth century and the accumulative effect of the improvements in commercial and financial organizations favoured a greater fluidity in international commerce. The results would be a further move towards the integration of international trade and, with it, a higher degree of competition between the various regions: these conditions brought about an unprecedented fight for markets. In these circumstances the capacity for reaction depended upon the flexibility of economies, which in turn was conditioned by their political and institutional systems.

France's economic situation by 1600–1620 was much healthier in general terms than that in most parts of Spain, particularly its interior, and Portugal. France, and its Atlantic coastal regions above all, enjoyed more benign ecological conditions, with Atlantic climates bringing greater humidity. It also enjoyed proportionally larger woodlands in many parts of the country, thus permitting a triennial rotation of crop cultivation. For these reasons the agriculture of the north was more easily able to overcome the productive blockades without having to employ revolutionary new technologies (Jacquart 1975, pp. 216–226).

But this was not France's only advantage. As we have seen, the aristocracy's need for economic innovation was higher in France than in Castile. This was not only evident in the management of aristocratic estates like that of La Trémoille but also in the development of agronomic theories to an extent unknown in countries such as Spain (Weary 1977). Ecclesiastic properties were less extensive in France than in Spain, especially after the alienations of the previous century. The reduction of the *taille* following Sully's reforms also allowed the peasants—and, in particular, the owners of small farms—much more room to manoeuvre (Jacquart 1975, pp. 213–215; and Holt 1995, p. 212). In complete contrast to the situation in Castile, cities in France still enjoyed a more fluid relationship with the countryside. The French urban network, centred around Paris and gravitating towards the great arteries of international trade in the north, would encounter problems in the course of the seventeenth century. These difficulties, however, were relatively minor in comparison with the complete collapse and dramatic shift towards macrocephalia of the urban systems that occurred in the interior of the Castilian plain. Taking into account the vicissitudes of the various centres, the structure, spatial division, and density of the French network became stronger, with some scholars even speaking of a period of growing urbanization (Benedict 1989, pp. 27–39). Even with the changes brought about by the lowering of the *taille*, the fiscal burden appears to have fallen more equitably between city and countryside; at the same time, the *paulette* favoured the better-off social groups but only to a relatively small degree (Bonney 1981, pp. 61–62). The close links between the cities and the great trade routes, the development of the *verlagssystem*, and the strong impetus given to the luxury goods industries by the demands of the international market, including that of Spain and more and more that of America, may help to explain the cities' dynamism and vitality, which was also a stimulus for the resistance of the rural areas.

The results were a more flexible economy, a more even distribution of incomes, and higher levels of productivity in France than in most areas of Spain. This was especially clear in the areas of the north—those above a line drawn from La Rochelle to Strasbourg. Here positive conditions were engineered, with both urban industry and rural production fed by Parisian demand. Here also the war with Spain and the integration of the area into international trade circuits had some positive effects on the textile production of Brittany, Nantes, and other zones. Papers, books, and other products were also positively affected (Lapeyre 1955, pp. 507–596).

The development of lines of commerce between the north and the south of Europe, the incremental advance of Atlantic trade, and the high levels of agricultural productivity contributed to generate a relatively flexible and competitive economy in this area.

In England the model of development that had emerged during Elizabeth's reign was gaining strength and momentum. The impetus afforded by the markets exerted its impact upon an economy which, in clear contrast to the Spanish model, appears to have been exceptionally receptive and flexible. One manifestation of this change was the growth of London in parallel to other urban centres. As we have seen, the much narrower political incomes of the aristocracy and the need to overcome their debts compelled them to diversify and increase their investments. These were channelled not only into agriculture but also, increasingly, into mining and commerce—a development without parallel in the other two countries (Stone 1979, pp. 335–384). England was progressing towards an open society in which entrance into the highest aristocratic circles was accessible to the gentry and even to businessmen (Stone and Stone 1995).

An old interpretation, advanced by Kerridge, is nowadays questioned: this held that the years 1560–1640 had witnessed the strengthening of agrarian capitalism and a period of great innovation on the large English estates. Later research has placed emphasis upon a 'first agrarian revolution', led by a vanguard of yeomen and whose bases would be the medium-sized farm, the intensification of work patterns, and connection forged with expanding local markets (Allen 1992, p. 310). These farms oversaw the 'prolonged transition from mainstream agriculture to alternative agriculture', characterized by the introduction of livestock fodder crops (among them clover and turnips) and made possible by a considerable degree of flexibility in the patterns of crop rotation (Thirsk 1997, pp. 24–25). Whatever the origins of the English agrarian transformations, they cannot be understood without taking into account the relatively high degree of mobility in the land market in comparison with Castile, thanks to a system, the strict settlements, which were less rigid than that of the *mayorazgos* (Habakkuk 1994). In complete contrast to what was occurring in Castile, this development allowed the redistribution of land towards the more dynamic and innovative sectors of the economy.

These shifts ran parallel to the greater orientation of the peasant economies towards industrial activities, which saw the emergence of the 'new draperies', in part thanks to commercial expansion towards the south of Europe. This development can be seen as the prelude to an 'industrious revolution', to use the terminology of Jan De Vries (2008). The fact that an important part of industrial activity was in the hands of peasants not only reduced costs but also avoided the emergence of very large cities (London being the exception), with all the provisioning problems that this entailed for cities such as those of Southern Europe. English changes were also in part made possible by merchants' willingness to invest in rural industries that were the bases for textile exports (Wrightson 1982, pp. 143–144). With a smaller tax system, the public debt was also more limited than in Castile—and, therefore, its capacity to attract private savings was also reduced.

This expansive model possibly led to a more even distribution of incomes than in Castile and, by extension, greater opportunities for the industrial goods market. It also offered greater resilience to increased fiscal demands. The growing demands of the parliamentary subsidies notwithstanding (by 1600 these revenues were worth more than those coming from the Crown lands and customs charges), fiscal burdens were easily met by a more flexible economy in which peasant multi-activity increased per capita wealth at the same time as it regularized income and the monetary flow coming from abroad facilitated tax payments. Far from thwarting productive activities, the growth of land rents and demographic pressure in fact led to an increase in auxiliary peasant activities (transport, peddling, domestic industry, etc.) as a means of overcoming these rising extractions. Even if this model reached a glass ceiling in the 1630s, still the cycle of expansion begun in the previous century had been a long one and may even have witnessed the most rapid phase of English economic growth in the early modern period (Snooks 1994; Allen 1992). There is no doubt that English goods were very competitive on the international market.

The evolution of the United Provinces followed a path similar to that of England. As in Castile, the fragmentation of the internal market was remarkable due to the uneven fiscal policies implemented by the different provinces. As has been said, both countries had similar tax systems, with heavy excises levied on basic goods. As in Castile, Dutch industrial production was mainly based on urban workshops under the control of guild regulation. The very high degree of urbanization and demographic pressure also provoked food supply problems, particularly for wheat, in both areas.

But the economy of the United Provinces was better prepared for these challenges. Its central role in international commerce—and particularly in the Baltic cereal trade—mitigated provisioning problems. For the reasons explained before, until at least 1650, the Dutch nobility displayed a widespread inclination towards investing in agrarian improvements (Van Nierop 1984, p. 138) and were, therefore, more immune than their Castilian peers to the attractions of rent-seeking and *rentier* practices until very late in the seventeenth century (Burke 1974, pp. 132, 139). Urban patricians who had made their fortunes in commerce tended to see high prices and increasing demand as a good reason to invest in the draining of relatively extensive areas and the introduction of productive improvements (De Vries and Van der Woude 1997, pp. 28–29). This contrasted with the avidity for land for purely *rentier* purposes that was so common in other parts of Europe, such as Castile. Furthermore, regional variation notwithstanding, it was the small and medium farms that were crucial in this regard, and the improvements in land productivity helped to smooth the negative effects of the increasing rents paid by peasants at the same time that growing economic multi-functionality and diversification widened sources of income and available resources.[34] The development of fishing and the attendant pickling or salting industry rounded off the incomes of the Dutch people (De Vries and Van der Woude 1997). The arrival of immigrant artisans from the southern Low Countries in the Hamburg region (Israel 1989, pp. 30–37) and subsequently in Holland provided the country with the main economic factor crucial to the industry of the time—human capital. This allowed for the production of high-value-added goods and, consequently, enhanced the taxpaying capacity of industry.

An economy of this sort—oriented to international demand, characterized by enhanced productivity and high-value-added activities—was able to withstand increasing fiscal pressure on family consumption. But this was not its only strength. The solidity, high commercial awareness, and relative wealth of the middle classes—both craftsmen and *bourgeois*—made possible the mass issuing of *renten*, public debt bonds, which facilitated the development of Europe's first financial revolution ('T Hart, Jonkers and Van Zanden 1997, p. 22). Very shortly, these conditions allowed the great commercial companies, the VOC and WIC, to sell off huge numbers of their shares. In turn these companies came to monopolize trade with the West Indies, the Mediterranean, and East Indies (Israel 1989).

---

[34] De Vries and Van der Woude (1997). A definition of these two terms can be found in Durand and Van Huylenbroeck (2003).

These practices led to the foundation of powerful commercial institutions supported by private capital and a multitude of small investors. A development of this sort, unthinkable in Castile despite occasional efforts in this direction, meant the creation of organisms whose prosperity was of direct interest and concern to large parts of the population and which, in addition to being directly involved in commercial development, would henceforth serve as the basis for the extension of Dutch trade across the face of the world (Israel 1989). Progress in sailing techniques would shortly culminate in the birth of a new type of ship, the *fluyt*, whose emergence was primarily possible thanks to the availability of capital, although mention might also be made of a variety of other factors, among them cheap wood from the Baltic (De Vries and Van der Woude 1997, p. 357). In 1621 the war with Spain again broke out. By this time Holland boasted one of the most versatile, solid, and competitive economies in Europe.

If less dynamic, the economy of the Spanish Netherlands was not entirely different, although historians have often dismissed it due to the unfavourable comparison with the prodigious Dutch advance. War did, of course, provoke enormous disruption, but the recovery was perceptible (Van der Wee 1994). As in Holland, the economy was based upon intensive farming, with crop rotation (specifically exploiting tuberous plants) increasingly significant in some areas. Reclaimed land, such as the former marshes between Dunkirk and Furnes, attracted capital investment from the nobility and businessmen as well as the efforts of a multitude of small family farmers. Another similarity lay in the flexibility of agriculture, which was innovative and less burdened by seigniorial restrictions than was the case in Southern Europe. Industrial activity was not confined to the cities but was also common to rural areas.

If the great Atlantic-Baltic trade routes increasingly passed around the southern Low Countries, then its political links with Spain allowed it to develop a flourishing trade with Seville and Madrid (Van Houtte and Stols 1973). The consequent external demand, in conjunction with the domestic markets, fed industrial production. After 1560 improvements in levels of industrial production were only marginal, but the demand for luxury goods elicited a quick response in many of the urban industries such as silk textiles, tapestries, jewellery, art, and so on. This demand coincided with the survival of the industries where the *verlagssystem* predominated and that provided popular manufactures (knitted or woollen fabrics) (Van der Wee 1988, pp. 347–351). The transfer of Spanish silver, which remained stable after reaching a peak in 1605 (Gelabert 1997, pp. 49–54), continued to give impetus and energy to the regional economy and the circulation of money, a crucial consideration for a dynamic and commercialized economy such as this one.

In Italy, even after the peace signed with Holland, Spanish demand fed the production of textiles, weapons, tapestries, and other expensive products originating in the north of the country and consumed in the Italian and Spanish courts. The flow of silver and spending provoked by war had a positive side also here. The war and the strengthening of these trade circuits provided impetus to cereal production in the South, a programme the Sicilian nobles enthusiastically sponsored as a means of escaping from their crippling debt problems (Cancila 2013). Even those Italian scholars who argue that the model for growth was broken in the last decades of the sixteenth century emphasize the ability to overcome the crisis and the resilience of trade networks. Florence made full use of Spanish wool and demand for luxury textiles, both of which were crucial to the restructuring of its industry towards the production of silk fabrics after 1575 (Ruiz 1990a, pp. 110–147; Malanima 1978, p. 237). In Milan this same sector, with others linked to it, continued to advance with considerable momentum, as did the Venetian woollen cloth industry.

Yet the indicators Ruggiero Romano used to measure Italian vitality until 1619–1620, like other sources explored more recently by scholars, offer clear evidence of problems. These studies do not, of course, reveal a recession of uniform depth and characteristics across the entire peninsula.[35] But, by 1620, the rigidity of the Italian economy was clearly greater than those of its northern rivals.

One of the problems was of a Malthusian character, manifest in the famines and high grain prices of the 1590s and resulting in a lowering of the demand for industrial goods. Skilled workers were being squeezed by rising costs of living. The result, as one Elizabethan traveller would note, was that grain was now more costly than in England—34% more expensive, according to Vigo (1998, p. 280). But this was not the only obstacle.

At the heart of everything stood the problem of market integration and economic structures. The extreme political fragmentation of the Italian Peninsula had meant that the numerous local economies had never properly integrated—a fact reflected in the concave distribution of the

---

[35] The high point of woollen cloth production was reached in 1591–1600; after this point the tailing off was unchecked. The fall of the 'tassa sull'ancoragio' is also evident from 1603 to 1605 (Romano 1962, pp. 492 and 501); the same can be said about urban production of silk fabrics (Ciriacono 1988, pp. 46–47; Vigo 1998).

urban network, which had not changed in this respect (De Vries 1984), and which raised the cost of the transport of wheat. In moments of dearth, the zones with a surplus found it difficult to provision the industrial areas of the north. Political disunity also posed an obstacle to the movement of primary materials for industry. An area with such an advanced technical division of labour, and with an industrial population that was clearly dissociated from food production, easily passed these additional costs onto prices (Vigo 1998, p. 280).

Another problem lay in the lack of flexibility and scope for innovation among the artisan sector, which reduced the degree of integration between city and rural areas.[36] Florence provides a good example. Throughout the seventeenth century, rural and urban industrial sectors remained separate (Malanima 1988). P. Malanima has stressed that the high opportunity costs and inherent risks were obstacles to change in mature economies such as these (Malanima 1998). Similar arguments gain strength if we factor in the existence in Italy of alternative investment strategies which, from the end of the sixteenth century, had attracted capital to purchase land (but not always to gain higher levels of productivity), fiefs, political offices, and so on. All of these considerations underline the fact that investors harboured profound doubts about the direction of imperial policy, which was very unlikely to be formulated for their benefit.

This structural rigidity appears to have had other consequences. The model of an 'Italian' agriculture unable or unwilling to change has been abandoned, at least in relation to the north of the peninsula. In Lombardy and even in Tuscany, efforts were made to improve fields and to extend the mulberry tree throughout the seventeenth century; these labours were sponsored by the great landowners who invested in them their fortunes, which had generally been obtained in commerce. Yet this trend could also lead to serious blockages, such as the one that overcame the Tuscan textile industry. Here the development of the *verlagssystem*, with a rural cycle, was obstructed by new farming techniques depending upon high-intensity labour throughout the year, thus reducing the time that peasants could devote to domestic industrial activities (Malanima 1988).

The eye-catching development of the financial and fiscal systems of the Italian city-states and kingdoms also had a negative effect. In the city-states of the north, as in the kingdoms of the south, these schemes resulted in a growth of public debt. In turn bankers and merchants came to see the option of loaning monies to governments as 'much more attractive than

---

[36] P. Malanima sees the lack of flexibility in the Italian industrial economy as a result of its excessive 'maturity' (1998).

investing in industry'.[37] These were, moreover, political systems that generated highly evolved patronage structures, offering numerous offices and incomes to elites, thus further reducing the attraction of risky investments in industry. Another attractive investment for the great noble and banking families was the purchase of works of art, buildings, and palaces or in financing diplomatic or military careers.

Clearly, improvement was possible in Italy or Southern Europe in general. But, when set in comparative terms, the disadvantages of this system in comparison to the changes taking place in Northern Europe were obvious. Set against Dutch arrangements (its chief competitor), the Italian 'crisis' of the first decades of the seventeenth century was one of relative recession and readjustment. The maps representing the European urban networks in 1600 and 1650 (Maps 6.1 and 6.2) as well as the map representing the European urban trends (Map 8.3) are very meaningful regarding the extent to which the shift of economic development towards Southern England and the Low Countries was taking place.

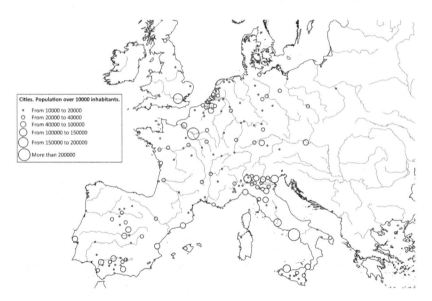

Map 6.1   European urban networks, 1600
Sources: My own elaboration with data from De Vries (1984) and my data of Spanish towns.

---

[37] The phrase comes from Davidson (1985, pp. 163–164) and refers to Venice. See also the case of Naples (Calabria 1991, pp. 104–147).

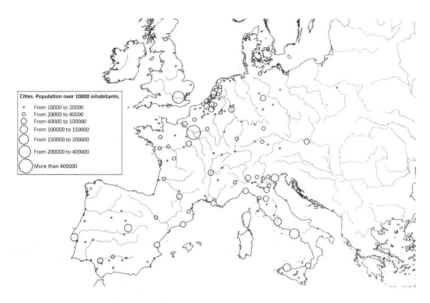

Map 6.2 European urban networks, 1650
Sources: My own elaboration with data from De Vries (1984) and my data of Spanish towns.

*   *   *

By 1600 European globalization had escaped the hands of governments. In truth, they had never controlled it. But by this point, a series of informal networks were beyond their reach. It is often remarked that the king in Madrid was unable to exercise his monopoly in the Indies, as well as in Africa and, even more, in Asia, to control emigration to them or the merchandise that was sent to—or received from—them. This failure was, however, nothing more than a reflection of how empires were—and are—unable to control the circulation of merchandise, goods, ideas, and persons. Understanding this incapacity is vital for what will follow.

At the same time and in spite of the small numbers that globalization meant in commercial terms, it was having profound effects on the life of Europeans. As we have seen in Chap. 4, its first steps had been crucial for the reproduction of the social order and institutional framework on the Iberian Peninsula. But the formation of global connections would be also decisive for many other areas of Europe: it enhanced the integration of international markets within Europe, thus increasing economic and political competition among European polities.

Here, we have tried to argue that, among other factors which fall out-side of our study, the capacity of the different countries to overcome tensions and, above all, of the dominant coalitions to reproduce themselves was indirectly tied to their position with respect to globalization and imperial connections. By analysing how the different challenges that those societies faced were addressed, one can better understand the role of their empires in Iberian societies and more in particular in Castile and Portugal.

The availability of silver and imperial resources in Castile and Portugal, which were also part of the globalizing process, was an important factor for the evolution of many Western European regions. And these factors, combining with internal ones, in which religion and religious confrontation were not negligible, were behind the breakdown (or survival and deep recomposition) of the different areas' dominant coalitions. Those factors were also behind essential changes—often forgotten in the study of European political economies—that affected the degree of efficiency in the use of resources in relation to economic growth. It should be emphasized—and should be clear from the previous pages—that the term political economy cannot be reduced to the simple working of formal institutions. Essential aspects—such as the creation of confidence—did not depend only upon such institutions: nor, in the short term, did growth and crisis. A range of aspects such as the position of each country in the transnational networks that distributed these resources, the different endowments of factors, and the way in which they were organized in agro-urban ecosystems were important and would continue to be so in the seventeenth century.

Open Access This chapter is licensed under the terms of the Creative Commons Attribution 4.0 International License (http://creativecommons.org/licenses/by/4.0/), which permits use, sharing, adaptation, distribution and reproduction in any medium or format, as long as you give appropriate credit to the original author(s) and the source, provide a link to the Creative Commons licence and indicate if changes were made.

The images or other third party material in this chapter are included in the chapter's Creative Commons licence, unless indicated otherwise in a credit line to the material. If material is not included in the chapter's Creative Commons licence and your intended use is not permitted by statutory regulation or exceeds the permitted use, you will need to obtain permission directly from the copyright holder.

CHAPTER 7

The Luso-Spanish Composite Global Empire, 1598–1640

The impact of globalization upon the Iberian complex becomes even clearer when we look at the way the imperial systems were created and interlinked, as well as at the evolution of the global forces in which they were embedded. This perspective also implies a study of the way imperial institutions operated and how social networks on a global scale interacted with the formal institutions created by the Crown to try to impose its authority and to control different agents' agendas.

THE IBERIAN COMPLEX IN A GLOBAL PERSPECTIVE

Two Empires and One World

Recent historiography has underlined, with good reason, the numerous inter-connections between the Spanish and Portuguese empires (Subrahmanyam 2007; Bethencourt 2013; Borges 2014; Herzog 2015). Certainly, in institutional terms both empires maintained the rule of their respective institutional systems and implicit codes of practice. Portuguese subjects of the Habsburgs could not enter directly into Castile's commerce with America; Castilians, like subjects of the peninsula's other kingdoms, were classified as foreigners in Portuguese territories ruled by the same dynasty.

The Council of Portugal, in Madrid, was charged with providing advice on the management of Portuguese overseas possessions, and the Council

© The Author(s) 2019

B. Yun-Casalilla, *Iberian World Empires and the Globalization of Europe 1415–1668*, Palgrave Studies in Comparative Global History, https://doi.org/10.1007/978-981-13-0833-8_7

of the Indies oversaw affairs relative to the Spanish colonies. The *Casa de la Contratación* of Seville and the *Casa da Índia* of Lisbon, two very similar institutions, operated, however, with total independence of each other. The same can be said of other institutions with colonial reach and impact, such as the Inquisition. Though one can recognize the sharing of an administrative culture similar in some respects as well as the exchange of information in some fields, the two organizations acted as separate bodies in Spain and Portugal (Bethencourt 2009). Likewise, the respective branches of the Catholic Church comprised separate organizations, in particular in regard to the exercise of patronage rights and the appointment of bishops, and so on. And the same can be said about the transfers of money and military resources between the two kingdoms, at least from a formal and juridical perspective. The problem of the transfer of funds between kingdoms in order to defend each other's interests had not abated.

Nevertheless, on occasions this formal separation could be overlooked. At the very beginning of the union of the two Crowns, in 1583, an expedition to the Azores had been financed with Castilian and Neapolitan money, while Portugal was involved in the Invincible Armada (Thompson 1976). Similar situations, in which joint contributions served the interests of one kingdom, would occur over the coming years, as in the recovery of Bahia in 1625. But combined operations would be a cause of controversy. In fact, the Portuguese, who had never previously been involved in this sort of venture, claimed that they contravened the terms of the Cortes of Tomar (1581). Moreover, in time the Castilians would make the same claim (Feros 2000, pp. 159–161).

This having been said, the binding or entwining of the Portuguese and Spanish empires would gather pace after 1580 (Herzog 2015). Thus, when in 1641 the governor of Buenos Aires received the royal order to expel the Portuguese for fear of 'contagion' of the rebellion in their homeland, a member of the city elite responded with a strong argument: this decree, he averred, broke up 'marriages', preventing husbands from 'living a marital life with our wives' (quoted by Trujillo 2009, 350).

This entwining of Iberians was in many respects the result of two global phenomena, which are normally studied as separate processes but which were in fact very much linked: the development of new avenues of Portuguese trade with Asia from the 1580s onwards and the silver mining boom in America after the 1560s.

The first process is well known thanks to the excellent studies of Boyajian (1983 and 1993). According to this author, even if pepper continued to be the most demanded product, a generation of New Christians emerged who took advantage of the Crown's need to broaden the trade into products such as Chinese and Indian cottons, silks, porcelain, diamonds, precious pearls, cinnamon, exotic perfumes, indigo, and even exquisite Asian furniture. This trade, it is important to note, was sometimes diverted from the African to the American coast, arriving in Brazil and, increasingly, in Río de la Plata (Studnicki-Gizbert 2007). The second process, the silver boom, was in a certain way a precedent and a cause of this new commercial development. Since the 1560s what Chaunu called the 'inter-cycle recession' of the fifties (Chaunu 1959, pp. 255–352) was overcome, and the discovery of new deposits, as well as technological advances, provoked a new boom in the production of silver in America that would last until the first decades of the seventeenth century (Bakewell 1990, p. 81 and Hamilton 1975, p. 47). The flow of American silver and the difficulty in matching Portuguese imports from Asia with African gold made the Portuguese more keen to secure this precious metal, which they were already using in their Seville connection. Thus, through Brazil, the Portuguese began to obtain a significant part of the available Peruvian silver in exchange for increasing quantities of African slaves, supplying the basis of the plantation economy. Then, shortly afterwards, a portion of this precious metal was diverted towards the Río de la Plata. In fact, these exchanges were not only based on the trade in slaves but also on that of other less well-known products, such as Indian cotton (Boyajian 1993; Russell-Wood 1992; Studnicki-Gizbert 2007).

The impact of these two trends was crucial, and some facets of it have been mentioned already. The silver boom came hand in hand with the development of the plantation economy and the increasing export to Europe of products from these ventures. For this reason, American trade was becoming richer and more diversified. But this development also enhanced, as we have seen, the connections with Northern Europe, from which increasing quantities of goods were brought to Iberia and exported from it to the colonies (particularly America), with more silver and Asian commodities being exported to the northern half of the old continent. It is not, therefore, surprising that the old theory about a decline in Asian trade in the second half of the sixteenth century is not accepted today (Boyajian 1993), and recent estimates of Portuguese shipping to Asia corroborate this revisionism.[1]

This same process facilitated the growing dynamism of a new route towards globalization: commerce between New Spain (Acapulco) and the Philippines (Manila) that completed the silver belt around the world and allowed Asian products to reach Mexico—whence some were sent on to Seville and Europe in general—in exchange for silver from New Spain. This route even skirted the Pacific coastlines of America, reaching down as far as Peru where Asian products were sold in return for that area's silver. American silver, being of greater purity—and therefore value—than Japanese silver, even allowed for the reduction of the importance of Japanese trade in China, thus adding to Portuguese power in the China Sea. This trade, like others of its time, did not only depend upon merchants in the strict sense of the word; rather exchanges were conducted also by soldiers, adventurers, and above all missionaries who obtained notable profits (Gasch 2012, Palomo 2016). And this was also the case in the commerce between the Philippines and Acapulco (Gasch 2012).

This new trend also impacted the Iberian Peninsula. The presence of Portuguese in Andalusia, and above all in Seville and Córdoba, increased (Studnicki-Gizbert 2007; Fortea 1981). The links between the Portuguese and the Duero Valley trade (connected to both Seville and Lisbon) were reinforced and were even one of the reasons for the positive reaction of the Castilian fairs, which prolonged their life until the end of the century in some cases (Yun 1987). By 1580 the circulation of Castilian silver in Portugal, and with it the influence of its economy, was bringing about a noticeable Castilianization of the Portuguese economy (Disney 2009).

All this explains how and why the interlinking of Portuguese and Castilians increased in this epoch in the colonial arena, as has been underlined (Subrahmanyam 2007). But—and this is often forgotten—the same interlinking occurred on the Iberian Peninsula. Both Castilians and Portuguese created settled personal relationships and trust networks based upon common interests. At this point the formal institutions of the two

---

[1] The available estimates show that the number of Portuguese ships sailing from Lisbon to Asia was revitalized from 1570, following a slight dip in numbers in previous years. This trend would reach its peak between 1601 and 1610 (despite attacks from the United Provinces) and was maintained at a very high level until 1620. Very meaningfully, Portuguese voyages therefore followed the same cycle as the arrival of American silver in Seville (Duncan 1986).

empires had more or less clearly defined frontiers. But the cross-border character of their connections was a fact. This does not mean that tensions were absent. On the contrary, contact itself was creating conflicts. But these were two empires in an increasingly interconnected world. As we shall see, this was not a closed system fully controlled from above; nor was it a massive trade grid capable of producing a strong convergence of prices at the global level (O'Rourke and Williamson 2002). Nevertheless, the ensuing connections would be decisive for the history of the Spanish and Portuguese empires and for the working of their political economies.

The Problem of Information

The issues outlined above are essential to identifying the great problems of the Luso-Spanish imperial complex, as well as the principles that governed its political economy and brought about a profound transformation in it from 1600 onwards.

One essential, recurring issue regarded information, the slowness of its circulation, the problems in obtaining it, and the consequent difficulties for government and business. Governors were perfectly conscious of these issues and dreamt of obtaining what they called the 'complete notice', ('la entera noticia') (Brendecke 2012). But they also presented a grave problem for the individuals and, above all, for the merchants who flowed through the arteries of this empire.

The slow circulation of news was caused, logically, by the distances involved. The voyage between the metropolis and the closest colonies in the Atlantic was, in the case of the Spanish empire, some 13 weeks on the way out and 18 on the return, while in the case of the English empire, it would be between 5 to 8 weeks and 3 to 8 weeks, respectively, according to the route chosen (Elliott 2006, pp. 177 and 181). The problem was even greater in the case of the Portuguese empire, where the voyage from Lisbon to Goa might last as long as 24 weeks. Yet this was not even the major problem or principal difference with the British colonies to the North. Rather, the great difficulties sprang from the rhythm and rigidity in the circulation of reports upon which the organization of the *Carrera de Indias* depended, which in turn was caused by the climate and rhythm of the seasons, winds and tides, and so on. While the English empire depended upon voyages that were much more staggered and frequent over the course of the year until at least the end of the seventeenth century, the Spanish depended upon fleets that could travel to the Caribbean only twice a year and return only at the end of the summer following the timetable already set out (Chap. 2). A similar situation affected Portugal on account of the monsoons (Parry 1990, chapters 6 and 7). For this reason, the communication systems (essential for political and business organizations) that crossed over and between these areas faced considerable difficulties. If ships departed from Lisbon in March, even with fair winds, they would not arrive in Goa until September, and they could only embark on their return journey towards January or February, arriving back in Portugal, if everything went well, in August or September of the year after their departure (Kellenbenz 2000, p. 602). That is to say that the information, instructions, and orders could be produced and sent from the headquarters of the *Estado da Índia* only once a year, and the arrival of responses in Lisbon might in theory take as long as 18 or 19 months.

Yet this was simply the first step, as within the colonies themselves, several weeks might be needed to communicate between the most distant parts of the empire and the Caribbean or Goa; for things to work well here, a perfect synchronization of voyages and climates and no little good fortune were necessary. It is not, therefore, surprising that letters written by emigrants were often filled with a terrible sense of isolation and disconnection. References abound to entire years in which communications with the Iberian Peninsula were interrupted, with insecurity flowing from the loss of correspondence or the unexplained disappearance of persons dispatched, while consternation was sometimes expressed about the plight of messengers sent to find people who were perhaps themselves in transit and therefore unlikely to be located. On 20 April 1592, one Pedro de la Huerta wrote to his nephew in response to a letter penned in September 1588, in which he complained of not having received any word from his uncle in almost four years. And in 1562 Diego Martín de Trujillo confessed that it had been more than 11 years since he had news of his family. These were two cases among hundreds that have survived (Otte 1988). And the same problem occurred in the royal administration that, despite a dense network of bureaucrats, informants, messengers, and mediators, still faced problems obtaining reliable and timely information (Brendecke 2012).

In this situation, the creation of oligopolistic circuits of privileged information gave their members certain advantages. One well-known example is that of the Dutch merchants who wrote their famous gazettes to Amsterdam recounting the details of American shipments to Spain even before the galleons arrived in Seville (Morineau 1985). The circuits created by consuls, nominally merchants, should be understood in the same light, and these were extended across many parts of Europe and very often operated according to an affinity based upon common origins, as was the case of the Italian or Jewish communities. For its part the Society of Jesus came to arrange an entire system for the exchange of information, the so-called 'Jesuit letters' (Broggio 2002). In reality many of these arrangements were alternatives to the existence of a postal or courier network, although something resembling one began to emerge in America at the beginning of the seventeenth century (Montáñez 1950). Throughout the sixteenth century, the letters of emigrants repeatedly refer to entrusting correspondence to the merchants and sailors who sailed the seas, a practice that entailed a high risk of loss and news blackout (Otte 1988). All of this can be taken as evidence of the high costs of information and the need to create networks of confidence based upon previous relations or mutual benefit that guaranteed the circulation and veracity of reports.

The consequences of this situation impacted governmental systems. Without doubt, government both depended upon and collected a multitude of reports, visits, and accounts, which presented a fuller picture of events than might otherwise have been obtained. The efforts of viceroys in both Asia and America provided a good demonstration of these phenomena (Merluzzi 2003, chapter 2). As we have seen, in both Crowns a number of centralizing projects were proposed, encompassing political organization as well as the news and information systems that facilitated the exercise of power. But the news that circulated through official channels was not always accurate, and many times the reports that reached Madrid (or Lisbon) provided 'not the truth, but rather indications of loyalty and disloyalty' (Brendecke 2012, p. 492). Because of these reasons, the result was a highly asymmetric information system that gave its mediators enormous power through its transmission and in particular favoured those who collected and advanced reports and news in situ, the price for which could only be paid through the cession of political capital which made it even more difficult for Madrid or Lisbon to implement the king's orders. The political economy of the empire would be highly affected by all of this.

Social Networks and Informal Institutions in a Cross-Border Perspective

The projection of elites across this global empire explains why, in part, imperial spaces across four continents very quickly became traversed by informal relationships that would prove decisive for their history. And this development was evident not only on the vast oceans, upon which historians have focused their attention, but also in Europe itself. This was, in many ways, a phenomenon that was unique to the period and of the fact that its politics had a corporate character.

The formation of these networks was often, but not always, an indirect consequence of possibilities for the social consolidation and extension of elites who had been present in the creation of the empire and in the process of globalization (Chap. 4). As we have said, these were social groups governed by two essential tensions—between solidarity and conflict and, at the same time, between the individual and the collective (see Chap. 1)—and as such could do nothing but project these same rules of play upon the empire itself. If there was a certain tendency towards rupture among the branches of each continent, there was also an intention to maintain contacts. In some cases this desire was expressed through networks, where contact was essential for the interests of individuals, as would be the case for the Jewish merchants and financiers (Studnicki-Gizbert 2007). These traders formed genuine dispersed coalitions, transferring capital and merchandise among their members, and their only chance of survival lay in avoiding rupture and atomization. At times personal interest surfaced, as would happen with the priest in Castro del Río who corresponded with his brother and retained the letters in the hope of proving his right to the family inheritance (Hidalgo 2006). At other times, as perhaps occurred with the American branch of the Borja, these connections served as a way of maintaining and conserving this immaterial capital that belonged to the house; this was also manifested in the use of the shield of that lineage on coats of arms and ornaments (Redondo and Yun 2008).

These networks were based upon familial links and kinship, upon forms of recognizing prestige and reputation in the ways described by A. Greif (2006) for the case of Medieval Genoa. Family connections and ties with more distant relatives were a way to create confidence and circulate information. In America, nearly all correspondents of the Corzo and the Mañara, the leading Sevillian businessmen, belonged to their family or ended up being related to it (Vila 1991, *passim*). And often this meant persons who, while related, resided on different sides of the Atlantic. Moreover, dowries, often transferred across the Atlantic, were a form of moving family capital from the bride's side to the groom's and from one side of the ocean to the other (Almorza Hidalgo 2011). Similarly, the practice of standing as a godparent, very common in America, allowed a person—usually a family member or associate—to bind himself to another family in the act of baptism itself, thus creating links of great value for business designed to reinforce personal trust (Nutini and Bell 1980).

Family relations were often strengthened through education and training with or near to relatives, with the intention being that the parties, having reached maturity, would eventually work, trade, or operate together (see some examples in Vila 1991). Permanent ties of culture, identity, and belonging could likewise be decisive. This was, of course, the case for the Jewish merchants. And it was not uncommon to find affinities of language binding Italians or members of the same 'nation'. Even in the world of lawyers, support networks were sometimes formed that could operate as genuine lobbies active on the Iberian Peninsula and in America or Asia. And this was very possibly the case for many Portuguese merchant adventurers who, like Bartolomeu Landeiro, operated as intermediaries between the Portuguese and the Chinese, sometimes even serving the latter in a military capacity (de Sousa 2010; Boxer 1959). No less important were the simple friendships that sprouted up in any number of situations. The lawyers who formed relationships of this sort in their school days or during undergraduate studies at Castile's universities provide an example of such a group, while merchants generally established similar friendship networks, sometimes basing them on nothing more than mutual necessity (García Hernán 2007, *passim*; Vila 1991).[2] Clientele and patronage relationships developed along similar lines, in particular between prominent persons such as viceroys and governors *da Índia*, who often belonged to the high aristocracy. In fact clientele practices—at times barely formalized in codes of external behaviour—could become decisive in a world much more inhospitable than that of the metropolis.

The result was often the formation of overlapping and flexible identities, as was logical in individuals who had two ways of conceiving themselves: as Jews and Portuguese, Castilians and Portuguese, or as belonging to a noble house, that is, to a lineage, while being subjects of a distant king in Madrid.

If the view from Europe necessarily entails the possibility of eurocentrism, then it is clear that the study of the connections within the colonies may provide a different perspective. The businessmen of the consulates of

---

[2] The case of J. de Solórzano is especially interesting (García Hernán 2007). In fact, if we review the contacts after his arrival in Peru, we find that, apart from extended family relations, a notable capacity to create 'friends', some of whom dated back to his time in Salamanca.

Lima and Mexico were often connected with groups based in Castile or Flanders, and they served at the other end of the network, as important as its European part and, indeed, crucial to its very operation, as is clear from a careful reading of the work of Studnicki-Gizbert (2007). In light of recent studies, something similar might be said of the creole elite that, little by little, formed in America and that, more than representing the periphery of a web, performed at times as the centre of a constellation of relationships that were projected out into Asia (or, at times, from Asia) and towards Europe. A similar degree of ex-centrality can be found in the networks of *converso* merchants who operated in the trade between the Atlantic, Africa, and Asia, at times working in a way that their most important connections did not pass through Lisbon and even, on occasion, attempting to impose their conditions on Madrid, where they negotiated *asientos* and rented monopolies (Boyajian 1983 and Studnicki-Gizbert 2007).

Precisely because of the distances involved and the consequent problems of communication, the relationships formed in this way between individuals and groups could be fragile and easily broken. The death of members, oversight, or a lack of communication could fracture them and render them transitory, something that frequently happened.[3] But these same dangers made these contacts even more necessary and led to their substitution and the replacing of defunct pacts and coalitions with great speed and efficiency. And these dangers afforded comparative advantages to the most solid networks, those based on family and those created by the Jews and which drew upon community identity, religion, social practices, cultural beliefs, and economic interests.

It is difficult to apply a single significance or historical effect to relations of this sort. Certainly, they were key to the conquest and functioning of empires. The lion's share of the available knowledge in military and economic affairs circulated through and along their branches, as did the political expertise that was crucial to making empire work. To give one example, military knowledge acquired in Europe by army captains and soldiers allowed for the wars of 'pacification' and conquest in America (Centenero 2009). And little remains to be said of the ability of Portuguese sailors to use the great advances of the incipient European military and naval revolution to serve their cause in Asia. Their knowledge of latest mining techniques allowed German emigrants to America to exploit the Peruvian and Mexican

---

[3] See different cases in Otte (1988).

deposits that would irrigate the world with white metals (Sánchez 1989). It was in part thanks to the projection into America of German families such as the Welser and the Fugger, or many others of Genoese or Portuguese origin, that the Habsburg wars and their political system could be sustained. And, of course, the emergence of a certain type of law and a specific juridical culture—certainly, in this regard Portugal and Castile followed a very similar course, both originating in essentially the same university world—that created shared codes of legal and political behaviour that were subsequently extended across enormous territories (Rivero 2011). In other words, relationship networks were largely responsible for allowing armadas to sail and armies to fight; *Audiencias*, mines, cities, and viceroyalties were in large part also the result of networks of personal connections that, if they had their propulsive niche in these institutions, were fed in reality by informal relations appropriate to these networks of weak ties and links (see some examples in Centenero 2009).

But our interest, in any case, is the interaction with formal institutions and the means by which they interfered in both realities.

'Perverting' 'Perverted' Institutions?

As we have seen, informal networks were crucial for initial contacts in the different areas of both empires. Their development to a certain degree would create, however, a tension with the royal administrative and judicial apparatus, whose development was crucial in a gradually more competitive world where violence among the different polities would be the norm. The following pages try to explain this very important change and how such a tension would be decisive in a context of increasing globalization.

Justice, Enforcement, and Distance

The Crown would try to control the exercise of coercion, understood primarily in terms of justice and military organization through the creation of formal institutions (described above). The military defence was attempted primarily through the system of fleets and colonial squadrons, such as the Atlantic fleet (*Armada del Mar Océano*), the squadrons such as the *Armada de Barlovento* established by the Spaniards in America, or the maritime system that the Portuguese set up in Goa. In any case, this resulted in a strategic military presence that was intended to control the trade, regulate economic and social relations, and, in the final instance, wield the power of the king (Goodman 1997 and Phillips (1986). In this regard, the institutions mentioned above, such as the House of Trade of Seville (*Casa de la Contratación de Sevilla*) and the *Casa da Índia*, exercised, in theory at least, a high degree of power of enforcement to the extent that the 'monopoly' was organized through them. The same was true of the Portuguese *Conselho da Fazenda* (Miranda 2010). Attempts were made to exercise control over justice through the *Audiencias* and the *Relaçoes*, respectively (Tomás y Valiente 1982, Schwartz 1973, Hespanha 2001). Both cases constituted an attempt to apply and uphold the law in the colonies through a group of bureaucrats trained in peninsula law or, in the Spanish case, in the Indian Laws too (Chap. 2). As mentioned above, both empires proceeded to compile laws in the hope that their application in a clear and uniform way would serve to reduce risks and transaction costs. In the cities and American municipalities, as in the Portuguese *câmaras* and *feitorias*, an attempt was thus made to apply the king's justice.

It is not, however, surprising that the assessment of this situation from the perspective of the new institutional economics has been very negative (Coatsworth 2008). As occurred in the Iberian Peninsula, the efficiency of these institutions in regard to the creation of a centralized, transparent and predictable system for the exercise of coercion was highly relative. Both empires saw a plurality of agents who applied overlapping and, very often, clashing forms of coercion (Hespanha 2001, pp. 181–2). This is very evident in Portugal, where a scholar has spoken of an 'estatuto colonial múltiplo' (a multiple colonial status) to underline the administrative and jurisdictional pluralism of the system (Hespanha and Santos 1998, pp. 353–61). This was in part a consequence of a diverse range of situations that even led to the creation of seigniorial estates in the colonies (Neto 1997, pp. 154–55). But, in the Spanish system, the plurality of agents active in the exercise of coercion and power, often clashing among themselves, was also present.

By the same standard, the exercise of coercion was closely linked to the practices of social agents. Despite the efforts of the Crown to preserve the superiority of its authority, it was impossible to prevent the *encomenderos* and the owners of mines, *mitas*, and *repartimientos*, as well as the *bandeirantes*, the owners of slaves and plantations and even the owners of *capitanias donatarias*, from exercising their capacity for coercion on a day-to-day basis. Even, indeed, a number of religious institutions such as the Jesuits retained notable use of coercion, to judge by the many examples and cases found in the seventeenth century. This fact would even emerge in debates in which institutions such as the *Audiencia* of Lima became involved about the ownership of 'personal services', a euphemism for practices that entailed the enslavement of the Amerindians (Díaz 2010, pp. 108–120 and *passim*). Above all in the frontier areas, violence between the Crown's servants, Jesuits (and other ecclesiastical orders), and parts of the Indian population remained common (Ariel and Svriz 2016 and Monteiro 1994). Cases such as that of the *bandeirantes* in Brazil demonstrate both the vigour and prevalence of these customs of violence—as well as the weakness of royal authority—which were basic to the working of the overall system and, in particular, to obtaining a slave workforce for the emerging plantation economy (Monteiro 1994, pp. 138 and ff). Even a very hierarchical institution, such as the Inquisition, though it was "mixed' in nature' (a tribunal of the Crown but also an ecclesiastical tribunal), did not become completely integrated into the state's machinery (Bethencourt 2009, pp. 316 and ff). Not only could the Holy Office act quite independently in the implementation of justice, it could even interfere with the king's regular justice. Though, in theory, the Inquisition did not prosecute economic crimes, it could exacerbate a sense of risk and uncertainty among economic agents, which could affect economic activities and trade in particular.

Merchant sectors in the Iberian Peninsula had clearly achieved a privileged position (Chap. 5). Yet by the same standards, their counterparts in the empire were not that much different; in particular, this was true of the very powerful Consulates of Lima (1613) and Mexico (1592), behind which stood extremely influential groups of businessmen involved in both Europe and Asia. A number of individuals, such as Juan de Solórzano, who helped to found consulates as 'justice courts for merchant affairs', saw how they evolved into 'professional corporations of merchants, thus becoming a lobby within the viceroyalty' (García Hernán 2007, p. 129). The information provided by J. L. Gasch (2015a) presents the modus operandi of the merchants of the Consulate of Mexico when faced with corruption in commerce with the Philippines. If the consulates themselves could positively reduce risks and transaction costs for their members, they could also fragment the map of conflict resolution and create barriers to the entrance of outsiders.

The forms of ownership established in the colonies were the opposite of what the new institutional economics considers the paradigm for efficiency. Although the Crown imposed and exercised its law in specific circumstances, a large part of property in both empires existed as a form of rights ceded by the king (Romano 2004). Moreover, property held in the privileged form of entailment was increasingly extended over time and led to the creation of lay and ecclesiastical elites in America. In this way a system was consecrated that not only placed obstacles before the circulation of land ownership but also advanced forms of management that were not always conducive to the implementation of productive improvements (Coatsworth 2008).

The political economy of the colonies was consequently characterized by the clash of forms of enforcement and by the importance of privilege and the opportunity to exercise violence as a substantial part of the productive relationships. All of this appears, on paper, a major problem for productive development and the efficient assignment of productive resources (North et al. 2009).

The imperial reality implied not only the adherence to local legal and normative codes but also systems that made distant institutions work and created forms of confidence and coercion in overseas spaces.

As occurred in the Iberian Peninsula, the Crown's scope for intervention as a third party in resolving conflicts was highly limited, although its role appeared to be guaranteed by the importance of the *Audiencias* and the authority of the viceroys and local authorities. In regard to lawsuits launched from the Iberian Peninsula, there were many problems. Enforcing compliance with contracts was sometimes complicated by the difficulty of locating persons or the time spent in doing so. In 1543 a Seville banker calculated that to prosecute a Fugger lawsuit in New Spain would require a year and a half (Kellenbenz 2000, p. 601). The execution of contracts by merchants involved in transatlantic trade was highly complex and required mechanisms of a mixed character. For example, Seville's merchants continually sent orders for unpaid debts to their operatives in America that appealed to the king's justice in the final instance (Cachero 2010). But, in order for them to arrive at that point, they themselves had to search for the debtors before these orders could be implemented. This revealed a form of justice that was accompanied by high transaction costs and that, by itself, had a limited capacity to reduce risks. And, if risks were fundamentally determined by other, more important factors (the chances of shipwreck, attack, appropriation by the king, the delay of the fleets, etc.), then forms of justice partly explain the high rates of maritime insurance (Bernal 1993). If, therefore, justice and enforcing compliance with contracts on the Iberian Peninsula were slow and there existed circuits outside of 'official' justice, to use the phrase of A. M. Hespanha, then the ramifications of this situation were even more emphatically felt in the immense world of global and local relations beyond it. For another thing, the very nature of a law that conceded a wide margin of manoeuvre to judges and entailed different jurisdictions meant that the problem was to know who was the 'best equipped to interpret and enforce the law' (Rivero 2011, p. 2011). In regard to the *Estado da Índia*, Hespanha has spoken of an extremely complex system in which seven areas of political jurisdiction were operative (Hespanha and Santos 1998).

The entwining of the two empires and their projection over extremely distinct societies increased the diverse range of moral and social codes, thus making it more difficult for official justice to penetrate the intricate social fabric and compelling it to highly complex cultural translations between the different social agents. This was the case in America, where the slow configuration of the 'caste society' (a term that is more a social representation than anything else) took place; it was also the case in the Portuguese dominions in Asia, where the frontier and the numerous cultures with whom they dealt was complex and porous.

Dominant Coalitions, Patronage, Rent-Seeking, Corruption, Fraud, and Contraband

These trans-frontier networks and webs cannot be understood as separate from the formation of elites and dominant coalitions of a local character. Indeed, the precise opposite was the case. Logically these webs acquired different characteristics according to the specific contexts in which they were born and their relations with the Crown.[4] Notable differences also existed in the weight they could bring to the negotiating table and their influence. They were especially powerful and influential in areas such as New Spain or the viceroyalty of Peru. Here minorities of powerful creoles concentrated, often being linked to the exploitation of mines, the great estates or *haciendas*, trade, and the bank that, enjoying strong connections with the royal bureaucracy, exercised an enormous decision-making capacity (Bakewell 1995; Kicza 1999). Its vast economic potential was complemented by its very considerable social capital and its influential and charismatic identity as a creole minority whose character was deliberately projected to distinguish it from both the indigenous population and the Spanish (Gasch 2014). In part exploiting norms of consumption that

[4]A series of case studies is found in B. Ch. Büschges and B. Schröter (eds.) (1999, pp. 10–82). The cases of Mexico and Río de la Plata, about which a great deal has been written, can be studied in Kicza (1999).

included the use of Asian products as a means of cultural differentiation, these creoles proceeded to invent their own tradition by underlining their hybrid but unique identity. Their powers were extended through the system for the transfer of funds between regions through the *situados*, which conferred a degree of pre-eminence upon them. Theirs were the areas which most frequently transferred resources to the poorer regions with the aim of not only oiling the bureaucratic machinery but also—and above all—priming defence forces (Grafe and Irigoin 2012).

A series of features were repeated in practically all local elites, although in different combinations. As perhaps had to be the case, one of these was the use of matrimony and family and kinship relations as a means of constructing power. Here in fact lies one of the reasons why the family has always been credited with enormous importance in the history of social relations in Latin America.[5] It could serve as a means of connection with the international networks mentioned above. In other instances relationships were based on occasional transfers of influence or of political and economic resources. The custom was that these networks of local relationships could call upon members who were strategically placed in politics, the bureaucracy, the magistrates, or business. This was a means of controlling diverse spaces that offered their different members a form of capital (economic, social, or cultural) that was easily interchangeable. And, despite there being no comparative study of this phenomena, the impression is that, if things were broadly similar on the Iberian Peninsula, the greatest weakness of the conception of a society of orders was that it conferred upon these elites a notable fluidity in the relations between their different component parts, above all through matrimony. It should be added that Portuguese colonial society in Asia passed through two phases in this regard. The first phase 'was characterised by the mobility of individuals' (Russell-Wood 1992, pp. 112–3). Figures such as Bartolomeu Landeiro or Fernando Mendes Pinto appear to have been continually on the move, being highly skilled and versatile operatives, blessed with a talent of obtaining information and selling it to the highest bidder while operating among local agents—a lifestyle and career, in short, indicative of their 'endemic individualism' (Russell-Wood 1992, p. 113; de Sousa 2010). But in a second phase, the presence of Jewish networks, marked by

---

[5] It is not surprising that the role of the family in the internal relationships between elites has been emphasized (Céspedes 2009, pp. 191–200).

a strong familial character, must have created a broader panorama in this area and proven more similar to what had occurred in the Portuguese colonies in Brazil, which in turn can be said to have been very similar in this regard to the Spanish case (Studnicki-Gizbert 2007, chapter 3). This sequence does not mean, however, that both models were not present in the whole period under analysis here.

This type of network based on family and kinship would be vital, as it would prove to be crucial to one of the essential developments in the history of the empire—the increasing perversion of its formal institutions. By this I mean a process whereby these social networks and informal institutions would be able to take over many different institutions, such as the *Audiencias*, the municipal and ecclesiastical councils, the consulates, and many other institutions, and then impose upon them—and therefore upon the rest of the society—their own interests, ways of creating trust, and forms of enforcement. It is important to note that, as in the metropolis, this was also possible due to the 'unmodern' character (in the Weberian sense) of these administrative and political bodies. In a context in which the boundaries between public and private domains were highly permeable, this brought about a very high degree of concentration of political and economic capital, thus forging one of the key characteristics of the political economy of the colonies. Elite Mexican families, for example, were able to accumulate and unify their influence in the mines, the agrarian sector, local politics, the royal bureaucratic machinery, the Church, and so on and at the same time they were establishing international connections with Seville, Lima, the Caribbean, or the Philippines. These networks of interest were highly successful in penetrating the institutional system created by the monarchy. In these circumstances, which were far from unique, their chances of applying practices of rent-seeking were very high, to say the least. They had access to privileged information; were able to wield 'public' power to their own ends, and marshalled a highly solid economic base that allowed them to make transfers to members through the exercise of political and even juridical authority; and, finally, if all else failed, they could even shift the legal framework if they acted together as genuine coalitions.

Equally, their chances of indulging in fraud and corrupt practices were extensive, given that their international connections offered them enormous scope for contraband and commercial fraud. Patronage, clientelism, and corruption, in fact, were tied to the very model of the Iberian state, the character of the composite monarchy as a group of powers and jurisdictions linked together only in the person of the king (Yun 1994b). The outcome was the reproduction in an amplified and perfected form in the Indies of practices of nepotism, patronage, and so on. One of the best studies of the theme has identified the viceroys who arrived in the New World 'with a large retinue of family members and creatures' as an epicentre of corruption. This was tied not only to the centre of the political system, but also extended out into the localities and "periphery of the administration" (Pietschmann 1989, pp. 163–182). Existing studies have also shown that strong solidarities existed between royal officials and the owners of sugar refineries, which led to similar situations (Schwartz 1973). And yet the problem of corruption did not reside only in the negative impact of the misuse of public funds. Nepotism, the promotion of clients—then, as today, but more so in those societies in which clientelism was rooted in the essence of the social fabric and was part of the moral economy of the elites—depended upon the use of human resources in the pursuit of private interest rather than that of the state. The dilemma between personal loyalty—so important in the codex of values of the period—and efficiency in state service was often resolved by placing the former ahead of the latter; obviously, this had important effects upon politics. In fact it was part of the political culture and practices of the epoch. At times corruption of this sort did not even necessarily require pre-existing family relationships, as it simply took root in the forms of payment and the cost of offices. Rather than focus on a very well-known field of study, such as the great bureaucrats who came to the colonies from the Iberian Peninsula, the example can be given of the *repartimientos*, which sometimes adopted a form of industrial *verlagssystem*. Patch's research has shown that the mayors (*alcaldes mayores*), being badly paid and in need of making good the money spent in buying their offices, fraudulently favoured the backer (*aviador*), a sort of *verlaguer* who had advanced money or primary material to the official and who thus obtained access to the forced labour of the Indians at a very low price (1994). Many variants of this sort of corruption can be found.

But the great problem—above all, as we shall see, in constructing a mercantilist empire or, simply, one based upon the control of the markets—was that one of the most important practices was contraband. This can be explained through the enormous power acquired by international networks of businessmen. But another factor was that these men, making use of their connections with local elites and functionaries, were able to pervert the working of the institutions. Moreover they found apt methods for doing so in the very institutions themselves. The renting of a state monopoly, the *asientos* of black slaves, and so on were means used by the very office holders themselves to facilitate fraudulent commerce; at other times these methods were exploited to exercise an unfair advantage over competitors, who might end up being removed or evicted from the sector in question (Studnicki-Gizbert 2007). Some time ago Zacarías Moutoukias provided information crucial to understanding another type of corrupt operation in the Río de la Plata and underlined the practical confusion that existed over what was legal and 'illegal' commerce. Indeed the multifunctional character of elites, in which functionaries mixed with merchants and their international connections raised smuggling to such levels that the monarchy had to 'legalize' it in return for money or the concession of privileges to its practitioners (Moutoukias 1988, chapter IV). The illegitimate thus became legal. A similar situation ensued in Cartagena and Veracruz where the collaboration of royal officials in the contraband networks has been very well described by J. M. Córdoba (2015). The same happened in Mexico, where members of the Consulate were awarded privileges in return for donations to the Crown of millions of pesos; these prerogatives granted them the right to discharge fiscal functions over their own shipments towards Asia (Gasch 2015a and 2015b). The method would also be applied in Seville and would be one of the keys to the so-called crisis of the *Carrera de Indias*, as we shall see. This admission—it might even be said, 'legalization'—of these practices in return for money testifies to the systemic character of corruption in the form of smuggling and contraband.

In these ways the networks of the empire had a series of characteristics: a pronounced family component, a marked prolongation of other forms of obtaining confidence, and a multilateral character spanning frontiers. It could also be made up of individuals belonging to many different 'nationalities' densely intermingled. In fact it is not difficult to see how in cases such as that of the Jewish networks of smugglers not only were the Spanish or Portuguese authorities involved in the subterfuge but so also were the English, Dutch, and French ones. In short, these were complex and multifunctional relationships. These agents had a notable capacity to prevent interference from the formal institutions which were, by their very nature, given to a sort of self-perversion; perhaps indeed, using the terminology built by Max Weber to describe modern societies, they can be considered as perverse. Though, the right way to express it beyond metaphors is to say that they were different and product of their own moment in history. In a global context, this would prove fatal to the state that sought to control this empire. All this does not mean that the Spanish and Portuguese administrative system was not subject to monitoring and control from the Crown. The *visitas* and other types of control were very common, and there are examples of major efforts against smuggling, fraud, and corruption (Bertrand 1999). But one needs to understand that contraband, fraud, rent-seeking, and corruption in general, often linked to nepotism and patronage as components of the prevalent political culture, were normal practices and a way to take advantage of previous investments in offices or to compensate poorly paid functionaries. In other words, corruption—particularly when it was 'legalized'—allowed the state to externalize a part of its very high protection costs.

CORROSIVE GLOBALIZATION

The great enemy of the Luso-Spanish imperial complex was its own creation: the process of globalization, understood not only as the discovery and contact with new worlds but also as the increasing intertwining of distant societies.

Globalization and Regional Economies

The result of the colonization and 'globalization' of the New World was to encourage the emergence of new internal circuits in it, all of them linked at some point with the transcontinental routes. These were regional economies that, if they obeyed their own rules, were thoroughly interwoven into processes of globalization.

The development of the cities and mining settlements, both manifestations of a world that was ever more global, activated the need to provision them with products from nearby areas. In the seaboard of the Pacific, a coastal complex emerged that served to feed Peru, whose growth was carried forward by its globally important role in the extraction and circulation of silver (Mörner 1990, p. 143). The increase in internal American demand, a consequence of its connections to the global economy, helped the development of the plantation economy. The great estates or *haciendas* of Mexico, Argentina, or Brazil supplied products such as maize, livestock, or sugar cane, without which it would not have been possible to feed or send primary materials to the areas connected to Atlantic trade. Phenomena such as the efforts to colonize new lands or, more simply, the hunt for slaves carried the frontier slowly forward into the interior of Brazil; certainly the formation of great livestock breeding farms there cannot be understood without reference to these international connections (Lockhart and Schwartz 1983). In this way the new plantation economy, shaped by production destined for internal American consumption and which would come to compete with—and complement—the mining economy, was also a consequence of its expansion and the global connections of America. The great fairs of Veracruz, Jalapa, or Portobello, which were crucial for the long-range commerce of the *Carrera de Indias*, also became the stage for a growing regional commerce in the Caribbean that operated according to its own rules (Macleod 1990, pp. 180–8). The connections between the west coasts of Brazil and Argentina encouraged not only these regional trade systems but also the global circuits between Peru and the Río de la Plata (Assadourian 1982; Garavaglia 1983), which in turn inserted themselves into other circuits of commerce.

These regional circuits in the American continent have been considered as key to a debate on the possible existence of a seventeenth-century crisis (Israel 1974; TePaske and Klein 1981; Kamen and Israel 1982). But similar situations can be found in other zones of the planet. The South Atlantic, between the coasts of Guinea and the Ivory Coast, on the one side, and the coasts between the Caribbean and the Río de la Plata, on the other side, constituted a subsystem within global commerce (Russell-Wood 1992; Boyajian 1993). Similar circuits had developed, sometimes being built upon regional economies already linked before the arrival of the Europeans, between the Cape of Good Hope and Japan, where there existed regional economies with a certain degree of autonomy and in which Portuguese penetration was necessarily limited (Subrahmanyam 1990). The China Sea was an area with its own logic, where the silver from Japan was secured in exchange for all types of product to feed regional commerce (Flynn and Giraldez 2002). An idea of the importance of the regional circuits (not separated from the very long distance trade) can be gained from calculations that postulate that even in the moment of peak export of American silver to the Pacific (1600–1640), it did not constitute more than 10–25% of the Japanese silver exported to China in compensation for its products (Barrett 1990, p. 246). Regional circuits were, therefore, more important in volume than long-distance and intercontinental trade.

Without doubt the penetration of American silver and the connection through the Philippines with America did more to open up these circuits, but they also had their own endogenous logic in many areas of Asia (Subrahmanyam 1990). The Indian Ocean and the Arabian Sea, from India to Madagascar, were replete with regional coastal circuits, many of them dating back to before the arrival of the Portuguese whose appearance in fact gave them a new dynamic. But, despite the connections with Portugal, the Asiatic economies had their own independence and a multitude of internal circuits. Today it is common to underline the fact that the portion of merchandise traded by the Portuguese—and, indeed, by the Europeans in general—was of reduced importance in relation to the total volume of traffic in these areas.

Globalization also implied the appearance of new routes. This was the case of the trade between Peru and the Río de la Plata (mentioned above) and that served to divert the route of the white metal that would not be channelled through the *Carrera de Indias*—and, therefore, that would not end up resting in the coffers of the King of Spain. It was also a zone whose base was smuggling, to which the Crown turned a blind eye, as we have seen. Moreover the Portuguese never came to control all of the commerce from Asia, as a significant part of it moved through the Red Sea and into the Ottoman Empire, thus creating another path of diffusion for these products. Carried through Greece and Venice, these goods often reached the north of Europe, usually passing through English hands (Fusaro 2015). The same effect was achieved by the inhospitable route that connected Persia with the north of Europe or travelled over Siberia towards the Baltic. The new commercial route between Acapulco and Manila strengthened these centrifugal commercial tendencies in the heart of the Luso-Spanish empire and, this way, increased the difficulties in controlling and maintaining the monopoly of Seville.

The impetus of both the regional economies, closely tied as they were to the expansion of international commerce, and the alternative routes of global trade can be interpreted as a symptom of the capacity of the world economy: it moved regional resources and generated new routes of economic development. It is also known that the fall in silver receipts in Seville and the crisis of Portuguese commerce with Asia would occur later than has been said. It certainly cannot be dated to before 1620–1630. But, on the other hand, it is also clear that these global mechanisms made it increasingly difficult to control the circulation of silver or maintain the extraction quota of the empire over a buoyant global economy that, even if it was in crisis in the short or long term, remained multipolar and with a very notable centrifugal component. As we shall see, this character would prove to be the Achilles heel of Madrid and of the empire. Would it also affect the economic agents who operated in it?

Problems of Regulation and Internal Conflicts

Historians have recently proposed that these empires might be described as polycentric (Cardim et al. 2012). The expression adds little to what we already know but has an undoubted graphic value as long as we do not forget that some centres had less power than others and that Madrid was in many senses 'the' centre of the empire. It is important to underline, moreover, that all empires in history have been polycentric in many ways. Furthermore, one of the problems of the expression is that so far it has been applied mainly, or only, on the political and jurisdictional levels and that it suggests a certain sense of exceptionalism of the Iberian world.

This multinuclear character is, in realty, the fruit of the plurality of points of negotiation and, therefore, of decision-making centres that affected not only themselves but also the system as a whole. Nevertheless, from the perspective of political and institutional history, it is often forgotten that this nodal character became more evident with the development of regional economies and globalization. In effect the development of the regional economies implied the transferal to each of these centres of an opportunity to convert economic capital into political capital. The case of the development, almost fraudulent, of the Río de la Plata is paradigmatic, although perhaps in this respect the Philippines, Macao, or other areas might also be mentioned. In such centres, as economic resources increased, a number of agents emerged—that is, new elites and institutions that very shortly would negotiate with the Crown and, over time, would become decisive for the defence of the American empire as a whole. By 1630 there were many poles of regional development: in the Caribbean, Mexico, Peru, the Río de la Plata, Chile gradually, the coast of Brazil, the factories of Africa and the islands of the Atlantic, Lisbon, Madrid, Seville, Naples, Milan or the Low Countries, the coasts of the Indian Ocean, Goa, Macao, the China Sea, the Philippines, and so on. Furthermore, these were just the most important points, and under each of them were concentrated other, lower nodes of negotiation within the hierarchy. In each case we find a group in which a variety of agents negotiated with the king and among themselves. The case of New Spain provides a valuable example of the complex web of institutional relations at play. Here a range of actors— the Consulate of Mexico, Mexico City itself, the freight shippers to the Philippines, the viceroy and the *Audiencia*—interacted among themselves, sometimes each pursuing its own agenda by recurring to institutional and economic privileges and yet, at the same time, also presenting claims for redress to the monarch in Madrid. Similar forms of rivalry and collaboration occurred under other types of institutional relations, for instance, in the European part of this composite monarchy (Chap. 5).

This situation ensued to the extent that the development of these new areas—and the deepening of the old ones—was based on the establishment of relations of *do ut des* with the Crown in which the concession of de facto jurisdictional or economic privileges played an essential role (these concessions and prerogatives came, nearly always, to assume a perpetual character); the system crystalized relations that were essential to its functioning. Still more important, privileges of this sort were seldom the fruit of a preconceived plan of imperial organization. On the contrary, these were relations borne of mutual necessity in specific conjectures between the king and local agents. And they responded to economic and political agendas marked by local concerns. The result was that the empire was configured as a group of different interests which were sometimes contradictory.

Many examples could be given. One study of the viceroyalties has arrived, with good reason, at the conclusion that 'jurisdictional conflict was the order of the day and formed part of the very nature of things' (Rivero 2011, p. 200). This author mentions another aspect of this situation, the collision of jurisdictions that formed part of the development of the European part of the composite monarchy of the Luso-Spanish empire. But the statement is also applicable to overseas territories, where institutions and an entire political philosophy had been exported and practices for the negotiation of privileges had been developed. For these reasons the Luso-Spanish complex existed during the first decades of the seventeenth century with a continual tension between placing more resources into the development of Pacific commerce—in which a large part of the Mexican and Lima elites were involved—and, alternatively, trying to limit and control it, as the businessmen of Seville and many who operated from Lisbon would have wanted and who saw in it a threat to their commerce with the Indian Ocean (Gasch 2015a). Even without resolving this question, the same phenomenon led to continual prohibitions being promulgated against the trade between Peru and New Spain that, if they appear not to have been entirely successful, did at least end the chances of uniting forces to proceed to the exploration and expansion into the South Pacific, a campaign that was left for English and French navigators (Céspedes 2009, p. 160). A similar conflict emerged over the development of trade through Buenos Aires, which infuriated the all-powerful Consulate of Seville, but was extremely remunerative for Peru's and the Río de la Plata's traders, as well as for the slave traders, many of them Portuguese, who connected this area with the Gulf of Guinea (Boyajian 1983; Studnicki-Gizbert 2007). The development of this route had strengthened the New Christians and Portuguese Jews who now, with the help of high-ranking governmental figures in Madrid, were coming into conflict with the Genoese over the control of the *asientos* (Ruiz Martín 1990b). Very similar conflicts were common in Asia. The opposition of institutions and Castilian and Portuguese corporations over China Sea commerce, or between enclaves such as Macao and Manila, and the disputes over the Moluccas, or over simple questions of naval protocol (and in this period, protocol was a means of setting the hierarchy of privileges that formed a part of political capital), are other good examples of this same tension (Valladares 2001, pp. 9, 20, 24, and 36). But, moreover, these conflicts could—and indeed did—have a markedly local character. Cases such as the dispute between the viceroy of New Spain and the bishop Palafox in Mexico have been considered as a clash of egos. But such episodes demonstrate a type of conflict between ecclesiastical power and civil authority that was present across the Iberian world (Álvarez de Toledo 2004). A good example can be found in the tensions between the Portuguese viceroy Linhares and the short-lived Portuguese East India Company, which decisively contributed to the failure of the latter (Disney 1978, chapter 9). Frontier zones, such as the region of Entre Ríos in Argentina, were the stage for conflicts between the Jesuits and the governor of Buenos Aires for long periods of time (Ariel and Svriz 2016). Numerous other examples could be given (Herzog 2015).

It is important to note that tensions of this type—and forms of lobbying— are present in any polity, from nation state to regional government. What makes this a special case are the scale and nature of the problems of distance, asymmetric information, and monitoring difficulties. But all of these disputes, and many others of a more local character, expressed what was in reality a problem of regulation and arbitration that, if common to all empires, was inherent to the very model of development of the Spanish and Portuguese systems. As would happen centuries later to the British Empire, part of the problem originated in the difficulties in the very centre of the empire (Darwin 2012). If it was by this point difficult to coordinate missions in the peninsula and in Europe (Chap. 4), it was even more challenging to do so in the distant spaces in an empire marked by the difficult circulation of information and the high degree of autonomy wielded by local agents. In 1625 a well-informed expert on American society, Gaytán

Torres, decided that the good government of the Indies required not only the purification of a thoroughly corrupt administration but also the reform of the various Councils in Madrid, whose rivalries and disputes were drawn out and debilitating (Amadori 2009). In the case of the Council of the Indies, clashes with the exchequer were especially frequent (Schäfer 2003, pp. 115–9 and 165–8). Joint actions involving the Council of Portugal and the Council of the Indies were not easy to coordinate. Moreover both councils (like all others) had more than one governmental function. As it has been said, they were also jurisdictional bodies and had to make sure that laws, customs, and rights (meaning therefore privileges) of each one of the components of the Iberian imperial complex were respected and upheld. And these were not always compatible. When Portuguese Jewish and Genoese bankers were in conflict, should the Crown back its traditional allies, who had mobilized the Republic of Genoa to serve the Habsburg cause of controlling Europe or its direct subjects from Portugal? In the majority of cases, when its own interest was at play, as was the case in debates about when or how it was to advance the exploration of the South Pacific that might well introduce even more centrifugal forces, the position of the Crown was to favour itself. But this, rather than correct the problem of regulation, only made things worse, and in fact it created a problem of arbitration from the centre.

WORLD WAR, MONEY, AND MEN

These features of the Luso-Spanish composite empire were also present at its European extreme. Moreover, the problems of regulation in the Habsburg domains were not an anomaly in themselves. As we have underlined, they were the logical outcome of social and political development in tune with the epoch's political systems.

Problems would arise, however, when increasing pressure was put upon the different nodes of the empire in America, Asia, Africa, and Europe. Such pressure was not only the outcome of Dutch and English actions in Europe but also a side effect of the development of other areas of the planet in which globalization had also progressed since the sixteenth century. The climax of the increasing tension on a world scale can be seen in an event that has always been considered either in a strict European dimension or in its different parts separately: the Thirty Years War (1618–1648), or to be more precise the Eighty Years War, which started with the Dutch rebellion and ended with the Peace of Westphalia and the Treaty of the Pyrenees (1568–1648/1659).

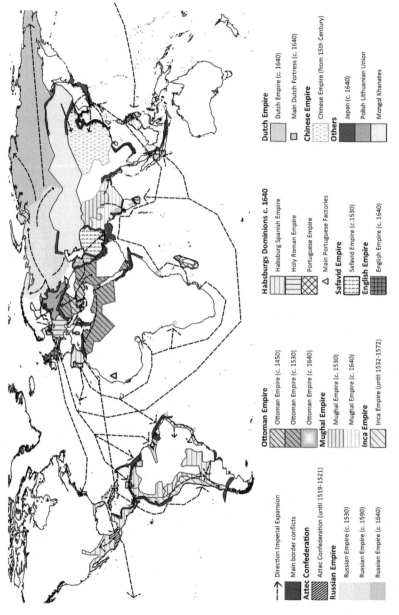

Map 7.1 Imperial expansions, until c. 1640

--> Direction Imperial Expansion

Main border conflicts

Aztec Confederation

Aztec Confederation (until 1519-1521)

Russian Empire

Russian Empire (c. 1530)

Russian Empire (c. 1590)

Russian Empire (c. 1640)

Ottoman Empire

Ottoman Empire (c. 1450)

Ottoman Empire (c. 1530)

Ottoman Empire (c. 1640)

Mughal Empire

Mughal Empire (c. 1530)

Mughal Empire (c. 1640)

Inca Empire

Inca Empire (until 1532-1572)

Habsburgs Dominions c. 1640

Habsburg Spanish Empire

Holy Roman Empire

Portuguese Empire

△ Main Portuguese Factories

Safavid Empire

Safavid Empire (c.1530)

English Empire

English Empire (c. 1640)

Dutch Empire

Dutch Empire (c. 1640)

☐ Main Dutch Fortress (c. 1640)

Chinese Empire

Chinese Empire (from 15th Century)

Others

Japan (c. 1640)

Polish Lithuanian Union

Mongol Khanates

Mars and Mercury on a World Scale

The years 1598–1621 were decisive. Fighting on against Holland until 1609 created an exhausting situation for the royal finances. The reforming instincts of Philip III and his favourite, the duke of Lerma, are recognized today (Feros 2000). This having been said, patronage, clientelism, and political corruption, which cannot be separated from their economic context and which were a constitutive part of the political regime, originating in Lerma and his family, appear to have reached unprecedented level (Feros 2000, chapter 8). The patronage system, the spine of the political economy, developed to the extent that it became impossible to recruit the best-qualified servants to government through the client network (Williams 2006, p. 355). The dilemma between, on the one hand, clientele loyalty achieved through side payments that kept lineages united and softened their internal conflicts and, on the other, efficiency in political management was being decided too often in favour of the former. The situation was even more disturbing for many as not only had the *millones* tax been increased, but the minting of *vellón* coinage had been allowed, a measure that was considered by many thinkers, such as Juan de Mariana, to be an act of tyranny—a rupture of the implicit agreement between the monarchy and its subjects since 1469 (de Mariana 1987).

If they could not provide figures to substantiate their claims, contemporaries were very much aware of what was happening. This was especially true of the *arbitristas*, who flooded the Cortes and the desks of governors with proposals for reform and remedies (J. Vilar 1974; Gutiérrez Nieto 1982). If the solutions proffered were very diverse in nature, then their diagnosis of the problems remains extremely valuable in regard to their analysis of the political economy. According to the *arbitristas*, when compared to its European competitors, the Spanish economy had clearly run out of steam. The empire had fallen into a type of bad government that was being taken advantage of by other 'nations', among whose number figured not only the Dutch, French, or English but also—and above all—the Genoese, the *Moriscos*, and the gypsies.[6] The Portuguese equivalent to the *arbitrista* literature, the so-called literature of remedies (la *literatura de remedios*), also dealt with similar topics and placed emphasis on the problems of the empire and of the *Estado da Índia*. The overall arguments

[6] See an example in Sancho de Moncada (1974 [1619]) and the introduction of Jean Vilar to his work (1974, pp. 78–81).

were very similar, but they were exactly the same in their consideration of foreigners and, above all, in taking the union of the Crowns as one of the main problems of the empire and of the country (Curto 2009 and Borges 2014). It is precisely this negative impression of foreign influence that led to the fluorescence of a sense of Spain and Portugal as a dual political identity that would be the basis of subsequent reform projects infused with a clear mercantilist character.

In the case of Spain, among the reasons for this new feeling were the difficulties in overcoming the United Provinces of the Netherlands, with which a truce had been signed in 1609.

By 1634 a painting was hung in the palace of the Buen Retiro in Madrid, which had been built for the greater glory of Philip IV (and, indirectly, for the Count Duke of Olivares). Its subject was an emblematic event: the recovery of Bahia in 1625. Laden with overt political symbolism (Brown and Elliott 1980, pp. 194–202), the work also appears today to reflect a number of elements that are crucial to understanding the political economy of the empire in these years: the likelihood of the Dutch attacking Portuguese areas of the empire, the fragility of Dutch efforts, and the considerable ability of the monarchy to react, despite its many problems. Without knowing it, the painting therefore confirmed the thinking of a group of Amsterdam merchants who, as we shall see, were increasingly convinced that the best way to penetrate the Luso-Spanish empire was by commercial infiltration rather than full frontal assault (Boxer 1973). Brimming with religious iconography and the representation of an imperial composite monarchy, the work of Juan Bautista Maíno perhaps demonstrates that the war with Holland was not a religious conflict. But neither was it a question of maintaining the unity of Habsburg patrimony; nor was it an economic war, despite its marked economic component, or one fought for reputation. Rather, it was all of these things at the same time. But, above all, this canvass allows us to understand that this was a global conflict fought by a geographically dispersed composite monarchy and dynastic world empire.

This unique combination of themes underlines the dilemmas of Spain when faced with its precise opposite, a small confederation of provinces: the Dutch Republic was a small and badly connected political system, an antistate (Elliott 1990); however, it drew strength from its spatial concentration and the high degree of interaction between its elites and government thanks to a system that permitted discussion and informal relations, in which conflict was often resolved with joint actions in defence of the economic bases of the country. It is not that corruption was inexistent in the Netherlands and even less the case that family networks were failing to penetrate its institutions in a similar way to what was occurring in Spain (Adams 2005). But its political skeleton was very different.

Any comparison between the Luso-Spanish empire and those that followed it, particularly the English and the Dutch, underlines this fact.

First, in contrast to the Iberian *imperio*, these were political formations in which the colonies were appendixes to proto-national states that comprised territorial unities and pursued a basically mercantilist agenda. In effect the great problem of the Spanish monarchy from 1598 to 1648, and more specifically from 1618 to 1648, lay in waging war on a number of fronts across Europe from a mosaic of polities that were governed by a very wide range of political agendas, with very strong geopolitical constrictions and constitutions, whose interests did not always fall in line with those of the king. To this must be added that the dynastic nature of this ensemble created the duty of serving the general strategy of the House of Habsburg, manifested—it is only one example—in the participation in the Battle of the White Mountain (1620) in defence of the Austrian branch of the family and then sending help to repulse the attacks of Gustavus Adolphus of Sweden in Central Europe (from 1630). This role also created strategic problems that led to actions which were not only absurd but also enormously exhausting. This was the case in the attempted conquest of Mantua, undertaken to prevent the Nevers, a family tied to the French branch of the Gonzaga and therefore to Louis XIII of France, from seizing power in the duchy.

Second, such difficulties resulted from being a composite monarchy and empire. In an international war fought on various fronts, the obstacles created by the political theory, inherent to the composite, states to the transfer of funds from one state to another would pose a crucial problem. But this was also the case when it came to colonial areas and the need to use Portuguese and Castilian resources in a coordinated way. This difficulty became even worse to the extent that it coincided with the first globalization, which made the Iberian complex extremely alluring to maritime and commercial states such as Holland and England. In Europe, the problem was even more serious because of the pincers around France created by the semicircle of the Pyrenees, the routes of the Spanish road and Flanders, which obliged the neighbouring country to a continuous fight against Habsburg interests.

Third, in many areas of the world, this was an empire of arteries and widespread neuralgic points. Its political and economic functioning depended upon a series of routes that tied together nuclei condemned to assist each other but whose local elites, bound by their separate and independent bargains with the Crown, found that their interests seldom coincided. For this reason, the geopolitical situation was implacable: the so-called Spanish road and the Mediterranean route from the East coast of the Iberian Peninsula was one of the most important but delicate routes, with an especially vulnerable point, the Valtellina pass in the Alps. The maritime connections between the Cantabrian coasts and the Low Countries were also vital. Along both routes men, military resources, and silver flowed, without which everything in the War of Flanders might have been lost. The connections between Lisbon and Brazil and their extension to the Río de la Plata were vital, as were the routes to Africa (where Guinea was also crucial) and the Indian-Pacific Ocean complex (in which Mombasa, Ormuz, Goa, Malacca, Manila, and Macao were stress points). Commerce was based in these sea lanes, as was the lion's share of Philip IV's income as King of Portugal and, most important, the loyalty of the Portuguese to Madrid. The other artery united Seville with the Caribbean, whence the fundamental routes to Mexico, Panama, and the coast of Tierra Firme ran; and in turn these points connected with the American Pacific and the links with the Philippines. Any enemy action against this artery threatened to interrupt the flow of silver to Castile, which in turn would endanger the financial nerve system of the empire. To give an idea of the distances involved, this network covered some 100,000 kilometres across oceans and along coastlines—two and a half-times the length of the equator.

Some of the fundamental characteristics of the Habsburg imperial system were, therefore, its dispersion and patrimonial nature, the obstacles to the mobilization of resources imposed by its character as a composite monarchy, and the strategic importance of some of the arteries and nodal points of the empire. Many empires have faced similar situations: their growth makes it more difficult to control frontiers faced with insupportable and continuous multilateral pressures, the variety of constitutions compels them to multilateral negotiations with local elites, military costs are always high, and so on. Indeed, some of these features have even been used to explain the failure of empires in general (Kennedy 1988). But the combination of all these characteristics in a moment of increasing globalization and fight for colonial markets would be decisive.

In these circumstances, the strategy used by the Dutch and English was to focus on delicate points to assault or infiltrate, thus taking advantage of the problems in co-ordination and negotiation between local agents and Madrid, as well as the attendant logistical constraints.

A quick glance at events between 1580 and 1635 is highly significant. From the end of the previous decade, the English corsairs (Drake, Cavendish, and Hawkins) had attacked a number of points on the coast of Peru, California, Cadiz, and the Caribbean. The point of outbreak was always a neuralgic node for the transport of silver and the expanding plantation economy. At the same time, the Dutch had increased their presence in the Caribbean and the coasts of Brazil, being especially drawn by smuggling sugar and slaves. The powerful network of Portuguese New Christians would prove a great help to them in the moment of a boom in the plantation economy. But the Dutch intention was also to gain access to Peruvian silver, which they obtained by selling their goods in the New World and more in particular in the Caribbean and along the Northern coast of Brazil. The truce of 1609–1621 also allowed the Dutch to sell their industrial products directly to Brazil, while 'dozens of Dutch vessels sailed from Portugal to Holland' and carried merchandise in the other direction (Israel 1990, p. 117). Access to Peruvian silver through Brazil was getting ever closer. In the 1590s, at the very height of the war, the Dutch also began their own expansion towards the Orient. According to Headrick (2010, p. 87), they drew upon a number of advantages that allowed them to build fortresses in the 'Spice Islands', where they ran into the Spanish, who were based in the Philippines (Israel 1990, chapter 3), and Portuguese. By 1617 the Dutch had established around 20 strong port fortresses and were 'the strongest European power in Asia', having supplanted the Portuguese, even if then they also had to face the English (Israel 1990, pp. 104–106), whose penetration into Lisbon's empire was more subtle, if no less inexorable. These were also the years in which the English defeated the Portuguese at Surat (1612) and obtained trading privileges from the Great Mogul in return for providing protection to Muslim pilgrims (1618).

For these reasons, it is possible to understand why, when the truce lapsed in 1621, the prowar Spanish faction had in mind not only religious and dynastic ideals. Many people, and not only nobles such as the Count of Benavente, thought that Spain needed a 'good war' to avoid the country becoming effeminate and to satisfy the proto-national feeling surging within Castilian society (Elliott 1990, pp. 86–99). The Iberian merchant communities also saw Holland and, to a lesser extent, England as a threat that had to be faced down. But the Dutch strategy persisted. Despite the problems that it would cause Dutch trade, the war also provided the pretext for a new offensive, an important early move being the seizure of Bahia and infiltration into Portuguese commerce between Africa and the Brazilian plantations (Brown and Elliott 1980, p. 195), a crucial road for the Luso-Spanish trade networks. The capture of Recife (7 March 1630) and the control of the large Portuguese region of Pernambuco (1630–1654) had the same meaning (Boxer, 1973).

A replica of events at Bahia was the help of the English to the Sha of Persia to conquer Ormuz (1622), which allowed them to forge the land route to Aleppo thus connecting with the Mediterranean, as we have said. At the same time, the Dutch established their headquarters at Batavia (Yakarta), whence they organized their entire military and commercial system, even nurturing the idea of 'becoming a territorial power' by attracting huge numbers of Dutch colonists to it; this plan was never implemented (De Vries and Van der Woude 1997, p. 386). After 1630 English and Dutch incursions into the trade of the Luso-Spanish empire only grew. These years saw the Dutch position at Pernambuco gain vigour under the government of Joh Mauritius (Boxer 1973). In Asia they gained a foothold in trade between China and Japan, taking Formosa (Taiwan) in 1641 and expelling the Portuguese from Ceylon and Cochin (Kochi) in the 1650s.

It is to be noted, however, that the Iberian complex was not stressed only by European agents. Some of these attacks or resistances, and those in Asia in particular, were the outcome of the alliance between the Dutch and the English with the polities in the region. But, more important, the multipolar process of globalization (Chap. 1) was also behind the situation in the seventeenth century. By then Russian expansion to the East was reaching a crucial point. The Rurik and then the Romanov dynasties (1613) had created an empire with many similitudes to that of the Iberians, where the tsar negotiated power with the boyars in exchange for access to economic resources and labour (mainly based on serfdom) as well as with state servitors, who were rewarded with conquered and confiscated land (Darwin 2008, p. 73). By the 1640s the new Romanov dynasty dominated land from the Asian Pacific to the coasts of the Northern Sea and the Baltic. This reinforced the fur trade from Siberia and also the trade from the Eastern Mediterranean and the Black Sea with the north of Europe, thus connecting to the different branches of the Silk Road (Fusaro 2015). As we have seen, since the sixteenth century, the pressure of the other big agent of globalization in Eurasia, the Ottoman Empire, on the Indian Ocean increased, and it became even stronger after the Battle of Lepanto (1571). The English-Ottoman alliance in Ormuz was part of this process. The rise of the Mughal Empire during the sixteenth century and its expansion in India would be another important trend. After the Second Battle of Panipat (1556) and with the conquest of the Deccan since 1590s, the Mughal created a new and more centralized political formation, which would be more reluctant to establish alliances with the Portuguese, in part due to religious reasons, and keener to befriend the Dutch (Costa 2014, pp. 176–181; Flores 2015). Equally important are the development of Japan and the rise of the Tokugawa shogunate during the first decades of the seventeenth century. This more centralized political system was especially disposed against the religious interference of the Iberian missionaries and sought to weaken the trade they established with the daimios (Findlay and O'Rourke 2007, p. 172).

It is to be noted that these trends are associated with the rejection of religious interference from the West, as well as with the spread in Asia of European warfare technology. Again, globalization elicited negative responses to the Iberian power, which would find crucial points in its nodal scheme under increasing stress.

The period until the early 1630s cannot, however, be considered one of implacable defeat for the empires of Philip IV, which retained a considerable capacity for reaction. But the strategy to hit its Achilles heel (i.e. its nodal arteries) was already designed.

What was happening? Some time ago J. Elliott drew attention to the way that the English adapted and adopted the legacy of the Spanish empire (2006). In the same way, the Dutch and English were imitating the methods used by the Portuguese in Asia since the fifteenth century: the foundation of factories and emporia trade—of long tradition in this area even before the arrival of the Portuguese (Chaudhuri 1985, pp. 105 and 107)—, the concentration of military force and commercial actions in strategic nodes, and the reduction of protection costs by balancing violence and negotiation on the local level. It is not the case that the Dutch did not try to conquer inland regions. The projects of Coen in Batavia (Israel 1989), where a vertical integration between spice production and trade led to the occupation of large territories, are good examples. The conquests of Bahia (1624) and then of Pernambuco (1630), with the intention of displacing the Portuguese from their continental dominium, are also a proof of this. But both campaigns showed that these were very risky and costly endeavours. The recovery of Bahia by the Spanish-Portuguese navy (1625) showed the inconsistency of this type of actions, and the fall of Pernambuco in 1654 was in part the consequence of the fact that in Amsterdam, 'the great merchant houses preferred an empire of trade and the expectations of quick profits to the uncertain and more distant returns from colonization' (Boxer 1957, p. 258).[7] This preference was, however, as old as the hills and provides one of the keys to understand what was happening. Although the Dutch could have been making a virtue of necessity, from the early years of the seventeenth century, many Dutch businessmen were very clear that major campaigns of conquest against the Spanish should be avoided because they 'involved large, open-ended financial commitments' (De Vries and Van der Woude 1997, p. 386). Behind this preference is the idea that conquering extensive regions, and so having to meet the high inherent protection costs, would have compelled them to maintain an expensive bureaucratic apparatus and therefore to open negotiations with colonial elites on the basis of the Spanish model and transfer political capital to local powers, thus giving rise to massive levels of contraband and political problems. At least in this period—as perhaps today—it was easier to infiltrate an empire than build one.

But it is important to note that the Dutch and English were also taking a step forward in the history of the colonization of the world and in the relations between formal and informal institutions. The key here lay in the commercial companies. As public and private enterprises (Chap. 6), they created internal mechanisms for the regulation of conflicts between merchant interests and political concerns. K. Chaudhuri expressed this perfectly when he wrote that the VOC 'symbolised one of the most powerful and prestigious combinations of trade and political objectives that the commercial world of Asia had witnessed' (1985, p. 83). Of course quarrels and fraud permeated all aspects of the companies (Chaudhuri 1985). But their capacity to resolve tensions was in sharp relief with the difficulties in reconciling the interests of merchants and monarch in the Iberian world. Their mixed character—simultaneously public and private—and their ability to finance their own military apparatus allowed them to create long-term

---

[7] The opinion of Boxer remains all the more interesting to the extent that he placed special emphasis upon the human factor as a cause of the re-conquest of the island by the Portuguese. But his account also makes clear that the resistance of the Portuguese and Spanish *moradores* (residents) and the difficulties in obtaining logistical help were crucial to remove the powerful Dutch interlopers (Boxer 1957).

strategies to resolve the classic economic dilemma of 'guns versus butter'. To be specific, in contrast to the Luso-Spanish empire, the Dutch were able to adapt and tailor their decisions in two senses: first, to delay the payment of dividends to their shareholders until their military power had allowed them to acquire and consolidate a solid position in the market (De Vries and Van der Woude 1997; Chaudhuri 1965) and second, and this was a crucial difference with the Luso-Spanish complex, to guarantee that the lion's share of available capital was used in costs that fed back into their own activities, something which emphatically did not happen with taxes paid by Iberian traders, an important part of which would end up in Flanders defending dynastic interests or, as Quevedo said, 'buried in Genoa', if not in the pockets of the bureaucrats, the aristocrats and what I have called the dominant coalition in general—let me add.[8] In addition the companies, acting as cartels, were able to regulate their competition and to lower the prices of the products that they bought (Chaudhuri 1965), something equally unthinkable in a system as unregulated as that of the Iberian world, whose independent companies—based on the model of the Italian medieval *compagnia*—tended to have a very short lifespan and compete among themselves.

What was the impact of Dutch and English competition? Was it able to provoke an immediate decline in Luso-Spanish trade? The prevailing interpretation has been that from 1600 all of this was having a devastating impact upon Iberian commerce. This view is quite logical, as when things are examined from the Dutch or English perspective, the impression is of an inexorable rise of both powers (Israel 1990; Brenner 1993), and the perspective from Spain has always underlined the enormous problems of the Catholic monarchy and the deep depression that accompanied them. But this idea deserves to be nuanced in degree and chronology.

The official figures of this trade are very revealing. The number of sugar refineries in Brazil increased during the first decades of the seventeenth century at the same rate as the figures for the official exportation of this product (Mauro 1960). Something similar can be said of the dimensions of the Portuguese merchant fleet in this region, which grew without interruption between 1583 and 1629 (Costa 2002, p. 173). All indicators invite us to conclude that the trade in these products, as in others such as indigo and cochineal for which only the merest hints exist in the archives

[8] This is obvious in the Spanish side of the empire, but even more in the Portuguese dominions, as Boyajian has pointed out (1993).

(Hough and Grier 2015, pp. 288–9), increased noticeably—or at least stabilized—during this period. A similar impression is conveyed by an analysis of maritime trade by the total tonnage of ships employed in the *Carrera de Indias*. Here a certain degree of Spanish resistance can be found, with figures remaining relatively high until the 1620s, with a notable fall occurring in this decade and a precipitous decline only in the 1630s and 1640s (Chaunu 1977, p. 255). This impression is corroborated by the evolution of the silver shipments arriving at Seville for private owners, a very important part of which were made up by consignments from emigrants and silver used to pay for merchandise sold in America (Bernal 1993). Figures for this sum, which provide a good reflection of the official commerce of Seville with America, reached their maximum proportions between 1616 and 1630 for the entire period 1500–1650.[9] If we add to this sum the value of the goods that came in these shipments, most of which was the fruit of colonial commerce (Bernal 1993), the impression is even more positive. And this is even more the case if the noticeable expansion of the commerce carried by the Manila galleon is taken into account, with the massive arrival of products from Asia in New Spain and a considerable reverse flow of silver (TePaske 1983, Gasch 2012). None of this can be considered strange if the upward cycle of silver production in the first decades of the century is added into the equation (Bakewell 1991); nor should it be forgotten that these years witnessed a marked expansion of the urban economy as well as the plantation economy and the linking together of economic networks in Latin America (Carmagnani 2011).

The same impression is given if we analyse the figures presented by Duncan some time ago for Portuguese trade in Asia (1986). Arrivals in Lisbon, as in Asia, without doubt the most reliable variable of the rhythm of commerce, remained high until 1620 and the more dramatic fall did not take place until 1630. Such a conclusion is reinforced by Boyajian's analysis, according to which private trade, particularly in the routes to Asia but also those to the Cape of Good Hope, 'did not collapse with the advent of European competition in Asia in 1600' and was in fact in its zenith during the two first decades of the seventeenth century (1993, p. 241).

---

[9] Using Hamilton's figures as a basis, I have calculated that these proportions constituted 85.5% between 1616 and 1620, 81% between 1621 and 1625, and 81% between 1626 and 1630; while in the overall period 1580 to 1650, only on one occasion, 1646 to 1650, did it reach the figure of 85% (and figures for this period are highly uncertain). In general the figure had moved between 60 and 75% (see Hamilton 1975, table on p. 47).

But what lies behind these figures?

It is worthwhile underlining that the infiltration of foreign businessmen and products into this commerce was highly important in the centres around which all else turned, Seville and Lisbon.

Contrary to the image of the *Carrera de Indias* as a monopoly system for the control of trade, it is to be noted that Seville was the main loading point for the shipping of non-Iberian products. The Crown's cession of the right to register products carried to America to the city's Consulate in return for sworn declarations of their worth and then, later, for fixed fiscal evaluations of the value of the contents of the shipments (see Chap. 5 above) was having its effects. This process continued during the seventeenth century. In return for a gift to the Crown (*donativo*) of 200,000 pesos (see below), in 1629 the system was changed to that of *avalúo*, in which tax assessment was made according to the weight of the crates and not the value of their content, a good deal of it being composed of high-value low-weight commodities.[10]

All of this acted in combination with the very system of financing the *Carrera de Indias*. Seville trade was predominantly based upon the 'loan at risk' (*préstamo a riesgo*) in which the lender, who assumed the risk, advanced money to a borrower who would repay the loan in America once he had sold his merchandise. Given that this restitution was made by an exchange of money between Spain and America and that considerable risk was involved in it, the interest rates of these loans were very high (normally between 80 and 100%). This meant that only the great merchants could undertake operations involving very large shipments and that, frequently, the loan consisted in the handing over of merchandise whose value, plus interest payments, would have to be returned to Seville after its sale in the colonies. For this reason this system ended up favouring operations among the great international merchants (inserted in networks with their epicentres in the Low Countries, England, Italy, etc.), who took advantage of Castilian front companies with presence in the Consulate to insert their products in America, using the main artery of this trade. This was an authentic example of 'legalized contraband', which allows us to understand why, despite the figures on commerce remaining relatively high until the 1620s, their positive effects on the Spanish economy in

---

[10] This is in itself a persuasive reason for thinking that figures produced by Hamilton and Chaunu should always be assumed to be lower than the real ones, as they referred in most cases to shipments of high-value fabrics.

general and its industry were less than could be expected. The system was aggravated—and this was the accusation of the Seville shipping merchants—by the presence in their city of the so-called peruleros, Peruvian traders who operated in the zone and who, after the foundation of the Consulate of Lima (1613), were able to defend their interests more effectively before the Crown. Their arrangement consisted of obtaining loans from private individuals in America and, having transferred the monies to Seville, the purchase in big quantities of products that would then be shipped back across the Atlantic (Oliva 2004, p. 36). The advantages acquired over the previous decades by the industries of the north of Europe, the lower prices of goods from these areas, and the strength of the foreign wholesale traders made them especially competitive in the markets of Seville and America.

It is interesting to underline some notable parallels with changes in Portuguese commerce. In contrast to the Castilian model, this was not a royal *estanco* ceded to national merchants, in which most royal income came from taxes paid on commercial activity and the taxes in America and mining activities. In Portugal it was the Crown itself that retained its rights to trade. But, in any case, the system of licences—which, as we have seen, proliferated from the end of the sixteenth century—implied that the Portuguese king's ships would be loaded by non-Portuguese merchants and that, by extension, the majority of the profits would not remain in the country or have a small positive impact on the sectors that might have created added value (Godinho 1982).

It is therefore evident that colonial trade from Seville and Lisbon remained very dynamic but also that part of it was already in the hands of transnational merchant networks.

Important as the infiltration of foreign merchants in the ports of both Seville and Lisbon was, evidence also suggests that direct smuggling between other countries and the colonies under Portuguese-Spanish control was also increasing and would gain momentum from the mid-1620s. To justify this assertion for the Asia trade, one can recur to a comparison between the ships arriving at Lisbon and Holland from Asia (Graph 7.1). But the fact is also obvious in the increasing losses of Portuguese ships—in a good deal due to Dutch and English attacks—during this period, as well as in the way 'the private traders conducted by royal officials, soldiers and private merchants' undercut the Crown's exclusive control of this trade (Schwartz 2007, pp. 27–28). Something similar can be said of American trade, if we take into account the marked increase in freight prices in traffic

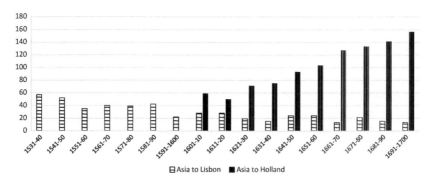

Graph 7.1   Ships arriving from Asia to Lisbon and Holland
Sources: My own elaboration with data from Israel (1989) and Duncan (1986).

to Brazil, a variable that was also partly influenced by the security of commerce.[11] The importance of smuggling, and the redirection of the trade at the expense of traffic in the *Carrera de Indias* between Seville and the Caribbean, is also clear in research on the Río de la Plata.[12] There is also the suspicion of a growing Dutch presence in the area, allowing more effective contraband from the 1620s onwards, something which is corroborated by qualitative data.

In conclusion, the most probable explanation of what was happening is that between 1580/1590 and 1630, America witnessed very marked growth, thanks to the coincidence of the last cycle of mining and an explosive burst forward of the export-orientated plantation economy.[13] Rates of urbanization, if rather crude and not directly dependent upon the development of plantations, endorse this view too. Similar deductions can be made from quite a few qualitative indicators. Thus, the strong growth of the American economy was able to sustain expanding trade within the New World and also an increasing official and contraband trade towards other continents at the same time until 1630. Something similar must have been happening in Asia, where Europeans as a whole were diverting

[11] According to the figures of Leonor Freire Costa (2002, pp. 76–7), it is clear that costs grew between 1580 and 1600, before stabilizing and even falling during the truce of 1609–1621. After this point they shot upwards.

[12] Moutoukias' study presents its most consistent figures for the period 1650–1700, but his data also underlines the dynamism of the early decades of the century in the formation of the Peru-Buenos Aires smuggling axis (Moutoukias 1988, Chapter 2).

[13] The growing number of slaves carried to the New World supports this analysis (Engerman and Genovese 1975; Curtin 1969).

towards the west a growing proportion of the local and interregional trade that, as Subrahmanyan says, was very voluminous and therefore allowed them to redirect greater quantities towards the old continent without suffering adverse effects.

From 1625 to 1630, the advance of Holland and England would be even clearer, and by 1648, when peace was finally signed with Holland, the system had reached a dramatic and ironic perfection. The policy of striking against weak points and infiltrating the trade of Lisbon, Seville, and other peripheral areas of the empire was yielding results. In both cities, the so-called monopolio now benefited many other countries. Moreover, smuggling was practised from strategic points in the Caribbean, Africa, and Asia. This situation was even more dramatically ironic if we take into account that the Catholic monarchy was seeing its spending rise for both the protection of these empires and the preservation of their markets (see below). Mercantilism was not only impossible but also benefited foreigners in proportion to the efforts to apply it. The outsiders had now found their 'Indies', as Thomas Mun would say in a work published posthumously in 1664 (Chap. 6). They had first imitated and then adapted the Portuguese techniques, at the same time as they learnt from the errors of the Spanish colonial system. Mun himself, as a director of the English East India Company, had been one of the protagonists in copying and perfecting existing practices and well knew the high cost that alternative experiments might entail. The Dutch and English were able to continue to trade in many American zones without having to take the trouble of conquest, thus saving themselves costs associated with social control, coercion, and administration.

Around 1620 Seville was brimming full with Flemish merchants and merchandise; representatives of other northern nations and Italians were equally prominent. The rise of the American market was now beginning to have a very positive effect on the industries of different areas of Europe, all of them more competitive than Castile. The English had gained access to the Mediterranean, and their 'new draperies'—light, fashionable, and adapted to the climates of the South—were starting to be worn by a good deal of the urban population both in the Iberian Peninsula and in the colonies (Brenner 1993; Coleman 1977). The Dutch, thanks to their multidirectional growth and expanding global markets (Israel 1989), were establishing a centre of information and exchange whose tentacles reached into every part of the world economy and through which data and intelligence were gathered, costs lowered, and predictions made as never before. Economic development and political independence—achieved through military efforts—meant that the Dutch hub was much more efficient than Antwerp had ever been (De Vries and Van der Woude 1997, p. 667). The French were a growing presence in Spanish and American trade and were setting down the basis for a system that would reach its full maturity and potential in the second half of the century. All of this was achieved at a time in which the presence of Italian industrial products in the international markets was declining, as these were now hindered by diminishing competitiveness in terms of their cost and capacity to adapt to market demands, as well as the inability of Italian political systems to exert influence successfully in a world increasingly shaped by mercantilist considerations and policies.

Global Wars and the Relevance of the Imperial Periphery

The traditional view of what was to occur is quite clear. The decline in American revenues, traditionally associated with the mining crisis, reduced the Crown's income precisely when the domestic economy was weakened and the Thirty Years War, understood as a European conflict with some colonial extensions, reached its climax. Under such circumstances, Castile would remain the only territory disposed to endure the conflict's enormous burden.[14] However, if a wider global perspective is adopted to analyse this period, the final impression may be very different. Any such attempt may even cast a great deal of light on processes that reshaped the empire and were essential in the long term.

Cash for the King on a Global Scale

It might be said that we are dealing here with an *economy of war* in many senses. This is evident in the fact that military spending, and the payment of debts contracted to meet it, by themselves constituted more than 60% of Castile's ordinary expenditures.[15] This stress provoked by war is also

---

[14] A number of excellent studies can be consulted, in particular Domínguez 1983, Ruiz Martín 1990b, and Gelabert 1997, 2001.

[15] By 1598 spending in Flanders and in general defence rose to 3.45 and 3.4 million ducats, respectively, more than 50% of total governmental expenditure as a whole, and in 1621 they reached 3.1 and 2.9 million, respectively, equivalent to half of the total. Moreover the second most important part of governmental spending concerned the servicing of debts, most of which derived from military spending. Payments on *juros* alone constituted 5.6 million in 1621, that is, 40% of the total cost and more than 50% of the income in this year (Thompson 1976, p. 288).

evident in the subscription of both *asientos* and *juros* and paved the way for the bankruptcies of 1607, 1627, and 1647 (Gelabert 1997; and Ruiz Martín 1990b).[16] The problems accumulated after 1580 with a cessation of growth in the interior zones of the Meseta and the end of expansion in Andalusia, the most highly taxed areas of the Crown, had a deleterious effect (Castillo 1965). Due to the limitations of what we have called the conflictive pact, the fiscal system was reaching the limits of its efficiency: clientelism, corruption in local and central management, disorder in the collection of taxes, and many other deficiencies were now becoming a problem (Domínguez 1983).

In this context, the war economy would reach its fullest extension. In the first decades of the century, the sale of *baldíos* and common lands had continued, as had those of jurisdictions and royal rents, reinforcing tax pressure upon the remaining royal domain. And if the *alcabalas* were hardly increased, these had now to be paid in some areas that contained a decreasing number of persons.[17] The outbreak of war in 1621 made things even worse. The decade would be marked by the negative effects of the minting of *vellón* coins, which brought about a rise of more than 40% in the premium of silver money in just eight years.[18] International payments (above all those effected in Flanders) could only be made in gold or silver: the result was a drastic reduction in the capacity of the monarchy to attend to the international dimensions of the war (Parker 1972, 247–65). These effects were even more prejudicial since between 1600 and 1640, the *guilder* rose in value by more than 30% in relation to the silver *real* (Graph 7.2). And from the 1630s, new payments of the *millones* taxes were introduced, their value quadrupling in many areas (Artola 1982). But, above all, this situation led the government to the *arbitrios*, or extraordinary measures, which on many occasions were not negotiated in the Cortes.

[16] The evolution of the *asientos* is indicative in this regard. They increased between 1602 and 1605, before falling, doubtless because of the bankruptcy caused in 1607. From around (approximately) 1616, a new growth cycle began, reaching a peak for the reign in 1623–1625, with the bankruptcy of 1627 on the horizon, after which a new dip can be seen. The war of Mantua, and specifically the entrance of France into the conflict, brought about a dramatic increase, which lasted until 1642 (Gelabert 1997, Graph 1.1, p. 323).

[17] In Segovia the *alcabalas* hardly rose between the 1570s and 1620s. But this quantity had to be paid by a population that had fallen by almost 25% and which now also had to pay the *millones* and other burdens (García Sanz 1987).

[18] It has been calculated that this led to an appreciation of up to 120% by 1648 as a result of the repeated minting of new *vellón* coin, with another royal bankruptcy in 1647 (Hamilton 1975, pp. 105–12).

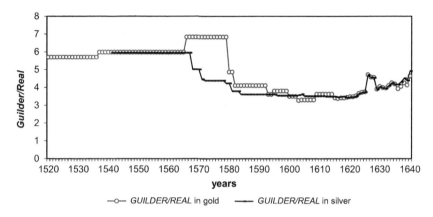

Graph 7.2   *Guilder/Real* ratio in gold and silver
Sources: Posthumus (1946, Tables VI to VIII) Feliu (1991, Table II.1), Hamilton (1975; p. 85, Table 4) and Yun (2004). For more details see Yun (2004; p. 142).

The complex constructed by Charles V was thus trembling (see our description in Chap. 4). The fiscal pact between the Cortes of Castile and the king was now weakened; the system for the consolidation of debt was taking on water like a sinking ship, and would continue to do so to the extent that the dynamism of the economy was falling. This was all the more evident since the other fundamental pillar, the royal American revenues, was also now cracking. The royal silver shipments, which had begun to fall in 1600, reached a level in 1616–1620 that did not exceed that of 1566–1570, when the Seville boom in metals began (Hamilton 1975, p. 48). Thus, the lubricant that served to obtain *asientos* and then to consolidate them as *juros* on Castilian incomes fell short. This would have very prejudicial effects, not only for the phenomenon in itself but also because it struck a blow to a fiscal system that was by now very highly indebted.[19] Even the other pillar, the credit provided by the Genoese, now began to weaken as did the difficult and fragile alliance with them. The bankruptcy of 1627 made it clear to Olivares and, indeed, to everyone else

---

[19] If in 1598 the *juros* absorbed approximately 45% of Crown incomes (4.6 million ducats from 10.22), in 1621 it had already reached 60% (5.6 million from 10.52). This is all the more revealing in that these years had seen a fall in the interest rate on debt from 7.1% to 5%, and many *juros* had been pledged by the Crown as security on these lower levels.

that now was the time to replace the Genoese or at least to counterbalance their enormous power (Boyajian 1983; Ruiz Martín 1990b). A policy of approximation to Portuguese Jewish bankers and *conversos* was therefore introduced. If the final result was not the credit monopoly falling into the latter's hands, then it did, over the century, produce a greater number and range of *asentistas* and agents, to whom the monarchy was much more closely tied for reasons of international political strategy (Sanz 1988).

But what was the real role of the colonies in this situation? Can we reduce the problem to a crisis of the Crown's colonial revenues, meaning a reduction of Asia's and America's capacity for sending money to the peninsula? Nothing could be further from the truth, although this interpretation has predominated when the problem has been viewed from a strictly peninsular perspective.

Certainly, the Portuguese system was facing difficulties. Here smuggling and the growing Dutch presence in Asia were bringing about a financial crisis in overseas incomes. But the other big problem was in the licence system, that is, in the fact that a big proportion of the colonial benefits were going to private hands, especially those of transnational and global agents. The kings of Portugal were seeing a fall in their income for this reason from 1588; by 1627 they hardly garnered a quarter of what they had at the beginning of the period, a sum that practically disappeared between 1632 and 1641 (Hespanha 1993b, pp. 197–205). Furthermore, as in Castile, a phase of sharp inflation in the 1630s eroded the buying power of the tax intake (Hespanha 1989, p. 112). Once again, the problem was the stress experienced by a global system that had functioned relatively well during the sixteenth century but that generated insuperable tensions not only at its centre, as is normally said, but, more important, on its periphery.

But the case of Castile is more meaningful. As we can see (Graph 7.3 and Table 7.1), the decade 1601–1610 saw a fall in the shipments of silver reaching the king from America that would continue until the 1640s, when a definitive collapse occurred. In these conditions it was extremely difficult to meet the needs created by the renewal of war in 1621 (Lynch 1969, pp. 71–6).

But, more than a crisis in the colonial tax system, what in reality was taking place in the long run was a downward trend in the proportion of the silver brought to Castile, with more remaining on the empire's periphery. Thus, if 64% of income in Lima were sent to Spain in 1591–1600, this proportion fell to 45% in 1601–1610 and 'to about one third for the next

368   B. YUN-CASALILLA

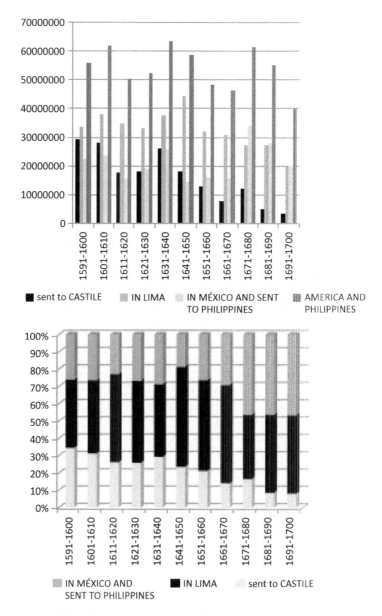

Graph 7.3 The distribution of the Spanish Crown American income
Sources: My own elaboration with data from TePaske and Klein (1982, Appendix).

Table 7.1 The distribution of the American Income (Spain)

	Sent to Castile	In Lima	In México and sent to Philippines	America and Philippines	% sent to Castile
1591–1600	29,290,549	33,683,302	22,270,657	55,953,959	52.35
1601–1610	27,960,747	38,006,115	23,772,246	61,778,361	45.26
1611–1620	17,816,355	34,664,082	15,720,600	50,384,682	35.36
1621–1630	18,159,998	33,319,795	18,939,319	52,259,114	34.75
1631–1640	26,217,176	37,686,150	25,844,488	63,530,638	41.27
1641–1650	17,937,904	44,162,913	14,411,753	58,574,666	30.62
1651–1660	12,912,496	32,077,933	16,182,019	48,259,952	26.76
1661–1670	7,559,713	30,655,309	15,796,262	46,451,571	16.27
1671–1680	12,056,228	27,249,881	34,104,600	61,354,481	19.65
1681–1690	5,078,377	27,166,234	28,013,250	55,179,484	9.20
1691–1700	3,422,516	19,606,978	20,199,095	39,806,073	8.60

Sources: TePaske and Klein (1982, Appendix)

two decades'. In the 1670s it hovered around 8%, and in the following decade, it had fallen to 1% (TePaske 1983, pp. 427–8). This tendency was repeated in Mexico, which moved from sending around 90% to Spain between 1581 and 1610 to almost 60% in 1641–1650. The remainder either stayed in America or was employed in the Philippines (being directed above all to defence, as we have seen) (TePaske 1983, Table 4, p. 444). These facts have even greater relevance given that in New Spain, in difference to Peru, mine production and, therefore, the incomes derived from it appear not to have diminished. Table 7.1 which represents the total income in America and the proportion sent to Castile is very meaningful. The total income fluctuated until 1680–1691 and only decreased in a very substantial way in the last decade of the century. But the proportion sent to Castile dramatically decreased during the century and more in particular after the big effort of 1631–1640, with the entry of France in the Thirty Years War.

There are a number of reasons for this, but one above all must be underlined: growing proportions of metal remained in the colonies to meet their own needs and above all the defensive costs that were rising in response to the Dutch and English attacks. Thus, one of the reasons for the growing military problems in Europe was the global character of the war and empire. In broader terms, the difficulty lay in the growing needs of a global empire that had to establish and defend a multitude of local interests and centrifugal forces spread across a vast geographical area and whose local elites demanded that the empire attend to their protection costs by spending a growing proportion of their taxes. It is important to note too that, if the silver collected in America remained at very high levels until 1681–1690, all available figures on mining production indicate an unbroken fall that began from 1620 to 1625 and continued until 1660–1670 (Barrett 1990, Figure 7.1, p. 238). In other words, a sizeable part of the shortfall was now coming not from the mines but from the pockets of the American population. It is not odd, therefore, that bigger parts of the budget were contributing to maintain the defensive system and the American colonial administration.

It should be noted that this is not only the case of America. In a revisionist study published years ago by Storrs (2006), this author made clear that the effort of the Habsburg empire's non-Castilian territories of Europe also increased during the last 30 years of the century. But this can be said also for the previous decades, in spite of the Union of Arms' failure. Thus royal incomes in Naples rose from some three million to almost six million ducats between 1600 and 1640, a 100% growth in nominal terms. This in fact meant a considerably larger contribution in real terms, since the fall of prices in the kingdom after 1620 also brought about a reassessment of the taxes levied, thus increasing the overall contribution of this state in real terms. In this kingdom, the consolidated debt grew by 65% between 1605 and 1638 (Calabria 1991, p. 91).[20] Something similar occurred in the territories of the Crown of Aragon, although on a somewhat lower scale (Bernabé 1993). Catalonia had already increased its extraordinary tax payments in 1599 up to 1,100,000 *lliures* a year (Elliott 1963). But, very importantly, in all of these kingdoms, new taxes were created on productive activities and commerce. These payments entailed contributions to the war or support for military units in situ. And, as in Castile, the municipalities had to impose *sisas* (sales taxes on items weighed or measured) to meet the costs of war (Bernabé 1993).[21] It is very difficult to work out the monetary contribution of the Low Countries. These monies remained in the treasury of the army, which in any case appears to

[20] According to figures presented by Calabria, the Crown incomes in 1638 were about 5.6 million ducats, whereas the public debt came to 3.2 million (1991, Appendix I, Tables 1 and 6, pp. 134 and 142).

[21] The viceroys of the Principality of Catalonia were able to extract more from towns, with Cervera's contribution rising from 5500 to 23,000 *lliures* between 1611 and 1618 (Elliott 1963, p. 145).

have acted as an extractive mechanism, and when taxes were raised by local authorities, they proved barely sufficient to cover the cost of their own defence. But G. Parker has calculated that from 1600 to 1640, the 'obedient provinces' contributed some 4,000,000 florins a year (almost three million ducats) (Parker 1972, 144).[22] In Milan the system of contributions by compensation (*compensazione*) and levelling off (*egualanze*) for the maintenance of troops was equally indicative of how war and the overall military system of this composite monarchy generated costs and how its 'peripheral states' were obliged to increase their incomes, as well as their contribution to warfare.[23]

But Not Only Cash: The Real Burden of the War
The contribution of the periphery of the monarchy to the imperial efforts on its many battle fronts is even clearer when the focus of attention moves from money to men. In effect, the economy of war was characterized by the use of forms of resource extraction that, in addition to taxes, resulted in the direct mobilization of troops and military units on the local level and battlefield. This is important in this case, since, as has been said in Chap. 4, the fiscal system is too often confused with the system for the mobilization of resources *sensu lato*. Yet this consideration is crucial to understanding the impact of war on the empire and not only—or so much—because of its weight but also because of its footprint on the political economy.

As expected, this type of contribution was very much present in Castile. Continuing the tradition set up in the precedent century, many cities—for example, Seville, Mérida, Segovia, Salamanca, and the coastal ones—came to contribute in this way with armies which were sometimes better paid than those of the king himself (Thompson 1976, pp. 134–5). There are some reasons to believe—though no overall figures can be provided—that

[22] This is, perhaps, an exaggerated figure. In fact, it comes close to the contribution of Castile itself to the war, if we follow the figures of Thompson (1976, p. 288). But other calculations hold that Flanders provided 25% of the resources for the war, which is at least one-third as much as Castile and not negligible (Esteban 2002, pp. 62–3). This makes sense if we add to the figures for 'Flanders' given by Thompson those relating to 'defence', some three million ducats in 1621.

[23] Buono (2008, pp. 35–48). The author describes 'compensation' as the right of local inhabitants to be compensated for the real cost, including the destruction of property, the lodging and keep of troops; in this arrangement zones that had not seen active fighting or billeting contributed to the costs of those that had.

efforts of this sort were extended in the 1630s, above all because of the war with France, which threatened the very Spanish territories (Mackay 1999, pp. 80–96). Thompson puts the value of the salaries and military equipment given by Seville at some 170,000 ducats during these years. In Murcia, the most exhaustively studied region, the city paid for armed men at its own cost and maintained its walls. It was also involved in skirmishes on the coast of Africa and even contributed to the maintenance costs of Orán (Ruiz Ibáñez 1995, pp. 227–9 and chapter VI.3). By the same standard, the city of Cartagena was directly involved in privateering offensive and defensive activities organized from its harbour (Ruiz Ibáñez and Montojo 1998).

Also like in the preceding century, this was not only a business of towns. Nobles were actively involved in raising men as a form of service paid for from their own pockets (or by advancing money). Troops of this kind were, at heart, a form of 'tribute in kind' rather than in liquid money, although at times this sort of contribution might be commuted for payment in metallic (Mackay 1999).[24] Thompson has argued that the fact that the treasury receipts of Philip IV did not exceed those of his grandfather 'is an indication not that the costs of government had remained unchanged, but that the central administration was now taking a smaller share in the management of the state' (1976, p. 141). In other words, the treasury figures do not provide us with the full picture, as has often been assumed. Moreover, all of these political actors contributed to the mobilization of troops, as was normal in a corporate composite monarchy.

But, as with the flows in cash, the contribution of other kingdoms was not negligible at all. The case of Milan, just mentioned, is perhaps one of the most expressive (Maffi 2009), as long as the compensations were associated with military mobilizations in situ, which opened the door to possible excesses related to the transfer of nonfiscal resources to the central power from the areas affected by the presence of troops. Moreover the levies of soldiers, their billeting, the forced purchase of provisions, and other actions, constituted a compulsory contribution that cannot be calculated but which should not be hidden behind the figures derived from treasury and exchequer accounts (Buono 2008). To the body of 60,000 men under arms, all paid for by the Crown, can be added the

---

[24] A meaningful evidence is that of the total number of *censos* taken out by a wide section of estates belonging to the titled nobility between 1580 and 1640, 18% were for military services (Yun 2002a, p. 175).

urban militias supported by the cities. This mechanism for the mobilization of resources, which often did not leave records in the central treasuries, was also employed in Sicily and Naples (Rizzo 1995, and Muto 2007). Though sometimes mixed with flows of cash, it also proved very common in the battlefield of the Low Countries (Parker 1972). We also know that local levies were raised in the Crown of Aragon, sometimes even as a result of forced agreements conceded by the Cortes (Bernabé 1993). The billeting of troops was especially costly in Catalonia during the war against France, to the point that this 'contribution' was another reason for the disaffection of the Catalans towards the House of Habsburg (Elliott 1963, chapter XIV).

Though there were differences and natural diversity, this type of mobilizations was very much present in America, from New Spain to the viceroyalty of Peru or Río de la Plata (Ruiz Ibáñez 2009). The formats employed ranged from the establishment of pacts between captains, Jesuits, and friendly Indians, who acted as sort of mercenaries in exchange for a range of concessions or advantages, to the formation of militias (Giudicelli 2009; Ariel and Svriz 2016). From the end of the sixteenth century, the urban militias were being rolled out in other territories and, indeed, across the Iberian world and its principal cities, most of them coastal, to the point that this was almost a global phenomenon (Ruiz Ibáñez 2009).[25]

The importance of all of this is difficult to exaggerate. As has been said (Chap. 4 above), it represented the military functioning of a composite monarchy. And it affects not only scholars' quantitative assessment of the war effort but also our understanding of the monarchy's overall debts— that is, not just those of the King of Castile. This was also because a sizeable part of these operations continued to be paid for not only by the incomes of these kingdoms and corporations but also by increasing their debts. This is also important because it was a crucial phenomenon that, regardless of its quantitative impact, underlay the configuration of pacts that definitively affected the institutions and the political economy of the different territories.

*　*　*

[25] See the works by Descimon (1993) and M. Prak (2005).

In less than a century, the Habsburgs had managed to put together the two greatest European empires. In both cases the expansion had produced great advantages. But in both cases, this expansion had also been possible thanks to the projection upon them of informal networks that, despite their going beyond the family and not being only or purely of a familial character, had their transcendental weight in this institution. It could not be any other way, as the networks of relatives and those that could be built upon them played an essential role in this society. In fact they served as the basis of the expansion itself, which was also the result of the needs for expansion of social elites for whom the themes set out in the previous pages—family and extended family relationships, clientele systems, patronage between groups, friendship understood as a political expression and an economic action, a sense of local and religious identity—provided the internal structural forces that shaped the strategies for the reproduction of the social order. This would be fundamental to all developments.

In a brilliant essay written in 2007, Stuart Schwartz set out the dynamic of Portuguese commerce as the product of the clash between public institutions and merchants' private interests. The idea is excellent, and the above pages have attempted to reformulate it. The argument does not serve simply for the Portuguese empire. Nor should it be limited to commerce and merchants, since networks of trade were on many occasions only a part of informal and multifunctional webs that were much more extensive and widespread. And the outcome was logical: to the extent in which the institutions of the monarchy were imbued in this same social and ideological structure, the history of both empires can be understood as a process of continual perversion of the efforts towards centralization by the Crown. All of this stood at the base of a political economy in which the practices of rent-seeking, the capture of privileges, corruption, the continual use of privileged information of a very asymmetrical character, and so on would be essential components. It would be these networks, the very agents that had contributed towards the establishment of the empires, which would weaken the power of the Crown, which without doubt must be seen as the most important and the most powerful of all agents but, in the final analysis, simply an agent in these pacts. And this was so much more the case to the extent that the very process of globalization would end by turning upon those who had created it.

The deficiencies in the system of the *Carrera de Indias* and commercial licences as well as the need to attend to the necessities of possessions in America, Africa, and Asia were leading to a fall in the Crown's revenues on the peninsula. This drop in revenues affected the sophisticated edifice constructed by Charles V. Yet this situation did not imply a long-term reduction of global commercial traffic. Under these circumstances, intra-colonial commerce grew, and even the official traffic centred on Seville and Lisbon resisted better and longer than has often been thought. At the same time, through these cities or through direct or indirect contraband with the colonies, commercial networks centred outside of the peninsula, in such centres as Amsterdam, Mexico, Manila, the coastal areas of Brazil, and others, increased their participation in this traffic. This change, moreover, also resulted from the fact that competitor states such as England or the United Provinces were conscious that it was easier and cheaper to infiltrate Iberian markets than to affront the risks and the costs of protection and administration that the conquest of such vast territories would have entailed. A tentacular empire is attacked at the nodes of its tentacles.

Such a subtle process of invasion took place during the conflicts of the first half of the seventeenth century. Though the Thirty Years War was lived in Europe with great intensity, its extra-European dimension would bring out key elements in the working of the empire and the construction of the state. Far from being a narrowly European conflict, the war was a global phenomenon that compelled this composite global empire to mobilize in its peripheral areas. The consequent mobilizations, moreover, were far greater than is usually recognized when attention focuses only on flows of cash. Precisely because of its dimensions and characteristics, this conflict brought to light the limits of the military revolution and its effects upon the system for the mobilization of resources, which unsurprisingly were more appropriate for a composite monarchy than for a modern state (this latter assumption being the starting point for most visions). And it led to mobilizations in peripheral areas of this composite global empire that would be far greater than is usually recognized when the European dimension is the sole focus of attention. For all these reasons, war would shape and mark the equilibrium of the dominant coalitions, the political economy, and the path taken by the Iberian world, which was very different from the direction embarked upon by countries such as England. But, above all, it would lead to a process of dispersion of resources and even decentralization that would be decisive for the future of the empire. Local elites, particularly in America, would find in this situation the bases for more and more power of negotiation with the centre and for increasing autonomy. The next chapter will explore this aspect.

Open Access This chapter is licensed under the terms of the Creative Commons Attribution 4.0 International License (http://creativecommons.org/licenses/by/4.0/), which permits use, sharing, adaptation, distribution and reproduction in any medium or format, as long as you give appropriate credit to the original author(s) and the source, provide a link to the Creative Commons licence and indicate if changes were made.

The images or other third party material in this chapter are included in the chapter's Creative Commons licence, unless indicated otherwise in a credit line to the material. If material is not included in the chapter's Creative Commons licence and your intended use is not permitted by statutory regulation or exceeds the permitted use, you will need to obtain permission directly from the copyright holder.

CHAPTER 8

Ruptures, Resilient Empires, and Small Divergences

The warfare and global tension to which the Luso-Hispanic complex found itself exposed undoubtedly posed the greatest challenge faced by the accords on which it had been based since the sixteenth century. This challenge would appear particularly in the system for mobilizing resources and in taxation in the different territories, which comprised an integral part of that system. It would, moreover, emerge most clearly in the extent to which the composite states' most important principle, that which limited the transfer of resources among their parts, continued to be violated.

The ensuing political ruptures, with many parallels elsewhere in Europe, would take the form of conflicts between the periphery—and the empire's different parts—and the logic of the government at the empire's dynastic centre. The result would be important for the history of these diverse territories, as well as for their political economies.

OLIVARES' CHALLENGE TO THE IMPERIAL ELITES

One of the most important reactions to the stress imposed upon the imperial system undoubtedly entailed the reformism and increase in fiscal pressure from Madrid. Although a well-known development, its fundamental landmarks merit consideration in relationship with this book's argument and, in particular, from the perspective of the relations between the Crown and the elites in the framework of the balance between accord and conflict consolidated during the sixteenth century (Chap. 4).

© The Author(s) 2019
B. Yun-Casalilla, *Iberian World Empires and the Globalization of Europe 1415–1668*, Palgrave Studies in Comparative Global History, https://doi.org/10.1007/978-981-13-0833-8_8

Reformism

The reforming spirit in Spain was most clearly embodied in the person of the Count Duke of Olivares (Rome, 1587–Toro, 1645). A member of the Guzmán family hailing from Andalusia and a lateral branch of the House of Medinasidonia, don Gaspar de Guzmán provides an exceptional portrait of the sort of noble who, without being the head of a major lineage, found—and took—his chance to advance in the fluid situation created by the circulation of elites (Chap. 4). In an episode that was typical of the internal tensions within these lineages, his family had found itself confronting the head of the lineage, the duke of Medinasidonia, over the claims of his grandfather, don Pedro de Guzmán, to the duchy (Chaps. 1 and 4). Thanks to his services in Seville and abroad, don Pedro had enjoyed the favour of Charles V. Like so many other families, this one carried the stigma of *conversos* in its past. Don Gaspar's father, don Enrique de Guzmán, made use of his notable political capital to marry a daughter of the Count of Monterrey, bringing him a dowry of 60,000 ducats and ties to one of the kingdom's most prominent families. His bride, doña María Pimentel de Fonseca, enjoyed the inestimable immaterial capital of having been miraculously made healthy by Teresa de Ávila, or so at least it was said. Don Enrique, Count of Olivares, served as ambassador in Rome and as viceroy in Palermo. His career meant that his income, drawn from important estates in Andalusia, was supplemented by extraordinary emoluments and also strengthened his political and personal capital by adding transnational qualities and ties. Thus the future Count Duke, despite being the youngest of three brothers, was baptized by the Cardinal Aldobrandini, the future Pope Clement VIII. Upon returning to Spain, don Gaspar was able to fritter away a large part of his fortune in a spending blitz at court that at least secured him a good marriage. This gesture was typical of the 'double economy' of the nobles' patrimonial management (see Chap. 5). 'The prodigality of his gestures', says Elliott, 'would strengthen his claims to the status of grandee of Castile'. The squandering of money was obviously a form of investment. After a few years in Seville, don Gaspar returned to Madrid and navigated the conflicts between court factions with considerable skill, eventually binding himself to the Zúñiga faction, the family of his wife, and thus securing access to the new king, Philip IV, on the death of his father (Philip III) in 1621. The future Count Duke had a solid humanistic training, in part acquired in Italy, and was well acquainted with the world of Spanish universities, having been sent to study at Salamanca precisely because of his status as third-born son. While a student at Salamanca, he had in fact served as the university rector (Elliott 1990, chapter 1).

His years in Seville gave Olivares a good understanding of the urban world and the internal conflicts and agreements between the oligarchies; Seville also taught him to understand the monarchy's global dimensions. Olivares' time in Madrid coincided with the outcry for reform. His solutions to the problems are well known and above all were set out in the scheme for the so-called Union of Arms, a sort of army agreement to be imposed upon the different kingdoms, and the establishment of local public banks (*erarios*) (Elliott 1982; Dubet 2003). The two schemes went hand in hand. The *erarios* were conceived as a means of financing the king and even of making credit circulate through society, as well as a way of sustaining a series of army units in the peninsula. But, also—this was the purpose of the Union of Arms—Olivares sought to engineer the creation of permanent army units in all kingdoms and provinces, including America, with the firm proviso that they would provide each other with mutual assistance. He also fully believed that a new merchant spirit should be encouraged among the aristocracy (without doubt this idea was a legacy of his life in Seville)—that the Crown should make better use of the non-Castilian nobilities and that trading companies, similar to those of Holland and England, should be established (Elliott and de la Peña 2013).

The modernity or character of this programme cannot be assessed here; what concerns us is the way that it affected the pillars upon which the dominant coalition had been built and its ulterior effects on the country's political economy.

Despite his maxim of *multa regna sed una lex*, Olivares was not a 'statist' in the modern sense, nor had he overcome the patrimonial concept of the monarchy. The Union of Arms implied, as has so often been stated, the ending of key aspects of the status quo, as it broke with the idea that the resources of each of the separate kingdoms should be employed only in its own defence. And, worse, this scheme would be implanted not only in Castile, where this precept had already been tacitly applied (even if the Castilians were loath to admit it), but across the empire. It also implied a strong displacement of the power of coercion and the administration of violence towards the monarchy, even when, as Olivares himself recognized, the local authorities were to be permitted to recruit troops.[1] Even more

---

[1] According to Elliott, 'Olivares was highly disposed to promise that the recruitment and payment of these troops would be managed entirely by local officials' (1990, p. 255).

destabilizing was the programme for the *erarios*, despite their being sometimes supported by the *procuradores* in the Cortes themselves. It at least made it very difficult to arrive at an agreement. This plan, which had been reformulated several times since its original version, fell short of a financial revolution of the sort that was cementing the success of the United Provinces (Chap. 4), given that Olivares' *erarios* operating with debt had nothing in common with a system of budget and debt bonds endorsed by the Cortes. Why, then, did the local elites resist them so bitterly? First, the deposits of these banks, far from being the outcome of the voluntary purchase of debt bonds (as was the case in Holland and, after 1694, England), were to originate in forced loans. On another level the plan also entailed an implicit attempt to remove decisive power from the urban oligarchies and the Genoese and to give it to the Crown. The oligarchies viewed the prospective eclipse of the Italian financiers with some relish but were rather less keen on the prospective loss of their capacity to control the king. Many patricians also resented the proposed reform of the tax system on the grounds that the abolition of the *millones* would entail their loss of power on the local level (Ruiz Martín 1990a). And these misgivings were often combined with others about the wisdom of Olivares' plan to substitute Genoese bankers for Portuguese financiers of Jewish *converso* origin, which added an element of religious prejudice into the equation. The Genoese at least benefited from the cultural capital afforded by their status as Catholics untainted by suspicion; this same concept or ideal provided a basis for the conflictive pact and, it could be said, the mortar that united this society.

If the Union of Arms also worried the nobility, then the arrogance of Olivares in seeking to overhaul its economic grounds was hardly the best balsam. The favourite probably allowed himself to be carried away by the image of a Seville aristocracy that tried to reconcile activities based upon commerce with its noble status (Pike 1978), of whom the most eye-catching example was, of course, the duke of Medinasidonia, up to his neck in illegal commerce in his estates in the lower Guadalquivir (Domínguez 1973). But trying to introduce merchants' habitus among the Spanish nobles went against not only their cultural beliefs but also against a form of moral economy that, if more complex than is sometimes believed, was at the heart of an economy of legitimation that fed the group's social capital. Despite the complaints of the Cortes that local banks were unfair because the nobility contributed little to them, the very existence of the *erarios* implied that a good part of the noble *auxilium* should not be understood in the context of the direct and personal service-favour (*do ut des*) exchange with the king that was the basis of their social consolidation and even survival as a class and power. Moreover, the Cortes themselves complained that 'this contribution is not voluntary, but forced and the nobility has never paid a personal contribution of this sort' (quoted by Domínguez 1973, p. 23). Something similar could be said about Olivares' plan to see the nobles educated at the universities, which was also a way of moving processes for the formation of social and cultural capital away from the family and lineage into the public domain. If this sort of measure might have had particular appeal to the second-born sons of noble houses—Olivares himself cannot have been entirely unaware of this element of it, as a third-born son—it would have broken with the idea that the best education for a member of the first estate was to be trained in court intrigues and knowing who was who. Rather than receive an intellectual schooling—which was not entirely absent from the aristocracy, as the biography of Olivares himself shows—the most profitable activity for the titled nobility was to acquire social and relational capital in Madrid. If this were not enough, in Castile the idea of further integrating the peripheral nobilities in the functioning of government was seen as spitting in the faces of those who extended their lineages and families precisely through these political resources, which were crucial to their social promotion.

The reaction to these proposals was quite varied. At one extreme stood the direct opposition in the Cortes of Aragon and Valencia, although this soon gave way to acceptance; at the other extreme was their total rejection in Catalonia; at other points they gave rise to struggles over specific aspects or projects and their general context. Some of these struggles elicited brutal criticism and biting satire from most refined practitioners of the Castilian language (Egido 1973). An army of wordsmiths, Quevedo among them, was mobilized against these plans. All of them made use of channels of communication that, if based upon the incipient public sphere, were the product of patronage and clientele systems that meant these quill-wielding soldiers ultimately served the interests of noble factions.

Fiscalism and Upheavals

Plans for reform were to be frustrated not only by resistance to them but also by the urgent and overwhelming need for money created by war, which compelled the government to take the existing status quo to the very limits of its possibilities and prioritize day-to-day solutions rather than the long-term reforms. Indeed Olivares brought the balance of this system near to the very limits of an absolutist regime—that is to say, to tyranny.

Olivares' measures would enrage all sectors of the Castilian elites, beginning with the urban oligarchies. This is the basis of the traditional interpretation that underlines the conflict between Olivares and this social sector. Thus the Cortes of Castile were urged to concede more services—*millones*, above all (Artola 1982)—and even to impose a levy on flour and salt, both of which would have had a major impact on the groups with the lowest incomes, or to create new taxes, like the so-called *cientos*, and the *media annata*, and withhold the payment of juros.[2] The impatience and determination that characterized Olivares led him to introduce measures that could only be justified by the assumption of *absoluta potestas*. This was emphatically the case in the manipulation of the *vellón* coins whose value was permanently reduced, despite many later efforts to reinstate their previous worth (Hamilton 1975, chapter 4). This course of action was first undertaken by Philip III. But the reign of Philip IV was marked by processes of currency devaluation and later revaluation that gave rise to a period of inflation and deflation whose effects were even worse than the simple minting of coins. Moreover, these acts were accompanied by the seizure of shipments from the Indies, forced loans, and so on. On top of all of these measures came frequent recourse to forced loans in the form of *donativos* that at times took the form of *asientos*.[3]

An additional problem lay in Olivares' treatment of the Cortes, over whose parsimonious processes and procedures he would trample, to the outrage of many. On top of this came the debate on the nature of the vote of the *procuradores*, which was alternatively understood to be *decisive* or *consultative*. The cities had previously sent their *procuradores* armed only with a *consultative vote*, that is to say a preliminary or advisory one, on the proviso that they would then return to the municipal councils for permis-

---

[2] (Domínguez 1983, pp. 295–309). The *cientos* consisted in a raising of the percentage of the theoretical rate of the *alcabalas*. The *media annata* was a tax on the inheritance of offices and other *mercedes*. Taxes were also created on the use of paper and so on.

[3] Domínguez Ortíz found 13 such *donativos* or general loans—that is to say ones that led to general campaigns for their collection across the kingdom—during the reign of Philip IV, with a noticeable intensification in the 1630s and, above all, from 1635, when war with France broke out (1983, chapter VII). In addition to these measures, there were individual or specific *donativos*, sometimes given to offset previous ones with individuals or corporations. These were grounded in the idea of *auxilium*, closely tied to the 'antidoral' theory present in the moral economy of the time (Clavero 1991).

sion to vote definitively (*voto decisivo*). The heart of the matter lay, logically, in Olivares's shortcutting of this second phase by taking the first vote to be decisive, thus saving time and giving the *procuradores*, who were more manageable than the oligarchies of the town halls, greater freedom of action and corruption (Fortea 2008).

But the absolutist methods of Olivares also affected the nobles. It is not certain that the Count Duke really sought to apply measures trying to limit the grants aristocrats received from the Crown (Yun 2002a, chapters 6 and 7), but any hint of a policy of this sort could create problems among a group who considered themselves to be the rightful recipients of royal largesse. That he began by awarding offices in Castile to the members of other aristocracies (Elliott 1982) should be seen in this light too. The high nobility saw its interests prejudiced by the currency devaluations, which considerably reduced its incomes in coin and made them more difficult to collect at a time when they were growing much more slowly than prices and even beginning to fall in real terms (Jago 1982; Valencia 2010, vol. I, pp. 542 and ff). The measures to reduce the official rates of interest the Crown paid for the *juros* may have followed market tendencies but also hit the pockets of many nobles, for whom they constituted an important source of income (the same was of course true for urban elites). Worse, on several occasions Olivares established criteria with regard to the conferral of favours based upon service that in many cases did not take into account what the high aristocrats considered to be distributive justice (in their view, considerations of rank meant more that offices and grants should be made mainly to them (Cárceles 1994)). The effects of such a policy could not be positive among a group that felt all of its interests to be threatened—its economic incomes, its political opportunities at court, and its access to the king, which the *valido* sought to limit or mediate. And the same effect was produced among the high aristocrats and the elites in general by the retention of half of the yields from *juros* (Domínguez 1973).

The fiscal absolutism of Olivares even touched the Church. On top of the Three Graces (*subsidio*, *excusado*, and *cruzada*; see Chap. 1) came a number of other voluntary donations (*donativos*; see Chap. 4) and services. If the fiscal weight of these revenues was being reduced by inflation, it was frequently the case that they (and above all the *cruzada*) were not used for the cause for which they had originally been granted, a 'misuse' which created considerable indignation among the clergy. But the principal problem was the *millones*, a service from which churchmen considered themselves to be exempt. For obvious reasons, they saw their interests prejudiced by the tax on franked paper, *papel sellado* (Gelabert 2001, pp. 150 and ff. 168). Their sense of injustice was even greater in relation to the war with France, which could hardly be presented as a fight for the defence of Christendom.

In this context, it is not difficult to understand why some have spoken of 'the convulsions of Castile' (Gelabert 2001). An uprising took place to protest the imposition of the salt tax in the Basque Country, whose fisheries and salting industry were badly affected (Fernández Albaladejo 1975). A long series of reactions against the taxes and the manipulations of the *vellón* currency occurred, and even after the fall of Olivares, there were altercations in cities such as Lorca and Palencia and in the Rioja region (Domínguez 1973, p. 20). Tensions would lead to risings between 1647 and 1652 in Andalusia, where even Córdoba and Seville were affected, when the poor harvests aggravated an already difficult situation and the local patricians were unable to control the people and in one case even incited them (Gelabert 2001; Domínguez 1973). Highly significant was the presence among these rebels of members of the local elites and clergymen; sometimes indeed it was they who led risings or encouraged them through their incendiary sermons.

If the cities broke with the *valido*, the nobles soon followed suit. They even went as far as a collective rebellion, a sort of a 'strike of the nobles', an inelegant but eloquent act—the abandonment of the political and constitutional functions of their class, specifically through their refusal to accompany the person of the king as a gesture of *auxilium* and *consilium*. The most serious noble protest was, however, the conspiracy led by two relatives of Olivares, the heavily indebted duke of Medinasidonia and the Marquis of Ayamonte, who took advantage of the rebellion led by João de Braganza in Portugal and, indeed, sought his help (Domínguez 1973; Salas 2013). In a certain way, this act provides yet another example of the tensions inherent in this sort of extended noble lineage frequent at court. But this episode had deeper roots and might even be profitably compared with events from as far back as the fifteenth century, when tensions of this sort were capable of combining with more general political processes to destabilize the entire political system. And this movement continued in 1648, being carried forward by the duke of Híjar in Aragon. Among the clergy things became so bad that a *cesatio a divinis* was sometimes proclaimed, meaning that they refused to administer religious rites. The bishops of Seville, Murcia, and Osma led acts of resistance or protest (Domínguez 1985, pp. 366–7). The wars of Mars were almost strangling the good works of Minerva; the grounds for complaint and rebellion were at times motivated by private interests but increasingly justified by the reigning political theory of the day.

CASTILE: CHANGE AND CONTINUITY

Reshaping the Conflictive Pact at the Core of the Empire

The protests discussed above would lead to important changes, but rather than rupture the conflictive pact, what emerged was a re-composition of it.

Despite these tensions, the Cortes and urban elites were able to resist the demands made of them. Many of Olivares' measures eventually led to—or, indeed, were from their very inception designed to achieve—more centralized forms of financing. Other proposals maintained and even, in some cases, strengthened the power of elites and their capacity to renegotiate with the Crown, even if—and this was the crux of the matter—they provoked a series of changes with the apparent agreement of both sides.

The negotiation over the *millones* and the subsequent *sisas* continued, and this was not necessarily bad business for the oligarchies, as an eighteenth-century text, Ruiz de Celada's *Estado de la Bolsa de Valladolid*, showed (Yun 1990; Ruiz Martín 1994). Even if urban tax systems were beginning to experience insolvency, the chance to exercise the dual roles of lender and manager of the debt, as a member of the town council, offered the elites notable advantages.[4] The sale of offices or the failure to abide by promises to absorb those already sold—a measure for which elites clamoured—meant that the oligarchies retained a social capacity to reproduce themselves. As in the previous century, the sale of noble titles continued to be seen as an opportunity and spigot for the ambitions of the oligarchies.

A very interesting part of this phenomenon lay in the *donativos*. This system was doubly useful for the elites in spite of their appearance of forced loans. In exchange for all manner of privileges, the king received a series of

---

[4]This mechanism has been set out in Chap. 4. It is worthwhile, however, to underline that the *censos*, unlike the *juros*, were not set on the debt of the treasury in general but on specific revenues. In this situation, whenever there were problems in claiming payment, they had to be resolved by the monarchy's administrators. For this reason a *regidor*, a member of the town council, always had a say on the order of payment, which was crucial in times of difficulties.

'donations' in money. In some cases, these were practically forced payments and provoked resistance, but normally it was not difficult to arrive at an agreement of some sort whereby the king provided important compensations. Only in the 1629 *donativo* Seville provided a loan of 500,000 ducats (5% of the income of the royal tax system at this point). In compensation it received, among other things, the return to its jurisdiction of towns or villages that had been recently sold and diverse judicial benefits; another privilege, which curiously benefited the patricians rather than the city itself, meant that officials (specifically, the *jurados* and *regidores*) of the municipal authority could not be arrested for having failed to pay their taxes (Martínez Ruiz 1992, pp. 266–7). In Andalusia, where extensive municipal properties existed, the towns asked for the right to privatize common lands to the benefit of a city or, sometimes, an individual (De Bernardo 1994). All of this constituted an attack upon the inalienability of the royal patrimony, a precept which the cities had so jealously guarded in the fifteenth century (Chap. 1). Also involved in trade-offs of this sort were monopolies on trade or on fishing, hunting, and taverns. Equally the municipal councils obtained privileges over their own jurisdictions: improved or extended scope to regulate the local market or the right of appointment to municipal offices which were previously of a royal prerogative, such as *alcaldías mayores* or *veedurías* (overseer of the local market) (Andrés and Lanza 2008). Given that normally these *donativos* were paid for by *sisas* (excise taxes) set on the consumption of basic products and that many of these political and economic resources were habitually employed to benefit the oligarchy, it is easy to see what lay behind all of this. But subscribers to the *donativos* were not only cities and towns. Moreover, many *donativos* were subscribed to by private individuals. As one royal decree put it, *donativos* were about 'speaking to all' (Domínguez 1983, p. 203). Among their subscribers we find nobles, who managed to obtain permission for *censos* to improve or sell parts of their *mayorazgo*. Equally some guilds and individuals of all kinds figure in the records (Domínguez 1983, chapter VII). In the final analysis, the *donativos* pulverized the relations between king and kingdom by making these relationships much more atomized and individualized. This was a genuine revolution that broke with the corporate force of the Cortes, even if this institution sometimes managed to intervene in their administration (see below).

Highly significant to this new relationship of atomized corporatism was the aforementioned Consulate of Seville, which would prove positive and, more important, comfortable for both parties and perpetuated an American commercial policy that would be highly harmful to the application of any sort of mercantilist programme, as we have seen.

Another crucial point in this new arrangement between the Crown and the kingdom was the resolution of the dispute over the consultative vote against the decisive vote. The kingdom, embodied in the Commission of the *Millones*, enjoyed a period in which it appears to have held a strong hand in negotiating with the king. This occurred, however, in parallel to a situation whereby each city with a vote in the assembly maintained its right to reach its own private agreement with the Crown in regard to both the concession of taxes and (especially) their method of collection (Fortea 2008). The end of this story would be crucial. The cities themselves, conscious of their power and influence, came to prefer to put an end to the Cortes, whose importance had in any case been declining. Everything indicates that they now preferred not to reconvene as an assembly, many of them being keen to establish a direct relationship with the king. The king, of course, seems to have been of the same opinion (Thompson 1993). This development, one of the keys to the evolution of Castilian constitutionalism, can be explained by the shift from a concept of the *procuradores* as representatives of the kingdom to one that, in practical terms, had them as representatives of each city with votes in the Cortes (Fortea 2008). This, of course, was a very different trajectory to the one followed by countries such as England.

Be that as it may, the result of the pressures generated by the Count Duke, and the need to relax them in order to reconstitute relations between king and kingdom after his fall, resulted in a greater degree of absolutism (evident in measures that went against the laws of the kingdom, such as the monetary manipulations) but which, without parliamentary mediation, would reinforce a growing localism.

The high aristocracy found itself in a similar situation. Despite the efforts of the Count Duke, it was impossible to sever the service-favours relationship, as it was essential to the patronage system and, indeed, to the political culture. A study (Yun 2002a) demonstrates that this group continued to receive many favours, privileges, and offices; in fact, no reduction in their conferral can be discerned. If, perhaps, comparison should be made with the concessions made to families from outside the titled nobility—something which in fact does not appear to have been frequent for this type of favour—then it is clear that the conferral of monetary payments (*ayudas de costa*), offices, positions at court, noble titles for family members, and estates and habits in the Military Orders was not only frequent but remained at the same levels seen in the previous period. In these decades the diplomatic service became ever more dominated by the aristocracy, as did the viceroyalties. Even measures such as the reduction of interest rates on *juros* or the minting of more money were cushioned: as the lowering of interest rates also affected the *censos* taken out on their *mayorazgos*, the nobles were able to substitute existing debts for new *censos* taken out at lower interest rates. Transfers of this sort were nearly always done with the permission of the Crown, which had few reservations about allowing them. Again, this policy can be seen as another form of royal favour and a means of relegating the mutual relationships. In other countries the sale of noble titles has been seen as a symptom of an 'inflation of honours' that prejudiced the high nobility; yet in Spain it also meant that many second-born sons and other members of these families acquired titles. For this reason its effects in Castile—and, perhaps, elsewhere—were perhaps not negative for the high aristocracy, even if they must have left some imprint or mark on the internal changes of this social sector. Despite the effects on the high aristocracy of new methods for raising troops (see Thompson's views above), the need to maintain a military mobilization system that had yet to eliminate private armies raised by contractors in fact strengthened the role of great nobles and the seigniors with peasants on their estates. It has even been said that as a result of the recruitment drives by nobles, 'the *señorío*, both as a source of soldiers and honorific *coronels*, and as a power structure that held administrative sway over much of Castile, assumed new importance in an age when its economic resources had never been so ill-fitted to the needs of the Crown' (Mackay 1999, p. 130). Far from the image of slumbering seigniors and great nobles who were finding their capacity for enforcement steadily reduced, what happened in Castile was a much more selective process; this having been said, it absolutely did *not* amount to the loss of power by the seigniors. If some cases can be found to suggest the 'fall of the nobility', these are more convincingly explained by absenteeism, the distances involved in managing estates, and the related problems of control and monitoring that were so common and exploited by stewards (*mayordomos*) and local agents. Perhaps it is not possible to speak of a process of 'refeudalization', but the relationship of symbiosis and conflict between nobility and Crown was strengthening the theoretical power of the former (Yun 1994a). And this was achieved on the basis of the disappearance from 1538 of a corporate institutional relationship in the Cortes. That is to say that, in the same way

that was happening in other sectors of society, an absolute king now negotiated and formed relationships not with a corporation but with each and
every noble house.

Something similar could be said of ecclesiastical institutions. Their
resistance to taxes was logical, and the mediation of two Popes, Urban
VIII, decidedly pro-French, and then Innocent X, in proroguing the *millones*, previously conceded to Philip II, was especially corrosive (Domínguez
1985, pp. 232–3). Yet the concession of some taxes was almost logical, as
the Pope also received a part of them. But it has also to be taken into
account that some contributions, like the *cruzada*, were not paid by the
clergy but rather were the result of bulls sold to the faithful. Moreover the
fraud was common in payments by the clergy, as became very clear in a
well-known case from Valladolid (Gutiérrez 1989; Yun 1990). The
Church was not deprived of the resources that originated in its special
relationship with the Crown. Ecclesiastical entitled properties, so criticized by the *arbitristas*, increased in number, the very opposite of what
was happening in many other countries of the time, France included
(Chap. 6).

In this context it is relatively easy to understand developments in the
king's justice and, specifically, the Chancelleries, as well as the fragmentation of the juridical system that we have mentioned before (Chap. 5). Very
possibly this situation did not serve to increase juridical security or to
reduce the transaction costs for many economic activities; on the other
hand, it certainly reflected the many means and varied methods of enforcement of the law and the clashing of jurisdictions, a legacy of the sixteenth
century that was growing in strength. This, inevitably, would have an
impact upon the allocation of resources and economic performance. As a
matter of fact, for some decades this *do ut des* paved the way for the managerial criteria less conducive to economic improvements (see Chap. 5).

Patrimonial Management, the Economic Resilience of Elites, and Property Rights

Very few of the changes for which the *arbitristas* had clamoured—and
were still clamouring—had been introduced. The quantity of *mayorazgos*
founded between 1600 and c. 1650 is not known. But we do know that
the institution not only grew in strength but also became increasingly
valued by local elites who saw in it both an economic strategy and a highly
rational way of conserving and recycling their social and political capital

(Hernández 1995). Many continued to invest massively in political resources and privileges, as can be seen in the rise in the price of the office of *regidor* in both Madrid and across Castile (Gelabert 1997, pp. 166–167). Putting money into the Military Orders—that is to say in social and political capital—remained at the same level and perhaps even grew, at least among urban elites (Hernández 1995, p. 226). The use of public properties, common lands, and *propios* lands (as we said those belonging to towns and villages) for private profit did not come to an end (De Bernardo 1994). As we have seen, such practices diminished the possibilities of agrarian innovations. As was by now commonplace, the traders of the Consulate of Seville continued to manage their businesses on the basis of their privileges, thus favouring both the arrival of non-Castilian products and the sky-high profits obtained by foreigners (Bernal 1993).

These practices, and above all those that allowed the acquisition of political capital, were not always—or only—implemented by *regidores* and direct members of the town councils but also by their relatives (Hernández 1995). This practice constituted an effort to maintain a logic of interfamilial relationships that would continue to resolve conflicts through lateral payments in the form of social promotion and that would corrode an institutional system which, by its very nature, was, according to new institutional economics, inefficient. Rent-seeking, which some historians have openly considered as corruption, was the great blight of the town councils and other institutions (see, among others, De Bernardo 1994; Cárceles 1994).

The halt in economic and demographic growth must have been one of the reasons for the reduction in the establishment of religious institutions (Graph 5.2). But the existing stock of foundations, nearly all of which had lands tied to them, and the large amount of entitled goods (a major bugbear for the *arbitristas*), was not reduced by an inch, and their weight now fell on an economy that was not growing or did so only very slowly. In other words, not only did they have a dissuasive effect on the development of productive investment, but they actually absorbed a growing portion of the GDP of Castile. Our existing knowledge of cases makes it clear that the religious order par excellence of the sixteenth century, the Jesuits, retained their capacity to absorb productive resources until at least 1620—or, indeed, even until 1640.[5] Viewed from the crisis at the end of the century, it is impossible to overlook the avidity of the ecclesiastical institu-

---

[5] Yun (1987, pp. 334–60), Lozano (2002, pp. 91–103), Mata (1987, pp. 171–8), Brumont (1993, pp. 296–97).

tions in extending their properties through purchases or the creation of *censos* that originated in the purchase of lands from heavily indebted peasants (Pereira 1991, pp. 84–101). Even if the demographic crisis reduced the internal pressure within the families of the oligarchies and the wealthier peasants, it is also evident that, for several decades, the ecclesiastical institutions continued to be capable of integrating into their ranks a sizeable number of members of these groups. Indeed they even helped advance the expansion of what F. Brumont called the 'peasant *mayorazgos*', that is to say the creation of chaplaincies and religious foundations that offered elite rural families the chance to settle a relative in them and were just one part of the broader strategies for the reproduction of the political and cultural capital of these lineages (Brumont 1993, pp. 289–99, and 32–33).

The sale of titles was also taken advantage of by new families originating in the urban patriciate, who found in it a means of access into the high nobility.[6] If many of them acquired or had acquired a seigniorial estate, sometimes with incomes of a jurisdictional sort, it is clear that land income was usually the most important component in their *mayorazgos*. Of course, this process occurred in regions such as Andalusia or Extremadura, where the character of the seigniors as great landowners and the abundance of large *latifundios* went far back. But it also became more common in the Duero Valley (Yun 1987). Rather than a seigniorial (or feudal) class, it appears to have been a group of landowners, in the literal sense. And, as in previous periods, some did invest in improving their *mayorazgos*, even if the requests for *censos* to this purpose appear to have been relatively few and marginal, barely touching 7% of the total (Yun 1999c). But, at the same time, this group was overcoming the fall in its incomes thanks to the replacement of *censos* (mentioned above) and by its service to the Crown, from which they acquired not only debts but also additional incomes and favours that, in certain cases, came to equal those generated by their estates (Yun 2002a).

[6] The advance of the number of title holders is the following:

Year	N° de of title holders	% growth	% yearly growth
1520	60	–	
1554	68	13	0.4
1581	100	32	1.2
1597	124	24	1.5
1631	241	194	5.7
1700	533	221	3.2

(Atienza 1987, p. 41)

Judged by the simplest and most vulgar gradient, the overview of these trends confirms the well-known Enlightenment view of the forms of management used by elites in Counter-Reformation Spain. Still it is worthwhile underlining that these economic strategies were not resistant to change or in any way irrational. Rather, what prevailed was a unique mastery in taking advantage of patrimonial resources during an age in which elites, like the rest of society, faced growing difficulties. They knew how to manage their *mayorazgos*, how to make good use of dowries, how to buy lands from peasants who were in beyond their depth, when—and when not—to free *censos*, and even when silver should be melted down to convert it into jewellery in view of its increasing value in respect to *vellón*. The land-purchase strategy employed by the ecclesiastical institutions was perfectly rational for their purposes and highlighted their intention to avoid the dispersal of plots of land (see, e.g. Mata 1987, p. 171 and Brumont 1993, p. 286). The fact that the price of the office of *regidor* increased more quickly than the value of land demonstrates that many buyers had good knowledge about where the best opportunities lay; but, by the same standard, the diversification of investments was very clear. We even know of efforts to introduce improvements to farms owned by the Jesuits in Villagarcía de Campos or by the Benedictine Monastery of La Espina (Yun 1987; López 1990). Of course, these measures did not keep the crisis from the door of the elites. And, worse, many of these strategies were the direct result of falls in agrarian income and prices, the declining profitability of *juros*, and the dip in rents paid on houses within the *mayorazgo* in which the temptation, though existing, of investment was not very high.

A Balance

The sense that the policies of Olivares were a total failure has created among historians a certain idea that the period was characterized by a complete absence of changes. The reasoning is logical: if the reforms failed, everything remained as before. But this line of thinking is incorrect. Many things did in fact change.

It is clear, on the one hand, that at times the arguments of Acemoglu *et alter* on absolutism present a reasonable view of the situation, particularly for the 1630s and 1640s. This having been said, it should be stressed that this is not really the case for Acemoglu's views on services, *donativos*, and other measures, as the majority of them 'were not, technically speaking, taxes that the Cortes had to approve' and were therefore acceptable on the juridical level (Fortea 2008, p. 249). But, certainly, Acemoglu is correct in that they, in themselves, were not particularly positive for economic development. Above all he is right in regard to the monetary manipulations—although rather absent in his reasoning—the seizure of shipments from the Indies, and the unilateral declarations of bankruptcy. But again, even here, it is impossible to forget that what was limiting the chances that the metropolitan economy might gain from its Atlantic empire were not acts of parasitic absolutism but rather pacts between the monarchy and the Consulate of Seville and the systematic sale of privileges in return for financial assistance.

In any case, attention should fall on the scale of resistance to Crown policies, the conflicts generated by them, and the fact that, in the heart of the empire, these disputes did not move beyond being phenomena of a purely local character. Historians have been much concerned by the (logical) question: why did Castile, the core of the empire, not witness a generalized upheaval similar to those of France or England? Certainly, there were conflicts—and many of them—but the 'Fronde' of Castile failed to become a massive and general movement. Instead it remained a bewildering and random series of uprisings, resistance, and isolated outcries of discontent. This failure to transform itself into something more substantial remains difficult to explain—this is, perhaps, always the case when it comes to saying why something did not happen in history. A posteriori, it is easy to fall into speculations, sometimes facile ones. Perhaps most important was that in 1643—the decisive moment—Philip IV chose to dismiss the Count Duke when faced with the rebellion of the duke of Medinasidonia in Andalusia, the revolt headed by Juan de Braganza in Portugal, and the insurrection in Catalonia. At a stroke, this measure removed the major grounds for complaint and perhaps ensured that additional risings were unnecessary. But if we want to speculate further on the effects of the political economy on politics, it might be possible to argue that the reformist 'acts of aggression' were bringing about a scenario in which these *Frondes* were increasingly undesirable. This was the case not only for the cities but also for the aristocracy and, in particular, for Madrid, where the immense possibilities offered by this empire could still unlock a flow of favours and patronage. And without Madrid—and here was the crucial difference, as Paris stood at the epicentre of the *Fronde*—it was difficult for the separate and isolated conflicts to coalesce into a general rebellion. By this point the Cortes—think of the leading role of the Parliament in England in the 1640s—was reasonably well controlled, and, indeed, its *procuradores* enjoyed both a certain degree of autonomy from the cities they represented and the favour of the Crown. Be this as it may, regardless of the Crown's ability to dissuade prospective rebels from rising in Castile, in the midst of this fight, the elites were sorting out their own problems or even gaining the upper hand in many battles, rendering an all-out war unnecessary. By this period, moreover, the role of the local institutions in politics and fiscal collection was proving an obstacle to the general processes of collective action. These battles took the form of isolated episodes between each city or group and the Crown, thus rendering any combined movement more difficult. Of course, one crucial element—the political culture of the day—is missing from this analysis; but, nevertheless, there are acceptable grounds for tentatively proposing these explanations for what is, without doubt, a very difficult issue.

The conflictive pact that had maintained the dominant coalition from the sixteenth century was being reformulated in many ways. It was no longer the same as it had been. The nobility had seen its military functions reborn for a while—indeed, they had even seen the traditional function of their seigniorial estates strengthened during the war with France. But the exit of Spain from the great stages of international war after the Peace of the Pyrenees (1659) made this role ever less important—at least this was the case for the old nobility—and gave rise to a change in the form of its military service. A new nobility would come to serve this function (and would consolidate its role during the eighteenth century). Rather than the mobilization of their vassals, this new system would be based on money, which allowed them to enlist and equip troops, purchase captaincies, or finance the establishment of army units in exchange for their military service; the seigniorial estates played only a very marginal role in the great majority of these cases (Andújar 2004). Although it retained its vigour in many senses, the seigniorial estate was less important in regard to military organization. The development of the colonial system itself would end up by establishing a nobility whose origins lay either in the American elites or in commerce or, very often, in both, thus changing the essential nature of the group (again, this development reached full maturity in the eighteenth century) (Yun, forthcoming). Many of these families came from the urban elite, and their relationship with the Crown would be direct and personal (Felices 2012). This would not be a corporate relationship in any sense.

The new fiscal system and, above all, the development of the *donativos* system with the disappearance of the Cortes—whose demise was an indicator of much more profound changes—were steps in the same direction. As set out above, the relationships between the king and the urban oligarchies—the need for an understanding between them—would continue to be present. The destruction of their corporate character brought about many changes, and, of course, this was important because it was altering a crucial element of the composite monarchy. This is also a decisive fact for the new institutional economics approach and the study of the political economy of this monarchy. It was to be a key phenomenon in the construction of a state that modulated a different type of conflictive pact. In this new model—without the Cortes—a financial revolution of the English style, where the role of the Parliament after the Glorious Revolution was crucial, was just unthinkable. It is also important for the historiography of political economies, which have made the revolution of 1688 the fundamental turning point (North and Weingast 1989). In Castile, the long-term evolution of the relationship between king and the elites was preventing any comparable process.

The overall result would be a system that for long periods fed the economy of legitimization and sustained the cost of a decentralized system of welfare, led by elites. This turned out to be relatively inefficient on the material level: helping the needy, preventing death and curing illness, and so on. But, as was fitting to a period and a form of Catholicism that understood welfare more in terms of the wellbeing of the soul than attending to the travails of the body, it perhaps served much more effectively as an antidote to growing discontent which might easily have manifested itself in massive conflicts. It might, therefore, serve to explain too the relatively low—in comparison with countries such as France or England—level of upheavals seen in Castile in this period.

The outcome would be the maintenance of property rights. Except for the alienation of communal and royal lands and the increasing concentration in land property, few substantial changes had occurred in the juridical nature of land property. And even these had a slow effect on the productive capacity of some zones. Moreover, in more than one case, there had not even been any sort of privatization; rather what had happened was that these lands were bought by the councils to be used henceforth solely for the benefit of the oligarchies and also obstructing any possibility for productive improvements in those lands. Privilege, in the sense of new institutional economics rather than as political prerogative, was now an important means of gaining access to wealth in a society that was closed rather than open and exclusive rather than inclusive; this was a society in which it was normal for personal networks to pervert even further the working of formal institutions, which were now very far from the Weberian ideal.

Yet this growing absolutism was based on a system that continued to be characterized by counterweights and balances in the exercise of power. In this period pacts, and not the all-embracing power of the king, were at the base of the most inefficient side of formal institutions (in the sense established by North and others).

Ruptures and Continuities: A Decadent Empire?

Approached from the viewpoint of the political economy, it would be an error to think that the various forms of conflictive pact established between elites and the Crown were determinative in the processes of rupture and continuity that were seen in the empire in the middle of the seventeenth century. An entire historiographical current, elegantly synthesized for Spain by X. Gil (2006), has rightly argued that the problem *also* needs to be seen from the perspective of intellectual history and political thought. But the perspective we are adopting here can (partially) illuminate the causes of the process as well as its effects on the political economies of the epoch.

Ruptures in the European Peripheral Kingdoms: Portugal and Catalonia

As all seventeenth-century European societies, those of the Iberian world witnessed political ruptures that are crucial in understanding its skeleton and history. Not only Castile, as we have seen, but also Naples, Sicily, Portugal, Catalonia, the American colonies, and so on went through similar experiences. Here we will consider the last three cases as a way to test how the relationship between the Crown and the elites affected the empire.

The Portuguese Rupture: Globalization Against the Composite Empire
Given their coincidence in time, it is normal for the crises of Catalonia and Portugal to be studied in parallel (although seldom are they placed in any sort of comparative framework).[7] There are good reasons for this, although the phenomena were very different. The crisis of Catalonia was another of the ruptures experienced by the composite monarchies of dynastic character on account of the pressure of war: Naples and Scotland, for example, followed a similar pattern. And Portugal had elements of this. But the

---

[7] See an excellent exception in Elliott (1963, pp. 489–522).

causes and the development of this latter conflict provide evidence also of the difficulty of maintaining a global empire such as the Luso-Spanish one in the context of a process of globalization and upon the basis of a composite monarchy, during the period that witnessed the dawn of the mercantilist policies of the seventeenth century.

Everything began, as is well known, in 1637 with the rising of the city of Évora and the regions of Alentejo, the Algarve, and Ribatejo. The work of local nobles and churchmen, the movement was suffocated without difficulty because of the lack of aristocratic support. But its second coming was decisive. After the Cortes of Tomar, an important tension had emerged over the efforts by the monarchy to involve the kingdom in the raising and lodging of troops (Schaub 2001). This tension had grown because of the attempts to implement the Union of Arms but reached its maximum intensity when Portugal and its *fidalgos* and nobility, Dom João de Braganza included, were asked to collaborate in the repression of Catalonia: on 1 December 1640, an uprising occurred in Lisbon that Braganza would soon take over and lead. As in Catalonia, the conflict quickly acquired an international character, with the involvement of France, attempts to interfere in Andalusia through the duke of Medinasidonia, and the arrival of help from England (Costa and Da Cunha 2006; Valladares 1998, pp. 37–45).

The Portuguese Restoration is understood as a rupture of the pacts formed with the Habsburg monarchy. As has been said, a sizeable part of the Portuguese aristocracy had formed unions with Castilian families which allowed it access to the favours of the empire. But, in complete difference to what happened in Catalonia, the most important family of the kingdom, the House of Braganza, though it had obtained economic awards, had remained rather outside the network of Madrid Court, something that afforded it considerable freedom of manoeuvre (Costa and Da Cunha 2006). Its ties to the Castilian aristocracy—Dom João's marriage to the sister of the duke of Medinasidonia, an outsider to the court dynamic of Madrid—rather than being a balsam for his discontent, was instead a help to the rebellion. Olivares had made great efforts—perhaps coming too late—to incorporate the peripheral nobilities into the government of the monarchy (Elliott 1982, pp. 513–6). But, 'to the extent that it was reducing the role played' by the Portuguese nobility, 'the solidarity of its nobles [with Madrid] was dissipating' (Bouza 2000, p. 229). Only one Portuguese—Braganza himself—had been granted membership of the Order of the Golden Fleece (de Ceballos-Escalera y Gila 2001,

p. 294).[8] No Portuguese noble had received the title of Grandee of Spain. If the royal favours had been fewer than desired, the Crown's attempts to revise the *Ley Mental* (a measure to return lands usurped up to the sixteenth century to the royal estates) were not the best antidote to discontent or, to be more specific, passivity when faced with open rebellion (Bouza 2000). Yet with all of this, the Portuguese aristocracy would remain the group most loyal to Philip IV: the revolt of 1640 produced a division within the high nobility rather than an unconditional support for Braganza (Schaub 2001; Bouza 2000). Moreover, some of the families that passed to the side of Dom João did so by a trans-frontier policy that, rather than pledge loyalty to a sole monarch, sought to maintain the interests of the houses on both sides of the border (Terrasa 2009).

As was the case across all of Europe, the rebellion had a fiscal component. In listing its causes, historians frequently mention measures which preceded the rebellion of Évora, such as the *real del agua* (a tax on the consumption of wine and meat), or the increase of the *sisas*. A number of taxes might be mentioned here: the *medias annatas* (introduced in 1631) was perhaps the most significant. On top of this came military mobilization after 1639 (Schaub 2001). But in reality the fiscal problem should be understood in the wider perspective of the tax systems of Portugal and Castile.

As we have seen, Portugal had created a tax state, but most of the incomes of the king originated above all in his empire, with the kingdom itself contributing very little. This remained the case until the seventeenth century, as can be seen in the budgets for 1607 and even 1621, which still maintained a surplus. The absence of costly overseas wars had prevented the development of public debt in the way that had occurred in Castile (Hespanha 1989, p. 198). But this arrangement was now unsustainable. The problems in the overseas empire meant that, from the 1620s, the *Estado da Índia* entered into a chronic deficit (Godinho 1982; Disney 2009). The reduction of commercial activity also provoked a fall in incomes derived from the overseas sector and the tolls on imports and exports. And this came at a time when defence costs were rising, something which, if not entirely the result of Habsburg policy, appeared to be the fault of Madrid to many Portuguese. All in all, from the third decade

---

[8]The honour was conferred in 1581 upon the sixth duke, Dom João de Portugal. His grandson, Dom João de Portugal (the eighth duke), was also made a member of the Order, although this would subsequently be annulled in light of his rebellion (de Ceballos-Escalera y Gila 2001, p. 341).

of the century, a historical change occurred, one unknown to the Portuguese: if until then a substantial part of the Portuguese Crown's expenditure had been afforded by the king's imperial revenues (Chap. 4), now the kingdom, and not the king, had to increase its contribution to the budget, deal with debt, and face growing military costs. The increase in prices, which devalued the income of the Crown, meant a doubling of these efforts (Hespanha 1989, p. 112). So the Union of Arms, in which Portugal was assigned responsibility for 16,000 soldiers, not only endangered the treasured principle of the 'kingdom's resources for the kingdom' but was also accompanied by a breaking of the rules of play between king and kingdom. To all of this can be added that, through a number of new forms of behaviour, Castilian interests were increasingly interfering in Portugal, creating notable conflicts of competence and jurisdiction (Schaub 2001).

It would be an error, nonetheless, to see the rebellion *only* from the perspective of the Iberian Peninsula. Its origins lay in the combination of a composite monarchy of many states and a global empire that characterized the monarchy as a whole. This is the principal difference with Catalonia, Naples, or Scotland and what gave the events in Portugal their specific and unique character.

Historians have usually placed emphasis on the political discontent with Madrid Court that, according to many Portuguese, governed only in line with the interests of Castile. The failure to defend Ormuz and the ridiculous campaign led by the Count of la Torre to save Pernambuco in 1638 further advanced these arguments (Elliott 1963). But, in reality, what lay behind all of this were problems that were more difficult to resolve.

One of these issues derived from the need to mobilize resources on a global stage that, to all extents and purposes, compelled the monarchy to undertake combined and complementary actions such as the recovery of Bahia. The drawback was that mobilizations of this sort were very difficult and were not always undertaken without problems. In fact, Castile complained of having to employ its funds in defence of Portuguese interests (Borges 2014). But the Portuguese, for their part, could take this problem as far as schizophrenia. Not only were they worried about the movement of resources out of the country to defend Castilian interests but also that help from Castile could lead to mistakes that might lead Castilians to make some claim upon Portuguese domains. The polemic on the 're-conquest' of imperial territories taken by the enemy and a

number of actions such as those in Asia in these years are highly significant in this regard (Cardim 2014; Valladares 2001). The appointment of
Castilians to colonial offices, as happened in Maranhão (Schwartz 1964,
p. 41), could only increase these concerns.

The abundance of cases in which the interests of Castilians and
Portuguese appeared to be in opposition moved things in the same direction. Certainly, the intertwining of both empires was more than evident.
But from Pernambuco (Schwartz 1973) to the Río de la Plata, to the
Chinese Sea, scenarios were created in which this relationship could lead
to conflicts between imagined communities of Portuguese and Castilian
or, simply, appear in this light and be transferred to Madrid or Lisbon in
their most problematic forms (when neither Madrid nor Lisbon was creating these issues). In this way the mingling of Portuguese and Castilians in
colonial spaces was producing a surge of feelings about imagined communities existing on top of one another. A point of convergence was found in
the condition of both peoples as Catholics, which led one observer from
Madrid to argue that they had the 'same nature' (Elliott 1963). But these
communities came into conflict with one another to the extent that each
also created itself through opposition to the other. This is not surprising if
we take into account that it was in the colonies, perhaps more than on the
Iberian Peninsula itself, that the seeds of imagined communities that
increasingly defined themselves as Portuguese and Spanish were sprouting
(Bernal 2007, pp. 324–325; Herzog 2015). The way that histories of
Castile (ever more closely identified with Spain) and Portugal proliferated
in this period underlined the apparently contradictory nature of the two
states and was a good symptom of this change (Cardim 2014). Such evidence reveals how the empire and the tensions that ran through its heartlands generated and reinforced imagined communities that were
suffocating the empire's very principles.

This clash of interests—or the way that elites, in both Madrid and
Lisbon and the overseas territories, conceived of them—did not only affect
the colonial world but also the relationships between it and Europe. The
Portuguese found it difficult to understand the prohibition on trade with
the Dutch, which meant that the salt trade with the Low Countries, which
had sustained their international commerce from the fifteenth century,
was now classified as contraband (Schaub 2001). Equally the critical phase
of the war, which obliged Madrid to concentrate forces in Europe, was
hardly compatible with the state of permanent attack in the colonies,
where Portugal faced powers which by now were practising a purely mer-

cantilist policy. If Portuguese perception was that the war in Flanders after 1621 had drawn attention away from Brazil, the outbreak of war with France in 1635 would only accentuate this feeling of suspicion. This situation was worsened to the extent that the defensive system, which was more effective in the Spanish colonies, deflected Dutch attacks towards Brazilian colonies, the weakest point militarily and also a very interesting one economically. If this were not enough, from the very beginning, the conflict between the Habsburgs and Portugal had a global root: if the war efforts imposed by Madrid's strategy were exhausting, in reality it was the decrease in colonial income from the *Estado da Índia* that rendered unviable a system that until this point had been more or less effective. Such factors went far beyond the Madrid's incapacity to resolve Portuguese problems—or, indeed, any insensitivity to them. This was a structural problem and one very difficult to resolve.

In this world of opposing interests, with an empire faced with enormous problems of regulation and arbitration, with expensive, slow, and asymmetric information, globalization—manifested in the intervention of outsiders into what the Spanish and Portuguese Courts understood as a monopoly—presented a daunting challenge. A river of ink has been spilt to try to justify the policies of the Habsburgs by the aggression of the English and Dutch against the Portuguese empire. But, can anyone really imagine Dutch merchantmen moored in Amsterdam waiting for permits to trade with a world—beginning with the Portuguese empire—that, as Grotius himself said, should be open to all countries? And, did this not mean, in any case, a peaceful and inevitable invasion brought about by infiltration into the very Portuguese monopoly and the system of licences?

In this way globalization, a multipolar phenomenon by definition, was an obstacle to keeping the two empires united. The composite and dispersed character of the monarchy moved things in the same direction. And together these things created a lethal combination that could only have been overcome—and even then it is debatable if any such programme could have been successful—by profound reforms in the political constitution of both kingdoms and their empires.

This global dimension of the composite monarchy was not only present in the causes of the conflict but also in its development. It is well known that the beginnings of the conflict had a multipolar and global character that was manifested in areas from Brazil to Angola, from New Spain to Cartagena de Indias and even Ceuta, Tangier, and as far as the coast of lower Andalusia (Valladares 1998, pp. 31–45). It has even been said that the rebellion began in 1634 in Asia, with the disobedience of the viceroy

Linhares, who, taking advantage of distance and the slow movement of information, refused to obey Olivares in the matter of agreements with England (Valladares 2001, p. 56). And this list does not include the confrontations in the Río de la Plata, the Philippines, and many other areas of Asia. Portugal's victory also had a great deal to do with the global dimensions of its empire, which quickly became a temptation that England could not resist, seeing in these dominions an area of potential indirect influence; London's help would be decisive in achieving independence from the Habsburgs and for the recovery of Pernambuco from an enemy—Holland—which in principle was much stronger (Boxer 1957). This same attraction would explain the marriage of Barbara of Braganza, the new monarch's daughter, to Charles II of England, which would seal the anti-Habsburg pact. The empire's multipolar structure also proved decisive, as revealed by Salvador Correia de Sá e Benevides' expedition from Brazil to seize Angola from the Dutch at a moment in which the peninsular war against the Habsburgs was decisive (Costa 2014, pp. 191–3). And, at the same time, the empire proved decisive in that it became money of exchange for peace with Holland (in the treaty of 1661–1663) when it was most necessary to concentrate forces on the peninsula against the Habsburg troops (Costa 2014, p. 208). Equally the victory of the Portuguese must be related to the Juan de Braganza's capacity to attract, over and above the attacks of the Inquisition, the financial help of the global networks of *conversos* and Portuguese Jews, at precisely the moment when the Spanish bankruptcy of 1647 brought to light the ill will and rancour towards them felt in Castile on account of their status as bankers and Jews (Sanz 1988). On the side of Castile, this was a demonstration that an informal and global network could—in specific circumstances—become a factor in the dissolution of political ties that it had attempted to restrict through the control of formal institutions.

As we have seen, at the heart of the matter stood the high degree of decentralization exhibited in these networks' economic and social organization. The combination of both characteristics, and the presence in them of actors with very different agendas, meant that it was very difficult for political power in Madrid to control them. One group of Jewish converts, for example, was able to adopt positions with totally different political effects in Madrid, Lisbon, or other parts of the empire—indeed, sometimes just one individual member of them was able to do so. This fact explains—in this case economic rationale had a lesser role—the case of the Jesuits, who were able to adopt political positions that, if well negotiated and never free of cost, were very different. In Asia, for example, the Jesuits supported the Portuguese side with no embarrassment (many of them being Portuguese in origin), while in America they fell on the side of Madrid. The only options for this empire were either disintegration or a high degree of negotiation and autonomy of the different nodes of these networks. And the outcome of these tensions could only be the split of the two imperial formations.

The Catalan Crisis or the Problem of a Composite Monarchy
In Barcelona in 1640 a rabble of harvest workers stormed the city, and the rebelling inhabitants were able to take control of it. In May 1652 groups of unemployed harvest workers from Galicia broke into the cities of Córdoba and Seville and sparked an uprising of the people against their governors and patricians. Although a part of the urban oligarchy and the well-off initially participated in these tumults, they then would suffocate the upheaval. The Barcelona revolt ended with the death of the viceroy Santa Coloma and was the opening of a civil war led by the elite of Barcelona and the *Generalitat*.

Neither conflict can be explained only by the attitudes of the urban elites. It would also be an error to look upon the Catalan elites as a counterpoint to their Castilian peers. Notable parallels can be found between these groups: their desire to control municipal life, their capacity to reach agreements with the king for the maintenance of order, the interest of some families to enter into the client networks of the court, and their use of dowries as strategies for social reproduction and similar practices (Torras 1998; Amelang 1986, pp. 86–91). Both groups had common aims and customs: the same affection for *rentier* incomes, their investment in public debt or in social and political capital, and their desire to marry into noble families, their use of ecclesiastical institutions as a means of reproducing family relationships. A careful reading of Xavier Torres' work demonstrates that all of them needed to promote their members and to give an outlet to their needs for social expansion (Torres 1994, pp. 201–23 and 234–40). The Catalan succession system, based on the *hereu* in which the main body of the inheritance passed to the eldest son, only increased this need. Many of these traits—with the exception of the inheritance system—were present in Castile and across Europe and, of course, throughout Mediterranean Europe (Delille 2003). Yet this does not mean that there were no differences in degree that, as we shall see, would have considerable importance. These differences were also conditioned by the different forms of relationship between elites and the monarchy and were mixed with the existence of differing constitutional practices and traditions. These points of divergence were superimposed upon other differences such as language, whose importance can never be overlooked, and even a process in which separate imagined communities were formed that in part owed their origins to the impression—confirmed by later research—that Castile was attempting to advance a growing sense of identification between the concepts of Spain and Castile.[9]

By 1585 the expansive wave of Catalan commerce appears to have reached its temporary ceiling. Catalonia's role as an important route for the dispatch of money towards the Spanish road had positive effects for the country's economy. But the difficulties of the Castilian fairs very possibly affected the Catalan merchants' capacity to introduce their products in Castile and even in America and reinforced the need to recompose the commercial networks towards *cabotage* trade in the Mediterranean (Elliott 1982, p. 52; García Espuche 1998). This was happening at a time of competition from products from other countries in Seville and in particular those channelled through the Consulate into America, which also went against the interests of the principality—and, of course, those of the industrial cities of Castile. As P. Vilar said, the decades that preceded the rebellion were not marked by economic crisis, as a recovery had occurred. But the Catalan economy gravitated less towards Castile than it had in the sixteenth century.

The progressive distancing of Catalonia from the Habsburgs, however, was not brought about by purely economic factors. In the Cortes of 1585, the fundamental conflicts came to light: on one side, the conflict between the king and the *Generalitat*, which Philip II sought to reorganize and control; on the other side, the Catalan claims to limit the number of familiars of the Inquisition and restrain the institution's power. The oligarchy of Barcelona, which at the beginning had been one of the closest sectors to the monarchy in Catalonia, found itself from 1586 in an open clash over the naming of *ciutadans honrats* (honoured citizens) which, far from daunting the Crown, led it to make a series of scandalous appointments. And, if a compromise agreement was eventually reached, an important short-term tension occurred (Amelang 1986, pp. 46–62). This came at precisely the moment when the Catalan Cortes increased their

---

[9]Elliott (1982, pp. 42–7); Simon i Tarrés (1999). For the idea of Spain as an extension of Castile, see Thompson (2005) and Cardim (2014).

RUPTURES, RESILIENT EMPIRES, AND SMALL DIVERGENCES   405

contribution to the king (500,000 libras in 1585 and as has been said 1,100,000 in 1599) and when they came to normalize the payment of the *quinto*, a tax on the fifth of taxes and municipal *sisas* (Hernández 1996, *passim*). In a country that had managed to maintain the principle that each kingdom should meet its own costs, the Union of Arms would be rejected by force. And the exasperation and rudeness of Olivares when faced with the slow proceedings of the Cortes would add fuel to this fire (Elliott 1982). In this context, during the 1630s Philip IV had preceded to the massive sale of positions of *ciutadans honrats* (Amelang 1986).

But, above all, the conflictive pact between the Catalan elites and the monarchy was different to its equivalent accord in Castile. Certainly, the great noble families—the Cabrera, the Cardona, or the Requesens—had formed solid ties with Castilian and Valencian families and, by this route, with the Crown. Absorbed by—and at times secondary within—the great Castilian lineages, some of these houses would be closer to the court and the king than to Catalonia's internal problems. And there was no shortage of patrician dynasties, such as the Franquesa, that managed to prosper thanks to their ties to the Court in Madrid. But the economic difficulties of the provincial nobility and their problems in reproducing their lineages, manifested in banditry (Elliott 1990, p. 117), provide evidence of their more problematic integration into the empire's patronage system and, consequently, the relative difficulty of this group in thereby achieving its social survival and promotion. It is very significant, for example, that only 14 of the 1400 members of the Military Orders in 1625 were Catalans (Elliott 1963, p. 74). This fact not only marked differences in respect to Castile but also to Aragon and, above all, Valencia, where the Military Orders and the presence of the mid-ranking nobility in them had been very significant. Various similarities existed between the elites of Castile and that of Catalonia, which played a vital role in the conflict of 1640. But, to an extent that was unthinkable in Castile, the Catalan elite was made up of lawyers and university graduates who had mixed with the semi-urban, mid-ranking nobility that was also increasingly university educated (Amelang 1986). This gave the elite economic independence and, more important, a type of constitutional vision of politics that sat badly next to the sort of absolutism that Philip IV and the Count Duke were so keen to promote.

The Catalan fiscal system, much less efficient in tying Crown and county than its Castilian equivalent, had not created a clear integration; nor had it forged as solid a conflictive pact between the king and urban oligarchies.

A part of the oligarchy of Barcelona had subscribed to the *censals* emitted upon the tax system of the city to pay for the king's debts. And the same had happened at a lower level in many towns of the principality (Elliott 1963, p. 139). But the independence of the *Diputació* with respect to the king, its 'dubious financial actions' (Elliott 1963, p. 141), and the temporary character of the services had prevented the Principality's tax system from becoming a continuous and systematic support for the debts of the king. It was impossible to imagine in Catalonia a single city becoming a 'pensionopolis'—a fount of pensions and offices—that, according to Fernández Albaladejo (1992), had been crucial for the fiscal pact between the king and kingdom (1992) in Castile. And it was also impossible to conceive of something of the proportions of the accord over the collection of the *alcabalas* or the *millones*, upon which the same pact had been established in Castile. As has been said, the very system of setting *censos* on *mayorazgos*, so important in binding nobles to king in Castile, functioned differently throughout the Crown of Aragon, where royal permission was not necessary (Abadía 1998). In certain circumstances in Catalonia, favours and privileges were granted to elites. Above all, this was done to continue or prolong the meetings of the Cortes. Nor did the Catalans entirely fail to secure appointments to positions in the administration. But the monarchical state was not as developed as in Castile and nor, therefore, was the scope for patronage and clientele arrangements. With the great offices and favours of the empire in the hands of the Castilians, the prospects of the Catalan elites were more remote, except for those members of families (mentioned above) belonging to the highest branches of the aristocracy (Vilar 1962, vol. I, p. 368; Molas 1996). In other words, the political system was much less efficient than in Castile at creating conditions that would have allowed the empire and the composite monarchy to become the solution to the dominant coalition's social development and expansion. On the contrary, the destabilizing effects of absolutism would make themselves felt (see Chap. 4).

The pressure exerted by the duke of Alcalá on Catalan towns, with the billeting of troops and the other measures introduced by Olivares, broke the previous pacts. Despite the Cortes refusing to back the Union of Arms, Catalonia's contributions to the defence of the monarchy also increased, as we have seen (Bernabé 1993). The sense that the Crown did not carry out its fundamental duty to control banditry and maintain order came to add to the negative effect of the devaluations of Castilian money that circulated in considerable quantities in Catalonia (Elliott 1963, Chapter 3). Yet the conflict that was unleashed in 1640 was much more than the sum of these parts and cannot be explained solely from this perspective. It had deeper political and even cultural components whose origins lay in traditions and also, importantly, in language. But, fundamentally, the political economy that created this weaker variant of the conflictive pact lay beneath these uprisings of 1640. This view can even in part explain the solution to the crisis. Catalonia—and above all its governing class—was divided into supporters of the French Bourbons and the Spanish Habsburgs. And after 13 years of war, the problems of both countries brought about an agreement that led to the domination of the latter over the principality. The conflict was very expressive of something shared with the Portuguese case: the mixture of civil war and international conflict found in both episodes.

What followed lies beyond the scope of this study. The result would be a very unstable conflictive pact between the Crown and the elites. Above all, the tension continued to manifest itself in the fight over the system for confiscation and the return to previous levels of self-government (Simon i Tarrés 2011, pp. 61–97). But it also resulted in a process of drawing together that passed through the renovation of a group of 'honoured citizens' of Barcelona thanks to the king's appointments, as well as those of the local aristocracy itself (Amelang 1986) that, if it did not lead to a total agreement with the Crown, at least put in place better bases for it and—according to some authors—even led to a greater presence in Madrid (Soldevila 1962; Vilar 1962).

From the perspective of this study, the differences with Portugal have a heuristic value. Both conflicts took an international character. Quite possibly the insertion of Catalonia and Portugal within Castile's social and economic life was to a similar degree. The benefits their elites received from the Spanish empire were also very limited in both cases. The elites of both countries had developed a sense of imagined community based on a linguistic distinction and so on. But Catalonia, without an empire, was less attractive to an exhausted France, than Portugal was for an England which, coming out from the ashes of the revolution, increased its aspirations over a very promising Portuguese empire. Catalonia lacked the international imperial webs almost impossible for the Habsburgs to control and which even allowed for expeditions like that of Salvador Correia de Sà. Nor had it the possibilities of obtaining international support in exchange for privileges and trade concessions, such as those obtained from the Dutch in 1661–1663, which allowed the monarch to concentrate forces on the peninsula. In part as a consequence of such factors, Catalonia could not even dream of dynastic alliances like that of Barbara de Braganza and Charles II.

It is impossible to know if, having met such conditions, Catalonia would have become independent. Furthermore, many more differences could be added. But reasoning in this sense helps to better understand to what extent globalization, again, was influencing the live of Europeans and more in particular of the Portuguese.

The Renewal of the American Colonial Pact

A Renovated and Difficult Agreement

The American colonies provided the opposite case to Catalonia, Naples, and Portugal. Here there were also confrontations. But, far from leading to a general rupture, a series of pacts was set down in depth and in the creation of a space of understanding with the Crown.

Until almost 1570 the general American fiscal burden, leaving aside the *quinto* of the mines, had been relatively light (Chap. 2). But the military commitments in Europe and the costs associated with the construction of the colonial state rendered the incomes from the mines insufficient and forced Madrid to try to increase its fiscal demands. The measures employed to this effect were to be the same as, or very similar to, those used in Castile and implied a relationship with elites that was formally very analogous. This led to the increase of the *alcabalas*, to the sale of wastelands and public offices and the introduction of the *media annata* (again, a tax on the succession to offices) and similar measures, the majority of these being part of bargaining with the colonial elites. To mitigate the increase in the *alcabalas* and the imposition of new tax burdens, the cities were given the chance to oversee their collection and management through the creation of *sisas* (Amadori 2012, pp. 10–15), something which, as in Castile, strengthened the power of the oligarchies and created areas of agreement with the Crown.[10] The same could be said of the creation of *juros*, to which the oligarchies subscribed (Adrien 1981). The municipal authorities even recurred to the seizure of Indian possessions to swell the *cajas* that, it was claimed, were to be used in the defence of the weaker areas of the empire (see below and Moutoukias 1988). They also developed the system of *donativos* that, as we have seen, was a form of exchanging resources in money, men, or equipment, for economic and political privileges (Amadori 2012).

---

[10]For a more specific list of the areas of fiscal income in America, see both TePaske (1983) and Amadori (2012, pp. 19–23).

Things were not, however, confined to fiscal level. In difference to Castile, the Crown did not yet recur to the sale of titles and jurisdictions. But the rhythm of legitimizing alienated lands (*composiciones de tierras*) continued or even increased, as did the granting of property rights to society in general and to the elites in particular. As Ruggiero Romano has shown in his excellent study (2004), the way that these grants were conferred meant that the Crown became the final guarantor of property rights. In this way, from the end of the sixteenth century, the emerging elites bought large tracts of land with which they established the great ranches of Mexico or the sugar or tobacco farms, to give examples from New Spain. And the same happened in Peru. Moreover the process of granting mining rights continued (Bakewell 1990, 1991).

On top of all of this came similar deals with the merchant and financial elites. The great traders of Lima and Mexico benefited from privileges to continue to feed their growing economic resources with this political capital. As we have seen, the Mexican elite involved in the Consulate were able, with the support of the town council, to secure advantageous accords with the Crown in exchange for money. Cases of this sort are very expressive of the type of practices that lay at the basis of this relationship. And similar practices can be found in the fiscal negotiations between the Consulate of Lima and the Crown (Gasch 2015a; Amadori 2012).

The development of colonial society brought about important changes in ecclesiastical organization. America—or the zones of greatest Spanish presence—became full of parishes, ecclesiastical councils, archbishoprics (five), and dioceses (thirty, plus four in the Philippines); these were allocated important sources of income: lands, tithes, and even industrial establishments in some cases. On top of this there were, from an early stage, charitable foundations and piety projects, confraternities, and other ecclesiastical institutions in whose government laymen played a very prominent role. And these were very wealthy institutions. In addition, an expansion of the religious orders took place from the moment of conquest itself. The evidence of this process (see, e.g. Céspedes 2009, pp. 250–63) can be used in an interpretation that comes close to the one presented here for Castile (Kicza 1999). The transposition into America of an economy of legitimation similar to that of the Iberian Peninsula fed these foundations and their growing wealth thanks to donations by elites. These endowments were the result not only of cultural beliefs very suitable to the political economy of this society, but also, and as in the peninsula, these institutions were soon to become an area into which elites would expand, one offering an outlet to many of their members. This development turned the Church into a 'less indigenous' institution, but it certainly did not reduce its enormous power over a population where Catholicism, often highly mixed in with older beliefs, exercised great influence (Céspedes 2009). It was precisely its proximity to the lowest ranks of society that gave religion its enormous stabilizing power upon the social system. But this is better understood if we take into account the notable control exerted by the Crown over ecclesiastical resources (Elliott 2006, p. 205).

The Church was also key to establishing and maintaining a certain social order in a world of enormous internal differences. But it was not the only factor. The *Leyes Nuevas* had created a framework in which the rights of the Indian were theoretically recognized. The establishment of Indian rural communities and towns enjoying a certain degree of autonomy and which, despite the usurpations, retained control over common lands (Coatsworth 2008) operated to the same effect. So did the recognition of misappropriated lands which, if elites took the lion's share, also benefited the lower echelons of society (see the figures given by Romano 2004, pp. 88–90) who, in this way, came to see the Crown as a guarantee of their claims on their possessions. And from the end of the sixteenth century, property rights were guaranteed increasingly by 'the application of Spanish laws' rather than by registers dating back to before the *conquista* (Elliott 2006, p. 203), thus tying them all to the king's decisions and creating dependence and loyalty. In the end, the possibility of flight, a common practice given the difficulty of controlling America's enormous spaces and huge range of available resources, acted at the same time as a safety valve against uprisings among the lowest levels of that society, be they Indians, slaves, *mulatos*, or any others.

The consequences of this conflictive pact in the colonies were not confined to the strengthening of the ties with the Crown and internal stability. We should also think of it being set down upon other values, among which religion—in opposition to the Protestant faith of the enemy—must have played a highly important role (Schwartz 2008). But, above all, the immediate consequence was the social amplification of the reproductive capacity of the elites. As in the Iberian Peninsula, the opportunity to move and circulate its members from the Church to commerce and administration and so on, and to provide an outlet to tensions, was established in its heart. It also offered them the chance to maintain their multi-functionality and to circulate different forms of capital within these networks which, at times, were dispersed in space (Chap. 7). What had been established was, moreover, for the moment a much more flexible elite than that of the metropolis, where the prejudices of honour, for example, were much more evident. As a result of all of this, America would be an immense space for the use of political, economic, and social resources, marked by a high degree of social mobility among the elites that could, in this way, satisfy aspirations for promotion with considerable ease and thus avoid the social and political ruptures that aborted institutional development and secured the prevailing political economy.[11] This process, at the same time, being based on vertical negotiations between the Crown and very dispersed and diverse groups, contributed to maintaining the empire's poly-nuclear character.

The colonial pact was not based only upon the hierarchical relationships between the Crown and the American elites. A system of interregional co-responsibility developed that strengthened the defensive capabilities of the colonies and, therefore, property rights when faced with other powers. In this way a step forward was taken in the organization of monetary flows between the different treasuries or *cajas* (Chap. 2). And, from the end of the sixteenth century, the regions of special sensitivity in the colonial defensive system, such as Puerto Rico, began to receive growing quantities of silver from other parts of the empire, such as New Spain (Vilar 1974; Pacheco 2012, pp. 115–24). The same was happening in other areas of strategic importance, such as the Philippines, where the figures are also highly indicative of how until 1645 defensive costs far outstripped all others (Alonso 2012, p. 282). This capacity to move sums in imperial circuits without many juridical problems, which constituted a fundamental difference in respect to what was happening in the European states of this composite monarchy, has been considered as the 'secret of the empire' or, put in other words, the key to its long survival (Marichal and von Grafenstein 2012).

Behind these developments was the growing decentralization in the use of imperial military resources and in the development of the local militias mentioned above (Chap. 7). These military efforts, which resulted in a high degree of local autonomy, did not prevent the capture of small islands in the Caribbean, and particularly in the West Indies, by the Dutch,

---

[11] One of the consequences of this situation lay in the enormous capacity of certain families of the Latin American elite who, being denied mechanisms for the preservation of their lineage and memory similar to those of European aristocrats, were in many cases able to survive until today.

English, and French, some of whose settlements would be recognized by Spain in the Treaty of Munster and then the Peace of Westphalia of 1648 (Céspedes 2009, map XIV, p. 277). But this form of decentralized military organization most definitely was one of the reasons—if not the only one, as we shall see—that prevented these European rivals from bursting into America and achieving control over huge dominions in the continent, as had happened at Pernambuco.

The colonial system had arrived at a status quo that would only gain strength and be further consolidated and reshaped in the following decades.

The relationships between the metropolis and the American elites had been consolidated. Despite there being some anti-fiscal movements—such as the revolt of Peru in the 1590s—a long series of local tumults and even a permanent situation of structural conflicts and of tensions within the elites, as in the case of México (Israel 1975; Ballone 2017; Álvarez de Toledo 2011), and many movements of resistance, nothing similar to the Catalan, or Portuguese events, happened in America.[12] There existed a sort of equilibrium that constituted a variety of the prevailing formula in Castile and in which tensions but not generalized rebellions were the norms. This is not to present a narrowly materialist interpretation of the reasons for the support and loyalty of American societies to the Crown. If recent views that underline the colonial pact from the perspective of the political economies have a fault, it lies in that they overlook the enormous importance of ideological factors that were implicit in it. They focus overly on demonstrating how this pact was *also* the result of a political economy that, as is generally recognized today, was based upon bartering and negotiation.[13] As in Castile, this relationship between elites and the monarchy lay upon transfers of immense volumes of economic resources and social and political capital in both directions. The result was a collection of accords and pacts with corporations and social groups who, without having a common representative body before the king similar to the Castilian Cortes, were arriving at an *entente* with Madrid. They had

---

[12] We still need a general study on the very complex social and political upheavals in Latin America which offers a typology and interpretation, but the reader can find a fast synthesis in Bennassar (1980, pp. 221–252).

[13] The phenomenon has been very clearly set out for the eighteenth century (see, among others, the works of Grafe and Irigoin 2012). Here our interest focuses on showing how the empire arrived at this situation.

established property rights over lands, mines, and even privileges in the use of political and fiscal resources that together conferred autonomy upon the American oligarchies. These same property rights and privileges afforded them a degree of security that raised the opportunity costs or the risks involved in any break with Madrid or drawing closer to other powers. Part of this accord was also based on the practice of turning a blind eye to smuggling and to the increasing presence of forced labour—camouflaged under different formulae—in America. This is not to present a cynical vision of the actions of elites but merely to show that the political economy of the empire would be *one* important component of its longevity.

At the same time, the investment in the military and protection system had been strengthened, thus assuring these elites of a certain level of confidence in relation to any possible attack by outsiders as well as a coercive system that, should the need arrive, would serve to maintain the colonial order. If such defences were not enough, the foreign powers that employed highly aggressive mercantilist policies had been able to seize enclaves that did not entail high protection costs and from which it was very easy to organize contraband with Spanish colonies. For the reasons we have explained, it was better for Amsterdam, London, and more and more Paris to infiltrate the empire rather than conquer it. The peace treaties signed in 1648 and afterwards consolidated this situation. Concessions such as the settlements in the West Indies, the *asiento* on black slaves to England, and so on would be, as 'legal smuggling' had also been, the recognition of a *fait accompli* that would frame the history of both the empire and Spain itself. The system guaranteed not only the longevity and political 'loyalty' of this empire—but also its economic consequences and specific place in the history of the empires, as we shall see.

Ecosystems, Globalization, and Plenty Versus Formal Institutions

This very delicate and unstable scheme was able to maintain itself thanks to one other fact: economic growth. This development may appear even more eye-catching to the extent that, as we have seen, a sizeable number of the institutions the Spanish implanted in America were scarcely conducive towards it. At least this is the case when viewed from the usual perspective of institutional economics (chapter 7; Coatsworth 2008).

Certainly, the economic history of Latin America has been viewed as a failure. And this impression, logically, has been extended to its capacity to generate economic growth. The more empirical forms of research have, however, pointed in another direction. In R. Romano's excellent comparison of the 'crisis of the seventeenth century' in Europe and America, it became clear that the iron century was not, in comparative terms, a period of recession in the American economy as a whole (1993). The same author has also provided additional proof to support his thesis, as well as further in-depth explanation of it (2004). Similar conclusions have been reached by Arroyo Abad and Van Zanden (2016), using more refined—and risky—calculations.[14] Taking both works together, it is fair to argue that, within regional differences, the American economy regained a path towards growth from the end of the sixteenth century, and this phase lasted until at least 1630–1640. After the establishment of the plantation economy, the boom in urbanization, and the intensification of regional economic circuits (Chap. 7) and despite a brief crisis of uneven regional impact, from 1640–1650 onwards, practically all indicators point towards (moderate) expansion. As a matter of fact, population figures in 1700 were higher than in 1600, in spite of the mid-century problems.[15] This is also reflected in the demographic recovery, due as much to internal factors as to migrations, within which an important role would be played by the forced movements of people associated with the trade in slaves (Romano 2004, pp. 63–7).

What were the reasons for this expansion, which came into its own from the midpoint of the century? In reality, rather than be a continuation of previous trends, it must be seen as a series of regional impulses with widely diverging roots. To understand it in its general framework, it is necessary to begin, to my mind, from various assumptions that acted in combination: (a) the limited impact of formal institutions—state institutions, if you wish—on the assignation of productive factors in an economy in which informal economy was so much developed, (b) the enormous abundance of resources per person derived from new regional ecosystems after the dramatic demographic recession of the sixteenth century, (c) the scope to put these resources to use through the introduction of European technology, and (d) the positive impact that international commerce and globalization would have in this context.

As we have seen, forms of property, the importance of forced labour regimes, the fragmentation and limits of the juridical system, the scope for using private violence, and so on appear in principle not to be very

[14] I must thank the authors for providing me with a copy of this study before its publication and allowing me to cite it.
[15] Following Romano's reconstruction of the figures, the population of Latin America had passed from 10 million in 1600 to 11.8 in 1700 and 19.3 in 1800 (Romano 2004, p. 61).

conducive to economic development—at least, this is the case from any perspective based upon the new institutional economics.[16] But in a territory as immense as Latin America, benefitting from such a positive relationship between resources and population, the (negative) effect of these institutions would have to be, necessarily, limited.[17] If the capacity for enforcement wielded by state institutions was reduced, then so was their scope for negative effects.

The collision of ecological systems had led to the destruction of the original ecosystems. But the result was the triumph of new variants drawing from a wide range of resources: large unpopulated zones belonging to no one (outside, therefore, of the property rights that appear to have been so negative for economic development), enormous herds of sometimes semi-wild livestock, thick and rich woods, minerals that could be readily exploited, and so on.

The primary sector underwent important changes. One of the most significant was the use of ploughs and agricultural iron tools of European origin, water mills, and other inventions whose effects remain unstudied and, therefore, unknown. But perhaps more eye-catching was the diffusion of mules as a beast of transport and burden.[18] According to Romano's calculations, in the eighteenth century, these would reach an animal-per-human ratio that was more than double the European level. This provided a source of exosomatic energy whose overall impact upon the productivity of work would be double that in the Old World. But, in addition, an outcome would be seen in forms of 'livestock breeding' that were not only based upon inexhaustible supplies of land (very often belonging to no one) but also on hunting and the herding of wild livestock for sale, as occurred in the Argentinian Pampas, to give just one example. Progressively the ecosystems destroyed by 'ecological imperialism' were substituted by others in which wheat was extended (and, little by little, the vine), as were sugar, cacao, tobacco, coffee, and many other products closely tied to

---

[16]To use Coatsworth's words: "as in most premodern states and empires, however, Iberian institutions were not designed to promote factor mobility, technological change, or frictionless transaction" (2006, p. 256).

[17]It is worth remembering that we are referring to a surface area of some 19,197,000 km², that until 1492 had supported a population of between 30 and 50 million (Livi Bacci 2008, 3–19).

[18]The phenomenon also gave rise to the development of a mule market of transcendental importance and trans-regional in scope, as Sempat Assadourian has shown in some of his studies (1982, pp. 18–55).

globalization. And there even took place a development in the use of products originally from America, such as the evergreen tree, maize, or the cassava tree, whose expansion European agents facilitated (Garavaglia 1983; Saldarriaga 2011).

The impact of these advances was not only felt in what can be called (according to today's classification) the primary sector. The expansion of the sugar industry, for instance, was also made possible by the chance to dedicate extensive land areas to graze the oxen and beasts of burden employed in these farms. But, in addition, the dynamism of this sector would be vital to the technological improvements. The expansive rhythm of the construction of windmills is proof of this, as is the diffusion of many of the Brazilian advances, such as the use of three vertical cylinders or the system of cauldrons for cooking (Gómez-Galvarriato 2006). Thus the existence of forced labour—and even the prohibitions that existed in some areas of Spanish America against it—did not necessarily abort productive expansion or technical improvements. The industrial growth was also seen in the textile sector and made evident in the development of the *obrajes*. These were workshops designed for large-scale production, based on the vertical integration of the distinct phases of production and represented an important advance on the production in small workshops that predominated in the Iberian Peninsula (Miño 1991). Their spread is evident between 1580 and 1630, both in New Spain and in Peru, although from this point they entered into crisis in the first of these areas and stagnation in the latter (Miño 1991, pp. 135–41). Even if they appear not to have led to continuous technological improvements, this was clearly a sector that also progressed despite being predominantly based upon forced repartitions and forced labour as a form of debt payment.[19]

Other important industries of the period, such as construction, are also highly significant in this regard. The sector played its part in a notable development between 1580 and 1630–1640. This ran parallel to the development of urban life (Kagan and Marías 1998) and the advance of religious institutions, whose vitality in building has been measured (Van Oss 1976). And this in turn was tied to the great cycle of the mining economy, the increase in the waves of immigration, and the branching out of elites into the ecclesiastical sector. The economic recovery can also be related to the diffusion of European building techniques and was undertaken despite the predominance of semi-forced salary systems, such as work to pay for debts,

---

[19]The system consisted in giving workers forced loans that they would have to repay with their labour and which thus served to retain them.

which were very much at odds with the rules of a free market (Romano 2004). The naval industry also expanded in some zones to the extent that they dedicated a greater portion of their budgets to defence and introduced European techniques in shipbuilding (Goodman 1997). If during the period 1551–1600 the vessels built in America constituted just 2.7% of those in the Old World, this proportion rose to 26.5% and then 22.06% during 1601–1650 and 1651 and 1700, respectively (Romano 2004, p. 261).

Mining, where the expansion of mercury-based systems of amalgamation provided a good example of the same march forward, also offers another dimension of this phenomenon: in spite of the well-established inefficiency of the Crown's chosen systems, growth in this sector would be a fact. The case of iron mining, vital for this growing economy, and of the use of potassium nitrate and sulphur, vital to the production of gunpowder, or salt, whose production was supposedly controlled by Crown monopoly systems, are very expressive (Romano 2004, pp. 145–8). If, perhaps, its development would have been still greater in another institutional context, still the production of these goods grew thanks to clandestine or semi-clandestine forms of production typical of an economy where informal networks and their capacity to generate confidence played a highly relevant role.

Contraband—an expression of the lack of efficiency of formal institutions—was, however, the cornerstone of a commercial growth that was pushing forward many of these sectors. These were illegal or semi-legal systems that by definition functioned on the basis that it was impossible to recur to the Crown as a guarantor of contracts and as a form of reducing risks and transaction costs. But at the same time, these were activities in which informal networks were able to generate forms of confidence through reputation, family, and extended family networks and formulas of a similar sort and so push forward an economic expansion.

All in all, the outcome of formal institutions that were in principle an obstacle for economic growth was not economic inactivity or recession. Rather the development of an informal sector of the economy that added to—and sometimes mixed with—activities more easily detectable by the authorities generated increasing quantities of wealth.[20] As a result, the so-called 'crisis of the seventeenth century' appears to have been more a coming together or super-

---

[20]This is not to say that state action did not have effects upon the economy. To give just one example, everything indicates that the crisis of the New Spain's workshops or *obrajes* after 1630 should be understood in relation to not only the momentary crisis of the mining sector in the region but also to the Crown's prohibitions of commerce with Peru, as a means of protecting the export of these goods from the metropolis (Miño 1991, p. 108).

imposition of alternate economic cycles which, since the middle of the six-teenth century, had brought about more or less constant growth. Of course, another matter was the type of society and political regime that generated this system, as well as its effect of exacerbating economic and social inequalities and intensifying the imperial exploitation of thousands of peoples.

REGIONAL RECESSION AND NEW GROWTH PATTERNS IN IBERIA, C. 1600–1668

As in other areas of seventeenth-century studies, the vision of the Iberian economy in this period has been very negative. Not only was it seen as being in crisis but also in recession and even in decline (Llopis 1994). From an international perspective, Spain and Italy served by their very nature as the stages for the crisis of the seventeenth century brought about to a large extent by the survival of feudal structures (Hobsbawm 1954).

A vision of this sort should, however, be set in the context of a wider lit-erature that has revised downwards the capacity of the state to extract resources from society (Collins 1988) and poses the question of the real impact of formal institutions upon the economy. It is also interesting to study the so-called 'crisis of the seventeenth century' in relation to the general changes occurring in Europe's economy, whose relationship with the process of globalization was very close indeed. In this sense, and as Jan De Vries has shown (1984), Europe passed from an urban model based on the develop-ment of the cities of the interior to one which, progressively but decidedly, was to unfold in the coastal cities, which were more directly affected by inter-national commerce. This process also combined with the shifting of urban dynamism towards the north of Europe and specifically into an area between Paris, Hamburg, and London. And this change was associated with the capacity of countries such as Holland, England, and, increasingly, France to build mercantilist political formations capable of capturing higher propor-tions of world commerce. See these trends in Maps 8.1, 8.2, 8.3, and 8.4.

The question, therefore, is: did the Iberian economies adjust to this scheme? And what were the transformations and factors that conditioned them?

Big Trends, Big Numbers: Recession in the Empire's Core

Recent studies on the Spanish economy of the epoch have shown that in the first half of the seventeenth century, a fall in real output per capita occurred that was even more intense and long-lasting than in other countries, Italy included (Álvarez Nogal and Prados de la Escosura 2013,

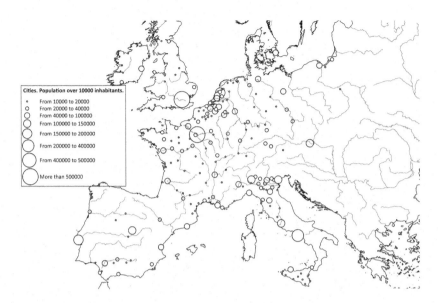

Map 8.1 European urban networks, 1700
Sources: My own elaboration with data from De Vries (1984) and my data of Spanish towns.

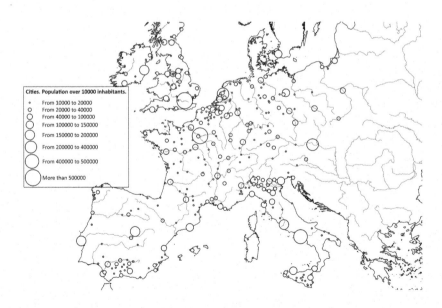

Map 8.2 European urban networks, 1800
Sources: My own elaboration with data from De Vries (1984) and my data of Spanish towns.

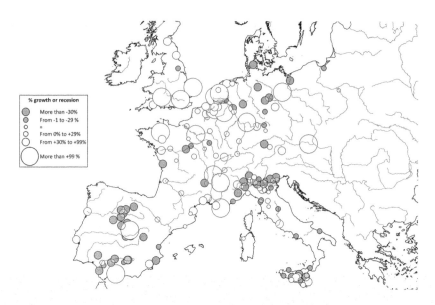

Map 8.3   Growth and recession of the European urban networks, 1600–1700
Sources: My own elaboration with data from De Vries (1984) and my data of Spanish towns.

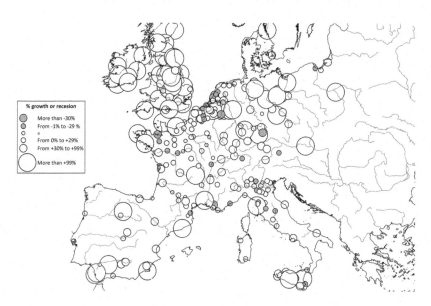

Map 8.4   Growth and recession of the European urban networks, 1700–1800
Sources: My own elaboration with data from De Vries (1984) and my data of Spanish towns.

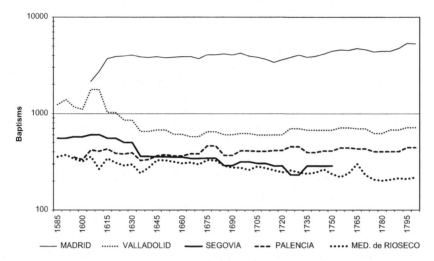

Graph 8.1 The demographic crisis—and recession—of the cities of the Duero Valley and the expansion of Madrid
Sources: Yun (2002b).

figure 7, table 1). This situation appears evident in the centre of the Iberian Peninsula, and above all on the Castilian plateau, where the end of the sixteenth-century crisis gave way to an economic recession accompanied by structural changes.[21]

The dismantling of the previous urban network continued, while Madrid's macrocephaly was reaching its zenith (Gelabert 1995. See Graph 8.1 in this chapter). The organization of an empire in which rent-seeking management and royal favour were good choices for palliating the rigidity in seigniorial incomes further accelerated the migration of noble and patrician families towards Madrid, where royal patronage was dispensed, information costs on the marriage market were lower, and informal lineage networks were more efficient. With the shifting of conspicuous consumption to the court, the service and construction sectors, the two most highly affected by elite spending patterns, entered into recession in the cities of the Duero Valley.[22]

---

[21] The reader can find some of the following arguments with more visible empirical evidence in Yun (1999c, 2002a).

[22] Cases such as that of Valladolid are highly expressive (Urrea 1996). Madrid, in contrast, underwent the very opposite process (Ringrose 1983a, pp. 112–4). On the migration of artisans to Madrid, see Nieto and Zofío (2016).

Without being the only cause of the problems (Chap. 6), fiscal pressure did not help industry while monetary manipulations negatively affected trade in one of the peninsula's more monetized areas. The peace settlements of the early 1600s facilitated the country's inundation by northern light fabrics, thus aggravating the difficulties of Castilian industries, which were unable in the short run to challenge the imports by imitating northern techniques. Yet this was not simply the result of political developments: it was, in many regards, a consequence of the function of international commercial networks. The growing need for silver and other colonial products for Dutch commerce in the Baltic intensified even further their interest in capturing these goods in Spain and America and, by this route, attempting to level out the commercial balance with Castile (Israel 1990, pp. 44–5, and 54). Despite the occasional blip, English commerce in the Mediterranean continued to expand, and increasing quantities of raw materials for industry, such as silk, travelled to the North, while ever greater amounts of British 'new draperies' were sold in the Mediterranean areas (Brenner 1993, table 1.3). Spain became the 'leading market outside northern Europe for English cloths', and by 1620 Albion's merchants were selling products at below their production price purely as a means of gaining access to goods from America (Brenner 1993, p. 30). It was no coincidence or accident that several regional industrial centres should have collapsed at this juncture or that the silk industry of Toledo was also running into difficulties. Granada had already entered into crisis and was now more focused on the export of raw silk. Furthermore, foreign competition in silk fabrics and other Asian products in the American market became more intensive.[23]

Madrid represented exactly the sort of marketplace that was relatively easy for foreign products to penetrate. Being a highly concentrated market, it involved relatively low transport and distribution and retailing costs, once foreign products had passed through its city gates; these were, precisely, the conditions most favourable to foreign goods, given the high proportion of their final price that derived from expenses incurred in their shipping and delivery. Research into the five great guilds of Madrid (the *Cinco Gremios Mayores de Madrid*) in later periods demonstrates the complex framework of competing interests that facilitated the distribution of imported goods (Pérez Sarrión 2016). Once Madrid had been taken, a very high percentage of the Castilian market had been won. The other important market,

---

[23]Gasch (2012), Boyajian (1993).

America (in other words, Seville), had similar characteristics (above all else, a high degree of spatial concentration) and operated according to rules that were highly favourable to foreign production (Chap. 7).

The restructuration of the interior urban network was accompanied by important changes in the rural sector. The demographic trends both in towns and the countryside of this area are of evident recession (Yun 2004). The trends discernible in the tithes show similar tendencies, and wheat production declined by some 30% between 1600 and 1630 (Yun 1999a, table p. 54). In previous centuries the slow movement of inhabitants towards the south had brought overall benefits (Chap. 3). This was no longer the case, as emigrants no longer relocated in order to farm high-quality soils; nor was this process as positive for the redistribution of land and labour as it was in the sixteenth century. On the contrary many displaced families flocked to Madrid, whose growth continued unabated until 1630–1640 due to the arrival of artisans but also of marginalized people. The new model of the urban network in the interior, with Madrid disproportionately large and influential, and a very weak urban network around, made this commercialization more difficult. It was also accompanied by a system of forced purchases exercised by Madrid (Ringrose 1983a) that, being focused on the large proprietors, redistributed the commercial benefits among a very small elite of the peasantry.

Similar trends occurred in Extremadura and the interior Andalusia, as well as, quite possibly, in the Alentejo, in part because of the relative drying up of the flow of emigrants from the North. There are reasons for suspecting that the level of resistance to collapse may have been greater in these regions. But an agrarian system based on large properties, many of them devoted to less demanding labour crops—or only requiring seasonal work, such as harvesting olives trees—or to livestock farming, retarded demographic recovery and at best provoked stagnation. In the interior of Spain, only New Castile retained any resistance to decline. To be specific, baptisms recorded in the rural areas of this region fell more slowly than those of the Duero Valley (at least this was the case until 1640), as did the tithes (until 1630).

Crisis and Adaptation in the Peninsula's Periphery

As we have seen, if the problems in the periphery should not be overlooked, then the depth of the crisis and recession in the Iberian interior has led to extrapolations on the overall peninsula position that are not at all correct. Above all, the calculations of Prados de la Escosura and Alvarez Nogal have to be nuanced. In a pioneering and seminal study, these scholars base their estimate of GDP on the evolution of the cities. This approach predominantly reflects the decline of the central areas where the biggest cities were concentrated and which was the largest of the country. Therefore, if in terms of 'Spain' the figures can be correct, these estimates do not represent the regional differences, which are crucial in an economy composed in fact by the aggregation of regional subnational circuits. The resulting figures fail to include a more precise vision of developments in the peripheral zones, where small population centres and reasonably active rural economies were very dominant. In fact, the crisis did not have the same chronology and outcomes in other regions of the peninsula, and whether or not the crisis led to a recession depended on many factors, ecological conditions among them.

The problems were very obvious in the region from Galicia to Navarre, roughly the so-called Atlantic Spain (Chap. 3). Here, again, there is the sense of a world that was full to the brink and was being punished for its demographic hubris with outbreaks of disease. The 'boom' of the Armada years was followed by a deep 'bust', in which naval construction ran into serious difficulties (Goodman 1997). The severing of trading links with the north of Europe, the outbreak of wars with Flanders and England, and the growing privateering threat in the Atlantic posed a range of problems (Fernández de Pinedo 1974, p. 31). These did not, however, end the Basque iron industry, although it was comparatively resistant to change and technical innovation and clearly affected by the contraction of internal demand. For these reasons the sector was unable to replace lost imports and reduce costs, thus forfeiting its competitive edge in relation to its overseas rivals (Bilbao 1987, pp. 52–7). And all of these setbacks came on top of the contraction of the trade that linked some of these areas to other regional economies in the interior of the peninsula (Lanza 1991, pp. 121–2; Yun 1987). Around 1600, then, many of the sectors that had facilitated the expansion of the previous century were in trouble. Contact with outside regions was limited, as is demonstrated by the fall in commerce with the Duero Valley from 1610 to 1620 (Yun 1987) meaning that it was increasingly difficult to gain access to specie. The scarcity of cash had always been crucial to economies of this sort, which needed it to overcome deficits in basic products. Though many nuances should be added, one could accept the proposition that the region went through a crisis between 1590 and 1615–1620.

Yet, the overall pattern would be very different from that of Castile. The region's ecological conditions meant that it was always able to turn slowly to new alimentary resources such as rye, the chestnut tree, and millet crops or those provided by the fishing industry or domestic livestock breeding. The abundance of forests guarantied the existence of a valuable cattle livestock and of a wide spectrum of food resources (Anes 1994). This ecosystem was receptive to the slow but continuous diffusion of maize from the beginning of the century, which greatly favoured its resistance to the food crisis.[24] And the fiscal burden took different forms here. The tax model based on *sisas* levied on commercial products would have a lesser impact in a region where family self-consumption was more common. Indeed even the products upon which taxes fell appear to have been less decisive—this was the case with wine, for example—and the final result was to avoid a recession of great intensity and scale (Saavedra 1993). The Crown had never sold lots of common lands in this region. The mid-term impact of the wars in Northern Europe was less than has been thought, and naval construction recovered sooner than has been thought (Grafe 2006; Valdez-Bubnov 2011, pp. 73–88). These features help to explain why, for all the problems of the early seventeenth century, in Galicia, Asturias, Cantabria, the Basque Country, and Navarre, the fall in the number of baptisms came later and was slower than in other regions of Spain to the extent that the impression is more that of a crisis with stagnation rather than recession (Yun 1999a; Lanza 2010).

A picture of similar balances and nuances emerges from the great arc that runs from the Catalan Pyrenees through the Levant coasts to Eastern Andalusia. The problems affecting this large strip of land were in part similar to those of Castile: the consolidation of the seigniorial system, the relative depreciation of landlords' incomes and the consequent struggle for produce, and the increasing indebtedness of the aristocracy and the rise of a peasant elite were also present here. As in the hinterland, landlord debts and pressure upon vassals were also factors (Casey 1983, pp. 135–6). In Valencia, for example, the uneven balance of pasture and arable lands posed considerable difficulties and was exacerbated by the crisis in transhumance livestock breeding (Casey 1983, p. 53). These problems were even clearer in Murcia. The expulsion of the *Moriscos* from 1609 also deprived these two areas of very valuable human capital with great skill in

[24] See Saavedra (1985), Barreiro (1984 pp. 296–303), Anes (1988 pp. 34–5), Fernández de Pinedo (1974), and Lanza (1991 pp. 158–77).

irrigation, intensive agriculture, interregional trade, and silk production (Casey 1983; Vassberg 1996). The urban economy, industry, and trade were also sailing into choppy seas. Partly this was because the money market did not favour the free flow of capital towards productive activities, as can be understood from the complaints about the *censals* levied on landlord incomes in Valencia (Casey 1983, pp. 95–7). The growth of the borrowing by municipalities and the *Generalitat* in Catalonia must have had a similar effect. The silk industry of Valencia was being squeezed out by more competitive rivals. As in Castile, silk was slowly being transformed from a primary material used in domestic industry into a raw material exported to other areas of Europe (Casey 1983, pp. 89–92).

There were, however, some differences with Castile, which affected both rural and urban dynamisms. The spiralling number of estates and *mayorazgos* was not present to the same extent as in Castile. Moreover, in this broad eastern arc (and in Catalonia especially), the lower participation of the nobility in the imperial endeavours limited the importance of rent-seeking strategies and the search for political rents in the court as a substitutive for better economic management.[25] This led, as we have seen, to banditry and insecurity in the countryside, which might have meant high transaction costs, but also improvements when the problem almost disappeared during the second half of the century. The agricultural sector was, moreover, notable for a certain dynamism in some areas. In Catalonia changes were occurring that saw the diversification of crops linked to the *masía* and a more intensive agriculture in relation to the interior of the peninsula.[26] Until 1620–1625 the French emigration into Catalonia and, to a lesser degree, Valencia continued, and Murcia was able to repopulate uninhabited areas in these decades.[27] Not even a blow such as the sale of the *tierras baldías y concejiles* had the effect that it might have done in areas of Castile.

Eva Serra's study (1988) also reveals a growing diversification of production which was part of an agriculture aimed at producing goods for the market and based upon wine, rice, the mulberry tree, and citric fruits (Vilar 1962, vol. I, pp. 389–90). These efforts not only allowed it to commercialize a greater percentage of its final produce but also to defraud

---

[25] Of course, this consideration did not include the *juros* in relation to Catalonia (Vilar 1962, vol. I, pp. 357–62).

[26] Vilar (1962, vol. I, p. 371), Durán (1998, p. 133), Serra (1988, pp. 404–5).

[27] On Catalonia see Nadal and Giralt (1960, p. 69) and Durán (1998, pp. 128–31). On Valencia, Casey (1983, pp. 6–7).

a higher proportion of rent due to landlords, thus reducing the pressure upon the peasantry. In both Valencia and Murcia, the expulsion of the *Moriscos* meant a lost opportunity for agrarian improvements but eventually resulted in the redistribution of economic activity and population, allowing for the emergence of a cereal-based agriculture in the dry lands. This switch entailed major changes. In Valencia the population was increasingly concentrated in littoral zones near the capital, a transformation which, it seems reasonable to assume, led to closer links between the countryside and city. As in Catalonia, hopes were founded on new commercial crops. This was the case for rice, the vine, maize, and *barilla*, a plant linked to the booming glass industry and the production of soap. These advances were matched by drives to expand the irrigation system and even efforts dating back to the previous century to break new grounds (Casey 1983, pp. 51–8; Pérez and Lemeunier 1984, pp. 115–119). The development of the market can be discerned behind all of these initiatives; other significant factors were the reorganization of property, leading to the concentration of lands in medium-sized farms which represented a greater balance between the available lands and the workforce (Furió 1995, pp. 324–6). Landlords of the sort found in Valencia, who drew their incomes from *partición de frutos* (the sharing of rent in kind) or farms leased over the long term in *enfiteusis*, could only encourage improvements in production: in this regard their interests coincided with those of their peasants or vassals. Property rights were positive here for economic recovery (Furió 1995, pp. 329–31). Combined with a greater flexibility in the land market and the lower impact of entitled lands, the overall result was a slow but clear recovery (Peris 1989, p. 501).

Cities too were in crisis but also far from collapsing. The arrival of new spices from Asia through Mediterranean trade (Chap. 7) would have a positive effect upon ports such as Alicante, which became a point of distribution towards the peninsula's hinterland. Alicante would also become a conduit into the Mediterranean for goods coming from America (Casey 1983, pp. 82–4). Until at least 1620, the benefits of American trade and the northern commercial networks were felt from Malaga to Almeria (Pulido 1993). Other sectors of the economy remained active. Even at the end of the sixteenth century, the silk trade continued to be relatively stable, with links stretching from Valencia and Murcia to Toledo. In Catalonia and Valencia, the fiscal burden had not grown here as much as in the *Meseta*, and the type of taxes was not as negative as the *millones*. Furthermore, the coastal regions of eastern Spain had suffered on account of the *censales*. But the more moderate character of institutional debts—if we compare with the Castilian state's *juros* and the municipal *censos*—meant that the deviation of capital from more productive investments like commerce was less intense (Vilar 1962, vol. I, p. 360). With bonds now providing lower yields and levels of seigniorial indebtedness having reached their natural limit, a more logical choice for investors was henceforth to plough their monies into commerce and productive activities. This conclusion was not entirely unexpected, for, as we have seen, in countries such as England, a similar process had occurred, albeit to a greater degree. The most important case was the textile sector of Barcelona. Here the problems of the guild-based industry would give rise the *verlagssystem*, more efficient and flexible at balancing offer and demand (Vilar 1962, I, pp. 383–387). Being situated on the coast, the eastern cities had the considerable advantage of a secure and regular provisioning system.

These positive forces also had an impact on the Mediterranean coasts of Eastern Andalusia. Although the crisis of the Granada silk industry was apparent, it did not disappear (Garzón 1972). More important, the coastal areas began benefiting from the slow but clear recovery of Mediterranean trade. The arrival of the Dutch and, above all, English animated small ports of the area and cities such as Malaga. Another part of this trade consisted of products arriving in Seville and connected with the rest of the Mediterranean. One effect was the beginning of the cultivation and trade of raisins, which would subsequently become the most dynamic sector from the end of the century.

In many respects Portugal and, specifically, its littoral zones were similar to the description of the coastal areas of the Mediterranean and Cantabria. The available measurements on GDP per capita, as well as those of agrarian production, show that growth slowed from 1570 but that, after a levelling-off until 1625, they experienced a slow but sustained expansion until 1700. This phenomenon should be tied to American commerce and left its mark in the expansion of cities such as Lisbon and, above all, Porto. The second half of the seventeenth century witnessed an agrarian expansion similar to that of the Spanish littoral: based on *enfiteusis*, it began with the development of commercial crops—wine would be the best example and the Porto zone the most important—and even exports (Barros 2007). Ties with England, more solid after the *Restauraçao*, were behind this expansive process and gained strength thanks to English interest in exports to Brazil. It has been convincingly demonstrated that due to this development, the empire's contribution to seventeenth-century Portuguese growth was very positive (Costa, Palma and Reis 2015).

Thus, the so-called seventeenth-century crisis came later in some of these regions and was smoother and shorter than in the centre of the peninsula.

A New Pattern of Growth

It is impossible to deny the drama of the problems of the first decades of the century, above all if one considers that it was accompanied by the enormous loss of lives and poverty and that the economy was unable to comply with its fundamental mission in *ancien régime* societies: to maintain population levels.

But this is only evident in some regions, and the crisis also set down the grounds for a new expansive model, which was characterized by the major dynamism of the Iberian periphery (Ringrose 1996). Though intensities varied, the economic recovery was also felt in the centre during the second half of the century. This is not the place to attempt an explanation of this revival.[28] As always in pre-industrial economies, it was due to readjustments of a Malthusian type, a better balance between livestock and crops, and the lowering of land rents (Anes 1994). The crisis also had positive effects as long as it provoked a redistribution of income. Variables such as the land rent-wage ratio, measuring the imbalance between landowners and workers, fell between 1590 and 1650 (Álvarez Nogal and Prados de la Escosura 2013, p. 9). These readjustments were also due to changes in the distribution of property. The concentration of land property and the emergence of new seigniorial estates in which land incomes rather than seigniorial rents were the basis of revenues activated the need to lease out lands thus creating better conditions for peasants able to rent those properties and for agrarian recovery. The concentration of capital in the hands of ecclesiastical institutions meant that they were increasingly able to offer *censos* and loans to farmers at interest rates below official levels. Beyond this, an even more complex bundle of factors was also at play. In any case, this explanation appears clear from this date when the evolution of baptisms is examined (Graph 8.2). And the same can be said of the development of tithes and even of the indicators of interior commerce (Yun 1999a).

---

[28]The reader interested in my own view can see it in Yun (1999a).

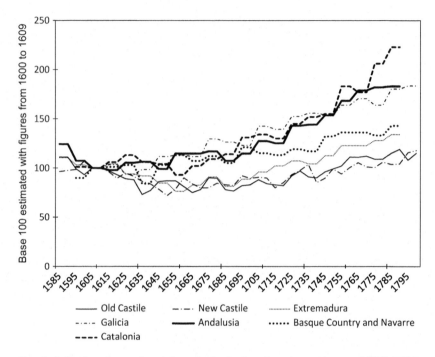

Graph 8.2 Interior and periphery in Spain: baptisms in rural areas, 1585–1800
Sources: Yun (1999b).

It is very possible that, looked at as a whole, the evolution of the Spanish economy of the period may have been very similar to the Italian one, as described by Federico and Malanima (2004). The existing studies on Portugal also point in this direction (Palma and Reis 2016). In the final analysis, Portugal was simply another peripheral region of the Iberian Peninsula. This having been said, the subalpine crisis was shorter and perhaps more creative than its Iberian counterpart (or, at least, that of Spain). But what happened in Spain was not different from the developmental model that was emerging in Europe, although perhaps its intensity or rhythm was. Maps on the density of town and city habitation demonstrate that Spain—though more slowly—did recover its sixteenth-century levels of urbanization (Álvarez Nogal and Prados de la Escosura 2013, table 2). As in the European model described by De Vries, peripheral cities such as Lisbon, Porto, Barcelona, Cadiz, Malaga, and Valencia replaced the dynamism of the centres of the interior such as Segovia, Salamanca, Toledo, or Valladolid. See Maps 8.1, 8.2, 8.3, and 8.4, which show patterns similar to the rest of Mediterranean Europe with urban recession between 1600 and 1700 and the slow but clear growth of coastal cities, with the exception of the Cantabrian coast.

In the second place, this recovery was achieved without a radical overhaul of the basic institutional framework, even if small rectifications had been made to it. This is all the more interesting to the extent that, as we have seen (Chap. 5), this framework was not in itself very positive for economic development. As in the American case, but at a much more modest level, the relative abundance of resources, ecological conditions, small changes in property rights, leasing systems (such as the spread of *enfiteusis* and long-term leasing), and international commerce could create conditions in which recovery and growth were possible. Also, the fact that the pacts among elites, and the institutional framework derived from them, were very different in each region, which was logical in a composite monarchy, reduced the chances of the obstructions presented by the institutional framework prevalent in Castile from affecting the peninsula as a whole in the same way. As a result, the recovery of specific regions was perfectly possible. And, with all its limitations, these were capable of generating stimuli to the extent that they consolidated a national economy. But this matter really belongs to the history of the eighteenth century (Ringrose 1996).

Around 1668, when the Treaty of Lisbon established peace between the Habsburg and the Braganza, the peninsular model of economic growth was already designed in a manner very similar to that of the rest of Europe.

This situation coincided, moreover, with a critical point at which both dynasties saw their own and their metropolitan territories' capacity to benefit from the possession of empires as very limited. The networks of international commerce operated in a way little favourable to such benefits (Everaert 1973) and globalization in Asia, Africa, and America were behind this circumstance. The institutions created in these processes were inefficient for such purposes, not by nature but, rather, because they were becoming obsolete. The paradox was evident: in a world like that of the eighteenth century in which growth would centre on the coasts and on ties with international commerce, two of the countries most oriented towards global circuits would grow slowly. Yet this is not the place to explain this situation. In any case, it is worthwhile to recall that Spain as well as Portugal witnessed important attempts at reform as early as the final decades of the seventeenth century, which demonstrate a certain capacity for adaptation (Storrs 2006). Many changes were still taking place. The increase in the number of noble titles was generating a new aristocracy, coastal areas grew to the rhythm of international exchanges, and cities like Barcelona or Cadiz benefited from the process and nurtured promising mercantile groups. Nevertheless, international competition would be fierce and the changes perhaps slower than desired. A new stage began in the history of empires and, therefore, of globalization.

*   *   *

Were these, then, decadent empires? From the moral perspective set out from a Whig view of history—in other words, the perspective of the Black Legend too—this was obviously the case. Corruption, as so many Enlightenment writers including Spanish and Portuguese thinkers claimed, was the order of the day in Iberian countries and their colonies. The same is true if we limit ourselves to the outcomes of international treaties, such as Munster (1648), Westphalia (1648), the Pyrenees (1659), and Lisbon (1668). Madrid was losing influence, and the European dominions of the Habsburgs were retreating, at the same time as the interference of other countries in the colonial monopoly was being legalized. Lisbon was starting to create a new state whose backbone, not by chance, would be a tax state with high implication of the kingdom but whose empire would very much depend upon English support.

On the other hand, neither today's moral perspective nor the first steps towards the disintegration of the imperial project provide the only viewpoints from which to assess the reality of the so-called Spanish and Portuguese empires and the composite monarchy that served as their bases. What the Enlightenment interpreted as corruption was part of a political system and a conflictive pact that afforded the empire its longevity. It flowed through its very heart, as a part of the need for the consolidation and circulation of elites. And this came at the same time as the American economy maintained a high capacity for recovery and the Spanish and Portuguese economy was passing through a long crisis but one that was not in any way exceptional in qualitative terms in the Mediterranean context and from which it would eventually recover, despite everything. On the other hand, a basis had been established in Spain that, once the separation from Portugal had been overcome, allowed the pact between the distinct centres of imperial power—and, above all, those between Madrid and the colonies—to survive for many years. That was also the case of Portugal with the very few remaining centres in Asia and Africa and, more important, with Brazil. The principal objective—and perhaps another way to assess the empires' success—was achieved: their own survival. No further essential disintegration would occur until the advent of the final crisis from 1808, nor would any major state succeed from it. The problem, as the epilogue will show, is that many things had changed in the international political landscape in or around 1668. And also a very important change had taken place in Iberia: the construction of absolutist systems in which negotiations between the Crown and the elites were based less and less on corporative bodies, such as the Cortes, and more and more on a tension, increasingly unequal, between the king, on the one side, and a myriad of social actors who often maintained different and clashing interests. This situation was not necessarily negative for some of these social actors but would make it more difficult to create wealth for the whole society.

Open Access This chapter is licensed under the terms of the Creative Commons Attribution 4.0 International License (http://creativecommons.org/licenses/by/4.0/), which permits use, sharing, adaptation, distribution and reproduction in any medium or format, as long as you give appropriate credit to the original author(s) and the source, provide a link to the Creative Commons licence and indicate if changes were made.

The images or other third party material in this chapter are included in the chapter's Creative Commons licence, unless indicated otherwise in a credit line to the material. If material is not included in the chapter's Creative Commons licence and your intended use is not permitted by statutory regulation or exceeds the permitted use, you will need to obtain permission directly from the copyright holder.

Conclusions Part III

ORGANIZING AND PAYING FOR GLOBAL EMPIRE, 1598–1668

One of the great problems in the history of Spain since the birth of the Black Legend has been that of exceptionalism. If less affected by the ideological tints of this hoary view, the history of Portugal has also been stained with this problem. A comparative history of this age underlines, however, that neither of these kingdoms constituted an anomaly in European history. Rather they are variants, shaped and determined by their imperial ventures, of a common model or ideal type. Other political formations of the time, including England, were characterized by the overlap, collision, and diversity of powers, by the existence of conflicting pacts with the elites, and by the coexistence of agents who exercised coercion. This is in fact the reason why, in the words of P. O'Brien, they were not efficient states 'that can be represented as sovereign authorities governing successful economies that provide high, stable and rising standards of welfare for their citizens.'

In England it has been possible to speak of a 'federation of counties, each with its individual ethos' (Smith 1997, p. 139). Phenomena such as royal patronage, rent-seeking practices, court corruption, monopolies that raised transaction costs for the outsiders, and so on were the order of the day. In France, the sale of offices is the best-known, but not the only, manifestation of how absolutism was maintained through pacts with the elites and by sharing—again not always peacefully—quotas of sovereignty. The same was true of the fiscal system and of French absolutism in general (see Mettam 1988; Beik 1985, and many other). The Frondes would bring to light the existence of privately owned armies whose importance has been emphasized by different studies on the seigneurial households (e.g. Béguin 1999).

This disavowal of exceptionalism does not mean that all societies are the same. What captures the attention about the Iberian ones in general, and of the Castilian and Portuguese cases above all, is their remarkable social stability and capacity to reproduce their political structures. This is all the more striking because they were connected to developed commercial and global circuits, something that stands in contrast to the historiographical tendency to see a link between commercial development and political change (as well as with a certain modernizing vision of globalization).

While not exclusive to Iberia, it was precisely this aspect of it that could provide the variant. The empires and the positioning of these societies in global networks served to stabilize them. This is not to claim that they did not change, and this is (one reason) why Pierre Vilar's notion that the Spanish empire represented 'the supreme phase of feudalism' (an affirmation that, mutatis mutandis, has also been applied implicitly to Portugal) cannot be accepted today. Furthermore, similar visions have been applied to countries such as France, in regard to which P. Anderson (1974), and Marxist historians in general, spoke of a form of feudal income centralized through the tax system, which also has its parallels in Castile and Portugal and which (supposedly) acted in the same sense while facilitating its elites' reproduction. It was in this context that religious phenomena acted. Catholicism was ingrained into the heart of the composite monarchy: it served not only to justify empires but also the system for the transfer and mobilization of fiscal and military resources. It is enough to reflect on the cases of England or the Netherlands and the way in which their religious fractures led to ruptures that would end up illuminating alternative forms of the state to underline the importance that religious orthodoxy had in the Iberian kingdoms and the way in which it contributed to the reproduction of an institutional framework that was important for the forms of allocation of productive resources.

From 1600 globalization—even if it still yielded insignificant trade figures in relation to overall European wealth—would coincide with a growing tension over market control and competition between European regional industries. In this context, the transfer of resources tying these two empires to Northern Europe, and in particular to the Netherlands and England, would also be important to spark decisive changes in these societies.

In all, the effects of Spanish silver and the expenses generated by war—the second of these being negative for the economy in the short term—would only be positive to the extent that the political and institutional systems evolved in a different way, especially in the cases of Holland and England. This occurred while in Iberia the capacity of the aristocracies to overcome the depreciation of seigneurial income both strengthened them and tied them more closely to the state. In other words, the capacity of trade and globalization to dissolve the fortunes of aristocratic elites and to erode their socio-economic bases was reduced and even reversed. The result would not be a recession—decline is still spoken of—as dramatic as the one successive generations of scholars conjured up; but it did lead to a loss of competitiveness of the industrial sector, even in the domestic market, and a re-composition of the economic map of the peninsula which, even if fell within general European patterns, would henceforth be so slow that the subsequent readjustments would not be able to achieve the same degree of efficiency as the Northern economic centre for a long time.

The great problem of the Iberian empires would originate in their own structure and context. Together they had launched European globalization, but soon things became rather more difficult. Empires were the springboard for the making up of informal global networks that did not always bend to the interests of rulers. In fact, they were so important precisely because the formal institutions created by these rulers were not efficient enough in generating trust among economic agents, who continued to resort to the same systems that their predecessors had been employing for many centuries: family, reputation, friendship, reciprocity, and so on. The result was that these networks, which had a transboundary character and were impossible for governments to control, would render obsolete and inoperable any imperial models based on the command of the most important commercial circuits, such as the Indies convoy (*Carrera de Indias*) or the State of India (*Estado da Índia*). In addition, the hybrid nature of these networks (merchants, officials, etc.) would encourage and foster patronage, clientelism, nepotism, rent-seeking, fraud, and even corruption, which would become constitutive of the system itself and would affect the functioning of formal institutions created in these empires. This fact, nevertheless, and in spite of the difficulties of political control from the centre of these empires, would not imply a reduction in the global networks' overall commerce, thus demonstrating, once again, the efficiency of informal mechanisms for creating confidence, even if they also rerouted a good part of the riches these empires generated to other political formations.

If the difficulties in states' control of colonial resources have almost always been viewed from the perspective of what happened in these two empires, the truth is that we need also to view those empires from the perspective of what happened in their peripheries and even outside them. This has much to do with the fact that the Iberian empires were, as has been said, one agent among many in this process of globalization. The expansion of the Ottoman Empire, its early projection to Asia in the fifteenth century, served not only to create an element of contention in the Indian Ocean from the mid-sixteenth century but also to promote globalization routes inaccessible to the Iberians. These routes came to be strengthened by the religious toleration practised by the sultans and the very nature of the empire as a collector of incomes generated by the mercantile networks that spanned its territories. From the early seventeenth century, the English routes that fed the trade of the Mediterranean Levant also had this function (Fusaro 2015). Moreover, to the extent that the Portuguese had only been able to control a small part of the Asian trade, their circuits could be redirected towards other actors, such as the Dutch, who operated with noticeable efficiency. From 1644, the new Qing dynasty, creator of another empire, limited European expansion in the South China Sea, while the trade of the *Estado da Índia* had already been subject to vampire-like attacks by non-Portuguese traders who proved difficult for Lisbon to control. In these same years, the Tokugawa consolidated an imperial system that would soon affect Portuguese trade in the South China Sea and across the Pacific system (Flores 1998). The problems experienced by both the *Estado da Índia* and the Crown revenues would be greatly affected by these changes. The incorporation of America into the process of globalization through the development of regional trade flows and alternative routes to those that linked the Caribbean with Seville also weakened the King of Spain to the same extent. And this occurred while the English colonies in North America expanded their illegal trade in the Caribbean and with Spanish and Portuguese colonies, with a concomitant impact upon the king's revenues. All this would also weaken the imperial pact between Lisbon and Madrid.

In this way and if, indeed, colonial commerce continued to provide a small part of the wealth of different European countries (in spite of its registered growth from the late sixteenth century), the important tensions generated around it would end up affecting political systems and would constitute one more factor that, in a context of general political competition, would accentuate the need for fiscal reforms and place unprecedented pressures upon composite states.

This was the case even if powers such as the Netherlands or England were undecided about whether to attempt to conquer territories controlled by the Portuguese and Spanish, suspecting that the post-conquest costs of protection would be exorbitant; these concerns, in conjunction with failed ventures such as those of Bahia and Pernambuco, ensured that the colonies remained under the Habsburg government of Madrid. But if these arrangements represented good political business for the Habsburgs, they were not sound commercial practice and became a problem from the standpoint of the fiscal system. Madrid and Lisbon paid for the costs of protection, externalizing the payments of their officials in the form of compensation for fraud, nepotism, patronage, and smuggling; but this came at the expense of a great deal of trade and economic resources eluding the monarchy.

The change in American ecosystems would allow a new phase of expansion that would also be beneficial for the king, who no longer claimed the lion's share of the general wealth generated by his dominions; indeed, his proportion was an ever-smaller part of it. To the extent that colonial elites had increased their economic capital, these same groups had also augmented their political decision-making capacity. Their increased ability to withhold resources—even military resources—at such a delicate time as the Thirty Years War was a good indication of the change underway in the balance between colonies and metropolis. What W. Maltby called the 'drift toward autonomy' was taking place: in reality, this was nothing more than an indication of the impossibility of applying a mercantilist policy in a composite monarchy, a formation that had none of the hallmarks of the proto-national systems typical of mercantilism (Yun 1999a). But this situation presents us with an image different from that of the immobile empires. Having separated in 1668, both the Spanish and the Portuguese empires constantly reconfigured themselves on new bases. The former depended upon a colonial pact that included a high degree of autonomy enjoyed by the Creole minorities and systems of interregional transfers of funds for their defence—and defence was no longer undertaken simply in the interests of Madrid but also on behalf of these elites who had resisted any loss of autonomy through conquest by other rival powers such as England or Holland. Portugal would turn to Brazil, where gold mining would create new bases for the development of the plantation economy. Moreover, at the very height of mercantilism and the war against Holland (after 1648 Amsterdam had allied with the Habsburgs), Lisbon would find in England an ally interested in maintaining an empire that brought it remarkable benefits. In both cases, areas of domination and influence were being lost, but the survival of very substantial parts of the colonial system was guaranteed.

Of course, all this was accompanied by ruptures in the composite monarchy of the Habsburgs. And again, these breaks cannot not be understood without considering the process of globalization and its overall effects. As the remittances of American silver arriving in Seville for the monarchs declined, and as American tax systems increasingly operated so that a (growing) portion of their resources remained in the New World, the composite monarchy began to be endangered. This failure of the global system allows us to understand the need to increase the fiscal burden on territories such as Catalonia, Portugal, Naples, and others, some of which were already used to a steady increase in their contributions. As we have emphasized, this reduction in the flow of Atlantic resources arriving at Seville did not happen because there was a lasting recession in the American economy as a whole but because Madrid's share of resources was limited by the centrifugal forces created by globalization and the pacts that this forced upon it. The rebellions in Portugal, Catalonia, and even Naples were more than fiscal movements. But they were also proof that one of the pillars of the pact between the Habsburgs and the European local elites over the mobilization of local resources was the efficiency of the royal revenue collection system of the empire and the functioning of a Portuguese system that was already unsustainable. In this case, moreover, the problem was not only the difficulty of maintaining the Portuguese fortress positions in Asia. It was also proof that these problems and developments strained relations between the king and elites in Goa and Lisbon until they were incompatible with the basic constitutional principle of the composite monarchy: that the resources of each kingdom (and by extension of each empire) should be employed for the benefit of its subjects. The far more drastic fiscal reforms that Dom João de Braganza would have to introduce after 1668 are a good symptom of what was happening: regardless of whether the Portuguese were right or wrong to see tyranny in the policy of Count Duke in the 1630s, the state could not be maintained with the existing parameters and basis; steps, therefore, had to be taken to strengthen the tax state within the kingdom.

Though gradually weakened, up until 1668 the Castilian elites had managed to preserve the essential components of the unstable pact made with Charles V within their frontiers. But the composite monarchy was no longer efficient, and neither was it an effective political system for this new world of globalization and mercantilism. These elites had succeeded in reproducing their status quo. Undoubtedly, the nobility was renewed to the extent that the circulation of elites (Yun 2004) allowed the ascent of new families. Now, at the end of the seventeenth century, a new Amerindian nobility was beginning to enter the peninsular social arena. The urban oligarchies of Castile had had to open up their ranks to new members. The asymmetry within the composite monarchy was creating a statist ideology and even an imagined Castilian community that was assimilated with Spain, as if Spain were a simple extension of Castile. But this political system would remain a composite state even after the disappearance from 1665 of the *Cortes* that represented the kingdom. And, more importantly, this coincided with the development of a model of absolutism in which, after the disappearance of assemblies, the territorial component of political representation was replaced by a system of direct and bilateral relations between the king and the oligarchies of each city or corporation. This model of constitutional development was similar to those of other European countries, such as France, but it was very different to the English model, which would prove itself capable of creating the most efficient state for the defence of markets and thereby reducing for its subjects the transaction costs of international trade.

In any case, from the beginning of the eighteenth century, the foundations of a new absolutism that depended upon a proto-national state with an empire, rather than a dispersed composite monarchy, were created in Spain and Portugal. In the case of Spain, this was achieved by the crisis and dismemberment of the Habsburgs' composite and dynastic monarchy. A new growth would emerge on this new foundation and the slow re-composition of the regional economies and relations among them; logically, this growth would be slow and limited in both countries. And this was a manifestation of another fact: the ability to generate economic expansion—at the levels prevailing in pre-industrial economies—might depend upon the institutional framework and property rights, but these were not the only variables. The performance of this institutional framework must be seen in the context of the availability of resources at any one moment. What could not be expected was that these institutions would witness a qualitative change of the scale of the Industrial Revolution, which would knock on England's door within a few decades. In other words, this eruption was difficult to imagine in political formations in which the state—not because of the Crown's parasitism but because of its political constitution and pacts with elites—systematically exploited private market activities rather than simply regulating them (Jones 1981, 2000).

The political reforms and consequent flexibility of the economies of France, Portugal, and Spain in the eighteenth century would be very favourable and serve to explain the growth in these countries. But they were still far from that of England. Meanwhile, the development of international trade, linked to globalization, would mark the geography of growth in the Iberian countries, which occurred mostly in the coastal regions. Such considerations do not imply that countries such as England were free from the corrupt and corrosive effects of informal networks. It only indicates that the relationship between such institutions and the state's capacity for enforcement would be different and that, at the same time, systems would be created for the canalization of state resources towards defensive systems more effective than those of the Iberian countries in the seventeenth century. It is very possible that the comparison between China and Great Britain that has been carried out by P. Vries (2015) is also applicable to the case of the Iberian empires.

EPILOGUE

Both the Spanish and Portuguese empires—as is almost a rule in the history of empires—have had bad press. From contemporary commentators to the current historiography, many authors have emphasized the most negative perspective or have made implicit comparisons with the present that have led to pessimistic assessments. When not seen as lost opportunities for the formation of national states, these empires are considered a drag on economic growth and even an obstacle to Spain's and Portugal's economic modernization.

From the political point of view, both empires—but above all the Spanish—have been considered as anomalous in the process of state formation. It has been generally accepted that the Spanish Empire was the key to an abortive process of constructing a Spanish nation state, which consequently could not evolve either on the English parliamentary model or according to the French Jacobin one (Bernal 2005). It can, however, be argued that other forms of state building were possible. Here it has been maintained that, at least until c. 1640, the Spanish empire was the key to the composite monarchy's high capacity for reproduction. We do not know what would have happened without it, but all available evidence leads us to think that this political system could not have survived, at least in the form that it did or for as long as it did, without the empire. The truth is that, as far as Spain is concerned, rather than an unfinished project (an argument that hides a certain anachronism tinged with pessimism), the empire allowed a composite monarchy consisting of diverse polities—

© The Author(s) 2019

B. Yun-Casalilla, *Iberian World Empires and the Globalization of Europe 1415–1668*, Palgrave Studies in Comparative Global History, https://doi.org/10.1007/978-981-13-0833-8

crowns, kingdoms, principalities, seigneurial and urban jurisdictions—with separate institutions and, above all, different parliaments, to reproduce itself. This political formula is not surprising for its time. Nor should it—viewed from the current perspective—be regarded as an aberration, in view of other, even longer, later and more complex processes of nation-building, such as those of Germany or Italy. As has been said many times, composite states are not the exception but the rule, in the history of early modern Europe.

In regards to its economy, the Portuguese empire has been considered the cause of its backwardness, which was based on the export of raw materials in exchange for industrial products. It has also been seen as the cause of the draining of human capital into the colonies, which, apart from other evils, aborted the formation of a solid bourgeoisie in the homeland.[1] In the Spanish case, the negative visions are curiously contradictory and bear the hallmark of monetarism. For many authors, the colonies were the cause of inflation, which rendered the goods produced in the homeland uncompetitive and, at the same time, led to an increase in wages, which reduced industrial profits. The result would be an unfavourable trade balance that would end up ruining Castile. On the other hand, it is still said—indeed, a number of contemporary theorists first noticed this trend—that the external payments of the monarchy in the European wars must have both encouraged the growth of other countries and limited the chances of domestic development.

As we have seen, recent studies on Portugal rather tend to strengthen the idea that the empire had a net positive effect on the economy. No similar estimates had been made for Spain. This having been said, in the above pages, it has been argued that the impact on the economies of both countries has to be studied from the viewpoint of institutions. In both cases, the empires contributed to—and were based on—the development of political economies that were efficient for a long period but, after 1600, were unable to feed domestic growth above a certain level of resource utilization and international competition. Furthermore, when this epoch's economic growth is studied, the impression is that it took place not because of the efficiency of the institutions—as the new institutional economic describes them—but in spite of them. This was largely because the empires contributed to accentuate the elites' capacities to acquire

---

[1] See a brief state of the art in Costa, Palma, and Reis (2015).

incomes rather than their interest in innovation, to use the binomial expressed by E. J. Jones. Moreover, the positive effect of Spanish silver on other economies—particularly the Dutch one (Chap. 6)—should be related to the fact that in these areas, with different institutional and social structures and with different ecosystems (particularly in the agricultural sector), the Habsburgs' expenditures increased their competitiveness. The result, in any case, was a series of readjustments in Iberia rather than an economic decline throughout the whole peninsula.

This being the case, it would be even more illusory to expect these empires to have produced a modernization of the Iberian economies or something similar to modern or intensive economic growth. Whatever the value of the concepts of the 'Great Divergence' and the industrial revolution, none of the current general interpretations of them have any heuristic significance from the perspective of Spain and Portugal in 1600. In Castile and Portugal, high salaries and emigration to America or Asia and Brazil did not lead to an investment in technology and the transition to a labour-saving and technologically intensive economy for obvious reasons that have to do with their political economy and institutional framework, the inexistence of an economically efficient state, and the still-limited nature of globalization.[2] It is important to stress how different the world of 1750 was from that of 1600: in regard to both foreign and interior markets, the state and globalization at the time of Philip III of Spain were far from those of England under Pitt the Elder. It is therefore clear that Iberian domestic growth of the sixteenth century had to be limited. Furthermore, to demand that industrial capitalism emerge from this growth and, though comparisons must be always welcomed, to judge the achievements of empires by their inability to sponsor and sustain intensive capitalist growth are simply an exercise in historical stupidity which few historians now posit.

Our view of Spanish and Portuguese imperial organization has also been dominated by an idea of exceptionalism. This is especially the case if the subject is approached from an anachronistic perspective based upon a simplistic understanding of the empires of the nineteenth century. But many of their supposed traits and failings are typical of almost all empires.

All empires have been based on a negotiation between centres and peripheries or on the plurality of decision-making centres, as is clear from

---

[2] For an interpretation along these lines for England, see Pomeranz (2001).

studies such as that of Burbank and Cooper (2010) and the relations they describe for empires such as those of the Ottomans, Chinese, Romans, and others. But this is also the case if we focus on post-Iberian empires. Darwin (2012) has seen the English empire as an unfinished one, partly because of the existence of very diverse decision-making centres and interests that did not always converge. Its experience in India and the transfer of sovereignty to the East India Company is very significant in this regard, as it is also the case of the Netherlands with the VOC and the existence of very diverse decision-making centres in its overseas domains (Adams 2005). Another weakness often highlighted for the Portuguese and Spanish empires, the high cost of war and the way in which the mobilization of military resources affected the chances of development, was set out long ago by P. Kennedy (1988) as a characteristic of all empires. By their extension all empires have experienced problems of communication and information, and they all must face the challenge of asymmetric information that affects the relations between their diverse centres, in particular in regard to those between the metropolis itself and its peripheries. Precisely because of the above, the negotiation between the centre and periphery—or between the different centres—led to transfers of not only political but also economic capital to the elites and resulted in rent-seeking practices among them, something that has often led to the use of the term corruption. And we could go on.

It is quite possible that the way to understand these empires better is by focusing on their specificities in their concrete historical context and in relation to their competitors of the day. Undoubtedly, their greatest rival until well into the seventeenth century would be the Ottoman Empire. This may be highly significant. Here Burbank and Cooper (2010) have offered very suggestive ideas. From the perspective of their respective political economies, there are many similarities. Like its Iberian competitors, the Ottoman Empire increasingly relied on taxation, especially after 1580, in part in response to the war efforts and in part because of its confrontation with the Habsburgs (Pamuk 2012). Like in the Portuguese and Spanish empires, this resulted in the local elites enjoying greater autonomy, which both increased their freedom of action and the decentralization of the tax state. But there was one fundamental difference: at no point before the eighteenth century did the Sultan try to implement a protectionist policy. Thus, there was never anything comparable to the *Carrera de Indias* in the Ottoman domains. On the contrary, the Sultan's principal concern was that commerce should flow through the various trade routes and networks—often under the control of non-Muslims—with the intention of collecting taxes and facilitating domestic supply systems, especially in Istanbul. Hence, the Sultans were able to meet, and even benefit from, the challenges of globalization that corroded the income of the Kings of Spain and Portugal. And the Ottoman Empire would also remain a very decentralized polity until the nineteenth century.

More important, however, was that the composite character of the Spanish empire and the monarchy hindered the transfer of funds from one state to another within it and that this occurred not only for technical reasons but also, and more importantly, because it created 'constitutional' frictions between those territories; this is to say that it affected the pacts with the various elites, especially in the European territories but also in the relations between Portuguese and Castilians, vital between 1580 and 1640. As I have repeatedly stressed, the Habsburg system was not a proto-state, a nation with an empire, but, rather, a network of polities, one of which, Castile, had created an empire (Yun 1998, 2012, 2015). The problem was not only that the Habsburgs had many theatres to attend to and deal with but also that their entire system was based on the theoretical precept that no transfer of resources could be made between their states. This system—based on a principle which was not always respected by the Crown—was efficient for the reasons set out above but only until political formations arose that, despite not being modern state units, increasingly resembled the formula of homogeneous proto-national states from the point of view of their territorial integrity and that, at the same time, built colonial systems of an eminently commercial character and sought to save costs in the administration of these colonies. This was the case for Holland and England in the seventeenth century. These political formations best fit the most efficient model in the emerging mercantilist world.

In both cases, Britain and Holland, this meant a territorial continuum which, despite its political fragmentation, allowed for a more efficient customs system, based upon a narrow fiscal space in the metropolis whose customs duties, fuelled by foreign and colonial trade, accounted for most of its income. This does not mean that those empires, including the British, were free from corruption, nepotism, smuggling, patronage, and the negative effects of informal social networks. The recent literature in this respect is very significant (see, e.g. Rothschild 2011). But, above all, these empires—and in particular England—also witnessed genuine financial revolutions which, from the end of the seventeenth century, supported more efficient tax systems and issued debt at interest rates even lower than those of Spain and with more payment guarantees. More importantly, from the late seventeenth century, the English empire would achieve all of this while a more efficient and competitive economy emerged and flourished. In this sense it is revealing that, although there was contraband in the English empire, it was often based on the fraudulent export of industrial products of high added value, which was positive for the country's economy as a whole.

There is another aspect to consider. The two Iberian empires belonged to an epoch in which family and extended kinships ties were crucial for the articulation of political, social, and economic life. They were in fact the DNA of those societies and therefore that of their empires. This is not new in history. On the contrary, family and kinship—in their very different variants—also had been crucial components of the social fabric and all primitive empires from the Romans to Tamerlane and even afterwards. As we have seen, imperial endeavours were in part a direct or indirect product of the dynamics of family and lineages and of the networks they supported, which were vital to the empires' constitution and functioning. This fact had many implications, and a very important one for our arguments is that one of the Iberian empires' key traits was the relative commercial efficiency of informal institutions that pivoted around kinship and went beyond it—and, in particular, of the mercantile networks that built trust upon mechanisms of enforcement that often operated on the margins of the state. Insofar as these networks had much to do with solidarities within the very extended family relationships and the political economy of the time, they not only corroded the monarchs' agenda for centralization but also contributed to the perversion (to our eyes) of the formal institutions and to the weakening of their states, making it more difficult to be competitive in the mercantilist world of the seventeenth century, particularly in America and even more in Asia. Above all, the Iberian empires could not maintain the primacy that they had enjoyed previously (in the sixteenth century), as states like England began to develop formal institutions more efficient in terms of protecting their markets. In short, the Iberian systems of the second half of the seventeenth century resulted in rich elites, weak states, and economies that found it inherently difficult to achieve expansion. The peninsula's tardiness in the implantation of a new regional model of growth based on the dynamics of the periphery is very meaningful.

Nevertheless, at the same time, attempts at reform and adaptation during the reign of Charles II (1665–1700) and the first Braganza kings—João (1640–1656) and Alfonso (1656–1683)—demonstrate that these empires were not inert bodies, unable to confront the many challenges they were facing. Indeed, it is not surprising that Storrs has been able to present a much more positive image of this epoch (Storrs 2006). Thus, the Spanish and Portuguese empires cannot longer be seen as subject to a fatal decay. Moreover, their skeletons, in the form of arteries, strategic enclaves, and positions with specific negotiating agendas, provided them with an enviable flexibility. To the extent that these points also gained—or maintained—autonomy, their survival was possible and could even increase the wealth they were able to generate for the various elites of the most important nodal points, both in the overseas territories and in Europe. Furthermore, although they were not administered by stupid or inexperienced statesmen, history shows that no one is immune to making serious mistakes. Then, in the following century, the Bourbon and Braganza reforms were a way of rethinking the pacts with elites in Europe, America, Africa, and Asia that allowed Madrid and Lisbon to fulfil the essential agenda of governments: that they and their empires survive, in spite of the trickle down of possessions captured by their competitors, above all in Asia and the Caribbean region.[3] Nevertheless, for well-known reasons, in the long run, these reforms would eventually break down the empires' internal equilibriums and pave the way for their fracture in the nineteenth century.

[3] Only after completing this volume could I consult the illuminating book by Storrs (2016) on the first decades of the eighteenth century.

REFERENCES

A. Abadía (1993) *Señorío y crédito en Aragón en el siglo XVI* (Zaragoza: Institución Fernando el Católico).

A. Abadía (1998) *La enajenación de rentas señoriales en el Reino de Aragón* (Zaragoza: Institución Fernando el Católico).

F. H. Abed Al-Hussein (1982) *Trade and Business Community in Old Castile. Medina del Campo, 1500–1575* (Ph.D. Thesis, University of East Anglia).

D. Abulafia (2011) *The Great Sea: A Human History of the Mediterranean* (London: Allen Lane).

D. Acemoglu, S. Johnson and J. Robinson (2005) 'The Rise of Europe: Atlantic Trade, Institutional Change, and Economic Growth', *The American Economic Review*, 95, 546–579.

J. Adams (2005) *The Familial State: Ruling Families and Merchant Capitalism in Early Modern Europe* (New York: Cornell University Press).

K. Adrien (1981) 'The Sale of Juros and the Politics of Reform in the Viceroyalty of Peru, 1608–1695', *Journal of Latin American Studies*, 13, 1–19.

R. Allen (1992) *Enclosure and the Yeoman: The Agricultural Development of the South-Midlands, 1450–1850* (Oxford: Clarendon Press).

A. Almorza Hidalgo (2011) *Género, emigración y movilidad social en la expansión Atlántica: mujeres españolas en el Perú colonial (1550–1650)* (Ph.D. Thesis, European University Institute).

L. Alonso (2012) 'La ayuda mexicana en el Pacífico: socorros y situados en Filipinas, 1565–1816' in C. Marichal and J. Grafenstein (eds.) *El secreto del Imperio Español: los situados coloniales en el siglo XVIII*, pp. 251–293 (Mexico: ColMex).

© The Author(s) 2019   451
B. Yun-Casalilla, *Iberian World Empires and the Globalization of Europe 1415–1668*, Palgrave Studies in Comparative Global History, https://doi.org/10.1007/978-981-13-0833-8

N. Alonso Cortés (1955) *Miscelánea vallisoletana* (Valladolid: Miñón).

I. Altman (2000) *Transatlantic Ties in the Spanish Empire: Brihuega, Spain & Puebla, Mexico, 1560–1620* (Stanford: Stanford University Press).

J. Álvarez (1987) *Rentas, precios y crédito en Zamora en el Antiguo Régimen* (Zamora: Colegio Universitario de Zamora).

J. Álvarez (1990) 'La contribución de Subsidio y Excusado en Zamora (1500–1800)', in E. Fernández de Pinedo (ed.) *Haciendas forales y hacienda real*, pp. 123–137 (Bilbao: Universidad del País Vasco).

C. Álvarez Nogal (2009) *Oferta y demanda de deuda pública en Castilla. Juros de alcabalas (1540–1740)* (Madrid: Banco de España).

C. Álvarez Nogal and L. Prados de la Escosura (2013), 'The Rise and Fall of Spain (1270–1850)', *The Economic History Review*, 66, 1–37.

C. Álvarez de Toledo (2004) *Politics and Reform in Spain and Viceregal Mexico: The Life and Though of Juan de Palafox, 1600–1659* (Oxford: Clarendon Press).

C. Álvarez de Toledo (2011) *Juan de Palafox. Obispo y virrey* (Madrid: Marcial Pons).

A. Amadori (2009) 'Que se de diferente modo al gobierno de las Indias, que se van perdiendo muy aprisa. Arbitrismo y administración a principios del siglo XVII', *Anuario de Estudios Americanos*, 66, 147–79.

A. Amadori (2012) "Fiscalidad y consenso en el virreinato de Perú, 1620–1650", *América Latina en la Historia Económica*, 19:2 (2012): 7–45.

J. Amelang (1986) *Honored Citizens of Barcelona: Patrician Culture and Class Relations, 1490–1714* (Princeton: Princeton University Press).

P. Anderson (1974) *Lineages of the Absolutist State* (London: NLB).

J. I. Andrés and R. Lanza (2008) 'Estructura y evolución de los ingresos de la Real Hacienda de Castilla en el siglo XVII', *Studia Historica. Historia Moderna*, 30, 147–199.

F. Andújar (2004) *El sonido del dinero: monarquía, ejército y venalidad en la España del siglo XVIII* (Madrid: Marcial Pons).

G. Anes (1988) *Economía y sociedad en la Asturias del Antiguo Régimen* (Barcelona: Crítica).

G. Anes (1994) 'The Agrarian 'Depression' in Castile in the Seventeenth Century', in I. A. A. Thompson and B. Yun (eds.) *The Castilian Crisis of the Seventeenth Century: New Perspectives on the Economic and Social History of Seventeenth Century Spain*, pp. 60–76 (Cambridge: Cambridge University Press).

B. Aram (2008) *Leyenda Negra y Leyendas Doradas en la conquista de América* (Madrid: Marcial Pons).

B. Aram and B. Yun (eds.) (2014) *Global Goods and the Spanish Empire, 1492–1824* (Basingstoke: Palgrave).

J. Aranda (1984) *Los moriscos en tierras de Córdoba* (Córdoba: Caja de Ahorros de Córdoba).

I. W. Archer (1991) *The Pursuit of Stability: Social Relations in Elizabethan London* (Cambridge: Cambridge University Press).

M. Ardit (1994) *Els homes; la terra del Pais Valencià (segles XVI–XVIII)* (Barcelona: Curial) vols. I–II.

F. Ariel and P. M. O. Svriz (2016) 'Defendiendo una frontera: La ciudad de Corrientes, milicias e indios chaqueños, siglos XVII–XVIII', *Jahrbuch für Geschichte Lateinamerikas*, 53, 59–86.

G. Arrighi (1994) *The Long Twentieth-Century: Money, Power, and the Origins of Our Times* (New York: Verso).

L. Arroyo Abad and J. L. Van Zanden (2016) 'Growth under Extractive Institutions? Latin American Per Capita GDP in Colonial Times', *The Journal of Economic History*, 76, 1182–1215.

M. Artola (1982) *La Hacienda del Antiguo Régiman* (Madrid: Alianza).

R. G. Asch (2003) *Nobilities in Transition, 1550–1700: Courtiers and Rebels in Britain and Europe* (London: Arnold).

C. S. Assadourian (1982) *El sistema de la economía colonial. Mercado interno, regiones y espacio económico* (Lima: Instituto de Estudios Peruanos, 1982).

A. Atienza (1988) *Propiedad, explotación y rentas. El clero regular zaragozano en el siglo XVIII* (Zaragoza: Departamento de Cultura y Educación).

A. Atienza (2008) *Tiempos de conventos. Una historia social de las fundaciones en la España Moderna* (Madrid: Marcial Pons).

I. Atienza (1987) *Aristocracia, poder y riqueza en la España Moderna. La Casa de Osuna, siglos XV–XIX* (Madrid: Siglo XXI).

I. Atienza and M. Simón (1989). '"Aunque fuese con una negra, si S.M. así lo desea": sobre la autoridad real, el amor y los hábitos matrimoniales de la nobleza hispana', *Gertae: taller de historia*, 1, 32–52.

A. Attman (1986) *American Bullion in the European World Trade, 1600–1800* (Göteborg: Kungliga vetenskaps).

L. Bagrow (1964) *The History of Cartography* (London: C. A. Watts).

A. Ballone (2017) *The 1624 Tumult of Mexico in Perspective (c. 1620–1650). Authority and Conflict Resolution in the Iberian Atlantic* (Leiden: Brill).

P. Bakewell (1990) 'La minería en la Hispanoamérica colonial' in L. Bethell (ed.) *Historia de América Latina 3. América Latina colonial: Economía*, pp. 49–91 (Barcelona: Crítica).

P. Bakewell (1991) 'Los determinantes de la producción minera en Charcas y en Nueva España durante el siglo XVII' in H. Bonilla (ed.) *El sistema colonial en la América española*, pp. 58–72 (Barcelona: Crítica).

P. Bakewell (1995) *Silver and Entrepreneurship in Seventeenth Century: Potosí: the Life and Times of Antonio López de Quiroga* (Dallas: Southern Methodist University Press, 1995).

C. Báncora (1959) 'Las remesas de metales preciosos desde Callao a España en la primera mitad del siglo XVII', *Revista de Indias*, 75, 35–88.

K. Barkey (2008) *Empire of Difference: The Ottomans in Comparative Perspective* (Cambridge: Cambridge University Press).

B. Barreiro (1984) 'La introducción de nuevos cultivos y la evolución de la ganadería en Asturias durante la Edad Moderna', in *Congreso de historia rural: siglos XV–XIX*, pp. 287–318 (Madrid: Casa de Velázquez).

A. Barrera-Osorio (2006) *Experiencing Nature: The Spanish American Empire and the Early Scientific Revolution* (Austin: University of Texas Press).

W. Barret (1990) 'World Bullion Flows, 1450–1800' in J. D. Tracy (ed.) *The Rise of Merchant Empires. Long-Distance Trade in the Early Modern World, 1350–1750*, pp. 224–254 (Cambridge: Cambridge University Press).

I. Barreto (2015) *A invençao de Goa. Poder imperial e conversões culturais nos séculos XVI e XVII* (Lisbon: Impresa de Ciencias Sociais).

M. Barrio (2001) 'La iglesia peninsular de los Reyes Católicos a Carlos V (1490–1530)' in E. Belenguer (ed.) *De la unión de coronas al Imperio de Carlos V*, vol. I, pp. 211–251 (Madrid: SECC).

M. Barrio (2004) *El Real Patronato y los obispos españoles del Antiguo Régimen* (Madrid: Centro de Estudios Políticos y Constitucionales).

A. Barros (2007) 'From a Natural Sage Haven to a Structured Seaport. Porto and the Atlantic System,' in A. Polónia and H. Osswald (eds.) *European Seaport System in the Early Modern Age: A Comparative Approach*, pp. 132–147 (Oporto: Instituto de História Moderna).

M. Basas (1994) *El Consulado de Burgos en el siglo XVI*, 2nd ed. (Burgos: Diputación Provincial).

H. Baudrillart (1878–1880) *Histoire du Luxe privé et public depuis l'Antiquité jusqu'à nos jours*, 4 vols. (Paris: Hachette).

K. Béguin (1999) *Les princes de Condé. Rebelles, courtisans et mécènes dans la France du Grand Siécle* (Seyssel: Champ Vallon).

W. Beik (1985) *Absolutism and Society in Seventeenth-Century France: State Power and Provincial Aristocracy in Languedoc* (Cambridge: Cambridge University Press).

E. Belenguer (1976) *València en la crisi del segle XV* (Barcelona: Edicions 62).

P. Benedict (ed.) (1989) *Cities and Social Change in Early Modern France* (London: Routledge).

B. Bennassar (1976) *Los españoles. Actitudes y mentalidad* (Barcelona: Argos Vergara).

B. Bennassar (1980) *La América española y la América portuguesa. Siglos XVI–XVIII* (Madrid: Akal).

B. Bennassar (1983) *Valladolid en el Siglo de Oro. Una ciudad de Castilla y su entorno agrario en el siglo XVI* (Valladolid: Ayuntamiento de Valladolid).

J. Bérenger (1990) *Histoire de l'Émpire des Habsbourg: 1273–1918* (Paris: Fayard).

A. M. Bernal (1993) *La financiación de la Carrera de Indias (1492–1824). Dinero y crédito en el comercio colonial español con América* (Seville: Tabapress).

A. M. Bernal (2005) *España, proyecto inacabado. Los costes/beneficios del Imperio* (Madrid: Marcial Pons).

A. M. Bernal (2007) *Historia de España. Monarquía e Imperio* (Madrid: Marcial Pons).

A. M. Bernal, A. Collantes and A. García Baquero (1978) 'Sevilla: de los gremios a la industrialización', *Estudios de Historia Social*, 5–6, 7–310.

D. Bernabé (1993) 'La fiscalidad en los territorios peninsulares de la Corona de Aragón durante la época de los Austrias' in J. I. Fortea and C. Cremades (eds.) *Política y Hacienda en el Antiguo Régimen*, vol. I, pp. 15–31 (Murcia: Murcia Universidad de Murcia).

M. Bertrand (1999) *Grandeur et misère de l'office. Les officiers de finances de Nouvelle Espagne (XVIIe–XVIIIe siècles)* (Paris: Publications de la Sorbonne).

J. M. De Bernardo (1994) 'Fiscal Pressure and the City of Cordoba's Communal Assets in the Early Seventeenth Century' in I. A. A. Thompson and B. Yum (eds.) *The Castilian Crisis of the Seventeenth Century: New Perspectives on the Economic and Social History of Seventeenth Century Spain*, pp. 206–219 (Cambridge: Cambridge University Press).

J. Bestard and M. Pérez (2010) *Familia, valores y representaciones* (Murcia: Universidad de Murcia).

F. Bethencourt (2009) *The Inquisition. A Global History* (Cambridge: Cambridge University Press).

F. Bethencourt (2013) 'The Iberian Atlantic: Trade, Networks and Boundaries' in H. Braun and L. Vollendorf (eds.) *Theorising the Ibero American Atlantic*, pp. 15–37 (Leiden: Brill).

L. M. Bilbao (1987) 'La industria siderometalúrgica tradicional en el País Vasco (1450–1720)', *Hacienda Pública Española*, 108/109, 47–79.

J. Bishko (1978) 'The Andalusian Municipal Mestas in the 14th–16th Centuries: Administrative and Social Aspects', *Actas I Congreso de Historia de Andalucía. Andalucía Medieval*, T. I, pp. 347–374 (Córdoba: Caja de Ahorros de Córdoba).

J. B. Black (1959) *The Reign of Elizabeth: 1558–1603*, 2nd ed. (Oxford: Clarendon Press).

M. Bloch (1968) *La société féodale* (Paris: A. Michel).

G. Bois (1976) *Crise du féodalisme: économie rurale et demographie en Normandie orientale du début du XIVe siècle au milieu du XVIe siècle* (Paris: EHESS).

G. Bois (1985) 'Against the Neo-Malthusian Orthodoxy' in T. H. Aston and C. H. E. Philpin (eds.) *The Brenner Debate: Agrarian Class Structure and Economic Development in Pre-Industrial Europe*, pp. 107–118 (Cambridge: Cambridge University Press).

J. A. Bonachía (1988) *El señorío de Burgos durante la Baja Edad Media (1255–1508)* (Valladolid: Universidad de Valladolid).

R. Bonney (1981) *The King's Debts. Finance and Politics in France, 589–1661* (Oxford: Clarendon Press).

J. L. Boone (1986) 'Parental Investment and Elite Family Structure in Preindustrial States: A Case Study of Late medieval-Early Modern Portuguese Genealogies', *American Anthropologist*, 88, 859–878.

G. A. Borges (2014) *Um império ibérico integrado?: União Ibérica, o Golfo Pérsico e o império ultramarino português, 1600–1625* (Ph.D. Thesis, European University Institute).

P. Borges (1983) 'La emigración de eclesiásticos a América en el siglo XVI' in F. Solano and F. del Pino (eds.) *América y la España del siglo XVI*, pp. 47–62 (Madrid: Instituto Fernández de Oviedo).

L. Bourquin (1994) *Noblesse seconde et pouvoir en Champagne aux XVIe. et XVIIe. Siècles* (Paris: Publications de la Sorbonne).

F. Bouza (2000) *Portugal no tempo dos Filipes: política, cultura, representaçoes (1580–1668)* (Lisbon: Cosmos, 2000).

C. R. Boxer (1952) *Salvador de Sá and the Struggle for Brazil and Angola, 1602–1686* (London: the Athlone Press).

C. R. Boxer (1957) *The Dutch in Brazil, 1624–1654* (Oxford: Clarendon Press).

C. R. Boxer (1959) *The Great Ship from Amacon: Annals of Macao and the Old Japan Trade, 1555–1640* (Lisbon: Centro de Estudios Históricos Ultramarinos).

C. R. Boxer (1963) *Two Pioneers of Tropical Medicine: Garcia d'Orta and Nicolás Monardes* (London: Wellcome Historical Medical Library).

C. R. Boxer (1965) *The Dutch Seaborne Empire 1600–1800* (London: Hutchinson).

C. R. Boxer (1969) *The Portuguese Seaborne Empire, 1415–1825* (London: Hutchinson).

C. R. Boxer (1973) *The Dutch in Brazil 1624–1654* (Hamden: Archon Books).

J. C. Boyajian (1983) *Portuguese Bankers at the Court of Spain, 1626–1650* (New Brunswick: Rutgers University Press).

J. C. Boyajian (1993) *Portuguese Trade in Asia under the Habsburgs, 1580–1640* (Baltimore: John Hopkins University Press).

F. Braudel (1976) *El Mediterráneo y el mundo mediterráneo en la época de Felipe II* (Madrid: Fondo de Cultura Económica) vols. I–II.

F. Braudel (1996) *Autour de la Mediterranée* (Paris: Fayard).

F. Braudel and F. Spooner (1967) 'Prices in Europe from 1450 to 1750' in E. E. Rich and C. H. Wilson (eds.) *The Cambridge Economic History of Europe, vol. 4 The Economy of Expanding Europe in the Sixteenth and Seventeenth Centuries*, pp. 378–486 (Cambridge: Cambridge University Press).

A. Brendecke (2012) *Imperio e información: funciones del saber en el dominio colonial español* (Frankfurt: Iberoamericana).

R. Brenner (1993) *Merchants and Revolution. Commercial Change, Political Conflict, and London's Overseas Traders, 1550–1653* (Princeton: Princeton University Press).

J. Brewer (1990) *Sinews of Power War, Money and the English State 1688–1783* (Cambridge: Harvard University Press).

P. Broggio (2002) *Evangelizzare il mondo. Le missioni della compagnia di Gesù tra eutropa e America (secoli XVI–XVII)* (Rome: Carocci).

J. Brotton (2002) *The Renaissance Bazaar: From the Silk Road to Michelangelo* (Oxford: Oxford University Press).

J. Brown and J. H. Elliott (1980) *A Palace for a King: The Buen Retiro and the Court of Philip IV* (New Haven: Yale University Press).

F. Brumont (1984a) *Campo y campesinos de Castilla la Vieja en tiempos de Felipe II* (Madrid: Siglo XXI).

F. Brumont (1984b) 'La laine dans la region de Nájera (deuxieme moitié du XVIe siécle)', *Actas del II coloquio de Metodología Histórica aplicada*. (Santiago: Universidad de Santiago), vol. II, pp. 317–32.

F. Brumont (1993) *Paysans de Vieille-Castille aux XVIe et XVIIe siècles* (Madrid: Casa de Velázquez).

O. Brunner (1992) *Land and Lordship: Structures of Governance in Medieval Austria* (Philadelphia: University of Pennsylvania Press).

J. Burbank and F. Cooper (2010), *Empires in World History: Power and the Politics of Difference* (Princeton: Princeton University Press).

P. Burke (1974) *Venice and Amsterdam: A Study of Seventeenth-century Elites* (London: Temple Smith).

A. Buono (2008) *Esercito, istituzioni, territorio. Alloggiamenti militari e "case herme" nello Stato di Milano (secoli XVI e XVII)* (Florence: Firenze University Press).

C. Büschges and B. Schröter (eds.) (1999) *Beneméritos, aristócratas y empresarios: identidades y estructuras sociales de las capas altas urbanas en América Hispánica* (Munich: Vervuert Iberoamericana).

A. Cabeza (1996) *Clérigos y señores. Política y religión en Palencia en el siglo de Oro* (Palencia: Diputación Provincial).

E. Cabrera (1977) *El condado de Belalcázar (1444–1518); aportación al estudio del régimen señorial* (Córdoba: Caja de Ahorros).

M. Cachero (2010) *Should we Trust? Explaining Trade Expansion in Early Modern Spain: Seville, 1500–1600* (Ph.D. Thesis, European University Institute).

A. Calabria (1991) *The Cost of Empire. The Finances of the Kingdom of Naples in the Time of Spanish Rule* (Cambridge: Cambridge University Press).

R. Cancila (2013) *Autorità sovrana e potere feudale nella Sicilia moderna* (Palermo: Mediterrania).

R. Canosa (1998) *Banchieri Genovesi e Sovrani Spagnoli tra Cinquecento e Seicento* (Rome: Sapere).

J. Cañizares-Esguerra (2006) *Puritan Conquistadors: Iberianizing the Atlantic, 1550–1700* (Stanford: Stanford University Press).

J. Cañizares-Esguerra (2017) "On Ignored Global "Scientific Revolutions"", *Journal of Early Modern History*, 21, 420–432.

R. Carande (1987) *Carlos V y sus banqueros* (Barcelona: Crítica) vols. I–III.

M. F. Carbajo (1987) *La población de la villa de Madrid. Desde finales del siglo XVI hasta mediados del siglo XIX* (Madrid: Siglo XXI).

B. Cárceles de Gea (1994) *Fraude y administración fiscal en Castilla: la Comisión de Millones (1632–1658): poder y privilegio jurídico-político* (Madrid: Banco de España).

P. Cardim (2014) *Portugal unido y separado: Felipe II, la unión de territorios y el debate sobre la condición política del reino de Portugal* (Valladolid: Universidad de Valladolid).

P. Cardim, T. Herzog, J. J. Ruiz Ibáñez and G. Sabatini (2012) 'Polycentric Monarchies. How did Early Modern Spain and Portugal Achieve and Maintain a Global Hegemony?' in P. Cardim et al. (eds.) *Polycentric Monarchies. How did Early Modern Spain and Portugal Achieve and Maintain a Global Hegemony?*, pp. 3–8 (Eastbourne: Sussex Academic Press).

M. Carmagnani (2011) *The Other West: Latin America from Invasion to Globalization* (Berkeley: University of California Press).

J. Caro Baroja (1978) *Las formas complejas de la vida religiosa* (Madrid: Akal).

P. Carrasco and G. Céspedes (1985), *América indígena. La conquista* (Madrid: Alianza Editorial).

J. M. Carretero (2000) 'Fiscalidad parlamentaria y deuda real' in B. García (coord.) *El imperio de Carlos V. Procesos de agregación y conflictos,* pp. 157–184 (Madrid: Fundación Carlos de Amberes).

J. M. Carretero (2001) 'La consolidación de un modelo representativo: las Cortes de Castilla en la época de los Reyes Católicos' in J. Valdeón Baruque (ed.) *Isabel la Católica y la política,* pp. 259–291 (Valladolid: Ámbito).

H. Carvalhal (2016) 'Lineage, Marriage and Social Mobility: the Teles de Meneses Family in the Iberian Courts (Fifteenth and Sixteenth Centuries)', *e-Journal of Portuguese History,* 14, 2–19.

G. Casale (2010) *The Ottoman Age of Exploration* (Oxford: Oxford University Press).

H. Casado (1985) 'Una familia de la oligarquía burgalesa en el siglo XV: los Alonso de Burgos-Maluenda', *La ciudad de Burgos. Actas del Congreso de Historia de Burgos* (León, Junta de Castilla y León,) pp. 143–162.

H. Casado (1987) *Señores, mercaderes y campesinos: la comarca de Burgos a fines de la Edad Media* (Valladolid: Junta de Castilla y León).

H. Casado (1997) 'De la judería a la grandeza de España. La trayectoria de los Bernuy, una familia de mercaderes. Sliglos XIV–XIX', *Bulletin of the Society for Spanish and Portuguese Historical Studies,* 22, 9–27.

H. Casado (2004) 'Guilds, Technical Progress and Economic Development in Preindustrial Spain', in P. Massa and A Maioli (eds.) *Dalla corporazione al mutuo soccorso. Organizzazione e tutela del lavoro tra XVI e XX secolo,* pp. 309–327 (Milan: Franco Angeli).

J. L. Casado Soto (1998) 'Flota atlántica y tecnología naval hispana en los tiempos de Felipe II' in L. Ribot (ed.) *Las sociedades ibéricas y el mar*, vol. II, pp. 339–364 (Madrid: SECC).

J. Casey (1983) *El reino de Valencia en el siglo XVII* (Madrid: Siglo XXI).

J. Casey (1985) 'Spain: a Failed Transition', in P. Clark (ed.) *European Crisis of the 1590s. Essays in Comparative History*, pp. 209–228 (London: Allen and Unwin).

J. Casey (1989) *The History of the Family* (Oxford: Basil Blackwell).

J. Casey (1999) *Early Modern Spain. A Social History* (London: Routledge).

J. Casey (2007) *Family and Community in Early Modern Spain* (Cambridge: Cambridge University Press).

A. Castillo (1963) 'Dette flottante et dette consolidée en Espagne, 1557 à 1600', *Annales ESC*, 18, 745–759.

A. Castillo (1965) 'Population et "richesse" en Castille durant la seconde moitié du XVIe siècle', *Annales ESC*, 20, 719–733.

J. Castillo de Bovadilla (1597) *Política para corregidores y señores de vassallos* (Madrid: Luis Suárez).

M. Cavillac (1994) *Pícaros y mercaderes en el "Guzmán de Alfarache": reformismo burgués y mentalidad aristocrática en la España del siglo de oro* (Granada: Universidad de Granada).

A. de Ceballos-Escalera y Gila (2001) *La Insigne Orden del Toisón de Oro* (Madrid: Palafox & Pezuela, 2001).

D. Centenero (2009) *Una monarquía de lazos débiles. Veteranos, militares y administradores en la Monarquía Católica 1554–1621* (Ph.D. Thesis, European University Institute).

G. Céspedes (1990) 'Cultural Contacts and Exchanges' in Peter Burke and Halil Inalcik (ed.) *History of Humanity: Scientific and Cultural Development*, Vol V, pp. 50–60 (New York: Routledge and UNESCO).

G. Céspedes (2009) *América Hispánica (1492–1898)* (Madrid: Fundación Jorge Juan and Marcial Pons).

F. Chacón (1979) *Murcia en la centuria del quinientos* (Murcia: Universidad de Murcia).

F. Chacón and J. Bertran (dirs.) (2011) *Familias. Historia de la sociedad española (del final de la Edad Media a nuestros días)* (Barcelona: Crítica).

K. N. Chaudhuri (1965) *The English East India Company: The Study of an Early Joint-Stock Company, 1600–1640* (London: F. Cass).

K. N. Chaudhuri (1985) *Trade and Civilization in the Indian Ocean: An Economic History from the Rise of Islam to 1750* (Cambridge: Cambridge University Press).

P. Chaunu (1959) *Seville et l'Atlantique (1504–1650)* (Paris: Armand Colin and SEVPEN).

P. Chaunu (1977) *La expansión europea (siglos XIII–XV)* (Barcelona: Labor).

F. Checa (1988) *Pintura y escultura del Renacimiento en España, 1450–1600* (Madrid: Cátedra).

B. Chevalier (1987) 'Fiscalité municipale et fiscalité d'état en France du XIVe à lafin du XVIe siècle', in J. H. Genet and M. Le Mené (eds.) *Genèse de L'État Moderne. Prélèvement et redistribution*, pp. 137–151 (Paris: CNRS).

B. Chevalier (1994) 'France from Charles VIII to Henry IV' in T. A. Brady, Jr, H. A. Oberman and J. D. Tracy (eds.) *Handbook of European History 1400–1600*, pp. 369–402 (Leiden: Brill).

W. R. Childs (1978) *Anglo-Castilian Trade in the Later Middle Age* (Manchester: Manchester University Press).

D. E. Chipman (2005) *Moctezuma's Children: Aztec Royalty under Spanish Rule, 1520–1700* (Austin: University of Texas Press).

W. Christian (1989) *Local Religion in Sixteenth-Century Spain* (Princeton: Princeton University Press).

C. M. Cipolla (1976) *Before the Industrial Revolution: European Society and Economy, 1000–1700* (London: Norton).

S. Ciriacono (1988) 'Mass Consumption Goods and Luxury Goods: the Deindustrialization of the Republic of Venice from the Sixteenth Century to the Eighteenth Century', in H. Van der Wee (ed.) *The Rise and Decline of Urban Industries in Italy and the Low Countries*, pp. 41–62 (Leuven: Leuven University Press).

E. Ciscar (1977) *Tierra y señorío en el país valenciano, 1579–1620* (Valencia: Del Cenia al Segura).

G. Clark (2007) *A Farewell to Alms a Brief Economic History of the World* (Princeton: Princeton University Press).

B. Clavero (1981) 'Institución política y derecho: acerca del concepto historiográfico de "estado moderno"', *Revista de Estudios Políticos* 19, 43–58.

B. Clavero (1986) *Tantas personas como estados. Por una antropología política de la historia europea* (Madrid: Tecnos).

B. Clavero (1991) *Antidora, Antropología Católica de la Economía Moderna* (Milan: Giuffrè).

C. G. A. Clay (1984) *Economic Expansion and Social Change: England 1500–1700* (Cambridge: Cambridge University Press).

J. Coatsworth (2006) 'Political Economy and Economic Organization' in V. Bulmer-Thomas, J. Coatsworth and R. Cortés (eds.) *The Cambridge Economic History of Latin America. Vol. I. The Colonial Era and the Short Nineteenth Century*, pp. 235–274 (Cambridge: Cambridge University Press).

G. Colás (1988) 'El régimen señorial en Aragón', *Revista de Historia Jerónimo Zurita*, 58, 9–29.

G. Colás (1994) 'La historiografía sobre el señorío tardofeudal' in E. Sarasa and E. Serrano (eds.) *Señorío y feudalismo en la península ibérica*, pp. 51–105 (Zaragoza: Institución Fernando el Católico).

G. Colás and J. Salas (1982) *Aragón en el siglo XVI: alteraciones sociales y conflictos políticos* (Zaragoza: Universidad de Zaragoza).

D. C. Coleman (1977) *The Economy of England, 1450–1750* (Oxford: Oxford University Press).

A. Collantes (1977) *Sevilla en la baja Edad Media. La ciudad y sus hombres* (Seville: Ayuntamiento de Sevilla).

J. B. Collins (1988) *Fiscal Limits of Absolutism. Direct Taxation in Early Seventeenth-Century France* (Berkeley: University of California Press).

F. Comín and B. Yun (2012) "Spain: from a Composite Monarchy to Nation State, 1492–1914. An Exceptional Case", in B. Yun and P. O'Brien (eds) *The Rise of Fiscal States. A Global History, 1500–1914*, pp. 1–35 (Cambridge: Cambridge University Press). pp. 233–266.

J. Contreras (1992) *Sotos contra Riquelmes. Regidores, inquisidores y criptojudíos* (Madrid: Mario Muchnik).

H. Cools, M. Keblusek and B. Noldus (eds.) (2006) *Your Humble Servant: Agents in Early Modern Europe* (Hilversum: Uitgeverij Verloren).

E. Cooper (1991) *Castillos señoriales en la Corona de Castilla* (Salamanca: Consejería de Cultura).

L. M. Córdoba (2013) *Guerra, imperio y violencia en la Audiencia de Santa Fe, Nuevo Reino de Granada, 1580–1620* (Ph.D. Thesis, Universidad Pablo de Olavide).

L. M. Córdoba (2015) '"Una grande máquina de agravios". Los oficiales reales y el comercio ilícito de esclavos y de mercancías en Cartagena en las primeras décadas del siglo XVI' in D. Bonet Velez (ed.) *Una obra para la Historia. Homenaje a Germán Colmenares*, pp. 101–131 (Rosario: Editorial Universidad del Rosario).

C. Corona (1958) 'España desde la muerte del Rey Católico hasta la llegada de Don Carlos', *Universidad*, 74, 343–368.

A. Cortés and B. Vincent (1986) *Historia de Granada Vol. 3: La época Moderna; siglos XVI, XVII y XVIII* (Granada: Don Quijote).

J. P. Costa (coord.) (2014) *História da Expansão e do Império Português* (Lisbon: A Esfera dos Livros).

J. P. Costa and V. L. Rodrigues (eds.) (2004) *A alta nobreza e a fundação do estado da Índia* (Lisbon: Universidade Nova de Lisboa).

L. F. Costa (1997) '*A Construção Naval*' in J. R. Magalhães (ed.) *História de Portugal. No Alvorecer da Modernidade, 1480–1620*, vol. III, pp. 292–310 (Lisbon: Ed. Estampa).

L. F. Costa (2002) *O transporte no Atlântico e a Companhia Geral do Comércio do Brasil (1580–1663)* (Lisbon: Comissão Nacional para as Comemorações dos Descobrimentos Portugueses).

L. F. Costa and M. S. da Cunha (2006) *D. João IV* (Lisbon: Círculo de Leitores).

L. F. Costa, N. Palma and J. Reis (2015) 'The Great Escape? The Contribution of the Empire to Portugal's Economic Growth, 1500–1800', *European Review of Economic History*, 19, 1–22.

P. Croft (1989) 'Trading with the Enemy', *The Historical Journal*, 32, 281–302.

A. W. Crosby (1988) *Imperialismo ecológico. La expansión biológica de Europa, 900–1900* (Barcelona: Crítica).

M. S. da Cunha (2003) 'Nobreza, rivalidade e clientelismo na primeira metade do século XVI', *Penélope*, 29, 33–48.

M. S. da Cunha (2005) 'Portuguese Nobility and Overseas Government: The Return to Portugal (16th to 17th centuries)' in E. Van Veen and L. Blussé (eds.), *Rivalry and Conflict. European Traders and Asian Trading Networks in the 16th and 17th centuries*, pp. 35–54 (Leiden: CNWS Publications).

M. S. da Cunha (2009) 'Títulos portugueses y matrimonios mixtos en la Monarquía Católica', in B. Yun (ed.) *Las redes del imperio. Élites sociales en la articulación de la Monarquía Hispánica, 1492–1714*, pp. 205–231 (Madrid: Marcial Pons).

M. S. da Cunha and N. G. Monteiro (2005) 'Governadores e capitães-mores do império Atlântico português nos séculos XVII e XVIII' in N. G. Monteiro, M. S. da Cunha and P. Cardim (eds), *Optima Pars. Elites Ibero-Americanas do Antigo Regime*, pp. 191–252 (Lisbon: Imprensa de Ciências Sociais).

S. Cunningham (2007) *Henry VII* (London: Routledge).

P. D. Curtin (1969) *The Atlantic Slave Trade: A Census* (Madison: The University of Wisconsin Press).

P. Curtin (1984) *Cross-cultural Trade in World History* (Cambridge: Cambridge University Press).

D. R. Curto (2009) *Cultura imperial e projetos coloniais (séculos XV a XVIII)* (Campinas: Editora Unicamp).

M. Danvila (ed.) (1861) *Actas de las Cortes de Castilla* (Madrid: Imprenta Nacional).

J. Darwin (2008) *After Tamerlane: The Global History of Empire since 1405* (London: Bloomsbury Press).

J. Darwin (2012) *Unfinished Empire: The Global Expansion of Britain* (London: Allen Lande).

N. S. Davidson (1985) 'Northern Italy in the 1590s', in P. Clark, (ed.) *The European Crisis of the 1590s. Essays in Comparative History*, pp. 157–176 (London: Allen and Unwin).

R. Davis (1976) *La Europa Atlántica. Desde los descubrimientos hasta la industrialización* (Madrid: Siglo XXI).

J. P. Dedieu (1986) 'Limpieza, pouvoir et richesse: conditions d'entrée dans le corps des ministres de l'Inquisition (tribunal de Tolède, XVIe–XVIIe siècle)', in *Les soicétées fermées dans le monde ibérique. Definitions et problematiques. Actes de la Table Ronde* (Paris: Maison des Pais Iberiques), pp. 169–187.

M. Defourneaux (1983) *La vida cotidiana en la España del Siglo de Oro* (Barcelona: Argos Vergara).

K. Degryse and P. Janssens (2005) 'The Economic Role of the Belgian Aristocracy in the 17th and 18th Centuries' in J. Janssens and B. Yun (eds.) *European*

Aristocracies and Colonial Elites: Patrimonial Management, Strategies and Economic Development, 15th–18th Centuries, pp. 57–82 (Aldershot: Ashgate, 2005).

G. Delille (1988) *Famille et propriété dans le Royaume de Naples, XVe–XIXe siècle* (Paris: EHESS).

G. Delille (2003) *Le maire et le prieur: pouvoir central et pouvoir local en Méditerranée occidentale, XVe–XVIIIe siècle* (Rome: École française de Rome).

R. Descimon (1993) 'Milice Bourgeoise et identité citadine a Paris au temps de la ligue' *Annales ESC*, 48:4, 885–906.

M. Diago (1993) *Estructuras de poder en Soria a fines de la Edad Media* (Valladolid: Junta de Castilla y León).

J. M. Díaz (2010). *Razón de estado y buen gobierno. La guerra defensiva y el imperialismo español en tiempos de Felipe III* (Seville: Universidad de Sevilla).

A. R. Disney (1978) *Twilight of the Pepper Empire: Portuguese Trade in Southwest India in the Early Seventeenth Century* (Cambridge: Harvard University Press).

A. R. Disney (2009) *A History of Portugal and the Portuguese Empire* (Cambridge: Cambridge University Press).

A. Domínguez (1973) *Crisis y decadencia de la España de los Austrias* (Barcelona: Ariel).

A. Domínguez (1983) *Política y hacienda de Felipe IV* (Madrid: Pegaso).

A. Domínguez (1985) *Las clases privilegiadas en el Antiguo Régimen* (Madrid: Istmo).

C. Donati (1995) "The Italian Nobilies in the Seventeenth and Eighteenth Centuries", in H. M. Scott (ed.) *The European Nobilities in the Seventeenth and Eighteenth Centuries*, pp. 237–268 (London: Longman).

B. M. Downing (1992) The Military Revolution and Political Change. Origins of Democracy and Autocracy in Early Modern Europe (Princeton: Princeton University Press).

M. Drelichman (2005) 'The Curse of Moctezuma: American Silver and the Dutch Disease', *Explorations in Economic History*, 42, 349–380.

M. Drelichman and H. Voth (2014) *Lending to the Borrower from Hell: Debt, Taxes, and Default in the Age of Philip II* (Princeton: Princeton University Press).

A. Dubet (2003) *Hacienda, arbitrismo y negociación política: el proyecto de los erarios públicos y montes de piedad en los siglos XVI y XVII* (Valladolid: Universidad de Valladolid).

T. B. Duncan (1986) 'Navigation between Portugal and Asia in the Sixteenth and Seventeenth Centuries' in E J van Kley and C K Phillapilly (eds.) *Asia and the West: Encounters and Exchanges from the Age of Explorations. Essays in Honor of Donald F Lach*, pp. 3–25 (Notre Dame: Cross Cultural Publications).

E. Duran (1982) *Les Germanies als Països Catalans* (Barcelona: Curial).

M. Duran (1998) '¿Excelencias de Cataluña?' in L. Ribot (coord.), *Las sociedades ibéricas y el mar*, vol. III, pp. 125–144 (Madrid: SECC).

G. Durand and G. Van Huylenbroeck (2003) 'Multifunctionality and Rural Development: A General Framework' in G. van Huylenbroeck and G. Durand (eds.) *Multifunctional Agriculture. A New Paradigm for European Agriculture and Rural Development*, pp. 1–18 (Aldershot: Ashgate).

C. Dyer (1989) *Standards of Living in the Later Middle Ages: Social Change in England c.1200–1520* (Cambridge: Cambridge University Press).

W. Eamon (2009) 'Nuestros males no son constitucionales, sino circunstanciales": The Black Legend and the History of Early Modern Spanish Science', *The Colorado Review of Hispanic Studies*, 7, 13–30.

J. Edwards (1977) 'Oligarchy and Merchant Capitalism in Lower Andalusia under the Catholic Kings: the Case of Cordoba and Jerez de la Frontera', *Historia, Instituciones y Documentos*, 4, 11–33.

T. Egido (1973) *Sátiras políticas de la España Moderna* (Madrid: Alianza).

R. Ehrenberg (1955) *Le Siècle des Fugger* (Paris: SEVPEN).

N. Elias (2000) *The Civilizing Process: Sociogenetic and Psychogenetic Investigations* (Oxford: Basil Blackwell).

J. H. Elliott (1963) *The Revolt of the Catalans. A Study in the Decline of Spain (1598–1640)* (Cambridge, Cambridge University Press).

J. H. Elliott (1965) *La España imperial, 1469–1716* (Barcelona: Vicens-Vives).

J. H. Elliott (1972) *The Old World and the New, 1492–1650* (Cambridge: Cambridge University Press).

J. H. Elliott (1982) 'El programa de Olivares y los movimientos de 1640' in J. M. Jover Zamora (dir.) *Historia de España fundada por Ramón Menéndez Pidal*, vol. XXV, pp. 333–524 (Madrid: Espasa Calpe).

J. H. Elliott (1986) *The Count-Duke of Olivares. The Statesman in an Age of Decline* (New Haven and London: Yale University Press).

J. H. Elliott (1990) *España y su mundo 1500–1700* (Madrid: Alianza Editorial).

J. H. Elliott (1992) 'A Europe of Composite Monarchies', *Past and Present*, 137, 48–71.

J. H. Elliott and J. F. de la Peña (2013) *Memoriales y cartas del Conde-Duque de Olivares, Vol. I, Política interior*, 2nd ed. (Madrid: Centro de Estudios Europa Hispánica, Marcial Pons).

G. Elton (1953) *The Tudor Revolution in Government: Administrative Changes in the Reign of Henry VIII* (Cambridge: Cambridge University Press).

S. L. Engerman and E. D. Genovese (1975) *Race and Slavery in the Western Hemisphere: Quantitative Studies* (Princeton: Princeton University Press).

S. R. Epstein (1998) 'Craft guilds, apprenticeship, and technological change in preindustrial Europe', *Journal of Economic History* 58, 684–713.

S. R. Epstein (2002) *Freedom and Growth: The Rise of States and Markets in Europe, 1300–1750* (London: Routledge).

T. Ertman (1997) *Birth of the Leviathan. Building States and Regimes in Medieval and Early Modern Europe* (Cambridge: Cambridge University Press).

A. Esteban (2002) 'Guerra y redistribución de cargas defensivas: la unión de Armas en los Países Bajos Católicos', *Cuadernos de Historia Moderna* 27 (2002): 49–98.

J. Everaert (1973) *Le commerce international e colonial des firms flamands à Cadix, 1670–1700* (Bruges: Tempel).

R. Fagel (2009) '"Es buen católico y sabe escribir los cuatro idiomas". Una nueva generación mixta entre españoles y flamencos ante la revuelta de Flandes' in B. Yun (ed.) *Las redes del imperio. Élites sociales en la articulación de la Monarquía Hispánica, 1492–1714*, pp. 289–312 (Madrid: Marcial Pons).

N. M. Farris (1984) *Maya Society under Colonial Rule: The Collective Enterprise of Survival* (Princeton: Princeton University Press).

G. Federico and P. Malanima (2004) 'Progress, Decline, Growth: Product and Productivity in Italian Agriculture, 1000–2000', *Economic History Review*, 57, 437–464.

M. Felices (2012) *La nueva nobleza titulada de España y América en el siglo XVIII (1701–1746)* (Almería: Universidad de Almería).

G. Feliu (1991) *Precios y salarios en la Cataluña moderna* (Madrid: Banco de España).

P. Fernández Albaladejo (1975) *La crisis del Antiguo Régimen en Guipúzcoa 1766–1833* (Madrid: Akal).

P. Fernández Albaladejo (1992) *Fragmentos de Monarquía* (Madrid: Alianza Editorial).

F. Fernández-Armesto (1982) *The Canary Islands after the Conquest: the Making of a Colonial Society in the Early Sixteenth Century* (Oxford: Oxford University Press).

F. Fernández-Armesto (2006) *Pathfinders: A Global History of Exploration* (Oxford: Oxford University Press).

A. B. Fernández de Castro (2015) *Juzgar las Indias: la práctica de la jurisdicción de los oidores de la Casa de la Contratación de Sevilla (1583–1598)* (Ph.D. Thesis, European University Institute).

E. Fernández de Pinedo (1974) *Crecimiento económico y transformaciones sociales del País Vasco* (Madrid: Siglo XXI).

A. Feros (2000) *Kingship and Favoritism in the Spain of Philip III, 1598–1621* (Cambridge: Cambridge University Press).

S. H. Ferreria (2015) *The Crown, the Court and the Casa da Índia: Political Centralization in Portugal (1479–1521)* (Leiden: Brill).

R. Findlay and K. O'Rourke (2007) *Power and Plenty: Trade, War, and the World Economy in the Second Millennium* (Princeton: Princeton University Press).

J. Flores (1998) 'Zonas de Influência e de Rejeição', in A. H. Marques (dir.) *História dos Portugueses no Extremo Oriente. Em torno de Macau. Séculos XVI–XVII*, vol. I, T. I, pp. 135–178.

J. Flores (2015) 'The *Mogor* as Venomous Hydra: Forging the Mughal-Portuguese Frontier', *Journal of Early Modern History*, 19, 539–562.

D. O. Flynn (1982) 'Fiscal Crisis and the Decline of Spain (Castile)', *The Journal of Economic History*, 42, 139–147.

D. O. Flynn and Arturo Giraldez (2002) 'Cycles of Silver: global Economic Unity through the Mid-Eighteenth Century', *Journal of World History* 13, 391–427.

J. I. Fortea (1981) *Córdoba en el siglo XVI: las bases demográficas y económicas de una expansión urbana* (Córdoba: Caja de Ahorros).

J. I. Fortea (1986) *Fiscalidad en Córdoba. Fisco, economía y sociedad: alcabalas y encabezamientos en tierras de Córdoba, 1513–1619* (Córdoba: Universidad de Córdoba).

J. I. Fortea (1990) *Monarquía y Cortes en la Corona de Castilla. Las ciudades ante la política fiscal de Felipe II* (Valladolid: Junta de Castilla y León).

J. I. Fortea (1995) "Las ciudades de la Corona de Castilla en el Antiguon Régimen. Una revisiópn historiográficas" en *Boletín de la Asociación de Demografía Histórica*, 3, 21–59.

J. I. Fortea (2008) *Las Cortes de Castilla y León bajo los Austrias: una interpretación* (Valladolid: Junta de Castilla y León).

J. Fragoso (ed.) (2001) *O Antigo Regime nos trópicos: a dinâmica imperial portuguesa, séculos XVI–XVIII* (Rio de Janeiro: Civilização Brasileira).

G. Frank (1978) *World Accumulation, 1492–1789* (New York: Monthly Review Press).

A. Furió (1995) *Història del País Valencià* (Valencia: Tres i quatre).

M. Fusaro (2015) *Political Economies of Empire in the Early Modern Mediterranean. The Decline of Venice and the Rise of England, 1450–1700* (Cambridge: Cambridge University Press).

G. Galasso (1994) *Alla periferia dell'Impero: il Regno di Napoli nel periodo spagnolo (secoli XVI–XVII)* (Turín: Einaudi).

J. C. Garavaglia (1983) *Mercado interno y economía colonial: tres siglos de historia de la yerba mate* (Mexico: Grijalbo).

A. García (2014) *Génova y el Atlántico (c. 1650–1680): emprendedores mediterráneos frente al auge del capitalismo del norte* (Ph.D. Thesis, European University Institute).

R. García Cárcel (1989) "Las Cortes catalanas en los siglos XVI y XVII", en *Las Cortes de Castilla y León en la edad moderna*, pp. 677–732 (Valladolid: Junta de Castilla y León).

J. A. García de Cortázar (1988) *La sociedad rural en la España Medieval* (Madrid: Siglo XXI).

A. García Espuche (1998) *Un siglo decisivo. Barcelona y Cataluña, 1150–1640* (Madrid: Alianza).

J. García Fernández (1975) *Organización del espacio y economía rural en la España Atlántica* (Madrid: Siglo XXI).

D. García Hernán (2010) *El gobierno señorial en Castilla. La presión y concesión nobiliaria en sus documentos (siglos XVI–XVIII)* (Madrid: Biblioteca Nueva).

E. García Hernán (2007) *Consejero de ambos mundos: vida y obra de Juan de Solórzano Pereira (1575–1655)* (Madrid: Fundación Mapfre).

J. García Mercadal (1999) *Viajes de extranjeros por España y Portugal: desde los tiempos más remotos hasta comienzos del siglo XX* (Valladolid: Junta de Castilla y León).

A. García Sanz (1987) 'Mercaderes hacedores de paños en Segovia en la época de Carlos V: organización del proceso constructivo y estructura del capital industrial', *Hacienda Pública Española*, 108/9, 65–79.

N. García Tapia (1990) *Patentes de invención españolas en el siglo de oro* (Madrid: Registro de la Propiedad Industrial).

A. García-Baquero (1986) *Andalucía y la Carrera de Indias, 1492–1824* (Seville: Editoriales Andaluzas Unidas).

A. García-Baquero (1992) *La Carrera de Indias. Suma de negociación y océano de negocios* (Seville: Algaida).

M. Garzón (1972) *La industria sedera en España: el arte de la seda en Granada* (Granada: Archivo de la Real Chancillería).

J. L. Gasch (2012) *Global Trade, Circulation and Consumption of Asian Goods in the Atlantic World: The Manila Galleons and the Social Elites of Mexico and Seville (1580–1640)* (Ph.D. Thesis, European University Institute).

J. L. Gasch (2014) 'Asian Silk, Porcelain and Material Culture in the Definition of Mexican and Andalusian Elites, c. 1565–1630' in B. Aram and B. Yun (eds.) *Global Goods and the Spanish Empire, 1492–1824*, pp. 153–173 (Basingstoke: Palgrave).

J. L. Gasch (2015a) 'Mecanismos de funcionamiento institucional en el Imperio Hispánico. El comercio de los galeones de Manila y el Consulado de Comerciantes de México en la década de 1630', *Revista de Historia Jerónimo Zurita* 90, 55–74.

J. L. Gasch (2015b) 'Transport Costs and Prices of Chinese Silk in the Spanish Empire: The Case of New Spain, c. 1571–1650', *Revista de historia Industrial* 60, 15–47.

R. Gascon (1972) *Grand commerce et vie urbaine au XVIe siècle: Lyon et ses marchands (1520–1580)* (Paris: Mouton) vols I–II.

R. Gascon (1994 [1977]) 'La France du mouvement: les commerces et les villes', in F. Braudel and E. Labrousse (dirs.) *Histoire economique et sociale de la France, 1450–1660*, T. I, pp. 231–482 (Paris: Presses Universitaires de France).

E. Gavilán (1986) *El dominio de Párraces en el siglo XV. Un estudio sobre la sociedad feudal* (Zamora: Junta de Castilla y León).

J. E. Gelabert (1994) 'Urbanisation and Deurbanisation in Castile', in I. A. A. Thompson and B. Yun eds., *The Castilian Crisis of the Seventeenth Century:*

New Perspectives on the Economic and Social History of Seventeenth-Century Spain, pp. 182–205 (Cambridge: Cambridge University Press).

J. E. Gelabert (1995) "Cities, Towns and Small Towns in Castile, 1500–1800" in P. Clark (ed.) *Small towns in early modern Europe*, pp. 270–294 (Cambridge: Cambridge University Press).

J. E. Gelabert (1997) *La bolsa del rey. Rey, reino y fisco en Castilla (1598–1648)* (Barcelona: Crítica).

J. E. Gelabert (2001) *Castilla convulsa (1631–1652)* (Madrid: Marcial Pons).

J. Gentil da Silva (1967) *Desarrollo económico, subsistencia y decadencia en España* (Madrid: Ciencia Nueva).

M. C. Gerbert (1979) *La noblesse dans le royaume de Castille: Étude sur ses structures sociales en Estrémadure (1454–1516)* (Paris: Université Paris IV).

M. C. Gerbet (1994) *Les noblesses espagnoles au Moyen Âge: XIe–XVe siècle* (Paris: Armand Colin).

B. Geremek (1987) *La Potence et la pitié. L'Europe des pauvres, du Moyen Âge à nos jours* (Paris: Gallimard, 1987).

X. Gil (1988) *De las alteraciones a la estabilidad. Corona, fueros y política en el reino de Aragón, 1585–1648* (Ph.D. Thesis, Universidad de Barcelona).

X. Gil (1991) 'Las Cortes de Aragón en la Edad Moderna: comparación y reevaluación', *Revista de las Cortes Generales*, 22, 79–119.

X. Gil (2006) *Tiempo de Política: perspectivas historiográficas sobre la Europa moderna* (Barcelona: Universitat de Barcelona).

F. Gilbert (1972) *The Progress of Society in Europe: an Historical Outline from the Subversion of the Roman Empire to the Beginning of the Sixteenth Century* (Chicago: University of Chicago).

C. Giudicelli (2009) '"Indios amigos" y movilización colonial en las fronteras americanas de la Monarquìa Católica (siglos XVI–XVII)' in J. J. Ruiz Ibáñez (ed.) *Las milicias del rey de España: sociedad, política e identidad en las monarquías ibéricas*, pp. 349–377 (Mexico: Fondo de Cultura Económica).

J. Glete (2000) *Warfare at Sea, 1500–1650. Maritime Conflicts and the Transformation of Europe* (London: Routledge).

V. M. Godinho (1963) *Os descobrimentos e a Economia Mundial* (Lisbon: Arcadia).

V. M. Godinho (1968) 'Finanças públicas e estrutura do Estado' in id. *Ensaios II. Sobre história de Portugal* pp. 25–63 (Lisbon: Sá da Costa Editora).

V. M. Godinho (1969) *L'Économie de l'empire portugaise aux XVI et XVII siècles* (Paris, SEVPEN).

V. M. Godinho (1982) *Les finances de l'état portugais des Indes Orientales (1517–1635): matériaux pour une étude structurale et conjoncturelle* (Paris: Fundaçao Calouste Gulbenkian).

V. M. Godinho (1982–1987) *Os descobrimentos e a Economia Mundial* (Lisbon: Presença).

J. Goldstone (1991) 'Monetary versus Velocity Interpretations of the 'Price Revolution': a Comment', *Journal of Economic History*, 51, 176–181.

R. Goldthwaite (1980) *The Building of Renaissance Florence: an Economic and Social History* (Baltimore: The Johns Hopkins University Press).

C. Gómez-Centurión (1988) *Felipe II, la empresa de Inglaterra y el comercio septentrional (1566–1609)* (Madrid: Naval).

C. Gómez Zorraquino (1987) *La burguesía mercantil en Aragon en los siglos XVI y XVV (1516–1652)* (Zaragoza: Fernando el Católico).

A. Gómez-Galvarriato (2006) 'Premodern Manufacturing' in V. Bulmer-Thomas, J. Coatsworth and R. Cortés Conde (eds.) *The Cambridge Economic History of Latin America: vol. I, The Colonial Era and the Short Nineteenth Century*, pp. 357–394 (Cambridge: Cambridge University Press).

J. Gómez Mendoza (1978) *Agricultura y expansión urbana. La campiña del Henares en la aglomeración de Madrid* (Madrid: Alianza Universidad).

B. González Alonso (1988) 'Poder regio, Cortes y régimen político en la Castilla Bajomedieval (1252–1474)' in *Las Cortes de Castilla y León en la Edad Media*, vol. II, pp. 201–254 (Valladolid: Junta de Castilla y León).

L. Gonzalez Antón (1989) 'Cortes de Aragón y Cortes de Castilla en el Antiguo Régimen', in *Las Cortes de Castilla y León en la Edad Moderna*, pp. 633–676 (Valladolid: Junta de Castilla y León).

Y. González de Lara (2008) 'The Secret of Venetian Success: A Public-Order, Reputation-Based Institution', *European Review of Economic History*, 12, 247–285.

D. Goodman (1988) *Power and Penury: Government, Technology, and Science in Philip II's Spain* (Cambridge: Cambridge University Press).

D. Goodman (1997) *Spanish Naval Power, 1589–1665: Reconstruction and Defeat* (Cambridge: Cambridge University Press).

R. Grafe (2006) 'Guerre, Trêve et marchés de l'Espagne du Nord dans la formation des empires mercantilistes européns, 1600–1660. Une histoire revisitée', in S. Marzagalli and B. Marnot (eds.) *Guerre et économie dans l'espace atlantique du XVIe au XXe siècle*, pp. 305–330 (Bordeaux: Presses Universitaires de Bordeaux).

R. Grafe (2012) *Distant Tyranny: Markets, Power and Backwardness in Spain, 1650–1800* (Princeton: Princeton University Press).

R. Grafe and A. Irigoin (2012) 'A Stakeholder Empire: The Political Economy of Spanish Imperial Rule in America', *The Economic History Review* 65, 609–651.

M. S. Granovetter (1973) 'The Strength of Weak Ties', *American Journal of Sociology*, 78, 1360–1380.

A. Greif (2006) *Institutions and the Path to the Modern Economy: Lessons from Medieval Trade* (Cambridge: Cambridge University Press).

E. Grendi (1997) *I Balbi: una famiglia genovese fra Spagna e Impero* (Turin, Einaudi).

R. Grier (1997) 'The Effect of Religion on Economic Development: A Cross National Study of 63 Former Colonies', *Kyklos*, 50, 47–62.

S. Gruzinski (2004) *Les quatre parties du monde: histoire d'une mondialisation* (Paris: Éditions de la Martinière).

A. Guerrero Mayllo (1993) *Familia y vida cotidiana de una élite de poder. Los regidores madrileños en tiempos de Felipe II* (Madrid: Siglo XXI).

A. Guevara (1994 [1529]) *Relox de Principes* (Madrid: ABL).

A. Guilarte (1987) *El Régimen Señorial en el siglo XVI* (Valladolid: Universidad de Valladolid).

A. Gutiérrez (1989) *Estudio sobre la decadencia de Castilla. La ciudad de Valladolid en el siglo XVII* (Valladolid: Universidad de Valladolid).

J. I. Gutiérrez Nieto (1973) *Las comunidades como movimiento antiseñorial* (Barcelona: Ariel).

J. I. Gutiérrez Nieto (1982) 'De la expansión a la decadencia económica de Castilla y León: manisfestaciones. El arbitrismo agrarista', in *El pasado histórico de Castilla y León*, vol. II, pp. 11–75 (Valladolid: Junta de Castilla y León).

J. Habakkuk (1994) *Marriage, Debt and the Estates System. English Landownership 1650–1950* (Oxford: Clarendon Press).

J. R. Hale (1985) *War and Society in Renaissance Europe, 1450–1620* (Baltimore: The Johns Hopkins University Press).

S. Haliczer (1975) 'The Castilian Aristocracy and the Mercedes Reform of 1478–1482', *Hispanic American Historical Review*, 55, 448–467.

S. Haliczer (1981) *The Comuneros of Castile. The Forging of a Revolution (1475–1521)* (Madison: University of Wisconsin Press).

T. Halperin (1980) *Un conflicto nacional; moriscos y cristianos viejos en Valencia* (Valencia: Institució Alfons el Magnánim).

E. J. Hamilton (1934) *American Treasure and the Price Revolution* (Cambridge, MA: Harvard University Press).

E. J. Hamilton (1975) *El tesoro americano y la revolución de los precios en España, 1501–1650* (Barcelona: Ariel).

T. Hampe and R. Honores (2004) 'Los abogados de Lima Colonial (1550–1650): formación, vinculaciones y carrera profesional' in R. Aguirre Salvador (ed.) *Carrera, Linaje y patronazgo. Clérigos y juristas en Nueva España, chile y Perú (siglos XVI–XVIII)*, pp. 151–175 (México DF: Universidad Autónoma de México).

D. R. Headrick (2010) *Power over Peoples: Technology, Environments, and Western Imperialism, 1400 to the Present* (Princeton: Princeton University Press).

J. Heers (1961) *Gênes au XVe. siècle: activité économique et problèmes sociaux* (Paris: SEVPEN).

H. Helpman (2004) *The Mystery of Economic Growth* (Cambridge, Ma: Harvard University Press).

B. Hernández (1996) 'Un assaig de reforma del sistema fisco-financier de la Monarquia a Catalunya: l'impost del Quint sobre les imposicions locals, 1580–1640', *Manuscrits. Revista d'Historia Moderna*, 14, 297–319.

M. Hernández (1995) *A la sombra de la corona: poder local y oligarquía urbana (Madrid, 1606–1808)* (Madrid: Siglo XXI).

R. Hernández (2007) *La industria textil de Palencia durante los siglos XVI y XVII: la implicación de una ciudad con la actividad manufacturera* (Valladolid: Universidad de Valladolid).

J. Hernández Franco (2006) 'El mayorazgo Moctezuma: reflexiones sobre un proceso de movilidad vertical con alternancias (1509–1807)', *Estudis: Revista de historia moderna*, 32, 215–236.

C. J. Hernando (1994) *Castilla y Nápoles en el siglo XVI: el virrey don Pedro de Toledo: linaje, estado y cultura (1532–1553)* (Valladolid: Junta de Castilla y León).

A. Herrera (1980) *El Aljarafe sevillano durante el Antiguo Régimen: un estudio de su evolución socioeconómica en los siglos XVI, XVII y XVIII* (Seville: Diputación Provincial).

M. Herrero (2009) 'La red genovesa de los Spínola y el entramado transnacional de los marqueses de los Balbases al servicio de la Monarquía Hispánica' in B. Yun (ed.) *Las redes del imperio. Élites sociales en la articulación de la Monarquía Hispánica, 1492–1714*, pp. 97–134 (Madrid: Marcial Pons).

M. Herrero, Y. R. Ben Yessef, C. Bittosi and D. Puncuh (eds.) (2011) *Génova y la Monarquía Hispánica (1528–1713)* (Genoa: Società Ligure di Storia Patria) vols. I–II.

A. M. Hespanha (1989) *Vísperas del Leviatán. Instituciones y poder político (Portugal siglo XVII)* (Madrid: Taurus).

A. M. Hespanha (1993a) *La gracia del derecho. Economía de la cultura en la edad moderna* (Madrid: Centro de Estudios Políticos y Constitucionales).

A. M. Hespanha (1993b) *História de Portugal. O Antigo Regime (1620–1807)* (Lisbon: Círculo de Leitores).

A. M. Hespanha (2001) 'A constituçao do Império português de alguns enviesamentos correntes' in J. Fragoso, M. F. Bicalho and M. F. Gouvêa (eds.) *O antigo regime nos trópicos. A dinâmica imperial portuguesa (séculos XVI–XVIII)*, pp. 163–188 (Rio de Janeiro: Civilização Brasileira).

A. M. Hespanha and Maria Catarina Santos (1998) 'Os poderes num Império Oceânico' in *História de Portugal. O Antigo Regime*, vol. IV, pp. 351–366 (Lisbon: Ed. Estampa).

T. Herzog (2015) *Frontiers of Possession: Spain and Portugal in Europe and the Americas* (Harvard and Cambridge MA: Harvard University Press).

P. Hidalgo (2006) *Entre Castro del Río y México: Correspondencia Privada de Diego de la Cueva y su hermano Juan, Emigrante en Indias (1601–1641)* (Córdoba: Universidad de Córdoba, 2006).

C. Hill (1969) *Reformation to Industrial Revolution, 1530–1780* (London: Penguin).

R. H. Hilton (1985) 'A Crisis of Feudalism' in T. H. Aston and C. H. E. Philpin (eds.) *The Brenner Debate: Agrarian Class Structure and Economic Development in Pre-Industrial Europe*, pp. 119–137 (Cambridge: Cambridge University Press).

E. Hobsbawm (1954) '*The General Crisis of the European Economy* in the Seventeenth Century', *Past and Present*, 5, 33–53.

P. Hoffman (1996) *Growth in a Traditional Society. The French Countryside, 1450–1815* (Princeton: Princeton University Press).

M. P. Holt (1995) *The French Wars of Religion, 1562–1629* (Cambridge: Cambridge University Press).

P. Horden and N. Purcell (2000) *The Corrupting Sea: A Study of Mediterranean History* (Oxford: Blackwell).

J. Hoock and P. Jeannin, eds. (1991) *Ars Mercatoria. Handbücher und Traktate für den Gebrauch des Kaufmans, 1470–1820* (Paderborn: Schöningh).

J. F. Hough and R. Grier (2015) *The Long Process of Development: Building Markets and States in Pre-industrial England, Spain, and Their Colonies* (Cambridge: Cambridge University Press).

A. Huetz de Lemps (1967) *Vignobles et vins du Nord-Ouest de l'Espagne* (Burdeaux: Institut de Géographie de la Faculté des Lettres).

S. Ibáñez (1995) *El pan de Dios y el pan de los hombres: diezmos, primicias y rentas en la diócesis de Calahorra (ss. XVI–XVIII)* (Logroño: Universidad de La Rioja).

P. Iradiel (1974) *Evolución de la industria textil castellana en los siglos XIII–XVI* (Salamanca: Universidad de Salamanca).

P. Iradiel and E. Sarasa (1989) *Historia medieval de la España cristiana* (Madrid: Cátedra).

A. Irigoyen (2001) *Entre el cielo y la tierra, entre la familia y la institución: el cabildo de la Catedral de Murcia en el siglo XVIII* (Murcia: Universidad de Murcia).

J. Israel (1974) 'Mexico and the "General Crisis" of the Seventeenth Century', *Past and Present*, 63, 33–57.

J. Israel (1975) *Race, Class and Politics in Colonial Mexico—1610–1670* (Oxford: Oxford University Press).

J. I. Israel (1985) *The European Jewry in the Age of Mercantilism* (Oxford: Clarendon Press).

J. I. Israel (1989) *Dutch Primacy in World Trade, 1585–1740* (Oxford: Clarendon Press).

J. I. Israel (1990) *Empires and Entrepots. The Dutch, The Spanish Monarchy and the Jews, 1585–1713* (London: The Hambledon Press).

J. I. Israel (1995) *The Dutch Republic: its Rise, Greatness, and Fall 1477–1806* (Oxford: Clarendon Press).

J. Izquierdo (2001) *El rostro de la comunidad. La identidad del campesino en la Castilla del Antiguo Régimen* (Madrid: CSIC).

J. Jacquart (1974) *La crise rurale en Île-de France. 1550–1670* (Paris: Armand Colin).

J. Jacquart (1975) 'Immobilisme et catastrophes, 1560–1660', in G. Duby (dir.) *Histoire de la France rurale, Vol 2, L'âge classique, 1340–1789*, pp. 185–348 (Paris: Seuil).

C. Jago (1981) "Habsburg Absolutism and the Cortes of Castile", *The American Historical Review*, 2, 307–326.

C. Jago (1982) 'La "crisis de la aristocracia' in la Castilla del Siglo XVII", in J. H. Elliott (ed.) *Poder y sociedad en la España de los Austrias*, pp. 248–286 (Barcelona: Crítica).

C. Jago (1985) "Philip II and the Cortes of Castile: the Case of the Cortes of 1576", *Past and Present*, 1, 24–43.

C. Jago (1989) "Crisis sociales y oposición política: Cortes y Monarquía durante el reinado de Felipe II" en *Las Cortes en la historia de Castilla y León en la Edad Moderna* (Valladolid: Junta de Castilla y León).

P. Janssens (1998) *L'evolution de la noblesse depuis la fin du Moyen Âge* (Brussels: Crédit Communal).

J. A. Jara (2000) *Concejo, poder y élites. La clase dominante de Cuenca en el siglo XV* (Madrid: CSIC).

E. L. Jones (1981) *The European Miracle: Environments, Economics and Geopolitics in the History of Europe and Asia* (Cambridge: Cambridge University Press).

E. L. Jones (2000) *Growth Recurring: Economic Change in World History* (Ann Arbor: University of Michigan Press).

A. Jouanna (1989) *Le devoir de revolte. La noblesse française et la gestation de l'Etat moderne, 1559–1661* (Paris: Fayard).

A. Jouanna (1991) 'De "gross et grass" aux "gens d'honneur"' in G. Chaussinaud-Nogaret (ed.), *Histoire des élites en France du XVIe au XXe siécle*, pp. 15–141 (Paris: Tallandier).

G. Jover (1997) *Societat rural i desenvolupament econòmic a Mallorca. Feudalisme, latifundi i pagesia, 1500–1800* (Ph.D. Thesis, Universidad de Barcelona).

R. Kagan (1981) *Universidad y sociedad en la España moderna* (Madrid: Tecnos).

R. Kagan (1991) *Pleitos y pleiteantes en Castilla* (Salamanca: Junta de Castilla y León).

R. Kagan and A. Dyer (2004) *Inquisitorial Inquiries. Brief Lives and Other Heretics* (Baltimore: Johns Hopkins University Press).

R. Kagan and F. Marías (1998) *Imágenes urbanas del mundo hispánico, 1493–1780* (Madrid: El Viso).

H. Kamen (1965) *The Spanish Inquisition* (London: Weidenfeld & Nicolson).

H. Kamen (1978) 'The Decline of Spain: A Historical Myth', *Past and Present*, 81, 24–50.

H. Kamen (2002) *Spain's Road to Empire: The Making of a World Power, 1492–1763* (London: Penguin, 2002).

H. Kamen and J. Israel (1982) 'The Seventeenth-Century Crisis in New Spain: Myth or Reality', *Past and Present* 97, 144–156.

H. Kellenbenz (2000) *Los Fugger en España y Portugal hasta 1560* (Salamanca: Junta de Castilla y León) vols. I–II.

P. Kennedy (1988) *The Rise and Fall of the Great Powers: Economic Change and Military Conflict from 1500 to 2000* (London: Unwin Hyman).

J. M. Keynes (1936) *The General Theory of Employment, Interest, and Money* (London: Macmillan).

J. E. Kicza (1999) 'Formación, identidad y estabilidad dentro de la élite colonial mexicana en los siglos XVI y XVII' in C. Büschges and B. Schröter (eds.) *Beneméritos, aristócratas y empresarios: identidades y estructuras sociales de las capas altas urbanas en América Hispánica*, pp. 17–34 (Munich: Vervuert Iberoamericana).

J. Klein (1979) *La Mesta. Estudio de la historia económica española, 1273–1836* (Madrid: Alianza Editorial).

P. Klep (1988) 'Urban decline in Brabant: the traditionalization of investment and labour (1374–1806)', in H. Van der Wee (ed.) *The Rise and Decline of Urban Industries in Italy and the Low Countries*, pp. 261–286 (Leuven: Leuven University Press).

R. Knecht (1996) *The French Wars of Religion. 1559–1598* (New York: Longman).

H. G. Koenigsberger (1971) *The Habsburgs and Europe, 1516–1660* (Ithaca: Cornell University Press).

H. G. Koenigsberger (1986) *Politicians and Virtuosi: Essays in Early Modern History* (London: Clarendon Press).

R. Konetzke (1976) *América Latina: La época colonial* (Madrid: siglo XXI).

K. O. Kupperman (2012) *The Atlantic in World History* (Oxford: Oxford University Press).

J. M. Lacarra (1972) *Aragón en el pasado* (Madrid: Espasa Calpe).

M. A. Ladero (1973) *La hacienda real de Castilla en el siglo XV* (La Laguna: Universidad de La Laguna).

M. A. Ladero (1982) 'Rentas condales en Plasencia (1454–1488)' in id. *El siglo XV en Castilla. Fuentes de renta y política fiscal*, pp. 168–189 (Barcelona: Ariel).

M. A. Ladero (1994) *Las ferias de Castilla. Siglos XII a XV* (Madrid: Comité Español de Ciencias Históricas).

REFERENCES 475

C. Laliena (1987) *Sistema social, estructura agraria y organización del poder en el Bajo Aragón en la Edad Media (siglos XII–XV)* (Teruel: Instituto de Estudios Turolenses).

D. Landes (1998) *The Wealth and Poverty of Nations. Why Some are So Rich and Some So Poor* (London: Abacus).

F. Lane (1973) *Venice. A Maritime Republic* (Baltimore: The Johns Hopkins University Press).

R. Lanza (1991) *La población y el crecimiento económico de Cantabria en el Antiguo Régimen* (Madrid: Universidad Autónoma de Madrid).

R. Lanza (2010) *Miseria, cambio y progreso en el Antiguo Régimen: Cantabria, siglos XVI–XVIII* (Santander: Publican).

H. Lapeyre (1953) *Simon Ruiz et les "asientos" de Phillippe II* (Paris: Armand Colin).

H. Lapeyre (1955) *Une famille de marchands: Les Ruiz* (Paris: Armand Colin).

H. Lapeyre (1981) *El comercio exterior de Castilla a través de las aduanas de Felipe II* (Valladolid: Universidad de Valladolid).

J. M. Latorre (1989) 'La producción agraria en el obispado de Huesca (siglos XVI–XVII)', *Jerónimo Zurita*, 59–60, 121–72.

J. M. Latorre (1992) *Economía y religión: Las rentas de la catedral de Huesca y su dustribución social (siglos XVI–XVII)* (Zaragoza: Instituto Fernando el Católico).

J. P. Le Flem (1972) 'Las cuentas de la Mesta (1510–1709)', *Moneda y Crédito*, 121, 23–104.

E. Le Roy Ladurie (1966) *Les paysannes de Languedoc* (Paris: PUF).

E. Le Roy Ladurie (1973) 'Un concept. L'Unification microbienne du monde (XIVe–XVIIe Siècles)', *Revue Suisse d'histoire*, 23, 627–696.

E. Le Roy Ladurie (1977) 'Les masses profondes: La paysannerie', in F. Braudel and E. Labrousse (dirs.), *Histoire economique et sociale de la France, 1450–1660*, vol. I, pp. 473–872 (Paris: Presses Universitaires de France).

G. Lemeunier (1998) *Los señoríos murcianos. S. XVI–XVIII* (Murcia: Universidad de Murcia).

G. Lemeunier (1977) 'Les estremeños, ceux qui viennent de loin. Contribution à l'etude de la transhumance ovine dans l'est castillan (XVI–XIXss.)', *Mélanges de la Casa de Velázquez*, 13, 321–359.

G. Levi (1985) *L'eredità immateriale: carriera di un esorcista nel Piemonte del Seicento* (Turin: Giulio Einaudi).

C. Lisón (1991) *La imagen del rey. Monarquía, realeza y poder ritual en la Casa de los Austrias* (Madrid: Espasa-Calpe).

M. Livi-Bacci (1988) *Ensayo sobre la historia demográfica europea. Población y alimentación* (Barcelona: Ariel).

M. Livi Bacci (2008) *Conquest: The Destruction of the American Indios* (Cambridge: Polity Press).

D. M. Loades (1994) 'England under the Tudors' in T. A. Brady, J. Heiko A. Oberman and J. D. Tracy (eds.) *Handbook of European History 1400–1600*, pp. 403–436 (Leiden: Brill).

I. Lobato (2013) *El sistema comercial español en la economía mundial (siglos XVII–XVIII)* (Huelva: Universidad de Huelva).

J. Lockhart and S. B. Schwartz (1983) *Early Latin America: A History of Colonial Spanish America and Brazil* (Cambridge: Cambridge University Press).

G. Lohman (1968) *Les Espinosa, une famille d'hommes d'affaires en Espagne et aux Indes à l'époque de la colonisation* (Paris: SEVPEN).

J. M. López (1990) *La transición del feudalismo al capitalismo en un señorío monástico castellano. El Abadengo de la Santa Espina (1147–1835)* (Valladolid: Junta de Castilla y León).

J. M. López (ed.) (1998) *El impacto de la corte en Castilla. Madrid y su territorio en la época moderna* (Madrid: Siglo XXI).

J. M. López Piñero (1979) *Ciencia y técnica en la sociedad española de los siglos XVI y XVII* (Barcelona: Labor).

J. López-Salazar (1986) *Estructuras agrarias y sociedad rural en la Mancha (ss. XVI–XVII)* (Ciudad Real: Instituto de Estudios Manchegos).

J. López-Salazar (1987) *Mesta, pastos y conflictos en el Campo de Calatrava durante el siglo XVI* (Madrid: Centro de Estudios Históricos).

E. Lorenzo (1979) *Comercio de España con América en la época de Felipe II* (Valladolid: Diputación Provincial) vols I–II.

A. W. Lovett (1977) *Philip II and Mateo Vázquez de Leca* (Geneve: Droz).

A. W. Lovett (1980) 'The Castilian Bankruptcy of 1575', *The Historical Journal*, 23, 899–911.

J. Lozano (2002) *La compañía de Jesús en el estado de los duques de Arcos: El colegio de Marchena (siglos XVI–XVIII)* (Granada, Universidad de Granada).

E. Llopis (1994) 'Castilian Agriculture in the Seventeenth Century: Depression, or 'Readjustment and Adaptation'?', in I. A. A. Thompson y B. Yun eds., *The Castilian Crisis of the Seventeenth Century: New Perspectives on the Economic and Social History of Seventeenth Century Spain*, pp. 77–100 (Cambridge: Cambridge University Press).

M. Lunenfeld (1987) *Keepers of the City: The Corregidores of Isabella I of Castile (1474–1504)* (Cambridge: Cambridge University Press).

J. A. Lynch (1969) *Spain Under the Habsburgs: Spain and America, 1598–1700* (Oxford: B. Blackwell).

M. Lucena (2006) *A los cuatro vientos: las ciudades de la América hispánica* (Madrid: Fundación Carolina).

L. N. MacAlister (1984) *Spain, and Portugal in the New World, 1492–1700* (Minneapolis: University of Minnesota Press).

K. B. MacFarlane (1973) *The Nobility of Later Medieval England* (Oxford, Oxford University Press).

A. Mackay (1972) 'Popular Movements and Programs in Fifteenth Century', *Past and Present*, 55, 33–67.

A. Mackay (1980) *La España de la Edad Media. Desde la frontera hasta el Imperio (1000–1500)* (Madrid: Cátedra).

A. Mackay (1981) *Money, Prices and Politics in Fifteenth-Century Castile* (London: Royal Historical Society).

R. MacKay (1999) *The Limits of Royal Authority: Resistance and Obedience in Seventeenth-Century Castile* (Cambridge: Cambridge University Press).

R. MacKay (2006) *'Lazy, Improvident People'. Myth and Reality in the Writing of Spanish History* (Ithaca: Cornell University Press).

M. J. Macleod (1990) 'Aspectos de la economía interna de la América española colonial: fuerza de trabajo, sistema tributario, distribución e intercambios', in L. Bethell (ed.), *Historia de América Latina, América Latina colonial: Economía*, vol. 3, pp. 148–189 (Barcelona: Crítica).

A. Maczak (1996) *Viajes y viajeros en la Europa moderna* (Barcelona: Omega).

A. De Maddalena and H Kellenbenz (eds.) (1986) *La repubblica internazionale del denaro tra XV e XVII secolo* (Bologna: Il Mulino).

A. Maddison (1995) *Explaining the Economic Performance of Nations: Essays in Time and Space* (Aldershot: Elgar).

S. Madrazo (2000) *Estado débil y ladrones poderosos en la España del siglo XVIII. Historia de un peculado en el reinado de Felipe V* (Madrid: Catarata).

D. Maffi (2009) 'Las milicias del estado de Milán: un intento de control social' in J. J. Ruiz Ibáñez (ed.) *Las milicias del rey de España: sociedad, política e identidad en las monarquías ibéricas*, pp. 245–267 (Mexico: Fondo de Cultura Económica).

J. R. Magalhães (1997) *História de Portugal. No alvorecer da modernidade (1480–1620)* (Lisbon: Ed. Estampa).

P. Malanima (1978) 'Firenze fra '500 e '700: l'andamento della industria citadina nel lungo periodo', *Societá e Storia*, 1, 231–56.

P. Malanima (1982) *La decadenza de un'economía cittadina: l'industria di Firenze nei secoli XVI–XVIII* (Bologna: Il Mulino).

P. Malanima (1988) 'An Example of Industrial Reconversion: Tuscany in the Sixteenth and Seventeenth Centuries' in H. Van der Wee (ed.) *The Rise and Decline of Urban Industries in Italy and the Low Countries*, pp. 63–74 (Leuven: Leuven University Press).

P. Malanima (1998) *La fine del primato. Crisi e riconversione nell'Italia del Seicento* (Milan: Mondadori).

W. S. Maltby (1983) *Alba: A Biography of Fernando Alvarez de Toledo, Third Duke of Alba, 1507–1582* (Berkeley: University of California Press).

W. S. Maltby (2011) *Auge y caída del imperio español* (Madrid: Marcial Pons).

J. A. Maravall (1970) *Las Comunidades de Castilla. Una primera revolución moderna*, 2nd ed. (Madrid: Revista de Occidente).

G. Marcocci (2012) *A Consciência de um Império. Portugal e o seu mundo (sécs. XV–XVII)* (Coimbra: Imprensa da universidade de Coimbra).

A. Marcos (1978) *Auge y declive de un núcleo mercantil y financiero de Castilla la Vieja. Evolución demográfica de Medina del Campo en los siglos XVI y XVII* (Valladolid: Universidad de Valladolid).

A. Marcos (1985) *Economía, sociedad, pobreza en Castilla: Palencia, 1500–1814* (Palencia: Diputación Provincial), vols. I–II.

J. de Mariana (1987 [1609]) *Tratado y discurso sobre la moneda de vellón* (Madrid: Instituto de Estudios Fiscales).

C. Marichal (2014) 'Mexican Cochineal and European Demand for a Luxury Dye, 1550–1850' in B. Aram and B. Yun (eds.) *Global Goods and the Spanish Empire, 1492–1824*, pp. 197–215 (Basingstoke: Palgrave).

C. Marichal and M. Souto (1994) 'Silver and Situados: New Spain and the Financing of the Spanish Empire in the Caribbean in the Eighteenth Century', *The Hispanic American Historical Review*, 74:4, 587–613.

C. Marichal and J. von Grafenstein (eds.) (2012) *El secreto del imperio español: los situados coloniales en el siglo XVII* (Mexico: ColMex).

B. Martínez (1993) *La emigración castellana y leonesa al Nuevo Mundo (1517–1700)* (Salamanca: Junta de Castilla y León).

J. Martínez and C. J. Morales (eds.) (1998) *Felipe II (1527–1598). La configuración de la monarquía hispana* (Salamanca: Junta de Castilla y León).

J. I. Martínez Ruiz (1992) *Finanzas municipales y crédito público en la España Moderna. La hacienda de la ciudad de Sevilla, 1528–1768* (Seville: Ayuntamiento).

C. Martínez Shaw (1994) *La emigración española a América (1492–1824)* (Colombres: Archivo de Indianos).

P. Martínez Sopena (1977) *El estado señorial de Medina de Rioseco bajo el Almirante Alfonso Enríquez (1389–1430)* (Valladolid: Universidad de Valladolid).

L. Martz (1983) *Poverty and Welfare in Habsburg Spain: the Example of Toledo* (Cambridge: Cambridge University Press).

R. Maruri (2007) *Repintar los blasones. El Marqués de la Casa Torre, un riojano en Indias (1662–1732)* (Logroño: Instituto de Estudios Riojanos).

R. Mata (1987) *Pequeña y gran propiedad agraria en la depresión del Guadalquivir* (Madrid: MAPA) vols I–II.

J. A. Mattoso (1997) *História de Portugal. A Monarquia Feudal (1096–1480)* (Lisbon: Ed. Estampa).

F. Mauro (1960) *Le Portugal et l'Atlantique au XVIIe siècle. Étude économique* (Paris: SEVPEN).

L. McAlister (1984) *Spain and Portugal in the New World 1492–1700* (Minneapolis: University of Minnesota Press).

W. McNeill (1977) *Plagues and Peoples* (New York: Anchor Books).

J. Menard (1991) "Transport Cost and Long-range Trade, 1300–1800: was there a European 'transport revolution' in the Early Modern Era?", en J. D. Tracy (ed.) *The Political Economy of Merchant Empires*, pp. 228–275 (Cambridge: Cambridge University Press).

M. Menegus (1991) 'La destrucción del señorío indígena y la formación de la república de indios en la Nueva España' in H. Bonilla (ed.) *El sistema colonial en la América española*, pp. 17–49 (Barcelona: Crítica).

M. Merluzzi (2003) *Politica e governo nel Nuovo mondo. Francisco de Toledo viceré del Perú (1569–1581)* (Rome: Carocci).

R. Mettam (1988) *Power and Faction in Louis XIV's France* (Oxford: Blackwell).

S. Mintz (1986) *Sweetness and Power: The Place of Sugar in Modern History* (New York: Penguin).

M. Miño (1991) 'La manufactura colonial: aspectos comparativos entre el obraje indiano y el novohispano' in H. Bonilla (ed.) *El sistema colonial en la América española*, pp. 102–153 (Barcelona: Crítica).

S. M. Miranda (2010) 'Organización financiera y práctica política en el estado de la India durante la Unión Ibérica' in Gaetano Sabatini (ed.) *Comprendere le monarchie iberiche. Risorse materiali e rappresentazioni del potere*, pp. 261–29 (Rome: Viella).

S. M. Miranda (2017) 'Coping with Europe and the Empire, 1500–1620' in D. Freire and P. Lains (eds.) *An agrarian History of Portugal, 1000–2000. Economic Development on the European Frontier*, pp. 71–100 (Leiden and Boston: Brill).

H. Miskimin (1981) *La economía europea en el Renacimiento tardío (1460–1600)* (Madrid: Cátedra).

H. Miskimin (1989) *Cash, Credit and Crisis in Europe, 1300–1600* (London: Variorum).

P. Molas (1996) *Catalunya i la casa d'Àustria* (Barcelona: Curial).

M. Mollat (1952) *Le commerce maritime normand à la fin del moyen âge* (Paris: Plon).

J. M. Monteiro (1994) *Negros da terra: índios e bandeirantes nas origens de São Paulo* (São Paulo: Companhia das Letras).

N. G. Monteiro (2003) '17th and 18th century Portuguese Nobilities in the European Context: A historiographical overview', *e-Journal of Portuguese History*, 1, 1–15.

J. Montemayor (1996) *Tolède entre fortune et declin (1530–1640)* (Panazol: Presses Universitaires de Limoges).

M. Morineau (1977) 'La conjoncture ou les cernes de la croissance' in F. Braudel and E, Labrousse (dirs.) *Histoire économique et sociale de la France, 1450–1660*, vol. I, pp. 873–1000 (Paris: Presses Universitaires de France).

M. Morineau (1985) *Incroyables gazettes et fabuleux métaux. Les retours des trésors américaines d'après les gazettes hollandaises (XVIe–XVIIIe siècles)* (Cambridge and Paris: Cambridge University Press and Éditions de la Maison des Sciences de l'Homme).

M. Mörner (1990) 'Economía rural y sociedad colonial en las posesiones españolas de Sudamérica' in L. Bethell (ed.), *Historia de América Latina. América Latina colonial: Economía,* vol. 3, pp. 122–146 (Barcelona: Crítica).

S. de Moncada (1974 [1619]) *Restauración política de España* (Madrid: Instituto de estudios Fiscales).

M. Montáñez (1950) *El correo en la España de los Austrias* (Madrid: CSIC).

R. Mousnier (1971) *La plume, la faucille et le marteau: Institutions et société en France du Moyen Âge à la Révolution* (Paris: Presses Universitaires de France).

Z. Moutoukias (1988) 'Power, Corruption, and Commerce: The Making of the Local Administrative Structure in Seventeenth-Century Buenos Aires', *The Hispanic American Historical Review,* 68, 771–801.

T. Mun (1664) *England's Treasure by Foreign Trade* (London: Thomas Clark).

J. Munro (1973) *Wool, Cloth and Gold: The Struggle for Bullion in the Anglo-Burgundian Trade, 1340–1478* (Brussels: Éditions de l'Université de Bruxelles and Toronto: Toronto University Press).

J. Munro (1994) 'Patterns of Trade, Money and Credit', in T. A. Bray, A. Oberman and J. D. Tracy (eds.) *Handbook of European History (1400–1600): Late Middle Ages, Renaissance and Reformation,* pp. 147–196 (Leiden: Brill).

G. Muto (1980) *Le finanze pubbliche napoletane tra riforme e restaurazione (1520–1634)* (Naples: Edizioni Scientifiche Italiane).

G. Muto (2005) "The Structure of Aristocratic Patrimonies in the Kingdom of Naples: Management Strategies and Regional Development, 16th–18th Centuries" in J. Janssens and B. Yun (eds.) *European Aristocracies and Colonial Elites. Patrimonial Management Strategies and Economic Development, 15th–18th Centuries,* pp. 115–135 (London: Ashgate).

G. Muto (2007) 'Apparati militari e fabbisogno finanziario nell'Europa moderna: il caso della Spagna "de los Austrias"' in C. Donati and B. R. Kroener (eds.) *Militari e società civile nell'Europa dell'età moderna (XVI–XVIII secolo),* pp. 23–52 (Bologna: il Mulino).

G. Muto (2009) 'La nobleza napolitana en el contexto de la Monarquía Hispánica: algunos planteamientos' in B. Yun (ed.) *Las redes del imperio: élites sociales en la articulación de la Monarquía Hispánica, 1492–1714,* pp. 135–172 (Madrid: Marcial Pons).

J. Nadal (1959) 'La revolución de los precios españoles en el siglo XVI: estado actual de la cuestión', *Hispania,* 19, 511–514.

J. Nadal (1984) *La población española (siglos XVI a XX)* (Barcelona: Ariel).

J. Nadal and E. Giralt (1960) *La population catalane de 1553 à 1717. L'immigration française* (Paris: SEVPEN).

H. Nader (1986) *Los Mendoza y el Renacimiento español* (Guadalajara: Institución Marqués de Santillana).

H. Nader (1990) *Liberty in Absolutist Spain. The Habsburg Sale of Towns, 1516–1700* (Cambridge: Cambridge University Press).

M. Nassiet (2000) *Parenté, Noblesse et états dynastiques, XVe–XVIe siècle* (Paris, EHESS).

M. S. Neto (1997) 'A persistência senhorial', in J. R. Magalhães (ed.) *História de Portugal. No alvorecer da modernidade (1480–1620)*, vol. III, pp. 165–175 (Lisbon: Ed. Estampa).

H. Neveux, J. Jacquart and E. Le Roy Ladurie (1975) *L'âge classique des paysans*, in G. Duby and A. Wallon eds., *Histoire de la France rurale* (Paris: Seuil) vols. I–II.

J. A. Nieto (2006) *Artesanos y mercaderes. Una historia social ybeconómica de Madrid (1450–1850)* (Madrid: Editorial Fundamentos).

J. A. Nieto and J. C. Zofio (2016) 'The Return of Guilds: A View from Early Modern Madrid', *Journal of Social History*, 50, 247–272.

D. C. North (1981) *Structure and Change in Economic History* (London: Routledge).

D. C. North (1991) 'Institutions, Transaction Costs, and the Rise of Merchant Empires' in J. D, Tracy (ed.) *The Political Economy of Merchant Empires. State Power and World Trade, 1350–1750*, pp. 22–40 (Cambridge: Cambridge University Press).

D. C. North and R. P. Thomas (1973) *The Rise of the Western World: A New Economic History* (Cambridge: Cambridge University Press).

D. C. North and B. R. Weingast (1989) 'Constitutions and Commitment: the Evolution of Institutional Governing Public Choice in Seventeenth-Century England', *The Journal of Economic History*, 49, 803–832.

D. C. North, J. J. Wallis and B. R. Weingast (2009) *Violence and Social Orders: A Conceptual Framework for Interpreting Recorded Human History* (Cambridge: Cambridge University Press).

L. Norton (1965) *A dinastía dos Sá no Brasil. A Fundação do Rio de Janeiro e a Restauração de Angola* (Lisbon: Agência Geral do Ultramar).

H. G. Nutini and B. Bell (1980) *Ritual Kinship: The Structure and Historical Development of the Compadrazgo System in Rural Tlaxcala* (Princeton: Princeton University Press).

P. O'Brien (1980) 'European Economic Development; the Contribution of the Periphery', *Economic History Review*, 35, 1–18.

P. O'Brien (1996) 'Path Dependency, or Why Britain Became an Industrialized and Urbanized Economy Long before France', *The Economic History Review*, 49, 213–249.

P. O'Brien and P. Hunt (1993) 'The Rise of a Fiscal State in England, 1485–1815', *Historical Research*, 160, 126–76.

S. Ogilvie (2007) 'Can We Rehabilitate the Guilds? A Sceptical Re-Appraisal', *Cambridge Working Papers in Economics*, 2007.

S. Ogilvie (2011) *Institutions and European Trade: Merchant Guilds, 1000–1800* (Cambridge: Cambridge University Press).

J. M. Oliva (2004) *El monopolio de Indias en el siglo XVII y la economía andaluza. La oportunidad que nunca existió* (Huelva: Universidad de Huelva).

F. Olival (2001) *As Ordenes Militares e o Estado Moderno. Honra, mercê, e venalidade em Portugal (1641–1789)* (Lisbon: Thesis).

F. Olival (2004) 'Structural Changes within the 16th-Century Portuguese Military Orders', *e-Journal of Portuguese History*, 2, 1–20.

J. W. O'Malley (1981) *A History of the Popes from Peter to Present* (Lanhan: Rowman and Littlefield).

K. H. O'Rourke and J. G. Williamson (2002) 'When did Globalisation begin?' *European Review of Economic History*, 6, 23–50.

K. H. O'Rourke and J. G. Williamson (2005) 'From Malthus to Ohlin: Trade, Industrialisation and Distribution Since 1500', *Journal of Economic Growth*, 10, 5–34.

J. Ortega (1974) *La transformación de un espacio rural: las montañas de Burgos: estudio de geografía regional* (Valladolid: Universidad de Valladolid).

T. Osborne (2002) *Dynasty and Diplomacy in the Court of Savoy: Political Culture and the Thirty Years' War* (Cambridge: Cambridge University Press).

A. C. Van Oss (1976) 'Mendicant Expansion in New Spain and the Extent of the Colony: Sixteenth Century', *Journal of Latin American and Caribbean Studies*, 21, 32–56.

E. Otte (1986) 'Il ruolo dei genovesi nella Spagna del XV e XVI secolo' in A. De Maddalena and H Kellenbenz (eds.), *La repubblica internazionale del denaro tra XV e XVII secolo*, pp. 17–56 (Bologna: Il Mulino).

E. Otte (1988) *Cartas privadas de emigrantes a Indias, 1540–1616* (Seville: Escuela de Estudios Hispano Americanos).

M. Overton (1996) *Agricultural Revolution in England. The Transformation of the Agrarian Economy, 1500–1850* (Cambridge: Cambridge University Press).

J. B. Owens (1980) *Rebelión, Monarquía y Oligarquía murciana en la época de Carlos V* (Murcia: Universidad de Murcia).

J. B. Owens (2005) *By my Absolute Royal Authority: Justice and the Castilian Commonwealth at the Beginning of the First Global Age* (Rochester: University of Rochester Press).

Z. P. Pach (1968) 'The shifting of International Trade Routes in the 15th–17th. Centuries', *Acta Historica Academiae Scientiarum Hungaricae*, 14, 277–319.

A. Pacheco (2012) 'Las transferencias fiscales novohispanas a Puerto Rico siglos XVI–XIX', in C. Marichal and J. Grafenstein (eds.) *El secreto del Imperio español: los situados coloniales en el siglo XVIII*, pp. 115–141 (Mexico: ColMex).

J-L. Palos (2016) 'Eleonora Álvarez de Toledo (1522–62): "A Spanish Barbarian and an Enemy of her Husband's Homeland": the Duchess of Florence and her Spanish Entourage' in J. L. Palos and M. Sánchez (eds.) *Early Dynastic Marriages and Cultural Transfer*, pp. 165–187 (Farnham: Ashgate).

F. Palomo (2016) 'Written Empires: Franciscans, Texts, and the Making of Early Modern Iberian Empires', *Culture and History Digital Journal*, 5, 1–8.

Ş. Pamuk (2002) *A Monetary History of the Ottoman Empire* (Cambridge: Cambridge University Press).

Ş. Pamuk (2012) 'The Evolution of Fiscal Institutions in the Ottoman Empire, 1500–1914,' in B. Yun and P. O'Brien (eds) *The Rise of Fiscal States. A Global History, 1500–1914*, pp. 304–331 (Cambridge: Cambridge University Press).

G. Parker (1972) *The Army of Flanders and the Spanish Road, 1567–1659* (Cambridge: Cambridge University Press).

G. Parker (1979) *Spain and The Netherlands, 1559–1659* (London: Collins).

G. Parker (1981) *Europa en crisis, 1598–1648* (Madrid: Siglo XXI).

G. Parker (1995) 'The Military Revolution, 1560–1660' – A Myth?' in C. J. Rogers (ed.) *The Military Revolution Debate*, pp. 37–54 (Boulder: Westview Press).

G. Parker (2001) *El éxito nunca es definitivo: imperialismo, guerra y fe en la Europa moderna* (Madrid: Taurus).

D. Parrott (2012) *The Business of War: Military Enterprise and Military Revolution in Early Modern Europe* (Cambridge: Cambridge University Press).

J. H. Parry (1990) *The Spanish Seaborne Empire* (Berkeley: University of California Press).

R. W. Patch (1994) 'Imperial Politics and Local Economy in Colonial Central America, 1670–1770', *Past and Present*, 143, 77–107.

J-M. Pelorson (1980) *Les 'letrados': juristes castillans sous Philippe III: recherches sur leur place dans la société, la culture et l'état* (Poitiers: Université de Poitiers).

A. Pelúcia (2009) *Martim Afonso de Sousa e a sua linhagem: trajectórias de uma elite no império de D. João III e D. Sebastião* (Lisbon: CHAM).

J. L. Pereira (1991) *Cáceres y su tierra en el siglo XVI. Economía y sociedad* (Cáceres: El Brocense).

J. Perez (1976) *La revolcuión de las Comunidades de Castilla (1520–1521)* (Madrid: Siglo XXI).

J. Perez (1989) *Los comuneros* (Madrid: Historia 16).

P. Pérez (1992) *América Latina y el colonialismo europeo. Siglos XVI–XVIII* (Madrid: Síntesis).

J. Pérez-Embid (1986) *El Císter en Castilla y León. Monacato y dominios rurales (s. XII–XV)* (Salamanca: Junta de Castilla y León).

J. Pérez del Barrio (1613) *Dirección de Secretarios de señores y las materias, cuydados y bligaciones que les tocan* (Madrid).

V. Pérez Moreda (1980) *Las crisis de mortalidad en la España interior, siglos XVI–XIX* (Madrid: Siglo XXI).

M. T. Pérez and G. Lemeunier (1984) *El proceso de modernización de la región murciana (siglos XVI–XIX)* (Murcia: Editora Regional).

G. Pérez Sarrión (2016), *The Emergence of a National Market in Spain, 1650–1800: Trade Networks, Foreign Powers and the State* (London: Bloomsbury Academic).

T. Peris (1989) *Propiedad y cambio social. Evolución patrimonial, sistema productivo y dinámica social en el realengo valenciano (Alcira, 1465–1768)* (Valencia: Diputació de València).

S. T. Perrone (1997) *Charles V and the Castilian Assembly of the Clergy* (Ph.D. Thesis, University of Michigan).

S. T. Perrone (1998) 'The Castilian Assembly of the Clergy in the Sixteenth Century', *Parliaments, Estates and Representation*, 18, 53–70.

L. Pezzolo (2012) "Republics and Principalities" in B. Yun and P. O'Brien (eds) *The Rise of Fiscal States. A Global History, 1500–1914*, pp. 1–35 (Cambridge: Cambridge University Press). pp. 267–284.

C. R. Phillips (1986) *Six Galleons for the King of Spain: Imperial Defense in the Early Seventeenth Century* (Baltimore: The Johns Hopkins University Press).

C. R. Phillips (1990) 'The Growth and the Composition of Trade in the Iberian Empires, 1450–1750', in J. D. Tracy (ed.) *The Rise of Merchant Empires. Long-distance Trade in the Early Modern World, 1350–1750*, pp. 34–101 (Cambridge: Cambridge University Press).

C. R. Phillips and W. D. Jr. Phillips (1997) *Spain's Golden Fleece. Wool Production and the Wool Trade from the Middle Ages to the Nineteenth Century* (Baltimore: The Johns Hopkins University Press).

R. Pieper (2012) 'Financing an Empire: The Austrian Composite Monarchy, 1650-1848' in B. Yun and P. O'Brien (eds) *The Rise of Fiscal States. A Global History, 1500–1914*, pp. 164–190 (Cambridge: Cambridge University Press).

P. Pierson (1989) *Commander of the Armada: the Seventh Duke of Medina Sidonia* (New Haven: Yale University Press).

H. Pietschmann (1989) *El Estado y su evolución al principio de la colonización española de América* (Mexico: Fondo de Cultura Económica).

R. Pike (1966) *Enterprise and Adventure: the Genoese in Seville and the Opening of the New World* (Ithaca: Cornell University Press).

R. Pike (1978) *Aristócratas y comerciantes* (Barcelona: Ariel).

A. de la Plaza (1980) *Archivo General de Indias. Guia del investigador* (Madrid: Ministerio de Cultura).

T. Pinheiro da Veiga (1989 [1605–1606]) *Fastiginia: vida cotidiana en la corte de Valadolid* (Valladolid: Ámbito).

H. R. Po-Chia (1998) *The World of Catholic Renewal, 1540–1770* (Cambridge: Cambridge University Press).

H. R. Po-Chia Sia (2010) *A Jesuit in the Forbidden City: Matteo Ricci* (Oxford: Oxford University Press).

K. Pomeranz (2001) The Great Divergence: China, Europe and the Making of World Economy (Princeton: Princeton University Press).

P. Ponsot (1986) *Atlas de Historia Económica de la Baja Andalucía (siglos XVI–XIX)* (Seville: Editoriales Andaluzas Unidas).

M. M. Postan (1966) 'Medieval Agrarian Society in its Prime: England' in id. (ed.) *The Cambridge Economic History of Europe: The Agrarian Life of the Middle Ages,* vol. I, pp. 548–632 (Cambridge: Cambridge University Press).

E. Postigo (1988) *Honor y privilegio en la Corona de Castilla. El Consejo de Ordenes y los Caballeros de Hábito en el siglo XVII* (Valladolid: Junta de Castilla y León).

N. Posthumus (1946) *Inquiry into the History of Prices in Holland* (Leiden: Brill).

L. Prados de la Escosura and C. Alvarez (2007) "The Decline of Spain (1500–1850): Conjectural Estimates", *European Review of Economic History,* 11, 319–366.

M. Prak (2005) *The Dutch Republic in the Seventeenth Century: The Golden Age* (Cambridge: Cambridge University Press).

J-P. Priotti (2004) *Bilbao et ses Marchands au XVIe siècle. Gènese d'une croissance* (Villeneuve d'Ascq, Presses Universitaires du Septentrion).

F. del Pulgar (1971) *Claros varones de Castilla* (Oxford: Oxford University Press).

I. Pulido (1993) *Almojarifazgos y comercio exterior en Andalucía durante la época mercantilista (1526–1740)* (Huelva: The author).

M. C. Quintanilla (1979) *Nobleza y señoríos en el reino de Córdoba: la Casa de Aguilar (siglos XIV y XV)* (Córdoba: Caja de Ahorros).

T. Rabb (1975) *The Struggle for Stability in Early Modern Europe* (Oxford: Oxford University Press).

F. Ramos (2012) "El papel de las instituciones en la españa del Antiguo Régimen. 'Castilla-León *versus* Cataluña: algunas notas sobre su evolución histórica, política y económica, 1500–1800" in F. Ramos and B. Yun (eds.) *Economía Política. Desde Estambul a Potosí: Ciudades estado, imperios y mercados en el Mediterráneo y el Atlántico ibérico, c. 1200–1800,* pp. 11–38 (Valencia: Universidat de València). pp. 259–302.

Á. Redondo and B. Yun (2008) 'Aristocracias, identidades y espacios políticos en la monarquía compuesta de los Austrias. La Casa de Borja (ss. XVI y XVII)' in J. L. Castellano and M. L. López Guadalupe (eds.) *Homejane a Antonio Domínguez Ortíz,* pp. 759–771 (Granada: Universidad de Granada).

Á. Redondo and B. Yun (2009) 'Bem visto tinha…" Entre Lisbon y Capodimonte. La aristocracia castellana en perspectiva "trans-nacional (ss. XVI–XVII)' in B. Yun (ed.) *Las redes del imperio. Élites sociales en la articulación de la Monarquía Hispánica, 1492–1714,* pp. 39–63 (Madrid: Marcial Pons).

J. Reglá (1966) *El bandolerisme català del barroc* (Barcelona: Edicions 62).

D. Reher (1990) *Town and Country in Pre-industrial Spain. Cuenca, 1550–1870* (Cambridge: Cambridge University Press).

D. Reher and E. Ballesteros (1993) 'Precios y salarios en Castilla la Nueva: la construcción de un índice de salarios reales, 1501–1991', *Revista de Historia Económica*, 1, 101–151.

J. Reis (2016) 'Gross Agricultural Output: A Quantitative, Unified Perspective, 1500–1850'. In D. Freire and P. Lains (eds.) *An Agrarian History of Portugal, 1000–2000. Economic development on the European frontier*, pp. 166–196 (Leiden: Brill).

L. Ribot (2008) "Las naciones en el ejército de los Austrias" in VV.AA. *Homenaje a Don Antonio Domínguez Ortíz* (Granada: Universidad de Granada). pp. 799–819.

D. Ringrose (1973) 'European Economic Growth: Comments on the North-Thomas Theory', *Economic History Review*, 26, 285–92.

D. Ringrose (1983a) *Madrid and the Spanish Economy* (Berkeley: University of California Press).

D. Ringrose (1983b) 'El desarrollo urbano y la decadencia económica española', *Revista de Historia Económica*, 1, 37–53.

D. Ringrose (1996) *Spain, Europe and the 'Spanish Miracle', 1700–1900* (Cambridge: Cambridge University Press).

M. J. del Río (2000) *Madrid, Urbs Regia. La capital ceremonial de la Monarquía Católica* (Madrid: Marcial Pons).

M. Rivero (2011) *La edad de oro de los virreyes: el virreinato en la Monarquía Hispánica durante los siglos XVI y XVII* (Madrid: Akal).

M. Rizzo (1995) 'Istituzioni militari e strutture socio-economiche in una città di antico regime. La milizia urbana a Pavia nell'età spagnola', *Cheiron*, 23–24, 144–171.

R. Ródenas (1990) *Vida cotidiana y negocio en la Segovia del Siglo de Oro. El mercader Juan de Cuéllar* (Valladolid: Junta de Castilla y León).

T.F. Rodriguez (1997) "Las estrutruas poblacionais" en J. R. Magalhaes (coord.) *História de Portugal. No alvorecer da modernidade* (Lisbon: Ed. Estampa).

M. Rodríguez-Salgado (1992) *Un imperio en transición. Carlos V, Felipe II y su mundo* (Barcelona: Crítica).

M. Rodríguez-Salgado (1998) 'Honour and Profit in the Court of Philip II of Spain' in M. Aymard and M. Romani (dirs.) *La Cour comme institution économique*, pp. 67–86 (Paris: Éditions de la Maison des Sciences de l'homme).

A. Rodríguez Villa (1905) *Ambrosio Spinola, primer marqués de los Balbases* (Madrid: Fortanet).

R. Romano (1962) 'Tra XVI e XVII secolo. Una crisi economica: 1619–1622', *Rivista di Storia di Italia*, 74, 480–531.

R. Romano (1992) *Conjonctures opposées: la "crise" du XVIIe siècle en Europe et en Amérique ibérique* (Genève: Droz).

R. Romano (2004) *Mecanismo y elementos del sistema económico colonial americano. Siglos XVI–XVIII* (Mexico: ColMex).

J. L. Rosenthal and R. Bin Wong (2011) *Before and Beyond Divergence: The Politics of Economic Change in China and Europe* (Cambridge MA: Harvard University Press).

E. Rothschild (2011) *The Inner Life of Empires: An Eighteenth-Century History* (Princeton: Princeton University Press).

A. Rucquoi (1987) *Valladolid en la Edad Media*, 2 vol. (Valladolid: Junta de Castilla y León).

J. J. Ruiz Ibáñez (1995) *Las dos caras de Jano. Monarquía, ciudad e individuo. Murcia, 1588–1648* (Murcia: Universidad de Murcia).

J. J. Ruiz Ibáñez, ed. (2009) *Las milicias del rey de España: sociedad, política e identidad en las monarquías ibéricas* (Mexico: Fondo de Cultura Económica).

J. J. Ruiz Ibáñez and V. Montojo (1998) *Entre el lucro y la defensa: las relaciones entre la monarquía y la sociedad mercantil cartagenera (comerciantes y corsarios en el siglo XVII)* (Murcia: Real Academia Alfonso X El Sabio).

F. Ruiz Martín (1965) 'Un expediente financiero entre 1560 y 1575. La Hacienda de FelipeII y la Casa de la Contratación de Sevilla', *Moneda y Crédito*, 92, 3–58.

F. Ruiz Martín (1975) 'Crédito y banca, comercio y transportes en la etapa del capitalismo mercantil', in *Actas de las I Jornadas de Metodología de las Ciencias Históricas*, Vol III, pp. 725–743 (Santiago: Universidad de Santiago de Compostela).

F. Ruiz Martín (1990a) *Pequeño capitalismo, gran capitalismo. Simón Ruíz y sus negocios en Florencia* (Barcelona: Crítica).

F. Ruiz Martín (1990b) *Las finanzas de la Monarquía Hispánica en tiempos de Felipe IV (1621–1665)* (Madrid: Real Academia de la Historia).

F. Ruiz Martín (1994) 'Credit Procedures for the Collection of Taxes in the Cities of Castile during the Sixteenth and Seventeenth Centuries: the Case of Valladolid', en I. A. A. Thompson and B. Yun (eds.) *The Castilian Crisis of the Seventeenth Century. New Perspectives on the Economic and Social History of Seventeenth Century Spain*, pp. 169–181 (Cambridge: Cambridge University Press).

F. Ruiz Martín (2005) *Los alumbres españoles. Un índice de la coyuntura económica europea del siglo XVI* (Madrid: Fundación Española de Historia Moderna-Ediciones Bornova).

J. Ruiz Rodríguez (1993) *Organización política y Económica de la Orden de Santiago en el siglo XVII: Los hombres, la economía y las instituciones en el Campo de Montiel* (Ciudad Real: Diputación Provincial).

F. Ruspio (2007) *La nazione portoghese: ebrei ponentini e nuovi cristiani a Venezia* (Turin: S. Zamorani).

C. Russell (1988) *The Crisis of Parliaments. English History, 1509–1660* (Oxford: Oxford University Press).

J. Russell Major (1980) *Representative Government in Early Modern France* (New Haven: Yale University Press).

J. Russell Major (1981) 'Nobel Income, Inflation and the Wars of Religion in France', *American Historical Review*, 86, 21–48.

J. R. Russell-Wood (1992) *A World on the Move: the Portuguese in Africa, Asia and America, 1415–1808* (Manchester: Carcanet).

I. dos G. Sá (1997) *Quando o Rico se faz Pobre: Misericórdias, caridade e poder no império português, 1500–1800* (Lisbon: Comissão Nacional para as Comemorações dos Descobrimentos Portugueses).

P. Saavedra (1985) *Economía, política y sociedad en Galicia: la provincia de Mondoñedo, 1480–1830* (Santiago: Xunta de Galicia).

P. Saavedra (1993) *A facenda real na Galicia do Antigo Réxime (As rendas provinciais)* (Santiago: Xunta de Galicia).

L. Salas (2013) *The Conspiracy of the Ninth Duke of Medina Sidonia (1641): An Aristocrat in the Crisis of the Spanish Empire* (Leiden: Brill).

G. Saldarriaga (2011) *Alimentación e identidades en el Nuevo Reino de Granada, siglos XVI y XVII* (Bogotá: Universidad del Rosario).

J. H. M. Salmon (1975) *Society in Crisis. France in the Sixteenth Century* (Cambridge: Cambridge University Press).

N. Salomon (1982) *La vida rural castellana en tiempos de Felipe II* (Barcelona: Ariel).

H. Samsonowicz (1973) 'Relations Commerciales entre la Baltique et la Méditérranée aux XVIe et XVIIe siècles, Gdansk et l'Italie' in B. Tenenti (ed.) *Histoire économique du monde méditerranéen, 1450–1650: Mélanges en l'honneur de Fernand Braudel*, pp. 537–546 (Toulouse: Privat).

C. Sánchez Albornoz (1976) *España un enigma histórico*, 5th ed. (Barcelona: Edhasa).

J. Sánchez (1989) *De minería, metalúrgica y comercio de metales. La minería no férrica en el reino de Castilla. 1450–1610* (Salamanca: Universidad de Salamanca) vols I–II.

C. Sanz (1988) *Los banqueros de Carlos II* (Valladolid: Universidad de Valladolid).

S. Sardone (2018) 'Forced Loans in the Spanish Empire: the First Requisition of American Trasures', *The Economic History Review*, forthcoming.

T. J. Sargent and F. R. Velde (2002) *The Big Problem of Small Change* (Princeton: Princeton University Press).

R. Savelli (1981) *La Repubblica Oligarchica. Legislazione, istituzioni e ceti a Genove nel Cinquecento* (Milan: Giuffré).

E. Schäfer (2003) *El Consejo Real y Supremo de las Indias* (Salamanca: Junta de Castilla y León).

E. Schalk (1986) *From Valor to Pedrigree: Idea of Nobility in France in the Sixteenth and Seventeenth Centuries* (Princeton: Princeton University Press).

J.-F. Schaub (2001) *Le Portugal au temps du Comte-Duc d'Olivares (1621–1640). Le conflict de jurisdictions comme exercice de la politique* (Madrid: Casa de Velázquez).

J. A. Schumpeter (1955) *Imperialism. Social Classes. Two Essays* (Cleveland: Meridian).

J. A. Schumpeter (1991) 'The Crisis of the Tax State' in R. Swedberg (ed.) *J. Schumpeter, The Economics and Sociology of Capitalism*, pp. 99–140 (Princeton: Princeton University Press).

S. B. Schwartz (1973) *Sovereignty and Society in Colonial Brazil. The High Court of Bahia and its Judges, 1609–1751* (Berkeley: University of California Press).

S. B. Schwartz (2007) 'The Economy of the Portuguese Empire' in F. Bethencourt and D. R. Curto (eds.) *Portuguese Oceanic Expansion, 1400–1800*, pp. 19–48 (Cambridge: Cambridge University Press).

S. B. Schwartz (2008) *All Can Be Saved: Religious Tolerance and Salvation in the Iberian Atlantic World* (New Haven: Yale University Press).

J. A. Sebastián (1999) 'Del fuero al arrendamiento: tenencia y explotación de la tierra en León entre la Edad Media y la Edad Moderna', *Revista de Historia Económica*, 17, 305–341.

T. Seijas (2014) *Asian Slaves in Colonial Mexico* (Cambridge: Cambridge University Press).

D. Sella (1957) 'Les mouvements longs de l'industrie lanière à Venice aux XVIe et XVIIe siècles', *Annales ESC*, 12, 29–45.

D. Sella and C. Capra (1984) *El ducato di Milano: dal 1535 al 1796* (Turin: UTET).

A. Sen (1981) *Poverty and Famines: An Essay on Entitlement and Deprivation* (Oxford: Oxford University Press).

E. Serra (1988) *Pagesos i senyors a la Catalunya del segle XVIII. Baronia de Sentmenat* (Barcelona: Crítica).

J. Serrão and A. H. Oliveira Marques (dirs.) (1998) Nova história de Portugal: Portugal do Rinascimento à crise dinástica (Lisbon: Ed. Estampa).

H. R. da Silva (2013) *O clero Catedralício português e os equilibrios sociais do poder (1564–1670)* (Lisbon: Univérsidade Católica Portuguesa).

A. Simon i Tarrés (1999) *Els orígens ideològics de la revolució catalana de 1640* (Montserrat: Abadía de Montserrat).

A. Simon i Tarrés (2011) *Del 1640 al 1705: l'autogovern de Catalunya i la clase dirigent en el joc de la política internacional europea* (Valencia: Universitat de València).

Q. Skinner (2002) *Visions of Politics. Vol II: Renaissance Virtues* (Cambridge: Cambridge University Press).

R. S. Smith (1978) *Historia de los Consulados del Mar (1250–1700)* (Barcelona: Ediciones Península).

A. G. R. Smith (1997) *The Emergence of a Nation State: The Commonwealth of England, 1529–1660* (London, Longman).

P. Slack (2015) *The Invention of Improvement: Information and Material Progress in Seventeenth-Century England* (Oxford: Oxford University Press).

E. Solano (2001) 'Las Cortes de Aragón: de Fernando el Católico a Carlos V (1490–1530)', in E. Belenguer (ed.) *De la unión de coronas al Imperio de Carlos V*. vol. 1, pp. 387–410 (Madrid: SECC).

F. Soldevila (1962) *Història de Catalunya*, 2nd ed. (Barcelona: Alpha).

E. Soria (1995) *La venta de señoríos en el Reino de Granada bajo los Austrias* (Granada: Universidad de Granada).

E. Soria (2000) *El cambio inmóvil. Transformaciones y permanencias en una élite de poder. (Córdoba, ss.XVI–XIX)* (Córdoba: La Posada).

E. Soria (2016) 'El negocio del siglo: los judeoconversos y la renta de la seda del Reino de Granada (siglo XVI)', *Hispania*, 253, 415–444.

L. de Sousa (2010) *The Early European Presence in China, Japan, the Philippines and Southeast Asia (1555–1590) – The Life of Bartolomeu Landeiro* (Macau: Fundação Macau).

L. de Sousa (2015) *The Jewish Diaspora and the Perez Family Case in China, Japan, the Philippines, and the Americas (16th Century)* (Macau: Fundaçao Macau).

P. Spufford (1988) *Money and its Use in Medieval Europe* (Cambridge: University Press).

G. D. Snooks (ed.) (1994) *Was the Industrial Revolution Necessary?* (London: Routledge).

L. Stone (1979) *The Crisis of the Aristocracy. 1558–1641* (New York: Harper and Row).

L. Stone and J. C. F. Stone (1995) *An Open Elite? England, 1540–1880* (London: Clarendon Press).

C. Storrs (2006) *The Resilience of the Spanish Monarchy 1665–1700* (Oxford: Oxford University Press).

C. Storrs (2016) *The Spanish Resurgence, 1713–1748* (New Haven: Yale University Press).

R. A. Stradling (1981) *Europe and the Decline of Spain* (London: George Allen and Unwin Publishers).

D. Studnicki-Gizbert (2007) *A Nation upon the Ocean Sea: Portugal's Atlantic Diaspora and the Crisis of the Spanish Empire* (Oxford: Oxford University Press).

E. Suárez (1975) *Nobleza y monarquía: puntos de vista sobre la historia política castellana del siglo XV* (Valladolid: Universidad de Valladolid).

S. Subrahmanyam (1990) *The Political Economy of Commerce: Southern India 1500–1650* (Cambridge: Cambridge University Press).

S. Subrahmanyam (2005) *Explorations in connected history. Mughals and Franks* (New Delhi: Oxford University Press).

S. Subrahmanyam (2007) 'Holding the World in Balance: The Connected Histories of the Iberian Overseas Empires, 1500–1640', *American Historical Review*, 112, 1359–1385.

S. Subrahmayam and L. F. Thomaz (1991) 'Evolution of the Empire: The Portuguese in the Indian Ocean During the Sixteenth Century' in J. D. Tracy (ed.) *The Political economy of Merchant Empires*, pp. 289–331 (Cambridge: Cambridge University Press).

J. TePaske (1983) 'New World Silver, Castile and the Philippines, 1590–1800' in J. F. Richards (ed.) *Precious Metals in the Later Medieval and Early Modern Worlds*, pp. 425–445 (Durham: Carolina Academic Press).

J. TePaske (1998) 'New World Gold Production in Hemispheric and Global Perspective, 1492–1810', in D. O. Flynn, M. Morineau and R. Von Glahn (eds.) *Monetary history in global perspective, 1500–1808*, Session B6 of *Twelfth International Economic History Congress*, Seville.

J. TePaske and H. S. Klein (1981) 'The Seventeenth-Century Crisis in New Spain: Myth or Reality?', *Past and Present*, 90, 116–135.

J. TePaske and H. S. Klein (1982) *The Royal Treasuries of the Spanish Empire in America* (Durham: Duke University Press).

A. Terrasa (2009) *Patrimonios aristocráticos y fronteras jurídico-políticas en la Monarquía Católica: los pleitos de la Casa de Pastrana en el siglo XVII* (Ph.D Thesis, European University Institute).

M. 'T Hart, J. Jonker and J. L. van Zanden (1997) *A Financial History of The Netherlands* (Cambridge: Cambridge University Press).

J. Thirsk (1978) *Economic Policy and Projects. The Development of a Consumer Society in Early Modern England* (Oxford: Clarendon Press).

J. Thirsk (1997) *Alternative agriculture. A History from the Black Death to the Present Day* (Oxford: Oxford University Press).

L. F. Thomaz (1994) *De Ceuta a Timor* (Lisbon: Difel).

I. A. A. Thompson (1976) *War and Government in Habsburg Spain* (London: the Athlone Press).

I. A. A. Thompson (1989) 'Cortes y ciudades: tipología de los procuradores (extracción social, representatividad)', in *Las Cortes de Castilla y León en la Edad Moderna*, pp. 191–248 (Valladolid: Junta de Castilla y León).

I. A. A. Thompson (1992) *War and Society in Habsburg Spain* (Norfolk: Variorum).

I. A. A. Thompson (1993) *Crown and Cortes. Government, Institutions and Representation in Early-Modern Castile* (Norfolk: Variorum).

I. A. A. Thompson (2005) 'La monarquía de España: la invención de un concepto', in F. J. Guillamón, D. Centenero and J. Muñoz (eds.) *Entre Clío y Casandra: poder y sociedad en la monarquía hispánica durante la Edad Moderna*, pp. 31–58 (Murcia: Universidad de Murcia).

I. A. A. Thompson and B. Yun (eds.) (1994) *The Castilian Crisis of the Seventeenth Century: New Perspectives on the Economic and Social History of Seventeenth Century Spain*, (Cambridge: Cambridge University Press).

C. Tilly (1990) *Coercion, capital and European States AD 990–1990* (Cambridge: Basil Blackwell).

F. Tomás y Valiente (1982) *Gobierno e instituciones en la España del Antiguo Régimen* (Madrid: Alianza Editorial).

F. Tomás y Valiente (1992) *Manual de Historia del Derecho español*, 4th ed. (Madrid: Tecnos).

J. M. Torras (1998) *Poders i relacions clientelars a la Catalunya dels Àustria* (Vic: Eumo).

X. Torres (1994) *Nyerros i cadells: bàndols i bandolerisme a la Catalunya moderna (1590–1640)* (Barcelona: Reial Acadèmia de Bones Lletres de Barcelona).

H. Touchard (1967) *Le commerce maritime breton à la fin du Moyen Age* (Paris: Plon).

J. Tracy (1985) *A Financial Revolution in the Habsburg Netherlands. Renten and Rentiers in the County of Holland, 1515–1565* (Berkeley: University of California Press).

O. Trujillo (2009) 'Facciones, parenesco y poder: la élite de Buenos Aires y la rebelión de Portugal de 1640' in B. Yun (ed.) *Las redes del imperio. Élites sociales en la articulación de la Monarquía Hispánica, 1492–1714*, pp. 341–358 (Madrid: Marcial Pons).

M. Ulloa (1977) *La Hacienda Real en Castilla en el reinado de Felipe II* (Madrid: Fundación Universitaria Española).

J. Urrea (1996) *Arquitectura y nobleza. Casas y palacios de Valladolid* (Valladolid: IV Centenario Ciudad de Valladolid).

J. M. Usunáriz (1997) *Nobleza y señoríos en la Navarra Moderna. Entre la solvencia y la crisis económica* (Pamplona: Eunsa).

J. Valdeón (1975) *Los conflictos sociales en el reino de Castilla en los siglos XIV y XV* (Madrid: Siglo XXI).

J. M. Valencia (2010) *El poder señorial en la edad moderna: la casa de feria (siglos XVI y XVII)* (Badajoz: Diputación de Badajoz).

B. Valle (1985) *Geografía agraria de Los Pedroches* (Córdoba: Diputación Provincial).

H. Van der Wee (1963) *The Growth of the Antwerp Market and the European Economy (Fourteenth-Sixteenth Centuries)* (The Hague: Nijhoff) vols I–III.

H. Van der Wee (1967) 'Anvers et les innovations de la technique financière aux XVIe et XVIIe siècles', *Annales ESC*, 22, 94–101.

H. Van der Wee (1978) 'Prices and Wages as Development Variables: A Comparison between England and The Southern Netherlands, 1400–1700', *Acta Historica Neerlandica*, 10, 58–78.

H. Van der Wee (1988) 'Industrial Dynamics and the Process of Urbanization and De-Urbanization in the Low Countries from the Late Middle Ages to the Eighteenth Century. A synthesis', in H. Van der Wee (ed.) *The Rise and Decline of Urban Industries in Italy and the Low Countries*, pp. 307–381 (Leuven: Leuven University Press).

H. Van der Wee (1990) 'Structural Changes in European Long Distance Trade, and Particularly in the Re-Export Trade from South to North, 1350–1750' in J. D. Tracy (ed.) *The Rise of Merchant Empires. Long-distance Trade in the Early Modern World, 1350–1750*, pp. 14–33 (Cambridge: Cambridge University Press).

H. Van der Wee and J. Blomme (1994) 'The Belgian Economy in a Long-Term Historical Perspective: Economic Development in Flanders and Brabant, 1580–1812' in A. Maddison and H. Van der Wee (eds.) *Economic Growth and Structural Change: Comparative Approaches over the Long Run*, pp. 77–96 (Leuven: Centrum voor Economische Studiën).

H. Van der Wee, R. Bogaert and G. Kurgan-Van Hentenryk (1991) *La Banque en Occident* (Antwerp: Fonds Mercator).

J. A. Van Houtte and E. Stols (1973) 'Les Pays- Bas et la 'Mediterranée atlantique' au XVIe. Siècle' in B. Tenenti (ed.) *Histoire économique du monde mediterranéen, 1450–1650 (Mélanges en l'honneur de Fernand Braudel)*, pp. 645–659 (Toulouse: Privat).

H. F. K. Van Nierop (1984) *The Nobility of Holland* (Cambridge: Cambridge University Press).

I. Valdez-Bubnov (2011) *Poder naval y modernización del estado: política de construcción naval española (siglos XVI–XVIII)* (Mexico: Iberoamericana).

R. Valladares (1998) *La rebelión de Portugal: guerra, conflicto y poderes en la Monarquía Hispánica (1640–1668)* (Valladolid: Junta de Castilla y León).

R. Valladares (2001) *Castilla y Portugal en Asia: 1580–1680: declive imperial y adaptación* (Leuven: Leuven University Press).

D. E. Vassberg (1983) *La venta de tierras baldías; el dominio público y la Corona en Castilla durante el siglo XVI* (Madrid: Instituto de Estudios Fiscales).

D. E. Vassberg (1986) *Tierra y sociedad en Castilla. Señores "poderosos" y campesinos en la España del siglo XVI* (Barcelona: Crítica).

D. E. Vassberg (1996) *The Village and the Outside World in Golden Age Castille. Mobility and Migration in Everyday Rural Life* (Cambridge: Cambridge University Press).

R. Vermeir (2009) 'Je t'aime, moi non plus. La nobleza flamenca y España en los siglos XVI y XVII' in B. Yun (ed.) *Las redes del imperio. Élites sociales en la articulación de la Monarquía Hispánica, 1492–1714*, pp. 313–337 (Madrid: Marcial Pons).

H. Viana (1968) *Capitulos de Historia Luso-Brasileira* (Lisbon: Academia Portuguesa da História).

J. Vicens Vives (1974) *Coyuntura económica y reformismo burgués y otros estudios de historia de España* (Barcelona: Ariel).

G. Vigo (1998), 'La economía en el Estado de Milán en la transición del siglo XVI al XVII' in L. Ribot (ed.), *Las sociedades ibéricas y el mar*, t. III, pp. 263–282 (Madrid: SECC).

E. Vila (1991) *Los Corzo y los Mañara: tipos y arquetipos del Mercader con Indias* (Seville: CSIC).

N. Vila-Santa (2015) *Entre o Reino e o Imperio: a carreira político-militar de D. Luís de Ataíde (1516–1581)* (Lisbon: ICS).

J. Vilar (1974) 'Conciencia nacional y conciencia económica' (estudio preliminar) de Sancho de Moncada (1616), *Restauración política de España*, pp. 5–81 (Madrid: Instituto de estudios fiscales).

P. Vilar (1962) *La Catalogne dans l'Espagne moderne. Recherches sur les fondamentes économiques des structures nationales* (Paris: SEVPEN) vols I–III.

P. Vilar (1969) *Oro y Moneda en la historia (1450–1920)* (Barcelona: Ariel).

P. Vilar (1974) *Crecimiento y desarrollo. Economía e historia. Reflexiones sobre el caso español* (Barcelona: Ariel).

P. B. Villella (2012) 'Indian Lords, Hispanics Gentlemen: The Salazars of Colonial Tlaxcala', *The Americas*, 69, 1–36.

R. Villares (1982) *La propiedad de la tierra en Galicia, 1500–1936* (Santiago: Universidad de Santiago de Compostela).

R. Villari (1973) *La rivolta antispagnola a Napoli. Le origini (1585–1647)* (Rome: Laterza).

C. Viñas (1970) 'Notas sobre primeras materias, capitalismo industrial e inflación en Castilla durante el siglo XVI', *Anuario de Historia Económica y Social*, 3, 339–421.

P. Volpini (2004) *Lo spazio político del "letrado", Juan Bautista Larrea magistrato e giurista nella monarchia di Filipo IV* (Bologna: Il Mulino).

J. de Vries (1984) *European Urbanization, 1500–1800* (Cambridge: Harvard University Press).

J. de Vries (1994) 'Population' in T. A. Brady, J. Heiko, A. Oberman and J. D. Tracy (eds.) *Handbook of European History 1400–1600* pp. 1–50 (Leiden, Brill).

J. de Vries (2003) *The Economy of Europe in an Age of Crisis, 1600–1750* (Cambridge: Cambridge University Press).

J. de Vries (2008) *The Industrious Revolution: Consumer Behaviour and the Household Economy, 1650 to the Present* (Cambridge: Cambridge University Press).

J. de Vries (2010) 'The Limits of Globalization in the Early Modern world', *The Economic History Review*, 63, 710–733.

J. de Vries (2011) 'Old and New Insights: a Personal Perspective', in F. Ammannati (ed). *Where is Economic History Going? Methods and Prospects from the XIIIth to the XVIIIth Centuries*, pp. 61–78 (Florence: Firenze University Press).

J. de Vries and A. Van der Woude (1997) *The First Modern Economy: Success, Failure, and Perseverance of the Dutch Economy, 1500–1815* (Cambridge: Cambridge University Press).

P. Vries (2015) *State, Economy and the Great Divergence: Great Britain and China, 1680s–1850s* (London: Bloomsbury).

I. Wallerstein (1979) *El moderno sistema mundial. La agricultura capitalista y los orígenes de la economía-mundo europea en el siglo XVI* (Madrid: Siglo XXI).

M. Walzer (1965) *The Revolution of the Saints: A Study of the Origins of Radical Politics* (Cambridge: Harvard University Press).

W. A. Weary (1977) 'The House of La Tremoille, Fifteenth through Eighteenth Centuries: Change and Adaptation in a French Noble Family', *Journal of Modern History*, 49, 1001–1038.

L. Weckmann (1993) La herencia material del Brasil (México: Fondo de Cultura Económica).

P. Williams (2006) *The Great Favourite: the Duke of Lerma and the Court and Government of Philip III of Spain* (Manchester: Manchester University Press).

P. Williams (2014) *Empire and Holy War in the Mediterranean: The Galley and Maritime Conflict between the Habsburg and Ottoman Empires* (London: I.B. Tauris).

C. Wilson (1959) 'The Other Face of Mercantilism', *Transactions of the Royal Society*, 9, 81–101.

M. Wolfe (1972) *The Fiscal Renaissance France* (New Haven: Yale University Press).

J. Wood (1980) *The Nobility of the Election of Bayeux, 1463–1666* (Princeton: Princeton University Press).

L. P. Wright (1982) 'Las ordenes militares en la sociedad española de los siglos XVI y XVII. La encarnación institucional de una tradición histórica' in J. H. Elliott (ed.) *Poder y sociedad en la España de los Austrias*, pp. 14–56 (Barcelona: Crítica).

K. Wrightson (1982) *English Society: 1580–1680* (London: Routledge).

E. A. Wrigley (1987) *People, Cities and Wealth. The Transformation of a traditional society* (New York: Basil Blackwell).

J. Yarza (1993) *Los Reyes Católicos. Paisaje artístico de una monarquía* (Madrid: Nerea).

B. Yun (1980) *Crisis de subsistencias y conflictividad social en Córdoba a principios del siglo XVI* (Córdoba: Diputación Provincial).

B. Yun (1987) *Sobre la transición al capitalismo en Castilla. Economía y sociedad en Tierra de Campos* (Salamanca: Junta de Castilla y León).

B. Yun (1990) 'Introducción', in J. Ruiz de Celada (1990 [1777]) *Estado de la Bolsa de Valladolid. Examen de sus tributos, cargas y medios de extinción. De su gobierno y reforma* (Valladolid: Universidad de Valladolid).

B. Yun (1994a) 'Seigneurial Economies in Sixteenth and Seventeenth Century Spain. Economic Rationality or Political and Social Management?' in P. Klep and E. Van Cauwenberghe (eds.) *Entrepreneurship and the Transformation of the Economy (10th–20th Centuries). Essays in Honour of Herman Van der Wee*, pp. 173–182 (Leuven: Leuven University Press).

B. Yun (1994b) 'Corrupción, fraude, eficacia hacendística y economía en la España del siglo XVII', *Hacienda Pública Española*, 1, 47–60.

B. Yun (1998) 'The American Empire and the Spanish Economy: an Institutional and Regional Perspective', *Revista de Historia Económica*, 1, 123–155.

B. Yun (1999a) 'Del centro a la periferia: la economía española bajo Carlos II', *Studia historica. Historia Moderna*, 20, 45–76.

B. Yun (1999b) 'Inventarios "post-mortem", consumo y niveles de vida del campesinado en el Antiguo Régimen: problemas metodológicos a la luz de la investigación internacional' in B. Yun and J. Torras (eds.) *Consumo, condiciones de vida y comercialización: Cataluña, Castilla, siglos XVII–XIX* pp. 27–40 (Valladolid: Junta de Castilla y León).

B. Yun (1999c) 'Valladolid en Castilla. Economía y consumo' in *Valladolid. Historia de una ciudad* (Valladolid: Junta de Castilla y León) T. II, pp. 457–490.

B. Yun (2001) 'Manufacturas, mercado interior y redes urbanas: recesión, reajustes y rigideces' in J. Alcalá-Zamora and E. Belenguer (eds.) *Calderón de la Barca y la España del Barroco*, vol. 1, pp. 111–128 (Madrid: Centro de Estudios Políticos y Constitucionales).

B. Yun (2002a) *La gestión del poder. Corona y economías aristocráticas en Castilla, siglos XV–XVIII* (Madrid: Akal).

B. Yun (2002b) 'City and countryside: Changing structures, changing relationships, 1450–1850. Views from Economics' in J. Marino (ed.) *Early Modern History and Social Sciences: Testing the Limits of Braudel's Mediterranean*, pp. 35–70 (Kirksville: Truman State University Press).

B. Yun (2004) *Marte contra Minerva. El precio del imperio español, c. 1450–1600* (Barcelona: Crítica).

B. Yun (2005a) 'From Political and Social Management to Economic Management? Castilian Aristocracy and Economic Development, 1450–1800' in J. Janssens and B. Yun (eds.) *European Aristocracies and Colonial Elites. Patrimonial Management Strategies and Economic Development, 15th–18th Centuries*, pp. 85–98 (London: Ashgate).

B. Yun (2005b) 'Economía moral y gestión aristocrática en tiempos del Quijote', *Revista de Historia Económica*, 23, 45–68.

B. Yun (2007) 'Imagen e ideología social en la Europa del siglo XVII: Trabajo y familia en Murillo y Martínez de Mata' in J. L. Palos and D. Carrió-Invernizzi (dirs.) *Historias imaginadas. Construcción visual del pasado y usos políticos de las imágenes en la Europa Moderna*, pp. 235–266 (Madrid: Centro de Estudios Europa Hispánica).

B. Yun (2009) 'Entre el imperio colonial y la monarquía compuesta. Élites y territorios en la Monarquía Hispánica' in B. Yun (ed.) *Las redes del imperio. Élites sociales en la articulación de la Monarquía Hispánica 1492–1714* pp. 11–35 (Madrid: Marcial Pons).

B. Yun (2010) 'Entre mina y mercado. ¿Fue América una oportunidad perdida para la economía española?' in D. García Hernán (ed.) *La historia sin complejos. La nueva visión del Imperio español*, pp. 204–229 (Madrid: Actas).

B. Yun (2011) 'Reading Sources throughout P. Bourdieu and Cyert and March. Aristocratic Patrimonies vs. Commercial Enterprises in Europe (c.1550–1650)' in F. Ammannati (ed.) *Dove va la Storia economica? Metodi e prospettive. S. XVI–XVIII.* pp. 325–337 (Florence: Firenze University Press).

B. Yun (2012) 'Introduction: the Rise of the Fiscal State in Eurasia from a Global, Comparative and Transnational Perspective' in B. Yun and P. O'Brien (eds) *The Rise of Fiscal States. A Global History, 1500–1914*, pp. 1–35 (Cambridge: Cambridge University Press).

B. Yun (2013) 'The History of Consumption of Early Modern Europe in a Trans-Atlantic Perspective. Some New Challenges in European Social History' in V. Hyden-Hanscho, R. Pieper, W. Stangl (eds.) *Cultural Exchange and Consumption Patterns in the Age of Enlightenment. Europe and the Atlantic World*, pp. 25–40 (Bochum: Verlag Dieter Winkler).

B. Yun (2014a) 'Transnational History. What Lies behind the Label? Some Reflections from the Early Modernist's Point of View', *Culture and History*, 3, 1–7.

B. Yun (2014b) 'The Spanish Empire, Globalization and Cross-Cultural Consumption in a World Context, c. 1400–1750' in B. Aram and B. Yun (eds.) *Global Goods and the Spanish Empire, 1492–1824: Circulation, Resistance and Diversity* (New York: Palgrave).

B. Yun (2015) 'El imperio español entre la monarquía compuesta y el colonialismo mercantil. Metodologías, contextos institucionales y perspectivas para el estudio de la fiscalidad y la movilización de recursos,' en M. P. Sánchez, E. Sánchez and M. Souto (coords.) *La ficalidad novohispana en el imperio español. Conceptualizaciones, proyectos y contradicciones*, pp. 29–68 (México: UNAM).

B. Yun (2016) 'Arbitristas, Projectors, Eccentrics and Political Thinkers. Contextualizing and "Translating" a European Phenomenon' in S. Rauschenbach and C. Windler (eds.) *Reforming Early Modern Monarchies: The Castilian Arbitristas in Comparative European Perspectives*, pp. 101–122 (Wiesbaden: Harrassowitz Verlag).

B. Yun (2017) "Social Networks and the Circulation of Technology and Knowledge in the Global Spanish Empire" in M. Pérez and L. de Sousa (eds.) *Global History and New polycentric Approaches. Europe, Asia and Americas in the World Network System* (Singapore: Palgrave Macmillan).

B. Yun and F. Ramos (2012) 'El Sur frente al Norte. Instituciones, economías políticas y lugares comunes', in F. Ramos and B. Yun (eds.) *Economía Política. Desde Estambul a Potosí: Ciudades estado, imperios y mercados en el Mediterráneo y el Atlántico ibérico, c. 1200–1800*, pp. 11–38 (Valencia, Universidat de València).

A. Zabalza (1994) *Aldeas y campesinos en la Navarra prepirenaica: (1550–1817)* (Pamplona: Gobierno de Navarra).

R. Zambardino (1980) 'Mexico´s Population in the Sixteenth Century: Demographic Anomaly or Mathematical Illusion?', *Journal of Interdisciplinary History*, 11, 1–27.

F. Zamora (2014) 'Interest and Curiosity: American Products, Information, and Exotica in Tuscany' in *Global Goods and the Spanish Empire, 1492–1824*, ed. B. Aram and B. Yun pp. 175–193 (Basingstoke: Palgrave).

C. Zanetti (2012) *Janello Torriani (Cremona 1500ca. – Toledo 1585): A Social History of Invention between Renaissance and Scientific Revolution* (Ph.D. Thesis, European University Institute).

J. C. Zofío (2005) *Las culturas del trabajo en Madrid, 1500–1650* (Madrid: Universidad Complutense).

L. Zytkowicz (1985) 'Trends of Agrarian Economy in Poland, Bohemia and Hungary from the Middle of the Fifteenth to the Middle of the Seventeenth Century', in A. Maczak, H. Samsonowicz and P. Burke (eds.) *East and Central Europe in Transition. From the Fourteenth to the Seventeenth Century*, pp. 59–83 (Cambridge: Cambridge University Press).

Index[1]

A

Absolutism, 2, 28, 42, 71, 146, 151,
  152, 157, 177–178, 180, 185,
  203, 216, 245, 250, 258, 263,
  264, 267, 273, 383, 387, 392,
  393, 396, 405, 406, 435, 441
  absoluta potestas, 245, 264, 382
Acapulco, 326, 344
Acosta, José de, 60
Africa, 7, 10, 14, 15, 22, 32, 33, 67,
  69, 79, 80, 83, 96, 147, 156n2,
  157, 161, 166n17, 200, 204,
  250, 259, 285–287, 290, 296,
  320, 345, 348, 353, 355, 363,
  374, 431, 433, 449
  coastline, 9
  coasts, 71, 96, 137, 146, 148
Agriculture
  agrarian development, 281, 290,
    308, 309

agrarian exploitation, 100
agrarian growth, 116, 117, 124n28,
  200, 205, 306
agrarian sector, 206, 339
Alba, duke of, 190, 281
Alburquerque, Dukes of, 24n21,
  199, 200
Alcalá, Duke of, 406
Alcázar (family), 176
Aldobrandini, Cardinal, 378
Alentejo, 16, 117, 118, 121, 302,
  397, 423
Aleppo, 83, 355
Algarve, 16, 117, 130, 147, 397
Alicante, 427
Alps, Valtelina Pass, 295, 353
Álvarez Cabral, Pedro, 69, 184, 222,
  248, 303n26
Álvarez de Toledo (family),
  190, 347, 412

---

[1] Note: Page numbers followed by 'n' refer to notes.

© The Author(s) 2019
B. Yun-Casalilla, *Iberian World Empires and the Globalization
of Europe 1415–1668*, Palgrave Studies in Comparative Global
History, https://doi.org/10.1007/978-981-13-0833-8

Printed by Printforce, the Netherlands